The Certainty of the Words

How the King James Bible Resolves the Ambiguity of the Original Languages

Kyle Stephens

DayStar Publishing
PO Box 464 • Miamitown, Ohio 45041

ISBN 978-1-890120-76-4

Library of Congress 2011941221

Printed by

Bible & Literature Missionary Foundation

713 Cannon Boulevard • Shelbyville, TN 37160

(931) 684-0304 • Email: officeblmf@bellsouth.net

www.biblelit.com

Table of Contents

Dedication

Humanly speaking, it is our privilege in this present hour to be able to discuss and elaborate on the matters contained in this book, threatened by precious little more than counter-opinions, adversarial debate, and perhaps scholarly condescension and dismissal. Such has not always been the case, and perhaps it will not always be the case.

This book is dedicated to the unnumbered masses of Bible-loving Christians, who in times not so distantly past, received, embraced, memorized, published, and proclaimed what were often little more than bits and pieces of paper which, should they be discovered, would cost those souls their homes, livelihoods, spouses, children and lives. This is written in honor of those who having lived in wretched spiritual darkness, who having been exploited mercilessly by the worst sort of sinister predator, were liberated by words written and spoken, which words came from outside this temporal domain - words from the Living God. These were words, which when trusted, enlightened them, delivered them, translated them, gave them a royal heritage, a birthright, a reason to live and a reason to die.

And die they did. They died merciless deaths - horrific deaths. In the end, it was all about words written on pieces of paper or leather, which when distributed or pronounced to the common man, became the most dangerous but blessed commodity to be found in this life. These words became integral parts of the spiritual makeup of the people that embraced them, and the "powers that be" - *dogs* and *bulls of Bashan* (Ps. 22) - would not abide such an infestation. So, the Bible-believers died. Those that did not die were threatened with death for their entire lives.

Many names we do know: Wycliffe, Tyndale, Erasmus, Huss, Jerome of Prague, Hubemaier, and Knox. Many groups we know: the Waldensians, Albigenses, Paulicans, Novatians and Donatists. Mainly though, there is a numberless lineage of largely nameless people which God used as pieces on a vast chessboard of history, through a mind-boggling maze of religion, politics, war, intrigue, culture, and satanic conspiracy. Out of this simmering pot of death, confusion and darkness emerged again and again, for each generation, the shining and eternal treasure: the words of the Living God.

What we write and debate about here from the comfort of our liberties and freedoms cost braver and better souls everything but their eternities. God forbid we lose perspective of the price they paid or the precious treasure they helped deliver to us

Preface

The Certainty of the Words is another of those books defending the AV 1611, King James Bible (KJV). This is certainly not a subject that has been ignored scholastically. Indeed, it has been addressed voluminously and loudly. Most of us who consider the issue vital to latter day Christianity have literally several feet of shelf space in our libraries that are dedicated to nothing but that subject, along with a few more linear feet of shelving that are home to authors not so appreciative of that unique 17th century accomplishment.

There is no desire here on the author's part to merely add another inch or so of *fill* to King James Bible lovers' (or detractors') bookcases. Many have put their hands to the plow and the pen in the erstwhile defense of the AV 1611. If I were unable to add legitimately to the body of knowledge and evidence in support of the KJV, there would be no purpose for this book. If I could not fill what I perceive as a void, and square off with particular aspects of the conflict that have not been addressed in certain details, I would gladly forfeit my inch on readers' bookshelves.

The reason for this book is that some years ago, I found myself troubled by a certain sub-issue contained within the larger King James Bible issue. Some AV 1611 detractors indulged in addressing the matter with disdainful glee – the joy of those certain that they held all the information they needed to properly expose and humiliate the weak minded in their quirky little King James Bible position. I found some insightful and helpful answers from the writings and audio sermons of certain KJV defenders, but the answers seemed scattered, and in general it seemed that no one really got around to specifically addressing the matter that troubled me. This statement is not intended to be critical. These defenders were staking out their own battle lines where the Lord had assigned them. Nonetheless, building on the seed of what a few others planted, I started keeping my eyes open as I read and studied my Bible for just such examples as might shed light on this topic that troubled me. The subtitle to this book describes that subject matter in brief. I hope the contribution made here justifies the venture into authorship.

I also wish to say that I know just how caustic and bitter debate over this issue can be. It is not possible in affairs where men have great convictions, feel great conscientious obligations, and where the devil is so insidiously interested, that exchange and debate will be lacking fire and acid. I enjoy the employment of sarcasm and wit as much as the next fellow, but I also know that there are shades and degrees among King James defenders. We have all neither begun at the same place nor arrived yet at where we are going. I know that many who do not agree 100% with me have made far greater contribution to the KJV cause than I ever will. May the reader be assured that I do present this material without the intent to divide, denigrate or alienate any of those in the KJV camp – or even those on the outside of it. I hope that even non-KJV people might consider the issues presented. The edge of the sword of the Spirit is sharp indeed. My desire is that the Spirit might make the incisions and not me.

For all those who have grasped that this war we fight is centered on the words of God delivered to us, I will first quote Abraham: *We be brethren* (Gen. 13:8). Thus, we should act like it. Then I say from my own heart: *The stewardship and trust given us is a sanctified and a holy one.* Don't sell it out.

Introduction

On a given Saturday, a Jehovah's Witness (JW), dressed all dapper, and distinguished in bearing, approaches the front door of a house outside of a large Midwestern city, rings the bell and awaits opportunity to enlighten whatever soul opens the door to his version of the "truth" regarding the coming kingdom. His sidekick and visitation partner is there to observe how it is done.

As happens only so often, the JW this particular morning does not encounter the mere vapid, religious zombie who only knows *what* he is supposed to believe, and not *why*. The doorbell is neither altogether ignored after a quick, flickering movement of the curtains, nor is it slammed shut in the middle of the JW's oft-rehearsed spiel. Further, the prospective convert does not stand with glazed-over eyes, shuffling feet and wistful glances over his shoulder at the beckoning recliner and a ballgame that is about to start.

No, instead of enduring further polite verbal skewering, the homeowner sallies forth and interrupts the JW elder's post-introductory procession of words, by announcing himself a born-again, Bible-believing Christian. He further disrupts the flow by informing the visitors that since he already knows what they believe down at the Kingdom Hall, he might as well cut to the chase and say outright what the issues at hand are. He then relates that he has already fully investigated those matters, and there are reasons that he could never come to an agreement with such doctrine.

He takes a short breath, giving the lead JW just a moment to adjust his tie and steal a glance at his now slightly wide-eyed partner-in-heresy. Unfortunately, the breath doesn't take long enough to allow him to jump in and regain the initiative in the conversation.

The Bible thumper proceeds to tell them that: 1) Hell is a real place that burns hot with God's wrath even on this fine Saturday morning, that Pilate has been there for 2000 years in torment and that the folks in today's obituaries are only beginning an eternal nightmare. 2) The Bible proves that Jesus Christ was literally God manifest in the flesh, quite unlike the JW idea, which was hatched by Origin and his buddies; and 3) Further, the blood of Christ shed for sinners was, thus, God's very blood; and only *the blood of Jesus Christ...cleanseth us from all sin* – and that completely by faith!

His timing all ruined, and disinterested now in continuing pursuit of such a theologically hardened yet well fortified aggressor, the still distinguished Arian frankly concedes that it does appear *unlikely* that he and his visitation partner will ever be able to come to any real agreement with the homeowner. So being willing to courteously disengage, he only wishes to say that the Bible-quoting saint should be aware that a great deal of truth is to be found in the Greek originals which is not contained in the fundamentalist's old outdated Bible. Naturally, it would be best if the born-again guy would come to some Kingdom Hall meetings to find out what the *bible* really says.

****

The young college student was riding a spiritual wave unlike anything he had ever known. He had been saved in a little country Baptist church at 10-years-old, and that meant that he had been saved for something like 10 or 11 years, but the personal revival he was experiencing in college was something else altogether! His salvation experience with Christ had been genuine as a boy, but he had grown precious little spiritually, and had become as lethargic as most of the people around him. As he grew older he had become more preoccupied with the world - school, sports, girls, cars and college.

Life had hit him like a cement truck in college. He had maintained a mostly conservative mindset, retaining at least some of his morals, but the misery of bad friends, a lack of real direction, and a sense of drifting and spiritual alienation had settled into his soul like the fog creeping across the creek-bottoms at dusk. Financial hardship, loneliness, lack of fulfillment and various circumstantial crises had brought him back to the realization of his manifold need for God. Life was too big to control and he had learned that there were unseen obstacles capable of sinking his ship.

For this, he had returned to the Savior of his youth, had genuinely turned from the sins that attached themselves to him like life-sucking leeches, and had given his miseries and burdens back to the One who had already borne them anyway. The precious promises were now sweeter than anything he had ever tasted. He felt free, and there was a certainty of God's plan for him, though he knew not where the path would lead. His part was to hold fast his hope and confidence, trust God, and do right.

On his journey back to the Father, he had wandered into a big, contemporary Baptist church in his college town. He was directed to the college-age department, and lo and behold, at the front of the class was an Elijah teaching the Bible in a manner he had never experienced before. The emphasis was on each word of the old Book and it was terribly plain that the words taught and believed as they stood in the text carried a punch that would put an All-American fullback on his backside. On occasion the teacher would bring in preaching tapes that were unlike anything that young Baptist had ever heard. The reverb from those messages would leave his soul afire until all hours of the night.

Though not *all* good things come to an end, a lot of them do, and it turned out that the excited young man's "KJV-only" Sunday School teacher was "found out". In effect, he had slipped between the cracks of church bureaucracy for a brief while, but his Bible emphasis fit neither with the conventionally-minded leadership of the church, nor with that of the pastor himself. The class was reorganized and reassigned to another teacher more fitted to the preconceived denominational mold. Almost from the opening bell, the theme of the reorganized "bible class" became, "Now in the originals…," "This is an unfortunate translation…," "A better rendering would be…," and "I think the NIV reading is particularly good here."

****

The young pastor had been in town for a few months, called to begin a new work. There was a drought of anything like a true Bible-believing Baptist church in the area, and there had been a good deal of success in making contact with folks committed to the King James Bible. Though the group was fairly diverse and would need some time and a steady hand to get them all on the same page, they all would have been categorized as extremely conservative Fundamentalists, and had all paid a certain price already in their advocacy of the old Book.

The backdrop was a Sunday evening fellowship after the service, held in the home of one of the enthusiastic attendees. Around food and conversation, talk turned to a certain matter in the scriptures. The query came from a middle-aged man, an established pro-King James Fundamentalist who had been very committed to the new church for months, both spiritually and materially. The pastor was asked what his thoughts were on the matter, so he proceeded to quote several passages of scripture that related directly, pointed out another couple of parallels and types in the Bible, and outlined what the negative logical alternatives were if it were not as he deemed it.

The response of the enthused Fundamental Baptist (who was so excited to *finally* be in a King James church where he would not have to worry about hearing the scriptures corrected from the pulpit anymore) was disappointing. "Well, I would sure like to find out what the sense of that scripture is in the original Hebrew," he said.

****

A young pastor embarking in starting a new Bible-believing work in a gospel-starved city received a call in response to a newspaper advertisement announcing the formation of the new Baptist church in town. The caller turned out to be another pastor from a few miles away who had seen the announcement. It turned out that both pastors were from the same native state, and the caller quickly stressed that he was a very strong King James man, and indeed, it turned out that his sending church was known for specific tracts and pamphlets that laid great stress on the AV 1611 and it's supporting Greek and Hebrew texts. However, the chit-chat didn't continue for long before it became obvious that the caller had something on his mind.

The caller said he had a couple of questions to ask to determine whether the two men and their churches could count on having fellowship together. It only took a question or two for the new man in town to see where the caller had drawn the line of fellowship. In the end they probably agreed on 95% of everything, including doctrine, standards of separation and church polity, but the caller was firm that they must see eye to eye on this one singular matter.

They discussed the relevant scriptural texts and tenets, could not really come to common ground on the subject and parted as gentlemen. Having given the caller his mailing address, the church planter received a package of literature a few days later, courtesy of the caller. All of the tracts and treatises in the mailing expanded on and expounded in detail the caller's position. The recipient felt that much of the information was poorly evaluated, biblically speaking, and led to mostly preconceived conclusions. Most noteworthy in the packet, though, was an exposition on a certain biblical text (remember, these men believed and defended the same English Bible) claiming that a critical preposition had been mistranslated from the Textus Receptus into the KJV English, having led thousands of Baptist churches through the years into apostate doctrine. The caller and his pamphlet held that the preposition should be changed.

****

Concerning the four separate incidents narrated above, it is important to make something plain. It should be noted that the incidents are neither hypothetical nor second-hand. I myself am the homeowner and the young college fellow in the first two stories, and the new church's pastor in each of the final two. These events occurred at different waypoints in the last 25 years of my personal experience, and there are many other such encounters, but I have chosen these four for a reason.

The four episodes offered are for comparison and contrast. The common thread that wends its way from scenario to scenario is that the new character introduced into each scene is in perfect agreement with the last, or the next; namely that the King James Bible believer really has no business placing his trust in the wording of his Bible. To each of them there is a higher appeal, and believing the old Book as it stands is *wrong*, or at best, the King James reading is *untrustworthy*. Now, the differing elements are fairly obvious, but troubling:

- The Jehovah's Witness out door-knocking was a lost man and could not be expected to have a lot of spiritual insight or discernment.
- The new Sunday School teacher (sent to replace the King James Bible-believing teacher) was an NIV user and had been, in effect, taught that bringing the wording of the Bible into question and offering his own fallen opinion was a noble and spiritual means of conducting God-honoring Bible study. He didn't know it, of course, but he was practicing *dynamic equivalence* and stood in defiance of Revelation 22:18-19.
- The born-again King James Fundamentalist who was so enthused to have his part in the founding of a new Bible-believing work, would readily shout "Amen!" whenever the old Book was exalted in preaching, and was always happy to show the uninitiated the woeful changes that had been introduced into the new versions. When push came to shove, though, with regard to the trustworthiness of the English grammar of his exalted Bible, he not only was in agreement with the teacher who used the NIV, but with the lost Jehovah's Witness as well! In h mind, his King James Bible needed "help" from the "original Greek."
- The Bible-believing pastor with the doctrinal bee in his bonnet came from a background of defending the 1611 Authorized Version, and was sent out by a church that

produced sheaves of information defending the text, translation, translators and tradition of that sacred volume. In the end, though, he and his circle of friends could not abide leaving the English as it stood because his doctrine required that the scriptures say something other than what they actually said and, incidentally, what they *still do say!*

The Jehovah's Witness was a real guy, just a regular fellow who happened to have staked his eternal claim in the wrong religious outfit. For the purposes here discussed, though, he represents an entire category of person as well. He is a lost man though he has a bible, a proponent of the Arian heresy, and a cult member. The text family of his *New World Translation* comes from Egypt, specifically Alexandria. The Greek text of his bible was grossly mutilated and corrupted by an apostate genius named Adamantius Origen back in the 200's AD[1], and Origen's adoring successors enthusiastically continued his work thereafter. The JW is an unregenerate man and represents a category of unregenerate man, which reads, studies and quotes a bible that is corrupt. He has a bible that comes from the wrong *text*! He further has the wrong *philosophy* about that bible. He believes, along with his church, that the scriptures are not inviolable and precise, but that the words are to be wrested, manipulated, and altered so that the people get the message, though they could never have the very words of the Living God. ***He is eternally lost and he has both the wrong text and the wrong philosophy about that text.***

The replacement Sunday School teacher discussed is a saved man. Mainline Christian bible studies are led by an army of men and women just like him. He has a stack of new

---

[1] "Origen | Christian History." *ChristianityToday.com | Magazines, News, Church Leadership & Bible Study*. Web. 3 Mar, 2009 <http://www.christianitytoday.com/ch/131christians/scholarsandscientists/origen.html>.

versions and a library of reference books, or failing that, a computer bible program with all the reference works a soul could want, right at his fingertips. In all his devotional reading and in all his training – formal or informal – he has been led and encouraged by example to view the new translations of the Bible as wonderful and enlightening developments. He does not realize that the new versions he so giddily quotes are rooted in the same degenerate Greek text as the Jehovah's Witness's bible, and further that his favorite English translations of that text reflect nearly all of the same perverted readings as the bible of those zealous, Arian heretics! The new Sunday School teacher is a saved man, he gives a good deal of time and effort to the Lord, and he loves God - but he, too, has the wrong *text.* That corrupt text follows in company with the wrong *philosophy* about the Bible, as well. None of the translators of any of his new versions held sacred the specificity of wording. Indeed, they all did their work knowing that there had to be enough changes in the English text of *each new translation* to justify a copyright for their work. They felt free to manipulate and recast the wording in the *word of God!* Wrong *philosophy!* ***The Sunday School bible study leader is a regenerated and decent man who has the same wrong text and the same wrong philosophy as the JW.***

The enthused church member so pleased to have a part in starting an Independent, Fundamental, King James-Only Baptist Church from scratch, is the type of person who has been the backbone of conservative Christianity for a long time. He is often old enough to have vivid and living memories of some of the legendary preachers of the past – Roloff, Norris, Rawlings, Rice, Hutson and Hyles. He feels a connection, a unity of spirit, with a generation of Christians that extends much further back in time. He understands that the old and good way (Jer. 6:16) has somehow been betrayed and sold out in the most recent generations. He has seen the fruits of the church's music sliding into Jazz and Blues rhythms, of down-spiraling standards of behavior and dress, and of preaching that somehow seems to contain more thunder than lightning. Naturally, he can see with perfect clarity that having six or seven different versions of the Bible dispersed in the congregation leads to confusion; that the heady Dr. Pastor's big game safaris into his Greek lexicon, his translational preferences, and his calisthenics in grammar are killing sheep.

If he ever had concerns about the scriptures of his fathers, Edward Hills, David Otis Fuller and J.J. Ray set him straight. The foundation for his Bible is a far cry from Alexandria, Egypt, and Origen never put his grimy, apostate pen to the Antiochian text! No, this Fundamentalist's copy of the scriptures is founded on more than 95% of all New Testament readings, the text of the Montanists, Cathari, Waldensians, the Reformers and the Anabaptists. He has the OLD Book and the OLD Faith! God bless them, the *old-time* men grounded in the *old way* assured that this *old-fashioned* Christian would endure Laodicea with the right *text!*

Alas, some traits of fallen human nature are hard to put away for good, and as moths to light, men are drawn to the wisdom of this world. The mantle and fraternity of scholarship appeals to the intellectual pride of the academic, and intimidates the rustic. The wise and scholarly are usually polarized to intellectualism and scholarship. The untitled tend to be insecure but deferential around the lofty heights of academia. The old powerhouse barnstormers trended toward acquiescence in certain degrees to high-minded scholarship, and the heady minds of Philadelphia-age Christianity had intellectual inclinations that left few unscathed by Alexandria. Their Antiochian text was undeniably right, but concessions were made to the wisdom of Egypt. That fine, Christian Independent Baptist had read the books, heard the sermons, and admired the men of God of old. ***He is saved, separated, eternally secure, has the right text, and the right Book in his native language,***

but he has been infected by the Egyptian tenet that there is a higher appeal!

Finally, the preposition altering pastor represents the category of God-called men in the ministry with whom most all conservative Bible-grounded Christians would agree to the tune of 95+% on matters of Bible doctrine and church polity. Ministerial tone and timber vary a fair amount, but these men are better read than most, biblically, have most often been trained either formally or informally, have a burden for souls and godly things, and labor under the weighty burden of leading God's people spiritually through this wilderness. There are varying degrees of extremity and zeal on various matters, but the category of men spoken of have openly publicized the positions of their churches and ministries as standing by the old King James.

Certainly, there are those who have merely leapt on the bandwagon blindly or for the wrong reasons, as the tradition-bound always have. Mostly though, a King James man has become one for a reason. If he compared the translations, studied the textual evidence, read the history, and discovered Satan's hand going back to Eden, then he knows he has chosen the right Greek and Hebrew text, and he knows he has the right Bible in English!

But...

But, the question to be asked is, does his English Bible - that blessed old AV 1611 - reflect all the meaning of the original languages? Does it say all it *should*? How about all it *could*? Does it communicate all that God would have us grasp? Are there particles of truth lost in translation? If so, did God see to it that these are mere unnecessary tidbits? If there are strands of necessary truth still entangled in that sieve of translation, *dear God, what floodgates of distrust and uncertainty that must open!*

In this pastor, laboring in my local area, I almost had another friend in the ministry. We agreed on nearly everything. We had a lot in common including a God, a Savior, a Great Commission, and a high calling. We even defended the same Bible. For him, the fly in the ointment was a doctrinal preconception that led him to alter a lowly preposition. He found in the Greek the latitude for an alternative translation that English would not allow. For other men the motive very well could be different and might be to cover personal or institutional sin, hatred for authority, the love of money, bitterness, ambition, or it might reflect plain old academic gall. Nevertheless, ***we could not have agreed more on the right Greek and Hebrew text, he and I, but regarding the words of our lofty and noble English Bible, he had another authority and a higher appeal.*** He was in agreement with the cult member and the new translation junky, that the King James English was *wrong*.

Brothers and sisters in Christ, there is a truth so true that it is now a cliché. That truth is that no two Christians will agree about absolutely 100% on everything. This little tenet can be used as an excuse and a justification for all manner of things; however the truth of the statement revolves around a whole bevy of variables like growth, maturity, lessons either learned or disregarded, poor training, good training, discipline, character, experience and study. I believe that honest, believing and enduring Bible study leads us much nearer the 100% agreement threshold than rabble-rousers and excuse-makers care to acknowledge.

This I will say: It is expected that "Christians" will have a difficult time agreeing 100% on all the Bible *means or teaches.* Such noble men as Paul and Barnabas came to an hour where they had a divisive disagreement on the proper scriptural course to take in the matter of John Mark (Acts 15:37-39). I do not know many Christians who expect their friends and fellow-soldiers to be in complete and unwavering agreement with them about absolutely everything. If it is expected that we may not agree perfectly about everything the Bible *means*, let me just say that it is a disgrace for Bible-believers to not agree 100% on what the Bible *says*. There is no point in talking about what it *means* if we cannot agree on what it *says*.

The brainwashed and unregenerate cult member said the old English Bible was just plain wrong. The new generation of Sunday School teacher blithely ricocheted from one new version to the next, quite sure that what he "preferred" was better than the old "King Jimmy". The Fundamental Bible-believing church member did not think the AV was wrong. He just thought it was *shallow* or *not expansive enough.* The "Bible-believing" pastor needed the text of his Bible to say something it did not in order that it might support his doctrinal preconceptions, so he opted for the charge that it was *unreliable* or *inadequate* in some of its translation.

Is the King James Bible *wrong*…even in a few places? Please do not be allured into a quizzical game of semantics with the word *wrong.* If it misleads, gives the incorrect sense or withholds a crucial truth, then it **is indeed *wrong*.** Is it *unreliable, untrustworthy, shallow, inadequate, or questionable* somehow, sometimes, or in some places? If one can interchange, substitute, or offer other more preferable words or more accurate words, then that must reflect something of a shortfall, does it not? Such an exercise in editing and altering speaks a great deal of the editor's attitude about the quality of work that either God or man (or both) accomplished in the translation of the AV 1611. Was it merely *man* that achieved that lofty standard of scripture and literature which has served so well for 400 years, and if not, what part did the Lord have in it? Did He *guide* the translators? Could He have *inclined* them to a certain form of wording? Did He ever *over-rule* them, *illuminate* their understanding, *lead* them, *dissuade* or *persuade* them? *Would* He do so?

Whom has God appointed as keepers of the words of God? To whom, if anyone, and by what decree, if any, has God given the latitude, the authority, to sit in judgment of the word choices, phraseology, and precision of the word of God? Surely a line must be drawn somewhere. If there is no such line, then anyone can claim the mantle. If there is such a delineation, then there must be some well-marked boundary or event in human affairs that serves notice that further meddling risks trespass into sanctified and holy things. Is there a line? If I am a cult member, do I get to change the Bible? No? How about if I have access to all the classic reference works and am able to speak by the authority of some of those heady commentators of the past? Still no? What if I am saved, godly, educated, orthodox, conservative, separated, and a Fundamentalist? Do I *then* have credentials enough to be allowed to reword and rephrase the English Bible? Where does the madness end? Where does the authority of God's Holy Word stand indivisible, insoluble, inflexible, unwavering, and adamant? Does it stand as such anywhere but in Heaven?

Men need answers to these questions. Many would prefer the questions were not framed in such a manner, but the fact remains that we need answers to questions that are unpalatable to some. The indispensable need for those answers lies in the affirmed reality that an entire range of people sit either in open rejection of the words of God, at worst, or in uncertainty and confusion, at best. It is expected that cult members and the ungodly would reject the wording of our Bible, but it is obviously incongruous that King James Bible-defending Christians, pastors and scholars would do the same.

Chapter 1

The Irksome Subject

> *Bow down thine ear, and hear the words of the wise, and apply thine heart unto my knowledge. For it is a pleasant thing if thou keep them within thee; they shall withal be fitted in thy lips. That thy trust may be in the LORD, I have made known to thee this day, even to thee. Have not I written to thee excellent things in counsels and knowledge,* ***That I might make thee know the certainty of the words of truth****; that thou mightest answer the words of truth to them that send unto thee?* (Prov. 22:17-21)

Whenever a Bible-believer undertakes to show the error of adopting the new English versions of the Bible, their mangled and corrupt texts, or the insidious satanic philosophy that engendered them, there are a great array of verses and biblical texts that readily present themselves. The word of God, itself a living entity (Heb. 4:12), almost literally *screams* out its protestations against the intrusive presumptions of the apostate bibles and their tainted scholarship. These passages are reviewed and revisited again and again by King James Bible believers as enduring and trusted assurances from the tongue and pen of the Living God, Who wanted us to know the absolute *certainty of the words of truth.*

> *The* ***words*** *of the LORD are* ***pure words****: as silver tried in a furnace of earth, purified seven*

times. ***Thou shalt keep them****, O LORD,* ***thou shalt preserve them*** *from this generation for ever.* (Ps. 12:6-7)

I will worship toward thy holy temple, and praise thy name for thy lovingkindness and for thy truth: for thou hast ***magnified thy word*** *above all thy name.*
(Ps. 138:2)

Every word of God is pure*: he is a shield unto them that put their trust in him.* ***Add thou not unto his words****, lest he reprove thee, and thou be found a liar.* (Prov. 30:5-6)

Therefore I esteem ***all*** *thy precepts concerning* ***all*** *things to be right; and I hate every false way.*
(Ps. 119:128)

For ever, O LORD, ***thy word*** *is settled in heaven.*
(Ps. 119:89)

Heaven and earth shall pass away, but ***my words*** *shall not pass away.* (Matt. 24:35)

And, behold, thou shalt be dumb, and not able to speak, until the day that these things shall be performed, because thou believest not ***my words****, which shall be fulfilled in their season.*
(Luke 1:20)

For whosoever shall be ashamed of me and of ***my words****, of him shall the Son of man be ashamed, when he shall come in his own glory, and in his Father's, and of the holy angels.*
(Luke 9:26)

For had ye believed Moses, ye would have believed me: for he wrote of me. But if ye believe not ***his writings****, how shall ye believe* ***my words****?* (John 5:46-47)

It is the spirit that quickeneth; the flesh profiteth nothing: ***the words*** *that I speak unto you, they are spirit, and they are life.* (John 6:63)

He that rejecteth me, and receiveth not ***my words****, hath one that judgeth him****: the word that I have spoken****, the same shall judge him in the last day.* (John 12:48)

Jesus answered and said unto him, If a man love me, he will keep ***my words****: and my Father will love him, and we will come unto him, and make our abode with him.* (John 14:23)

If any man teach otherwise, and consent not to ***wholesome words****,* ***even the words of our Lord Jesus Christ****, and to the doctrine which is according to godliness; He is proud, knowing nothing, but doting about questions and strifes of words, whereof cometh envy, strife, railings, evil surmisings, Perverse disputings of men of corrupt minds, and destitute of the truth, supposing that gain is godliness: from such withdraw thyself.* (1 Tim. 6:3-5)

For the prophecy came not in old time by the will of man: but holy men of God ***spake*** *as they were moved by the Holy Ghost.*

(2 Pet. 1:21)

> *And that from a child thou hast known the **holy scriptures**, which are able to make thee wise unto salvation through faith which is in Christ Jesus. **All scripture** is given by inspiration of God, and is profitable for doctrine, for reproof, for correction, for instruction in righteousness: That the man of God may be perfect, throughly furnished unto all good works.*
>
> (2 Tim. 3:15-17)

Most of us are able to hearken back to the day when we first became aware of the insidious conspiracy against the Bible. Whether the scriptural evidence was unceremoniously deposited in our laps all at once by an informed believer who was loaded for bear, or whether through a more circuitous process of time, study, and subsequent guidance from the Father, we became more fully enlightened about Satan's predatory ambush of Eve and his continuing preoccupation and obsession with corrupting the eternal, life-giving seed. The verses cited above appeared to us to be so plain and their implications so evident, that it seemed patently ridiculous and blatantly unreasonable to reach beyond the plain meaning of the texts. The simple truth is written there right before our very eyes! ***God inspired His word, spake and wrote His words to us, preserved them all for us, and therefore we have them...all of them.*** Simple stuff. Rudimentary. Done deal.

Such forthright simplicity and sincere faith have borne their own sweet and evident spiritual fruits. Though these texts listed represent a mere fraction of the weight of emphasis that the Lord placed upon His very words throughout the testimony of the scriptures, they have proven themselves to be the ballast that has kept many a Christian's ship upright in the storm tossed seas of Laodicea. They have fueled the courage of many who would have been mere spiritual cowards without them - those simply who would not have ever entered the arena. They have kept the fires burning in many hearts during stone-cold apostasy. They have sounded the trumpet that has led many onto the right field of battle and into the right fight. They have represented a perpetual, unmoving and unalterable landmark in the shifting sands and eroding waypoints of moral relativism, intellectual double-mindedness, and encroaching spiritual perdition.

Most people that carry a King James Bible for a reason can recite a goodly portion of God's promises about His word by heart. They heartily *amen* the advocacy of the old Book from the pulpit, and it is laughable to most to think of shifting allegiance to another kind of bible. After all, it is plainly seen by anyone who takes the time that the new English versions major in omitting crucial and indispensable words, phrases, verses, and indeed, entire passages of the scriptures. The *words,* which God Himself so stresses, are routinely and flippantly interchanged with other words, often wrongly called synonyms. These are oft found in long lists put together by men who appear to have impeccable academic credentials, who speak in sonorous and spiritual tones, and whose sense of sacredness is not the least disturbed by altering the *holy words* of their so called "*Holy Word.*"

Unfortunately, as many have learned, there is a certain sad awakening that awaits those of simple faith, who commerce in plain and evident truth, and reach reasonable and obvious conclusions. A long time ago, the apostle Paul pronounced a dire cautionary admonition, *Beware lest any man spoil you through philosophy and vain deceit, after the tradition of men, after the rudiments of the world, and not after Christ* (Col. 2:8). He preceded this warning a few books earlier with a sister passage, *But I fear lest by any means as Satan beguiled Eve through his subtlety, so your minds should be corrupted from the simplicity that is in Christ* (II Cor. 11:3). These verses, backed by many others, concisely reveal the fact that the simplicity and plainness of real spiritual truth, and the adoption, acceptance, and profit of that truth in the minds and hearts of unassuming believers, will be exposed to spoilage and corruption of both man and the devil. This is accomplished through ***subtlety***, the first revealed trait of the devil in the word of God (Gen. 3:1). The avenues of this insidious subtlety are:

- ***Philosophy*** (Col. 2:8) – Man's long, encyclopedic system of rhetorical detours around the spiritual truths of sin, depravity, judgment, retribution and redemption, Philosophy is excuse-making and spiritual blindness clothed in the ornate robes of intellectual verbiage.
- ***Vain Deceit*** (Col. 2:8) – The devil's grand accomplishment will be having *deceived the whole world* (Rev. 12:9). Men having gone whole-heartedly after the bait, and having sold themselves to complete deceit, will receive in return for that eternal price…*nothing!* Vanity. Emptiness. They gaze mesmerized into the mirror of self-interest so intently, that they give everything that matters away for *nothing!*
- ***The Tradition of Men*** (Col. 2:8) – Man's longstanding historical habit of doing something, or believing something, or embracing something, merely because "that's how we've always done it". "What did so-and-so say or write", they ask, "for he, she, or they are people whom we like, trust and admire".
- ***The Rudiments of the World*** (Col. 2:8) – The men of Saul's day longingly wanted to *be like all the nations* (I Sam. 8:20). They wanted to be subject to the same principles and rules of operation as the world, instead of being ruled by God. Spiritually blind or unwary men of the 21st century still follow in their footsteps. Human nature never changes.

In magnificent simplicity *the Lord gave the word…*(Ps. 68:11) and *…the faith which was once delivered unto the saints…* (Jd.

3), for *faith cometh by hearing, and hearing by the word of God* (Rom. 10:17).

Peter called this word *incorruptible seed* (I Pet. 1:23), and so, incorruptible it is! Once given, those words of the Living God did what they were supposed to do. They shined their plain and luminescent truths into our dank darkness. They beamed their profound and rudimentary concepts into our hearts, and even as they exposed our transgressions, ignorance, and vileness in the naked light of God's judgment, they also illuminated a straight and narrow passage by which we alien and unacceptable miscreants could step into the presence of a smiling and welcoming God.

Further, those words showed us the ways of God that extend far beyond the necessity of salvation itself. Though the temptation is to stop with the gift of eternal life and pronounce the spiritual journey complete, we must continue in His word. The babe must eventually crawl, then walk, then run. He must graduate from diapers and pap. He must mature, grow strong, and put on the armor of the seasoned soldier for Jesus Christ. Each of these steps and developments is governed by plain, simple words that flow from the heart of a holy, eternal Father, through the instruments of His penmanship, into the receptive and good ground of the honest heart of a child that loves his Father and wants to grow up to be like his Dad.

For some of us, the salvation stage and the growth stage were separated by unfortunate and fallow years. We learned a good deal about the corruption of the mind of which Paul spake in II Corinthians 11:3 and about the foul spoilage of entire segments of a life wasted. We forsook the simplicity of that lofty and honorable way for a time, thinking that the flashy tinsel and the fluorescent pleasures of the low and dirty road held for us the true satisfactions of life. In time, the stench of moral sewage and the sometimes more subtle agonies of heart, led us to raise our eyes once again to a way once forsaken, a byway where a lamp actually lighted the placement of the feet, and where a light illuminated the subtle textures of our respective paths through this life. We discovered anew the straight-from-the-shoulder plainness of the statutes of God. Those clear and unalloyed words discerned and examined us far more than we examined them. The sharp edge of the Lord's sword pierced deeply but precisely, and though the incisions were painful in their own right, the backside of that blade laid down a soothing balm into the depth of the wounds that left us knowing that the Physician well understood the pain and that we were better for having endured the steely edge. We fell in love again with a guide that spoke with the profound power of an eternal voice, yet in such elemental and unsophisticated terms that perception and understanding was a function of the heart, not of the intellect.

We found its unwavering, unblinking, stone-steady clarity an anchor in our lives, casting every situation, every conundrum, every crossroad into the light of objective and eternal truth that supersedes the earthy and carnal variables that cloud the issues and spoil the judgment of the inattentive.

Thus, as we ought, we returned to the fountain of truth again, basking in the sublime and plain light. We rested in its clear truths, labored to implement them in our lives. There was no "shadow of turning" or obscurity in our understanding that the scriptures quoted to open this chapter authorized us, admonished us, *commanded* us to render our hearts in complete subjection to the watch-care of the volume that contained the words delivered to us.

In summary, at some juncture of our Christian lives, we "King James people" were made aware that a Bible version issue existed, and then in time, and by whatever route, we became convinced of the verifiable superiority of the

Authorized Version of 1611: the King James Bible. This superiority is seen, and has been wonderfully documented and expanded upon in several categories by writers, authors and speakers, all defending the KJV.

First, there is the great body of omitted words in the new versions. It is not difficult for an honest heart to see the travesty of calling a book *The Bible* when that book simply omits – nay, *rejects and dismisses* - the number of words that the new versions do. It takes neither special training nor spectacular achievement of scholarship to discern such truth and error. In spite of the new version advocates' obsessively repetitious propaganda that nothing of doctrinal import is omitted or changed in the new versions (perhaps they protest too much), even the most rudimentary inventory reveals that Satan not only catches away the seed that is sown in the heart (Mark 4:15), but he also introduces mildew and rot even before it is sown!

Secondly, neither is it hard to apprehend how the phrasing of the new versions is without edge, impotent, enfeebled and vapid. We, of course, have heard how it is just our preference and our subjectivity of taste that prejudices our opinion against the readings of the new versions, however, the Author of the Book lives within us, and the clumsiness and awkwardness of the perversions is not something to which the Spirit bears witness. The incessant, unrelenting practice of softening hard truth, dulling sharp insight, and weakening powerful phrasing can no more be masked than can the eclipse of the sun. These two reasons are actually sufficient in themselves to allow these corruptions to decompose on the store shelves of the apostasy merchants; nevertheless we learned we had not yet been acquainted with all the shining virtues of the old Book.

Thirdly, a good many men gave the balance of their lives to explore and investigate the supremacy of the text of the King James Bible. This encompasses its Hebrew and Greek origins, its subsequent translation into the widespread languages of the Middle East, Europe, Africa and the world. It turns out that all of Plato's Gnostic cronies, the Alexandrian Cult, and the Roman Catholic spoilers never succeeded in their quest to eradicate the true lineage of God's word. Satan's little helpers with their scissors and pens did indeed manage to help turn the light out for the Dark Ages. With all their allegorizing, philosophizing, conjecturing and prevaricating, they certainly did throw up enough dust and ash to obscure the truth for vast multitudes, but as the Prince of Life could not *be holden* of death (Acts 2:24), neither could God's word be entombed in obscure antiquity. By Wycliffe's time, the true text was shining its light around the seal of the door of what Satan had hoped was its eternal tomb, and after Erasmus ransacked the libraries of Europe and cracked the Roman Catholic Church a good one, the light broke forth to illuminate the paths and inspire the hearts of an army such as the devil had never seen: Luther, Tyndale, Knox, Hus, Jerome of Prague, the Waldensians, the Albigenses, Hubemaer, and the Anabaptists. The royal and regal nature of the Antiochian Text (Byzantine, Traditional, Majority or Received Text are other somewhat interchangeable names for it) from which the King James Bible springs is not substantively deniable, and its proponents have not been reasonably answered to this hour. The widespread adoption of the text of the modern versions (the Alexandrian text) is not a product of heavenly power or of the witness of the Holy Spirit, but of perversion, marketing, deceit and ignorance.

Fourthly, no such company of spiritual and brilliant men as the King James translators has ever been assembled, before or since. The actual scholastic and intellectual achievement that qualified these men to be worthy of the work set before them is of such an extraordinary nature, that it is hard for us modern men - so bound to our conveniences and electronic gizmos – to even grasp. These men were without word processors or flash memories except for that which resided between their ears. No doubt they had much information at their fingertips, but it was not accessed by a keyboard. To embark on telling of their astonishing intellectual qualities is to tempt oneself to recite, in whole, a number of books already written. Lancelot Andrews humored himself on his annual month-long vacations by learning a new language, and thus after a mere few years had mastered most of the modern languages of Europe.[2] Andrews was said to be conversant in 15 languages at his death.[3] Further, Andrews was given the sobriquet, the "star of preachers."[4] Then there was William Bedwell, the author of a three volume Arabic Lexicon, and a Persian dictionary.[5] John Reynolds was so skilled in arts and sciences as to leave the impression that he had spent an entire lifetime in each of them.[6] He was said to be "most excellent in all tongues."[7] Far from being a mere heady intellectual, Reynolds was known and despised by the papists for his zeal and spiritual successes against them. As for Miles Smith, so expert was he in the Chaldee, Syriac and Arabic languages that they were almost as familiar as his native tongue.[8] Lawrence Chaderton left audiences to whom he preached for two hours straight pleading that he would not yet cease his sermons.[9] This is a mere sampling of the academic and spiritual qualifications of the 47 learned and spiritual men whose names we know on the AV translation committee.

---

[2] McClure, Alexander, *Translators Revived* (Maranatha Publications, Worthington, PA) p.78

[3] Ibid., p.87

[4] Ibid., p.85

[5] Ibid., p.101-102

[6] Ibid., p.133

[7] Ibid., p.132

[8] Ibid., p.143

[9] Ibid., p.115

Brethren, our trust as Bible believers is in God. Yet a King James Bible believer has the not-too-common privilege of enjoying the best of both worlds, in this case. When it comes to the spiritual side of the matter, we put our faith in the Incarnate Word and not man. Surely, Jesus Christ can word and phrase things as He pleases, and He did in the King James Bible. On the other hand, as the reward of our trust in Him, he convened a company of 47 men whose names we know who were of such unsurpassed academic excellence as to embarrass and overshadow whatever other scholarly assemblage mortal man could ever again draw together.

Fifthly, the *technique* or *method* the translators employed in their translation of the AV 1611 marks the King James as a work of extraordinary accuracy and fidelity. Though 54 men were originally chosen, 47 of their names are positively known. They were divided into six different companies and worked in three different locations: Westminster, Oxford and Cambridge. In the scripture portions assigned to them *each individual* made his own separate translation, at which point the members of his company reviewed the work. When each company completed their work, it was sent to each of the five other companies. When the entire Bible was translated, a committee of 12 selected from all the companies, reviewed the translation. Finally, what was to be known as the King James Bible came before a committee of two men to be assembled and "polished" just before being sent to the royal printer. Dear Christian, by this process, each passage of your Bible was reviewed and scrutinized ***14 times*** by what is likely the most academically accomplished assembly of men ever convened! Intellect and training aside, Sargent summarizes what is the yet loftier characteristic of their work thus, "...the ***one binding conviction*** shared by all was that they were dealing with God's sacred Truth, and that the Scriptures were the inspired, inerrant, and authoritative Word of God."[10]

Of paramount importance in understanding the superiority of the AV translators' ***technique*** is to know that there is a certain spectrum of translation philosophies that affect exactness of wording in any Bible translation work. One end would include loose, free-reading and inexact translation with regard to strictness of word meaning. The other end would seek to carry into the other language meaning, tone, emphasis and wording that is precise as possible. ***Paraphrasing*** would hold down the liberal and inexact end of the scale. Though some users of paraphrases would object to the verbiage of this summary, there is little if any reverence for precision of wording in a paraphrase. It is chiefly concerned with communicating *ideas* as opposed to *words*. The 1971 version entitled *The Living Bible* remains one of the corrupt monuments of this technique of translating. Because God inspired and preserved His every word, there is no faithful example of a paraphrased translation. The somewhat-less-corrupt method of translation is called ***Dynamic Equivalence***. Some translators would dispute that paraphrases and dynamic equivalence translations are of any significant distinction. I would not desire to dispute such a claim as they mark the method(s) of translation for all of the corrupt new bibles, and whether distinct from one another or merely a matter of degree, both are tools of corruption. For simplicity's sake here, I will present them as distinct from one another.

Dynamic Equivalence translations are known by other names: thought or idea translations, impact translations, idiomatic translations, functional equivalence translations, and common language translations. Dr. Eugene Nida of the United

---

[10] Sargent, Robert J., *Landmarks of English Bible: Manuscript Evidence* (Bible Baptist Church Publications, Oak Harbor, Washington, 1989) p.223

Bible Societies is known as something of an apostle of this method of translating the scriptures.[11] This technique is based on the idea that the scriptures must be rendered in easily understood lingo of every language and culture. This does not sound too bad on the surface, but it has led to the ridiculous idea that every cultural or ethnic subset deserves a bible in their own peculiar language including slang and euphemisms. Here in the States, we have even been cursed with a movement to put the Bible into "Ebonics" (a slang of African-American origins). One translator in India is reported to have reasoned that since a particular tribe had only sacrificed roosters to their gods and never lambs, that thus the proper dynamic equivalence translation must be rendered, *"Behold the Cock of God which taketh away the sin of the world."*[12] In his book *Christianity In Culture,* Charles Kraft says that if a missionary should find himself in a culture where a lamb is vulgar and a pig is sacred, that a translator would be compelled to translate John 1:29 as... *"Behold the pig of God."*[13] Obviously, while dynamic equivalence is concerned about *sense* and *meaning*, it is not particular about individual words and does not consider doctrinal typology sacred at all (Exod. 8:26).

While the mainstream modern English version has not resorted yet to translating the *Lamb* as a *pig*, the obsessive preoccupation of the modern translators with regard to our changing language, and the unending insistence upon putting the Bible into common daily language - no matter how degraded - is suddenly exposed for what it truly is: a translating philosophy that *would* (and actually *has*) altered vital and indispensable doctrine. How long before some evangelical doctor decides that the average city kid has no real knowledge of farm life and lambs, and thus decides to remodel the concept of the sacrificial Lamb? It should alarm any Christian that

---

[11] Ibid., p.309
[12] Ibid., p.309
[13] Ibid., p.309

people with such loose verbal boundaries, such pitiful spiritual discernment and such low esteem for accuracy should consider themselves divinely called to remold what God said. They delusively consider this a great service!

Formal Equivalence is the technique used by the King James translators, and could be described as a translation method which is as faithful to individual word meaning and sense as possible, while still maintaining readability. Most people have heard how stilted and incomplete a word for word translation from one language to another can be. You can't really use a French dictionary to translate an English sentence into French that is acceptable to a Frenchman's ear. There are great differences in word meanings, depths and tones, and the grammatical construction of sentences varies greatly from language to language. However, in formal equivalence, the idea is not to merely translate the *gist*, but the *literal words* and *sense* insofar as possible, including the *style* and *emphasis* of the words. A translator of this type wouldn't dream of translating a lamb as a pig. The AV translators put words in italics that were required in order to complete the meaning. They retained the much maligned *thee's, thou's, thy's* and *ye's* for pronouns, as well as the *–est's, --eth's* and *–edst's* for verb endings in order to be exact with regard to person, number, and time. Indeed, in spite of much noise made to the contrary, Harvard University's *Literary Guide to the Bible* pronounces that the King James translation "…is still arguably the version that best preserves the literary effects of the original languages," that what most unthinkingly describe as archaic, ought best be assumed to reflect "an attempt to reproduce the original's word or phrase order," that "the Authorized Version translators have taken care to reproduce the syntactic details of the original," that "its overall effect is still much more Hebraic than English," and that "the Authorized Version has the kind of transparency which makes it possible for the reader to see the original clearly."[14]

The stringency and precision of ***Formal Equivalence*** did not produce what many might expect: a stilted, awkward and dry translation. Indeed, one of the first things out of the mouths of most of the King James Bible's worst detractors is the acknowledgment of the AV's poetic flow and the majestic and unsurpassed beauty of its language.

Returning to the narration of our diverse individual journeys back to the Bible, there came a day when we knew we held the Holy Scriptures in our hands. Whether having digested the whole of the material above, or having been of a less informed yet more childlike faith, we knew there was a God that loved us, Who had sent His Son to atone for us, and Who had given us His inspired and preserved words to bear record to His will and His deeds. We held God's words in our hands, and all those words were contained in a well-proven, long fruitful, majestic old Book: The King James Bible - the AV 1611.

It was royal and beautiful in its language. It was accurate and it contained every word that it was supposed to have. It was powerful and incisive, and this was evident by how the world of lost men, and even a great many saved ones, hated its unveiled judgments and its shocking assessments. It came from the correct roots of language and history, had the proper textual pedigree, and could be traced back into antiquity by following the blood trail that told its own gruesome tale of true Christian fidelity, love for Christ, grace under fire and almost unimaginable courage. These deeds were all accomplished by saints and martyrs of old while being haunted, tracked, hated and tested by all the torment and terror that Satan could devise. The King James Bible was translated by

---

[14] Riplinger, Gail, *The Language of the King James Bible* (A. V. Publications, Ararat, VA, 1998) p.133-134

genuinely spiritual men who were the best of the best, academically. From Wycliffe's genius and courage, to Erasmus' profound labors, to Tyndale's linguistic excellence, the translators added their own, and being blessed by God, it was enough. With God's help they did things the right way, made wise decisions, exercised discretion, held themselves to rigid standards, and delivered to the world the King James Bible. It was a polished and purified work. It was, by anyone's standards, monumental. It spoke to the world in its last days in the universal language of the last days. It was authorized by a king (Ecc. 8:4), the king had a Jewish name, and he ruled a land that the world would set its clocks by in time to come. That same world would have to locate its position on the globe by orienting itself longitudinally on a British "zero."

It is sad to say that a certain naiveté accompanied the esprit de corps, the élan, and the perceived unity that animated us in those first days after we found our Bible. The sense of being under the full and manifest authority of the King of Kings made our hearts swell, and the sense of brotherhood with fellow believers who were under the same umbrella gave us a sense of belonging and inspired us to straighten our backs, tuck our chins and suck in our guts. The *goodly heritage* of Psalm 16:6 had true substance, and we were conscious of its weight under our arms and of its swelling presence in our hip pockets and purses. We were King James Bible Believers and we had a Book! We had finally found our crowd. It was good to stand in holy purpose with fellow soldiers in the right army. We had joined the ranks of the faithful. We were living Jude 3 and Proverbs 4:20-22. Our shelves were as loaded as an armory with books by men defending the faith found in the AV. Our cassette players, and in time, our CD and MP3 players were fed tapes and discs by those whose ardency for the Old Book seemed utterly without any wavering or question. We appreciated pulpits and scholastic chairs occupied by men whose words were bold and strong, their stand seemed so clear, their arguments so unfaltering. We looked up to those who had so assisted us in triangulating on the truth. It was good to be on the right team, shoulder to shoulder with the right people!

Alas, many people have had the experience of beginning employment at a company whose image and reputation was immaculate, only to learn that the workings day to day within fell short of the image projected and the utopia expected. Many, too, have had the experience of finding the "perfect church", which in time revealed itself to be inhabited by the less than perfect. Of course, in time most people learn life's precept that these disappointments are to be expected. Indeed, this principle applies to many things in life: friends, spouses, children, romance, dreams, etc. On the road of life, preconceived idealistic notions usually are "T-boned" by reality on a regular basis. In spite of the idealistic mottos and assurances cited at the recruitment office, no army achieves battle readiness without casualties, insubordination, bitter failure, ambitious self-service and predation within the ranks. No corporation's pay scale, benefit package, and public image will ever stifle completely the baseness of the fallen nature of its workforce. The precept is that, except for Heaven and Christ Himself, all of the romanticism of idealistic notions and expectations are disappointed at one point or another in this temporal domain.

Tragically, it also applies to the King James crowd. Some learned what it was to be suddenly and bitterly disappointed. For others there was more of a gradual dawning of comprehension that in spite of the public stand and pulpit rhetoric of some, not everyone who waved an AV 1611 or penned a passionate defense of it actually held it in the same esteem they so openly stated. In our simplicity, we had guilelessly accepted that a man who condemned the new versions for their omissions and corruptions, while endorsing the King James for its accuracy and purity, was actually of the same mind as we were. Why should we not think so? The manifestly evident promises of God's word in our language said that God preserved those very words for us, and that we were responsible as stewards to keep those very words and *to earnestly contend* (Jd. 3) for the faith that they imparted. We had taken at face value that a church advertising itself as a King James church would rigorously believe and defend every word of the King James Bible. It seemed incongruous that a church which was founded on the AV and advertised itself as a King James church would be sheepish or reserved about its stance. Why should we have doubted the forthrightness or fidelity of that pastor, who with such inflamed and impassioned eloquence, waved the Old Book, pledged his allegiance to it, and magnified it as the unchanging word of the Living God, the only hope and the only light for a world of sinners? Should we have actually been able to anticipate that the same man sitting behind his desk would so seamlessly transition from the adamant pronouncements of his pulpit to the semantic world of doublespeak and dual authorities when away from the scrutiny of his congregation? How is it that we should have fortified ourselves, only to learn that the trumpeted slogans and carefully forged reputations of conservative Christian educational institutions that professed such unwavering love for the old faith, were mere facades that hid the same machinations of infidelity in their classrooms as other liberal schools which at least were honest about *their* positions?

It was with gradually opened eyes and a certain crestfallen dread that we realized that some of the authors and AV defenders who had restored the foundations of our faith, had somehow themselves failed to come to the logical end they had helped us reach. Indeed, we did have to consider the possibility that our own line of reasoning had led us to ill-balanced conclusions; that some sequence of mistakes in logic or discretion had short-circuited the soundness of the position at which we had arrived. This honest possibility must be acknowledged, but so must its opposing counterpoint. Lofty-minded, sincere and spiritual Christian academics are sinners just like common men, and they are indeed just as apt to make mistakes in reasoning as any other mortal. Every scholar does still have a fallen nature, in spite of his intelligence or his academic accomplishments, and he is just as capable as any of us of arriving at some conclusion of a spiritual nature detrimentally influenced by the subtleties of motivation, pride, presumption or ambition. Sadly, many of us woke one day to discover that some that had assisted us out of darkness into such clear and plain light had somehow themselves become mired, entangled, or perhaps enamored by something in the shadows, never emerging to the same position as we held, and do still hold.

It is important at this juncture to once again reiterate that the motivation here is not to alienate, humiliate or divide. The purpose is not to make old wounds bleed, to resurrect old disputes, or to disparage embattled saints either dead or alive. Many of these were, or even are, soldiers on the battlefield of the truth of God, and where they have helped and built the believers, they deserve commendation and gratitude. Importantly though, where their constructive contributions need to be recognized and honored, their failures in reasoning and faith also must come to light. The spotlight of accomplishment and honor also reveals blemishes and oversights. Openly publishing a position is an act of invitation for scrutiny and critique of the author's facts, logic and conclusions. Those who have proved to be a help to Bible believers need not be cast in a harsh nor adversarial light, nor should we cheapen the monumental value of the contributions of some of those whose work we must here evaluate. Nevertheless, to look objectively at where their work led them is critical to the understanding that perhaps their final conclusions with regard to the words of God were not all what they should and could have been. Each generation of Christians has its own responsibility before God for the *faith once delivered unto the saints* (Jd. 3). Each generation, in some respects, must refine the imperfections of their fathers as well as building on their true foundations. If this is not the case, then we should just go purchase the works of the earliest church fathers and blithely live by their 2nd and 3rd century conclusions!

A perfect example of such a profound and bona fide work is the book *Believing Bible Study* by Edward F. Hills. Most King James Bible believers have been greatly affected by this book either directly or indirectly. It remains one of the groundbreaking works and very few pro-King James theses are written which do not make some reference to it. In 225 plus pages, Dr. Hills makes the classic and yet substantively unanswered case for the AV 1611. The entire book is a tribute to God's greatness and faithfulness, and it greatly magnifies and glorifies God's processes for delivering to us the masterwork of English Bible translation: the Authorized Version of 1611. It is greatly edifying, devotionally inspiring and very enlightening in respect to the technical aspects of the transmission of the biblical text. First copyrighted in 1967, it came at a crucial time in the battle for the Bible in these last days. However, a third of the way through the book, a very critical issue is broached and discussed. It is still a very critical issue today, but Dr. Hills' treatment of the subject sounds a note that is discordant with the spirit of the rest of the book and is disharmonious with the spirit of faith he has helped instill in so many King James Bible believers. He says:

> **Is the King James Version Perfect? – Not Ideally but Practically**
>
> Admittedly the King James Version is **not ideally perfect**. **No translation ever can be**. But it is the product of such God-guided

> scholarship that it is practically perfect. Its **errors are very few and very minor**.[15]

To those who have been exposed to the double-tongued semantics of the anti-King James crowd, hearing one of our own resort to the Clintonesque distinctions of "ideal perfection" vs. "practical perfection" is more than a little bit repulsive. To then concede to the enemy the issue of perfection, the imperfection of all translations, and errors of the AV, though he categorizes them as "minor," is in a manner a denunciation of all he had, and would, establish in the book. It does not mean that Hills was apostate. It means there was an inconsistency in his own faith, and as such, it becomes a fly in the ointment that we have to deal with. He goes on to say a bit later:

> It is possible, of course, that in the future the English language will change so much that **a new translation of the Bible will be absolutely necessary**. But in that case any version that we prepare today would be equally antiquated.[16]

Again the concession, even hypothetically, of a complete abandonment of the AV after all that has been researched and written to elevate it and magnify it – after all that has been done to identify it as preserved and God-ordained – is unthinkable. So, why did he reason thus? Why would he concede this?

In another of his undeniably profound works, *The King James Version Defended,* Dr. Hills makes a very impassioned, very learned and very inspiring argument in defense of the AV, but once again batters his foot against the stumbling-stone of translation. He acknowledges the providential guidance of the

---

[15] Hills, Edward F., *Believing Bible Study Key to the Space Age* (The Christian Research Press: Des Moines, Iowa, 1967, 1977), p.83.
[16] Ibid., p.85

AV translators and remonstrates for retaining the present form of the King James Bible, but again he makes a disturbing concession saying

> Hence we receive the King James Version as the providentially appointed English Bible. Admittedly this venerable version is **not absolutely perfect, but it is trustworthy**.[17]

In the next paragraph he continues along this line:

> It is possible, if the Lord tarry, that in the future the English language will change so much that a **new English translation** of the Bible will be **absolutely necessary**.[18]

Earlier in the book, yet in this same vein, he elaborates on archaic words:

> There are several ways to handle this matter of obsolete words and meanings in the King James Version. Perhaps the best way is to place the modern equivalent in the margin... Another way would be to place the more modern word **in brackets beside the older word**.[19]

Most King James Bible believers are accustomed enough to marginal notes in various publications of the King James Bible to understand that they are opinions of man, whether they are correct or incorrect. However, should the matter of archaic words be dealt with as Hills suggested secondly – placing the up to date word beside the archaic word

---

[17] Hills, Edward F., *The King James Version Defended* (The Christian Research Press, Des Moines, Iowa, 1956, 1973, 1979), p.230

[18] Ibid., p.230

[19] Ibid., p.218

within the scriptural text – most every believer who venerates the scriptures knows that that action would be an invasion of sacred territory: the very text of the Holy Scripture! Again, it is regrettable to hear such a valuable contributor to the Bible's cause yield such important ground.

In his noble and worthwhile argument on why the King James should be retained in our modern world, Dr. Hills enumerates six things, which are all very good points, yet in his sixth reason, he says:

> ...the King James Version is the historic Bible of the English-speaking Protestants. Upon it God, working providentially, has placed the stamp of His approval through the usage of many generations of Bible-believing Christians. Hence, if we believe in God's providential preservation of the Scriptures, we will retain the King James Version, for in doing so we will be following the clear leading of the Almighty.[20]

Granted, Dr. Hills did not intend for the final of his six reasons to stand alone as an all-sufficient reason to retain the Kings James; however, pounding the pulpit for historicity's sake, while actually denying the argument for perfections sake, is not exactly the soul-stirring trumpet call that boils the blood of the saints to do battle for their Lord. This is especially true when the Lord did actually and plainly go on record as promising perfection.

Dr. David Otis Fuller is another defender of the King James Bible to whom many of us openly profess to owe a debt of gratitude for his great labor and manifest courage as a writer and editor. His works go quite hand in hand with the labors of Dr. Hills. He is much remembered for publishing edited works

---

[20] Ibid., p.219-220

of textual experts who resolutely defended the AV 1611 and the Hebrew and Greek texts from which it was translated.

It is important to set forth at the very outset that after the publication of his works, Dr. Fuller in personal conversation with Dr. Sam Gipp, as related to me by Dr. Gipp, revealed that he had advanced significantly beyond his published position, and came to hold the King James Bible, not merely as a faithful translation, but as the very word of God itself! A Bible-believer's heart rejoices in this, for while his published works were of great import there were again troublesome echoes of discord to an attuned ear:

> *Which Bible?* is not a repudiation of scholarship. **It is not an argument for the inerrancy of a translation.**.. It is a long-overdue defense of the worth of the old Authorized Version...[21]

If the flyleaf is representative of Dr. Fuller's position at the height of his publishing career, the AV needed to be defended, but was not inerrant Fuller's then-held position can be ascertained in the following:

> ...the reader is encouraged to maintain confidence in the King James Version as a **faithful translation** based upon a reliable text.[22]

We cannot help but notice Fuller's assessment that the King James is merely a "faithful translation", and for that matter that the text of the Greek is merely "reliable".

---

[21] Fuller, David Otis, *True or False?* (Grand Rapids International Publications, Grand Rapids, Michigan, 1973, 1975) flyleaf

[22] Fuller, David Otis, *Which Bible* (Grand Rapids International Publications, Grand Rapids, Michigan, 1970) p. 6

In his book *Which Bible,* Fuller published a work by George Sayles Bishop, a man who was very critical of the English Revised Version of 1881, which, of course, began the avalanche of new versions, and which also provided a stage and a spotlight for the scripture altering atrocities of Westcott and Hort. Though defending the AV, Bishop nonetheless exposes his own shaky foundation in saying

> That **a few changes might be made in both Testaments** [of the King James], for the better, no man pretends to deny...[23]

Bishop plainly is unopposed to changing certain portions of the New and Old Testament in the KJV.

Reading Sir Robert Anderson, who was obviously appalled by the travesties of the RV of 1881, a Bible-believer today knowing the kind of mileage Satan has gotten out of the issue, must grind his teeth when Anderson says,

> But **what concerns us here is not the changes in the translation** [of the AV], **but the far more serious matter of the changes in the text** [the Greek text].[24]

Anderson may have defended the King James in a measure, but he is not as troubled by changes in it as he is in changes in the Greek text. We are not for changing the Greek text, by any means, but Anderson unwittingly shows us his lack of esteem for the AV in comparison to the Greek.

Dr. Benjamin G. Wilkinson wrote *Our Authorized Bible Vindicated*, which volume has become a mainstay in the battle for the King James and for the *Textus Receptus* NT Greek text.

---

[23] Ibid., p.106
[24] Ibid., p.120

The battle for the right Greek text was one that had to be fought, and we thank God for those who were engaged on that battlefield during the 19th and 20th centuries, but it is painful to hear the acquiescence to the enemy that reads thus:

> The friends and devotees of the King James Bible **naturally wished** that **certain retouches** might be given the book that would **replace words** counted obsolete,...**correct** what they considered a few and **clear blemishes** in the Received Text, so that its bitter opponents...might be answered.[25]

It is plain that Wilkinson considered retouches to the AV, replacement of words, and correction "natural".

The learned Phillip Mauro was a Supreme Court Justice and a King James defender. He was on the Lord's side in respect to his Christianity and the Bible issue, and he was thus a friend to our cause, *BUT*

> ...it became increasingly evident that, notwithstanding the excellencies of that great and admirable work (the AV), there were particulars wherein, for one cause or another, **it admitted of (and indeed called for) correction....** It was found also that **corrections in translation were demanded here and there, particularly in regard to the tenses of verbs**...[26]

---

[25] Ibid., p.283-284

[26] Fuller, David Otis, *True or False?* (Grand Rapids International Publications, Grand Rapids, Michigan, 1973, 1975) p.59

Unfortunately, Mauro's comments are self-explanatory to real Bible-believing Christians.

John W. Burgon is a name recognized by nearly all who have attempted to even scratch the surface of the King James issue. His well deserved fame is not only for excellence of scholarship, great power in authorship, and thorough defense of the Received Text of the AV 1611, but more especially for the head to head battle that he fought with Westcott and Hort. Those appalling reprobates both attempted, and frankly, succeeded in commandeering the Revision Committee of 1881 into accepting a debauched textual theory, grossly corrupt manuscripts, and eventually, a perverted bible text that has "done Satan proud." Burgon, though a champion of the Received text, disappoints in one respect, and it is also interesting to note the aforementioned Edward Hills introduction of the statement made by Burgon:

> In his controversy with the revisionists of 1881 Burgon stood forth as the uncompromising champion of the King James (Authorized) Version. "As a companion in the study and for private edification: as a book of reference for critical purposes, especially in respect of difficult and controverted passages – **we hold that a revised edition of the Authorized Version of our English Bible** (if executed with consummate ability and learning) **would at any time be a work of inestimable value**..."[27]

Burgon did go on to say that the idea of undertaking a translation intended to supersede the AV was not to be entertained. Hills clarifies that Burgon's purpose was to defend

---

[27] Fuller, David Otis, *Counterfeit or Genuine Mark 16? John 8?* (Grand Rapids International Publications, Grand Rapids, Michigan, 1975) p.23-24

the Byzantine Text of the AV. It is hoped that the reader might ascertain that this is a dangerous dance of semantics with the devil. First, an uncompromising championship of the King James Bible is not the exact same thing as championing the Textus Receptus (TR). Truthfully, Burgon championed the TR, not the King James. Secondly, Burgon was quite open to a revision of the AV, but did not want the old superseded by the new. If it was not clear to this acknowledged old warhorse *then*, it is perfectly clear to any clear-minded soul *now*, that granting latter day Bible-correctors latitude to *revise* the King James Bible is the equivalent of giving them utter license to *corrupt and pervert.* It should further be stated that countenancing a Bible for "private edification" and as "a book of reference for critical purposes" versus a Bible for public and non-critical purposes is short-sighted, hypocritical, and smacks of the doctrine of the Nicolaitanes.

Jasper James Ray soundly affected the faith of many in his book *God Wrote Only One Bible,* copyrighted first in 1955. Its sister pamphlet, the *New Eye Opener* is found tucked behind the front or back Bible covers of countless Bible-believers, and is still passed on to many an inquirer seeking light on the Bible version issue. An unquestioned help, and a work of profound effect since its publication, it still trumpets forth a sour note for someone who is not a Greek student, yet who still knows that the King James Bible emanates a power inexplicable by mere accurate translation. Ray says:

> **The Bible God wrote has been providentially preserved for us in the Greek Textus Receptus**, from which the King James Bible was translated in 1611.[28]

And a few pages later:

---

[28] Ray, Jasper James, *God Wrote Only One Bible*, (The Eye Opener Publishers, Eugene, Oregon, 1955) p.106

> HELP SAVE OUR GOD-GIVEN BIBLE
> Let's pray, plan, work and pull together to help save **our God-inspired Bible** from the "scrap-heap" of this modern hodge-podge of corrupted Revised Bibles. **The Greek Textus Receptus ought to be used in our Bible Schools** instead of the text of Westcott & Hort.[29]

It is plain that Ray held that the actual Bible that God wrote was the Greek Textus Receptus of the New Testament, and that it, and not the AV 1611, was the ultimate appeal.

These above-mentioned men, having fought a good fight, have undoubtedly ascended to be present with the Lord, and are quite soon to receive their well-earned rewards. They are our brothers and our friends, and their laurels await the heavenly reunion. So, let us move a bit forward in time and take just a sampling of a few of the contemporary defenders of the King James. After all, it is unlikely that even as astute a man as Burgon could have quite predicted the expansive havoc and extensive damage wrought by the insidious philosophies that won the day in the RV committee of 1881. Men residing in the late 20th and early 21st century have seen some things in fulfillment that even Hills and Fuller could not fully predict.

In his work, *Touch Not the Unclean Thing*, David Sorenson writes what is a sound review of the material found in nearly all the major 20th century works attesting to the historical and textual facts and characteristics of the Textus Receptus and the King James Bible. His position is not uncommon at all among AV 1611 defenders, but he makes a point to distinguish his position from the following:

> ...the advocates of **the King James only position** have a severe problem. Most of **them**

---

[29] Ibid., p.117

> hold the view that the King James Version of 1611 as a *translation* was inspired and thus has no need for further *translational* revision.[30]

It probably should be mentioned that King James Bible haters throw the "King James Only" nomenclature at just about anyone who stands in disagreement with them in hopes that they will be scared away. The animal equivalent is that of a Chihuahua with its hackles up: the opposing dog is humored, but doesn't feel particularly threatened. Sorenson would be considered "King James Only" in many circles. In a later chapter we will discuss the ramifications of whether it is so wrong to consider that something originally "inspired" might still be "inspired." To make a long story short, if *all scripture was given by inspiration of God (II Tim.3:16)*, and what you have in your hand is the scripture, then that is still *inspired scripture*, for all scripture was given by inspiration! For now, the main point is that yet another helpful voice in the battle for the AV 1611 obviously holds that the sanctity of the King James, as translated, is contestable.

In the publication of Donald Brake's Master's thesis, as referenced by David Otis Fuller in *Counterfeit or Genuine*, Brake's final word on the doctrine of the preservation of the scriptures is to simply quote the Westminster Confession:

> The Old Testament **in Hebrew**, and the New Testament **in Greek**, **being immediately inspired by God**, and, by His singular care and providence, kept pure in all ages, are therefore

---

[30] Sorenson, David H., *Touch Not The Unclean Thing The Text Issue and Separation* (Northstar Baptist Ministries, Duluth, MN, 2001) p.18

> authentical; so as, in all controversies of religion, **the Church is finally to appeal to them**.[31]

According to Brake, the Church's final appeal is to the Hebrew and Greek. Many undoubtedly agree, but is that what you mean when ***you*** magnify the King James Bible as the word of God?

Floyd Nolen Jones wrote an excellent work called *Which Version Is The Bible*. It is a very fine resource and exalts the AV 1611. He is consistent in his theme of exalting the King James Bible throughout the book, and it is a shame to have to mention one disappointing juncture where, in discussing one of the great neck-breakers in the King James Bible (the archaic words), he says:

> There are only several hundred obsolete or archaic words remaining within the 1611 King James Bible... These few **could and should** be brought up to date. **The "eth" endings could also easily be changed**... although care must be taken as to its rendering else many times the actual meanings may be lost.[32]

The idea that bringing up to date certain words – presumably "several hundred" according to his statement – ***could*** be done, is latitude that cannot be granted. Indeed, it should be argued that a Christian would do well to elevate his vocabulary and reading comprehension instead of degrading the word of God to his own level of ignorance and lack of initiative.

---

[31] Fuller, David Otis, *Counterfeit or Genuine Mark 16? John 8?* (Grand Rapids International Publications, Grand Rapids, Michigan, 1975) p.214

[32] Jones, Floyd Nolen, *Which Version Is The Bible* (KingsWord Press, Goodyear, AZ, 1989, 2006) p.78

Even unsaved people deepen their vocabularies for their careers and for financial gain. Should not Christians, then, broaden their vocabularies for their Savior? Jones goes another disturbing step further, though, and states that changing those words ***should*** be done!

Jones, after suggesting that the "eth" endings on verbs could be changed as well, does an odd thing and subsequently defends the AV's old-fashioned usage of pronouns like "ye", "thee", "thou", "thy" and "thine" as being much more accurate than the modern equivalents because they denote singulars and plurals. While he says the "eth" endings have served a "vital function" in the AV, he seems strangely unresolved about the fact that the old verb endings are themselves a logical extension of the distinctive accuracy of the pronouns, and he leaves the door very much open for Bible correcting camels to stick their noses through the door, and to subsequently assume permanent residence.

Dr. Donald A. Waite is perhaps one of the premier scholars of our day with regard to traditional Bible texts. He has had a long career in defense of the texts from whence our AV 1611 is born, and is an earnest defender of the King James as a translation. He is the President of the Dean Burgon Society, the Founder, President and Director of The Bible For Today, and is the Pastor for the Bible For Today Baptist Church in Collingswood, New Jersey. Dr. Waite's material is quite helpful and informative. He has done a mule's burden of work in research and publishing, and he is a voice for Baptistic principles in doctrine and in history, separation from the world, and conservative music. On the cover of his book, *Defending The King James Bible A Fourfold Superiority*, the subtitle on both the cover and the title page is *God's Word Kept Intact In English*. A novice, unaccustomed to the specificity and fine distinctions of wording, might draw from the title and subtitle that the King James Version would be unequivocally defended in the book. It is defended in the book only in a measure, for Dr. Waite has reservations regarding The AV 1611. In fielding whether the King James is without translational errors, Waite answers,

> Yes, I would say regarding translation errors that I haven't found any either in the Old Testament Hebrew or in the New Testament Greek. **I don't like to use the word "inerrant" of any English (or other language) translation of the Bible** because the word "inerrant" is implied from the Greek Word, *theopneustos* (2 Timothy 3:16) which means literally, "God-Breathed."[33]

Continuing, and in regard to the King James translators,

> There are **many other choices in English they could have used**, but what they did pick was within the rules of both Hebrew and Greek grammar and English grammar. Therefore, I have not found any translation errors in the King James Bible.[34]

Most true Bible-believers would be a good deal less reserved than Waite in response to a direct question about translation errors in the AV. The good Dr. has not found any errors yet, but leaves the door open to the possibility! Here, once again, we find a respected old warrior shying from the prospect of inerrancy in translation. Further, in reference to his book subtitle, we are confident that the inspired writers of the originals were not accorded a tremendous amount of latitude as far as word choices were concerned since, all agree, those were

---

[33] Waite, D.A., *Defending The King James Bible A Fourfold Superiority* (The Bible For Today Press, Collingswood, N.J., 1992) p.239-240

[34] Ibid., p.240

the words of God. If the King James does indeed keep God's word *intact* in English, as Waite's subtitle purports, and if God did preserve His word in the AV, how is it that the translators of the King James had so "many other choices in English" that they "could have used"?

We cannot help but observe that our list of King James defenders spend a great deal of time establishing biblically how inspiration and preservation are God-ordained, God-honoring, and God-mediated processes, with the hand of God manifest at the critical junctures of Church history. Further, they all, without fail, go into the extraordinary qualifications of the AV translators; the hand of God being evident in the care, the fervency, the excellence, the scholarly discretion, the technique, and indeed the unequaled distinction of their combined assemblage. Having thus established the providential momentousness of the AV committee's qualifications and accomplishments, and having sold their audience on God's wonderful handiwork within that committee, they then proceed to run as scalded cats from the reasonable deductions to which they have led their readers. If God was so much "in" the machinations of the AV committee, why is even the idea of discussing *inerrancy* or *perfection in translation* so outlandish and unthinkable?

In the end, the reason that Dr. Waite is so non-emphatic about the King James (despite his book's title and subtitle) is because, to him, the King James is not actually the word of God. According to him, the words in the Masoretic Hebrew and Received Greek texts are the words of God.

> …it is my own personal conviction and belief, after studying this subject since 1971, that **the WORDS of the Received Greek and Masoretic Hebrew texts that underlie the King James Bible** are the very WORDS which

> God has PRESERVED down through the centuries, being the **exact WORDS of the ORIGINALS themselves.**[35]

We do not dispute that God preserved the correct Greek and Hebrew texts, but ultimately it is plain that for Dr. Waite authority is derived from the Greek and Hebrew texts in finality, and that the AV 1611 is only authoritative in a measure. In fact, on pages 247-248 of his work, Waite advocates the use of various lexicons and theological dictionaries,

> … if you really want to see what the various Greek word meanings are.[36]

Waite's Dean Burgon Society Statement on Preservation reads in part,

> The [AV] translators did such a fine job in their translation task that we can without apology hold up the Authorized Version of 1611 and say, **"This is the word of God!"** while at the same time realizing that, in some verses, **we must go back to the underlying original language Texts for complete clarity**, and also compare scripture with scripture.[37]

So how *intact* is the word of God kept in the English language in Dr. Waite's view? Not *intact* enough to be the final appeal. While Waite advocates returning to the original language texts for "complete clarity", many of us have had the experience of seeing the process of appealing to Greek and

---

[35] Ibid., p.48

[36] Ibid., p.248

[37] Cloud, David W., *Myths About The Modern Bible Versions* (Way of Life Literature, Oak Harbor, Washington, 1999) p.112-113

Hebrew yield nothing but a deafening cacophony of confused noise, further uncertainty, and greater obscurity of truth than when the seeker began his multilingual journey. Perhaps "scripture with scripture" should be Waite's first resort instead of mere afterthought. In the end, God's word has ***not*** been kept *intact* enough in English for Waite to rely upon it when push comes to shove. *Intact*, in his mind, turns out to be a very relative term instead of an exact one. This position is a disappointment to those who can read plain words and promises from the scriptures, but it is also a different stance than the title and subtitle of his book imply.

Another valuable, contemporary defender of the AV 1611 is David Cloud. A missionary to Nepal, Cloud has been a prolific author of very helpful material. He is a well reasoned voice for Baptistic principles and separation. He has written very fine material which dissects the Rock & Roll and Contemporary Christian music movements. He writes for the Fundamental Baptist Information service, has published *O Timothy* magazine for years, and heads the Way of Life ministries. Again, a good deal of his material is written in the defense of the King James and its underlying texts, and is truly good resource material.

In his book, *Myths About the Modern Bible Versions*, Cloud says this:

> I do not believe there are mistakes in the King James Bible.
>
> I do believe **there are places that could be translated more clearly for readers today**. I do believe **there are antiquated words that could be brought up to date. There are words and passages that could be translated differently. (Note I did not say *should* be, but**

> ***could* be.)** To say, that there are changes that **could be made** in the KJV is entirely different from saying it contains mistakes.[38]

As much as we try to appreciate the distinction between *mistakes* versus *translating something differently,* and the further delineation between *could* and *should,* the fact is that we, on scriptural grounds, are still dealing with the precept: *Man shall not live by bread alone, but by* ***every word*** *that proceedeth out of the mouth of God* (Matt.4:4). The concession by Cloud that the AV *could* be translated differently in some to-this-point indeterminate places, is an open revelation that in Cloud's judgment, the very inviolable words of the Living God are not contained in whole in the King James Bible, but in the Greek and Hebrew that underlies the King James Bible.

In like manner, Cloud reiterates his position in his 2006 book, *The Glorious History of the King James Bible.* David Cloud gets two distinct concepts tangled in his arguments, and therefore we can conclude that he has them entangled in his mind, as well. These two distinct and separate concepts are inspiration and the perfection (or inerrancy) of the King James Bible. He thinks, as do most scholars who are not particularly interested in representing a King James Bible believer's position accurately, that claiming inerrancy or perfect accuracy for the AV is the same as claiming that it was *given by inspiration.* We will address the often intentional sophistry of intermingling the two concepts at a later time. Cloud posits this:

> **I do not say that the KJV could never be changed** or that its words are always the very best that they possibly could be (though I do not believe it will ever be replaced in this apostate hour)… I also know that I am not scholar enough

---

[38] Ibid., p.111

> to correct them…I have only begun to learn what the KJV translators can teach me.[39]

Cloud's defense of the King James is appreciated, as are his humbly worded sentiments regarding his own abilities, but again, the specter of a future "revision" of the AV still is evident in his thoughts. Note again that the possibility does abide as some sort of prospect, though he feels it unlikely:

> I do not believe that a better English language translation of the Masoretic Hebrew and the Greek Received Text could be made in our day… **As for a new revision of the King James Bible, we are not opposed to it in theory** if it were done after the fashion of the previous revisions in the 18th century… This type of revision has been made before, and **we see no reason in theory why it could not be done again**.[40]

Cloud, as a KJV defender, first hands us a providential treasure, and then smashes our fingers when we reach for it. This characteristic is actually quite typical of the vast majority of AV defenders, for they readily acknowledge its excellence and the hand of God - to a point. The critical issue, though, is whether there is something truly providential about the specific wording of the King James Bible in total. To these gentlemen, there is no genuine "hands off" policy about the AV 1611. For practicality's sake, they are willing to leave it as it is and defend it - to a point. As the brother stated, however, they are theoretically open to editing and opposed to proclaiming it perfect as it stands. To remind the reader, the purpose of this book is not to skewer these men verbally for disagreeing in

---

39 Cloud, David W., *The Glorious History of the King James Bible* (Way of Life Literature, Port Huron, MI, 2006) p.213.

40 Ibid., p.214.

measure with us. For that matter, it is not to disparage their persons nor the main body of their research and work The purpose is to point to some specific matters they have not discussed or evaluated insofar as is known.

In like manner, Dr. Thomas Strouse from the Department of Theology at Tabernacle Baptist Theological Seminary in Virginia Beach, Virginia, states as follows:

> **THE KJV IS THE WORD OF GOD IN THE ENGLISH LANGUAGE.** It has no errors in it because it carefully reflects the original language texts closest to the autographs. **The AV**, like all translations, **has 'language limitations'**, **but these are not errors**.[41]

So then, to Dr. Strouse, the King James Bible is the word of God. It has *no errors*. It has "language limitations," but these are *not errors*. These limitations leave us with a Bible that has *no errors*, ***but neither he, nor these other men, can bring themselves to defend the AV as "inerrant"*** **and totally perfect!** Indeed, they recoil reflexively from such an idea. If it has no errors, how is it not inerrant?

Let it be said yet again: these men are not God's enemies, nor are they the enemies of the Bible. Just the opposite is true. We are brothers. They are the friends of Jesus Christ. We all can stand in appreciation of a large body of their work. On a percentage basis, we agree more with them than the Sinaiticus and Vaticanus manuscripts agree with one another! This is not written to disparage or to bloody a brother. It is written to document their positions regarding the perfection of God's words. On the subject of the inspiration and the preservation of those words, these are their published

---

[41] Cloud, David W., *Myths About The Modern Bible Versions* (Way of Life Literature, Oak Harbor, Washington, 1999) p.163

statements, and the views and judgments reached by these men have been carefully reasoned, worded and crafted. They have drawn fine lines of distinction, and have undoubtedly measured their verbiage with much forethought. They are unashamed of their conclusions and have published them because they believe them to be right, and to be a help to Christians.

But, are they right?

Somewhere along the ongoing path of growing spiritually, many of us discovered that the person of Jesus Christ was the great divisive issue in this life. *Yea, and all that will live godly in Christ Jesus shall suffer persecution* (2 Tim. 3:12). Christ came to set *at variance* (Matt. 10:35) and *there was a division among the people because of him* (Jn. 7:43). In many cases friends have parted, families have sundered, and bitter words and accusations have opened breaches that remain unclosed. Then again, it is ***the Bible*** which shows and manifests Jesus Christ to us. The only Jesus that is true ***is the Jesus of the Bible***. The modern Church is perhaps the greatest of idol factories in its unending modifications made to the person of Christ. To some He is a hippy, to others a vegetarian, to others an animal rights activist, and to some, a liberal humanist. As the Lord so aptly said, *every imagination of the thoughts of his* [man's] *heart was only evil continually* (Gen. 6:5). Since we truly only know Christ by and through His word, that means that the first crucial, and thus, divisive issue is the words of God - even more so than the person of Christ!

With Eve, Satan attacked the words of God in order to cast aspersions on the person of God (Gen. 3:4). The Jews of Jesus' day saw clearly His person and the open manifestation of His power, but it was plainly what He *said* that moved them to judicial murder. In fact, even before Christ's words could be believed by the men of His day, He plainly stated that they had to believe something else first – Moses' written words! *For had ye believed Moses, ye would have believed me: for he* ***wrote*** *of me. But* ***if ye believe not his writings, how shall ye believe my words*** (Jn. 5:46-47)?

So, the written word of God is a divisive and contentious subject. It always has been. For deep spiritual reasons men have always had an unending struggle with just how much and to what extent they could, would or should believe what God said or wrote. As the mass of the moon works its forces upon the tides of the seas, man's dark, corrupt and unbelieving nature tends to ceaselessly draw him by increments back to shadows of infidelity. The convoluted history of exactly how God preserved His words through time adds confusing obstructions to the picture. No living man for many generations has set eyes on an original writing from God. Through the chaotic centuries of the Church Age, the genocidal murder of whole segments of populations, the fires that burned history as well as martyrs' flesh, the fact-obscuring villainy of the Catholic Church, and the rotating doors of heathen empires, we are quite certain that God did preserve His word - but the exact means and machinations by which He did so are not absolutely and at all times apparent. Much of what God hath wrought can be seen, but the precise methods He used can at times be a mystery. He did not always use whom *we* would have used, and it is likely that He used some whom *we would not* have used. He used the efforts of some and refused the services of others. Men still argue about whether it was God who used some or whether it was the prince of darkness.

Most importantly – above and beyond all else - we have our Father's promise of what He would do. Without fail, all that we either see or do not see, all that we understand or do not comprehend, all abundance of evidence or lack thereof, all that is explicable and manifestly obvious or obscure, must be trumped by the promises of His word. *We have also a more sure word of prophecy...* (2 Pet. 1:19), and in the passage the word we have is surer than *...such a voice... from the excellent glory* (2 Pet. 1:17). What we have is surer than a voice from Heaven! The Lord never intimated that He required man to discover each incremental progression of Bible preservation and transmission along the pathway of history. He told us to trust His providence and power to preserve it. One cannot find a commission for men to reconstruct the body of the "original language text" of the New Testament after the devil and the Roman Catholic Church tag-teamed to try to destroy the Bible from the face of the earth. Is it good we have as much historical light as we do? Surely! Are the labors and sacrifices of those who uncovered it appreciated? Absolutely! Is all the genuine manuscript evidence and discovery to be discounted? Certainly not! All that being granted, God promised to inspire, preserve and keep His ***words*** whether we discovered all the secrets of the process or not. ***We would still have the Bible even if we were obstructed from exploring its lineage.*** God promised us His ***words***, not an exhaustive log of each progressive step of preservation. *So then faith cometh by hearing, and hearing by the word of God* (Rom. 10:17). We walk by faith, not by *science*; not by *archeological discovery*; not by *manuscript evidence*. We walk by faith, not by the *linguistic excellence* of Dr So-and-so.

This ought not be too hard to swallow for an English-speaking Bible-believer who has, quite rightly, centered himself on the King James Bible. Nonetheless, it may come as a surprise just how many AV 1611 proponents would look upon the contents of the cup of that last paragraph with dismay – nay, disdain – and refuse to drink.

All of this leads us to the issue that is so polarizing within the camp of those who recognize the hand of God upon the King James Bible. It is a thin line, but it divides us significantly. We brotherly adversaries are agreed on almost all facts of history pertaining to the AV. We are decidedly in accord on most every critical doctrine of consequence in the Bible.

But…

But, there is an issue between us, and it reveals itself to be an irksome subject. It is where the rubber meets the road and the fur hits the fan. The fulmination, the vitriol, and the name-calling that it generates are not particularly edifying, but the heat radiated from it alerts the wary of the fiery nature of the conflict. Neither camp has shown much hesitation in the hearty use of various forms of the words *heretic* or *cult* in describing their opposition. *Cranks, quacks, church splitters* and *divisive* are other readily applied diagnoses. Those of us who believe the King James is word perfect might just as well wear *Ruckmanite* tattooed on our foreheads in the eyes of our counterparts, nor does it take long in a town for a church holding an adamant position regarding the inerrancy of the King James Bible to be referred to as, *"Oh… THEM!"*

No, it is not good for brethren whose respective positions reside so nigh unto one another to be divided or at adversity. I suppose it could be called "a shame". One of the profound issues, though, that drew us to the Bible was the matter of ***final authority***. It is the issue that Satan originally instigated with the Lord. It is the issue that caused the conflict in Eve's heart and subsequently deposited us all into this sinful sewer in which we still reside. It is the lesson that took so long for some of us to learn out in the world, and it is the issue of final authority that remains ***the issue***, even in the King James camp.

It has been noted that some of the King James defenders in this chapter have been a disappointment to those of us whose esteem for the AV rises beyond its textual roots and mere "reliability" in translation. It is worthy of emphasis that several of them were very skittish around the idea that *the translation* of the King James was anything more than reliable or accurate. Indeed, they prove themselves very emphatic that *no translation* is, or can be perfect and therefore they hold that the King James is not. Even further, some of them are not at all hesitant to go on the offensive against such believers that proceed beyond their own lack of confidence in the old Book as a translation. A brief review suffices:

> Admittedly the King James Version is not ideally perfect. No translation ever can be.
> – Edward Hills[42]

> It is possible, of course, that in the future the English language will change so much that a new translation of the Bible will be absolutely necessary.
> – Edward Hills[43]

> *Which Bible* is not a repudiation of scholarship. It **is not** an argument for the inerrancy of a translation... It is a long-overdue defense of the worth of the old Authorized Version.[44]

> That a few changes might be made in both Testaments (of the King James – author's note), for the better, no man pretends to deny...
> –George Sayles Bishop[45]

---

[42] Hills, Edward F., *Believing Bible Study Key to the Space Age* (The Christian Research Press: Des Moines, Iowa, 1967, 1977), p.83.

[43] Ibid., p.85

[44] Fuller, David Otis, *True or False?* (Grand Rapids International Publications, Grand Rapids, Michigan, 1973, 1975) flyleaf

[45] Fuller, David Otis, *Which Bible* (Grand Rapids International Publications, Grand Rapids, Michigan, 1970) p. 6

> ...it became increasingly evident that, notwithstanding the excellencies of that great and admirable work (the AV), there were particulars wherein, for one cause or another, it admitted of (and indeed called for) correction.... It was found also that corrections in translation were demanded here and there, particularly in regard to the tenses of verbs...
>
> – Mauro[46]

> ...we hold that a revised edition of the Authorized Version of our English Bible (if executed with consummate ability and learning) would at any time be a work of inestimable value..."
>
> - Dean Burgon[47]

> ...the advocates of the King James only position have a severe problem. Most of **them** hold the view that the King James Version of 1611 as a *translation* was inspired and thus has no need for further *translational* revision.
>
> – David Sorenson[48]

> There are only several hundred obsolete or archaic words remaining within the 1611 King James Bible... These few **could and should** be brought up to date.
>
> – Floyd Nolen Jones[49]

---

[46] Fuller, David Otis, *True or False?* (Grand Rapids International Publications, Grand Rapids, Michigan, 1973, 1975) p.59

[47] Fuller, David Otis, *Counterfeit or Genuine Mark 16? John 8?* (Grand Rapids International Publications, Grand Rapids, Michigan, 1975) p.23-24

[48] Sorenson, David H., *Touch Not The Unclean Thing The Text Issue and Separation* (Northstar Baptist Ministries, Duluth, MN, 2001) p.18

> I don't like to use the word "inerrant" of any English (or other language) translation of the Bible because the word "inerrant" is implied from the Greek Word, *theopneustos* (2 Timothy 3:16) which means literally, "God-Breathed."
>
> - Donald Waite[50]

> I do believe there are places that could be translated more clearly for readers today. I do believe there are antiquated words that could be brought up to date. There are words and passages that could be translated differently. (Note I did not say *should* be, but *could* be.) To say, that there are changes that could be made in the KJV is entirely different from saying it contains mistakes.
>
> – David Cloud[51]

> The AV, like all translations, has 'language limitations', but these are not errors.
>
> – Thomas Strouse[52]

The issue of translation will be taken up in greater length in a later chapter, but for now suffice to say that, plainly, the King James Bible as a translation is a stumbling block as a standard of final authority to these men. This is because they believe that the ultimate appeal for what the Bible says is the

---

49 Jones, Floyd Nolen, *Which Version Is The Bible* (KingsWord Press, Goodyear, AZ, 1989, 2006) p.78

50 Waite, D.A., *Defending The King James Bible A Fourfold Superiority* (The Bible For Today Press, Collingswood, N.J., 1992) p.239-240

51 Cloud, David W., *Myths About The Modern Bible Versions* (Way of Life Literature, Oak Harbor, Washington, 1999) p.111

52 Ibid., p.163

original Greek or Hebrew from whence the AV comes. This is in no way a cheap shot at these fellows. It is their considered and published opinion. Though they have strong connections and affections for the King James Bible, it is equitable to point out that in this respect, they hold the same opinion that most, if not all, of the new version proponents and liberal bible scholars hold: ***there is no perfect translation of the Bible.*** They believe that there is no inerrant other-language translation of the Bible: not the King James Bible: not any Bible.

Truth being told, the tenet that there has not been and cannot be a perfect translation of the Bible, has become generally accepted as a fundamental truth of the faith. It is more widely held than the Deity of Christ. The range of "Christians" (a term loosely used in this case) which hold to this *philosophy* extends from the very most apostate liberal theologians to many of the Fundamental "Bible-believers" whom we hold as friends. This is not written in a frothing tirade. It is an observation of fact. Deists believe in God as do I, and Catholics believe in the virgin birth as do I. In these cases, the Catholics, the Deists, and I all are right, though we would agree together on little else. Heretics and the faithful often rightly hold certain isolated and limited truths in common. It is worthy of note though, that God's saints also sometimes grow to embrace the same untruths as the lost. Fundamental King James Bible defenders often believe, along with much ranker liberals, that no translation is perfect. It is with no intent of slandering them that I resolutely ask, ***"ARE THEY RIGHT?"*** If so, *why are they right?* How do you know they are right? Even better, *how do* ***they*** *know they are right?*

This is the irksome subject. It is grievous and acrimonious to many. It has rendered the Christian fellowship of some a bare respectful avoidance of the issue, and it has sundered the communion of others into far less tranquil coexistence. To ask the question - to even inquire into the matter at any depth or in any detail - is to invite a combative, foul response. Soul winners often recognize that a combative response from a "Christian" who resents being asked the details of his conversion usually marks a spiritual illness that is either severe backsliding, or far worse, a lack of conversion altogether. What would short-fused, aggressive resentment and irritation mark in a "Bible-believer" who is asked for details about what exactly his ***final authority*** is, and why he holds it as such? I am not put off by being asked the "what's and why's" of my personal final authority.

It is an irksome, irritating subject to raise. It is *...as vinegar upon nitre* (Prov. 25:20).

The idea that the translation - the King James Bible - could be the final authority and ultimate appeal in all matters that we hold as Christians is attacked by various forms of rhetoric. One of the most childish and expected forms is to pontificate and bluster about *lack of scholarship* or *anti-intellectualism.* The Christian who comes to the prayerful and informed conviction that the words of God actually reside in a volume written in English, will have to resolve to accept that he is a rather stupid hick in the estimation of nearly all Greek and Hebrew scholars, as well as in the eyes of all those who wish to belong to that very elite "Greek and Hebrew scholar's club."

It is also unlikely that the aforementioned Christian will escape the Laodicean diatribe which accuses him of *worshipping the Bible*, charges him with saying *nobody can be saved but by reading out of the King James*, and labels him as being *overcritical, hateful,* or a *church splitter.* In the process of corrupting the word of God, the devil slandered the character of God to Eve. A true Bible-believer can count on being lied about and misrepresented in his quest to stand for God against that very same corruption and that very same enemy.

Dr. Peter Ruckman has long been in the bitter battle for the AV 1611. A Bob Jones University graduate of voracious intellect and reading, and one of the most prolific writers on scriptural topics of the 20th and 21st centuries, Ruckman broke the mold of intellectual and scholarly sophistication. In halls oft inhabited by sequestered and reclusive academics, he has proven to be an unchained beast in style and ferocity. Indeed, he has on many occasions recited as his calling from God to be "the Lord's junkyard dog" with respect to the King James Bible. However it is that one looks at this self-described commission, his style certainly has not enamored his critics. His pugilistic, blue-collar verbiage is often rejected as "un-Christian" and base, though many hail his bluntness and incisiveness as a welcome and much-appreciated change. Ceaselessly combative, and with invective and brimstone, he has unendingly called upon what he terms the "scholar's union" to account for their inconsistencies, their infidelities regarding the written word, and their haughty condescension toward the common man. His readily self-acknowledged two divorces and remarriages have been fodder for his many critics. A Bible teacher of the first order in the eyes of many, his dispensationalist views, dogmatism in doctrine, antagonistic language and high visibility have predictably left him open to an encyclopedic volume's worth of quotes (some contextual and some not) and criticisms used against him.

I state all of this to prepare the unsuspecting for the fact that if they believe the King James Bible to be the word of God, they will undoubtedly at some juncture be called a *Ruckmanite*. An oft-raised charge in connection with Dr. Ruckman is the accusation, *"He believes the English corrects the Greek and Hebrew."* Thus, it will be insinuated that any accused *Ruckmanite* also believes this. As discussed above, this belief is very literally an abomination in scholastic circles. Ruckman has pointed out many cases in the AV where it can be trusted to render the correct reading to the mind and heart, in contrast to the scholars who perpetually return to the Greek or Hebrew for deeper meanings, or more insidiously, to change what is actually clearly stated. I have had occasion to review volumes worth of Dr. Ruckman's monthly publication, the *Bible Believer's Bulletin,* in which he has through the years produced many examples of what is termed, *"...the English correcting the originals."* Interestingly, I found that much of the time his point is that the AV, in giving the correct English reading, also points back to the correct and proper Received Greek Text reading, as opposed to the Alexandrian Text of Origin, Westcott and Hort. This should not be unpalatable to the advocates of the Received Text, but only flies in the face of those who constantly harp on about the "originals," while changing the Bible with corrupt Alexandrian manuscripts, the Vatican manuscript, Sinaiticus, or other Gnostic or Catholic corruptions of scripture.

Those so labeled as *Ruckmanites* will be further hassled with whether they believe the King James Bible has *advanced revelations.* Akin to *the English correcting the originals* charge, this is a reference to Ruckman's other broad range of examples where he claims that the AV 1611 English introduces truths to the hearts and minds of believers that are not contained in the original languages – or at least are not perceived by the scholars of the those languages. Again, that a translation of the Bible could reveal truths to the hearts of men that are not found in the Hebrew and Greek is, to them, akin to blasphemy. More to the point, many who otherwise adhere to and defend the King James Bible, still glower, murmur and pronounce anathemas on such ideas. Detailed review and discussion of the merits (or the lack thereof) of Dr. Ruckman's position is beyond our purview at this juncture, but hear this informative warning: whether you have ever heard of Peter Ruckman or not (many have not), if you believe your King James Bible to be inerrant and to have all the words of God in it, you will be called a *Ruckmanite.*

There are other stones slung at a Bible-believer, as well:

Where was the Bible before 1611?
King James was a homosexual.
The translators never claimed to be inspired.
There are archaic words we cannot understand today.
Many godly men have used other versions as well as Greek and Hebrew.
This issue is dividing the body of Christ.
Such belief comes from a cultic mentality.
The majority of Christians do not believe as you do.
There are contradictions in the King James Bible.
Believing a translation can be perfect is not a "Historic Position".

The list could well go on and on.

This book is not written to humiliate and lambaste our brothers who are adverse to the perfection of the King James Bible. It is written out of a personal search that began over twenty years ago when I, as a new, young King James Bible believer, was made aware of the disparity in the King James camp. To me it mattered that conservative, fundamental Christians would, in the most rousing and adamant fashion, be taught that the King James Bible was the "very word of God," only to find that such was a relatively superficial position. In far too many cases, that position was, and is, only a *front*. The *front* was only good for so long as it took to ask a handful of incisive and direct questions about final authority in the pastor's study. The same can be said of writers who somehow in the midst of defending the Bible, wind up tearing it down only a certain percentage less than their Alexandrian counterparts.

We are taught, exhorted, admonished and challenged to believe each blessed word of the grand old Book, but that is not the end of the matter. *That* is the facade erected to impress the observer with the impassioned fidelity of the church, school or ministry of the barker. In the end, to them, *the man of God* **is not** *throughly furnished unto all good works* (II Tim. 3:17) until he has learned Greek and Hebrew, and has studied the Bible in the original language in which it was written. Even in the camp holding to the correct Greek and Hebrew texts, in the end it is still a *priest-class* of scholars who are the true keepers of the faith, not the common men and women of the New Testament Church, the Body of Christ, the Priesthood of Believers. There is no way around it. To them, any individual must be both well-schooled and well-exercised in Greek and Hebrew to have a chance at actually accessing the ultimate final authority. To be blunt, in many of their minds, the common "layman" does not really need access to the ultimate final authority. Such endeavors should just be left to the heady fellows who know Greek and Hebrew. Only they are truly qualified to sort through all that really complicated, deep stuff. Common bread (the King James) is to be your spiritual fare. The princely lords will allow some of their kingly meat (the Greek and Hebrew) to trickle down to the common Christian if he remains properly subjugated, and acknowledges a scholarly man of God when one comes by. In their minds, the AV 1611 is a landmark and a faithful and reliable translation – but it is not inerrant. It is not untouchable. It is neither beyond scrutiny, criticism, updating or – let us face the word manfully – ***correction.***

There are a number of connected issues to delve into, and with God's help, we will delve. The Bible issue is a multi-layered subject of both great simplicity and great depth all at once. The skeleton and sinew of this book is built around answering a simple question apart from the clamor of rhetorical objections, name-calling and historic positions: ***Does the English of the King James Bible reveal truth that the Greek and Hebrew do not?*** Asked again, framed slightly differently: ***Is there a clarity achieved, is there truth settled, in the AV 1611 in a way that it is not achieved in the Greek and Hebrew of even the proper original language texts?*** Even as a possibility, ***is there inherent obscurity in the Greek and Hebrew texts and languages that actually require an Arbiter*** (God, in this case) ***to decisively settle by translation?*** If so, ***did this process actually occur in the King James Bible?***

If the answer to any of these questions is, "Yes," then such fruit should be able to be empirically and actually demonstrated from those scriptures, so that anyone can see it if they are willing to honestly explore the issue. It should not be like shuffling through the semantics and rhetoric of mere philosophical positions and schools of thought. We are not seeking whether Aristotelian philosophy or Platonic philosophy holds more virtue. We are not investigating Chevy versus Ford. Either the King James English reveals to the believer's heart and mind more truth than the Greek or Hebrew, or it does not.

Let us see…

Chapter 2

The Language of Love

So when they had dined, Jesus saith to Simon Peter, Simon, son of Jonas, lovest thou me more than these? He saith unto him, Yea, Lord; thou knowest that I love thee. He saith unto him, Feed my lambs. He saith to him again the second time, Simon, son of Jonas, lovest thou me? He saith unto him, Yea, Lord; thou knowest that I love thee. He saith unto him, Feed my sheep. He saith unto him the third time, Simon, son of Jonas, lovest thou me? Peter was grieved because he said unto him the third time, Lovest thou me? And he said unto him, Lord, thou knowest all things; thou knowest that I love thee. Jesus saith unto him, Feed my sheep. (Jn. 21:15-17)

Sometimes in life, and even in the realm of scriptural faith, there are certain ideas that come to be considered old "standbys." These are presumed "truths" that are accepted without much question or thought. An example of this in life is that in the minds of many, after high school, "you have to go to college." College can certainly be God's will and the next rightful step in a high school graduate's life, but it is also quite often a step taken in ill-preparedness. Many college students are without real direction or real decisiveness about their futures. I know – I was once just such a student. Though college often marks the first time away from home, though there are clear faults in self-discipline and character, though wolves lie in wait in the hallowed halls, anticipating tender and susceptible intellectual prey, the kids are 18, fresh out of high school, and college is the time-honored and traditional standby.

There are "old standbys" spiritually, too. When asked what fruit Eve ate in the garden, many would say, "an apple," without blinking an eye. How can one be so sure it was an apple? What scriptural precept exists to suggest it was an apple? When asked where the devil is right now, many would say, "Why, in Hell, of course." Yet, is this truly the case? For most of my young Christian life, I heard that Christ was crucified on a dogwood tree. Due to the frequency of its repetition, I thought that the saying, "the eye is the window to the soul," was a Bible verse until I was far too old to admit here.

Some things become standbys.

Some elements of Christian doctrine have become standbys, as well. They are so common that once a preacher or teacher embarks on a certain line of thought in certain passages, it is almost assured that certain things are about to be said. It is habitual and predictable. It is like watching and listening as a child cranks away on his jack-in-the-box: *here it comes!*

Beginning in the passage from John 21 cited at the opening of this chapter, "Christian" men and women have quite habitually, and as a matter of course, committed one of the great, unprofitable debacles of Bible exposition of our time. Oftentimes, radio teachers and preachers, pastors and Sunday school teachers can hardly complete the quotation of the passage before hasting to the Greek, which in fact mires them in the fool's bog, though they do blithely slog onward to apply their ill-fated and blind precepts to other related passages. This practice has become a most predictable standby.

It was this passage in the 21st chapter of John, that God used to begin to open my eyes in answer to the question of whether there was a final court of appeal besides the Greek and Hebrew of the "originals" (which "originals" no one living has ever seen). Perhaps I should say that it was here, in this passage of scripture, where I began to observe a few facts about the translation of the King James Bible as compared to the blind and careless machinations and contortions of those who so confidently revert to the Greek and Hebrew for finality.

I am happy to mention that Dr. Samuel Gipp was the one who really tore away the curtain for me. Dr. Gipp has for years in his Bible conference seminars and in his writings, laid open the material contained in the interplay between Christ and Peter in John 21. He has clearly demonstrated the shallow pretentiousness and great carelessness of those who commence to play the "Greek game" with *agape* and *phileo* love. Beyond that, Bro. Gipp, by his example, gave me both a template and the inspiration by which to search out more of these matters on my own, and thus draw further conclusions about just how the King James Bible as a translation relates to its Greek and Hebrew roots.

For the sake of simplicity, let me reformat the passage with the commonly used Greek insertion in question in this way:

> John 21:15-17
> *15 So when they had dined, Jesus saith to Simon Peter, Simon, son of Jonas,* ***lovest*** **[agapao]** *thou me more than these? He saith unto him, Yea, Lord; thou knowest that I* ***love*** **[phileo]** *thee. He saith unto him, Feed my lambs.*
> *16 He saith to him again the second time, Simon, son of Jonas,* ***lovest*** **[agapao]** *thou me? He saith unto him, Yea, Lord; thou knowest that I* ***love*** **[phileo]** *thee. He saith unto him, Feed my sheep.*

> *17 He saith unto him the third time, Simon, son of Jonas,* ***lovest*** **[phileo]** *thou me? Peter was grieved because he said unto him the third time,* ***Lovest*** **[phileo]** *thou me? And he said unto him, Lord, thou knowest all things; thou knowest that I* ***love*** **[phileo]** *thee. Jesus saith unto him, Feed my sheep.*

Note that I have supplied the associated Greek transliteration of the word "love" beside its English counterpart in the passage, as is found in the Greek text. For simplicity's sake, and to avoid confusion, I have left the Greek word in its transliterated root form, instead of its specific tense, and will make it a habit to do so throughout the rest of this book.

The Old Standby

The way this passage is approached by a mainstream Christian Bible teacher is nearly as predictable as the sun's rise: ***agapao*** love is a deep, eternal, abiding, infinite and unconditional love. This is how God loves. This is how Christ loves. It is in this way that a man should love his wife and children. Indeed, this is how God wants Christians to love Him, and also one another. Greater love hath no man than this: *agapao* love. ***Phileo*** love, on the other hand, is a brotherly love. Philadelphia, by definition, is the city of "brotherly love". Brotherly love is desirable, companionable and commendable, but it is understood to be a good deal shallower and more superficial than *Agapao.*

It takes our friends who think there is so much to be gathered from the Greek very little effort to find fodder for their cannon. The following are the merest samplings of the standard line of definition, description and exposition.

Under John 21:15, *Robertson's Word Pictures of the New Testament* says:

> *[I love thee] [filoo (grk 5368) su (grk 4771)]. Peter makes no claim here to* ***superior love*** *and passes by the "more than these" and* ***does not even use Christ's word [agapaoo] (grk 25) for high and devoted love, but the humbler word [fileoo] (grk 5368) for love as a friend.*** *He insists that Christ knows this in spite of his conduct.*[53]

From the Adam Clarke Commentary:

> *It is remarkable that in these three questions our Lord uses the verb* ***agapaoo (grk 25), which signifies to love affectionately, ardently, supremely, perfectly****-- see the note at <Matt. 21:37>; and that* ***Peter always replies, using the verb phileoo (grk 5368), which signifies to love, to like, to regard, to feel friendship for another. As if our Lord had said, "Peter, dost thou love me ardently and supremely?" To which he answers, "Lord, I feel an affection for thee-- I do esteem thee-- but dare, at present, say no more."***[54]

From Vine's Expository Dictionary of Biblical Words:

> *In respect of* ***agapao*** *as used of God****, it expresses the deep and constant "love" and interest of a***

---

[53] Robertson, A.T. *Robertson's Word Pictures of the New Testament* (1998) P C Study Bible (Version 2.11) [Computer Software]. Seattle, WA: Biblesoft.

[54] Clarke, Adam. *Clarke's Commentary.* (1998) P C Study Bible (Version 2.11) [Computer Software]. Seattle, WA: Biblesoft.

> ***perfect Being towards entirely unworthy objects, producing and fostering a reverential "love" in them towards the Giver, and a practical "love" towards those who are partakers of the same, and a desire to help others to seek the Giver.*** *See BELOVED.*
> *2.* ***phileo ^5368^ is to be distinguished from agapao in this, that phileo more nearly represents "tender affection."***[55]

Zondervan's *Pictorial Encyclopedia of the Bible* puts it this way:

> ***Phileo… means to love in the sense of being friendly,*** *to delight in or long for, to love to do, or to do with pleasure. On the other hand* ***agapao properly denotes a love founded on admiration, veneration, and esteem.***[56]

If the definitions for these two Greek words as presented by the above scholars were stringently adhered to, the spiritual applications would be profound. The brief bulleted points below represent the everlasting profundity that many commentators and leaders believe they have unearthed.

- In John 21:15, Jesus asks Peter if Peter loves (*agapao*) Jesus with a deep, reverential, ardent and supreme love. Peter replies that he loves (*phileo*) Jesus with a brotherly, affectionate and friendly love.

---

[55] *Vine's Expository Dictionary of Biblical Words* (1998) P C Study Bible (Version 2.11) [Computer Software]. Seattle, WA: Biblesoft.

[56] Tenney, Merrill C., Zondervan's *Pictorial Encyclopedia of the Bible* (Vols.1-5). Grand Rapids, MI: Regency Reference Library. Vol.3, pg.989.

- In John 21:16, Jesus asks Peter, at least as far as his love is concerned, the same question, which Peter answers in the same way as before.
- Thus far, the lesson from Greek is that Jesus sought a deep, eternal, intimate and reverential love from Peter, but to this point, Peter has only been able to summon something like brotherly affection. Or, perhaps, Peter is just a "guy" and is unable to express passions quite as intimate and deep as is being asked of him.
- Whatever the case, Jesus condescends and rescues Peter from his discomfort by asking in John 21:17 if Peter *phileos* Jesus, to which Peter replies for the third time that indeed he does *phileo* the Lord.
- This marks a departure from the previous line of questioning, for Christ changed the verb He used, and settled for the shallower and less noble form of love, while Peter retained the one he used and held to the line of brotherly affection.
- At this point, the commentators devotionalize, elaborate, and draw expansive lessons about Jesus meeting a sinner "where he is at." They speak of Jesus' humbleness and understanding and His patient nature. They point out Peter's failings, his need for maturity and his shallowness of love for Christ at this juncture in his life. It is all very touching.

There is no doubt as to the loving, tender and condescending attributes of the Lord Jesus Christ toward sinners, and the scriptures make very obvious quite a number of Peter's failings and flaws. With so much of the above material, however, built upon definitions that presumably can be only accessed by going back to the Greek, it must be contended that English speakers and Bible-believers should be allotted the following blunt question: ***are these conclusions and lessons from "the Greek" actually true?*** These lessons taken from the supposed definitions of these Greek words; these lessons found only in Greek: ***are they really true?***

If true, then the ramifications are clear and it should be plain that the English does not contain these *deeper meanings*. The AV English, after all, simply uses the various verb tenses of the single word "love," while the Greek uses two separate words with all the implications and distinctions of meaning. If true, the manifest need is for Christians to equip themselves to refer to the Greek or else submit themselves to someone who can fully inform them about these deeper Greek meanings that are otherwise inaccessible. If true, the King James Bible would indeed be much inferior to the Greek of the New Testament. In fact, with such an inferior source of knowledge, one would very much run the risk of being an "inferior" Christian. After all, a Christian with such a shallow base of knowledge and Biblical authority would be left in ignorance as to the deeper truths of the Christian life - the fine, subtle truths of the scriptures. It is reasonable, if these things are true, to view the non-Greek-equipped Christian as ill-equipped, unprepared and only partially enlightened.

Behind the Facade

The entire basis of these alleged *deeper lessons* from John 21 is the respective definitions of the two Greek words for love. Since so much is drawn and inferred in this passage from the distinction between those two forms of love; and since the King James Bible only uses the single word – *love* – and is thus "inferior," it probably should have occurred to someone to take into account the other places in the Greek New Testament where the words *agapao* and *phileo* appear. Perhaps it would be worth their while to check to see if the "scholars" respective definitions of the two words are consistent with how the words are used in other passages.

To reiterate, the authoritative Greek scholars say that ***agapao*** love is deep, lasting, reverential and intimate. It is how God loves Christ and Christians. It is how Christians are to grow to love God and Christ, as well as each other. ***Agapao*** is the goal, the high mark and calling of the Christian life. ***Phileo***, on the other hand, is friendly, brotherly, affectionate love. It is desirable, but second best. ***Phileo*** makes buddies, but nobody gets carried away.

Now there are places in the New Testament in which the distinctions between these two Greek forms of love hold true to the definitions which the scholars propose. In the following table, each word translated "love" in the AV is from either the Greek verb *agapao*, or the noun form *agape*. Incidentally, from this point, we will generally allow ***agape*** to stand for both noun and verb forms, and ***phileo*** to do so as well, since most readers are familiar with these terms.

Agapao *–Verb Form;* ***Agape*** *– Noun Form*

Matt 22:37	*Your love for God*	*Jesus said unto him, Thou shalt* ***love*** *the Lord thy God with all thy heart, and with all thy soul, and with all thy mind.*
Matt 22:39	*Your love for neighbour*	*And the second is like unto it, Thou shalt* ***love*** *thy neighbour as thyself.*
John 3:16	*God's love for you*	*For God so* ***loved*** *the world, that he gave his only begotten Son...*

John 3:35	*God's love for Christ*	*The Father **loveth** the Son, and hath given all things into his hand.*
John 11:5	*Jesus' love for others*	*Now Jesus **loved** Martha, and her sister, and Lazarus.*
John13:34	*Your love for one another*	*A new commandment I give unto you, That ye **love** one another; as I have **loved** you, that ye also **love** one another.*
John15:13	*Your love for one another*	*Greater **love** hath no man than this, that a man lay down his life for his friends.*
Rom 5:8	*God's love for us*	*But God commendeth his **love** toward us, in that, while we were yet sinners, Christ died for us.*
Rom 13:8	*Our love to man*	*Owe no man any thing, but to **love** one another: for he that **loveth** another hath fulfilled the law.*

Thus, *agape* love thus far is contextually consistent with the kind of devoted, deep, and God-like love as the scholars define it. Notice the same is also true of *phileo* love in the chart below.

Phileo *– Verb Form;* ***Philos*** *– Noun Form*

Rom 12:10	*Brotherly love*	*Be kindly affectioned one to another with brotherly* ***love***
1Thes 4:9	*Brotherly love*	*But as touching brotherly* ***love*** *ye need not that I write unto you*
Titus 1:8	*Loving hospitality and men*	*But a* ***lover*** *of hospitality, a* ***lover*** *of good men*
1Pet 1:22	*Brotherly love*	*Seeing ye have purified your souls in obeying the truth... unto unfeigned* ***love*** *of the brethren*
1Pet 3:8	*Brotherly love*	*Finally, be ye all of one mind...* ***love*** *as brethren*

Thus, all seems quite consistent with the teachings that have been circulated for all these years. *Agape* love certainly seems to be a deeper, nobler, more intimate brand of lasting and godly love. *Phileo* love gives the appearance of a mere affectionate and brotherly fondness. Where would we be without the depths of the original Greek?

The problem with this picture just painted, which is consistent with what has been presented by both scholars and Greek-going Bible study and Sunday school teachers for a very long time, is the same problem as so often lies with a great deal of the falsehood in this world. What has been presented is merely *part* of the information. It is only what someone wanted the reader to see. It is information carefully pared and filleted of the rest of the facts, which facts would have presented a much different picture, and might have led to a very different conclusion.

The definitions of the *Agape* brand of love versus the *Phileo* brand of love are presented by Greek scholars, or those pretentiously posing as Greek scholars, as if written in stone. Meanings are stated as hard, cold facts that allow no latitude or argumentation. We are accustomed to going to an English dictionary as an authoritative reference to what a certain English word means. When a Greek linguist says with authority, "The Greek word means thus and thus," those of us who have not devoted a fair portion of our lives to the intricacies of Greek, feel the strong compunction to acquiesce and defer to them. After all, he is the expert and most of us are not! But, what if the expert's information is faulty? Do we not all know cases where highly trained, brilliant medical specialists have been very wrong about a diagnosis? Engineers, mechanics, and chemists whose expertise is unquestioned have proven to be wrong once in a while, at least. What *should* be asked is, ***"Does God understand these words to mean what the scholars are so adamant that they mean"?*** Does God use them as the scholars do, or as they say that He used them? The answer to that is: ***hardly!***

When studying what is actually contained in the Greek of the New Testament, Bible believers are suddenly faced with the fact that the ***Agape-Phileo Doctrine*** of Christian radio teachers and seminary students is not so much a deep insight as it is a foolish debacle. The Christian finds a much-frayed end of a tragically woven doctrine when he observes first that the two following verses are clear statements of God's love for Jesus Christ. Notice the Greek word for that love which I have supplied, and remember that for simplicity's sake, I am grouping both noun and verb forms of each Greek word simply as *agape* or *phileo*, respectively.

> *The Father* ***loveth*** **[agape]** *the Son, and hath given all things into his hand.*
> (Jn. 3:35)

> *For the Father* ***loveth*** **[phileo]** *the Son, and sheweth him all things that himself doeth: and he will shew him greater works than these, that ye may marvel.* (Jn. 5:20)

If any kind of consistency is to be observed, what must the lesson here mean? Did the Father indeed love Jesus in a deep, eternal, intimate and profound way in John 3:35, but digress to a mere brotherly type of affection in John 5:20, only two chapters later? Is the Christian to seriously make the same kind of application here as has so freely been exercised by the scholars in John 21? If so, it is fortunate that by John 10:17 that Christ has found His way back into the *agape* love of His Father in Heaven!

> *Therefore doth my Father* ***love*** **[agape]** *me, because I lay down my life, that I might take it again.* (Jn. 10:17)

It is unavoidable but to conclude that in "the Greek," at least by the commonly accepted definitions, God's love toward His Son was rather unstable and fluctuating. After all, we cannot hold Simon Peter to one standard in John 21 and not make the application in the passages just listed. If this were true, needless to say, it would have the greatest implications for the saints here in this world.

At this juncture, though, the doctrine has only just begun to unravel. Jesus, in the two sister-passages below, is in the midst of taking the Pharisees to task. He uses the same key wording in each passage, addressing the same people.

> *And* ***love*** **[phileo]** *the uppermost rooms at feasts, and the chief seats in the synagogues...*
> (Matt. 23:6)

> *Woe unto you, Pharisees! for ye* ***love*** **[agape]** *the uppermost seats in the synagogues, and greetings in the markets.* (Lk. 11:43)

Obviously, Jesus uses a different Greek word for "love" in the two passages. Were the Pharisees just *affectionate* about those chief seats in Matthew, later having grown to love those uppermost seats with a *reverential* and *eternal love* in Luke? Is that the deeper truth that is to be drawn? Again, a discerning disciple cannot hammer Peter for his lack of depth, passion, and commitment in John 21:15-17 if he cannot make application of those very same passions as they resided in the hearts of the Pharisees in Matthew 23 and Luke 11.

Consider this as well: what if Luke 11:43 is a quotation of the very same incident as in Matthew 23:6? What if Luke's quotation is the same exact quote as Matthew's, only inserted at a different point and in slightly different order than the Holy Spirit instructed Matthew to quote it. This would mean that each of the originals – Matthew's and Luke's – had a different word for *love* in Greek, even though the writers were inspired by the Holy Ghost to write them so.

Academically and reasonably, it cannot be both ways. If the Greek safari hunters are right about the definitions, then either the Pharisees grew to really, really, really love those seats between Matthew 23 and Luke 11, or each of the accounts have a different Greek word which mean **the same thing!**

The reasonable and sane explanation would be that the two Greek words for *love* are synonyms (words with the same meaning), just like there are many English words that are synonyms, and that Jesus was *making the exact same accusation in each case*, and that the two inspired writers were equally as inspired in putting down one word as the other.

Let us explore more of the *Agape-Phileo Doctrine.* In the book of John, no commentator that I am aware of argues with the fact that John's method of referring to himself in the narratives is denoted by the phrase, *the disciple whom Jesus loved.* It should indeed be gripping to the reader of John's gospel that John's heart and spirit seems entirely captivated by the fact of Jesus Christ's love for him personally. God's love extended to the world as a whole is touching, but to a genuine Christian, His love for ***you*** personally should be all-consuming! Noticc the following complete sequence of John's references to himself in his gospel, beginning with the last supper in John 13, all the way through the final post-resurrection scene by the fire in John 21:

> *Now there was leaning on Jesus' bosom one of his disciples, whom Jesus* ***loved*** **[agape].**
> (Jn. 13:23)

> *When Jesus therefore saw his mother, and the disciple standing by, whom he* ***loved*** **[agape]**, *he saith unto his mother, Woman, behold thy son!*
> (Jn. 19:26)

> *Then she runneth, and cometh to Simon Peter, and to the other disciple, whom Jesus* ***loved*** **[phileo],** *and saith unto them, They have taken away the Lord out of the sepulchre, and we know not where they have laid him.*
>
> (Jn. 20:2)

> *Therefore that disciple whom Jesus* ***loved*** **[agape]** *saith unto Peter, It is the Lord.*
>
> (Jn. 21:7a)

> *Then Peter, turning about, seeth the disciple whom Jesus* ***loved*** **[agape]** *following;*
>
> (Jn. 21:20a)

For those preoccupied by the implications and definitions of Greek words, what lessons are to be drawn from the fact that John was loved by Jesus with *agape* love in four of the five occurrences, but merely with *phileo* love in the midst? If the Holy Spirit inspired John to write individual Greek words, and if there is a definite distinction between *agape* and *phileo* love in the Greek, just exactly what are the lessons in this? On resurrection morning, how is it that Christ could only summon brotherly affection for John? Was He so tired and exhausted by His conquest of the devil, sin, death and hell that He was unable to summon a greater love than *phileo*? What is to be drawn from the use of the word *phileo* in John 20:2, if not that? Brothers and sisters in Christ, I have been teaching and preaching the English Bible for 24 years as of this writing, and I have never been led from the KJV to tread the breeding grounds of this type of speculation. It should be emphasized that these slavishly, Greek-loving scholars cannot reasonably make the kind of authoritative application of *agape* and *phileo* in John 21, as they do, and then flippantly ***not*** make *any* distinction or application in the above passages. They do not make such application in John 20:2 because they know that it would be nonsensical and ridiculous. Why then are they not more cautious in John 21?

Let us see more.

> *Husbands, **love*** **[agape]** *your wives, even as Christ also loved the church, and gave himself for it;* (Eph. 5:25)
>
> *So ought men to **love*** **[agape]** *their wives as their own bodies. He that **loveth*** **[agape]** *his wife **loveth*** **[agape]** *himself.* (Eph. 5:28)
>
> *Nevertheless let every one of you in particular so **love*** **[agape]** *his wife even as himself; and the wife see that she reverence her husband.* (Eph. 5:33)
>
> *Husbands, **love*** **[agape]** *your wives, and be not bitter against them.* (Col. 3:19)
>
> *That they may teach the young women to be sober, to **love*** **[phileo]** *their husbands, to **love*** **[phileo]** *their children,* (Tit. 2:4)

As stated several times, *agape* love as defined by scholars, is the deep, eternal, intimate love by which the Father loved Christ, with which He loved us, and as we are to love Him. Plainly, as the earthly, familial relationship reflects the Heavenly, husbands, wives, mothers, fathers and children are to love each other with a love that is supposed to magnify that which is in Heaven. The scriptures state it clearly. The biblical typologies all are consistent with this fact. Born-again Christians' eternal security in Christ and the impossibility of separation from the love of God in Christ (Rom. 8:35-38), paired with our being pictured as sons of God, the Bride of

Christ, and the body of Christ all make the relationships between husbands, wives and children a sacred and honored picture of our relationship with God in Christ.

However, *Dead flies cause the ointment of the apothecary to send forth a stinking savour* (Eccl. 10:1), and that is the precise circumstance left to us by those who have decided to *meddle to their own hurt* (2 Chron. 25:19). Notice above, that the husbands are exhorted thoroughly and repeatedly to love their wives. This is a much needed exhortation today as the corrupt spiritual decline of the latter days continues its insidious down-spiral in the hearts of men. Christians, as never before, though indwelt by the Holy Ghost, must be constantly admonished to keep the *sacred* sacred and the *holy* in matrimony. So, husbands are to love their wives as Christ loved the church - as their own bodies and as they love themselves.

Perhaps there is a profound set of lessons in that the man is admonished so often to love, and that the wives are not. Nonetheless, from Genesis 3:16 we know her desire should be to her husband, from Ephesians 5:22 that she is to *submit* herself to him, and from Ephesians 5:33 that she is to *reverence* him. Only in one place is she actually admonished to *love* him, and we see that in Titus 2:4 above. ***Oh, what a tangled web is woven, though,*** by those who have incessantly carped on the distinctive applications of the Greek definitions of *agape* and *phileo*! Christianity – itself in crisis over the statistically high failure of marriages – must deal with the heretical nonsense that a man must *agape* his wife, but she in return only owes him a brotherly *phileo* brand of love! And what of the children, dear people? Why, Mom is only required to love ***them*** with *phileo* love!

Mary Pride is the author of a book called *The Way Home* wherein she makes a fair biblical attempt, in some respects, to rescue Christian wives and mothers from the nefarious and insidious heresies of feminism. The book is undoubtedly well-intentioned, and it has high points that are valuable enough for the truths they hold; however, Pride while seeking to uncover spiritual keys for rescuing families and biblical womanhood, dips her bucket in the wrong well:

> ...***God requires young wives to "love their husbands"*** (Titus 2:4) and the "love" he asks from us is ***phileo*** **love: brotherly love**. It is based on our *relationship*, not our emotions.[57]

She continues along this line of reasoning and lays out her idea of a "Sister-Wife" as she expands on this "nugget" (*phileo* love) that she dug out of the Greek:

> Under God, brotherly love is the sustaining ingredient of marriage. Sisterly love is the same as brotherly love... **All these passages describe *phileo* love, and they all apply to Christian marriage**.[58]

The whole Sister-Wife concept, so called by her, is Greek-inspired weirdness that leads to the perversion of the truth. The "passages" Pride references in the quote above, and the lessons she draws from them are acceptable and profitable enough from a biblical viewpoint, but she is quite hypnotized by the falsehood implanted by preoccupation with Greek that they may be categorized under the heading, *phileo* love. Further, because of the Greek behind Titus 2:4, she feels compelled to say later,

---

[57] Pride, Mary, *The Way Home: Beyond Feminism, Back to Reality* (Wheaton, Illinois: Crossway Books, 1985) p.20.

[58] Ibid. p.20

> The **love of children** that young mothers are supposed to be trained in **is *phileo* love, brotherly love, natural affection, liking, friendship**.[59]

Thus we see that the preoccupation with the Greek definitions implanted by the Greek lexicographers, leads to a doctrinal prejudice that should be easily discerned as not only detrimental to marriages and families, but it is also a justification for unnatural affection within the marriage and in motherhood! Imagine teaching that husbands must *agape* their wives, but that wives and mothers need only *phileo* their husbands and children! It turns out that the treasures and secrets of the Greek are, in actuality, imaginary nonsense - offal, in reality - that undermine the truth and the very foundations that Mary Pride seeks to defend. Is there a better way to describe the product here described than *deceit* and *delusion*?

For this debauched counsel and perverse exegesis we are truly indebted to Greek scholars and Greek expositors. Charles Darwin will go down in eternity for having fostered a truly bad and thoroughly false theory that it seems today has swallowed the real and obvious truth in almost its entirety. In like manner, they who are so jubilant to trumpet their triumphant findings from the Greek of John 21:15-17, will be exposed at Judgment as having wielded the tools of fools and committed spiritual malpractice.

> Is there more? Oh, yes.
> *I in them, and thou in me, that they may be made perfect in one; and that the world may know that thou* [God] *hast sent me* [Christ], *and hast **loved*** **[agape]** *them, as thou hast **loved*** **[agape]** *me.*
> (Jn. 17:23)

---

[59] Ibid. p.39

> *And I have declared unto them thy name, and will declare it: that the* ***love*** **[agape]** *wherewith thou hast* ***loved*** **[agape]** *me may be in them, and I in them.*
>
> (Jn. 17:26)

What a wonderful thing! We Christians are loved by the Father in the very same way as He hath loved the Son, Jesus Christ! In fact, that same love is in us. Naturally, when the ***Agape-Phileo Doctrine*** of mainline Christianity is applied, this should make it all the more wonderful because *agape* love is the particular kind that is in view… unless, that is, we take into account what had just been stated in the previous chapter:

> *For the Father himself* ***loveth*** **[phileo]** *you, because ye have* ***loved*** **[phileo]** *me, and have believed that I came out from God.*
>
> (Jn. 16:27)

So are we loved with *agape* love by the Father, or merely with *phileo* love? Christ Himself tells us that first it is one and then the other. Again, as applied by the rule of the scholars, there must be a distinction, for the lessons we have learned from the Greek, back by that seaside fire in John 21, have been taught for too long for there ***not*** to be a distinction. However, if there is a distinction, what must it be? Does God's love fluctuate? Cannot Christ make up His mind? Incidentally, it would seem quite alright for us to *phileo* Christ if we are to believe John 16:27. Why then is it taught that Peter's *phileo* love of John 21 is inferior and worthy of reproof?

The inconsistencies between the scholars' definitions of the two words and the way we see the words are actually used in the scriptures, abound; and yet, those same inconsistencies are unaddressed and unnoticed by those who seem to be aghast by what they perceive as the slightest inconsistency in the King James Bible. Apparently, there is only a certain species of gnat at which to strain.

Phileo, as we have frequently repeated, is the oft-cited Greek word for brotherly love. It should seem that people's curiosity would at least be aroused by the fact that in so many of the "brotherly love" admonitions, that *agape* love is the active verb:

> *Honour all men.* ***Love*** **[agape]** ***the brotherhood.*** *Fear God. Honour the king.* (1 Pet. 2:17)

> *He that* ***loveth*** **[agape]** ***his brother*** *abideth in the light, and there is none occasion of stumbling in him.* (1 Jn. 2:10)

> *In this the children of God are manifest, and the children of the devil: whosoever doeth not righteousness is not of God, neither he that* ***loveth*** **[agape]** ***not his brother.***
> (1 Jn. 3:10)

> *We know that we have passed from death unto life, because we* ***love*** **[agape]** ***the brethren.*** *He that* ***loveth*** **[agape]** ***not his brother*** *abideth in death.* (1 Jn. 3:14)

Though justifiable by the explanation that we are, of course, supposed to grow to love our brethren in Christ with *agape* love, the following should again give some pause to the runaway *agape-phileo* train.

> *But as touching brotherly* ***love*** **[phileo]** *ye need not that I write unto you: for ye yourselves are*

> *taught of God to **love** [agape] one another.*
> (1 Thes. 4:9)

> *Seeing ye have purified your souls in obeying the truth through the Spirit unto unfeigned **love** [phileo] of the brethren, see that ye **love** [agape] one another with a pure heart fervently:*
> (1 Pet. 1:22)

We realize that if the mainstream Christian Greek fruit punch drinkers might well try to justify a distinction in the two previously cited verses, but would the reader just please notice that Paul writes in I Thessalonians 4:9 *as touching brotherly **love*** **[phileo]**, so that is what his subject is in the verse. Thus, *as touching brotherly **love*** **[phileo]**, Paul has no need to write unto them because they are taught of God to, what? *(T)o **love*** **[agape]** *one another*! Brothers and sisters in Christ, the two loves are the same! They are interchangeable in speaking. As touching one, Paul goes right on to speak of the other. In light of that, it is easier to see that in I Peter 1:22, Peter is not speaking of two different kinds of love so much as he is urging a continuation in growth of love from mere *unfeigned* love, to *pure* and *fervent* love. It is not a different *kind* of love. It is merely a growth of the same love. The emphasis is not on differing Greek words. It is the growth and fervency of love clarified by blunt and plain English words!

If this be not true, then the following statement made by Paul seems an odd choice of words considering how brethren in Christ are to love on another.

> *All that are with me salute thee. Greet them that **love** [phileo] us in the faith. Grace be with you all. Amen.* (Tit. 3:15)

If *agape* love were the high calling that the scholars represent it to be, why would Paul be satisfied to acknowledge mere *phileo* love?

To add one final nail, no one is surprised to learn that God in almost all cases which refer to His love for us uses the word *agape* in Greek. Naturally, this would fit with the definition of deep, eternal, sacrificial love. It is evident that the love He commended to us through Christ must have been a deep and sacrificial love. I wonder why none from the *Agape-Phileo School of Bible Exposition* have mentioned anything about the following:

> *But after that the kindness and* ***love*** **[phileo]** *of God our Saviour toward man appeared...*
>
> (Tit. 3:4a)

According to Titus 3:4, God's truly great and sacrificial love that appeared to us in the sacrifice of Christ was merely *phileo* love. This doth not match at all with what we are taught by those who would render us dependent upon the Greek and its impertinent consort of scholars. In other words, the Bible's use of words does not correspond with what Greek scholars say the Greek reveals to us. Are the scholars blind to these discrepancies, or do they simply not tell us what they know? If they know, why would they not tell us?

Unavoidable Conclusions about *Agape-Phileo*

1) Mainline (and often Fundamentalist) Christian definitions of *Agape* and *Phileo* are inconsistent and contradictory to their true Bible meanings. In general terms, both noun and verb forms of *agape* and *phileo* are translated by the King James translators into the appropriate English noun and verb forms of *love* around 250 times in the New Testament.

In the first place, as cited earlier, there are ready and abundant sources of Greek language and biblical reference materials that very distinctively define the two Greek words as two very different and characteristic forms of love. Much is made of their presumed distinguishing attributes, and application based on those distinctions abound. The problem is that, as demonstrated in this chapter, the scholars' definitions and applications of those words routinely contradict themselves when studied in many of the passages where they appear. Secondly, the step is taken by commentators, writers, leaders and speakers to rigorously and bountifully apply those definitions of the words into their biblical courses of study, teaching or preaching. It seems that few, if any, of these effusive users of Greek have troubled themselves to verify *in Greek* whether the definitions they have borrowed from the reference materials actually are verified by scriptural context. **What the Bible does say and teach is in this way subjugated to the *word of men*.**

It is simply a mockery to any kind of reasonable theology that is built *precept upon precept; line upon line* (Isa. 28:13), to try to reconcile God loving *Christ* at one point with *agape* love (Jn. 3:35) as defined by the scholars and at another time (Jn. 5:20) with *phileo* love as defined by the scholars. What a three-ring circus it is to try to rectify John being the disciple whom Jesus loved with *agape* love those four times, but the one whom He loved merely with *phileo* love in John 20:2.

What sober, godly lesson is to be implemented into family life where the husband is to *agape* his wife even as he loves himself, but she has only to *phileo* him and the children (Tit. 2:4)? How secure are we in the love of God when He most usually bestows *agape* love upon us, but on some occasions, like John.16:27, we are regarded with mere *phileo* love?

Before claiming that no well educated theologian would teach such wayward and skewed "love," remember that it has been documented that Mary Pride, in her own writings, teaches that the woman only need *phileo* her husband. It is hoped that any well-reasoned Fundamental Bible-believer would be able to discern and avoid such ridiculous false doctrine. Really, though, that is the point. Most would not dare teach such corrupted forms of love mentioned above because it is obviously crack-brained theologically. However, if one subscribes to that whole *agape-phileo* interplay in John 21 as exposited so often by these pseudo-theologians, then it is inconsistent and hypocritical to fail to apply those same rules and distinctions throughout the rest of the New Testament! If a Fundamental pastor accepts the insights from the Greek in John 21, as delineated by the reference materials on his bookshelf, then he *should* be fastidious and courageous enough to go right ahead and make the consistent application in the rest of his Bible.

Incidentally, with the encroachment of the Emerging Church, the Purpose Driven Church, the New Evangelicals, and every green student-preacher being applauded for "going to the Greek" as a mark of spirituality, it would be no surprise to find that theological insanity should become perfectly orthodox.

2) The Greek *Agape* and *Phileo* of the New Testament mean the same thing! There seems only one feasible and sane conclusion to be drawn from the Lord's abundant usage of the noun and verb forms of *Agape* and *Phileo*: **they mean the same thing!** They do not distinguish two separate forms or two different depths of love. They both mean *to love*. It is for this reason that they are used in interchangeable fashion in Greek, and that is why they were translated as one word – *love* – by the AV translators. They are synonyms. To take the separate and distinct meanings of the two words as they are defined by so many, and to try to apply those definitions in a consistent manner throughout the New Testament, is to make a theological disaster of anything resembling the truth. Imagine *Laurel and Hardy* or *The Three Stooges* transitioned from the silver screen to the theological chair, and one would hardly be exposed to more of a disreputable sideshow than what is being taught about this very theological matter today.

If one were to hypothesize that the two word forms meant two separate things, a sincere and scientific scriptural search would simply overthrow the hypothesis due to the abundant and overwhelming conflicts of the biblical evidence with the hypothesis. Evolutionists routinely ignore the scientific conflicts with their hallowed hypothesis because they do not wish to be led where the truth leads. Creationist "Fundamentalists" rip them "up one side and down the other" for their prejudice and insincerity. Have so called "Bible-believers" lost the desire and ability to objectively evaluate the affairs of their own theological house?

If there is any doubt that *agape* and *phileo* mean the same thing, first go back through the verses printed in parallel with one another in this chapter and compare contexts and statements. Secondly, return whence we started the chapter in John 21. Notice again the conversational parrying of Peter and the Lord with the Greek verbs *agape* and *phileo.* Also, notice this time that the Holy Spirit marks the three separate exchanges by His use of the words *the second time* in verse 16, and *the third time* in verse 17.

John 21:15-17

> *15 So when they had dined, Jesus saith to Simon Peter, Simon, son of Jonas,* ***lovest*** **[agape]** *thou me more than these? He saith unto him, Yea, Lord; thou knowest that I* ***love*** **[phileo]** *thee. He saith unto him, Feed my lambs.*

> *16 He saith to him again* ***the second time****, Simon, son of Jonas,* ***lovest*** **[agape]** *thou me? He saith unto him, Yea, Lord; thou knowest that I* ***love*** **[phileo]** *thee. He saith unto him, Feed my sheep.*
> *17 He saith unto him* ***the third time****, Simon, son of Jonas,* ***lovest*** **[phileo]** *thou me? Peter was grieved because he said unto him the third time, Lovest* **[phileo]** *thou me? And he said unto him, Lord, thou knowest all things; thou knowest that I* ***love*** **[phileo]** *thee. Jesus saith unto him, Feed my sheep.*

The second time (vs.16), Jesus questioned Peter about his love using the word *agape* just as He had in the first query in verse 15. But, the third time in verse 17, Jesus, as has been so much written about, asked Peter about his love using the word *phileo*. If the two Greek words mean something so different, then we must acknowledge that Jesus actually asked Peter a *different question* in the third exchange. So why does the scripture read that Christ said the question for the ***third time***? The reason why is because Jesus asked Peter the very same question (at least with regard to Peter's love) all three times! ***1) Lovest thou me… 2) Lovest thou me… 3) Lovest thou me…***

Not only are the questions all the same in English, but they are also the same in Greek, because *agape* and *phileo* are used interchangeably as synonyms throughout the New Testament. If the Greek student had been anything but superficial, he would have discovered this demonstrable fact. He thus would have uncovered the verity that the King's English simplified the truth of *love* in the Greek, by avoiding the confusion of two differing words by translating them with the same word in English. No student of the King James English was ever misdirected for a moment by the pseudo-intellectual complications and confusion presented by the two Greek words and all the train of false propaganda that followed them. No AV 1611 reader was ever allured into the unprofitable pursuit of unraveling in Greek what God had already settled in English.

Agape and *phileo* mean the same thing.

3) The definitions of *agape and phileo,* as represented in the mainline Christian material, are man-generated, not scripture-generated. It is most insightful indeed to watch the almost automatic machinations of the expositors when it comes time to teach or preach from John 21. The primary and seemingly robotic exercise is to take the English word *love* back to the Greek's *agape* and *phileo.* Of more monumental importance though, is the fact that the very next action is to ***import*** the definitions of *agape and phileo* out of various Greek reference works, commentaries and word studies instead of using even the Greek New Testament. There is no real, purposeful attempt to even survey how the two words are used on the whole in the Greek New Testament. The only explanation for the continuing existence in contemporary teaching, preaching and devotional studies of the flagrant and ridiculously obvious inconsistencies and contradictions set forth in this chapter, can only be that those guilty of such teaching never even bother to see if the definitions consistently mesh in other places. They are entirely tunnel-visioned. Where they do make application of the definitions to other passages, they yet again do not circumspectly look beyond the immediate passage in question. The pervading ideal seems to be along the line of, "The *Agape-Phileo Doctrine* worked great back in John 21. It'll work fine here too."

The precept placed into practice here can hardly be overemphasized. In making man's conclusion of the definition the first and last order of appeal, man becomes the arbiter of truth – the first appeal and final authority. The King James Bible is perfect, infallible and inerrant, and as such it is my final appeal. Importantly though, the travesty of the *Agape-Phileo Doctrine* is obvious even if one uses the Greek as the final appeal! A Junior High School graduate with a *Strong's Concordance* running the references by the numbers is able to find every contradiction that has been highlighted in this chapter.

These scholars' and teachers' tragic set of errors with *agape* and *phileo* is magnified in that they failed to research the matter in the Greek texts which they consider to be the final authority, thus they do not discover the glaring discrepancies. But this is not their primary error. Their first and principal error is that even the scriptures they so adamantly claim to believe are not truly their final authority. ***Man was and is their final authority.*** Their first inclination is to appeal to the definitions of words as conceived by men. They seek not to understand how words are used even in their own Greek bibles. They appeal immediately to what other men have thought and written. Their theology is determined from the start by appealing to men for "what this means," and apparently nothing much upsets the applecart of their theology because they blithely continue teaching the *Agape-Phileo Doctrine* while naming their churches *Agape Baptist Church* and *Agape Fellowship.* All the while, these flagrant inconsistencies are nestled in and await discovery within the very reference materials they herald.

In the end, the whole sad travesty of the *Agape-Phileo Doctrine* is that from the opening bell it is a man-generated teaching. Men originated the definitions, commandeered the actual meanings of the words away from their contexts, and then other men came along and applied the misleading falsehoods as Christian truths and deep devotional insights. In the end, the words of Christ must reverberate through the hollow souls of the careless and guilty: *Making the word of God of none effect through your tradition, which ye have delivered: and many such like things do ye* (Mk. 7:13).

The teaching is man-generated not scripture-generated.

4) The definitions of *agape, philos, agapao and phileo* are artificial definitions. This, of course, is akin to being man-generated, but man often needs to be put in his place and with authority. Only what God has to offer is real. Whether speaking of life, light, salvation, a Savior, or the scripture, only what God offers is real. Man has developed the same bad habits as his first father, the devil: he thinks his own opinion and input into the affairs of God matters. Man tends to think that he can alter his commission and orders in any way that he deems is constructive or better, and that God will receive his little opinion as some valued source of intelligence. Like the children of Israel in Deuteronomy 1:21-22, man receives words from God and then thinks that when he has a "better idea," it is a good thing. That is not how it worked out in Deuteronomy chapter 1.

Every time man sets his hand to meddle in God's affairs in a way that God did not ordain, he generates a spurious substitute for what God intended us to have. Man "blesses" us with an artificial, carved or molten image, melted down in the *strange fire* of Nadab and Abihu, formed and fashioned with the utmost care and ingenuity of a sincere *idolator!*

So it is with God's word. God said what He said, had men write down what He said, preserved what He said, and then providentially guided the hearts and intellects of chosen men to put His words into the languages of the earth. On one hand, God guides men. On the other hand, many men presume to insert themselves into the process very much as Israel did in Deuteronomy 1, as Aaron did in Exodus 32, and as Jeroboam did in 1 Kings 12. The result is a cheap, artificial, spurious and powerless product. It may be sacred to the idol makers and idol lovers, but it is abomination to the Lord.

The smiths who carved and engraved the *Agape-Phileo Doctrine* formed something that "sounded good" and seemed to work very well within the context of John 21. They thought and molded and chiseled away at the definitions of these two Greek words for *love*, and when they were done, the congregation was altogether wowed by the apparent spiritual depths of their work, and was no little bit impressed by how scholarly and intelligent were the minds that discovered such treasure from the scripture.

The problem turns out to be that the so called treasure is a cheap substitute for the truth. Conceived in the mind of man instead of the heart of God, it may look pretty good in certain surroundings and in limited light, but up close and with just the smallest sprinkling of sincere, studious investigation, it turns out to be plaster, tin foil, spray paint, and glitter. Against the backdrop of the rest of the scriptures, it is exposed for what it is: just something men dreamed up and ran with under the guise of intellectualism and spirituality. Those pseudo-definitions have prejudiced the minds of preachers and teachers to the extent that they take the definition as the gospel truth and do not even bother to check the actual gospel scriptures.

The mainstream definitions of *agape* and *phileo* are artificial, inconsistent and, thus, false.

Consider the Scholars

Before detailing the ramifications that all this has with respect to the superiority of the King James Bible, there are first two things that need to be seriously considered in light of what we have seen. One of the things is appalling and the other is tragic.

First, the "scholars" responsible for the propagation of the pathetic *Agape-Phileo Doctrine* as taught and embraced by so much of Christianity today, need to be addressed. This shall not be addressed as "scholarship" for that would be a misappropriation of terms. Further the term "scholarship" insinuates to the mind that scholarship is an entity unto itself. It is not. "Scholarship" is produced by "scholars" - mere men. Scholarship springs from the minds and hearts of men. It is a product of their spirituality (or lack thereof), and is subject to motivations, ambitions, fears, imbalances and sins. Scholarship may well be brought forth of blatant stupidity, as well as insightful brilliance. It may set forth profound spiritual light, but has been known to arise from and engender gross blindness and darkness. This matter came from "scholars." Men are responsible for it.

The plain intent of this book is not to open wounds unnecessarily nor devolve to caustic rhetoric and name-calling. Nevertheless, it most necessary, in light of the flagrant and obvious contradictions and inconsistencies found in this *Agape-Phileo* issue, to turn attention for at least a few moments upon the scholars who have proven themselves altogether deserving of this scrutiny. It is necessary that they should be held accountable for how such a doctrinal travesty as the *Agape-Phileo Doctrine* managed to find expression from their pens, and then afterwards, for all its manifest falsehood, to escape their attention for all this time.

Three utterly inescapable conclusions regarding the scholars' oversights seem to present themselves, and assessment and reassessment only seems to deepen the resolve that there can be little else that explains this doctrinal shipwreck:

1) Carelessness. It is emphasized again that the game with the two Greek words works very well if limited to John 21 and a few other passages that would support the preconceived definitions. It most definitely does not work, as has been shown, when the entirety of the Greek passages are considered. Christians are constantly regaled with the eminent academic qualifications and degrees of these "scholarly" men and women. We hear of their great familiarity with the Greek New Testament, their memorization of it, their meditation in it, their brilliance, their godliness, their teaching experience and their authored works. Indeed, the "common folk" are made to feel the ponderous weight and power of the scholastic and intellectual excellence of such people to the extent that it seems both preposterous and disrespectful if anyone should even question their conclusions or put their methods to the test.

Nevertheless, the falsehood and unjustifiable discrepancies of the *Agape-Phileo* issue lead Bible believers to ask how this matter could have escaped the attention of such lauded theologians and linguists. Certainly, much lesser academic luminaries, with such simple tools as a *Strong's Concordance* or a Bible program, have proven themselves capable of discovering these discrepancies. This we know: whichever scholar first gave birth to this *doctrine*, and however many subsequent "scholars" have signed on to it and helped propagate it, the doctrine itself has enjoyed continuance due to a truly profound and sustained ***carelessness!***

Think about it. There have been generations of professors, linguists, theologians and academics who have devoted their lives to studying the Greek New Testament in one form or another. They have matriculated and trained generation after generation of "soldiers of the Cross" who have spread the matter abroad and pontificated on and on about *agape* and *phileo*. Could it truly be that ***nobody*** caught the errors and discrepancies and raised an alarm? To many, though they are wrong, these people are considered the watchdogs and caretakers of biblical faith. How is it then that those who are reputed to be as familiar with the Greek as their own native languages, completely missed God's interchangeable use of the words?

If these who are reputed for their godliness, devotion and excellence simply overlooked these matters out of incontrovertible carelessness, then what does that mean for thousands of other doctrines and insights into the word of God? If other such cases of oversight, negligence, and obliviousness in those to whom most all of Christianity looks for finality can be shown, what would that mean? If those who propagate and support the *Agape-Phileo Doctrine* would check their reference sources, their Greek sources and their Bibles, they would swiftly discover the bogus nature of it. They do not discover it because they are ***careless.*** Perhaps *laziness* enters, or *naiveté*, or, undoubtedly at times, *ignorance.* In the end, the Christian must *...<u>study</u> to shew (himself) approved <u>unto God</u>, a workman that needeth not to be ashamed*... (2 Tim. 2:15). If he does not do so, he is ***careless.***

Perhaps, brethren, God gave believers a Bible by which to judge the scholars instead of giving us scholars by which we judge the Bible.

2) Cowardice. If one was not careless; if he did catch the inconsistencies in the *Agape-Phileo Doctrine*; if he knew the ramifications, and then if he did not raise the alarm, what would THAT mean? It could well mean that he is a ***coward.*** The number of less than noble factors that can influence the human heart is truly amazing. In a society of tightly bound academics, for whom the reputation of their expertise, the respect of their colleagues, and the tenure of their positions could theoretically mean much, is it possible that some might see something contradictory, and yet speak not? Before a very similar group to that one just described, Jesus said this: *How can ye believe, which receive honour one of another, and seek not the honour that cometh from God only* (Jn. 5:44)? Though some did genuinely believe Christ, they were driven to anonymity for a reason: *Nevertheless among the chief rulers also many believed on him; but because of the Pharisees they did not confess him, lest they should be put out of the synagogue* (Jn. 12:42). *The fear of man bringeth a snare* (Prov. 29:25a). It always has brought a snare. The snare is cowardice.

Whether the fear be that standing for Christ and the truth would cost life, wealth, career, social standing or respect, in the end cowardice is the name for the reason such an one would not act.

3) Crookedness. If a respected Greek scholar or a pastor were not careless, knew that what was being taught about *agape* and *phileo* was wrong, but then did not raise the alarm, it might mean he was a coward. Another possibility exists. He may not be a coward. He may be ***crooked.***

I personally am in no way convinced that the contradictions have been overlooked and remain utterly unseen, considering the number of seminary professors, authors and language scholars in this country. I believe there are many that do know the truth about the *Agape-Phileo* travesty and simply choose not to rock the boat. They are willing to allow untruth to be taught. Without raising an alarm, they are willing to allow the Bible to be falsely preached to God's people. At the very least, on their watch, they do not say anything when the Bible is said to teach something that it does not. An accountant who does your taxes in such a dishonest manner is a ***crook***! A policeman who ignores similar corruption is said to be "bent." He is ***crooked.*** What other conclusion could then be drawn about a professor or scholar who similarly chooses to further a lie by refusing to voice the truth?

Consider the Samuels

Samuel was born out of a heartbroken mother's prayers and the blessing of an old man of God. At a tender age he was delivered to the hand of that very same old man, the high priest, Eli, and in his care Samuel spent the remainder of his childhood serving God and firming his foundation for the future. Samuel represented for God the next generation of useful men. Eli's reprobate and wanton sons would not be among that generation. Samuel watched the villainous behavior of the hypocrites, learned to recognize the voice of God, and developed the character to deliver even the worst kind of news when called upon to do so.

By the time he was a young man, something was evident:

> *And Samuel grew, and the LORD was with him, and did let none of his words fall to the ground. And **all Israel from Dan even to Beersheba knew that Samuel was established to be a prophet of the LORD**. And the LORD appeared again in Shiloh: for the LORD revealed himself to Samuel in Shiloh by the word of the LORD.*
> (1 Sam. 3:19-21)

Samuel would go on to represent the very presence of God to Israel. It was he who was called upon to anoint Saul, to rebuke Israel for that ill-fated idea, and to eventually judge and condemn Saul in his kingdom. It was his honor to anoint King David, and having poured the oil on the head of the Messiah's genealogical father, and having blessed the throne that would one day be the throne of King Jesus, Samuel went the way of all flesh, yet he went a victor. Some would say he had an unmatched "career."

In his boyhood, Samuel stood in the presence of old Eli, and was ordained to be the prophet for the next generation. He *...did let none of his words fall to the ground, ... all Israel from Dan even to Beersheba knew that Samuel was established to be a prophet of the LORD,* and ... *the LORD revealed himself to Samuel in Shiloh by the word of the LORD* (1 Sam. 3:19-21). Who will the next generation be if the Lord tarries? What will that generation of "prophets" be like who, in many cases, have for their entire lives been exposed to Laodicean scholarship, if not to the world itself?

In recent months, a Fundamental Independent Baptist church near the Independent Bible-believing Baptist church which I pastor had an evening in which some of their "preacher-boys" preached for the Sunday evening service. These young men were high-school-aged and the service was an outgrowth of the Christian day school of that church. Having no desire to embarrass the youngster, I will refrain from certain specifics, but one of the young men ascended to the pulpit for his turn, opened his text from John, the first epistle, and promptly proceeded to drive directly off into the Greek to expand on the type of love which was the subject of his address. Naturally, the species of love was the *agape* variety. In succeeding weeks the young man went to represent his school in the preacher-boy competition at a gathering of other Christian sister schools. He was the only kid who went to the Greek. He went into much detail regarding the depths of the *Agape-Phileo Doctrine*. He won first place in the youth preacher competition between Fundamental Baptist schools.

This particular generation of preachers, educators and scholars have not been thorough or vigilant enough in their study of that which they consider their final authority, to detect the gross discrepancies that exist and await discovery for anyone who shows the least bit of initiative. One looks in vain for the merest shred of unction that should have been exercised at least to the extent of verifying a few simple cross references. These men are awarding ribbons to young preachers who are the puppets and mouthpieces of "scholars" who have been demonstrably careless, hopelessly crooked, or abashed cowards. They are training, matriculating, and rewarding your Samuels, the leaders and feeders of the flock of God for the next generation.

Agape and *Phileo* vs. *Love* in the AV 1611

Having thus laid the groundwork necessary to be able to intelligently weigh the ramifications, consider what it means to have a time-tested, God-honored and fruitful old Book whose translators rendered the *agape* and *phileo* of the Greek into, most usually, (with a few exceptions to be discussed in a later chapter) *love* in the English. Scholars of most all stripes, including even the majority of the very most conservative King James defenders, believe that no translation can be superior to its Greek or Hebrew roots, and that Christians do not (cannot) gain more light and understanding from the King James Bible than they would from the Greek or Hebrew. To contend with them on this point is to guarantee a vociferous and quite active response.

In light of the material in this chapter: **how *is not* the English *Love* of the King James Bible Superior to the *Agape-Phileo* of the Greek Manuscripts?** It has been meticulously shown that despite the Greek scholars' insistence that the two Greek words are exemplary of the wonderful depths of the Greek language, and the deeper understanding to be gained by studying the characteristics and distinctions of those two words, the *actual* reality is that the two words are interchangeable in Greek. Not only did God interchange them in Greek, it was actually man who artificially inserted the false definitions of *agape* and *phileo*, and the scholars' precious "hypothesis" does not stand under the least amount of reasonable scrutiny. The word *love,* as used in the King James Bible is a superior translation because the believer no longer has to juggle two words that mean the very same thing. There is a providential clarity in English that the confused scholars have shown is not so evident in the Greek. The confusion of two words identifying the very same concept is thus eliminated and represents a simplification of the truth.

It is worthwhile at this juncture to mention that God is the Author of His own Book, and He has license to use whatever words He wants and to lead men accordingly. We do not charge that God does not use synonyms, for He does. Nor do we presume to say that His work is always to simplify the truth. God can weave His truth with whatever simplicity or intricacy that He wishes.

It may be safely said that the scholars in this case erected a straw man of false doctrine. They did so of their own downfallen ingenuity by imparting meanings and distinctions in the Greek that God never intended. In the King James Bible, God effortlessly knocked their straw man down. It is perfectly clear to an English reader what God meant by *love* in John 21 and throughout the New Testament. There is no indication that the Greek readers of, say 200 A.D., were confused by the Greek usage of two words for love, but it is certain that the scholars have since inserted confusion into the whole affair. The matter *cannot* be confused in the AV.

Is it possible that the obscurities of meaning which exist in the original languages were actually cleared up in the AV 1611? All language scholars, linguists and translators are very quick to inform everyone that it is impossible for man to render perfect and exact meaning from one language to another. Words which are packed with meanings, implications, tones and inferences in one language, are so often maddeningly impossible to render exactly in another language. Thus, the scholars insist that all translations of the Bible must be inferior to the original languages, because in translating them, men could not possibly have rendered all the meaning found in the Greek and Hebrew.

This mentality has led the way for every doctrinal crackpot around to be able to "go to the Greek" and come up with some variance of what is written in his Bible. It is a profoundly wonderful excuse to offer for **not being subject to *what God said***, since one can always find a different way to translate *what God said.*

In the case of *agape* and *phileo,* let it suffice to point out that while men read meanings and distinctions into the words that God did not intend, God erased whatever obscurity existed, or was imagined, with the translation of the King James Bible! Consider the ramifications, first, for this one strand of truth. In the case of *Agape-Phileo*, the English cleared up whatever obscurity might have existed in the original languages. That clarification, by the hands of the AV translators, is situated for every English reader to see and prosper in without the assistance – *no, in spite* of the assistance – of the "scholars" of our day.

If the Sun of Righteousness burned off the fog of obscurity in this case, and He did, then it should be considered that it may have been a regular exercise throughout the AV 1611. In fact, one must at least contemplate that it may have been the entire purpose of the King James Bible.

It is the purpose of this book to show that while all translators face "choices" of wording when it comes to translation, God led the King James translators in their choices in such a way that those choices of words and phrasing are demonstrably superior to the Greek and Hebrew by virtue of the fact that they clarified meaning and erased the inherent obscurities of the language differential. Though a lengthier discussion of this will follow later, there is no reason to read God's providential oversight of the translation as some form of "re-inspiration" or "double-inspiration," as detractors are anxious to accuse. Every King James defender believes God oversaw the preservation of His word as well as the inspiration of His word. Without fail, each King James defender will heartily endorse the idea that God led Erasmus in certain respects. Every single one will laud and thank the Lord for leading Wycliff, Tyndale and Coverdale providentially. Did not God, in some measure, lead those men in word choices? Do we preachers not often beg God to guide our thoughts, hearts and judgments? Do we not pray that He would set a guard upon our lips and "give" us answers? How is it such an alien and abominable concept that God would affect the word choices of the *Authorized Version* translators in 1604-1611 in such a way that those choices would be to His own pleasing? How is it that honor may be routinely lauded upon the providential courses of the lives, merits and accomplishments of these men, but only up to the point of what they mutually agreed should be put on the sacred page of the King James Bible? If we give God glory for His use of men in both the inspiration and preservation of the scriptures in Hebrew and Greek; if we gladly extol Him for His guidance in the noble work of Wycliff, the brilliance of Erasmus, and the ingenuity and excellence of Tyndale; if the lives, times and works of Bois, Reynolds, Savile, Smith and Andrews are praiseworthy heavenward in other respects, why should we imagine that it should instantly become heretically abominable to consider that God affected their corporate choices of wording in translating the AV 1611?

No light or depth of understanding whatsoever has been attained by going to the Greek in this matter. Again, as has been demonstrated, all of those highly espoused insights from the "original languages" in the case of *Agape-Phileo* have been a complete waste of breath and ink. Indeed, in view of what has been seen in this chapter, the AV 1611 seems to have been the final authoritative word about the matter, and no English reader who believed and studied what he read has ever been misled for a single moment. In fact, one important consideration that will undoubtedly be a nightmarish specter to many, is the observation that reverting back to the Greek in this case should be viewed as a ***regression***. That exercise did not assist men's understanding. It ***thwarted*** it. It was not progress. It was a ***hindrance***. Importantly, it actually unraveled what God had already accomplished in the truth of the English Bible. Every time a man ran back to play the Greek game with *agape* and *phileo*, he was actually traveling *backwards* into a less clear and more ill-defined source of doctrine than was contained in his majestic, pure old English King James Bible.

Chapter 3

Charity Cases

> *Though I speak with the tongues of men and of angels, and have not charity, I am become as sounding brass, or a tinkling cymbal. And though I have the gift of prophecy, and understand all mysteries, and all knowledge; and though I have all faith, so that I could remove mountains, and have not charity, I am nothing. And though I bestow all my goods to feed the poor, and though I give my body to be burned, and have not charity, it profiteth me nothing. Charity suffereth long, and is kind; charity envieth not; charity vaunteth not itself, is not puffed up, Doth not behave itself unseemly, seeketh not her own, is not easily provoked, thinketh no evil; Rejoiceth not in iniquity, but rejoiceth in the truth; Beareth all things, believeth all things, hopeth all things, endureth all things. Charity never faileth: but whether there be prophecies, they shall fail; whether there be tongues, they shall cease; whether there be knowledge, it shall vanish away.*
>
> (1 Cor. 13:1-8)

The analysis of the Greek word ***Agape*** cannot yet be left for other subjects. While the verb form ***agapao*** shows up a great many more times, the noun form ***agape*** appears around 115 times in the New Testament and is usually translated *love* by the King James translators, which is expected. There is a curiosity though, in that, 29 times, ***agape***, one of the now famous Greek words for *love,* is translated ***charity*** or ***charitably*** in the AV.

The Dismissal of *Charity*

The word *charity* has been a burr under the saddles of bible scholars and commentators for a long time. First, in all 29 occurrences in the AV 1611 where *agape* was translated *charity* or *charitably*, the new versions of the Bible are unfailing in translating it *love.* The survey of the new versions that do so includes, among others, the New American Standard Version (NASV), the New International Version (NIV), the Revised Standard Version (RSV), the New American Standard Update, the Living Bible and the New King James Version (NKJV). As a point of emphasis, the NKJV, which some like to tout as the King James without the *thee's and thou's*, did unapologetically fall in step with the other apostate versions in this matter.

Reference works in the form of linguistic tools and commentaries are very quick indeed in disposing of, or disregarding, *charity.* In *The Companion Bible,* E. W. Bullinger, without even a hiccup, referred the reader of 1 Corinthians 13:1 to his margin where, with no preamble or explanation, he identifies ***charity*** as *love*[60], and from thence the reader is sent to Bullinger's appendix[61], where *charity* is not so much as mentioned and *agape* is merely equated with *love.* In like manner, *The Zondervan Pictorial Encyclopedia of the Bible,* dismissing the 350 year old translation of 1 Corinthians 13, says Paul declared love to be the greatest of the Christian

---

[60] Bullinger, E.W., *The Companion Bible* (Humphrey Milford Oxford University Press, London, New York, Toronto & Melbourne) p.1718

[61] Ibid., Append.135, p.164

graces in 1 Corinthians 13:13.[62]

It is obvious from the "scripture" quotations contained in this work that Zondervan has no commitment to the KJV, but the *charity* of the majestic old Book is haughtily shunned – actually, not recognized at all. Its translational invalidity in the eyes of Zondervan's editors is almost palpable. In eight pages of discourse on the subject of love, the reader would never know that *agape* was ever translated *charity,* for once again the Authorized Version's rendering of the word is resolutely ignored in Zondervan's work thus:

> Paul likewise subscribes to the eternal quality of **love** in declaring that "**Love** never ends" (1 Cor. 13:8a).[63]

> After listing a number of interpersonal virtues, Paul admonished, "And above all these put on **love**, which binds everything together in perfect harmony" (Col. 3:14).[64]

> ...he (Paul) concluded by pointing out "a still more excellent way" (1 Cor. 12:31b) with his immortal classic on **love** (1 Cor. 13).[65]

Robertson's Word Pictures reflects some of the disdain that Bible *charity* has endured from the pens of the learned:

> This is the crux of the chapter. **Love** is the way par excellence of <1 Cor. 12:31>... The word is rare in the Gospels, but common in Paul, John,

---

[62] Tenney, Merrill C. ed., *The Zondervan Pictorial Encyclopedia of the Bible* (Regency Reference Library, Grand Rapids, Michigan, 1975, 1976) Vol.3, p.989.
[63] Ibid., p.990
[64] Ibid., p.993
[65] Ibid., p.994

> Peter, Jude. Paul does not limit [agapee] (grk 26) at all (both toward God and man). **Charity (Latin caritas) is wholly inadequate**.[66]

Vincent is no less condescending when expositing 1 Corinthians 13:1:

> **The change in the English Revised Version (1885) from "charity" to "love," is a good and thoroughly defensible one.** "Charity" follows the "caritas" of the Vulgate, **and is not used consistently in the King James Version** On the contrary, in the gospels, [agapee] (grk 26) is always rendered "love," and mostly elsewhere, except in this epistle, where the word occurs but twice**. "Charity," in modern usage, has acquired the senses of "tolerance and beneficence," which express only single phases of love**. There is no more reason for saying "charity envieth not," than for saying "God is charity;" "the charity of Christ constraineth us;" "the charity of God is shed abroad in our hearts." The real objection to the change on the part of **unscholarly partisans** of the King James Version is the breaking of the familiar rhythm of the verses.[67]

We shall see within the next few pages how "defensible" is the Revised Version's change of the wording of the old Book. Perhaps the heady conceit which drips from Vincent's pen will prove to be indefensible, as well. It is possible that even the

---

[66] Robertson, A.T. *Robertson's Word Pictures of the New Testament* (1998) P C Study Bible (Version 2.11) [Computer Software]. Seattle, WA: Biblesoft.

[67] *Vincent's Word Studies of the New Testament* (1997) P C Study Bible (Version 2.11) [Computer Software]. Seattle, WA: Biblesoft.

"unscholarly partisans" – read that "hicks" – might be able to glean a crumb or two from the Bible without Mr. Vincent.

Adam Clarke, in his classic commentary, marches in lockstep with the sentiments of the scholars who are opposed to the idea of *charity* being a translation in which God's hand was present.

> Before I proceed to the consideration of the different parts of this chapter, it may be necessary to examine **whether the word agape (grk 26) be best translated by charity or love. Wycliff**, translating from the Vulgate**, has the word charity**; and him our authorized version follows. **But Coverdale, Matthews, Cranmer, and the Geneva Bible, have love**; which is adopted by recent translators and commentators in general; among whom the chief are Dodd, Pearce, Purver, Wakefield, and Wesley; **all these strenuously contend that the word charity, which is now confined to almsgiving, is utterly improper; and that the word love, alone expresses the apostle's sense**. As the word charity seems now to express little else than almsgiving, which, performed even to the uttermost of a man's power, is nothing if he lacks what the apostle terms as agapee (grk 26), and which we here translate charity**; it is best to omit the use of a word in this place which, taken in its ordinary signification, makes the apostle contradict himself;** [68]

[68] Clarke, Adam. *Clarke's Commentary.* (1998) P C Study Bible (Version 2.11) [Computer Software]. Seattle, WA: Biblesoft.

Again, as a point of emphasis, the quality that seems to be missing in these fellows' discourses and "learned" opinions is the humble attribute of hallowed and contrite reverence in dealing with God's word. Moses was told he had better kick off his shoes before the bush (Exod. 3), and the men of Bethshemesh learned the price of presumptuously peering into the Ark of the Covenant (1 Sam. 6:19). Flippancy and presumption are very grave and sober failings before the God of Heaven. Behind the lofty language and the linguistic display of these editors and correctors, resides an ungodly comfort in altering holy things, and a detectable lack of awe and humility in the liberal application of Jehudi's pen-knife (Jer. 36:23). If it were true that the King James translators were imperfect in their monumental labors, it would seem that the terrible awe by which they proceeded in their work, and the unmatched credentials of their combined assemblage might at least inspire those who labor to disassemble their accomplishments to do so with just a hint of tremulous reverence. Alas, it is not so.

It is plain that there is overwhelming sentiment amongst the scholars that *charity* should be discarded as a legitimate translation. Unfortunately, these ideas have succeeded in infiltrating the King James camp more than is wont. Lester Roloff was a much beloved soul and a courageous Bible-believer. Famous for founding homes for troubled children, for his battles with the authorities, for his down-home, yet inspirational singing and preaching, Lester Roloff sparks cherished and sometimes tearful memories for those that remember him as a brave, true and uncompromising soldier of Jesus Christ. I believe Brother Roloff was all those things, as well, and I admire him greatly. Yet in a cassette tape (one which I am sad to say gave up the ghost after much play) of his group of girl singers, the Honeybee Quartet, in a song taken directly from 1 Corinthians 13 – the *charity* chapter – the quartet changed the word from *charity* to "love." This, of course, does not mean that Lester Roloff was an apostate. It does mean that changing the wording of the Holy Bible is a subtle and insidious leaven! A word (*charity*), which is the theme of an entire chapter of the Bible (1 Cor. 13), was changed and altered to another word (love), and that egregious trespass (Rev. 22:18-19) was overlooked by as vigilant and valiant a warrior as Lester Roloff! To this hour, many are the King James Bible-believers who do not think to bristle when 1 Corinthians 13 is referred to as the ***"Love Chapter."***

Yes, as Messr.'s Vincent and Clark above point out, *charity* has come, in most recent generations, to mean almsgiving and beneficence to the common mind. To the forefront of men's thoughts, *charity* sparks little else besides the United Way, the Red Cross, and the Girl Scouts. It might be worthwhile to note that that is the case with many words. *Gay* hardly means *cheerful* anymore, nor is a *faggot* a burning bundle of sticks. *Conversation* only means "talk" now, and the *"lover of good men,"* in Titus 1:8, suggests vileness to us upon which we need not elaborate. It does not seem to register with men that when, to the inattentive and simple-minded, meanings of words fall to disrepair and drop from common usage, that it is men that are deprived of precious treasure, not God.

Charity Suffereth Long (1 Cor.13:4)

It is worthwhile here to highlight to the reader the philosophy that afflicts the minds and defiles the works of so many scholars and translators. They think that the Holy Scriptures must constantly adjust to the changing and evolving languages of men. In a measure, this is certainly true, but there are a two points worth bearing in mind: 1) Man's languages, as does his nature, tend toward degradation and deterioration over time. 2) God never promised to pursue man all the way into the depths of the sewer with constantly and perennially *down*-dated bibles! It must not be forgotten that *...the LORD said, My spirit shall not always strive with man...* (Gen. 6:3), nor should the important sequence found in Romans 1:24, 26 & 28 be overlooked:

> *Wherefore God also* ***gave them up***...(24)
> *For this cause God* ***gave them up***...(26)
> *God* ***gave them over*** *to a reprobate mind*...(28)

It may seem a terribly bold suggestion to the modern mind, but perhaps man should expend a bit of effort and aspire to retain the depths and the textures of the words that God gave him. Plainly, from the standard that God set at Pentecost in Acts 2, He did not necessarily intend all men to learn Hebrew or Greek. It is reasonable that the message borne by those who left Jerusalem after that monumental day would be guarded and cherished in the language of the bearers and the subsequent hearers. As we have noted before, men and women with gallant hearts sally forth to technical school, college or university to acquire, in large part, acquaintance with the technical language of their chosen field: pharmacology, dentistry, medicine, computers, electricity, realty, graphics, etc. To the uninitiated, much of the dialogue between two trained technicians in a common field is a barrage of indiscernible techno-speak. These career-oriented souls very readily "stay up" on the shifting language and technical developments of their fields so they can make money. And yet, the average Christian considers it a monumental inconvenience to seek out the true root meanings of a handful of words in his own English language. Christians expect their holy and exalted God to publish and print a new downgraded bible every six months to keep pace with the cultural and the individual's slothful deterioration!

To the average American Christian, *charity* does not mean what it used to, but is that not approaching the matter from the wrong perspective? After all, it *was* God that inspired the scriptures and wrote the Bible. Believing that *all scripture is given by inspiration of God* (2 Tim. 3:16), and by faith concluding that the King James Bible is still to be considered *scripture,* in spite of the naysayers, what does the word *charity* mean to God? How did God use the word *charity*? How did God intend for ***you*** to understand the word *charity*? If it is possible that God actually was responsible for – even pleased by - the translation *charity,* from the Greek a*gape*, what significance might He have intended you to draw from translating it in such a manner? Could there be a providential method and design to the English translation, *charity*?

The Vindication of *Charity - A More Excellent Way* (1 Cor. 12:31)

It seems so arbitrary to the modern scholars that of the 115 times that *agape* appears in the Greek New Testament, 29 of those times *agape* is translated *charity* or *charitably*. So "arbitrary" is it, in fact, that in many cases it is blown off and replaced by *love* without even an explanation. Carelessness in the presence of the living words of the Living God is not unlike walking a tight-rope on razor wire. Perhaps a bit of care may have discovered a context that would have discouraged such a flippant and presumptuous heist of words.

> *We are bound to thank God always for you,* ***brethren****, as it is meet, because that your faith groweth exceedingly, and the* ***charity*** *of every one of you all* ***toward each other*** *aboundeth.*
> (2 Thes. 1:3)

One will notice here that the *charity* of the verse above is exercised in the context of *brethren*, and that *charity* abounds among those brethren ***toward each other.*** Note this again,

> *And above all things have fervent* ***charity among yourselves****: for charity shall cover the multitude of sins.* (1 Pet. 4:8)

The clear context of 1 Peter 4 is redeemed believers and brethren. With the discovery of such verses where *charity* actually seems an earmark and a distinctive affection between Christians, a bit more investigation would not hurt. While it is not feasible to record the entirety of all the contexts where *charity* is found, notice in the table below that the rightmost column either provides a flash sampling of the context or briefly categorizes it.

Reference	*Agape* translated as *charity*	Context
Rom.14:15	…walkest thou not *charitably*	*…brother…* grieved with thy meat… *for whom Christ died.*
I Cor. 8:1	…*charity* edifieth	…as touching things offered unto idols, *we know* that *we all have knowledge.*
ICor.13:1-13	*Charity* (9 times)	…covet earnestly the best *gifts:* and yet…more excellent way. (1 Cor.12:31) Though *I speak with the tongues* (1 Cor.13:1)
I Cor. 14:1	Follow after *charity*	…desire *spiritual gifts…* rather that *ye may prophesy*
1Cor.16:14	…done with *charity*	brother Apollos… you…brethren (12) Watch ye, stand fast in the faith (13) I beseech you, brethren…ministry of the saints. (15)

Col. 3:14	…put on *charity*	Forbearing one another…forgiving… as Christ forgave you (13)… peace of God rule in your hearts…ye are called in one body (15)
1 Thes. 3:6	…your faith and *charity*	Timotheus came from you unto us (6)… brethren (7)… your faith (7)… ye stand fast in the Lord (8)
2 Thes. 1:3	*Charity*	Brethren…your faith groweth… every one of you all toward each other aboundeth;
1 Tim. 1:5	End…is *charity*	…thou mightest charge some that they teach no other doctrine,
1 Tim 2:15	…if they continue in faith and *charity*	Christian marriage
1Tim. 4:12	…in *charity*	Timothy – Paul's son in the faith (1 Tim 1:2)
2Tim. 2:22	…follow righteousness, faith, *charity*…	Christian sanctification
2 Tim. 3:10	thou hast fully known my… *charity*	Paul's testimony
Tit. 2:2	…sound in faith, in *charity*	Christian testimony – aged men (2)
1 Pet. 4:8	Have fervent *charity*…for *charity*…	among yourselves…

		as good stewards of the manifold grace of God. (10)
1 Pet. 5:14	kiss of *charity*	Greet ye one another… are in Christ Jesus… church that is at Babylon, elected together with you (13)
2 Pet. 1:7	to brotherly kindness *charity.*	…to them that have obtained like precious faith with us (1)
3 Jn. 1:6	thy *charity*	before the church
Jude 12	your feasts of *charity*	…to them that are sanctified by God… and preserved in Jesus Christ… (1)
Rev. 2:19	I know thy… *charity*	unto the angel of the church in Thyatira (18)

The nine occurrences if *charity* in 1 Corinthians 13 are obviously all within the same context. Thus having all the occurrences of the translation *charity* accounted for and immediate contexts summarized, it is most interesting to note that absolutely every occurrence of this ill-esteemed translation falls within a context of purely Christian affection and sentiment toward one another. The word *charity,* absolutely never occurs in the AV 1611 in a context outside of Christianity. In the scriptures, the King James Bible, *charity* is not a sentiment directed toward the lost or toward the world, and neither is it a particular affection that the unregenerate exude or share among themselves.

Take care here! Do not leap to conclusions. It is inarguable that God did indeed love *(agape)* the world enough to die for all of mankind. It is also inarguable that we Christians are to love our fellow man, to pray for them and to try to get the gospel to them. Indeed, we must! Men should also love *(agape)* their wives. But, it is also true that according to the English scriptures of the AV 1611, *charity* is a particular species of affection that God differentiated from all other forms, and confined entirely to a Christian context. ***It is how God chose to distinguish and categorize a particular and peculiar sentiment***. God did tell us we were to be a *peculiar people* (Tit. 2:14) since He has given us a peculiar rebirth, a peculiar commission, and a peculiar and distinct destiny from all other categories of mankind. Is it really so strange that we would share a peculiar form of love amongst ourselves, and that the Lord would differentiate it from other forms by naming it distinctively?

After years of hearing derogatory commentary on the "antiquated language" of the old "King Jimmy," and knowing further that this is probably utterly foreign to the ears of even the most entrenched Fundamentalist, it is probably best at this point to ask what (or whom) is the reader's genuine final authority for determining what he or she believes. If you found a one-thousand dollar bill behind your bathroom mirror today, would it matter that you and the people that lived in the house before you had been in that bathroom and looked in that mirror thousands of times without having discovered the thin edge of that bill behind that mirror? I trow not. You would rejoice that it was you who had finally seen it! Why are Fundamentalists often ***not*** that way at all when it comes to biblical truth?

Even King James defenders have held their noses at certain translations of certain words in the AV. In the case of *charity* many now just dismiss it with a haughty sniff, change the word to another (love) with no explanation extended or even deemed necessary.

In truth, if the scriptures are allowed to dictate Christian beliefs instead of one coming to the Bible with those beliefs and prejudices entrenched behind the battlements of presumption and academically fortified conceit, there are some reasonable and balanced conclusions that might well be reached:

Charity **is not the correct scriptural terminology for the trait of beneficent almsgiving or relief agencies**. In no way are these condemned where they are legitimate, nor is the sentiment of mercy which inspires them being criticized. It is merely that such worthwhile activities have been misnamed as far as the scriptures are concerned. Biblically, *charity* is not that in which the Red Cross and Salvation Army commerce. *Charity* is a Christian sentiment extended toward Christians. When it was still true to General William Booth's vision for it, the Salvation Army may have been the ideal for love, beneficence, Christian mercy and help, but ***biblically*** such ideals are not defined by the word *charity!* *Charity* is a Christian characteristic exercised amongst and toward Christians.

The contexts of the 29 occurrences of *charity* are completely consistent as being Christian in nature. Every single person in the scriptures admonished to have *charity* was a believing disciple of Jesus Christ. They were each being instructed and exhorted regarding their relationships and fellowship with other Christians. *Charity* is a particular trait unique among Christians!

The English of the King James Bible distinguished and illuminated this truth by its distinctive usage of a word not otherwise used in the AV, and not used at all in the new versions. Had the illustrious scholars paid more attention to the context and the actual lines of the Bible they often defend and magnify with their mere lip-service, they may actually have learned something worthwhile about *love* and *charity*. Instead, they dismissed the context of the AV because they disdained the translation of the word *charity*. In their contempt, God blinded their eyes to such an extent that Christianity is bereft of any scholar, in any age past, that seems to have grasped the distinction that God set down on paper. It is a blessing that Dr. Gail Riplinger saw and published the truth about charity in her 1998 book, *The Language of the King James Bible*.[69] Yet, where are the many voices and the volumes of writings of the Bible-believing students of the scriptures for whom the scriptures are the first appeal and the last? Why have the oft-unregenerate writers of lexicons and oft-compromising theologian commentators not been taken to task substantively on their own grounds for their carelessness and presumptuous oversights?

The perpetual chiding of the scholars regarding the AV 1611 and its "outdated language" is devastated as an argument in this matter. In this case, a word was needed and found that was distinctive from the many other times that *love* was used. It needed to be different for it is a different species of love and affection: *charity*. The scholars, all too ready by the tenets of their philosophy to jettison and discard what they consider an outdated word in favor of a common one, rejected a higher, nobler, more distinguished precept and truth from the

---

[69] Riplinger, Gail, *The Language of the King James Bible* (A.V. Publications Corp., Ararat, VA, 1998),p.73-74.

word of God. Were it not so sad, it would be humorous that this assemblage of learned men have crowed for years about the magnificent depths of two distinctive Greek words (*agape* and *phileo)* - which distinction has been shown to be nonexistent. At the same time, they have flippantly dismissed a distinctive English word (*charity*) which carries a demonstrably different scriptural meaning than the word they insert in its place: love. A serious Bible student stands again face to face with the specter of the Greek not holding as profound a meaning as is advertised, while the English shows a great deal more of the hand of God than the good doctors can bring themselves to admit.

The lesson to be learned is that if God chooses a word that is antiquated or uncommonly used, He has a prescribed and intentional purpose for doing so. One of the genuine differences between Bible-believers and those who the Bible identifies as having *a form of godliness, but denying the power thereof* (2 Tim. 3:5) is that a Bible-believer fears to alter the word, while the pretender finds a "godly" reason for doing so at his pleasure. *Let them alone: they be blind leaders of the blind. And if the blind lead the blind, both shall fall into the ditch* (Matt. 15:14).

Charity in the KJV: Some Thoughts and the Import of it

It is, perhaps, odd and ironic that one of the characteristics of *charity* is that it… *Rejoiceth not in iniquity, but rejoiceth in the truth* (1 Cor. 13:6). Since, *thy word is truth* (Jn. 17:17), it seems unavoidable that we must point out several observations that this matter illuminates, while realizing there are profound ramifications in the broader scope of the 1611 Authorized Version's translation in English. One question which remains to be answered will be whether the reader *rejoices* in the truth to which he is led.

The King James English makes distinctions not found in the original Greek. *Charity* is a clearly distinct concept contained in the AV and not in the Greek or in the new versions. It is translated from *agape* these 29 times, while the remaining balance of the occurrences of *agape* are generally translated, *love.* The distinction of *charity,* as a separate ideal, is primarily accomplished by its usage as a separate word, but once impressed upon the mind, one can easily see that the contexts of these occurrences support it as a separate concept. No such distinction exists in the Greek, for it requires translation to a different word in order to be able to apprehend the difference.

The Greek scholars and the Greek scholar-pretenders blithely storm past the AV English translation, back to their Greek, which contains no distinctions in this case. They walk right past the expansion of meaning and the deepening of understanding already provided in the English, in order to blunder around in ignorance in the original language. Thus, the King James Bible contains theologically definable and differentiated concepts that wise men have not even gotten a whiff of in the Greek. It very literally contains doctrine in this case, that is not discernibly contained in the Greek manuscripts.

Who is responsible for making the distinction by translating *agape* as *charity*? We feel that we must haste to this point due to the profoundness of its import. *Somebody* bears the responsibility of translating *agape* to *charity* 29 times, while leaving the remaining occasions it occurs to be translated *love.* In doing so, this "*Somebody*" is responsible for delineating and illuminating in the English scriptures an entirely diverse concept distinguishable from *love.* *Who* is responsible for that?

It should be anticipated that the scholars' union may well conceive and give birth to kittens at the very mention of all this, because there are only so many possibilities for the answer to the question, and none of these do anything but devastate the philosophy and mode of operation by which scholarship has proceeded for these many years.

One must first anticipate chaff, smoke and evasion. Denial that there is any distinction between *love* and *charity* will be the first tactic used. Remember that it is genuinely heretical to this particular fraternity of men that deeper truth might reside in a translation, rather than in their absent yet exulted originals. It is predetermined dogma to them that nothing could ever supersede the Greek or Hebrew. Thus, since it is a doctrinal precept to them that no greater light could come from English, then it follows that anyone who produces evidence of such light is a doctrinal heretic. If one is a heretic, it will naturally follow to pin various woeful descriptives and monikers upon him. Hence, right after the chaff, spin and evasion, what follows will be various sobriquets and epithets that are designed to force the guilty heretic to flinch and dive for cover. Once their target of humiliation ducks, the "orthodox," scholarly aggressor will turn up the juice, will keep calling names, and the presumptuous nonconformist will flush and run. Common Bible-believers are *ignorant hayseeds* – "unscholarly partisans" is what Vincent called us. Make no mistake, to them, we are *sectarian, divisive, bibliolators, rabble-rousers, extremists,* and last but not least, *Ruckmanites.*

Should one "keep his head," and reach this particular juncture in the lofty and *spiritual* exchange of ideas without flinching, diving and flushing, he might notice that "*Somebody*" yet still remains responsible for the English translation which rendered *charity* as a distinct characteristic separate and different from *love.* In Greek, *agape* is *agape* is *agape*, **but in English *agape* is *love* quite often, but it is also *charity* 29 times!** Those 29 instances of *charity* are demonstrably dissimilar theologically from *love.* "*Somebody*" is responsible for masterminding the translation thus, and for distinguishing the two in translation. Scholarly evasion and name-calling does not answer the question: ***Who is responsible for this translation?***

Supposedly, one might say that Satan is responsible for it, but one cannot readily think of any real strategic advantage which he gains by this. We will leave the Satanic possibility as one to be expanded upon by those who can produce a reason. In the meantime, there seem to be only two feasible possibilities for the question, "***Who is responsible for "charity" in the King James Bible?***"

1) The King James Translators could be responsible. Now, it is understood that they are obviously responsible in the respect that *charity* is what proceeded from their pens. However, if the material presented earlier in this chapter be carefully digested, it must be concluded that there was a process and a plan to translate *agape* as *charity* those 29 times. It was a premeditated, cognitive and consistent exercise to translate it so. The contexts were too consistent and the distinctions too uniform to have proceeded out of arbitrary happenstance – the mere mindless interchanging of synonyms. This bears all the marks of *design* and *intention.* Design requires a *Designer* or *designers.*

It must, then, be considered a possibility that the King James translation committee, 47 men whose names we know, "put their heads together," and through an intricately organized and repetitive sequence of checks and balances, corporately agreed to translate *agape* as *charity* those 29 times. They would have had to conceptualize the distinction between *love* and *agape.* They would have had to do so in spite of there being no particular differentiation in Greek, where *agape* is the singular concept presented. Humanly speaking, they would have had to agree universally throughout their assemblage, subcommittees, and processes, that *charity* was to be the uniform translation of *agape* in those 29 occurrences.

If this is how it came about, the Bible believer should be most happy to rejoice in the excellence of the accomplishment. It is elemental and obvious that the academic and spiritual qualities of the King James translators are not only unsurpassed in history, but that they will never be approached in the present or future. In what measure we must rest on the attributes and works of men, we are most happy to rest in the accomplishment of that exalted group.

However...

This possibility does not bode well for those who would even be slightly critical of the translators, for if the translators, by their human ingenuity and wisdom, were in and of themselves able to pre-plan and design such an intricate web of depth and distinction as is represented by *love* and *charity*, how would one be able to honestly critique any of the rest of their work in a critical fashion? If they were so insightful and attuned as to be able to accomplish what has been outlined here, so that modern scholars even now miss the import of the accomplishment, why would one think they were less insightful elsewhere in the AV 1611? How could an honest man, who had not till now even grasped the distinctions they set on paper 400 years ago, presume to sit in judgment of the AV translators ever again? At the very worst, that brotherhood of 17th century men is far and away the master of this modern gaggle of careless and shallow puppets today. At best, humanly speaking, what the King James translators set forth is several shades of genius and design beyond the accomplishments – and apparently, the apprehension – of those who have presumed to so uncomprehendingly criticize them.

Perhaps the translators of the Authorized Version are responsible for the light set forth by translating *charity* from *agape.* On the other hand…

2) God Himself could be responsible. Logically, it seems that the only other legitimate possibility for the responsibility of the translation, *charity*, aside from the AV translators themselves, would be God! Either the translators are responsible for the insight, clarity and instruction imparted by the English translation – and only by the English – or else God is responsible.

Now, the primary rule in the fraternal vows of this convocation of modern scholars is that God does not involve Himself in translation in any kind of intimate way. Their dogma says that He inspired the original writings, preserved the manuscripts in such a way that we know what the original writings were in the original languages (Greek and Hebrew), but God could never, ever, ever involve Himself in a translation of the scriptures to the extent that He should affect and determine what the wording of the translation would be. They would hold that if God providentially guided men producing translations, His providence never, ever was so intrusive as to appoint specific words. In the scholars' view, that would be ***inspiration* again** or ***re-inspiration***. Out of that could be drawn the reasonable inference that, with God having involved Himself in a translation, such involvement would make the translation perfect and without error. That would be *heresy*! God would never do that. They have a rule about that.

If God did involve Himself in translation, some translations, or even one particular translation, it would change the ground rules that have dictated scholars' philosophies for generations. At this moment, if the reader is faint-hearted about dismissing one of the scholars' cardinal rules, he need only for the time answer one question honestly: *Who was the active agent – who bears the responsibility – in translating* ***agape*** *as* ***charity*** *those 29 distinct times in the KJV?*

A Christian is spiritually benefited in having *charity* distinguished from *love* in the King James. There is greater insight supplied, and greater spiritual understanding of the nature of things, due to the translation, *charity*. This understanding is not available in Greek, for there is no distinct difference in Greek. A Christian is a new creature, has a new nature and the spirit of Christ sealed inside his body. He is destined for a new home, is a child of God, will one day be a new bride, is a member of the priesthood of believers, is an ambassador for Christ and is a minister of the New Testament. That in the midst of his new heritage and newly fashioned relationships, he would also be the beneficiary of a new and clearly distinguished attribute of affection should be a great blessing to him!

In this regard, the King James English clarifies and expands meaning. Greek scholars make no distinctions in Greek between *"agape" love* and *charity* for they do not exist in Greek. Again, we are nigh unto buried with all the laudatory exultation that the "Greekers" can muster when it comes to the depth of meaning represented by the differences in *agape* and *phileo* in the Greek New Testament. It is ironic that those distinctions have proved to have no basis whatsoever, as seen in the last chapter. God overruled the scholars' traditions and *suppositions* and drew no distinction between *agape* and *phileo.* On the other hand, in an astounding display of God's stated practice in 1 Corinthians 1:27-28, the Lord defied all the rules and boundaries that biblical scholastic academia reveres: God took the one word in Greek, *agape*, and expanded its meaning and its impact on New Testament doctrine, in differentiating two different forms of affection in English, though no such distinctions were made in Greek.

> *But God hath chosen the foolish things of the world to confound the wise; and God hath chosen the weak things of the world to confound the things which are mighty; And base things of the world, and things which are despised, hath God chosen, yea, and things which are not, to bring to nought things that are:*
>
> (1 Cor. 1:27-28)

There are, therefore, ambiguities in Greek that the King James English settles and clarifies. The first portion of this statement should not be too hard for folks to swallow for scholars hold that there are such profound treasures and depths of meaning in Greek, that said scholars are commissioned to spend a lifetime digging out the profundities of the original language - which are, of course, inaccessible to the common English reader. Following on the heels of this justification for what they do with their time and resources, believers are subjected to various forms of learned lecture, which is intended to drive home the notion that there are tones, shades of meaning, and concepts in the original languages which are very difficult to grasp. They are even harder – impossible, really - to express in another language. Apparently, Christians are stuck until the return of Christ with a class of men and women who have by their own confession, labored ceaselessly, tirelessly and sacrificially to, 1) conceive what God said in Greek, and 2) communicate it to us, as perfectly as possible, in the language in which we converse daily. To this hour, after several hundred years of labors over the Bible in the English language, most scholars still are mortified at the idea that their task is - or should be – finished. Even the King James defenders, who hold the AV 1611 to be the representative Bible in English, are territorially defiant and pugnacious at the suggestion of a completed and perfect translation in English.

We believe that it can now be safely concluded that this body of men, containing such a diverse variety of extremity in both fidelity and fallacy, will never decide that they have accomplished their task of rendering to us the words of God perfectly. The liberals and heretics among them obviously will not, and it does not seem that those who hold conservative, orthodox positions most like ours show any more of a proclivity to declare their work accomplished. It simply is not going to happen. *For ever, O LORD, thy word is settled in heaven* (Ps. 119:89) say the scriptures, but to them it will never be settled *down here*! With the tiniest exception, the vast majority of New Testament Greek scholars believe their work is anything but finished, that the body of Christ is incessantly dependent upon them for the *real truth*, and that their tenure as princely arbiters of what God *really meant* is ensconced in everlasting security as long as Christians abide on earth.

On the other hand, to consider another possibility, since it is plain that the modern scholar's and translator's work is never done, what if God already finished it for them? Or, even, ***in spite of them***? It is plain that there are ambiguities and difficulties in Greek and Hebrew; else our heroic scholars would have nothing to wrestle. Presumably, if the meanings were not so obscure to apprehend and so difficult to translate, our scholars would have long ago accomplished their task. Being as it has proven such an insurmountable venture to these fellows, does that not perhaps suggest that if God intended us to have all the light and truth from the Bible that He, Himself, might just have provided it in bypassing the mainstream, accepted scholarship of our day?

A case in point: The concept of *agape* contains within it – indistinguishable in Greek – a distinction that God chose to make in English. He separated the idea of *love*, in a broader sense, from *charity*, which is a peculiarly Christian ideal set forth for the benefit and edification for the Body of Jesus Christ

– the Church. That which was, and is, indiscernible in Greek was set forth distinctively by the Lord in plain English. He used the King James translators' hearts, labors, judgments and pens to accomplish what Greek scholars have not even discerned.

So, in this respect, the English produces light and revelation to the Christian heart and mind that the Greek (original or otherwise) does not. It can only be pointed out, once again, that the Greek *agape,* when studied in its New Testament setting, and when traced linguistically back to its very roots by lexicographers and gifted Greek language experts, does not "ring a bell" or produce any insightful light of understanding. This is shown by the fact that said scholars are bereft of any reference or comment which would indicate that they saw a distinction in Greek for those passages where, in English, the Bible reader was *taught by the Holy Ghost* the difference between *love* and *charity.*

Further, reverting back to the Greek in this case is a regression from revealed truth. All that is necessary to understand the concept of *charity,* which the Lord imparted, is to believe what is written in English, and to genuinely study the contexts. In doing so, the reader is given more light in the English of the AV than he could have ever drawn from Greek. The act of blithely and habitually reverting to the Greek in this case, even in ignorance, is to overlook what the Author of the Bible has already accomplished in the KJV, and it is a retrograde return to darkness and increased ambiguity.

These men insist that Christians must lean on them for understanding and help. *Wherefore by their fruits ye shall know them* (Matt. 7:20). The fruit produced by the academics and scholars that insist upon our acquiescence to their brand of wisdom, seems to point to a lack of insight, a great deal of bumbling, and a plague of biblical powerlessness and ignorance. Perhaps, since we must accept that sometimes the guidance of man is from the Lord (Acts 8:31), we will accept the fine guidance of the AV translators whose work seems a testament to wisdom, the Spirit of God, and the handiwork of the Lord.

Understanding fully that the next observation and point will be "where the fur really hits the fan," it is crucial that the Bible-believer does not "bail out" when the import of the evidence is displeasing and upsets the applecart of his favorite teacher's presumptions. From the evidence that has been seen in the occurrences of *charity* in the old King James:

It is undeniable that the English of the King James Bible, in this case, is an example of the revelation of truth, doctrine, and instruction not contained in the Greek Texts. In this case then, truth was revealed in English, which was not revealed in Greek. The revelation that came was a product of a sequence in which Greek words were translated into English words. By the Lord's providence, at the hands of the AV translators, what was revealed to man was ***advanced*** in a substantive and observable way by the process of translating Greek to English – *agape* to *charity*. You and I understand in English the distinct and different concepts of *charity* versus *love* because our translation reveals the difference. Those relying on the Greek - scholars, students, Textus Receptus advocates alike – do not apprehend the difference. The difference does not exist in Greek. If this is not ***advanced revelation*** in English, what would you prefer it be called?

This evaluation of *charity* in the Authorized Version will be concluded by asking a simple question. **In what way is the English of the King James Bible *not* superior to the Greek in this matter?**

Chapter 4

Distinguishing the Deacons

> *I commend unto you Phebe our sister, which is a servant of the church which is at Cenchrea:*
> (Rom. 16:1)

To Eve, the fruit that Satan offered, aside from being forbidden by the Lord, must have looked to be pretty unimpressive and harmless. The variety of color shades of the liquids represented on the liquor store's shelves hardly speaks of the deadly poison hidden beneath the seals. A pack of white little cylinders packed with finely minced tobacco hardly bears the threatening menace of bonds and chains, nor does it advertise truthfully the agonizing and horrific death that it so oft delivers to the unwary and naïve. Clinically viewed as a specimen, or prodded gently with a dental tool, the tongue does not impress as a murderous instrument, or a bodily member that could produce disaster on a massive human scale. Nevertheless, the scriptures testify that *Death and life are in the power of the tongue* (Prov. 18:21), and *...the tongue is a fire, a world of iniquity: so is the tongue among our members, that it defileth the whole body, and setteth on fire the course of nature; and it is set on fire of hell* (James 3:6).

All this is mentioned but to illustrate that hidden beneath the robes of the commonplace and unimpressive sometimes lies that which may prove to be dangerous, infectious, or even deadly.

Romans 16:1 does not look like much of a candidate for a verse out of which to build heresy or support a usurpation of

God's intended plan or structure. A faithful sister of the church at Cenchrea is commended by the Apostle Paul for her service to the church, and the church is urged to receive her, for she had been a *succourer of many* (vs.2), including Paul himself. Phebe was a blessing and there is no indication that she was ever anything but a blessing. Unfortunately, Phebe's reputation and testimony, through no fault of her own, has suffered a good deal of revision, and her name is now used at the forefront of a movement that has done the Lord, sound doctrine, and the body of Christ a great disservice. She and Mary, the mother of the Lord, are two ladies who, should they be given an opportunity like that of the *queen of the south* (Matt.12:42) to speak at judgment, may leave scald wounds on their hearers for the injustices done to their Christian names and testimonies.

Though Romans 16:1 appears to be a verse of small content or import, it has been turned into another tragic debacle at the hands of our friends, the Greek scholars and their make-believe scholar accomplices. It is a verse that has proven to be the entry point and the justification for much nonsense that has greatly contributed to the *falling away* of churches today. It is a most important observation, that there was no issue or snag whatsoever in this verse until someone opted to go to the Greek, at which point the can of worms was opened.

In Greek, the verse looks like this:
Συνίστημι δὲ ὑμι□ν Φοίβην τὴν ἀδελφὴν ἡμῶν, οὖσαν [καὶ] **διάκονον** τῆς ἐκκλησίας τῆς ἐν Κεγχρεαι□ς, (Rom. 16:1)

The English translation counterpart for the bold-faced word can be seen thus:

> *I commend unto you Phebe our sister, which is a* ***servant (διάκονον)*** *of the church which is at Cenchrea:* (Rom. 16:1)

The Anglicized transliteration of the Greek word doesn't look remarkably different than when it is written in its native Greek. The word is ***diakonon***. If this does not yet ring a bell, this is the base word for the word ***deacon***, which of course is one of the scriptural offices ordained by the Lord in the local churches.

The Sister is a *Deacon?*

This passage happens to be one of those delectable verses that make careless and overconfident Bible study and Sunday school teachers salivate. If they have been schooled and brainwashed into the idea that just about anybody with a computer Bible program is equipped to translate the Bible for themselves, this is a most wonderful opportunity to wow the saintly guinea pigs with their linguistic expertise.

It is also one of those made-to-order verses that show so plainly, in their minds, that no translation of the scriptures (especially the King James Bible) can compete with a thorough knowledge of the Greek language.

You see, the English of the AV – oh, those backwards and ill-equipped translators! – relegates Phebe's position in the church as that of a "servant." Yes, in the old "King Jimmy" she was *merely* a faithful and highly reputed lady that served God in the church. But the depths of the "original Greek" reveal something far different and more sublime! Indeed, the Greek plainly shows that the root Greek word translated *servant* in the AV 1611, is the very same Greek word translated *deacon* in other passages in the New Testament such as Philippians 1:1 and I Timothy 3:8, 10, 12 & 13, where the Bible outlines the *church office of a deacon.* Let all Christians now do back-flips because it is now known from the Greek (not the English) that Phebe was actually an office-holding *deacon*! We are all breathless with the discovery.

Quite expectedly, Adam Clarke leaps aboard the *deaconess* bandwagon:

> ...Phoebe is here termed "a servant", diakonon (grk 1249), **a deaconess of the church** at Cenchrea. **There were deaconesses in the primitive church**, whose business it was to attend the female converts at baptism; to instruct the catechumens (persons who were candidates for baptism); to visit the sick, and those who were in prison, and, in short, to perform those religious functions for the female part of the church which could not be performed by men with propriety. They were chosen in general out of the most experienced of the church, and were ordinarily widows, who had borne children.[70]

Clarke's comments seem quite adamant, considering that the Bible itself makes no such mention of a specific office of "deaconess." Many feel compelled to take his unwavering statement as an oracle from God. Jamieson, Fausset, and Brown cannot resist the opportunity for presumption, as did Clarke:

> [I commend unto you Phebe our sister, which is a servant, [diakonon (grk 1249), or, `**deaconess, '] of the church** which is at Cenchrea.]... That in the earliest churches **there were deaconesses**, to attend to the wants of the female members,

[70] Clarke, Adam. *Clarke's Commentary.* (1998) P C Study Bible (Version 2.11) [Computer Software]. Seattle, WA: Biblesoft.

> **there is no good reason to doubt**. So early at least as the reign of Trajan...[71]

Barnes falls in line with the other commentators:

> [Which is a servant] Greek,"**Who is a deaconess**." It is clear from the New Testament that there was **an order of women** in the church known as **"deaconesses."** Reference is made to a class of females whose duty it was to "teach" other females, and to take the general superintendence of that part of the church, in various places in the New Testament;[72]

What is "clear from the New Testament," according to Barnes is that the NT he is alluding to is the Greek NT, for the AV's English makes no such distinction. The Wycliffe Commentary sees no reason to call the assumption into question:

> In recommending Phoebe, Paul tells who she is and where she comes from. **She was a deaconess** of the church in Cenchrea. Her duties, **like those of the deacons**, were quite general. Material needs and also spiritual needs of others were met by believers like Phoebe ...[73]

The Wycliffe commentators are followed by Nelson's Illustrated Bible Dictionary, and it sounds not a note of discord

---

[71] *Jamieson, Fausset, and Brown Commentary*. (1998) P C Study Bible (Version 2.11) [Computer Software]. Seattle, WA: Biblesoft.
[72] Barnes, Albert. *Barnes' Notes* (1997) P C Study Bible (Version 2.11) [Computer Software]. Seattle, WA: Biblesoft.
[73] Pfeiffer, Charles and Harrison, Everett, ed. *The Wycliffe Bible Commentary*. (1962) Moody Press. P C Study Bible (Version 2.11) [Computer Software]. Seattle, WA: Biblesoft.

with the rest of the respectable scholars and commentators with regard to the *Deaconess Doctrine*:

> **DEACONESS**
> **A female believer serving in the office of DEACON in a church**.
> The only New Testament reference to **deaconess** as a church office is Paul's description of **Phoebe as a deaconess of the church** in Cenchrea <Rom. 16:1>, (RSV). The Greek word translated as deaconess in this passage is rendered as deacon and servant by other versions of the Bible. **The office of deaconess was similar to the office of deacon.** Their spiritual responsibility was essentially the same, except that **deaconesses probably rendered a ministry exclusively to women**, particularly in the early years of the church.[74]

Once again, a Bible-believer finds himself at a fork in the road as far as what his Bible says, versus what other men say that his Bible should say. Or, perhaps, even more insidious is men's speculation over what the Lord really meant when He said what He said. If the scholars are correct, then the old English Bible does Christians a disservice and is underpowered when it comes to transmitting meaning. According to them, the true riches of understanding reside in the Greek, and one does not have to be too sharp a tack to see that if what they are saying is accurate, then the Greek *diakonon* does appear to hold more sway in the New Testament churches than the *servant* of the King James. Consider the fork in the road carefully, dear believer. It has already been seen in the case of *agape* and *phileo* that these Bible editors and commentators are none too

---

[74] *Nelson's Illustrated Bible Dictionary*. (1998) P C Study Bible (Version 2.11) [Computer Software]. Seattle, WA: Biblesoft.

thorough in their research, nor do they seem much interested in presenting the saints any substantive body of evidence that does not coincide with their superficial, and perhaps predetermined, evaluations.

Diakonon: Never Waste a Good Opportunity

A remark was once made by Dr. Sam Gipp in one of his sermons, which most likely is repeated in some of his written work. The remark was to this effect: "It takes genuine character and resolve to build something. Any dope-smoking hippy can tear something down!" This is a profound observation for our particular day in age, because while various historians might mark the commencement differently than others, our country and culture have apparently been overrun with *dope-smoking hippies* – in spirit, if not actuality. As Americans advanced past the age of the World War I generation, the Great Depression generation, and the World War II generation, a cultural, moral and spiritual transformation occurred. It seems that any of the established institutions which were founded in the blood, sweat, tears and wisdom of our forebears, became the mocking and disdainful targets of the privileged and spoiled progeny of that earlier, nobler generation of men and women. Marriage, self-control, basic morality, government, respect, hard work, character, the Bible and faith are but an abbreviated list of the pillars of strength and health that wound up spray painted, graffiti-ed and adorned with urine and feces.

This is not the time for a lengthy socio-political discourse, but all mankind proceeds on a basic degenerative down-spiral, and it seems that American society never recovered from the effects of the "free love," peacenik, dope-smoking hippy generation. We are able to see that at this moment in the USA, anyone can find online a support group or a fraternal society to join that would justify and promote just about every perverse and despicable activity or taste imaginable.

It seems almost a trivial development in some people's minds today, as we not only face the ever increasing perversity of apostasy, but as we have adapted and adjusted to certain changes that would have been repulsive a few generations ago. These have now become commonplace and accepted. To a more reserved and spiritually conservative generation, the proper order and place of the man and the woman in both society and the church was part of the strength of the interwoven fibers of our lives. There were always exceptions and those who refused to be part of the weave, but there was an order and a hierarchy of leadership, authority, and service understood by most. That we as a nation prospered under those ideals is not surprising, for they had their foundations in God's Book which was of profound effect upon the foundations of our nation and society. We were a paternalistic and masculine society, not only because those qualities were utterly necessary in pioneering the continent, but because the Bible is primarily paternalistic. The husband, the father, the pastor, the king, and the captain of the armies are all given to be the point of the spear and the leaders of the people in the scriptures. This was reflected in our society. The ladies, in accord with the tenets of the scriptures, had their honored place and were to be loved and cherished by husbands and fathers as in no other form of civilization in the world. However, there were certain bounds of authority and oversight which were not to be overrun. Usurpation of paternal guidance in the home and in instruction, rejection of the man's spiritual leadership, and rebellion from beneath the man's beneficent care in the marriage were not flippant hobbies practiced by most of our grandmothers and grandfathers.

Though immorality is much older than Sodom, it was not an accepted norm for much of American history, nevertheless one day we awoke to a societal revolution consisting of "shacking up" and free love, bell-bottoms and dope, an obsession with civil rights and equality, and along with it: Women's Liberation. No known historian can truthfully document a time in American history where women as a gender were enslaved or in bondage, though there will always be statistical exceptions of exploitation and abuse.

The scripture does say that *the Spirit speaketh expressly, that in the latter times some shall depart from the faith, giving heed to seducing spirits, and doctrines of devils* (1 Tim. 4:1). It is always only a matter of time before the world's degeneracy finds its way into the church, insinuates itself into the church's doctrine, and eventually transforms itself into the puppet master of church polity.

At some juncture, some open-minded and liberal spirited soul peered into the Greek text that stands behind a seemingly innocuous Romans 16:1, and said, "Hey! The Greek word for *servant* here is ***diakonon***! Phebe was a deacon! No, a ***deaconess***! Why don't we have ***deaconesses*** on our churches? We need ***deaconesses*** in our churches! Hey, everybody…" The rest of the story can be puzzled together with little difficulty.

Some of our "Fundamentalist" brethren have been compromised for years in the idea of the deacon's office being shared by men and women alike. This is the heritage passed on through the habit of *going to the Greek*, for one cannot draw such a conclusion by abiding by the AV English. Thus, the proverbial camel, once his nose is in the door, proceeds to take over the tent. Every mainstream "Christian" denomination at this point is facing an onslaught of women who clamor for office within "the ministry," but not just as deaconesses. They want to be pastors and bishops as well.

The Demise of *Deaconesses*: Bitter Pills from the Greek

It may seem a bit startling to discover that the Greek word behind the English Bible's *servant* in Romans 16:1 is *diakonon*, the same Greek word translated *deacon* in Philippians 1 and 1 Timothy 3. There are those that exploit the reality that many Bible-believers would be startled by the revelation of this fact. They gladly take advantage of the inevitability that some would be taken aback and would not have a ready answer. The average person is basically intimidated when challenged by an adversary with an unfamiliar language.

On the other hand, when a Bible-corrector is on the aggressive in seeking to throw a Bible-believer off balance, one sound bit of advice is that the Bible-believer should keep his head, remember what the Lord promised about His words, and understand something very important: all one has to do is survey a mere few of the pages of the *Greek and Hebrew Dictionary* at the back of a *Strong's Exhaustive Concordance*, to learn that it is a common occurrence that the translators had quite a number of options of how they could translate many words into English out of Greek or Hebrew. Indeed this is exploited enthusiastically by the King James Bible detractors, since, given all these choices, why should we be "stuck" with a Bible that just says something one way, when translating it another way might be a better way? It does not take long before one becomes comfortable with the idea and is inclined to view all these choices as mere interchangeable options. In this way, there is almost a Mr. Potato Head mentality that begins to insinuate itself, where one has a Bible with interchangeable parts and accessories that can be added or subtracted at one's pleasure and in accord with one's preferences.

So, was Phebe a "deaconess"? Well, in Greek she was a *diakonon*. That much is certain. On the other hand, this is just one verse. The Greek, if it teaches that Phebe was a church officer and held that office of a *deacon,* overthrows an entire school of thought, not to mention the broad and deep precepts laid in scripture. The English Bible reading stood for hundreds of years as a standard. Did the English mislead churchmen and Christians for all these years? Has the Christian womanhood among us been cheated, circumvented, and subjugated by improper translation in the grand old Book?

Since this particular breed of scholar to whom we refer is not abashed to make Phebe a *deacon*, let us see if there may be other deacons hidden in the Bible, which we may discover by "going to the Greek." In each of the verses below, the word in boldface is translated from a form of the Greek word, *diakonos*, just as was *servant* in Romans 16:1, and as was *deacon(s)* in Philippians 1:1 and in 1 Timothy 3:8 & 12.

> Matt. 22:13 - *Then said the king to the* ***servants****, Bind him hand and foot, and take him away, and cast him into outer darkness; there shall be weeping and gnashing of teeth.*

> Matt. 23:10-11 - *Neither be ye called masters: for one is your Master, even Christ. But he that is greatest among you shall be your* ***servant.***

> Mark 10:43 - *But so shall it not be among you: but whosoever will be great among you, shall be your* ***minister:***

> John 2:5 - *His mother saith unto the* ***servants****, Whatsoever he saith unto you, do it.*

> Rom. 13:3-4 - *For rulers are not a terror to good works, but to the evil. Wilt thou then not be afraid of the power? do that which is good, and*

> *thou shalt have praise of the same: For he is the* ***minister*** *of God to thee for good. But if thou do that which is evil, be afraid; for he beareth not the sword in vain: for he is the* ***minister*** *of God, a revenger to execute wrath upon him that doeth evil.*

> Rom. 15:8 - *Now I say that Jesus Christ was a* ***minister*** *of the circumcision for the truth of God, to confirm the promises made unto the fathers:*

> 1 Cor. 3:5 - *Who then is Paul, and who is Apollos, but* ***ministers*** *by whom ye believed, even as the Lord gave to every man?*

> 2 Cor. 3:6 - *Who also hath made us able* ***ministers*** *of the new testament; not of the letter, but of the spirit: for the letter killeth, but the spirit giveth life.*

One will first note that in each of these cases the word in boldface, which comes from the Greek's *diakonos,* is translated either *servant(s)* or *minister(s).* This is most usually the case throughout the New Testament. In fact, occurring just over 100 times in the New Testament, all forms of the root word *diakonos* are almost all translated as the nouns, *minister(s), servant(s), ministry, ministration, administration, service* and *relief*; and as the verbs, *serve, served, serveth, serving, minister, ministered, ministering.* **The only exceptions to these listed are the isolated five occasions when these Greek words are translated using the words *deacon* or *deacons.***

If one becomes too delirious in going to the Greek, he may well see a *deacon* behind every bush. Notice in the references above, that by these pseudo-scholars principles, *deacons* would cast people into outer darkness in Mathew. 22, and the *servants* at the marriage in Cana in John 2, were actually *deacons*! Further, our secular rulers in Romans 13 are *deacons* too, and Jesus, as well, was a ***Deacon*** *of the circumcision* in Romans 15:8. You probably knew that Paul was the Apostle to the Gentiles, but according to 1 Corinthians 3:5, he and Apollos were *deacons*, and they were *deacons of the new testament* in 2 Corinthians 3:6. That is…according to the Greek.

For just a sampling of how your Bible might have read should we carry forward consistently what the scholars themselves are willing to do to poor Phebe, I have taken liberty to insert into the verses below a form of the word *deacon* after each word in the verses where *diakonos,* in one form or other, appears in the Greek.

> Matt. 8:15 - *And he touched her hand, and the fever left her: and she arose, and* ***ministered (deaconed)*** *unto them.*
>
> Matt. 4:11 - *Then the devil leaveth him, and, behold, angels came and* ***ministered (deaconed)*** *unto him.*
>
> Matt. 20:28 - *Even as the Son of man came not to be* ***ministered (deaconed)*** *unto, but to* ***minister (deacon)****, and to give his life a ransom for many.*
>
> Luke 10:40 - *But Martha was cumbered about much* ***serving (deaconing)****, and came to him, and said, Lord, dost thou not care that my sister hath left me to* ***serve (deacon)*** *alone? bid her therefore that she help me.*

Rom. 15:25 - *But now I go unto Jerusalem to* ***minister (deacon)*** *unto the saints.*

Acts 1:17 - *For he was numbered with us, and had obtained part of this* ***ministry (deaconship).***

Acts 1:25 - *That he may take part of this* ***ministry (deaconship)*** *and apostleship, from which Judas by transgression fell, that he might go to his own place.*

Acts 6:4 - *But we will give ourselves continually to prayer, and to the* ***ministry (deaconing)*** *of the word.*

Acts 12:25 - *And Barnabas and Saul returned from Jerusalem, when they had fulfilled their* ***ministry (deaconing)****, and took with them John, whose surname was Mark.*

2 Cor. 3:7-9 - *But if the* ***ministration (deaconing)*** *of death, written and engraven in stones, was glorious, so that the children of Israel could not stedfastly behold the face of Moses for the glory of his countenance; which glory was to be done away: How shall not the* ***ministration (deaconing)*** *of the spirit be rather glorious? For if the* ***ministration (deaconing)*** *of condemnation be glory, much more doth the* ***ministration (deaconing)*** *of righteousness exceed in glory.*

2 Cor. 5:18 - *And all things are of God, who hath reconciled us to himself by Jesus Christ, and hath given to us the* ***ministry (deaconship)*** *of reconciliation;*

> Eph. 4:11-12 - *And he gave some, apostles; and some, prophets; and some, evangelists; and some, pastors and teachers; For the perfecting of the saints, for the work of the* ***ministry (deaconship),*** *for the edifying of the body of Christ:*
>
> 1 Tim. 1:12 - *And I thank Christ Jesus our Lord, who hath enabled me, for that he counted me faithful, putting me into the* ***ministry (deaconship)****;*
>
> 2 Cor. 11:8 - *I robbed other churches, taking wages of them, to do you* ***service (deaconship)****.*
>
> Rev. 2:19 - *I know thy works, and charity, and* ***service (deaconship)****, and faith, and thy patience, and thy works; and the last to be more than the first.*

The "scholars" dissenting from the King James translation of the word *diakonon* in Romans 16:1, have proven themselves quite rash, even precipitous, in their haste to replace *servant* with *deaconess*. In their celerity, they have championed Phebe as something of a forerunner of the more modern feminist concept of how things should be. We cannot help but wonder when was the last time in "going to the Greek," a student or teacher actually noticed that forms of the word *diakonos* appear in the Greek over 100 times and routinely continue to be rendered *serve, served, serving, servant, minister, ministered, ministering, ministration* and *administration.* By what reason and authority would one proclaim Phebe a deacon when Christ, Paul, Apollos, and various other personages, were described by the same word in the Greek? Why are we to arbitrarily assign a posthumous deaconship upon Phebe and not make the same applications across the board? If we are to remake Phebe, why would we not revamp the entirety of the concept of servanthood and ministry?

The fact is that, as described in our discussion of *agape* and *phileo*, the specter of pseudo-scholarship's carelessness and capriciousness once again rises to haunt them. With all the haughtiness of sinners who believe their dirty works are covered and hidden, these "scholars" have proceeded in their gleeful rampage through God's Holy Bible, falsely assured by the sheer numbers of other trifling imposters and by the conceit that no one would actually research the Greek for themselves. They count on God's people being too intimidated by the personage of the scholar and the insecurity of handling reference materials in another language. They also know that people are as lazy as they themselves are. Thus, they make sloppy incursions into the Greek, draw indolent and hasty conclusions, depend upon 75 cent words to lend the impression of deep knowledge, and in the end they know full well that most people will be too intimidated and slothful to actually check their work.

Deaconesses? Deathblows from the English

God never insinuated, much less did He state, that a Christian need be fluent in, or even familiar with, more than one language in order to apprehend all of the truths of God. Sometimes it is wise to withdraw from all the noise and tempest of the issue and just contemplate for a moment the very first principles. Where in the Bible is the precautionary warning, the solemn qualification from the Lord, that truth would not (could not) be wholly and completely transmitted and transported from Greek and Hebrew to the subsequent languages of the Bible? No such written precept exists. Yet, with precious few exceptions, this is a foundational principle of just about every Bible scholar that can be named, no matter how conservative their doctrine proves to be.

Bible-believers are often left with jaws slightly agape, unprepared to answer, and intimidated at heart when they hear their Bible criticized, corrected and edited by folks doing so on the basis of Greek and Hebrew roots, rules and rubbish.

One of the great and wondrous attributes of our God is His foresight. Yes, He is all powerful. Yes, He is omnipresent. He also knows everything, and that means that He *foreknows* everything, as well! Knowing everything, when He wrote and commissioned His word, He was already fully apprised of all of man's past, present and future shenanigans. He was all too familiar with man's predilection to satanic deceit. Man is proud, conceited, avaricious, dishonest and ambitious. Man is a fool, but he thinks he is wise. He is a man, but he thinks he is a god. Man is ever prone to stray after his wicked heart and imaginations no matter how intelligent he is. He is simultaneously prone to both tyranny and bondage. In short, man is corrupt, and to God, quite predictable. God's foresight is one of His great attributes because when He left us the Faith, the Gospel, and the Bible, he knew full well that men would foul up and corrupt all three were it not for His own intervention and oversight. It is well worth remembering that the Lord foresaw these various generations of crackpot "scholars." In His great foresight, what did He do to combat the effects that they would have on Christianity – on you and on me? Very simply, He over-ruled them. He went over their heads. He overthrew whatever they tried and gave His people the truth in spite of them. He did not honor their fabricated traditions and rigid rules any more than He honored the traditions of the Pharisees in Jesus' day. God gave His people the Bible in spite of the efforts and fulminations of many of His people's own "Bible scholars."

No better example exists than the dispute over whether Phebe was a "deaconess." Simply put, Bible believers had the truth in the King James English without respect to what anyone said that the Greek said. Observe:

> 8 *Likewise must the* ***deacons*** *be grave, not doubletongued, not given to much wine, not greedy of filthy lucre;*
> 9 *Holding the mystery of the faith in a pure conscience.*
> 10 *And let these also first be proved; then let them use the* ***office of a deacon****, being found blameless.*
> 11 *Even so must* ***their wives*** *be grave, not slanderers, sober, faithful in all things.*
> 12 ***Let the deacons be the husbands of one wife, ruling their children and their own houses well.***
> 13 *For they that have used the* ***office of a deacon*** *well purchase to themselves a good degree, and great boldness in the faith which is in Christ Jesus.* (1 Tim. 3:8-13)

Without preamble, the *deacons* were men only, since they had wives. They were to be the husbands of only one wife. If you believe the Bible for what it says, nothing could be clearer. Further, the *deacon* was to rule his own house well. Scripturally, only a man can fulfill that verse. This is indisputable on any kind of genuine Biblical grounds.

> *Let the woman learn in silence with all subjection. But I suffer not a woman to teach, nor to usurp authority over the man, but to be in silence. For Adam was first formed, then Eve.*
> (1 Tim. 2:11-13)

> *Likewise, ye wives, be in subjection to your own husbands; that, if any obey not the word, they*

> *also may without the word be won by the conversation of the wives;* (1 Pet. 3:1)
>
> *For after this manner in the old time the holy women also, who trusted in God, adorned themselves, being in subjection unto their own husbands:* (1 Pet. 3:5)
>
> *Wives, submit yourselves unto your own husbands, as unto the Lord. For the husband is the head of the wife, even as Christ is the head of the church: and he is the saviour of the body.*
> (Eph. 5:22-23)
>
> *Wives, submit yourselves unto your own husbands, as it is fit in the Lord.*
> (Col. 3:18)
>
> *Children, obey your parents in all things: for this is well pleasing unto the Lord.*
> (Col. 3:20)

True, the fallacy of the entire idea of *deaconesses* is exposed in the Greek. Most importantly, this truth would have already been evident to anyone who was resigned to the truth of the King James Bible and to the providence of the God who preserved it. It is the English that is the true compass in the matter, for once again, it is the English that makes the distinction indisputably plain, while the Greek leaves one to try to differentiate between the truths of various passages that use the same Greek word.

Office of a Deacon: The Handiwork of a Designer

It is important, before moving on to the next examples, that justice be done to God's handiwork. *The heavens declare the glory of God; and the firmament sheweth his handywork* (Ps.19:1). Most mature Christians have had occasion to reflect on the paths of their lives and have been able to track the manifold interventions of the Father at specific junctures along the way. It is wonderful indeed to be able to discover and contemplate the sometimes subtle handprints and the signs that show that God really did, and does, lead His people in a singular and sacred way.

Except for our lives as individual Christians and our service in Christ-honoring, scripture-based New Testament churches, it is difficult to think of a more obvious place to find the handiwork of God but in and upon the Bible. We would expect to find God's thumbprints there.

The richness of God's providence and oversight throughout history; His oversight through the Dark Ages, in Wycliffe's work, followed by Tyndale and Coverdale, and culminating in the work of the AV translators, is nothing short of astounding. Try as he might, no supporter of the Revised Version of 1881 can ever erase the despicable dishonesty nor deny the mutinous spiritual betrayal that marks its publication. The American Standard, the Revised Standard, the New American Standard, the New International all lend the appearance of being unescorted by the providential and inexplicable blessing of the Almighty. The reprobate apostasy of so many of the scholars involved, the ecumenical involvement of the publishers and editors, the spiritual seediness and rancid associations of the new versions' Greek text, the shenanigans in publication, the haughtiness and ambition of editors, and the sheer unending procession of ever-newer versions - all these speak of an absence of God's hand in the process.

To be plain and forthright, most of the New Testament Textus Receptus and Old Testament Masoretic Text proponents are very quick to point out how the hand of God was obvious in the preservation and oversight of those two cornerstones of the Bible, as we know it. They are laudatory, and do recognize, as well, that the Lord plainly had His hand on Erasmus, Wycliffe, Tyndale and others. As they recite the progression of events and recount the mighty labors and the imminent qualifications of the translators of the AV, these King James men continue to be enthused about the involvement of God in the process. But, as the final product comes into fruition in 1611, there is a marked cooling of that exuberant enthusiasm. Suddenly the superlative language earlier used to magnify the hand of God in the labor, seems to be replaced by a cooler academic need to qualify the final product as, yet still, the work of men. Very qualified men, we are reminded, but fallible men nonetheless. Somehow, the spirit of glorious exultation and swelling wonder at the providential intervention of God in the giving of the old English Bible, seems to bleed off for many of the writers between the beginning of the work in 1604 and the culmination of the work in 1611.

You see, as these men approach the juncture where their logical processes naturally lead them to the acknowledgment that the final product and fruit of 1611 actually supersedes the capacity and capability of men alone, they flee from the responsibility of bearing witness to it. As they approach the target, the horrible specter of perfection and inerrancy in translation rears its ghastly head, and they are dissuaded from their course. They know that to "go there" is to defy one of their principal dogmas: *No translation can be perfect.* It is not a foundation of scripture, but it is an ironbound precept of their scholarly fraternity. To defy that principle, and to speak out or acknowledge that God may have governed the choices of words, is to risk uttering scholastic heresy. Academically, it is the unforgivable sin. Even worse, it is to risk being categorized a *Ruckmanite*, being marginalized, mocked, and cast out of the intellectual synagogue.

So let us be plain. The handiwork of God not only exists upon the providential preservation of the Masoretic Text and the Textus Receptus. It is indeed evident that God used the minds, eyes, hands and intellects of Erasmus, Wycliffe and Tyndale; but God's handprints are also all over the King James Bible as a translation as well. It bears exclusive marks of the Lord, not merely in its corporate existence, its general quality as a reliable translation, its fruit borne through generations or its majestic language, but in the individual words of the translation. It is earmarked by the superlative quality and superiority of those words over even the languages from whence they came.

In spite of over 100 times in which one form or other of the Greek word *diakonos* occurs, the King James Bible only renders it *deacon, deacons,* or *office of a deacon,* **five** singular times. In every other instance *diakonos* is translated as relating to service, servants, ministry or ministers. The five distinct instances, which are the fractionally small exceptions to the habit the translators otherwise followed, were for the express purpose of distinguishing the church office of the *deacon* from the rest of the ministry and service which were separate from that church office.

The term *deacon* is, then, a sanctified term in scripture – a term that God set in place to clearly denote the church office. It means something special. It draws a clear and observable line. Different words so often mean different things, and in this case, it is inarguable, that the Lord clarified, illuminated and sanctified the *office of the deacon* by the language He chose to use. Phebe was not a *deacon.* She was never called a *deacon.* She did not qualify for the office in Greek or in English. God sanctified the use of the word *deacon* in English, and set it apart where it could only be confused by the incautious, the insincere, or by those driven by motives other than reverence for the truth.

This *deaconship* is only clearly differentiated and indisputable in English. The church office could have been, and is, confused with other aspects of Christian service in Greek, for *diakonos* forms the root word for various terms that were not so plainly separate in meaning in the Greek. In this case, the AV 1611 does differentiate in its translation of English words what the "original" does not reveal in its Greek state.

There are, then, ambiguities in Greek that the English clarifies and settles. One gets more light from the English than from the Greek. The Greek, in this case and in other cases already shown, is more ambiguous and uncertain than the final product of the translation of the King James Bible. The reason men can confuse Phebe's role in the church in Greek, is because God did something in English that He did not do in the Greek: He clarified the truth. He drew distinctions that are unavailable in the "original language."

Knowledge derived from the AV's English is significantly advanced beyond the knowledge that is found in Greek. More information is revealed from the English than from Greek. There is more accurate and definitive Christian instruction in the English than in the Greek. This might or might not be termed ***advanced revelation***, but what English reveals is more detailed and finely tuned than the mere *diakonos* of Greek

In this way, a Christian that reads and studies the English of the AV 1611 would be better equipped as a Christian than a mere student of the original language. This is a profoundly difficult pill to swallow for those who have fought against this precept for so long, nevertheless, the precept is undeniable in this example.

The English translation in the KJV is thereby superior to any existing Greek that we have with respect to

this passage. This fact has likely never been acknowledged by any scholar who leans on the original language for final authority. Perhaps one should lean in another direction. In any case, the Greek is demonstrably more obscure in meaning and does indeed lead to confusion and heresy. The fact that the King James Bible proves itself to be replete with these types of examples may prove a continuing burr under scholars' saddles. If English is clearer in meaning, less obscure, more definite, more exact, more accurate, less confusing, and more enlightening – in what way is it not superior to Greek? That is a question worth asking: **just exactly how *is* the AV 1611 not superior to the Greek in this case?** And why would pointing out the specifics and asking the question make one a disreputable heretic?

Referring to the Greek is a step backwards in understanding and demonstrably unravels work that God has accomplished. No one would have been in the least confused about Phebe, or the *deaconship,* in reading and studying only the English of the King James. Said another way, and with a more deservedly accusatory tone, **"going to the Greek" confused the doctrinal matter at hand.** The act of "going to the Greek" obscured and undermined clear and concise meaning in English. It is the source of insubordination, false leadership and heresy in the local church. It has contributed greatly to apostasy. It has falsely justified unscriptural sentiment and disorder in churches and families. It has enabled rebels and those who seek an excuse to marginalize and make relative the precision of the truth of God. Where is that proverbial *great treasure* from the Greek in this case? Has any decent fruit ever been borne of it?

Who is/are the active agent(s) in the translation, as found in the AV 1611? An honest and reasonable student must acknowledge the clear supremacy of the King James English in this case, along with the *agape-phileo* issue and the *charity* issue of past chapters. As in those cases, it is necessary to ask, **who is responsible for the superior translation?** If the answer is "the King James translators," then Christians must again ramp up their appreciation and respect for their profound discretion and insight. If by mere linguistic and spiritual expertise, they have accomplished this feat, it must again be proposed that the arrogant assembly-line scholars of our day should cease their chiding and niggling of the AV translators and take their seats in the student gallery.

On the other hand, what if God is actually the responsible agent for the translation of *diakonos* as it stands in the KJV? Somebody ***is*** responsible! If the translation is superior (and it is), then someone is responsible for it. Either Bois, Andrews, Reynolds and company are responsible for it, or God is responsible for it. Could it be that God used the translators in a much more intricate and elaborate fashion than even some KJV defenders are willing to consider? What would we label this ornately complex and intertwined involvement of God with His human instruments?

Deacons, Evolutionists, and Hippies

Creationists rightly disparage evolutionists for their incredible and self-willed obstinacy in refusing to acknowledge that where there is design and order, there must be a Designer. There must be One who put things in order. Art requires an artist. It does not just "happen." Engineering marvels require a marvelous engineer. The evolutionist is blinded, not because of either the abundance of or lack of evidence for creation, but by his preconceived notions and philosophy which prejudice him against acknowledging God's hand. Unfortunately, many Biblical scholars suffer from the same strain of pride and prejudice in a different arena.

No translation is perfect, therefore the KJV cannot be perfect.

God's inspiration and preservation of scripture does not extend with precision to the words of another language.
The translators were fallible men, therefore they must have done fallible work..
Only the originals were God-breathed.
Only the originals were perfect.
God did not involve Himself in translation as He did in inspiration.
God would never overrule a translator's fallible opinion.
Inspiration could never extend to translation.
The whole truth and treasure of the scripture lies in the ancient originals, thus it is heresy to appeal in finality to an other-language translation.

When they see the handiwork of God upon a translation, does this change their opinion? When they have the manifest guidance of God exhibited before their eyes, do they reevaluate?

Dr. Sam Gipp, as noted previously, preached that it takes men of character and discipline to build, while any dope-smoking hippy can tear things down. There is no question regarding the intelligence, zeal, prayer life or moral character of many of the men whom have thus far been mentioned and referenced in these few chapters. It has been readily admitted that many of their labors and accomplishments far exceed what this author's will ever be. I have taken upon myself the role of critiquing some of the ultimate opinions and conclusions of those for whom I have respect. Obviously, there are those whom I do not respect, as well. The ultimate vision here is not so much to divide, as it is to move some, by manifest evidence and example, to consider whether they have gone far enough in their thinking. Might some otherwise good men have fallen into a philosophical rut and adopted unfaithful precepts rather than scriptural ones? Might they be defending a treasure and dishonoring it all at the same time?

The questions must be asked, although not without respect: if the Greek is the real answer to scriptural dilemmas and mysteries, why has such disparity been found so far? If the New Testament Greek is presented as the ultimate authority, but it is not so in truth – as in the cases displayed so far – what damage is being done by perpetuating the myth? If some, in the name of Christ, are supposed to be building the people of God by the knowledge of God, but by certain prejudicial tradition they are actually withholding light from them, what would that make such shepherds? If in the name of feeding the flock, they actually are withholding vital nutrients and starving them, who are the disciplined men of character in this scenario, and who are the rebels and hippies? In spite of boldly standing beneath the mere banner of "Christianity" and "biblical scholarship," who is doing the building, and who is tearing down?

Chapter 5

A Little Lower Than the Angels

> *What is man, that thou art mindful of him? and the son of man, that thou visitest him? For thou hast made him a little lower than* ***the angels****, and hast crowned him with glory and honour.*
> (Ps. 8:4-5)

> *But one in a certain place testified, saying, What is man, that thou art mindful of him? or the son of man, that thou visitest him? Thou madest him a little lower than* ***the angels****; thou crownedst him with glory and honour, and didst set him over the works of thy hands: Thou hast put all things in subjection under his feet. For in that he put all in subjection under him, he left nothing that is not put under him. But now we see not yet all things put under him. But we see Jesus, who was made a little lower than* ***the angels*** *for the suffering of death, crowned with glory and honour; that he by the grace of God should taste death for every man.* (Heb. 2:6-9)

In this chapter, the original languages will intermingle just a bit. The cases documented thus far, and the precepts which have sprung from them, apply as much in the Hebrew language of the Old Testament as in the Greek of the New

Testament. A superficial perusal of the *Hebrew and Chaldee Dictionary* in the back of *Strong's Analytical Concordance* will affirm that there are a dizzying array of ways in which Mr. Strong holds that a Hebrew word may be (and was) translated. Most linguists acknowledge that there is a depth and esoteric quality to the Hebrew language that even the Greek does not contain. This is the reason that some have been honest enough to confess that Bible translation in any language is far more of an art than a science. This is a tidbit worth remembering, because the English reader of the KJV sometimes finds the reading of his Bible disparaged and rejected by scholars, and he himself can be sometimes overwhelmed by the academic bullying of those who make adamant pronouncements about how Greek or Hebrew absolutely *must* be translated. These statements are made with all the finality and authority of hard scientific certainty. Translation is far from hard science. It is not as simple as plugging the coefficient of friction into a physics equation or *pi* into a geometry equation and solving for *x*. Water may freeze at 32 degrees Fahrenheit at mean sea level, but translating Hebrew to English is a far cry from reading a thermometer and an altimeter.

The testimonies of the scriptures which open this chapter mark the only occasions that the "*little lower than the angels*" quotations occur in the King James Bible. It is not difficult to find from whence in the Old Testament that God drew the Hebrews 2 quotation, since there is only one place it could have come from: Psalms 8:5. Things do get a little interesting from there if one chooses to see what new versions say in English, or if one investigates any of the Hebrew and Greek support for the passages.

An *Angelic* Nightmare

The new versions, while translating the crucial phrase in Hebrews 2:6 and 2:9 in close accord with the AV, truly give us some eye-opening renditions of the verse from Psalms 8. A handful of examples will suffice:

Psalm. 8:5
Yet Thou hast made him ***a little lower than God****,*
and dost crown him with glory and majesty!
(New American Standard)

Yet you have made him ***a little lower than God****,*
and you crown him with glory and majesty!
(New American Update)

You made him ***a little lower than the heavenly beings*** *and crowned him with glory and honor.*
(New International Version)

Yet thou hast made him ***little less than God****, and dost crown him with glory and honor.*
(Revised Standard Version)

Remember now, dear reader, that this is the "greater light" directly from the original Hebrew! As stated, this makes for some interesting reading and has some theological ramifications that underscore the need for uniform and exact translation. A few things best be addressed at this juncture:

1) There is a destructive quality to these ill-thought and poorly advised translations. Though all the scholars agree on the translation of *angels* in Hebrews 2, by diverging from the wisdom of the AV translators and not translating the corresponding word of Psalms 8:5 *angels*, as well, the modern translators have destroyed the Old Testament source for the New Testament quotation in Hebrews 2. In 1 Corinthians 2:12-13, we are given the key to grasping the things of God:

> *12 Now we have received, not the spirit of the world, but the spirit which is of God; that* ***we might know the things that are freely given to us*** *of God.*
> *13* ***Which things also we speak, not in the words*** *which man's wisdom teacheth, but which the Holy Ghost teacheth;* ***comparing spiritual things with spiritual.***

It is impossible to overlook the idea set forth in 1 Corinthians 2:12-13, that *the things of God* are grasped and *known* by *comparing spiritual things with spiritual*, and that those *spiritual things* are ***words.*** You see, there is a link between Psalms 8:5 and Hebrews 2:6-9 that is destroyed by the translation of most of the new versions. The link between the two passages is a certain ***word.*** When that singular ***word*** is altered, then the chain linking the two ideas in two diverse passages is thus destroyed. The key word of Psalms 8:5, *angels,* is cast off and another is substituted in its place. In losing the link, the unsuspecting soul has lost the comparison, and in losing the comparison, he lost what the *Holy Ghost teacheth*!

Unavoidably, by the mere act of making this observation, the gauntlet is again cast down for those who think the real treasure rests in Greek and Hebrew as opposed to English. The slap in the face for those who so zealously pursue this apparition is the fact that it took the English translation of the AV to link the two passages together. The chain that links them is the English. The reader will be required to choose whether indeed the final, whole and complete truth lies in the original languages or in the English translation in this case. Nonetheless, it has been Bible-believing defenders' continuing anthem that by the act of blithely changing and altering words in the Bible, the dissenting translator is disconnecting truths, fouling the keys of knowledge, and destroying God's method of teaching His ways to His children.

2) Changing words changes the meaning and understanding of scripture. In this case, nothing could be plainer than the fact that changing *angels* to *God* in Psalms 8:5 marks a change in message, connotation, apprehension, and doctrine. *Angels* are plainly not the same as *God*! New version advocates have been long-exercised in spinning all the changes in the new bibles as having resulted in no change whatever to doctrine or truth. We Bible-believers have been long-exercised in rolling our eyes at such preposterous propaganda and in watching to see which Eskimo steps to the front of the line to buy the ice-maker.

3) Man is *a little lower than the angels*, and a lot lower than God! It is unclear whether any of these translators think about the ramifications of what they write, or if they truly understand the responsibilities that they take upon their heads when they change the words of God, but if they do think, it must be along different lines than the average child of God. When Psalms 8:5 is changed to read *…yet Thou hast made him **a little lower than God*** (NAS), it is a mockery doctrinally. Man is a lot lower than God! The false translation is completely disreputable scripturally.

> *For my thoughts are not your thoughts, neither are your ways my ways, saith the LORD. For as the heavens are higher than the earth, so are my ways higher than your ways, and my thoughts than your thoughts.* (Isa. 55:8-9)

> *If thou seest the oppression of the poor, and violent perverting of judgment and justice in a province, marvel not at the matter: for he that is*

higher than the highest regardeth; and there be higher than they. (Ecc. 5:8)

For such an high priest became us, who is holy, harmless, undefiled, separate from sinners, and made higher than the heavens; (Heb. 7:26)

...surely every man is vanity. (Ps. 39:11b)

Man is like to vanity: his days are as a shadow that passeth away. (Ps. 144:4)

Every man is brutish in his knowledge... (Jer. 10:14a)

O LORD, I know that the way of man is not in himself: it is not in man that walketh to direct his steps (Jer. 10:23)

Though the LORD be high, yet hath he respect unto the lowly: but the proud he knoweth afar off. (Ps. 138:6)

Psalms 8:4 precedes our verse in question, and says, *What is man, that thou art mindful of him? and the son of man, that thou visitest him?* While man is made a *little lower than the angels* in 8:5, the scriptures make plain that man is fallen a vast distance beneath God's plateau: *Every one of them is gone back: they are altogether become filthy; there is none that doeth good, no, not one* (Ps. 53:3). Man is much lower than God. The AV is correct in that we are at least only a little lower than the angels and that there are a vast number of angels that have fallen (Jude 6) and more yet that will fall (Rev. 12:7-8). Man is so low that members of his unconverted populace will go into everlasting fire *...prepared for the devil and his angels* (Matt. 25:41).

4) Jesus Christ is *not* lower than, or less than, God! One other doctrinal aberration that results from the acceptance of the fraudulent reading of the new bibles in Psalms 8:5 relates to the fact that Hebrews 2:7 applies the *little lower than the angels* reading of Psalms 8:5 to man in general, and rightly so. It is critical to note that the author of Hebrews then bridges the application of *a little lower than the angels* in Hebrews 2:9 to apply to Jesus Christ as well. This is crucial on two counts:

a) Christ is clearly foreseen prophetically in Psalms 8, for verse 2 is applied to Christ in Matthew 21:16. Jesus our Lord is further seen in the title *son of man* in verse 4, one of His many names in the New Testament. Further, Psalms 8:5-6 is eventually fulfilled in Christ as the One *crowned with glory and honour* and as having *dominion over the works* of God's hands.

b) Since Christ is part of the greater fulfillment of Psalms 8:5, how atrocious and heretical is a translation that thus translates *...Yet Thou hast made him* ***a little lower than God*** (NAS) or *...Yet thou hast made him* ***little less than God*** (RSV)? Since Hebrews 2:7 and 2:9 are dually applied to first, man (vs.7), and then, Jesus Christ (vs.9), Psalms 8:5 absolutely must say *...For thou hast made him a little lower than* ***the angels*** (AV 1611), instead of *...Thou hast made him* ***a little lower than God*** (NAS), ***because Christ was and is God!*** He was not made lower than God. He could not be made lower than God. He was God manifest in the flesh (1 Tim. 3:16). He was *the Word ...and the Word was God* (Jn.1:1). He was indeed made *lower than the angels* in the days of His flesh down here on earth, but He was never made less than God or lower than God, for He was, and still is, God!

Christians are called to love God and Christ with all their hearts, souls, minds and strength. It is an auspicious calling since men's very hearts and nature are wicked (Jer. 17:9). They are further called to *live by... every word that proceedeth out of the mouth of God* (Matt. 4:4). It is difficult to express the depth of the disgust and distain felt by a Bible-believer when either Christ or the word is attacked by fools, but the sentiment is particularly virulent and deep when they both are disparaged and soiled at the same time. Many names and adjectives could be, and have been, applied to the men and women who do so, but the reader should rest assured that *scholar, godly, earnest, honest,* and *faithful* are not among those that are applicable.

Angelic Nuggets from the Original

With all of the propaganda and sophistry that is employed by so many of the Greek and Hebrew scholars, it would be altogether easy to refuse to even gaze into the well from whence they drink their stale and foul water. It is my own position that no Christian with a King James Bible needs to employ himself in the Greek or Hebrew to attain new light or deeper nuggets. The originals are needed neither for preaching, teaching, nor study. The light is no brighter there and the nuggets are no more golden. Contrary to the scholarly rhetoric with which Christian radio listeners are constantly bombarded, final certainty, ultimate truth, and eternal clarity are no more evident in the original languages than they are in English. As has already been made plainly evident, there is often more confusion and ambiguity in the original languages than the self-serving academics will ever admit. On the other hand, for someone who is not interested in overthrowing the authority of the AV and only wants to marvel at the handiwork and the finished accomplishments of God within His word in English, peering into the ancient biblical languages yields sights and wonders unappreciated by most linguistic doctors. These marvels confirm the King James Bible instead of overthrowing it.

There is no controversy concerning the translation *angels* in Hebrews 2:7 and 2:9. The translation comes from the word *ἀγγέλους* in Greek, or for our purposes, *aggelos*. The controversy, as discussed above, comes from the Old Testament Hebrew where the translation *angels,* comes from the Hebrew word *elohiym.* Usually in the Old Testament, the Hebrew word from which comes *angel(s)* is *malak*, but not this time. Of the approximate 120 times that the words *angel or angels)* are translated in the Old Testament, only one singular time does the word *angel(s)* come from the Hebrew root word *elohiym.*

What is the significance of this? The significance is that ***elohiym*** is most usually translated ***God*** in English. A listing of facts at this point might be helpful to see the dilemma and the resultant blessing for a King James Bible believer.

- ***Elohiym* occurs around 2700 times in the Hebrew Old Testament**[75]
- **The vast percentage of times *elohiym* is translated *God* in the English Bible**
- **About 7% of the time (just over 200 times) it is translated *gods*.**
- **It is translated *judge(s)* 5-6 times**
- ***Elohiym* is translated *goddess* 2 times.**
- **Thus, well over 90% of the time *elohiym* refers to God Himself.**
- **Only once is *elohiym* translated *angels* (Ps. 8:5).**

---

[75] Bullinger, E.W., *The Companion Bible* (Humphrey Milford Oxford University Press, London, New York, Toronto & Melbourne) Appendix 4, p.6.

Obviously, 2700 occurrences of a word is quite a large number. It is equally obvious that being translated *God* something near 2500 times is also a very high number of times. The vast majority of times you read *God* in your KJV Old Testament, you are reading a word that is translated from the Hebrew *elohiym.* It is fair to say that the context of most all the cases makes clear whether the translation should be *God*, *gods* or *goddesses*. In the cases where *elohiym* is translated *judges*, it is again plain that the word *God* or *gods* would not satisfy the context.

Psalms 8:5 sticks out about as much as an occurrence can stick out amidst 2700 other occurrences. It is highlighted due to its singularity: the fact that it is the only time out of 2700 that *elohiym* is translated *angels*. It also sticks out because it is the only Old Testament source in our written canon of scripture for the New Testament quotation in Hebrews 2. It sticks out because there would be no obvious grounds for translating *elohiym* as *angels* for this one singular time out of 2700 times. There is no precedent whatever for translating it *angels.*

We have explored what a terrible theological mess is made by the alternative translations of the new bible versions. As we have the finished product in front of us and as we see the fruit of the reading as it is in the KJV, and since we have further noticed the splatter made by the modern scholars' attempts to do a better job than the AV translators, let us evaluate what we actually have before us.

The Glory of *Angels*

It could well be argued that the AV translators retrospectively translated Psalms 8:5 as *angels* since they plainly knew that Hebrews 2:7 and 2:9 were translated *angels* from Greek. After all, it is evident that the quotation in Hebrews 2 used Psalms 8:5 as the source. In other words, it is conceivable that the AV translators did not really know what to do with Psalms 8 from the Hebrew, but when they saw how Hebrews 2:7-9 was translated, they put *angels* into Psalms 8 because they had that quotation clearly from the New Testament Greek.

This is an interesting theory, though what argues against it is the number of times that the translators did not translate Old and New Testament quotations as exact word for word matches. Anyone who looks up cross-references in the Bible knows fully well that many NT quotations of OT passages do not match word for word. Why would the translators be preoccupied with forcing this one to match?

Now, if that is indeed what they did, the AV translators' actions in doing so prove to be a great deal wiser than the modern scholars' precipitous translations which begin a chain reaction of doctrinal and theological debacles as discussed earlier in this chapter. Thus, even if we lay the responsibility for the translation of *angels* from *elohiym* at the feet of these men, **the AV translators' actions, reasoning and fruit more than justify the 1611's translation when compared to the alternative.** If the translators are responsible for the translation, then they are responsible for the superiority represented by the translation, and deserve the deference of the comparatively slipshod amateurs of this hour.

It is, however, reasonable to consider that **perhaps man is not responsible for the translation, *angels*, in Psalms 8:5.** Perhaps God is responsible. *Again.* This possibility of course torments the sensibilities of the naysayers whose minds have long been hardened to the idea, but consider the possibilities. The horrific mess that is made if the AV translation of Psalms 8:5 is altered has been seen, so one is forced to choose between two possibilities. 1) Either the King James translators were not the gifted yet backwards bumblers they are represented as today by every slovenly commentator with a computer bible program, or 2) God Himself is responsible for the manifestly correct translation of the verse.

The Bible commentators' and scholars' predisposition to anti-scriptural prejudice must once again be raised here. Almost universally, a primary dogma held by scholars is that no translation can be perfect and that God Himself would never press beyond the initial inspiration of the originals to affect the language in a translation. It seldom seems to occur to such scholars that they should compare the precepts of their work for the Lord with the precepts found in the word of the Lord!

• Moses and Pharaoh spake one to another in the Egyptian language, and yet the OT scriptures themselves were written in Hebrew. That constitutes one translation from the original Egyptian into the original Hebrew. So, does or does not God ever involve Himself in a translation?

• In Acts 21:40 and 22:2, Paul addresses the mob in the Hebrew tongue, but it is recorded in Greek. So, there was one translation that occurred *before* it was ever written in the inspired, original Greek! Does God ever involve Himself in a translation?

• In Acts 2 the men of diverse speech in Jerusalem heard the word of God in their own languages. One may look at this in several ways. 1) Perhaps God spake to the apostles that day in the diverse tongues in which they spake. In that case no translation would have been necessary, but if this is true, then God *gave* the inspired originals in languages other than Greek or Hebrew! 2) On the other hand, if God spake to the apostles in one language (the original), then the apostles had to speak it in yet other languages to be understood by the men who heard. Were these translations faulted? 3) The men of Acts 2:8 said, *And how hear we every man in our own tongue, wherein we were born?* Perhaps one apostle spake in one tongue and the men around him understood him in the multiplicities of their own tongues. Wow! An apostle speaks in Hebrew, for example, and ten men surrounding him hear him in ten different languages. What would that be called? Did the men who went back to their native lands, carry back a gospel message that was imperfect and errant in their own respective languages? Can one be sure that God did not insert Himself in the translation process?

• In Genesis 42:23, Joseph spake unto his brethren by an interpreter, and yet all that he said is recorded in Hebrew in the originals. Again, that constitutes a translation before even being written in the original language! Was God in that?

How can a man, professing to live by the Bible and seeking for the principles of life from the Bible, claim as a foundational precept of his scholarly profession that God simply does not lead in translation to the point of perfection or inerrancy? What Biblical example can he cite that would convince us that he was actually following a Biblical pattern of thought or consideration in arriving at that conclusion? And, finally, how as a corporate entity, can an entire body of men (scholars in general), teaching, preaching and professing to study the Bible, all be so adamantly sold on a principle ("no translation can be perfect") that is adverse to what the Bible truly teaches? We have no choice but to conclude that such Bible scholars in fact do not read or study their own Bibles sincerely nor singularly.

To the common, Bible-reading Bible believer it is manifestly evident that God has at many junctures providentially intervened in the translation of His Book. After considering the fruit borne and the present line of reasoning being advanced here, why should one balk at the idea that God was responsible for *elohiym* being translated *angels* in Psalms 8:5 of the King James Bible?

Returning to the original Hebrew as the primary appeal causes a great deal of trouble, and undermines clarity and sound doctrine. The English translation of the two passages in the AV 1611 is 100% plain, and could not be any clearer. Any confusion that may have existed was resolved in English. Any conflict or obscurity was made perfectly plain. What most scholars consider something of a sacred act – referring to the original – actually is the cause of all the problems here. It leads to the misapprehension of Christ's Deity, it is misleading as to man's position before God, and it destroys a plain linkage between two verses in the Old and New Testaments, which are necessary for understanding.

It cannot be understated that the act of referring back to the original language, presuming to translate directly from the original, and in doing so ignoring how the AV translators in their wisdom translated *elohiym,* is an act that quenches the light of already perfect clarity in the verse. Changing the King James' translation here is the undoing of accuracy and truth already achieved, and simply draws us back into darkness, obscurity, and confusion. No one is made better for the exercise. In fact, if we lend credence to the exercise and yield to it, we are all the worse off for it, because we understand less than when we started. No one leaning upon the English of the KJV would have been in any wise mislead, nor would they have been left in the dark.

How is it that we allow the authority for what we understand spiritually in truth (the AV English) to be trumped and undermined by an "authority" that leads us to darkness, false readings, unclear doctrine and confusion (the "original Hebrew")? The only reason any English reader of the Bible could have been confused in this affair is by the fact that so many give weight to the idea that only the original languages bear the seal of ultimate authority. Every Christian has the privilege of perfectly clear understanding attested to by the authority of the AV English, yet so many have allowed that authority to be made subservient to a "higher authority" – the Hebrew. Scholars have condemned the understanding of many as "not being good enough" because, for them the Bible we have is not good enough. The academics and scholars have a higher appeal with which they attempt to subvert a common Christian's final authority: the King James Bible. So they worked the marvels of their wisdom, appealed to the source of "greater understanding," and what is the product? *Confusion.* Where there was once accord, there is now discord. Where there once was apprehension, there is now ignorance. Darkness and uncertainty have superseded light and the *more sure word of prophecy* (2 Pet. 1:19). Where once there was the fruit of understanding, there is now only a mess.

In the end, going back to the Hebrew *undid* and *destroyed* what God had already accomplished.

The real light in these passages is in English, not Hebrew or Greek. This fact is detailed in previous chapters, as well. The average reader would be "lost" if required to translate the two passages under scrutiny in this chapter from their original languages. Most have no legitimate working knowledge of Greek or Hebrew whatever. Some may feel this places them at a great disadvantage scripturally, since the Bible was originally written in Hebrew and Greek, a fact of which so many with fingers in the mix are very ardent to remind all who lend ear. I would challenge the reader to recognize that this feeling of being at a disadvantage, in most cases, did not exactly originate at the initiative of the individual's conscience. The fact is that a person's intimidation in this affair is a seed largely planted, watered and nourished by men whose life "calling" is to labor in those languages, and who are both quick and zealous about calling a simple Bible-believer's attention back to his insufficiency in another language. They consider themselves the authorities and experts, and all less qualified Bible readers are among the intellectual peons and the pitifully ignorant. If the reader will search his own heart, he likely will discover that he has been to the Garden of Eden himself, stood in the shadow of a certain tree of knowledge, and heard the Satanic pitch, "Yea, hath God said"?

I am not an economist and am happy to defer to an expert in macroeconomics when such a matter arises. I have never pretended to be a pharmacist, or for that matter, any other of a number of specialists or professionals that might be mentioned. Two things are important to recognize, though:

1) I do not need a macroeconomist to balance my own checkbook and to handle my own financial affairs. I do not need a pharmacist to know when to take 3 Advil.

2) God is the Expert, and the Author of the Bible. He promised to keep and preserve the words, and He commissioned me to *earnestly contend for the faith* (Jude 3), and said to me, *My son, attend to my words; incline thine ear unto my sayings. Let them not depart from thine eyes; keep them in the midst of thine heart* (Prov. 4:20-21). The fact is that God did not commission scholarly institutions nor academic chairs to keep, defend, spread and exposit the words of God. He commissioned Bible-believing Christian soldiers. He commissioned the body of Christ, the Church (Col. 1:18). He commissioned you and me. Nobody appointed Dr. So-and-so a general officer or commander-in-chief. The fact is that a great deal of evidence points to the fact that God has equipped you and me very well indeed, and that we are intended to go to war with what we have. This fact merely points out the inferiority of the sword with which a good number of men parading as masters and experts of war would like to equip Christian soldiers. Consider that you may be trading with the enemy's quartermaster. Further remember, that David rejected the use of Saul's armor in going to battle against Goliath.

One characteristic stands out that is worthy of mention. The scholars and Christian academics seem all too quick to do two things: 1) criticize what the King James Bible says, and 2) correct it out of the Greek or Hebrew. Who notices that they themselves seem always to be at odds on what exactly the Bible should say in the places they are so quick to alter? Our lack of expertise in the original languages is supposed to cripple us as Christians and obligate us to the experts, but the "experts" themselves seem never to agree on what the Bible says! Or else, as we have seen, they offer Christians an alternative that can be proven manifestly inferior to that with which we started. The act of referring to the original languages is represented as some sort of sacred, holy and superior act, but as shown here, it actually disarms Bible believers of certainty, clarity, and understanding, and rearms them with uncertainty and confusion.

The ambiguity and uncertainty of the Hebrew is resolved in the AV's English. There is a lack of clarity and an uncertainty of meaning contained in the Hebrew texts that is evident even to those who know Hebrew. I know this is true because the Hebrew experts translate the critical portion of the verse under scrutiny in different manners. Notice:

- ***…a little lower than God***
  (New American Standard)
- ***…a little lower than the heavenly beings***
  (NIV)
- ***…little less than God***
  (RSV)

If Christians are supposed to acquiesce to them as experts, if the incorrectness of the AV is so certain, and if the Hebrew is so deep and studded with treasure, why is it so common that there is so little consensus among so called experts about what the Bible should and does say? The raw facts are that *elohiym* occurs close to 2700 times in the Hebrew

Old Testament, and for all its usages, Psalms 8:5 stands out as an anomaly when compared to the other occurrences. Given all the possible choices for translation, it is a matter of opinion among those experts about what it should be. Where is the science and certitude in that? Whatever uncertainty and ambiguity exists in the Hebrew is utterly resolved and clarified in the King James Bible where:

- 47 magnificent and humble scholars did agree on what it said in 1611
- God has blessed what it says in English for nigh unto 400 years
- Its context and doctrinal implications are consistent with what the rest of the scriptures attest.
- English readers are not the slightest bit confounded by its meaning or application.

What reason is there to go back to the Hebrew?

Man proves again that he is careless. The scholars who are reported to have built their lives and disciplines around the originals of the Biblical languages are again careless and unheeding of the ramifications of changing the Bible. They are impetuous in flippantly overthrowing the work of men whose learning and credentials should give, of all people, the degree-conscious modern scholars pause. They are negligent to notice the damage they do in doctrine. They are slipshod in the truths they obscure, undermine and disconnect from other truths. Their egotism leads them to think that they are eminently qualified to adjust and modify, but their haughtiness and pride guarantees not only their fall (Pro. 16:18), but that God will distance Himself from their work and their persons (Ps. 138:6). These men are careless. They have not a detectible concern about holy ground (Ex. 3:5), strange fire (Lev. 10:1) or their *part* in *the book of life* (Rev. 22:19). They are rash, and at the same time slovenly, in that they take no pause at God's stated adversity to the type of wisdom they employ:

- *For it is written, I will destroy the wisdom of the wise, and will bring to nothing the understanding of the prudent.* (1 Cor. 1:19)

- *...hath not God made foolish the wisdom of this world?* (1 Cor. 1:20)

- *For the wisdom of this world is foolishness with God. For it is written, He taketh the wise in their own craftiness.* (1 Cor. 3:19)

- *That your faith should not stand in the wisdom of men, but in the power of God.* (1 Cor. 2:5)

In the end, there are far better reasons – academically, reasonably, and spiritually - for retaining the readings of the King James Bible, than they have for modifying it.

The *English translation* of this passage in the King James is manifestly superior to its Hebrew roots. It is more accurate. Guessing at one meaning in 2700 occurrences is not accurate. The old English Holy Bible is doctrinally consistent. The newfangled translations, in wresting the scriptures, pervert the doctrine of the scriptures and of Christ! The English is clear. It is concise. It resolves the Hebrew's ambiguity. It overrules the poor judgment of bad translations and bad translators. It sheds light on the New Testament passage spawned from it, and does not confuse the reader. It is superior in every way.

Chapter 6

God Will Provide Himself

> *And Isaac spake unto Abraham his father, and said, My father: and he said, Here am I, my son. And he said, Behold the fire and the wood: but where is the lamb for a burnt offering? And Abraham said, My son, God will provide himself a lamb for a burnt offering: so they went both of them together.* (Gen. 22:7-8)

There is not a more bitterly or more hotly contested spiritual battleground than that of the Deity of our Lord Jesus Christ. In Genesis 3:15, against the backdrop of the first man's shattered destiny, the Lord endued Adam and Eve with the life-giving promise of hope, assuring them of a *seed* that would come and that would bruise the sinister and subtle serpent's head. No doubt, many was the saint of God that clung to that promise down through the centuries of Old Testament history, but that knowledge was also shared by one who had no inclination to yield his pate to the heel of the Messiah without a death battle. So, while God's people hoped and anticipated, the old red dragon strategized and laid in wait.

The minefields, the ambuscades, and the mazes of deceit that he laid in place for both sinners and the Savior were impressive indeed. In a day when there was no media as we think of it today, no medium that quite compared to our machines by which we communicate now, and no printing press which made mass production of information the curse or blessing that it is, the devil still managed to *blind the eyes of them that believe not* (2 Cor. 4:4) and to have a sequence of artful defenses in place which deceived the masses and led the sinners to crucify the promised *Seed* and Savior, the Son of God. He was called just about every name in the book, but all too few saw Him for who He really was: God.

One would think that a resurrection from the dead would turn the tide, and for many of us, that is exactly what happened. Nevertheless, the old serpent has shown a resilience that is most frightful. Even though the Lord delivered him a resounding defeat, Satan has never lessened his hold upon the deluded minds and hearts of those he has mesmerized. The devil succeeded in "spinning" Jesus Christ as a blasphemous imposter while Christ was here on earth, and the fallacious campaign fomented by that fallen cherub only accelerated and grew more successful after the Lord ascended.

It is remarkable that every worldly and religious philosophy makes a place for Jesus, but none ever accord Him His rightful place. Every religion, sect, or cult must find a place for Jesus Christ somewhere in its system of deceit. This is remarkable because we Christians, for instance, make no place of honor whatsoever for Mohammad, Buddha, or any of the 325 million gods of the Hindus. *(A)ll the gods of the nations are idols* (Ps. 96:5). The only place a Bible-believing Christian allots to the deities of the heathen is to acknowledge them as unclean spirits and devils. This they cannot do with Christ. Excepting the Jews, for whom He died and who castigate Him more ruthlessly than any other group on earth, almost every category of men, when it comes to their fallen spiritual inclinations, must allot some place of honor for Christ. Even the worst of the ungodly – sodomites, pagans, witches, Nazis, pedophiles, New Agers – adorn Christ with the despicable characteristics of their own reprobate natures. Would it not just be easier to ignore Him entirely? Would it not be easier to merely discount Him? We Christians discount Krishna in approximately three nanoseconds and give no thought to him again. Why are others unable to do this with Christ?

The reason why, is that Jesus Christ is embedded in the conscience of even the most hardened pagan religious soul. He is *...the true Light, which lighteth every man that cometh into the world* (Jn. 1:9), and men have to *do something* with Him! So, what men do is twist and mold Him into what they want Him to be. They cannot truly do away with Him, so they adorn Him with deceitful falsehoods and cheap, tinsel ornamentation. They can accept Him being a prophet or a miracle worker. They consider Him sublime as a philosopher, a social activist and a humanist. However, ***they can never abide the concept that He is God.*** It is okay for Him to be denominated the *son of God*, as long as being the *son of God* does not mean that He is the ***S****on of God – God...manifest in the flesh* (1 Tim. 3:16).

The church was born into a world where the god of this world (2 Cor. 4:4) had the battleground arranged to his own choosing and all armaments were "cocked and locked." Some would say that the decks were stacked. Platonic and Gnostic philosophies were at the pinnacle of power, and the Roman Empire was a multicultural admixture of heathen men with all their divergent ideas of gods. Add to that mix that the Roman government was overbearing and intrusive in its power and scope. There were legal religions, and then there were illegal ones.[76] The legal ones were state sponsored, registered, and were not allowed to proselytize. It was a crime against the state for one man to press upon another individual the need for conversion, and to express that his religion and his God were true in exclusivity to others was an act that placed one in adversity with the entire Roman Empire. It was such a system that sought to tempt, and failing that, to impose upon

---

[76] Cairns, Earl E., *Christianity Through The Centuries: A History of the Christian Church.* Zondervan Publishing House, Grand Rapids, Michigan 49506, 1954, 1981, p.87.

Christianity a requirement to abandon the singular truth of its doctrine and its Savior, and place them upon the shelves of honorable religions beside 1000 other idols and dogmas. The field was ripe for men setting forth scores and scores of different views on the nature of Jesus Christ as it related to God the Father.

Christ was barely conceived before questions arose about His Father's identity. The church was borne into a world where hundreds of philosophical midwives all laid different claim to knowing the truth of Jesus' precise relation to God. The deity of Christ has never ceased to be one of the chief controversies on any given day among *"Christians."* To this very hour, in the 21st century, the deity of Christ remains bloody and divisive ground. Jehovah's Witnesses and Mormons are common cults that deny Christ's deity, though they spend a great deal of time trying to show themselves orthodox by sophistry and rhetoric. There are a number of so-called "Protestant" groups and sects that have a less than Biblical view of Christ's Godhood, when one stops to examine their dogma in detail. Further, as the mainstream "church" continues to play footsy with the world and to intertwine herself with New Ageism, Eastern Mysticism, philosophy and humanism, the end result is inevitable: she will depart, and so often already *has* departed, from the Godhood of Jesus Christ.

The new bibles continue collectively to be the greatest monument and attestation to the insidious power of Satan. It was inevitable that he who questioned God's motive and character in Genesis 3, would question His very nature once it was revealed that God Himself would shed His own blood (Acts 20:28) for sinners. A nearly blind prophet could see that the one who undermined the woman's confidence in the word of God from his first utterance (Gen. 3:1), would surely alter the testimony to the fact that God *became a man*, but remained God while He *was a man*, and is God today *as a man*, though He *ever liveth to make intercession* for us (Heb. 7:25).

The Sublime Prophecy in the King's English

The profound depth of Abraham's faith in God is awe-inspiring to all who consider it today. God made a promise to Abraham about Isaac being the promised seed (Gen. 17:19). It would have been a soul-shattering experience for most of us had we been in Abraham's position, for that doting and loving father subsequently heard God direct that he should sacrifice Isaac (Gen. 22:2). However, Abraham was no shallow believer, and the Bible testifies that Abraham obeyed God to the letter and journeyed to Moriah with Isaac, having the resolute intent to obey God's command to the letter. Abraham's reasoning in the matter is not recorded until Hebrews 11:19, where his readiness to follow through and actually kill his son Isaac as a sacrifice is explained thus: *Accounting that God was able to raise him up, even from the dead; from whence also he received him in a figure.* James 2:23 bears witness that it was at this point that Abraham earned the revered title, *the Friend of God.*

In one of the dramatic moments of this God-inspired narrative, the Holy Spirit testifies that

> *...Isaac spake unto Abraham his father, and said, My father: and he said, Here am I, my son. And he said, Behold the fire and the wood: but where is the lamb for a burnt offering?*
>
> (Gen. 22:7)

Abraham's reply must go down in history as one of the most sublime pronouncements that ever proceeded from the lips of a mortal man. Faithful, God-fearing, a father himself, a mere man, one who would have to live with himself as well as having to explain his actions to Isaac's mother, Abraham replied to his promised and beloved son,

> *My son, God will provide himself a lamb for a burnt offering...* (Gen. 22:8)

The Lord is able to pour profound meaning and import into just a few words. That fact testifies to the verity that God is the Author of the Book and that the word of God is alive (Heb. 4:12) and not a mere book whose boundaries are limited by fragile paper, ink, leather and cloth (2 Tim. 2:9). For our purposes, we will be looking past the personal ramifications for Abraham and Isaac, their faith in God, Abraham's supreme confidence in the Father, and all that this subsequently means for our faith. Instead, let us consider the import of the phrase: ***God will provide himself a lamb*** (Gen. 22:8).

God *did* make provision for that day. Isaac certainly was seeking no deep prophetic insight or revelation when he inquired after the lamb. It is also certain that as he lay bound before his broken-hearted yet determined father, he was looking for no greater fulfillment of his father's promise than that something with wool and hooves would arrive on the scene very soon!

For Abraham's part, who can say just how deeply he understood the prophecy he made to his son at that moment? We know that Christ testified that, *Your father Abraham rejoiced to see my day: and he saw it, and was glad* (John 8:56). At the precise moment Abraham pronounced the words to Isaac, it is questionable whether he wholly foresaw the ultimate fulfillment in the person of Jesus Christ upon those same mountains 2000 years later. One plain and evident view of the promise is clearly that Abraham's meaning was that Isaac himself was the lamb. Had Abraham hesitated at that altar and fumbled a bit with the knife, it could be argued that he was waiting for God to come through with other provision, but that is not the impression the scriptures leave.

> *And they came to the place which God had told him of; and Abraham built an altar there, and laid the wood in order, and bound Isaac his son, and laid him on the altar upon the wood. And Abraham stretched forth his hand, and took the knife to slay his son.* (Gen. 22: 9-10)

It is clear and heart-rending that Abraham, in promising God's provision to Isaac, first meant that *Isaac was that provision.*

But, Abraham learned something about the provision of God that day, and thank God that he did. It turned out that God made His own provision for the offering, and to Abraham it was unexpected. At the crucial split second that divided life from death, the Lord stopped Abraham cold.

> *And the angel of the LORD called unto him out of heaven, and said, Abraham, Abraham: and he said, Here am I. And he said, Lay not thine hand upon the lad, neither do thou any thing unto him...* (Gen. 22:11-12a)

It was then that Abraham learned that while he had prophesied rightly regarding God making provision for the sacrifice, it was not as Abraham apprehended the meaning at the first. Isaac was not to be the sacrifice, but God provided for Himself another.

> *And Abraham lifted up his eyes, and looked, and behold behind him a ram caught in a thicket by his horns: and Abraham went and took the ram,*

> *and offered him up for a burnt offering in the stead of his son.* (Gen. 22:13)

Thus, God provided in that critical hour a sacrificial lamb for Himself in a way that Abraham had not understood at the first. Nevertheless, the prophecy was fulfilled that day: *God will provide himself a lamb*.

Or was it?

God left a loose end dangling to alert us all – and perhaps to alert Abraham and Isaac too – that there was a great deal more to the prophecy than that one isolated event in the desert was able to fulfill by itself. Notice in the reference to Genesis 22:13, that the animal caught in the thicket was a ***ram***. Now, we understand that a lamb is a young sheep. The ewe is the female sheep and the ram is, of course, the male. Usually, when the reference to "ewe" or "ram" is mentioned in isolation, that reference will be to a mature sheep. A mature sheep is not normally categorized as a "lamb". A lamb is a young sheep.

My own life experiences revolve around cattle rather than sheep. Among cattle, the nomenclature is similar to that above. A "calf" is always young, and when one says "calf", no gender is implied. A "cow" is mature, and a "bull" is mature. (For the record, a heifer is a young female nigh maturity.) One would never say, "the bull is caught in the fence", if it was a male calf caught in the fence. You might say that it is a "bull calf" caught in the fence, but to say that about a "bull," is to understand instinctively that you have your work cut out for you, because the animal in the fence is a grown animal, or at least, nigh grown.

So, why would God, who designated through Abraham's prophecy that a "lamb" was to be provided for sacrifice, then, specify that what was caught in the thicket was a

ram? A lamb would be a young lamb with unspecific gender, though obviously it would be a young ram or ewe. Let us be reminded that God really is a stickler for details. A ram is a mature male sheep. While the ***ram*** could have technically been a ***lamb***, why would the Lord not use the same terminology as used in the prophecy to clarify the fulfillment beyond any question?

I believe that God fulfilled the immediate prophesy of that day, but left a detail just slightly askew – not incorrect, but technically a curiosity; a clue, if you will – so that you and I could see that there is something far deeper in the prophecy.

God literally provided *Himself* a lamb, in 34 AD, in the Lord Jesus Christ. The reason a big deal is made out of the long, vicious conflict over the Godhood of Christ is closely examined in opening this chapter and is to show that often what is debated in the translation conflict is a conspicuous continuation of that same conflict. It is a secret to few who read this book that *God was manifest in the flesh* (1 Tim. 3:16) when Christ came to this earth. *In the beginning was the Word, and the Word was with God, and the Word was God,* says John 1:1. The deity of Christ is proven readily and easily, and yet many works could be written on the subject. Suffice to say, at this time, that when John Baptist declared, *Behold the Lamb of God, which taketh away the sin of the world* (Jn. 1:29), the implications reached all the way back to Mount Moriah in Genesis 22, and indeed all the way back to the lamb slain for Adam and Eve.

What is evident is that there are few doctrines more often affected by the new translations of the scriptures than the doctrine of the deity of the Lord Jesus Christ. The new version editors and defenders make application of every bit of sophistry they can muster to try to fortify against the charges and to maintain respectability for their moth-eaten perversions, but a Bible reader will not be fooled by their ploys.

The beauty of the King James Bible is seen in high resolution here. In a singular, simple phrase, the Lord commends to the world two magnificent and wonderful prophecies which are yet distinct from one another. 1) *God provided Himself a lamb* in that there was a ram supplied for the sacrifice that day in place of Abraham's son, Isaac. 2) *God provided Himself a lamb*, in that there was a day that God came in the flesh in the person of His own son and made the ultimate sacrifice for our sins forever. **He provided *Himself!***

Through the two applications of this prophecy, it is plain that in saying one thing, the Lord actually said two distinct and separate things!

The scriptures are multifaceted. What is seen in Genesis 22:8 is a ***dual application*** of the scriptures in time. One application is rather immediate historically; the other is far-reaching and much more grandiose and glorious. Yet still, the two distinct prophecies, with far different meaning and application, abide couched together in the very same phrase in the scripture. The scripture says two absolutely different things spanning thousands of years in prospect, and it manages to do so in a singular phrase, recorded only once! This is a remarkable trait of scripture, and yet it is routinely seen in the King James Bible. In the almost mindless and baseless interchanging of words in the new versions, this is one of the treasures that is cast off, rejected and destroyed in so many cases.

A cousin of this trait is one of ***double meaning*** as in John 11:50-51, where Caiaphas the High Priest of the Jews is trying to convince the Jews that they should kill Christ. His clear intention was that the people would be better off politically and religiously if Jesus were out of the way. What he said was,

> *Nor consider that it is expedient for us,* ***that one man should die for the people****, and that the whole nation perish not. And this spake he not of himself: but being high priest that year,* ***he prophesied that Jesus should die for that nation;***

He meant it one way, but in the end, it was prophetic in another way, because Jesus did die for the nation as a substitutionary sacrifice for sins. That was not how the old murderer intended it, but there was a deeper meaning than he intended.

Another form of ***double application*** is seen in Hosea 11:1 and Matthew 2:15. The phrase *called my son out of Egypt* is applied to two distinctly different things: 1) Israel called out, and, 2) Christ called out. Add to that the application that as sons of God in Christ we are called out of Egypt (the world), as well. This means there are actually ***three applications*** to the one phrase instantly visible.

There are many variants of this phenomenon in the scripture, one being that of ***partial fulfillments of scripture prior to complete fulfillments***. Joel 2:28 and Acts 2:17 are examples of this. At Pentecost, in Acts 2:16, Peter declared, *But this is that which was spoken by the prophet Joel,* and yet what followed in the chapter was barely a smidgen of a greater and more complete fulfillment in the future. In that day God indeed ...*will pour out my spirit upon all flesh; and your sons and your daughters shall prophesy, your old men shall dream dreams, your young men shall see visions* (Joel 2:28). Thus, at Pentecost in Acts 2, it was hardly a percentage that actually came to pass as stated in Joel 2. The fact is that there were a lot of "could have been's" at that particular transitional juncture of the New Testament, nevertheless we see today that the fuller and more magnificent fulfillment awaits the Second Coming of Christ.

Having barely scratched the surface of this subject, yet with this profound characteristic of the true scriptures in mind, let us consider something else.

The Sorry Excuses for Bibles

One does not have to seek very long or far to discover what shallow work the new version translators have done. This characteristic is but one that marks them as the inept pretenders and poor excuses they are, though they parade themselves as spiritual men and women of depth and insight.

Consider their renditions of Genesis 22:8:

> And Abraham said, "God will ***provide for Himself*** the lamb for the burnt offering, my son." So the two of them walked on together.
>
> (New American Standard)

> Abraham said, "God will ***provide for Himself*** the lamb for the burnt offering, my son." So the two of them walked on together.
>
> (New American Update)

> Abraham answered, "***God himself will provide*** the lamb for the burnt offering, my son." And the two of them went on together.
>
> (New International Version)

> And Abraham said, "My son, God will ***provide for Himself*** the lamb for a burnt offering." So the two of them went together.
> (New King James Version)

> "***God will see to it,*** my son," Abraham replied. And they went on. (The Living Bible)

It takes no linguist to see that these new bibles, including the much-lauded New King James, restrict by their phrasing the fulfillment of Abraham's prophecy to that single day on Mount Moriah when Isaac was spared a tragic death. Plainly, The Living Bible says nothing of consequence, but of the other four listed, God is either going to provide ***for Himself*** the lamb, or else ***God Himself will provide*** it. May the reader mull over the phrasing and see for himself that either of those sequences of words limits the fulfillment of prophecy to that singular day.

By rephrasing and shuffling words into different positions in the sentence, the new versions effectively blot out the fact that God, through Abraham, was also prophesying of a far grander fulfillment, for a far distant day, when the God of Heaven Himself would become both the Provider of the Lamb as well as the actual Sacrifice itself.

The fact is that it is possible to omit truth and obliterate light in the scriptures by means other than merely removing words or verses altogether. Without a doubt, removing words, phrases, verses, and at times, entire passages, is the more common and more obvious way in which the new versions' translators and editors have committed sacrilege against the Holy Scriptures. Anyone can, if they would, investigate words and phrases merely being removed, and this is one of the usual methods of showing the uninformed that there is a bible version issue. Here, though, it is seen that the act of shuffling and rephrasing largely the same words is also a means by which the truth of the scriptures is altered, the prophecies obscured, and the light effectively snuffed out.

The Scholars' Superficiality

The scholars and classic commentators, whose "calling" is to expound the scriptures, seem a little quiet on the subject. There first is an over-riding emphasis on the personal aspects of the trial for Abraham and his son. This is certainly justifiable for it is necessary to see the extraordinary example of Abraham's faith under fire. The treatment of the critical phrase (*God will provide himself a lamb)* and the grander fulfillment to which it attests (the deity of Christ and the fact that God Himself came, shed His own blood, and made sacrifice for sins forever) seems rather sparing on the part of those who are so wordy and expansive on other less critical themes.

The notes in Ethelbert Bullinger's *Companion Bible* specify in the margin that the meaning of God's provision was ***for Himself***[77] as opposed to God ***providing Himself***.

Matthew Henry sees that God provided Christ as the future sacrifice, but makes no real mention of the even greater truth that Christ was God Himself! [78]

> Thus, First, **Christ, the great sacrifice of atonement, was of God's providing**; when none in heaven or earth could have found a lamb for that burnt-offering, **God himself found the**

---

[77] Bullinger, EW, *The Companion Bible* (Oxford University Press, London, New York, Toronto, Melbourne) Genesis 22:8, p.31, margin.
[78] Henry, Matthew. *Matthew Henry's Commentary on the Whole Bible*. (1998) P C Study Bible (Version 2.11) [Computer Software]. Seattle, WA: Biblesoft.

> **ransom,** <Ps. 89:20>. Secondly, All our sacrifices of acknowledgment are of God's providing too. It is he that prepares the heart, <Ps. 10:17>. The broken and contrite spirit is a sacrifice of God <Ps. 51:17>, of his providing.

Adam Clarke's insight into the verse is similarly limited.[79]

> ...the patriarch spoke prophetically, and referred **to that Lamb of God which HE had provided for himself**, who in the fullness of time should take away the sin of the world, and of whom Isaac was a most expressive type. All the other lambs which had been offered from the foundation of the world had been such as MEN chose and MEN offered; but THIS was the Lamb which GOD had provided-- emphatically, THE LAMB OF GOD.

If Jameson, Faucet, and Brown, Barnes, or the Wycliffe commentators found the fulfillment of Christ being *God Himself* in this passage they masked their discovery well, for it was not mentioned.

The many-faceted truths of the Holy Scriptures are actually layered. One can liken Biblical truth to be akin to the old-fashioned transparency projector. A clear, transparent sheet with a picture on it is projected onto a screen with light from beneath the platform on which the picture sheet lies. The fact is that multiple transparencies may well lie on the platform, each contributing its own details, colors, or shading to the landscape of the picture. The transparencies may individually be peeled

---

[79] Clarke, Adam. *Clarke's Commentary.* (1998) P C Study Bible (Version 2.11) [Computer Software]. Seattle, WA: Biblesoft.

off or laid on, removing or adding, one at a time, the varying details of the picture.

Dual applications have been addressed already, but the applications often go beyond duality. As stated before, God providing Himself a lamb, was a prophetic verity that came to pass with a ram tangled in the thicket. Looking more deeply, there is the obvious application to Christ being the Lamb that God provided. Yet there is further truth layered beneath that, for in providing Himself a Lamb for the sinners' sacrifice in the person of Jesus Christ, God provided ***Himself*** a Lamb. **God Himself** was the Lamb provided in Christ! So the truth and application of a single phrase of Genesis 22:8, winds up being a tri-fold revelation.

1) God provided the ram.
2) God provided Himself the Lamb. The Lamb was Jesus Christ.
3) God provided Himself the Lamb. He Himself was the Lamb since Christ was God.

As one might imagine, there are variations of this sort of multiple application principle throughout the Holy Bible. In fact, there are times where there are more than three applications in truth. The important thing that should be impressed upon all honest hearts at this juncture is that the Bible is truly an astounding book and deserves the wonderment of mankind for the depth of its truth, the incisiveness of its applications, and its capability to communicate the truth of God in the simplest and most economic fashion imaginable.

What is the point in this? The point is that it seems the commentators and scholars do not fire on all cylinders. The fulfillment of the scripture is plainly evident when the ram is substituted for Isaac. Most seem to see that God's provision for the sins of the world was Christ, the Lamb that God provided, though many of the learned men seem rather more reserved than could be expected when a 2000 year old prophecy is fulfilled by a personal Savior. Even more subdued, and in some cases nonexistent, is the glorious revelation that the Lamb will not merely be Christ, but God Himself. It seems that the learned men could not differentiate or discover the majesty and depth of the layering of the truth. Usually quietude in a commentator either means he did not see or grasp a certain aspect of the matter, or else he is uncertain of it and wishes not to commit himself in print concerning it.

How could one miss – how could a saved scholar not uncover – that God Himself provided *God Himself:* Jesus Christ? How, having seen the deity of Christ in the New Testament, could one not have the insight that opens the passage in Genesis 22:8? How could one not shout the matter unto the heavens if he did see it?

These men have painted themselves into a philosophical corner. They are between "a rock and a hard place," so to speak. They are conflicted or deceived about what the Bible says and means, because they are uncertain - or blatantly wrong – about what to believe with regard to final authority. They believe that they can be dismissive of some varying number of passages in the King James Bible (the exact number depends on how liberal or conservative they are). Their response to what the English Bible says is to check to see what the Hebrew or Greek says, or better, to check what their huddle of favorite scholars says that the Hebrew or Greek says. Their first instinct is not to delve deeply into the English Bible. Their first inclination is to never, ever allow the King James wording to stand unassailable. The depths of truth, to them, reside in the original languages. Their instinct and training is not to believe the words, wording, and word order of the Holy Bible. They have been taught to look at those particular characteristics of the Bible as preferential and fluid, instead of absolute and eternally static. If they did see a phrasing in the KJV that impressed the mind as having a dual or tri-fold meaning, they would be quick to subject that particular form of wording or phrasing to what they, or someone else, could discern from the Greek or Hebrew.

These men have, wittingly or not, proceeded to comment on, exposit and correct the Holy Bible, while defying at heart one of the most foundational principles in seeking light from the Lord.

> ***But without faith it is impossible to please him:*** *for he that cometh to God must believe that he is, and that he is a rewarder of them that diligently seek him.* (Heb. 11:6)
>
> ***But let him ask in faith, nothing wavering.*** *For he that wavereth is like a wave of the sea driven with the wind and tossed.* ***For let not that man think that he shall receive any thing of the Lord.*** (Jas. 1:6-7)

It is worthy of notice that seeking God Himself in Hebrews 11, and seeking wisdom from God Himself in James 1, are both exercises which, in order to be fruitful, require ***faith***. While that particular required attribute is not likely to be a thunderclap of theological insight for most, it is worthwhile to say that Biblical faith has a fountainhead and a streambed in which it flows. Men have been exceedingly careless in that they have all but lost their vigilance over what species of faith they possess. After all, every religion in the world requires a certain brand of faith, as does every conceivable social and political ideal. God requires a certain brand of faith. It is reasonable that an errant and twisted faith will not be rewarded in finding God.

> *So then faith cometh by hearing, and hearing by the word of God.* (Rom. 10:17)

The right kind of faith comes from the word of God. Again, this is rudimentary to the Christianity of most people, but it must be asked, what kind of faith is it that leads a certain scholarly man to dismiss and personally ignore certain and clear light? After dismissing that light (the KJV reading), he then turns to a form of ancient scriptures (the Hebrew) from which he is unsuccessful in acquiring the understanding and insight that someone receives who has not dismissed that first set of scriptures (the KJV). What kind of faith does the scholar have?

It is worthwhile to mention here again that it is not known all that Abraham was able to understand about the prophetic depths of God's promise to him in his native language, nor do we know all he apprehended when he answered Isaac's question about the provisional lamb. Whatever depths of meaning Abraham grasped in that day, we have been given no reason whatever to invest any real confidence in the modern scholars' grasp of the Hebrew language. We are not dismissing God's inspired biblical Hebrew. We are dismissing the modern scholars' professed understanding of it in light of what the Lord has subsequently allowed to shine forth in the English of the King James Bible.

Isaiah 55:6 says *Seek ye the LORD while he may be found, call ye upon him while he is near.* Sometimes though, people have difficulty grasping the significance and interconnection of scriptures a few verses apart. For instance, Isaiah 55:11 says *So shall my word be that goeth forth out of my mouth: it shall not return unto me void, but it shall accomplish that which I please, and it shall prosper in the thing whereto I sent it.* Seeking God is not an exercise that anyone can do in depth without attending carefully to what God said in His word, and graciously acquiescing along the way to this next statement from the same passage: *For my thoughts are not your thoughts, neither are your ways my ways, saith the LORD. For as the heavens are higher than the earth, so are my ways higher than your ways, and my thoughts than your thoughts* (Isa. 55:8-9). Presumptuous persons think that they can subject the holy words of a holy God to their fallen intellect and inferior judgment, and have it come out a viable and blessed product. They reject the light that God has given them, go to another source that the Lord has demonstrably improved upon, exhibit inability to see what we already have seen, yet they expect God's people to join them in enjoying Esau's pottage. No, sir! *Seek ye out of the book of the LORD, and read* (Isa. 34:16)!

> *Stay yourselves, and wonder; cry ye out, and cry: **they are drunken**, but not with wine; **they stagger**, but not with strong drink. For the LORD hath poured out upon you the **spirit of deep sleep**, and hath **closed your eyes: the prophets and your rulers, the seers hath he covered**. And the vision of all is become unto you as the **words of a book that is sealed**, which men deliver to one that is learned, saying, Read this, I pray thee: and he saith, I cannot; for it is sealed:* (Isa. 29:9-11)

The Sure Significance in Laodicea

*And Abraham said, My son, **God will provide himself a lamb** for a burnt offering: so they went both of them together* (Gen. 22:8). Here is a scripture that reaches across 4000 years to all Christians today. A wayfaring tent-dweller gives a word of assurance to his son somewhere (we know where) on the backside of a Canaanite wilderness. That statement is transmitted to every generation since that time, possessing special value and sweetness to those of the last 2000 of those years. A very personal, and to anyone else, a very insignificant conversation between a man and his boy is recorded in an eternal Book, and today blesses the heart of a 21st century American Gentile, who is as far from the Judean wilderness as it is possible to be!

But that American finds in the verse not only the promise of personal provision from the God of that old Hebrew man, but he finds assurance that there is the provision of a substitutionary sacrifice for his sins as well. As an added bonus, in a sequence of merely six words, along with the first two promises, that man also learns that the sacrifice was far more than a pitiable sacrificial substitute. The prophecy foresaw the substitute as not merely the Son of God, as the Jehovah's Witnesses and Mormons would concede. ***The Lamb that was slain was God Himself!***

Such significance and hope comes to us from a 4000 year old sentence. This is no particular stumbling block for a Bible-believer, for we are assured that *...the prophecy came not in old time by the will of man: but holy men of God spake as they were moved by the Holy Ghost* (2 Pet. 1:21). It seems little understood today that the God who was the Initiator of the statement, would also be the One who would ultimately be responsible for being the Transmitter and the Communicator of it. It is not just that ***Abraham*** was inspired when he said what he said. It is that God inspired ***what he said***, and what he said bore very profound and intimate import to the Lord who inspired it. The statement was not only God's blissful promise to a Bedouin tent-dweller for that day, but it was a prophetic promise to sinners everywhere of a Lamb from God who would redeem our sins. The saying was extended further by the fact that God also revealed within those very words something about the nature of that Lamb. The Lamb would be God Himself.

Again, it is impossible to say just how much of this prophetic truth Abraham understood when the words were spoken. It is plain from 1 Peter 1:11 that all the prophets did not understand the full import of all they spake when they spoke or wrote by the Holy Ghost. What is plain is that the Lord having said it wanted *us* to see, grasp, apprehend and embrace it. He wanted the words He gave to bear the full import and weight of His intention and provision. He wanted a pronouncement by the one who was to become a father of faith to all believers (Rom. 4:11-16), to blossom forth, flower, and burst with color and fragrance upon the understanding of us who live *forty centuries* after the original statement. From a life lived in tents and by campfires, sleeping on the ground while surrounded by sheep, goats and asses, a six word phrase leaves the lips of a traumatized and broken old man, survives 4000 years of Satanic subterfuge, and comes to us in a land of microprocessors, IPods, fast food, space stations and Wal-Mart. It is supposed to bless our hearts and prosper our souls. It is supposed to give us confidence that the God of Abraham would make provision for us as well as Abraham. It is supposed to communicate the fullness of what our redemption cost the Lord. It is intended to communicate to us all the meaning of all the words that God spake, affirming for us that God communicates just as thoroughly and personally today as He ever did when He spake mouth to ear with Abraham and the prophets.

With this in mind, let it be stated that in the King James Bible, God succeeded in His mission. This has been demonstrated and shown. It would be delinquent not to point out that the new versions fail miserably in this respect. Many of the classic commentators are guilty in apparently overlooking the full flower of the prophecy. If a bible does not communicate all that God intended, what does that make that bible? If a coven of "men of God" routinely overlook in their translations and their expositions all that God said, what does that make them?

God said plainly and clearly in the King James English what, it would appear, no one in modern times sees in the Hebrew. It is obvious that generally the new versions largely miss the implications of Genesis 22:8, even if they do retain the deity of Christ in other places. That means that the "brilliant Christians" and "godly Fundamentalist scholars" of our day, and in past centuries, miss it as well.

Objectively considering this, it can truthfully be said that ***our Holy Bible in English is thus superior to the Hebrew.*** It is superior at least insofar as that none of the self-aggrandizing and publicly lauded scholars seem to be able to draw the depth of truth from the Hebrew as we have plainly before our eyes in English. I question not that the treasures of the meaning abide in the Hebrew, for God inspired Abraham in Hebrew, but the capacity of Hebrew scholars to discern it from Hebrew is what stands in question. One thing is plain, and that is that the evidence points to the fact that God seems to have impressed the fullness of the truth on our minds when the passage was translated out of the Hebrew into the English of the King James. If this statement is not true, then point out who discerned the depths of truth from another source.

If this phenomenon is due merely to the ineptness, blindness or misapprehension of our relatively modern scholars, well, so be it. Christians are still better off with the King James Bible than with those fellows bumbling around in the dark and swinging a Greek or Hebrew broomstick at the eternal truths of God. King James Bible believers have indeed been *throughly furnished unto all good works* (2 Tim. 3:17).

Again, someone is responsible for this demonstrable superiority of the AV translation over original language. Were the King James translators, in all their discipline and academic brilliance, able to discern linguistically what more modern scholars could not, or cannot, ascertain? If mortal intellect saw the fine distinctions of meaning that have been evaluated here, and if that brilliance was then ingenious enough to couch all these layers of truth into the translation, our confidence should rest in the King James translators being able to do so above and beyond all others, past or present. If confidence is required to be placed in man, then judgment must fall in favor of Bedwell, Bois, Reynolds and company!

However, it is not so certain that the magnificently overlaid, intertwined, and adorning truth herein seen can be justifiably credited to the ingenuity of mortal intellects. Many, though not all, scholars acknowledge that God is the Author of the Bible. He inspired men to speak and write. Most conservative scholars agree that He is the preserver of scripture, and that He has routinely led and directed men in the preservation of His word. Is it really so hard to see that if God preserved His word after inspiring it, that there is a manifold necessity that He would have to personally intervene at times, to preserve certain, specific word choices? In fact, considering the insidious persistence of the devil and the corruption of man, is it not more likely that He had to intervene, literally, all the time?

To tie the rag on the bush, it must be asked once again, where in scripture is found the tenet that God would never, ever avail Himself the opportunity of preserving and advancing His word in *translation,* as opposed to merely limiting Himself to the original languages? Where in scripture is it ever set forth that the true treasure and all genuine authority reside in the originals? The fact is that there is no such precept in the Bible. This is as much a tradition of men as is the perpetual virginity of Mary or the observance of "Christ's birth" on December 25th of every year.

We should credit and glorify God Himself for the written revelation by which *God... provide(d) Himself a lamb.* God knows what He said at the first, as well as what He intended for us to understand from His revelation. Since He is the Author of the Bible, being the Word Himself, omniscient, omnipotent, omnipresent, and *the Faithful Witness* (Rev. 1:5), there is just no reason why God's people should abide reticent, intimidated, and discouraged from giving God the Father and the Lord Jesus Christ direct credit for the manifold and demonstrable truth that we have in the AV 1611.

The English, again, serves to clarify and expand truth that is ambiguous and more obscure in the original language. The English speaking Christian has a choice to make. On one hand are the manuscripts written in Hebrew (there are no original writings extant). The average Bible-believer cannot read them. When referring to Biblical resource and reference material on the Hebrew language, one must entrust one's quest for truth to men who often were unsaved and at adversity to the doctrines of Christ. Even if they were or are true men, one is still overwhelmed with choices and linguistic details one can hardly be expected to wade through with any verifiable certainty. Further, if he leans on the understanding of the experts of Hebrew language and exposition, the student finds an alarming lack of agreement and uniformity in their opinions. The certainty offered by the Hebrew scholars is disturbingly variable, and the reported treasures of the Hebrew are either disappointing, more tarnished than expected, or apparently inaccessible.

On the other hand, there is a proven Bible in hand in our own language. It is admitted by most to be exceedingly accurate, majestic, and faithful to the truth. It says what it says, and *glory to God*, it is understandable! It yields more light, spiritual beauty and truth to you and me than the Hebrew yields to its proponents and advocates. It proves itself to be multi-layered and multi-faceted with respect to the truth, yet at the same time it is simple and direct to the point of being painful.

What is a soul to do?

The choice is not a difficult one. In fact, were it not for the propaganda of the scholars and publishers, the fear of man, and the believer's own natural insecurities, the average Christian's money would be spent in such a way that the publishing companies would be forced to keep the bookstore shelves stocked with King James Bibles or else go out of business.

These facts are consistent with the idea that the English translation of the verse advances our understanding beyond what scholars are able to mine from the Hebrew texts. To be direct, if one purports that there is light in the Hebrew not found in the English, then it would seem that the "proof is in the pudding." Some cruder souls might pipe in that such a one should "put up or shut up." If there are truths in the Hebrew that are utterly inaccessible to the English Bible reader, what are they? Perhaps scholars of Hebrew today simply cannot truly discern the depths of Hebrew as Abraham might have been able to do with God's help. Whatever the reason, we are given clear light today.

Genesis 22:8 offers clear proof of the superiority of the AV 1611. The fulfillment of Christ as the Lamb is shrouded at best in the new versions, and Christ being *God Himself* in Genesis 22:8 is obliterated altogether. That the deity of Christ can be found elsewhere in the scriptures is irrelevant to our discussion. It should be prophesied and ultimately fulfilled from Genesis 22:8. It ***is clearly and manifestly*** prophesied in the King James Bible. It ***is clearly and plainly <u>not</u>*** prophesied in the new versions cited, as well as most other versions not specifically referenced in this chapter. In this case, the Hebrew, as translated, exposited and understood by our stable of scholars, obscured truth that was made clear in the AV. In fact, the King James Authorized Version set forth information that men have apparently not found in Hebrew, that is missing from the new versions, and upon which the commentators make no comment. Indeed, we will find in succeeding chapters, as we have in the preceding, that as here, the old English masterpiece exceeds the hidden revelations of the originals - as men apprehend them, anyway - by several country miles.

Let the reader hold onto his hat, for there is no other way to say what needs to be here said. This particular example constitutes an example of the English containing ***advanced revelation*** over the original language. Though we do not know all exactly that Abraham understood from the passage, we do know that it is revelation hidden to the eyes of lauded scholars, yet it is plainly revealed in the King James Bible. It is information that advanced the revelation from the limited application evident to scholars in Hebrew, to what all English readers of the AV can see. Call it what you like, but it seems that ***advanced revelation***, far from being a disturbing heresy, is a descriptive term accurately depicting a reality that this chapter has sought to illuminate.

It is worthwhile to call attention to the possibility that all the light the so called "scholars" purportedly receive from the Greek and Hebrew may well be much ado about nothing. For what it is worth, I myself have been a Christian now for 40 years as of the writing of this book. I landed in the King James camp about 27 or 28 years ago, and have been a pastor for over 24 years, as of this writing. In the wandering years of being ungrounded and without anchor, I had the great privilege of being exposed to quite a lot of nonsense, a good deal of which was biblical nonsense. I heard men and women get up and make claims about the nuggets of the original languages to which we peons were not privy. After all their secret treasure had been spread out before me, there proved to be nothing new or anything containing any deeper discernable substance to be learned, or else what they sought to teach actually contradicted what the Bible plainly says. The fact is that when such a scholar proceeds to gush and spew about the treasures in the originals, most discerning Bible-believers have observed,

> 1) That what the scholar gushes about is already revealed in English.
> 2) That the scholar is stretching and pressing because he wants to find a golden nugget, and the "treasure" is discovered to be of no discernible substance.
> 3) That what the scholar finds is actually contradictory to other tenets of the scriptures. (Isaiah 8:20 gives command on how to handle such matters).
> 4) That the scholar wants to play a condescending game with "the commoners," and proceeds to elucidate verb and noun forms, endings and tenses. This is to establish his scholarly superiority, but there is no reason whatever to believe otherwise than that the AV translators, with the help of God, were fully apprised of the translational complexities and complications, and already have successfully overcome those obstacles in the King James Bible.

Further, it shows that what is oftentimes falsely considered *archaic* vocabulary or verbiage in the KJV, actually contains depths of truth and revelation that modern vernacular does not. It is the rare King James Bible believer that has not heard the haranguing of critics concerning the vocabulary and wording of the AV. Even her defenders, after exalting her beauty and accuracy, are quick to yield again the ground they have defended by saying that there are places in the King James that could be improved.

Is the King James Version Perfect? – Not Ideally but Practically

Admittedly the King James Version is **not ideally perfect**. **No translation ever can be**. But it is the product of such God-guided scholarship that it is practically perfect. Its **errors are very few and very minor.**[80]

That **a few changes might be made in both Testaments** [of the King James], for the better, no man pretends to deny. [81]

...the advocates of **the King James only position** have a severe problem. Most of **them** hold the view that the King James version of 1611 as a *translation* was inspired and thus has no need for further *translational* revision [82]

There are only several hundred obsolete or archaic words remaining within the 1611 King James Bible... These few **could and should** be brought up to date. The "eth" endings could also easily be changed... although care must be taken as to its rendering else many times the actual meanings may be lost.[83]

---

[80] Hills, Edward F., *Believing Bible Study Key to the Space Age* (The Christian Research Press: Des Moines, Iowa, 1967, 1977), p.83.
[81] Fuller, David Otis, *Which Bible* (Grand Rapids International Publications, Grand Rapids, Michigan, 1970) p. 106
[82] Sorenson, David H., *Touch Not The Unclean Thing The Text Issue and Separation* (Northstar Baptist Ministries, Duluth, MN, 2001) p.18

[83] Jones, Floyd Nolen, *Which Version Is The Bible* (KingsWord Press, Goodyear, AZ, 1989, 2006) p.78

> I do not believe there are mistakes in the King James Bible.
>
> I do believe there are places that **could be translated more clearly for readers today**. I do believe **there are antiquated words** that could be brought up to date. There are words and passages that could be translated differently. (Note I did not say *should* be, but *could* be.) To say, that there are changes that could be made in the KJV is entirely different from saying it contains mistakes.[84]
>
> **THE KJV IS THE WORD OF GOD IN THE ENGLISH LANGUAGE**. It has no errors in it because it carefully reflects the original language texts closest to the autographs. The AV, like all translations, has **'language limitations'**, but these are not errors.[85]

The information laid out in this book shows that there may be another side to the story which is quite the opposite of the common rant. The reader should be reminded that the *thee's, thou's* and *ye's* of the AV actually denote the person and number of the pronouns which the *you's* and *your's* of colloquial speech do not supply. The same is true of the *–eth, -est, -edst* endings found in the verbs of the King James. These *archaic* forms supply more light and information than does the form used in modern versions.

By the same token, in Genesis 22:8, the AV's *God will provide himself a lamb*, is replaced by *God will provide for Himself the lamb* in the NASV and *God himself will provide the*

[84] Cloud, David W., *Myths About The Modern Bible Versions* (Way of Life Literature, Oak Harbor, Washington, 1999) p.111
[85] Ibid., p.163

lamb in the NIV. The sense of the two readings from the NIV and NASV are entirely different; however, in the NASV you can still see the fulfillment in the ram in Genesis 22 and that God will provide the Lamb (Christ) in the New Testament. The same two conclusions could be read into the NIV as well. The sense that is not contained in those two versions' readings is the great truth that the New Testament Lamb will be *God Himself!* ***The AV 1611's so called "archaic language" and word structure provided all three senses and communicated all three truths at once!*** In shameful ineptitude, the scholars and translators of the new versions destroyed the theologically most important of the three senses altogether. The same translators then continue even now to rail and complain about how hard the KJV is to understand. Perhaps individuals and "experts" who obscure and delete at least 33% of the truth in a select passage such as this (that truth relating to the very nature of Jesus Christ) should realize that even ***Satan himself did not edit out as much of the truth in Genesis 3.*** Perhaps these scholars should consider a new line of work.

To lean on the Hebrew, in this case, is to regress into shallower understanding and backdated ignorance. Aside from the possibility of profound cultural and societal upheaval, it is very unlikely that we will go back to plowing fields with horses and oxen. Propeller-driven aircraft are unlikely to be the wave of the future in air travel, and Civil War era medicine probably will not be making much of a comeback. The reason why, is that man has advanced a good deal in nearly every aspect of industry, manufacturing, travel, communications and medicine from just about any given point in the past. To go backwards would be retrograde and regressive - just the opposite of progress. It is doubtful that anyone today is very interested in going back to old IBM 286's or to candles and oil lamps for domestic lighting, for that matter. What we have is better, and to revert to those things of the past would be viewed by the average person as the opposite of progress.

If a Hebrew speaker of 1000BC or 1000AD was of shallow perception and apprehension regarding the knowledge and foresight that was revealed in Abraham's curt assurance to Isaac, there is no excuse now. The Hebrews are notorious for their blindness and various oversights of the truth regarding their Messiah. The blindness is a prophetic reality (Rom. 11) that clouded their vision in 30 AD and does so still to this hour. Without controversy, the greatest portion of that blindness has its cause in the generalized Hebrew peoples' motivations, insincerity, rebellion, and lack of love for the truth. In other words, much of the issue of the Jews dark spiritual world resides in their own hearts. Is it not interesting though, that the experts in the Hebrew language, Jew and Gentile alike, seem to be unable to unearth the critical fact of the deity of the Lamb as prophesied in Genesis 22:8? The indispensable verity that *God provided Himself* seems lost on the Christian commentator as much as it is lost upon the Jew, though the Christian usually finds Christ's deity elsewhere. What is the nature of this shadowy shroud of non-recognition? Perhaps God so arranged it that the Hebrew of the Old Testament was capable of shrouding and veiling the deeper truth of that Lamb within the folds of its language. Maybe the light and power abode undetected behind the nouns, verbs and articles of the original dialect. Perhaps it took another unrelated language to catalyze the truth hidden there into a fireworks display of recognition.

This we do know: to us, it was in English that the brilliant light suddenly shone forth. The Hebrew obscured the light and the deeper truth that we are able to revel in. Why do some prefer the shadows? Why do they insist not only on going back to the Hebrew, but on also dragging other undiscerning Christians back to the Hebrew with them?

In the end, the decision will rest squarely upon the individual conscience of the reader. One can follow the party line of the seminaries and the traditions of the scholars, and abide safely in the majority opinion. There will be little disdain or mockery there, and one may reside in that sanctuary with the comfort of being where most *settle on their lees* (Jer. 48:11; Zeph. 1:12). On the other hand, there is a place outside the camp (Heb. 13:13) where certain aspects of Christianity abide that are, to most, less respectable, but far more magnificent. Jesus Christ is among those things that are outside the mainstream camp of religion, tradition and respectability. He will not mind at all that you found in the English of the AV 1611 His deity and glory tucked away in Genesis 22:8.

> *To the law and to the testimony: if they speak not according to this word, it is because there is no light in them.* (Isa. 8:20)

> *Now I beseech you, brethren, mark them which cause divisions and offences contrary to the doctrine which ye have learned; and avoid them. For they that are such serve not our Lord Jesus Christ, but their own belly; and by good words and fair speeches deceive the hearts of the simple.* (Rom. 16:17-18)

Chapter 7

The Shirts on Baalites' Backs

And Jehu sent through all Israel: and all the worshippers of Baal came, so that there was not a man left that came not. And they came into the house of Baal; and the house of Baal was full from one end to another. And he said unto him that was over the vestry, Bring forth vestments for all the worshippers of Baal. And he brought them forth vestments. And Jehu went, and Jehonadab the son of Rechab, into the house of Baal, and said unto the worshippers of Baal, Search, and look that there be here with you none of the servants of the LORD, but the worshippers of Baal only.

(2 Kings 10:21-23)

Jehu was quite the terror to the Baal worshippers of his day. In a bold and convincing move, under the guise of tolerance and goodwill, he congregated all the Baalites at one central point, and then, in a bloody and deceitful move, he had the men of his army kill all the Baalites assembled together in the house of Baal. It brings to mind the saying about shooting fish in a bowl. This is a difficult passage for Christians of our day to swallow, and Jehu's actions may be viewed as either zealous, despicable, or some combination of the two. Notwithstanding the issue of the advisability of King Jehu's actions, the disciples of Baal were among the cancers in the Lord's earthly and literal theocratic kingdom of the Old

Testament. Baal was the kingpin of the gods of the people of Canaan, which placed him in the center of the railroad tracks before God's oncoming engine of destruction. In reality, before the omnipotent God that *made heaven and earth, the sea, and all that in them is* (Exod. 20:11), Baal fared about as well as Dagon in 1 Samuel 5. Nevertheless, Baal remained a force in the corrupt imaginations of his foolish subjects, and his only real capability of competing with God was due to the corrupt, idolatrous nature of the lemmings who were led by the pipers of the piercing serpent.

Perhaps due to its bloody and intolerant nature, Jehu's exploit is not one of the more commonly repeated tales on the lips of Christians. It is, thus, relegated to a degree of obscurity that, unfortunately, also masks one of the remarkable things that the Lord accomplished in His use of the language of the King James Bible. Note in 2 Kings 10:22, the following:

> *And he said unto him that was over the vestry, Bring forth* ***vestments*** *for all the worshippers of Baal. And he brought them forth* ***vestments.***
> (2 Ki. 10:22)

According to the AV, Jehu specified that the ***vestments*** for the Baalites be brought forth. It turns out that the word ***vestments*** is quite the curious choice of nouns, for 2 Kings 10:22 is the only occasion in the King James Bible that the word is used.

Eat Your Spinach, or Else No Dessert

Many Bible-believers have been driven to a palpable antipathy due to the practice of teachers, preachers and scholars making a headlong retreat to the Greek or Hebrew at every crucial juncture in the scriptures. This disdain is not, as some believe, the product of the mere jealousy and envy of the uneducated and uninformed towards the ultra-illuminated and enlightened priest-class of oh-so-sincere light-bearers. The fact is that many Bible-believers have found very little light shining forth from this much overrated exercise of linguistic calisthenics. The disdain and revulsion is more often the result of the sheep being unfed and unimpressed by the spiritual water and substance drawn by the academics from that particular well. The fact is that a fair segment of the Lord's mal-fed flock feels an aversion to the constant practice of having what their Bible plainly says undermined and wrested into something else entirely.

It is hoped that the lovers of the pure, true scriptures might be convinced that there is another method of investigating the Hebrew and Greek, which instead of undermining what God has accomplished in the AV 1611, instead exalts and magnifies it all the more. This does not mean that it is necessary, or even acceptable, to refer to the "original languages" to get more light on the English, as is the scholars' habit. It means, rather, that peering into those first languages of the Bible actually reveals to us that we have more light in English than even scholars can draw from Greek or Hebrew. If anything, an objective and faithful query into these languages will actually more than justify the words and letters that we have in the King's English. In the end, this means that Greek or Hebrew could indeed benefit a Bible-believer because it would verify and bolster his confidence in the King James Bible. Such an exercise illuminates and justifies the wisdom and providence of the translation of the King James Bible; it does not tear it down nor subvert it.

Thus, if the reader abhors, and is repulsed by, the age-old practice of mini-Hebrew lessons every time he goes to Sunday school or turns on Christian radio, he should note that in this case, "going to the Hebrew" is unto an entirely different end. Neither Hebrew nor spinach are all that palatable to most, but in this case the reader is urged to just take a bite or two.

Inserted below, are the Hebrew transliterations of the words translated *vestments* in the King James. The numbers beside the words are the *Strong's Exhaustive Concordance* numbers, which will help the reader locate them in the Hebrew dictionary in the back of *Strong's* should one desire to look them up.

> *And he said unto him that was over the vestry, Bring forth* ***vestments*** **(lebuwsh-3830)** *for all the worshippers of Baal. And he brought them forth* ***vestments*** **(malbuwsh-4403).** (2 Ki. 10:22)

Even transliterated, it is easy to see that the two words are akin to one another and from the same root. *Strong's* cites that both forms of the word are from **3847-labash**. *Labash* is defined as:

> a primitive root; properly, wrap around, i.e. (by implication) to put on a garment or clothe (oneself, or another), literally or figuratively: (Strong's).

The general meanings of all three of these numbered and related words are given as: *apparel, clothed with, clothing, garment, raiment, vestment, vesture, array (self), clothe, wear.*

The three forms of those words (3830, 4403, & 3847) are used approximately 200 times in the Old Testament. That is, those three forms are words that are translated into the English of the King James Bible around 200 times. Again the words are translated into English in various forms of the following words: *apparel, clothed with, clothing, garment, raiment, vestment, vesture, array (self), clothe, wear.* It should be plain to the reader that there are, then, many forms of the differing words used to describe the attire of what all manner of people in the Bible wore then, and do (or should) wear now.

Nuggets in the King James English

Two words that are very much akin to each other in English are *vesture* and *vestments*. Yet, what a vastly different connotation and context mark the two words as the Holy Spirit used them in the AV. In the following table, note the abbreviated reading in the center column and a brief contextual description in the rightmost column.

Vesture	**AV Reading**	**Context**
Gen. 41:42	*Pharaoh...arrayed him in* ***vestures*** *of fine linen*	Joseph – type of Christ
Deut.22:12	*...make thee fringes upon the four quarters of thy* ***vesture***	Israel – kingdom of priests (Ex.19:6)
Ps. 22:18	*They part my garments among them, and cast lots upon my* ***vesture***	Christ's clothes
Ps. 102:26	*...all of them (heavens) shall wax old like a garment; as a* ***vesture*** *shalt thou change them,*	God's clothes: The Heavens!
Mt. 27:35	*They parted my garments among them, and upon my* ***vesture*** *did they cast lots...*	Christ's clothes
John 19:24	*They parted my raiment among them, and for my* ***vesture*** *they did cast lots...*	Christ's clothes
Heb. 1:12	*And as a* ***vesture*** *shalt thou fold them up...*	God's clothes: The Heavens!
Rev. 19:13	*And he was clothed with a*	Christ's clothes

	vesture *dipped in blood: and his name is called The Word of God.*	
Rev. 19:16	*And he hath on his* ***vesture*** *and on his thigh a name written, KING OF KINGS, AND LORD OF LORDS.*	Christ's clothes

Note that the forms of the word ***vesture*** are used,

- To designate that the Heavens themselves are God's clothes.
- To denote Christ's clothing at Calvary and the Second Coming.
- To point out Joseph as one of the greatest types of Christ in the scriptures. He was second ruler in Egypt, only behind Pharaoh.
- To describe Israel's clothing. Israel was a peculiar nation among all the nations of the earth, a kingdom of priests (Ex. 19:6). They foreshadowed the body of Christ and the priesthood of believers (1 Pet. 2:9).

One must admit that this is a particularly sanctified usage of the word *vesture*. *Vesture(s)* is not used in any other manner. In the scriptures, the Philistines, I am sure, wore clothing. Rebekah placed *raiment* on Jacob to deceive poor, old, hungry Isaac (Gen. 27:15), and wolves wear *sheep's clothing* in Matthew 7:15. However, the Bible never designates that what they wore was a *vesture*. God sets aside certain words for ***sanctified usage***, just as He has certain sanctified vessels that He uses (2 Tim. 2:21). *Vesture(s)* is like fine china or crystal, and it is only used under specific and closely guarded circumstances.

In contrast, the word ***vestments*** is another matter, and the way it is used denotes something quite far from sanctified. To reiterate, the term *vestments* only occurs two times, and that in one single verse:

> *And he said unto him that was over the vestry, Bring forth* **vestments** *for all the worshippers of Baal. And he brought them forth* **vestments.**
>
> (2 Ki. 10:22)

The only souls in the scriptures to wear vestments were Baal worshippers. These *vestments* were even brought out especially for them to wear during their "services." Over 200 times, the root word forms in Hebrew that were translated *vestments* in this verse were variously and distinctively translated otherwise throughout the Old Testament English scriptures. On the other hand, a word closely akin, and sharing some of the same Hebrew roots, *vesture*, was only translated to signify what God and Christ wore, or else the clothing of sanctified types.

So, out of a pool of the same Hebrew words, the Lord saw fit to distinguish *by **different and distinct English words*** the sanctified vesture of God and Christ, as opposed to the garments used in false worship by the Baalites. Neither God's people nor God's priests were ever said to wear *vestments*, though they had garments patterned, ordered and sanctified by the Lord. ***The distinction is not in Hebrew, but in English!***

Baal's Little Helpers Lend a Hand

It should come as no surprise that most of the translators of the new versions seem to miss any implications that might be the result of specific wording. Specific wording for them is of little or no import for a couple of reasons.

1) In contrast to the **Formal Equivalence** of the King James Bible, which honors and elevates the specific meaning of individual words when translating from the original languages, the new versions are sprouted from a much baser "philosophy" of translating. It is called **Dynamic Equivalence**. Read "dynamic" as "flowing," "changing" or – oh, here's one – "evolving." Formal Equivalence would attempt to bring singular and individual words through the translation to the extent of precise and exact meaning, though not at the expense of readability. Why? Well, a man in the Sudan needs to know as exactly what God said as does a Hebrew or a Greek. Dynamic Equivalence is an ambivalent surfer-dude in comparison to Formal Equivalence. He just wants to get ideas across, because, "You know, man…dude, it ain't the individual words that matter, man, you know, because… like, we just wanna get the *idea* across; dude… 'cause that would be, like…cool." If some should take exception to the beach bum simile, it should at least send chills up the reader's spine to know that Dynamic Equivalence disciples have no regard whatever for specific and distinctive wording.

2) The second reason specificity in words and terms is not an issue in new versions, is that wording contained within the new versions has to justify their copyright. Translators *have* to change some words of the King James Bible or else what they publish would be a King James Bible. For that matter, they have to have enough changes between an NIV, and say, an NASV to justify distinguishing between the two with respect to their copyright. Again, the chilling realization should be that, ***a) They have every intention from the very beginning in changing the words of the Bible, and, b) They change the Bible for money!***

Suffice to say that the Baalites do not wear *vestments* in most of the new bibles:

2 Kings 10:22
And he said to the one who {was} in charge of the wardrobe, "Bring out ***garments*** for all the worshipers of Baal." So he brought out ***garments*** for them. (New American Standard)

He said to the one who {was} in charge of the wardrobe, "Bring out ***garments*** for all the worshipers of Baal." So he brought out ***garments*** for them. (New American Update)

And Jehu said to the keeper of the wardrobe, "Bring ***robes*** for all the ministers of Baal." So he brought out ***robes*** for them.
(New International Version)

He instructed the head of the robing room, "Be sure that every worshiper wears one of the ***special robes***." (The Living Bible)

If Matthew Henry, Adam Clark, Jameson, Faucett & Brown, Barnes, the Wycliffe commentators, or Keil & Delitsch saw any indication of anything that has been pointed out here, it was not mentioned in their works on 2 Kings 10:22. They did not regard these specific words as distinguishing anything of particular detail in English, so they wandered right on past them in their comments, without even knowing what they had bypassed.

The Baalites Know What *Vestments* Are

If a Bible-believer is not careful, he will think as little in passing inattentively by the Lord's critical word choices as some of the Lord's adversaries. We should not make this mistake. If the noteworthy commentators miss the implications and direct references in the King's English, one can be certain that the Baalites themselves still use the term for the clerical garments of false religion today, just as Jehu, Jehonadab, and the mass-murdered false worshippers in 2 Kings 10 used it in that day.

From Wikipedia:

> **Vestments** are **liturgical garments** and articles associated primarily with the Christian religions, especially the **Latin Rite and other Catholics, Eastern Orthodox, Anglicans, Methodists, and Lutheran Churches.** Many other groups also make use of **vestments**, but this was a point of controversy in the Protestant Reformation and sometimes since - notably during the Ritualist controversies in England in the 19th century.[86]

Mirriam-Webster Online defines *vestment* as,

> 1 a: an outer garment ; *especially* **: a robe of ceremony or office** b *plural* **:** clothing , garb
> 2**:** a covering resembling a garment
> 3**:** one of the **articles of the ceremonial attire and insignia worn by ecclesiastical officiants and assistants as indicative of their rank and appropriate to the rite being celebrated**.[87]

From the Catholic Encyclopedia is read:

> **By liturgical vestments** are meant the **vestments** that, according to the rules of the

---

[86] "Vestment." *Wikipedia, the Free Encyclopedia*. Web. 11 Dec. 2010. <http://en.wikipedia.org/wiki/Vestment>.
[87] "Vestments." *Merriam-Webster Dictionary. Dictionary and Thesaurus - Merriam-Webster Online*. Web. 13 Dec. 2010. <http://www.merriam-webster.com/dictionary>.

> Church or from ecclesiastical usage, are to be **worn by the clergy in performing the ceremonies of the services of the Church,** consequently, above all, at the **celebration of the Mass**, then in the administration of **the sacraments**, at **blessings**, the **solemn recitation of the canonical hours, public services of prayer, processions, etc.**
>
> The **pope has the most elaborate and the greatest number of liturgical vestments**… The **vestments of the priest** are…Besides the **vestments worn by the priest the liturgical dress of the bishop includes**…those of the **archbishop** include further... The **subdiaconal vestments** consist of …those of the **deacon** of... Finally, the **lower clergy** wear the surplice as **a liturgical vestment**, a **vestment** that belongs to all the **grades of ordination**.[88]

Naturally, the Orthodox Church did not stray far from "Mother" in its definition:

> The Orthodox **clergy** wear two kinds of **robes, non-liturgical and liturgical**. The non-liturgical robes are the ordinary daily clothing of the clergy, worn underneath **'liturgical robes'. Liturgical robes, or 'vestments', are worn during church services.** [89]

---

[88] Catholic Encyclopedia, Vestments, In Western Europe. http://www.newadvent.org/cathen/15388a.htm

[89] By the Way. "Orthodoxy's Liturgical Vestment Colors." *Al's Web Niche*. Web. 13 Dec. 2010. <http://aggreen.net/vestment/liturgical_colors.html>.

It is quite the impressive display of insidious mind-bending by Satan when one stops to consider the ramifications. *(T)he god of this world hath blinded the minds of them which believe not* (2 Cor. 4:4) to the extent that the archaic, outdated, and dismissed terminology of the AV 1611, used by an Israelite king in 900BC, is still used to this hour in the 21st century by the descendents of that very false religion in order to describe their ceremonial garments! Very much a part of the irony is the fact that the enlightened "Christian" scholars and commentators, disregard the word *vestments*, use other terms, and thus miss the extraordinary fact that the Baal worshippers have not exchanged their archaic terms for more modern substitutes. The Baalites still unknowingly and blindly identify *themselves* by calling their clerical garb what the AV translators called them: ***vestments.*** Modern scholarship, just as unknowingly and blindly, walks right past the remarkable identifiers. Those identifiers are ***words.***

Vestments: Lessons From Jehu to You

To summarize, the word *vestments* is found only twice in the King James Bible, and that in one verse: 2 Kings 22:10. The roots from which come the Hebrew words used for *vestments*, are translated in other fashions over 200 times in the KJV. It seems curious that *vestments* would occur in such isolation and contrast if there were not some method or means involved. As it turns out, the only people to wear those *vestments* in the entire Bible were worshippers of Baal. Linguistically speaking, those *vestments* could have been otherwise "rendered" from the Hebrew into English in other fashion: *garments, raiment, robes, vesture*, *clothing*, etc. Importantly, though, the words were *not* otherwise translated. For as long as the AV 1611 remains, it (even if no other bibles do) will bear record that the liturgical costumes the Baalites wore were identified and referenced as ***vestments*** - and they still are.

Even the usage of its cousin word, *vesture,* draws a careful line of demarcation between the Holy and the unholy. *Vesture* is used only for what God and Christ wore or wears. Otherwise, the occurrences of *vesture* distinguish *typologically* what Christ wears. When we see these traits and qualities displayed, we cannot help but be reminded of Exodus 11:7,

> *But against any of the children of Israel shall not a dog move his tongue, against man or beast:* ***that ye may know how that the LORD doth put a difference between the Egyptians and Israel.***

Given that He was incarnate as the Word of God, we have a genuinely hard time concluding that God is incapable of making the very kind of distinctions as are being documented here. One really cannot help but believe that the Lord is perfectly competent to conceal knowledge (*It is the glory of God to conceal a thing* – Prov. 25:2a.), or reveal light when He sees fit, and in any language and manner that He chooses. All things considered, it is hard to accept that He is as ***disinclined*** to involve Himself in the translation process as the scholars and scribes of Fundamental orthodoxy insist. With the utmost sobriety, a Fundamentalist Bible-based Christian should carefully consider whether or not God actually is bound by the stringencies and boundaries that Fundamentalist scholars have set for Him. As one contemplates this matter, it is worthwhile to point out that what the Christian reader concludes about it will profoundly and deeply affect how he views the authority of the Bible in his life. The fact is that if one does not philosophically believe that God can give an inerrant translation in one's own language, such a one will be forever stuck in the misconception that he does not have a final authority he can lay his hands on. This is particularly true of the King James Bible, which has established itself as the authoritative oracle in the language of the last days, has endured 400 years of attack, has a magnificent textual lineage, and is unsurpassed in its scholarship, language, fruit, and accuracy. As this study shows, it also bears the marks of the manifold providence and guidance of God.

If an English reader does not choose the AV as his final authority, such a one will be stuck in the same indistinct bible netherworld in which so many find themselves. Some of the more scholarly card-carrying citizens of this community of esoteric authority will raise their voices in outrage and indignation at this plain statement, but it is nonetheless true. If a Christian's confidence in the AV 1611 is complete and established in his own heart, then he has the issue of final authority settled, and his final appeal in all matters is no further away than the resting place of his Bible in his own home or car. Otherwise, his ultimate appeal is a set of writings that are written in a foreign language of which most Christians will never have a working knowledge. Such a Christian will lean on men to tell him what the writings say. Those men on which he leans will have diverse doctrinal learning and convictions which affect their perception of what the writings say. Just as dangerously, they will have different philosophies about the meanings and interpretation of those words. Perhaps the man on whom one leans today will prove to be an utter fool. How will a Christian student know? The judgment of these mediators and interpreters will be affected by their own training, prejudices, motives, ambitions and sins. They may have undue personal loyalty to certain academics or unwarranted preference for the views and philosophies of certain men who adversely affect their opinions. Their reference materials may lead them wrong. The ultimate appeal of a Christian who enters this world of varying authority will not be his Bible, but will waver from person to person, as the Christian is forced to query first one scholar and then another about what the Greek or Hebrew says *here* and means *there*. It is also inevitable that the scholars will always quibble amongst themselves about the details of the meanings. For such a Christian whose final appeal is man, a quotation from the Bible will never again fall for him as a judge's gavel upon the sound block of God's bench. It may more closely resemble the sound of a ceaselessly dripping faucet. He may settle it in his heart that he will never again hold in his hand *the actual Bible* which he personally can read and understand; by which he personally can measure all matters of truth. There will be a screen and an obstacle ever between him and what his God says. He will spend the rest of his mortal days asking his little coven of scholars at his side, "What did He say?" Such a one will never again truly be able to say, "Thus saith the Lord." Instead, his most ardent and dogmatic conviction will be sealed by the words, "Thus saith Dr. So-and-so, who said that the Lord said…"*…(Y)et shew I unto you a more excellent way* (1 Cor. 12:31), said the apostle Paul when he evaluated the work and fruits of the haughty and fatally gifted among the Corinthians. There truly is a more edifying and expedient alternative to the academic's endless and debilitating practice of unceasingly presuming he is qualified to judge and alter the words of the Holy God. The *more excellent way* is clearly manifest when we evaluate the example of the *vestments* of Baal's buffoons.

The very narrow, yet still common, usage of *vestments* as Baalite garb is not a distinction that can be made in Hebrew. Much is the talk of all the light and hidden treasure that the original languages contain, but there is no indication whatsoever that any of the modern scholars or commentators found such distinction as has been uncovered here in English. It could well be argued that the King James translators found it. If so, this is a sure indication that their work should be left unmolested by linguistic scavengers no matter how sincere or "godly" they are.

The distinction is seen only in our old English Bible - or else one that parodies it. The Bible scholars' lot in life sometimes seems to consist of little more than being obsessed by the theory of the unmined depths and treasures of the original languages. Their penchant for "going to the Hebrew" seems at times to be reflexive, and very often after doing so, the writer or speaker seems blind to the fact that the exercise did nothing to illuminate the passage or understanding beyond the English reading. People under certain pressures, or who are otherwise preoccupied, sometimes develop "ticks" or nervous habits that are unplanned, unconscious and reflexive. Such, it seems, is the scholars' habitual and compulsive reflex of referring to the original languages. The scholars verifiably prove little, and do demonstrably obscure the light, as has been shown. Nevertheless, they continue with unending zeal and ferocity to exult in these reportedly profound treasures from the originals. Queen Gertrude's line in Shakespeare's Hamlet comes to mind, "The lady doth protest too much, methinks."[90]

The fact is that contrary to the avalanche of rhetoric, it is the King James English in this case that makes the edifying distinction that has survived both the passage of time as well as the linguistic looters of academia. They would remove *vestments* and replace it with something else. They *have* done so. In their haste and haughtiness, they missed the definitive distinctions made in English. These distinctions are not seen in Hebrew. They also seem to have overlooked that the Baalites still call their garments what the King James Bible calls them, rather than what the NIV or NASV call them.

This would mean that we do indeed get light from the English that we do not receive from the Hebrew. This also exposes the fact that the King James English reveals certain details that the Hebrew does not. This being the case, English then *advances* our knowledge beyond the point where the Hebrew ceased to manifest clear light and knowledge. Thus,

[90] William Shakespeare, *Hamlet, Act 3, scene 2, 222–230*

the English of the King James Bible can be said to be ***advanced revelation*** above and beyond the Hebrew of the "originals."

I am conscious of the bile that rises to the throats of those who have denounced and denigrated this concept for so long. Such revulsion has become reflexive due to training and association. I would be perfectly satisfied if another form of nomenclature could be used to describe and define this particular attribute of the scriptures. The questions that remain are, 1) Does one recognize the fact that there are demonstrable cases where the AV English advances the knowledge of the student past what the Hebrew reveals, and, 2) What would one call such phenomena?

This would, in turn, indicate that in this case the English is superior to the Hebrew. Of course, we have already learned that this superiority is not merely limited to certain isolated passages to which those nasty *Ruckmanites* can so cunningly apply their prejudices. In fact, we are fortifying an ever-stronger beachhead with respect to this matter, since the cases and examples of this are starting to add up.

Further, the archaic terms of the AV prove not be archaic at all. They prove to be accurate and very much active today. If there is anything to be said of the archaic nature of the English words, it is that where archaic words are used, they actually help to illuminate and highlight the truth. They stand out to the contrast of more common and mundane words.

Think for a moment. Who would be interested in covering the fact that it was the Baalite idolaters who tugged on *vestments* to worship? Why in the world would a NIV or NASV translator, "loving the Lord" as he does, be so free in changing such a clear identifier of a false religion – Satan's religion? If the translator made the change completely unaware of the ramifications, is it not still profoundly sobering that Satan would be able to affect such changes without alerting his puppet of a translator?

The responsibility and credit for the accuracy and enlightenment of the KJV translation, *vestments*, must be laid at the feet of the individuals or individual to whom it belongs. Does the credit belong to the translators who were of such magnificent insight as to be able to discern this matter? After all, it is their *translation into English,* which reveals this wonderful bit of wisdom and understanding. If credit does belong to them, and since it appears that the brand of wisdom which they wield makes foolish the wisdom of the modern Jannes and Jambres of our day (2 Tim. 3:8), perhaps our up-to-date scholarship is too demonstrably blind and compromised to have the honor of seriously critiquing those extraordinary 17th century translators.

Should not the direct credit belong to God, the Author of the Book? Are we really to lay all the laurels and bouquets at the feet of mortal intellect, insight and accomplished excellence in the translation committee? Were those men really so brilliant as to be able to engineer even the fine distinctions that have been explored thus far? Should not the most adamant Fundamentalist scholar, at some juncture along this portion of the roadway, begin to fathom that the hand of the Almighty may well have led and guided these men at a depth of intricate detail which mainline and Fundamentalist theology has not recognized or acknowledged heretofore? If God were as involved as suggested, would it matter that even Masoretic and Textus Receptus scholars insist that He could not have, and would not have, been so engaged?

Chapter 8

Fallen Man, the god of this World, and the Holy Bible

Psalm. 50:15-23

15 And call upon me in the day of trouble: I will deliver thee, and thou shalt glorify me.

16 But unto the wicked God saith, What hast thou to do to declare my statutes, or that thou shouldest take my covenant in thy mouth?

17 Seeing thou hatest instruction, and castest my words behind thee.

18 When thou sawest a thief, then thou consentedst with him, and hast been partaker with adulterers.

19 Thou givest thy mouth to evil, and thy tongue frameth deceit.

20 Thou sittest and speakest against thy brother; thou slanderest thine own mother's son.

21 These things hast thou done, and I kept silence; thou thoughtest that I was altogether such an one as thyself: but I will reprove thee, and set them in order before thine eyes.

22 Now consider this, ye that forget God, lest I tear you in pieces, and there be none to deliver.

23 Whoso offereth praise glorifieth me: and to him that ordereth his conversation aright will I shew the salvation of God.

With the exception of an undisclosed period of time when Mr. and Mrs. Adam abode in a state of perfection in Eden, a garden none of the rest of mankind ever set eyes upon, man has shared his entire temporal, earthly existence in company with a malevolent and insidious fallen entity. Not one single day has passed in man's diverse history that he has not been conspired against, hunted and haunted by a vile and malignant creature that not only sought man's mortal demise, but also his eternal agony. It is very difficult, if not impossible, to summarize Satan's goals and motivations and still, somehow, communicate the depth, tragedy, and reality of the truth of it. The horrors are beyond the capability of words in man's literary treatment of the subject.

The word "conspiracy" hardly does the matter justice. Yet a conspiracy is what it is. To coin a phrase, the devil's plan against God and man is "the mother of all conspiracies." We are certainly aware that there is more than a fair portion of people who are of the broader "conspiracy mindset" that operate in a world of imaginative paranoia. Most Bible-believing pastors have had the blessing of trying to pastor a few such paranoid souls. While some obsess and become unbalanced in their preoccupation with conspiracies, there are also many who recognize that there are legitimate and real forces at work "behind the curtain" that are of a profoundly virulent nature. The problem with detailing the depths of conspiracies is that they are by nature secretive and masked, and it is often hard to tell where substantive truth and verity ends and where imagination and paranoia begin. *Nevertheless, the foundation of God standeth sure* (2 Tim. 2:19), and the fact remains that behind all of the fallacious lies and all the assorted partial truths to be found in all the conspiracy theories in this world, rests the very real and very true concept of the devil - that great red Dragon, the piercing serpent. A murderer from the beginning is he (Jn. 8:44), a liar, and a deceiver (Rev. 12:9). To him *the power of death* (Heb. 2:14) has been allotted. In fact, it is of him that the natural, unregenerate man is born into this world (Jn. 8:44), and the unconverted have the humiliation of being animated by his spirit which *worketh in the children of disobedience* (Eph. 2:2).

When the Lord put the Bible together, He chronicled many different strains of truth all in one interlaced and intertwined flow of scripture. The threads invariably weave themselves between, over, under and through a multitude of other themes, and usually run literally from the beginning of the Bible all the way to the end. Plainly, Jesus Christ is the preeminent topic and glorious theme that wends its way through the grand old Book. Sin, man's corrupt nature, redemption, God's longsuffering, God's sufficiency and provision, the divine nature of the word of God – all these are a mere sampling of literally scores and scores of themes that can be traced through the scriptures. The person and influence of Satan is very much one of those continuous theses that flows through the holy oracles. The sordid saga of the serpent affects, infects and insinuates itself throughout all the comings, goings, successes and failures of man. A sinister presence, he always lurks, both seeking and engineering opportunities. His thumbprint is almost as evident in the history of man as is the Lord's, considering man's proclivity and habit of catastrophic failure. When we investigate the history of all man's foolhardy failings, we find that surrounding each one there lingers the slight scent of brimstone and the fading echo of soft but mocking laughter.

The Author of the Bible charts in faithful detail the old dragon's movements and tactics through the course of the Bible for a reason. The first direct mention resides early in the Book: Genesis 3:1. However, there proves to be more to the story since Isaiah 14:12-14 indicates that the devil and the Lord had a run in well before Genesis 3:1, chronologically. The universe will not be done with Satan until Revelation 20:10, when he is finally restricted to his eternal fiery fate. In an odd "coincidence," the devil's first mention is a mere three chapters from the beginning of Genesis and his final citation is in the third chapter from the end of Revelation. In between these two bookends of this satanic saga is 7000 years of intrigue, deception, misery and death. The Lord narrates in historical detail and prophetic accuracy the fact that the devil hounds, hunts and haunts man for his entire earthly history, excepting the millennial reign of Christ through which the devil is handcuffed to a post in the pit.

It seems astounding that men would be blessed with so thorough a treatise and be so forewarned of the pervasive presence and the malevolent motives of such an entity as Satan, and that they would yet sally forth into their individual and corporate lives so unconcerned, ill-equipped and incautious. Almost everyone has heard of the devil, and most have assigned him some place in the appendix of their personal theology. It is to man's everlasting discredit that Satan most usually is accorded the innocuous and fabled role of being merely "the boogeyman." In men's minds, he is cartoonish; a goofy caricature of some ill-defined evil. In some vague way, he is blamed when bad things happen. Man has to credit evil to something or someone, and a pointy-tailed, goateed, goofily-dressed, devilish character seems to fit the bill well enough. Forty thousand baseball fans at a Yankee game are willing to acquiesce to the sentiments (pass the beer, please) expressed in "God Bless America," and they are equally happy to let the devil have the blame for certain ills and sore fortunes, but those sentiments are neither deeply held or seriously considered. They occupy a place where theology and life never really collide. The masses are blithely unaware of the truly debauched and malevolent nature of him with whom they deal. A 500 pound African lion may be disregarded until faced in the bush and on his home turf. A dragon is not that scary when restricted to fanciful children's tales or even the cinematic visuals in *Harry Potter*. Most have no concept of what *behemoth* or *leviathan* might be (jackals, hippos or crocs, the scholars say), so the threat of either seems rather distant here in the land of iPhones and *American Idol*. All the imaginative genius of man has failed to capture the truly unfathomable horror of the conspiratorial instruments that Satan brings to bear upon the souls and minds of men.

Inexcusably, "Christians" themselves are some of the most naïve and careless. Many notable and well-known Christian figures have forsaken the concept of a personal devil altogether, along with the actual fiery hell which was prepared for him. Seeker-friendly, mega-church and Emerging Church goals do not coincide very well with theology that describes the devil as the father of the seekers, the originator of their vile lusts, the author of their deceit, and the one who will be eternally comforted over the multitude of his weeping, wailing, and agonized spiritual progeny (Ezek. 32:31). Mainline Protestant churches sometimes still adhere hypothetically to theological truths about the insidiousness of Satan, but in a spiritual atmosphere where positivity and humanistic appeal rule the day, practice does not leave much room for a working theology that paints a horrifically negative and frightening picture. Southern Baptists, the so-called largest "Protestant" denomination, excepting for a few holdouts have bought into the new bibles, the new theology of "non-negativism," and seem generally poised to eat all the pottage that Esau can possibly secure from Jacob. For them too, Satan poses a theoretical threat, but practically the evidence of his presence yields way to other more pressing concerns.

The apostasy of these last moments in Church History is a vile, creeping and infectious thing. The *falling away* (II Thes. 2:3) prophesied by Paul is currently a blind but maddened stampede. Commenting upon they who bring in the *damnable heresies* of 2 Peter 2:1, Peter, saddened, comments …*And many shall follow their pernicious ways* (2 Pet. 2:2). *Lukewarm* (Rev.

3:16) is now the new orthodoxy, and ignorance of the fact that *thou art wretched, and miserable, and poor, and blind, and naked* (Rev. 3:17) is the actual course of study in masters and doctoral programs. The tendrils of that poisonous vine invaded scholarship and biblical academia a long, long time ago. *Falling away* to the *damnable heresies* that undermine the true faith of God also means a departure from the true doctrines that illuminate the work of Satan and the debased and defiled nature of man.

It is seldom properly weighed and appreciated just how invasively and deeply the influences of Satan and the corrupt nature of man have affected all the minute affairs and issues that surround the Holy Bible. The very finest among Christians still tend to lose perspective of just how horribly corrupt and debased we are down at the root of our mortal nature. We speak lamentably of our depravity, but we have lived with it all our lives and have gotten accustomed to the stench. Further, while most Bible-believers hold a sound and detailed formal theological position concerning Satan, it is almost inescapable but that we, in our fallen condition mortally, would lose the crucial edge in our vigil and knowledge of just how profoundly *subtil* (Gen. 3:1) and insidiously invasive Satan is.

These two variables, man's corrupt nature and Satan's influences, have the most monumental effects upon not only our society, culture and lives, but upon our attitude, perception and understanding of the scriptures. For many of the best among us, the mind has been tainted (2 Cor. 11:3) by corrupt fallen nature and by the pervasive influences of *the god of this world* (2 Cor. 4:4). For the unregenerate, the reprobate, and even the backslidden, the mind is sometimes altogether and wholly compromised in its integrity (Rom. 1:28).

Long before an unsaved or saved sinner takes upon himself to critique the scriptures and, perhaps, to recommend that they be updated, upgraded or corrected, he would do well to consider what foundation of thought and reason led him to such exercises. Does he fully apprehend the ground on which he treads? People all proceed logically, think and reason, from foundational precepts and principles laid in their minds. Evolutionists proceed from foundations laid in Darwinian principles. Sodomites and Platonic philosophers think along lines proceeding from their respective underpinnings of thought. As for a Christian, *The fear of the LORD is the beginning of knowledge: but fools despise wisdom and instruction* (Prov. 1:7), and *The fear of the LORD is the beginning of wisdom: and the knowledge of the holy is understanding* (Prov. 9:10).

This sinner-saint-scholar, this individual who presumes to think it his role to critically appraise the scriptures, from what foundations of reason doth he proceed? Did he yield his mind at some point to influences that are capable not only of corrupting it but of virtually commandeering it? *To whom hast thou uttered words? And* ***whose spirit came from thee?*** (Job 26:4)

The Terrible Triad: Blessed Be the Tie That Binds

It is no new thing to most who have received even rudimentary discipleship and teaching that the three noteworthy enemies of a Christian are ***the world*** (Jas. 4:4), ***the flesh*** (Rom. 7:18), and ***the devil*** (1 Pet. 5:8).

The Devil

In the most simplistic terms, Satan is man's natural spiritual father (Jn. 8:44). He is every individual's very own personal liar and deceiver (Gen. 3). He also is the *god of this world* (2 Cor. 4:4) and eventually he *deceiveth the whole world* (Rev. 12:9).

The Flesh

Briefly summed up, the flesh is pretty much mankind, individually in mortal terms. Born again unto salvation, the flesh still remains unchanged in its nature until *...the adoption, to wit, the redemption of our body* (Rom. 8:23). New creatures in Christ (2 Cor. 5:17), we are given a new man (Col. 3:10) which is a treasure that we have *in earthen vessels* (2 Cor. 4:7), and actually is *Christ in you, the hope of glory* (Col. 1:27). The flesh is the fallen and unregenerate part of man with which we will not be wholly finished until the Rapture.

> *16 This I say then, Walk in the Spirit, and ye shall not fulfil the lust of the flesh.*
> *17 For the flesh lusteth against the Spirit, and the Spirit against the flesh: and these are contrary the one to the other: so that ye cannot do the things that ye would.* (Gal. 5:16-17)

The flesh is what one serves before salvation, and it is what one lives and walks in (Eph. 2:3). The flesh is basically human nature. It is unregenerate man. It is what man *is* without spiritual conversion and regeneration. After salvation, the tenet remains that until the *redemption of our body* (Rom. 8:23) the *old man* must be resolutely *put off* (Col. 3:9) and mortified (Col. 3:5). The resounding truth for all Christians still living on the mortal side of the veil ever remains *...For I know that in me (that is, in my flesh,) dwelleth no good thing* (Rom. 7:18).

The World

For simplicity's sake, the world is basically man in the conglomerate. It is the sum to which all the fleshly carnal individuals in the population come. It is society, culture, politics, economics, populations and ethnicities all summed up in one five-letter word: ***world***. The world is our enemy as Christians, because far from the adversity of an individual's singular fleshy nature, the *world* represents all the malignant mischief and iniquity of mankind's corporate flesh. It moves as a ponderous and powerful entity, its character defined in all the trends, pressures and vilifications of the vast pooling of man's wretched fallen nature all put together. The world is a monster. It is six and one half billion polluted human beings, excepting only painfully few regenerated and separated Christians, all bearing the fallen nature with all its lusts, debaucheries and perversions. Those 6.5 billion fleshy, fallen souls all interact and move together in explicitly complicated fashion, giving rise to an exponential combination of unregenerate attributes, behaviors, trends and developments which are altogether foreign and abominable to the God of heaven.

So much could be said of the world, but the summation is here limited to our brother, John's, admonition in I John 2:15-16:

> *15 Love not the world, neither the things that are in the world. If any man love the world, the love of the Father is not in him.*
> *16 For all that is in the world, the lust of the flesh, and the lust of the eyes, and the pride of life, is not of the Father, but is of the world.*

The Interplay

The world is, in a general sense, run by the devil. He is the *god of this world* (2 Cor. 4:4), and in the context of the kingdoms of this world and the power that he exerts over them, Satan offered the whole kit and caboodle to Christ … *for that is delivered unto me; and to whomsoever I will I give it* (Luke

4:6). With respect to the individual unsaved man, he is also ...*a king over all the children of pride* (Job 41:34). The lot and heritage of the unregenerate is well described by the following reminder from our past,

> *And you hath he quickened, who were dead in trespasses and sins; Wherein in time past ye walked according to the course of this world, according to the prince of the power of the air, the spirit that now worketh in the children of disobedience:* (Eph. 2:1-2)

Thus, Satan holds vast sway over the souls of man both individually and corporately. The dragon and his minions have shown themselves to treat the flesh, man's old nature, much as a master puppeteer manipulates the strings of the impotent and hapless dummy. In holding power over the individual, he also holds far-reaching power in the world at large.

The natural man, as an individual, has a great deal stacked against him. Whether he realizes it or not, his very own human nature works against him to undermine his well-being in ways he often does not even apprehend. Satan uses the brutish and corrupt nature of the flesh to gain power over the man, and thereby, exploits and manipulates him. Where the prince of darkness does not use the man's individual flesh directly, he still has the colossal resources of corruption in the world to exert titanic pressures, both internally and externally, upon the man. The individual man then adds his deeds and miniscule contributions to the corruption of the whole, and on and on the cycle goes. The darkness deepens and the manacles of spiritual bondage bind fast the hands and feet of all but the most vigilant and alert Christian.

The ***world*** is made up of man's flesh in conglomerate, and is administrated by the great red dragon. The ***devil*** is both *the god of this world* and *the spirit that worketh* in each child of disobedience. The ***flesh*** is affected by both the unclean spirit that haunts it (the devil), and the world of which it is a part and to which it makes its contribution. The relationship is, in this way, similar to a sick chemical molecule made up of three elements, each element being bound to the other two by spiritual bonds that are intimate, horrible and unbreakable but for the grace of God.

The Simplification

There is one slight simplification that will help us in our evaluation. The ***devil*** himself is very obviously an independent entity. When we see that the ***flesh*** is essentially just a man's fallen, corrupt nature, and that the ***world*** is, in elemental terms, just all the flesh in a population of men as a whole, it is easy to then see that all the power and evil of sin in this life is a result of two entities: man and the devil. By no means is the world disregarded, but plainly, if there were no men, then there would be no fodder for the world. There would be no world. The world is made up of men.

The Examination

The goal of this chapter is to examine how that which came to us perfectly from the great God of heaven, the word of God, has been corrupted. More specifically, it is to show how subtly, insidiously, and potently corrupting elements have entered. Further, its purpose is to show how he who trafficked in a form of knowledge that spiritually wrecked the first Adam and his spouse, continues still with the treachery of a supernatural deceit, to compromise the very minds and reasoning of even men who labor consistently in ...*the word of God, which effectually worketh also in you that believe* (1 Thes. 2:13).

The Malevolent Master

Adam's Fair Wife

It is open to the eyes of all just what tactics the serpent employed in the garden when he compromised by his subtlety his very first earthly victims. In an account regarded by many as a fable altogether, and by others as an allegory, Satan achieved exactly what he wanted. It was not a partial victory, but one complete and fulfilling to him. He accomplished the spiritual murder (Gen. 2:17) of two of God's children, clearly affecting the death of their individual spirits (Eph. 2:1) and achieving a new leverage upon their eternal souls. Henceforth, the soul of man would be the eternally treasured spoil over which the Lord and the devil would wrestle and plan.

It seems that the import of some of the lessons taught and recorded on that fateful day are all but lost to a generation of people who have been taught to look upon the narration account of man's fall as dubious, at best. The serpent's *subtlety*, an attribute of lore, was and is, in reality, a characteristic which enables him to affect the thoughts and deceive the minds of men. It was with sophistry and artful guile that he manipulated Eve's thoughts (and she a perfect and unfallen woman, at that) and inserted false premises into the progression of reasoning. It may be said in Adam's case, that in duplicity, Satan trapped him into making a fateful decision by exploiting his emotions and affections for the woman. If *Adam was not deceived* (1 Tim. 2:14), and indeed he was not, then it can only be concluded that the man loved the woman and decided to "bite the bullet," come what may. The dragon's manipulative powers ought to be a most sobering wake-up for the sinner and saint alike.

It should not ever be overlooked that the devil went after

the souls of the man and the woman by attacking what and how *they thought*! It must never be overlooked that within the first four words he spake, he raised the subject of God's own words - *Yea, hath God said...?* (Gen. 3:1). **He is obsessed with the Lord's words.** The very next words from his lips were a blatant contradiction of what God had indeed said: *Ye shall not surely die* (Gen. 3:4). **He will ever and always deny the complete truth of what God said.** He next misrepresents the knowledge of God - what God knows: *For God doth know that in the day ye eat thereof, then your eyes shall be opened...* (Gen. 3:5). **He misrepresents God to seduce the sinner.** He, then, makes a pitch for a certain brand of knowledge that God had forbidden, but it is indeed "knowledge" that the devil trafficked in that day. *...(A)nd ye shall be as gods, knowing good and evil* (Gen. 3:5). If in doubt about this, one need only look at the next tragic statement regarding the woman's frame of mind. *And when the woman saw that the tree was good for food, and that it was pleasant to the eyes, and a tree to be desired to make one wise, she took of the fruit thereof, and did eat* (Gen. 3:6). ***Satan's appeal has always been to involve man in knowledge and wisdom best left alone.***

Satan's Reasoning		Implications & Insinuations
Step 1:	*Yea, hath God said?*	The attack is on the words of God.
Step 2:	*Ye shall not surely die*	What God said is untrue.
Step 3:	*For God doth know*	God has secret or ulterior motives.
Step 4:	*knowing; make one wise*	There is special, hidden knowledge elsewhere to be had.

It should be highlighted with eternally luminescent ink that the devil inserted himself into how the man and woman thought and reasoned about their circumstances. He contaminated and fouled the content of their minds and the processes by which they reasoned. They were responsible for it, but it was he that introduced the corruption and spoilage.

In Step 1 of the scenario, it is plain that the prime issue with the devil is the words of the Living God. Whether it is the fact that he hates those words above all else, and that his prime goal was to destroy those words, or whether it is the idea that he hated that man and woman (or even God) more than anything else, and the perversion of those words was the most efficient means of reaching the goal, the reader must determine. Either scenario as a possibility still yields the same conclusion. Satan goes after the word of God as a rabid wolf – a very subtle and devious rabid wolf.

Step 2 is plainly not just an attack upon the integrity of the God of the Bible, but also an attack upon the certainty of what the Bible said. Importantly, in attacking the scripture (what God said), the devil was certainly attacking personally the God that said it. There is no question that Satan would be happy if people believed utterly nothing in the Bible at all, but it appears that that is not his goal. He did not say, "Ye shall not die," or "Ye shall not die at all," or "Surely, ye shall not die." He said *Ye shall not **surely** die.* Though acknowledging the possibility of death, what Satan undermined was the ***certainty*** of it. Not to be overlooked is the fact that he assaulted the ***inflexible accuracy*** of what the Lord had said, and convinced Eve that it was worth the gamble.

Today, this peculiarly satanic characteristic is found even among God's people, and sometimes particularly among God's "trained" men, who are responsible for teaching and preaching the word of God. It almost seems at times that the more dogmatically and unequivocally something is stated in the scriptures, the more likely it is to be scrutinized by the scholars as something all the more dubious and uncertain.

This trait is particularly evident among textual scholars and Bible critics. From the infidels and the scholars who think Genesis is a myth and that Christ was a sodomite, to the comparatively much more faithful Textus Receptus scholars, who hold that the King James is the best, but by no means perfect, translation, there is one thing certain to them: God did not, could not, and would not actually do what He said He would do! God did not keep every word pure (Ps. 12), and give each word to individual Christians so that they might live by them (Matt. 4).

Step 3 is perhaps the prince of darkness's most perfidious artifice. He ascribes ulterior motives to the Creator and Savior, the Author of our God-given scriptures. He implies there are things about God that one should know, but that the Lord has not been forthright enough to tell. Satan holds that God manifested Himself to us in certain ways and said certain things to us, but He did not tell us all He could have or should have. Our God, it is insinuated, is in some measures faulty and guileful in that He did not give us a complete account of how things really are. The insinuation is that they who trust the words of the Lord are being cheated and shortchanged. Since, by the devils implications, God did not "come clean" with man, man must look out for number one and take necessary action by which his needs may be met and so that he might be truly fulfilled as a person.

Step 4 seals the deal, has fueled a thousand movements through history, and is the foundational precept at the vast majority of institutions of Biblical learning. Here it is: *"One cannot trust what God said as He said it, no matter how simple and straightforward it seems. Only by taking the next step can one attain true knowledge and know true wisdom. The truth is not as it seems on the surface. That type of truth is for superficial people, common people, and for mere public consumption. There is another, much more sublime layer of truth that lies beneath and behind what is simplistically recorded. If one wants to be a shallow stooge, a mere boob, a follower that accepts everything on face value, let him just go ahead, read his Bible and remain a second class Christian. If one wants to be on the inside, a part of those who really know and who are truly wise, he cannot merely accept what God said on the surface."* With regard to God's words, this mindset basically represents *Satan's Manifesto.*

It was a terrible dialogue that Eve involved herself in that day. She would have been wise never to have entered the conversation. She became entangled, mired, insecure and confused. She left the tree that day *dead in trespasses and sins* (Eph. 2:1), having lost her soul until the Lord should later intervene.

She also set the ball rolling in another part of her being. With a spirit now dead, and a soul hanging in the balance, she had also allowed herself to be deceived and degraded in mind and heart. Unknowingly, she set the stage for a day not too distant, when for all her progeny it could be said, *that every imagination of the thoughts of his (man's) heart was only evil continually* (Gen. 6:5). A precedent was set from which the human race has never recovered.

The *roaring lion* (1 Pet. 5:8) loved every minute of it.

Christ's Chaste Virgin

You may be certain that the devil did not forget the kind

of success he had with that fair young lady in that garden. Many other women in time would follow their predecessor down a slippery and sordid trail. Of course, many are the men, as well, that had altogether as little success as Eve in fencing with the serpent. Just as the first Adam learned that the serpent presented a horrific threat to his bride, so too, the Last Adam (1 Cor. 15:45) has spent two millennia undertaking to help his bride properly fortify against the wiles of the devil. On this wise, the apostle Paul said,

> *For I am jealous over you with godly jealousy: for I have espoused you to one husband, that I may present you as a chaste virgin to Christ. But I fear, lest by any means, as the serpent beguiled Eve through his subtilty, so your minds should be corrupted from the simplicity that is in Christ.* (2 Cor. 11:2-3)

It is insightful that Paul chooses to mention the *subtilty* of Satan in the passage, as that was the first attribute mentioned of him back when the first Adam's wife had her shoot-out with him. As already outlined above, the bride of Christ will be, and has been, attacked with the identical tactics and strategy as was revealed to us in the garden. It is pitiful that our success, on a practical basis, has not been substantially better than Eve's.

There are two other important tidbits of information. ***In the first place***, notice that for a Christian, the danger is that *your minds should be corrupted* (vs.3). The word *corrupted* is an important word and indicates that Eve's mind was indeed corrupted. The word *mind* denotes the fact that a Christian must be ever-vigilant and on guard, lest his mind be corrupted, and being thus corrupted, he is unable to think and reason as he should. Our minds are given us to think, reason, apprehend and understand. If the mind should be corrupted, what other possible conclusion is there to reach but that we would be unable to think as intended?

In the second place, note that the danger is that we will be moved away *from the simplicity that is in Christ.* Simplicity. Apparently, the finely honed skills of the devil revolve around making complicated things that are simple. This certainly is consistent with what happened in Genesis 3. There was nothing complicated about, " *...of the tree of the knowledge of good and evil, thou shalt not eat of it: for in the day that thou eatest thereof thou shalt surely die"* (Gen.2:17). But, the devil did cloud the issue with his sophistry, and exploited the woman's naiveté, discontent and failure to prepare for such an assault.

It is worthwhile to point out that complicating what is nothing more than an elemental and simple command or precept, could easily be masked behind a façade of intellectualism, education, and academia. The act of complicating the matter could well be called education, higher learning, or even, scholarship. Adultery is called many things, but somebody had to take courses and do research in order for it to be called "adult consent." One can get a doctorate in various "culture studies," but a ten year old in a good church Sunday School class knows that it is simply "heathenism" by another name. The world does not want simple truth from God; they prefer intricate and convoluted philosophies. This allows "wiggle room" in their lives since men love *darkness rather than light, because their deeds were evil* (John 3:19).

The minds of Christian men and women are corrupted from the simplicity that is in Christ by being drawn into elaborate and sophisticated convolutions that were in no way designed by God. How oft have we heard complaints about all the *thou shalt's* and *thou shalt not's* in the Bible, quickly followed by the most enlightened opinion that, "It just isn't that simple"?

I cannot help but remember the time I received one of many complaints I have fielded about the 4x8 foot, changeable scripture panel that we have as part of our church sign here in the Minneapolis area. The scripture verse is usually changed once and sometimes twice a week. I received a call from a very irate man whose closing comment before slamming down the phone was, "I have been driving by that _____ ______ church for seven years, and I haven't understood a single thing you have had on that sign!" The scripture that was on the sign at the time was *Thou shalt not commit adultery.* A very complex sentence and concept, I admit.

Just take note of how each simple moral imperative that the Lord sets forth in the scripture is somehow complicated by a score of things ranging from culture, to interpretation, to the "evolution of society," to "paternalistic ethics," or – how about this one – the meaning in the "original Greek or Hebrew." It seems almost impossible for modern man to simply allow the word of God to speak, and from thence obey or heed the word without entering into some serpentine, philosophical meandering concluding that the meaning cannot be the simple and elemental concept as stated.

With respect to the Bible itself, it is absolutely ***not*** acceptable to even Fundamentalist scholarship that we should receive the simple and oft repeated promises of the purity and perfection of the Bible, and apply those promises to the translation of the Bible that rests in our laps. Proverbs 4:20-21 absolutely ***cannot*** mean what it says as applied to our Bible:

> *My son,* ***attend to my words****; incline thine ear unto my sayings.* ***Let them not depart from thine eyes****; keep them in the midst of thine heart.*

Most all of the scholars profess to be in agreement in this matter. So, here is the question: ***is it the Bible-believer who***

accepts the word in its simplicity that bears the attributes of Satan, or is it the scholar who resolutely and adamantly insists that it is not as simple as it seems?

God's Tempted Son

Matthew 4 and Luke 4 both bear the account of the tempter's frontal attack upon the Lord Jesus Christ on the Mount of Temptation. In Matthew 4 we read,

> *3 And when the tempter came to him, he said, If thou be the Son of God, command that these stones be made bread.*
> *4 But he answered and said, It is written, Man shall not live by bread alone, but by every word that proceedeth out of the mouth of God.*
> *5 Then the devil taketh him up into the holy city, and setteth him on a pinnacle of the temple,*
> *6 And saith unto him, If thou be the Son of God, cast thyself down: for it is written, He shall give his angels charge concerning thee: and in their hands they shall bear thee up, lest at any time thou dash thy foot against a stone.*
> *7 Jesus said unto him, It is written again, Thou shalt not tempt the Lord thy God.*
> *8 Again, the devil taketh him up into an exceeding high mountain, and sheweth him all the kingdoms of the world, and the glory of them;*
> *9 And saith unto him, All these things will I give thee, if thou wilt fall down and worship me.*
> *10 Then saith Jesus unto him, Get thee hence, Satan: for it is written, Thou shalt worship the Lord thy God, and him only shalt thou serve.* (Matt. 4:3-10)

Note the following bare-bones parts of the exchange between Satan and Christ

The Devil	The Lord Jesus
If thou be the Son of God, command that these stones be made bread.	*But he answered and said, It is written...*
If thou be the Son of God, cast thyself down...	*Jesus said unto him, It is written again...*
All these things will I give thee if thou wilt fall, down and worship me.	*Get thee hence, Satan: for it is written...*

Much has been preached and written on this narrative of the great clash between the Son of God and the formerly-anointed cherub. There are some observations and lessons that are insightful into the tactics of our adversary.

First, without microscopically dissecting all of the manna found in this passage, please note that ***the devil urges and prods the Lord to take presumptuous and precipitous action.*** This checks with what he did with Eve in the garden, as well. This is what he does to every man, woman, boy and girl. Satan desires man to go beyond his bounds, to take upon himself the foolhardy initiative to do what he ought not, when he ought not. He urges haste and boldness – unholy boldness. As Nadab and Abihu, and as King Uzziah, he urges men to rush to ground that they ought not to tread. As with Achan, he admonishes the fool to snatch and hide some abominable and forbidden thing. It is presumptuous and precipitous decisiveness and action that he wants. A further description of the type of actions he desires of man includes the words *incautious, irreverent, hasty, impetuous* and *brash.* The stench of effrontery emanates from what the devil wants from man.

Secondly, ***even One so powerful and imperial as Jesus Christ did not take that bait!*** The Son of God Himself, God manifest in the flesh refused to go there. Why is man so quick to advance where even the Lord Himself would not?

Third, with one singular exception, ***the only thing that God's Anointed had to say to Satan was quoted from the scripture itself.*** Three times He said, *It is written.* The only addition Christ made to the quotation of scripture, was that in verse 10, Christ commanded, *Get thee hence, Satan.* Otherwise, nothing proceeded from the mouth of the Lord in those moments except the very oracles of God previously written. If anyone ever trod upon the earth equipped to give the devil a thorough and complete tongue lashing, it was Jesus Christ. The Lord could have pinned the serpent against a rock and "skinned him alive" for as long as He pleased, but He did not. Even for Christ, the scripture more than sufficed.

The devil finds men in scenarios where he can take the advantage of them by herding and driving them into making impetuous and brash decisions. In doing so, he is essentially "running" and controlling man. Whether he frightens, intimidates, humiliates or drives men to this action by ambition or rebellion, it makes little difference. The end is the same. Man makes foolish and precipitous decisions. The issue can be fornication, dope, running off with a sleazebag, hooking up with the wrong religious outfit, or taking a job where there is no Bible-believing church. Importantly, the issue may also be yielding ground on *the faith which was once delivered unto the saints* (Jude 3), all the while knowing that that very faith *cometh by hearing, and hearing by the word of God* (Rom. 10:17). It would truly be foolhardy to think that the serpent does not patrol the territory of Biblical scholarship, and that the same ambushes he laid for Eve, the bride of Christ, and the Lord

Himself would not be sprung upon textual or expository scholars.

The People of God

There is a much longer scenic tour of doctrinal insights into the devil's tactics against the redeemed, but for the sake of relative brevity, we will just add to our record of the devil's devices the following brief attributes:

Improperly *"savouring"* what God said gives foothold to the devil.

> *From that time forth began Jesus to shew unto his disciples, how that he must go unto Jerusalem, and suffer many things of the elders and chief priests and scribes, and be killed, and be raised again the third day. Then Peter took him, and began to rebuke him, saying, Be it far from thee, Lord: this shall not be unto thee. But he turned, and said unto Peter, Get thee behind me, Satan: thou art an offence unto me:* ***for thou savourest not the things that be of God****, but those that be of men* (Matt. 16:21-23)

"Satan cometh immediately, and taketh away the word" **where it is received into a heart that is not an *"honest and good heart"* (Luke 8:15)!**

> *The sower soweth the word. And these are they by the way side, where the word is sown; but when they have heard,* ***Satan cometh immediately****, and taketh away the word that was sown in their hearts.* (Mark 4:14-15)

Men - Judas in this case - make decisions that open them further to Satan's influence.

> *Jesus answered, He it is, to whom I shall give a sop, when I have dipped it. And when he had dipped the sop, he gave it to Judas Iscariot, the son of Simon.* ***And after the sop Satan entered into him.*** *Then said Jesus unto him, That thou doest, do quickly.* (John 13:26-27)

Nothing opens men to Satan's influence more than failing faith. The source of faith is the word of God (Rom.10:17)!

> *And the Lord said, Simon, Simon, behold, Satan hath desired to have you, that he may sift you as wheat: But I have prayed for thee,* ***that thy faith fail not****: and when thou art converted, strengthen thy brethren.* (Luke 22:31-32)

Our vigilance and steadfastness against the serpent is *"in the faith."* Again, the fountainhead of our faith is the word of God (Rom.10:17).

> *Be sober, be vigilant; because your adversary the devil, as a roaring lion, walketh about, seeking whom he may devour: Whom resist stedfast* ***in the faith****, knowing that the same afflictions are accomplished in your brethren that are in the world.* (1 Pet. 5:8-9)

Satan uses our inmost sins to his *"advantage."*

> *To whom ye forgive any thing, I forgive also: for if I forgave any thing, to whom I forgave it, for your sakes forgave I it in the person of Christ;*

Lest Satan should get an ***advantage*** *of us: for we are not ignorant of his devices.*
(2 Cor. 2:10-11)

Such inward sins essentially subvert us to the devil's use.

Be ye angry, and sin not: let not the sun go down upon your wrath: Neither ***give place*** *to the devil.*
(Eph. 4:26-27)

Satan *"fills"* the heart so he can use the tongue (or pen).

But Peter said, Ananias, why hath ***Satan filled thine heart*** *to lie to the Holy Ghost, and to keep back part of the price of the land?*
(Acts 5:3)

The devil leads people (even scholars) to speak things they ought not.

And withal they learn to be idle, wandering about from house to house; and not only idle, but tattlers also and busybodies, ***speaking things which they ought not****. I will therefore that the younger women marry, bear children, guide the house, give none occasion to the adversary to speak reproachfully. For some are already turned aside after Satan.* (1 Tim. 5:13-15)

The "light" gotten from Satan is false light!

Thy word is a lamp unto my feet, and a light unto my path (Ps. 119:105), and Christ is *the light of the world* (John 8:12) and *the true Light, which lighteth every man* (John 1:9), but Satan destroyed Eve spiritually with *knowing* (Gen. 3:5) and is responsible for wisdom that *is*

> *earthly, sensual, devilish* (James 3:15). *And no marvel;* ***for Satan himself is transformed into an angel of light*** (2 Cor. 11:14).

It will take the entire armory of God for you to even STAND!

> *Put on the whole armour of God,* ***that ye may be able to stand*** *against the wiles of the devil. For we wrestle not against flesh and blood, but against principalities, against powers, against the rulers of the darkness of this world, against spiritual wickedness in high places. Wherefore take unto you the whole armour of God,* ***that ye may be able to withstand*** *in the evil day, and* ***having done all, to stand. Stand therefore,*** *having your loins girt about with truth, and having on the breastplate of righteousness;*
> (Eph. 6:11-14)

There are those who are ready and usable tools to the serpent anytime, and as often as, he chooses.

And that they may recover themselves out of the snare of the devil, ***who are taken captive by him at his will.***
(2 Tim. 2:26)

It is important to say, here, that these tactics and tools are used in very many areas of the spiritual lives of lost and saved people alike, both individually and in mass. However, it is most needful that one should realize that these are devices and movements that the tempter uses in his quest to destroy and decimate the words of God and Christ. It would be a terrible mistake to apply these precepts to the moral and spiritual lives of men without seeing that if Satan can tactically, and primarily, bring the Bible into disrepute, then picking off men is like shooting fish in a bowl.

An indispensable question is this: After fully six millennia of this war over God's Holy Word, just how compromised and imperiled is the integrity of mind, heart and doctrine of your favorite Bible scholar, teacher or commentator? How much of the devil's bologna has he bought? The committee of men or board of trustees that administrates your denomination, fellowship, favorite Bible college or mission board, do they, or do they not, bear the characteristics of such as have been compromised to the devil's philosophy when it comes to the perfection of the Bible?

The Haughty Hand Puppets

The Old Man

Men often have quite a hard time realizing just how the very innate and instinctive nature of man plays directly into the hands of the old dragon. The very thoughts, imaginations, and inclinations of man tend more toward corruption than toward godliness. *And GOD saw that the wickedness of man was great in the earth, and that* ***every imagination*** *of the thoughts of his heart was only evil continually* (Gen. 6:5), and *the* ***natural man receiveth not*** *the things of the Spirit of God: for they are foolishness unto him* (1 Cor. 2:14).

In following with the purely natural, *Ye are of your father the devil, and the lusts of your father ye will do* (John 8:44), man born only after the manner of the flesh is in a terrible way: *dead in trespasses and sins* (Eph. 2:1). His course in this world is walked in accordance *to the prince of the power of the air, the spirit that now worketh in the children of disobedience* (Eph. 2:2). Not only is his soul lost and his being literally "devil possessed," but his mind and heart are in concord with the spirit of the prince of this world, and thus his thoughts and affections lean that way.

Much changes when a lost soul is born again. *Therefore if any man be in Christ, he is a new creature: old things are passed away; behold, all things are become new* (2 Cor. 5:17). Suddenly the blood of Christ is real, Heaven is certain, and the promises of our adoptive Father sure. One does embark upon a new course, but in many ways it is a more challenging and frustrating one than the new Christian has ever before experienced. A Christian must deal with two natures. The old nature in man is not eradicated during the new birth, but it awaits the *manifestation of the sons of God* (Rom. 8:19) at the Rapture. Paul expounds on the interplay between those two natures in several places in the New Testament, but there is no better place to see how contrary the two are than in Ephesians 4:22-24:

> *22 That ye put off concerning the former conversation* ***the old man, which is corrupt*** *according to the deceitful lusts;*
> *23 And be renewed in the spirit of your mind;*
> *24 And that ye put on* ***the new man, which after God is created in righteousness and true holiness.***

Another synopsis of this elemental fact about the Christian life is found in Galatians 5:16-17.

> *16 This I say then, Walk in* ***the Spirit****, and ye shall not fulfil the lust of* ***the flesh.***
> *17* ***For the flesh lusteth against the Spirit, and the Spirit against the flesh: and these are contrary the one to the other****: so that ye cannot*

do the things that ye would.

The thesis here is not about the dual nature of regenerate man, so it is not profitable to delve into the depths of the scriptures regarding it. It *is* both profitable and necessary to understand that the answer to how Satan so effortlessly manages to undermine, compromise, and exploit man, lies in the existence of the fallen and corrupt nature in all men. That is the only nature that a non-Christian knows, but it is also a very powerful and ever-present part of a converted saint's make-up.

As long as there have been men, there have been failings due to this corrupt nature. For as long as there have been Christian men, there have been failings due to the presence of the old man. In the hour of the most fiery revival and sanctification, the old man is relegated to the shadows while the new man exults in his Savior and is mightily strengthened. History has shown that some of the fervor of the new man will invariably wane in some measure due to a thousand different combinations of circumstances. When this happens, the fallen nature will be there to do all it can to reassert itself.

The very best and most ardent of Christian men struggle to keep off the ever-rebounding old man. Because that old man is such a persistent presence, it has proven difficult for Christians to keep the vigil as zealously as they ought. The ever-present character of our fallen nature tends to breed familiarity and a sense of amicability. The tendency is to grow to view the old, fallen man as a pest and a hindrance rather than a debauched and perverse enemy to all we are supposed to be as Christians. The unvarnished truth is that the more one allows the old man to edge and insinuate himself back into one's life, the closer he comes to giving place to the devil (Eph. 4:27), and the more advantage one allows him (2 Cor. 2:11). The old nature, the natural man, is the most insidious and useful avenue the devil has to work his devices in any Christian's life and heart.

A Dark Judgment

A resounding and profound denunciation of man's nature is found in a singular verse in the book of Proverbs, though there are many other verses much akin to it. This verse applies to many facets of life. It applies to lost men, but it also applies to the pervading fallen nature of regenerate man as well. The verse is a magnificent commentary on Hollywood and the fashion industry. It explains the whorish nature of politics and why kids emerge from college with a degree, yet somehow are more ignorant and degraded than before their entry. It explains environmentalism, evolution, atheism, sodomy, the Gothic movement, the Emerging Church, Barak Obama's agenda, and it also is an explanation of why the average doofus with a Greek text, a concordance, and a two-bit Bible college education cannot allow the words of God to stand as written. The verse says,

> ***The foolishness of man perverteth his way: and his heart fretteth against the LORD.***
> (Prov. 19:3)

By nature, man is a fool. By nature, man resents boundaries and restrictions. An object that looks like an upside-down lampshade is placed around a dog's neck when he has particular kinds of injuries. This action is taken because it is in the dog's nature to "fret" the injury so that it will not heal. He will lick, bite and worry it into a greater sore than in its beginning. So it is that man's *heart fretteth against the LORD.* As Israel stood at the base of Mount Sinai, frightened to death at the terrible display of flashing lightning and roaring thunder, in their mortal terror it was easy for them to say unto Moses,

Speak thou with us, and we will hear: but let not God speak with us, lest we die (Exod. 20:19). Still occupying the base of that terrible smoking and rumbling mountain, it was only a short time later that God's people had adjusted to the ominous sights and sounds and were prepared for a descent into apostasy. *Up, make us gods* (Exod. 32:1), said they unto Moses brother, Aaron. Waving a hand past the face will shoo the mosquitoes, but its effectiveness is counted in fractions of seconds, not minutes or hours. Even so it is that man's *heart fretteth against the LORD.* The spiritual nature of a man's heart does not really allow for a plateau, a flat place, where the man may rest and relax after a season of spiritual victory or fruitfulness. The heart always rebounds and awakes with unrelenting fretting. It is a millstone around the neck of the spiritual man. *The heart is deceitful above all things, and desperately wicked: who can know it* (Jer. 17:9)? *He that trusteth in his own heart is a fool* (Prov. 28:26).

It is certain that the hearts of men fret against God in all of the various expectations He has for man. It certainly applies to matters of sexual purity, friendships, idols, and gambling along with all the more carnal lusts that come so readily to our minds when a listing of sins seems needful. It is important to acknowledge that this fretting is at work not only in the categories of sin involving open carnality, but also in the more subtle classes of spiritual exercise requiring true faithfulness, such as scholarship, wisdom, professorship and learning. Human nature is neither eradicated by entering the pulpit, nor the study, nor the classroom, nor the Christian institution of learning. The textual scholar's heart is a fretting heart just like the heart of the mechanic or pawn broker.

The fretting of man's heart is, of course, related to and a contributor to, his foolishness, and that foolishness ***perverteth his way.*** That is strong language. The place to where man's foolish nature and his fretting heart lead him is a much lower and debauched place than he usually understands. His way is *perverted*! The natural, fallen, inner workings of his own sinful being literally wrests, twists and distorts what he is and what he is to become. This invariably places a man who is following the inclinations of his own heart independent of God's word in a very dark spiritual place. *He that walketh in his uprightness feareth the LORD:* ***but he that is perverse in his ways despiseth him*** (Prov. 14:2). No matter how much a man following the leadership of his own heart professes that he loves the Lord, the scriptures, which *discern the thoughts and intents of the heart* (Heb. 4:12), declare otherwise.

For this reason, contradictory to what mainline Christians are regularly taught, the child of God is admonished in blessed forthrightness, *Hear thou, my son, and be wise, and* ***guide thine heart in the way*** (Prov. 23:19). The heart is not the guide of man, but man the guide of his heart. Following one's own heart will transform him into a pervert. Unhindered and unchecked, this inclination can well lead a man to a place where he is an active agent in the perversion and distortion of God's truth and work. It was Paul that said, *O full of all subtilty and all mischief, thou child of the devil, thou enemy of all righteousness, wilt thou not cease to pervert the right ways of the Lord?* (Acts 13:10)

When Wise is Foolish

Though man often believes and professes himself wise, this is far from the Lord's view of the matter. Man has invented cool stuff, and he now travels and communicates in novel, technologically advanced ways. Man has made vast leaps in demonstrable scientific knowledge and development, but this is not the Lord's standard for judging wisdom.

> *Let no man deceive himself. If any man among you seemeth to be wise in this world, let him*

become a fool, that he may be wise. For the wisdom of this world is foolishness with God. For it is written, He taketh the wise in their own craftiness. (1 Cor. 3:18-19)

Where is the wise? where is the scribe? where is the disputer of this world? hath not God made foolish the wisdom of this world? For after that in the wisdom of God the world by wisdom knew not God, it pleased God by the foolishness of preaching to save them that believe.
(1 Cor. 1:20-21)

Foolishness is bound in the heart of a child (Prov. 22:15), and that foolishness often lingers on well into adulthood, and endures even higher education and doctoral programs. Professorship and tenure by no means indicate victory over foolishness. No social class or age group has a particular corner on the market for foolishness, and probably every one of us has painful memories to prove that we all have the unenviable capacity for playing the fool. There are fools for money, fools for women, and the general population has far too many Elvis impersonators and professional wrestling fans for man to be accounted truly wise. It is worthwhile to consider though, that a man or woman who traffics in wisdom is a frontrunner for trouble in this area. There are many warnings of being wise in one's own conceit (Pro. 26:12) and being *highminded* (2 Tim. 3:4), but they who merchandise in wisdom, education, learning, philosophy, academics and scholarship, to name a few, are truly prime candidates for being taken *in their own craftiness.*

(T)he wisdom of this world is foolishness with God (1 Cor. 3:19a) says the Lord, but man has shown that he has tremendous difficulty in discerning and holding the line of distinction between the wisdom of this world and that of God.

As a moth to light, so it seems that man, once he has his taste set to wisdom, is drawn and enamored by wisdom of just about any sort, including that which is inadvisable. It is a historical fact that early Christianity was terribly - almost fatally - seduced by the "wisdom" of the unregenerate Platonic philosophers and Gnostics. During the Renaissance of the 1300-1400's, Aristotelian philosophy was revived, and once again the "Christian" scholars dashed themselves to their own demise against the mesmerizing brilliance of the wisdom of this world. Wave upon wave of philosophical claptrap has hammered upon the levies of God's wisdom, a wisdom found only in the Bible. Formally named philosophies like Materialism, Deism, and German Rationalism have all risen in turn and swept Christians out into the open seas. Modernism, the Emerging Church Movement, Contemplative Mysticism and others all exhibit a certain *shew of wisdom* (Col. 2:23), and each in turn draws from the flock alarming percentages of those who have not *their senses exercised to discern both good and evil* (Heb. 5:14).

The problem is that the heart of a man, when left to itself, always leads that man into foolish and corrupt pursuits. Man is fallen; therefore his base tastes are corrupt as well. ***The foolishness of man perverteth his way: and his heart fretteth against the LORD!*** *The heart is deceitful above all things, and desperately wicked: who can know it?* (Jer. 17:9) *He that trusteth in his own heart is a fool* (Prov. 28:26). A man who has tasted and seen that the Lord is good, and that God's wisdom is exceedingly good, will almost invariably be desirous to try other more vulgar and variant forms of wisdom. Even Eve, a sinless woman in pristine surroundings, still was drawn to a form of knowledge and wisdom that killed her. Proverbs 18:1 sets forth a deadly pronouncement: *Through desire a man, having separated himself, seeketh and intermeddleth with all wisdom.* It is also an honest epitaph that could be engraved on many a wise man's headstone. Man was never intended to *meddle with **all wisdom**.* The wisdom found in philosophy is urgently condemned: *Beware lest any man spoil you through* ***philosophy*** (Col. 2:8a). Just as off-limits is the idol of 21st century America – Science: *keep that which is committed to thy trust, avoiding profane and vain babblings, and oppositions of* ***science*** *falsely so called* (1 Tim. 6:20). That is the open and obvious meaning of an oft- overlooked statement by Paul: *I would have you wise unto that which is good, and simple concerning evil* (Rom. 16:19). Nevertheless, since man's heart is corrupt and his inclinations base, he desires to taste all fruit, even that which is forbidden.

To the law and to the testimony: if they speak not according to this word, it is because there is no light in them (Isa. 8:20). Without the absolute most stringent adherence to the precepts of the scriptures, the wisdom of the world, and thus of Satan, is readily embraced. As in all things, only the Bible can truly distinguish for a man whether the wisdom he receives is of God, or from elsewhere.

The Hottest Battleground

There will always be influences that feed the carnal fires in the hearts of men, no matter what their occupation or calling; but there can be little doubt that the devil has more of a vested interest in leading a man to defile and wrest the word of God, than he has in getting him to morally fall with a floozy. Satan went for Eve's soul, but he attacked the Bible to do so. The indispensable ground we defend is the word of God. Satan has never lost view of the fact that that ground is the goal. Capturing that flag and seizing control of that parcel of spiritual territory would spell disaster for all, without exception. Dope, gambling, hatred and sex are terrible tools that the devil uses to bring havoc upon the lives of men and women, their families, their friends and all that an individual may influence. On the other hand, Satan is perfectly happy to leave his victims with sterile and uneventful lives, without addiction, if he can but entice them into disavowing and dismissing the words of God from their lives entirely.

Those words are the fount of all pure heavenly truth. They are how one discerns what the truth is. Those words are foundational and indispensable to the knowing of Christ. Jesus Christ is the singular most important facet of life, but it is only through the Bible that any can know the true Christ. Again, *To the law and to the testimony: if they speak not according to this word, it is because there is no light in them* (Isa. 8:20). Mainline "Christianity," at this juncture, is one of the most idolatrous populations on earth. The leaders and partakers of this mainline "Christian" movement take the Lord Jesus Christ of the Bible, but they have determined that they do not like certain aspects of His revealed nature. Therefore, they remove, box and store those particular traits. They then take the traits that appeal to them the most, and magnify and elaborate on those traits even above the balances found in the scriptures. In a pinch, they will make up certain virtues out of thin air, or search for them in some non-canonical imposter's epistle. In this way, they construct a Christ of their own making, embellished by their own adornments. This is the grossest and most blasphemous form of idolatry!

In this way, the intermingling of the wisdom of the world and the wisdom of God is a guaranteed recipe for disaster.

Oddly, while many sound fundamental Bible-believers are quick to see that these precepts must necessarily be applied to Rock music, dope and illicit sex, they often seem to suffer a certain blind spot nearer to home. Obviously, Solomon played the fool in his admitted experimentations with sin throughout the book of Ecclesiastes. Ecclesiastes 1:17 is an admitted, though prideful, expedition into darkness and delusion. *And I gave my heart to know wisdom, and to know madness and folly.* Solomon paid dearly for those adventures. He thought he would be wiser for having experimented with the wisdom of the world and that it would contribute to the wisdom God had given him. He was wrong. Only fools would think they could be profited by experimenting with addictive activities, imagination-rotting pornography, or a couple of months of training in Zen Buddhism. The wisdom of the world and the wisdom of God are oil and water, and do not mingle well.

As mentioned before, Satan's first strategic and tactical move against the soul of Mrs. Adam was recorded as, *Yea, hath God said* (Gen. 3:1). The rule of first mention, the testimony of the remainder of the scriptures, and the history of the battle for the Bible shows that, without a doubt, Satan is still doing absolutely everything he can to overthrow the wisdom and knowledge of God by inserting the contamination of the wisdom and knowledge of the world into the hearts and minds of man. There is much that is omitted of God's word in the new bible versions, but a profound amount is also reworded, interchanged, and jumbled.

There is, thus, a crossing point for several different critical issues to both God and the devil:

1) The word – 1st thing Satan attacked. He still does.
2) Wisdom – the wisdom of God vs. the wisdom of the world (Satan)
3) Knowledge – the knowledge of God vs. what Satan offered to Eve (and to us)
4) Man's fallen nature - *his heart fretteth against the LORD* . (Pro.19:3).
5) Man as a tool, used either of God (Paul) or the devil (Eve).

The crossing point mentioned above is not only a mighty crossroad of tumult and vicious spiritual conflict, but much of the fight is fought in the hearts and heads of the men and women who have lofty titles in institutions of biblical academia. Theological scholars, linguists, writers of Greek and Hebrew grammars, lexicographers, textual experts, tenured-for-life seminary professors and learned editors of technical manuals related to biblical studies are all some of the main participants in the shipwreck of faith (1 Tim. 1:19).

Few seem to take seriously how compromised the true wisdom of God in these areas has become, and how sorely infected is that wisdom with the wisdom of the world. Biblical scholarship, so often spoken of in noble and reverent terms among Christians, has been for many years a stagnant incubator for the Satan-inspired wisdom of this world. Few who have superficial interest in such matters, realize how much of what most scholars claim to *know*, is actually founded on the work and *discernment* of unconverted and unregenerate adversaries to the plainly stated truths of God in the scriptures. Most common Christians would be shocked, and ought to be *outraged*, by how profoundly the self-appointed defenders of biblical scholarship have allowed the foundations of truth to be undermined and jeopardized. Gail Riplinger elaborates thus,

> The lexicons and grammars of *unsaved liberals* are at the foundation of *all* Greek and Hebrew studies today. Current lexicons are either reprints of the works of 19th century liberals or highly plagiarized and slightly edited re-typeset editions. The *few* study aids that have been written by "Christians" were compiled *using* the corrupt lexicons of unbelievers. These unsaved men cannot discern spiritual things.[91]

---

[91] Riplinger, G.A., *In Awe of Thy Word, Understanding the King James Bible,* (A.V. Publications, Ararat, VA, 24053, 2003) p. 508.

For example, Wilhelm Gesenius (1786-1842) is principally known for his Hebrew *Grammar,* and is reputed for being one of the greatest of the Hebrew and biblical scholars. Honey-dipped endorsements by blind admirers or fellow-apostates are truly of little value. A Bible-believer ought not to be deceived by nepotism and self-serving accolades among thieves and those whose profession it is to eviscerate the integrity and content of the words of God. Of Gesenius, it is stated,

> He …aroused bitter opposition. He was one of the first to open Semitic to scientific study, because of his point of view that Hebrew and its sister languages were not sacrosanct, as most contemporary Christians thought them to be.[92]

In other words, Gesenius was a reprobate in his approach to the Hebrew Bible. He did not view God as having been the author of the Hebrew scriptures. Naturally, that did not stop him from making a living in handling and vilifying the word of God. Riplinger adds, "All Hebrew grammars and lexicons merely echo his bias," and, "Gesenius' Hebrew Grammar begins by saying that, 'the Hebrew of the Old Testament' comes not from God, but from the pagan 'Canaanitish' people (p.2)."[93]

When we name the names of Gesenius, Kittel, Strong, Thayer, Robertson, Hodge, Lake, Brown, Driver, Briggs, and others, we are essentially listing the master roll of the authors of reference works that occupy the libraries of biblical scholars, academics and pastors. Among those men rests some of the

---

[92] "Definition of Gesenius, Wilhelm in the Free Online Encyclopedia." *Encyclopedia*. Web. 11 Dec. 2010. <http://encyclopedia2.thefreedictionary.com/Gesenius, Wilhelm>.

[93] Riplinger, G.A., *In Awe of Thy Word, Understanding the King James Bible,* (A.V. Publications, Ararat, VA, 24053, 2003) p. 516.

worst biblical theology imaginable. Besides Gesenius, another example is Joseph H. Thayer, mentioned above. A lexical writer, he was a Unitarian, and his publishers gave warning that some of his explanatory notes were compromised by his apostate theology.[94] Thayer is known for other gross errors in doctrine.[95] While there are biblically sound writers and editors of biblical reference materials, it is shocking to most to realize how much the foundation of what even Fundamentalists consider sound biblical scholarship, rests squarely upon the work of some of the worst apostates "Christianity" ever produced. As Riplinger stated above, the works by sound men in the faith are often highly plagiarized and only slightly re-typeset, the foundational work being based on the writings of some of the worst liberals, some of the most adversarial to the doctrines of inspiration and preservation, and these who were definitively unregenerate.

It is worthwhile to take a moment to say that it is undoubtedly true that reference works by men with whom one is not in 100% agreement doctrinally, may still be of good value. There is no just reason for advocating the destruction of reference works by anyone who was/is not devoted to the precepts of eternal security, dispensationalism, and the pre-tribulation Rapture. If one reads only those with whom one agrees in everything, he would have precious little reading material. The AV translators, for instance, would not have been in 100% agreement with you or me theologically, though it should be stated that they were our intimate brethren compared to what Gesenius and Thayer believed. So having established that there is a balance to such criticisms, let us see if we can find the crucial tipping point.

1) Lost men handling biblical material, linguistically or

---

[94] Cloud, David W., *The Modern Bible Version Hall of Shame,* (Way of Life Literature, Port Huron, MI 48061, 2005) p.122

[95] Ibid. p.123.

theologically, are still unregenerate and natural men, no matter how brilliant and well trained they are. The earnest contention for the faith was allotted to the body of Christ, not heathen men, scholars though they be. Handling holy things requires a sanctification of which the lost are bankrupt, and work for God needs desperately to be blessed of God. These men would have to be discerning men, and *the natural man receiveth not the things of the Spirit of God: for they are foolishness unto him: neither can he know them, because they are spiritually discerned* (1 Cor. 2:14). The unconverted are unequipped to make the discriminating judgments required of true biblical scholars or scriptural theologians.

2) Besides the necessity of the new birth, the foundations of understanding the things of God are based upon precept, and are sequential in nature. Just as it is necessary to grasp the principles of algebra before proceeding to trigonometry or calculus, so there is a certain sequence to the building of spiritual knowledge, understanding and discernment. Isaiah 28:13 words it this way: *But the word of the LORD was unto them precept upon precept, precept upon precept; line upon line, line upon line; here a little, and there a little.* 1 Corinthians 2:13 adds, *Which things also we speak, not in the words which man's wisdom teacheth, but which the Holy Ghost teacheth; comparing spiritual things with spiritual.* Notice that it is ***words*** which *the Holy Ghost teacheth*, and the method is by *comparing spiritual things with spiritual.* The things which are to be compared are those ***words!*** On what does an unregenerate man (or even a regenerate one) have to build, if he has rejected the inspiration of the Bible, the creation account in Genesis, the Deity of Christ, or the efficacy of the blood of God's own Son? How can anyone accept the viability and verity of these men's necessarily precise and distinctive judgments about minute and complicated matters when they have proven themselves untrustworthy in matters that even 10 year old school children who are saved and nourished up in the

word can grasp?

3) It seems that there is a difference between accepting, as an example, James Strong's work in his *Exhaustive Concordance of the Bible*, where he is merely giving account, detailing and referencing how often and in what places this word or that appears in the Bible. It is quite another thing to accept his judgment, or lack of it, with respect to his interpretation of Greek or Hebrew words in his dictionary. A lost man might be counted on to document how often a word appears and where. However, when a lost man's labors become interpretive, or where they are based in the necessity of grasping truly spiritual principles, that unregenerate man is unequipped for such labor. If that man does not even grasp that God's hand would be providentially involved in the very material with which he works; if he believes that God's hand was never involved in it; if he disdains the whole idea and intentionally works to overthrow such a concept, are we to expect that God would use him to buttress the foundations of our faith?

4) Having granted that one does not necessarily expect 100% agreement to one's doctrine among reference writers, a Christian should weigh carefully how much the foundations of "biblical scholarship" can be undermined by completely humanistic and profane philosophies before the structure collapses. Gesenius and Thayer did not merely part from the faith on assorted, though important, matters of doctrine. These are not men laboring in Greek and Hebrew manuscriptology and grammar, whose personal theologies are tainted by Calvinism, who have not embraced pre-millennialism, or who deny dispensational theology. We are speaking of men who reject and renounce the very elemental and fundamental building blocks of biblical faith: the inspiration, preservation and integrity of the word of God, the Deity of Christ, and the need of man for a Savior! They deny Christ and the Word of God, and yet they are the grandfathers and foundation layers for all

that our ministerial prospects receive in seminaries around the world. How do they, of all people, set the rules and standards for biblical scholarship?

An informed, cautious, and vigilant man, knowing the weaknesses and failures of these reprobate men's positions, may be able to wend his way carefully around the apostates' teachings, and conceivably learn *something* from them. At least that is how it could work hypothetically. But, what happens in the 10th, 20th or 30th generation of Bible students and scholars for whom the reprobates' falsehoods have become a virtually lost fact of history? What happens when the apostates' writings have become the standard and the foundation for their particular branch of "Christian" learning? What happens when the old deluded scholars' works have become the *definitive works* in their respective fields? Some of the works of these notoriously compromised infidels still form the very scholastic foundations of academia that *supposed* Bible defenders base their discipline upon.

Again, this is not an appeal to pastors or students to throw out their concordances, dictionaries and lexicons, but a reminder that the pastor or the student had better realize that it is the foundation of the words of God that standeth sure, not the foundations of *man's wisdom!* Man's scholarship, within the realm of biblical scholarship, at no time overthrows the Bible's potency or authority. A man's opinion, learned or not, is still a man's opinion and never approaches unto the word of God. A man's writings on the Bible, though festooned with the laurels of degrees and academic titles, are still only a sinner's corruptible opinion. The fact is that a Bible-believer can do altogether without men, and works of men, such as Gesenius, Thayer, Lake and Kittel. One cannot do without his Bible, but one can do wholly without those men and be only profited by their absence.

If it be the objection of some that God uses the minds and pens of men, the point proves to be true enough. God did indeed use men such as Erasmus, Luther, Wycliffe, Tyndale, and the AV translators. He used and blessed their work, scholarship and discipline. It should also be noted that Satan uses men as well. Satan uses men's minds and pens, their scholarship, and their sacrificial labors. The devil uses men just like Kittel, Gesenius, Aland, Metzger and Thayer – in fact he uses *those particular men!* How can one tell the difference?

> *To the law and to the testimony:* ***if they speak not according to this word, it is because there is no light in them.*** (Isa. 8:20)

> *Sanctify them through thy truth:* ***thy word is truth.*** *(John 17:17)*

> *For* ***the wisdom of this world is foolishness with God. For it is written, He taketh the wise in their own craftiness.*** (1 Cor. 3:19)

This essay is about how the word of God is acted upon by the combined and coordinated effects of the fallen nature of man and the insidious working of Satan.

The Spoils of Sophistry

In the section on **The Malevolent Master**, earlier in this chapter, the deceitful nature of Satan's work in man's heart is briefly but carefully documented. In the end of his appointed time here on the topside of the earth, he *deceiveth the whole world* (Rev. 12:9). A *murderer from the beginning, ...he is a liar, and the father of it* (John 8:44). He sought Eve's soul and apparently won brief control over it. Since that fateful day, every child born onto this earth, excluding Jesus Christ, was born a child of the devil (John 8:44).

It is utterly certain that on an individual basis, the greatest prize for Satan is the eternal soul of a man, and the old dragon has won a staggering number of that everlasting booty. The game Satan plays so well, however, is not a win all, lose all game. If a soul is won to the eternal and irrevocable embrace of Jesus Christ, it by no means assures that the devil then packs his wares and goes to trouble another. In fact, it means anything but that, for there is spoil yet to be won! Christians have come to view salvation more and more as something like the final chapter and ultimate goal. Granted, nothing ever could be more important than settling the destiny of the eternal soul, but once born again unto Christ, the fight is anything but over. Heaven may be home, and the soul may be God's, but the devil is still out to win what is next best.

2 Corinthians 4:4 gives an insight into what is second place, the silver medal, for the devil. It is not the gold, but it is still much prized. *(T)he god of this world hath* ***blinded the minds*** *of them which believe not, lest the light of the glorious gospel of Christ, who is the image of God, should shine unto them.* The context for 2 Corinthians 4:4 makes plain its application to the lost, however we shall learn soon enough that the mind and heart is a much sought after prize in the regenerate Christian as well.

To reiterate earlier points, 1 Timothy 2:14 makes plain that the devil ***deceived Eve***. In Matthew 4, he obviously tried to maneuver the Lord Jesus into precipitous action by his subtlety and cunning, trying, though without success, to deceive even Him. In 2 Corinthians 11:3, in the case of saved, redeemed and regenerated children of God, Paul's fear was that their ***minds should be corrupted from the simplicity that is in Christ.*** Paul's fear was not for our souls, but for our minds. Let the reader be certain, that the devil wants to insert himself into the processes of mind and heart whereby man thinks, reasons, feels, decides, discerns and comes to conclusions. As stated earlier, the devil uses man in the individual sense in an attempt to accomplish this purpose, and he uses man in the collective, as well. This collective is known as *the world.*

The Mind: A Treasure Second Only to the Soul

Obviously, the worst thing that a man can fritter away is his soul. *For what shall it profit a man, if he shall gain the whole world, and lose his own soul* (Mark 8:36)? It is also obvious that both the Lord and the devil have the most intense interest in the minds and hearts of men. Plainly, the Lord intended that the entirety of our hearts and minds be poured into loving and serving Him.

> *And thou shalt love the Lord thy God with* ***all thy heart****, and with all thy soul, and with* ***all thy mind****, and with all thy strength: this is the first commandment.* (Mark 12:30)

In the bad old days of being lost, Christians' minds were blinded according to 2 Corinthians 4:4. This truth is elaborated on in other passages. Before salvation *we all had our conversation in times past in the lusts of our flesh,* ***fulfilling the desires of the flesh and of the mind****; and were by nature the children of wrath,* even as others (Eph. 2:3). To this hour, the unregenerate Gentiles walk *in the* ***vanity of their mind*** (Eph. 4:17), **Israel's *minds were blinded*** (2 Cor. 3:14), and *to be* ***carnally minded*** *is death* (Rom 8:6). The maniac, once the devils were cast out of him, was found at *the feet of Jesus, clothed, and* ***in his right mind*** (Luke 8:35). Evidently, there was, and is, a tremendous spiritual conflict in the lives of the mortal, and that battle is for the mind. This makes sense considering that the devil can secure the soul by deceiving, deluding or merely distracting the mind and heart long enough. A decision for Jesus Christ, on the other hand, secures the soul forever in the body of Christ. The redeemed still face a profound conflict, because the new birth is merely the first step in the remainder of the mortal life of the Christian.

The born-again are given a great promise: *For God hath not given us the spirit of fear; but of power, and of love, and of a sound mind* (2 Tim. 1:7). It is, however, plain from the scriptures that follow, that the spirit of a *sound mind* given us, is both a perishable and renewable resource. It is something over which we are stewards. It is something that we are entrusted with, and we are to nurture it and invest in it.

The Purpose for a Christian's Mind

In this increasingly secular society, and as Christianity slides ever deeper in the lukewarm Laodicean swamp, Christians are more and more satisfied to camp and settle on the fact that the soul is saved. Israel did not stop on the eastern bank of the Red Sea and Paul did not recline in the dirt of the road to Damascus after his conversion, but today's Christians tend to view salvation as the crowning achievement of the Christian life. Salvation certainly is the singular most monumental moment spiritually in anyone's life. Nothing whatever exceeds the importance of that one profound instant of conversion, when old things pass away and all things become new. Notwithstanding all this, salvation is not the crowning achievement and it is certainly not the end of the road! *For we are his workmanship, created in Christ Jesus unto good works, which God hath before ordained that we should walk in them* (Eph. 2:10). *...(Y)e turned to God from idols to serve the living and true God* (1 Thes. 1:9).

The Lord did not save any who have yet a portion of their candles still to burn to be mere memorials of God's grace. He did not save us so that He could serve us. He did not send His Son to die and rise just so He would have cause for pouring out health, wealth and blessings on us for the balance of our mortal lives. There is a definitive purpose for each Christian, and without respect to relative health, wealth, youth or talent, we are all called to ***serve Him***. In order to serve Him, we have to be on the same page as He is. ***We cannot be of a different opinion or of a different mind***. How you and I think, how we process information and make judgments, what precepts and principles affect how we assess incoming information, and what sort of knowledge and wisdom animates us to action is of prime concern to the Almighty God in heaven who saved our souls. God did not just save your soul to take you to paradise. He saved you so you would, and could, think as He thinks. Now you can meditate and assess things in life and eternity in accord with the God of Hosts.

Let us be certain that this is a just conclusion:

- *And be not conformed to this world: but be ye transformed by the* ***renewing of your mind****, that ye may prove what is that good, and , and perfect, will of God.* (Rom. 12:2)

- *...that ye all speak the same thing, and that there be no divisions among you; but that ye be* ***perfectly joined together in the same mind and in the same judgment.*** (1 Cor. 1:10)

- ***Let this mind be in you****, which was also in Christ Jesus...* (Phil. 2:5)

- ***Be of the same mind*** *one toward another.* ***Mind not*** *high things...* (Rom. 12:16)

- *That ye put off concerning the former conversation the old man, which is corrupt according to the deceitful lusts; And* ***be renewed***

in the spirit of your mind; *And that ye put on the new man, which after God is created in righteousness and true holiness.*
(Eph. 4:22-24)

• *And the peace of God, which passeth all understanding,* ***shall keep your hearts and minds*** *through Christ Jesus.* (Phil. 4:7)

• *Young men likewise exhort to* ***be sober minded.*** (Tit. 2:6)

• *Wherefore gird up the* ***loins of your mind, be sober****...* (1 Pet. 1:13)

• *For* ***consider*** *him that endured such contradiction of sinners against himself, lest ye be* ***wearied and faint in your minds.***
(Heb. 12:3)

• *That ye be not soon* ***shaken in mind****, or be troubled, neither by spirit, nor by word, nor by letter as from us, as that the day of Christ is at hand.* (2 Thes. 2:2)

• *And seek not ye what ye shall eat, or what ye shall drink, neither be ye of* ***doubtful mind.***
(Luke 12:29)

• *...they received the word with all* ***readiness of mind****, and searched the scriptures daily...*
(Acts 17:11)

• *Serving the Lord with* ***all humility of mind****, and with many tears,* (Acts 20:19)

• *For to be* ***carnally minded is death****; but to be* ***spiritually minded is life and peace****.*
(Rom. 8:6)

• *This I say therefore, and testify in the Lord, that ye henceforth walk not as other Gentiles walk****, in the vanity of their mind****...* (Eph. 4:17)

• *Fulfil ye my joy, that* ***ye be likeminded****, having the same love, being of one accord,* ***of one mind****.*
(Phil. 2:2)

• *Nevertheless, whereto we have already attained, let us walk by the same rule,* ***let us mind the same thing****.* (Phil. 3:16)

It is relatively common knowledge among Christians that the Bible says that *we have the mind of Christ.* Many do not know where to actually *find* the passage in the scriptures, nor do they know its context, but they know it is there and they think they know what it means. The sad fact is that most people view the passage quite mystically. To be brief, they infer that having *the mind of Christ* basically means that at some juncture or another, or some point in time – whether momentarily in a critical second or for a longer spread of time – the mind of Christ exerts its presence and its potency over our own. It is not by any sequence of discipline or training that we attain access to the mind of Christ, but instead, it comes upon us and, for lack of a better word, *overwhelms* our own mind and its faulty judgments, ignorance or foolishness.

This supposed mystical and metaphysical imputation of Christ's mind into, or over, our own is convenient and desirable to the modern mega-church or Emerging Church "Christian." First, it justifies and rewards laziness and spiritual sloth among believers. With no particular precepts or principles for attaining the mind of the Lord, the "Christian" gets to sit by and await the enlightening moment to come, or for the more energetic, they may pursue any number of paths after their own willful and corrupt hearts by which they may hope that they shall attain the mind of the Blessed. Secondly, in the mystic lack of genuine pursuit of the Lord's mind, should wisdom or knowledge fail the expectant "Christian," or should the counsel or wisdom that "comes to mind" prove faulty, then that more or less leaves the Lord at fault for not supplying the poor seeker with the promised supply. This is a very convenient and valuable excuse for a Christianized victim to be able to fall back on in a pinch. By such a method, a modern 21st century child of God could feel just as cheated and just as victimized as Eve felt when the devil offered her the fruit! *And the serpent said unto the woman, Ye shall not surely die: **For God doth know** that in the day ye eat thereof, then your eyes shall be opened, and ye shall be as gods, knowing good and evil* (Gen. 3:4-5). Don't you see? According to this line of reasoning, God shortchanged you!

> *(A)nd there is no new thing under the sun.*
> (Eccl. 1:9)

Suffice to say this esoteric and uncertain impartation is not the method by which *we have the mind of Christ.* Notice the verse we refer to, 1 Corinthians 2:16, quoted in its context:

> *9 But as it is written, Eye hath not seen, nor ear heard, neither have entered **into the <u>heart</u> of man**, the things which God hath prepared for them that love him.*
> *10 But God hath **revealed them unto us by his Spirit**: for the Spirit searcheth **all things**, yea, the **deep things of God**.*
> *11 For what man **knoweth** the things of a man, save the spirit of man which is in him? even*

so the things of God ***knoweth no man****, but the Spirit of God.*
12 Now we have received, not the spirit of the world, but the spirit which is of God; that we might ***know*** *the* ***things that are freely given to us*** *of God.*
13 ***Which things also we speak, not in the words which man's wisdom teacheth, but which the Holy Ghost teacheth; comparing spiritual things with spiritual.***
14 But the natural man receiveth not ***the things of the Spirit of God:*** *for* ***they*** *are foolishness unto him: neither can he* ***know*** *them, because* ***they*** *are spiritually discerned.*
15 But he that is spiritual ***judgeth all things****, yet he himself is judged of no man.*
16 For ***who hath known the mind of the Lord****, that he may instruct him? But* ***we have the mind of Christ.*** (1 Cor. 2:9-16)

Ignoring the boldfaced portions just for a moment, please note that according to verses 9-12, a spiritual conversion is required to have access to the mind of Christ in verse 16. There is indeed a certain mystical quality to understanding the things of God in the respect that the Spirit of God is a necessary agent in helping our spirits and minds to grasp and apprehend God's things - *the deep things of God* (vs.10). Plainly, from verse 14, the natural and unregenerate man is not of the same nature as the Lord, and requires a regenerate and spiritual nature in order to be able to receive *the things of the Spirit of God* (vs.14).

Having acknowledged the spiritual, somewhat mystical, aspect of understanding the things of the Spirit, there is plainly a very practical and disciplined aspect that is necessary, as well. First, see in the underlined portions of the passage in verse 9 and verse 16, that these things are matters of the ***heart*** and ***mind.*** Secondly, the entirety of the boldfaced portions of the passage drives home the fact that the ***things*** of which we speak are the ***things*** of knowledge and wisdom. These are things taught and received, given and spoken; things to be compared and judged.

Having established *that*, follow now the parentheses inserted into the passage establishing the things to which the pronouns refer. Mind you, I am not changing the scripture, nor am I advocating insertion of words in a Bible text. I am expositing the text, while trying to make it as visually simple as possible.

> *12 Now we have received, not the spirit of the world, but the spirit which is of God; that we might know the things* ***(what things? Things God prepared; revealed things; deep things; given things – vss. 9-12)*** *that are freely given to us of God.*
> *13 Which things also we speak* ***(words are spoken!)****, not in the* ***words*** *which man's wisdom teacheth, but* ***(in the words)*** *which the Holy Ghost teacheth* ***(in words!)****; comparing spiritual things* ***(the words)*** *with spiritual* ***(the words).***
> *14 But the natural man receiveth not the things* ***(those words of vs. 13)*** *of the Spirit of God: for they* ***(the things; those words)*** *are foolishness unto him: neither can he know them* ***(the things; those words)****, because they* ***(the things; those words)*** *are spiritually discerned.*
> *15 But he that is spiritual judgeth all things, yet he himself is judged of no man.*
> *16 For who hath known the mind of the Lord, that he may instruct him?* ***But we have the mind of Christ.***

Simply put, the conclusion to be drawn from the passage with regard to the mind of Christ is not that the mind of Christ is some esoteric, metaphysical thing that might exert itself over our thoughts, imaginations and faulty judgments. The mind of Christ is, quite literally, the words which the *Holy Ghost teacheth.* It is not obscure thoughts or lessons. The mind of Christ ***is*** the words of God. The *mind of Christ* sits in your lap, contained in 66 books, written in the King's English! The more of the Bible you truly know, have digested and have stored away in your heart, the more of the *mind of Christ* you will have attained unto.

If there is doubt as to whether this is the correct meaning, notice what follows.

> *11 And the Israelitish woman's son blasphemed the name of the LORD, and cursed. And they brought him unto Moses: (and his mother's name was Shelomith, the daughter of Dibri, of the tribe of Dan:)*
> *12 And they put him in ward**, that the mind of the LORD might be shewed them.***
> *13 **And the LORD spake unto Moses, saying,***
> *14 Bring forth him that hath cursed without the camp; and let all that heard him lay their hands upon his head, and let all the congregation stone him.* (Lev. 24:11-14)

The *mind of the Lord* was *shewed them.* The *mind of the Lord* was what the Lord said unto Moses. The Bible, the word of God, *is the mind of the Lord*!

The purpose of the Christian's mind is that it may be conformed to the thoughts and mind of God. The Christian is to grow to think like the Lord. His goal should be to judge, discern, appreciate, meditate and think like Christ. This is verified in a verse most of us have tucked away in memory: *And be* ***not conformed to this world****: but be ye* ***transformed by the renewing of your mind****, that ye may prove what is that good, and acceptable, and perfect, will of God* (Rom. 12:2).

Satan has a similar but more insidious purpose. Satan wants you to think like him. He was successful in getting Eve to board his train of thought. 2 Corinthians 4:4 verifies that he has led a very successful brainwashing campaign indeed, for he *hath blinded the minds of them that believe not.* Certainly more success is yet to follow: *And the great dragon was cast out... the Devil, and Satan, which deceiveth the whole world* (Rev. 12:9).

In order to keep the lengthy essay at hand on focus, consider for a moment the Bible scholar. Presuming that the scholar is not merely a Christian in name only, God's plan for the scholar's mind is altogether consistent with His expectation for any other Christian. The scholar's mind is to be conformed to the mind of Jesus Christ, as is every other Christian's. Is that indeed the case with the main body of scholars? Why is it that all the questions, the gainsaying, the naysaying, and the oppositions to the plain meaning of the scriptures seem to trickle down to us "unlearned" peons from the nests of scholars and lofty seats of scholarship? Why is it that the scholars are not as plainspoken and direct in their faith and their thinking as Christ? When did Christ ever speak in roundabout sophistry with respect to the word of God? When did He ever cast aspersions or doubtful shadows upon the holy words which the disciples had in hand? Why do the scholars' speeches and writings abound in doublespeak? Why do they make profound and boisterous proclamations about the perfection and inerrancy of the Bible, and then just as quickly pronounce the Bible imperfect and errant? Why do the scholars seem to speak more after the fashion of Satan than after the fashion of the Savior?

The Blueprint of Blinded Minds

If the Lord has thus faithfully warned us of the malevolent campaign that is being led against our very minds and hearts, then it is evident that He will be just as faithful to reveal the plans, cogs and machinery of the warfare at hand. The depravity and corruption of human nature falls into categories and patterns of behavior and thought. Plainly, the Lord Himself is both organized and ordered in His great designs of creation, and once we know the *mind of the Lord* (see above), we also learn that His knowledge is attained *precept upon precept* and *line upon line* (Is. 28:10). Our God definitely had, and has, a plan. Isaiah 1:18 shows that the Lord is *reasonable*, and thus, there is a certain ordered sequence to how God does things. It only follows that there would be a certain order and pattern to how Satan accomplishes his ultimate goal of deceiving *the whole world* (Rev. 12:9).

The Various Schools of Sophistry

By all scriptural implications, it is not until the Great Tribulation that the Dragon more or less just shows up on the TV, unmasked and fully manifested, to lay all his cards on the table. That would not be too *subtle* (Gen. 3:1), but by the time the Antichrist is fully empowered as Satan incarnate, there will be no need for subtlety. Subtlety is the particular trait however, at this moment in time, that is still the name of the game for the devil, since Paul testifies that the threat in this hour remains *...as the serpent beguiled Eve through his subtilty* (2 Cor. 11:3). The serpent, then, must channel his deceit and delusions through other entities or institutions that mask and camouflage the actual exercise of spiritual murder and mind-bending.

These institutions among men are revealed in the scriptures and are highly spoken of and much esteemed by the world and a good proportion of "Christians." These institutions are the holy sanctums and fountainheads for the all-encompassing ***wisdom of this world***, which God hath *made foolish* (1 Cor. 1:20), *that come to nought* (1 Cor. 2:6), and that are *foolishness with God* (1 Cor. 3:19). The devil's great schools are found here:

> Col. 2:8
> *Beware lest any man spoil you through* ***philosophy*** *and vain deceit*[96]*, after* ***the tradition of men****, after* ***the rudiments of the world****, and not after Christ.*
>
> 1 Tim. 6:20
> *O Timothy, keep that which is committed to thy trust, avoiding profane and vain babblings, and oppositions of* ***science*** *falsely so called:*
>
> Acts 26:5
> *Which knew me from the beginning, if they would testify, that after the most straitest sect of our* ***religion*** *I lived a Pharisee.*

In this way, then, the schools of sophistry and deceit are Philosophy, Tradition, the Rudiments of the World, Science, and Religion.

Philosophy. Ever straight-from-the-shoulder, the Apostle Paul sounded an alarm to the Colossians to which the ancient and modern worlds should well have hearkened. They

---

[96] It may be justifiable to argue for the inclusion of ***vain deceit*** in the list, although in the author's mind this quality denotes a quest by the devil and the world to deceive for no other reason than just to deceive - to deceive for vanity's sake. As such, it may not be a particular discipline of deceit as much as it is to deceive in any way, for any reason. Eph.4:14 is a commentary on the trait. ***Vain deceit*** fits in, as well, with the ***vain babblings*** of 1 Tim.6:20, and for our purposes will not be included in the "Schools."

did not, and neither has the Christian population as a whole today. *Beware lest any man spoil you through* ***philosophy***...(Col. 2:8), he said. *Philosophy* has been an avenue by which the devil has exported to this world a spiritual drug that will kill most of the population of man. *Philosophy* is one of the principle conduits of the wisdom of this world by which the serpent *hath blinded the minds of them that believe not.*

In its Greek origins meaning *love (philo) of wisdom (sophy)*, there is utterly no question in history, or in the scriptures, which of the two types of wisdom mentioned in the scriptures that *Philosophy* falls under. The wisdom loved, is with absolute certainty, the wisdom of the world. Fueled by a fallen supernatural being feeding false information to fallen, mortal minds, urged and prodded on by an unregenerate nature *fulfilling the desires of the flesh and of the mind,* man's quest for illicit and unprofitable wisdom, having begun in the garden, has unceasingly continued to this very hour. *Philosophy* is a multifaceted conglomeration of knowledge and wisdom as man has conceptualized it. Every conceivable extremity of morality, persuasion and discipline is represented by the word. It encompasses all the formalized and officially recognized schools of thought, yet still includes that *philosophy* which informally exists in the alleys and streets, in the cultures of the naked savages, in the barnyards, rice paddies, steppes and Quonset huts. A lost man may or may not attain a formal doctorate in *philosophy*, but he will adopt one of the many variant forms of *philosophy* that infects the hearts and minds of man like some virulent, festering pandemic.

Philosophy is how the lost mind - intelligent or not, educated or not - deals with the moral questions, and the dilemmas of the heart and soul. Man is all too impressed with his own intellectual capacity for handling some of the great and ultimate questions in life. Man thinks that because he can address these matters, and manage in matador-type fashion to confront and yet avoid all in the same movement, that he in some way has successfully achieved something. From the *Epicureans* and the *Stoicks* mentioned in Acts 17:18, to Platonic *philosophy*, which attempted to hijack Christianity in its infancy, *philosophy* has been a plague to the spiritual and moral truth in men's lives. Socrates, Aristotle, Buddha, Rationalism, Materialism, Deism, Pantheism, Existentialism – all these and their unlisted variants have perverted the truth that the Creator revealed to His creatures (Rom. 8:20-21). In the end, *philosophy* – formalized or casual – is merely man's long, encyclopedic system of rhetorical, hypothetical and semantic detours around the spiritual truths of sin, depravity, judgment, retribution and redemption. *Philosophy* is excuse making and spiritual blindness clothed both in the ornate robes of intellectual verbiage and in the homespun, fireside pseudo-wisdom of ma and pa.

Little known is the fact that two of the great modern intellectual idols – Psychology and Psychiatry – are far more philosophical in nature than they are anything else. Even less appreciated is how completely entangled and enmeshed with vile philosophy biblical and textual scholarship has become. As related before, some of the heralded masters of scholarship, whose works and textbooks are the very foundation on which "Christian" education and the principles of scholarship are founded, have not only been lost and unregenerate spiritually, but have been almost wholly compromised intellectually by the wisdom found in the philosophical ramblings of satanic intellectual degeneracy. Their speech and their writings betray them. Their attitudes about the word of God do not even remotely resemble that of the prophets or of Christ Himself. *To the law and to the testimony: if they speak not according to this word, it is because there is no light in them* (Isa. 8:20).

Tradition. Somewhat akin to *philosophy*, *tradition* has proven itself a powerful adversary arrayed against God's truth. Paul designates by the Holy Spirit that it is one of the great spoilers: *Beware lest any man spoil you through philosophy and vain deceit, **after the tradition of men**...*(Col. 2:8). Jesus Christ provided a blunt and accusatory evaluation: *Full well ye reject the commandment of God, that ye may keep your own **tradition*** (Mk. 7:9), and then He adds, *Making the word of God of none effect through your **tradition**, which ye have delivered: and many such like things do ye* (Mk. 7:13). The *tradition of men* is man's longstanding and verifiable habit of doing something, or believing something, or embracing something, merely because "that's how we've always done it." Jeremiah commented on the characteristic using slightly different terminology, *For the customs of the people are vain...* (Jer. 10:3).

By no means are the educated exempt from the truth-defiling traits of *tradition*, but time and history have shown that where a formalized and deeply intellectual *philosophy* is unattainable by the common folk, all too often habits and customs have been generationally established which entrap the prey with bonds nigh unbreakable. Loyalties, precepts, habits, customs and beliefs are formed and rigidly upheld, for no other reason than to carry on a custom began by some distant, previous generation. In many regards, the much heralded and esteemed *Culture* so oft spoken of today, is really little more than *tradition*.

For many, the "truth of God" has more to do with the fact that for generations they have followed, without thinking, the same rote and unthinking customs, than with anything God ever said or established by example. For those ensnared by tradition, concise meanings of Bible words do not matter. Reason and logic do not matter. Whence we came, where we started, or how we progressed to here, often do not matter. All that matters is that there is a linkage to the past by which friends and family, and their friends and families before them, held to these customs and traditions. The great comfort lies in familiarity, not in a true foundation. The bonds of this source of spoilage (Col. 2:8) rest in the tranquility of knowing that others near to us, dear to us, whom we respect, and whom we want to respect us, believe and act upon all the same traditions.

This is animal-like behavior. One lemming or buffalo runs off the precipice, so a thousand or ten thousand others follow. One crazy steer bolts and a thousand cattle stampede. This synopsis is obviously a superficial scratch upon the vast body of material that spans all the cultures and subcultures of the world, traditions of social interaction, food, worship, marriage, family, etc. Notwithstanding this necessarily shallow and short appraisal, *tradition* is plainly a stupendous resource into which the serpent has tapped. He can entrap and ensnare entire peoples into habits of behavior and thought, if he can only prime the pump and get the tradition started. They will follow like sheep, and once a cultural momentum is attained, sinners very rarely pause to think twice about it. Men are lazy and they want to be with their own kind.

To focus on the matter at hand, biblical and textual scholars are not one iota less likely to fall for the subtle comforts and familiarity of *tradition* than any of the rest of mankind. Their education and academic discipline does not serve to better equip them against this failure of human nature. Many is the upright and conservative Bible scholar who loves the Lord, but nonetheless longs for the recognition of his fellow academics, and who is horrified at the prospect of diverting from an accepted and honored school of thought. To challenge or disparage the character or work of one of the gurus of his particular discipline is virtually unthinkable. To depart from the wisdom and works of Gesenius, Thayer or Alford – what might be the results? A career might actually be sacrificed by such action! One could wind up a scholastic outcast! One's fellows would write disparaging critiques of the dissenter. This could have tremendous implications for a professor's tenure, for one's pastorate, for one's *next* pastorate.

In the end, the question will not necessarily be, "Have you or has your favorite scholar sold out the entirety of our biblical heritage?" The question will be, "How many of the opinions of the scholar in question have been affected and altered by adhering to the wisdom of this world? How much has the devil corrupted such a scholar's opinions due to the fallen nature of the man, and Satan's subtly employed avenues of approach? Is the faith of the scholar truly a scriptural faith, or has he compromised parts of his discipline so that, in a measure, his opinion reflects that of the devil more than that of his Lord?"

Rudiments of the World. Another vast stream that floods the plain with the wisdom of the world is denominated by the Lord as *the rudiments of the world. Beware lest any man spoil you…* ***after the rudiments of the world*** (Col. 2:8). If there be any question about whether those rudiments are bad, Colossians 2:20 informs us that one of the accomplishments of Calvary was that in being both buried and risen with Christ, *…ye be dead with Christ* ***from the rudiments of the world!*** Webster defines *rudiment* as,

> *A first principle or element; that which is to be first learnt; as the rudiments of learning or science. Articulate sounds are the rudiments of language; letters or characters are the rudiments of written language; the primary rules of any art or science are its rudiments. Hence instruction in the rudiments of any art or science, constitutes*

the beginning of education in that art or science.[97]

The *rudiments*, principles, precepts or elemental rules of how the world works can destroy a man if that man adheres to them. Again, there is a kinship with *philosophy* and *tradition*, but this world has a set of rules just as God has elemental rules. God's basics include among many others, *thou shalt have no other gods before me, thou shalt not commit adultery, thou shalt not steal, thou shalt not bear false witness, and man shall not live by bread alone but by every word that proceedeth out of the mouth of God.*

The world basically has its own bible, imprinted upon the minds of the lost by the *god of this world*, assisted by a fallen nature, desperate to justify one's own self and actions. A sampling of these rudiments follows.

- *There are many paths to God.*
- *It is OK if you love him/her.*
- *If it is "natural," it cannot be bad.*
- *I was born this way.*
- *Follow your heart.*
- *What matters is that you are true to yourself.*
- *You've gotta make a living.*
- *Jesus came to show us how to live and die.*
- *If you do the best that you can, you will be all right.*
- *You've gotta do what feels right.*
- *Man wrote the Bible.*
- *Religion is personal and should be kept to one's self.*

---

[97] *Webster's 1828 Dictionary.* Christian Technologies, Inc. version 2 (Build 20040406), 2004.

- *It is all in how you interpret the Bible.*
- *God isn't in any kind of organized "religion."*
- *Peter was the first pope and the Catholic Church is THE church.*
- *It is a sin to kill a mockingbird.*
- *An axe-murderer cannot just repent, believe and get saved.*
- *A little bit doesn't hurt.*
- *I'll know when to quit.*
- *All sin is the same.*
- *No translation of the Bible can be perfect.*
- *All that matters is that you are happy.*
- *No harm, no foul.*
- *Jesus drank wine.*
- *Mohammed was a prophet.*
- *There is value in all religions.*
- *What really matters is that you are sincere.*
- *Everybody does it before they are married.*
- *There are other holy writings besides the Bible.*
- *You've gotta do what you've gotta do.*
- *All good people go to heaven.*

It is true that a true Christian's life should not be terribly affected by these things, and since a Christian is stated to be dead with Christ *from* these *rudiments* (Col. 2:20), it is plain that God considers him to be spiritually dead to them. If the Christian is fully engaged in serving God in his church, surrounded by God's people, Bible preaching, and fellowship with the Lord, it is true that the effects of these things in his life should be minimized. Nevertheless, we all still abide in this *present evil world* (Gal. 1:4), so these things are part of the darkness that our light must continually drive back. The real danger is that in being delivered from these things, for one reason or another, men often find themselves yearning for them, nonetheless.

> *Howbeit then, when ye knew not God, ye did service unto them which by nature are no gods. But now, after that ye have known God, or rather are known of God, how turn ye again to the* ***weak and beggarly elements****, whereunto ye desire again to be in bondage?*
>
> (Gal. 4:8-9)

Sometimes God's own people find themselves back in the world, living by the same rules, *elements* and *rudiments* as they did in the old life. For some reason, parts of the incomplete list previously given continue to appeal to man's fallen nature. The term *profane* in the Bible does not necessarily denote "dirty" as much as it denotes "secular," "common" or "worldly." With that in mind notice,

> *If thou put the brethren in remembrance of these things, thou shalt be a good minister of Jesus Christ, nourished up in the words of faith and of good doctrine, whereunto thou hast attained. But refuse* ***profane and old wives' fables,*** *and exercise thyself rather unto godliness.*
>
> (1 Tim. 4:6-7)

A Christian should be careful lest his mind return to the old secular and *profane* things from the old life. Notice that we all have to fend off and parry *fables*. These *fables* are *rudiments* and *elements* that some people attempt to frame and build a life upon, but they are falsehood and lies. Note too, in verse 6, that these things are the opposite of godliness, and thus opposite to God. This is driven home yet once again in 2 Timothy 4:3-4:

> *For the time will come when they will not endure sound doctrine; but after their own lusts shall they heap to themselves teachers, having itching ears; And they shall turn away their ears from*

the truth, and ***shall be turned unto fables.***

The fables are the opposite of *sound doctrine* (vs.3), and the ears have to be turned away *from the truth* (vs.4) of the Bible and good doctrine in order to *be turned unto fables* (vs.4). This marks a return to the *rudiments of the world.*

To repeat, a Bible scholar is no more awarded immunity against this natural tendency toward degradation than any of the rest of humanity. If a Bible scholar allows his faith, his Bible beliefs, Bible reading and fellowship with the Lord to deteriorate, he will be altogether as susceptible to this regression as any other common sinner. This is true even though his livelihood is earned by trafficking in "biblical" things. The Lord pointed out this very thing through Jeremiah in the days of Israel's apostasy: *For both prophet and priest are* ***profane****; yea, in my house have I found their wickedness* (Jer. 23:11).

Has the scholar that casts aspersions on the inerrancy and purity of the Bible a Christian holds in his lap, been re-infected with some of the old "fundamentals" from the unregenerate life? Is his mind truly sanctified unto the Lord's precepts, or has he given some of the ground dearly won at Calvary back to the devil? *Beware of false prophets, which come to you in sheep's clothing, but inwardly they are ravening wolves.* ***Ye shall know them by their fruits****. Do men gather grapes of thorns, or figs of thistles?* (Matt. 7:15-16).

Science. Ah, yes, *Science*: the all-pervading idol of our day. All are expected to swoon before it, bow and pay homage. Let every man scramble and scuttle about to make sure that all that he believes and knows can be verified by and aligned with *science*! *Science*, which says that all order came from a disorderly explosion. *Science*, which dictates that all life and all men came from inanimate non-life. All hail *science.* Are the glaciers advancing or are they melting? Is the earth cooling or warming? It does not matter, for *science* will change its position on these matters every 7-10 years, at the most. Is coffee health food, or is it poison? It does not matter – the scientific evidence will lead to different conclusions next week.

God bless the apostle Paul, who relieved Bible believing Christians of the shackles of a great deal of nonsense by the following admonition: *O Timothy, keep that which is committed to thy trust, avoiding profane and vain babblings, and* ***oppositions of science falsely so called*** (1 Tim. 6:20).

These statements require some qualifications. Certainly, there is a legitimate *science* which explores and studies God's creation and uses the acquired knowledge in a way that benefits man and glorifies God. Physical and chemical laws are studied, quantified, understood, and then applied to useful purposes. Frictional coefficients, thermodynamics, laws of combustion and the chemical makeup of substances have obvious profitable and godly applications. Genuine principles discovered in biology, astronomy and mathematics are not the targets of 1Timothy 6:20. Regardless of the extraordinary uses and encyclopedic amount of knowledge uncovered by true *science*, there is still yet an intermingled strain of *science* that is one of the great bastions by which the dragon hornswoggles the entire world. Grasping the precepts of combustion, condensation and molecular bonds, which God set in place, is one thing. Perverting the processes of inquiry and commandeering data and conclusions to "prove" the monstrosity known as Evolution, or to justify Sodomy as a natural affection, is quite something else. During the thousand years of the Dark Ages, the devil, with the Pope's assistance, held men in the bondage of ignorance by withholding knowledge from them. Nowadays, men are just as ignorant as Dark Age men, bound just the same, but this time held in the shackles of false knowledge: *science falsely so called.*

In the world's eyes, the ultimate credibility for anything in this life in these latter days is that it should be *scientifically* credible. This is held as truth in spite of the blunt warning of the Lord through Paul, and in spite of failings and exploitations that rival anything that the worst of the cult religions ever set forward. "Scientists" have foisted upon the whole world the theory of *Evolution.* "Scientists" have ranted about global warming, experimented on helpless Jews by the thousands in Nazi concentration camps, and subjected 3,500 of the mentally sick to trans-orbital lobotomies under the madman, Walter Freeman (1895-1972)[98]. In the name of Science, sexual perversion, drunkenness and addiction have all been excused from categorization as *Sin* by calling them "genetic" maladies. "Scientists" have now drugged entire generations of people who instead needed Jesus Christ, a boost of character, and a kick in the backside. What they received instead was addiction to psych-medications. "Science" claims to be able to look backward 300 million years to tell us with accuracy what actually happened then. *Science falsely so called* has become very much like statistics – one can make it say pretty much what one wants. Countless millions of people have been deluded out of their eternal souls because *science* has misinformed and misdirected them. It has led them down fruitless and perverse paths. It, in large part, denies faith, sin, eternity and God, for none of those fit in a test tube. Of course, evolution does not fit in the test tubes either, but the key is that the *god of this world* (2 Cor. 4:4) is directing a great many of the fields of *science* as well as the other schools of deception.

Psychology and Psychiatry have lobbied and pandered for years to be blessed with the honor of being called *sciences.* They are not *sciences* so much as they are *philosophies* and

---

[98] "Walter Freeman." *Wikipedia, the Free Encyclopedia.* Web. 11 Dec. 2010. <http://en.wikipedia.org/wiki/Walter_Freeman>.

even *witchcraft*, but they have succeeded in their quest, and they are now more or less officially, *Science*. A simple Google search will reveal that witches consider their craft a *science*, as do astrologers, necromancers and practitioners of the paranormal.

That same Google search will reveal that the biblical translators and textual critics are nearly desperate to have their disciplines recognized as *science*. They salivate to be identified with "scientists." Understanding that in these areas, there is a quest for knowledge and a form of inquiry that requires a scientific approach, it is not to be forgotten that in every area of man's knowledge, *the god of this world* hath inserted both himself and his nefarious and perverse strain of knowledge and *science*. *Science* is now the authority by which man justifies every abomination, and Bible correctors desperately and acutely long to be perceived as objective scientists given no choice but to defile the words of the living God. After all, they are "just doing their jobs." They want the cover and the protection that *science* provides. If God's people knew that these "scholars" are oftentimes apostates in part, or wholly so, and that their sources and teachers are indeed apostate, then there is little chance that their work would be honored. But, if they are presented and perceived as hard laboring, objective-minded *scientists*, "well-trained and dealing with absolutes in the science of textual criticism and biblical translation," the people of God are more likely to be intimidated by their credentials and reputations and leave well enough alone.

Brethren, we would not consider taking algebra from a teacher who never learned to add, subtract or do long division. There is utterly no excuse for the body of Jesus Christ to accept the academic authority of men who merchandise in the *faith which was once delivered* (Jude 3) to *US*. Especially when these so called academics often do not believe the simplest, most rudimentary and most necessary precepts of the scriptures: the godhead, the Deity of Christ, the blood atonement, the historicity of creation, the narrative accounts of the Bible, or the preservation of the Bible.

Religion. Paul's testimony about his pre-conversion institution is forthright. *Which knew me from the beginning, if they would testify, that after the most straitest sect of our* ***religion*** *I lived a Pharisee* (Acts 26:5). By his own testimony, Paul was as rigorous a Pharisee as he could be, but he was still lost. He elaborates in the details a bit more in Galatians 1, and the reader should notice from the following that Paul was a rising star.

> *For ye have heard of my conversation in time past in the Jews'* ***religion****, how that* ***beyond measure I persecuted the church of God, and wasted it:*** *And profited in the Jews'* ***religion above many my equals*** *in mine own nation, being* ***more exceedingly zealous*** *of the traditions of my fathers.* (Gal. 1:13-14)

> *Though I might also have confidence in the flesh. If any other man thinketh that he hath whereof he might trust in the flesh, I more: Circumcised the eighth day, of the stock of Israel, of the tribe of Benjamin, an Hebrew of the Hebrews; as touching the law, a Pharisee; Concerning zeal, persecuting the church;* ***touching the righteousness which is in the law, blameless. But what things were gain to me, those I counted loss for Christ.*** *Yea doubtless, and I count all things but loss for the excellency of the knowledge of Christ Jesus my Lord: for whom I have suffered the loss of all things, and do count them but dung, that I may win Christ,*
> (Phil. 3:4-8)

Paul excelled in the discipline and zealousness of his religion, but he was a lost, hell-bound sinner. Paul was a rising star within the ranks, but his ***mind and heart*** were completely blinded to the truth of Christ and the gospel – that is, the word of God – until after his salvation in Acts 9.

It is often overlooked that man is by nature a spiritual creature. *God is a spirit* (Jn. 4:24), and though man by sin fell from the honor of being made *in the image of God* (Gen. 1:27), natural man, born after the flesh still carries with him the innate and natural conscience of his spiritual being. This is one of the profound weaknesses of the character of man which Satan so easily exploits. Man, by nature, is a religious creature. He is drawn to "spiritual" things. The devil has worked to make certain through the years that there are a great variety of appealing choices of "religion" from which man may choose. There is a religion to suit every taste and fetish of corrupt man. What God ordained for salvation and worship is not a brand of religion which "tickles the fancy" of man's corrupt nature. God's way is Truth! *I the LORD speak righteousness, I declare things that are right* (Isa. 45:19). Satan has made absolutely certain that there is a variety of religious belief and fervor which appeals to the debauched fancy of the corrupt nature of every man. In this way, the truth of God is often rejected in favor of tasty religious morsels that appeal to man's prejudices and self-righteousness, and do not so crimp his style.

Though many make much ado about rejecting religion, it remains a rather humorous, though tragic, fact that often they who so boisterously reject "religion" proper, nevertheless remain zealously religious. Where men grow weary of what they consider orthodox religion, such as Catholicism or Protestantism, they nevertheless oft fall prey to Eastern Mysticism or New Age nonsense. Naturally, Muslims are profoundly "religious," but then so are Buddhists and Hindus. Should a man see through some of the fables of the above mentioned, he often still falls subject to one of the great religions of our time: Evolution. All evolutionists grasp after and pursue a faith that is much more fleeting and despairing than anything Christianity has to offer. Atheists often are brash and pugnacious. In their rejection of Christianity, they fill the void from whence they booted out God, with a most ardent and religious zealotry trumpeting that there is no God. This becomes their religion! Environmentalism, Animal Rights Activism, and Secular Humanism are all movements as equally religious and spiritual as that of the more orthodox branches.

Religion is most often a combination of Philosophy, the traditions of men and the rudiments of the world - usually with a little *science falsely so called* thrown in for good measure. The true earmark of religion is that it has no real higher authority than the four aforementioned schools of deceit. Though religion is likely to give the Bible a salute once in awhile to preserve the appearance of something high, noble and godly, religion has very little to do with any kind of consistent adherence to the scriptures. It is the pursuit of man's religious nature after spiritual things, but not in any way after the statutes of the Bible.

Again, the truth of these matters as revealed from the scriptures catches up to our particular focus group: biblical and textual scholars. These people reside in blatantly "religious" places: Chairs, halls and schools of theology, departments of manuscriptology, and various other places of spiritual entitlement. They accept as authoritative certain philosophies, rudiments, traditions and scientific "findings" that are not scripturally verifiable, and are often in distinct contradiction to what the Bible does actually say. Theologically, many of these have proven themselves to be errant children with the Bible that they do hold, yet all are expected to yield to their expertise in correcting the very authority which they could not decipher correctly to begin with.

Whence do these men and women draw their errant ideas? Who planted those thoughts and conclusions? When they offer counsel to correct the Bible, one must ask, *whose spirit came from* them (Job 26:4)? These men and women of considerable academic renown are no better fortified against the wiles of Satan than any of the rest of Christianity. Indeed, if their studies and "vast learning" have endued them with the hardly concealable haughty pride of scholastic condescension, they are not fortified *at all* against being taken and ensnared by the devil! *Not a novice, lest being lifted up with pride he fall into the condemnation of the devil* (1 Tim. 3:6).

Philosophy, the Traditions of men, the Rudiments of the world, Science and Religion – these are the subtle and powerful schools by which Satan will accomplish his assault upon the minds of men, the lost and the saved, both scholar and common man alike.

How Blinded Minds Work

What follows is documentation from the scriptures on the function of the minds of men which *the god of this world* has successfully blinded. It is rather an amazement that a Book that says as much as the Bible does about the minds of men, could be so blithely ignored by all. Christians today are almost rabid in their pursuits of the psychobabble that so permeates modern "Christendom," yet the Bible, which authoritatively and copiously addresses the mind and heart of man, lies mostly unopened amidst the rubble of their lives.

In two verses previously referred to at some length, note again the boldfaced words, and the concepts that they communicate.

Col. 2:8
Beware lest any man ***spoil*** *you through philosophy and vain deceit, after the tradition of men, after the rudiments of the world, and not after Christ.*

2 Cor. 11:3
But I fear, lest by any means, as the serpent beguiled Eve through his subtilty, so your ***minds should be corrupted*** *from the simplicity that is in Christ.*

In Colossians 2:8, notice that the danger of philosophy, tradition, and the rudiments of the world, is that they can and do ***spoil*** a Christian. It does not take a seminary theologian to be able to see that it is the Christian's mind and heart that would be ***spoiled***. Indeed, if these postulations are correct, the seminary theologian would be likely to overlook the point entirely, for he long ago discarded any reservations he once might have had about the philosophy and traditions that he serves.

In 2 Corinthians11:3, Paul is very specific in saying that it is the Corinthians' ***minds*** that are at stake, and the categorization of damage would be that the ***minds should be corrupted***.

Corruption. With particular attention to *corruption,* notice a survey of what the Bible says about the matter.

The Corruption	***The Cause***
2 Cor. 11:3 – *minds... corrupted*	*beguiled* by the serpent
1 Tim. 6:5 - *corrupt minds*	not consenting to words of Christ (vs.3)

2 Tim. 3:8 - *corrupt minds*	*resist the truth; reprobate*
Jude 1:10 - *they corrupt themselves*	*things... they know not... know naturally*
1 Cor. 15:33 - *corrupt good manners*	*evil communications.*
Eph. 4:22 - *old man corrupt*	*deceitful lusts;*
Matt. 7:17 - *corrupt tree... evil fruit.*	What false prophets think and say (vs.15)
Ps. 14:1 - *They are corrupt*	What *(t)he fool hath said in his heart.*
Ps. 38:5 – *wounds... corrupt*	*because of my foolishness.*
Rev. 19:2 - *corrupt the earth*	*great whore... fornication.*

A word about Revelation 19:2: it is important to recognize the Great Whore as a religious cult called Roman Catholicism. Avoiding any argumentation on that point, it should be plain that the fornication spoken of has to be other than the carnal variety. The only way the "spiritual" variety of fornication could be achieved, would be by the religious cult compromising the minds and hearts of her subjects to the extent that they concede to her way of thinking, her religious regimentation and principles. Thus, the *corruption* spoken of is the corporate corruption of kings and peoples

Having seen the scriptural testimony and evidence for *corrupt minds*, consider for just a moment the concept of personally possessing and employing a ***corrupt*** *mind.* The devil, *the anointed cherub that covereth* in Ezekiel 28:14, is said to have *corrupted thy wisdom* in Ezekiel 28:17. That is, in falling from his earlier exalted position, the devil corrupted his wisdom. In other words, the information, understanding and usage of that over which his mind labored, somehow became pernicious, perverse and abased. It was *corrupted.* In the same fashion, we are often forewarned of the degenerate forms of knowledge and wisdom that continually present themselves to us in this life. Presumably, the acceptance of enough of the debauched, degenerate and corrupt wisdom will literally *corrupt* the mind.

It does not seem too great a leap to conclude that a *corrupt mind* would not function properly. Thought processes, judgments, discernments and conclusions would be affected and compromised. Certainly, affections and passions would follow suit, and the processes of logic and reason of such a person would be severely compromised.

Defilement. Another concept akin to corruption of the mind is found in Titus 1:15.

> Unto the pure all things are pure: but unto them that are ***defiled*** and unbelieving is nothing pure; but even their ***mind and conscience is defiled.***

Certainly one can see both mind and conscience can not only be hardened, but that both can be defiled. In these cases, there is no choice but to conclude that the makeup of such a mind is grossly compromised. When the integrity of a boat is "compromised" enough, it will no longer float. If the integrity of the mind and conscience is ***defiled***, what might that mean for its function and capabilities? In 1 Timothy 4:2, the conscience is *seared*, and thus presumably, malfunctions or is dysfunctional.

With respect to defilement and the mind, note that the

Lord Jesus straitly clarified in Matthew 15:18-19, that the *defilement* of man proceeds from *the heart.* As verse 19 distinctly mentions *evil thoughts,* it is clear that the mind of man is included in this concept.

> *But those things which proceed out of the mouth come* ***forth from the heart****; and they* ***defile the man****. For* ***out of the heart*** *proceed* ***evil thoughts,*** *murders, adulteries, fornications, thefts, false witness, blasphemies:*

In Hebrews 12:15, note again that defilement originates in the heart and mind, since that is where *bitterness* springs.

> *Looking diligently lest any man fail of the grace of God; lest any* ***root of bitterness springing up*** *trouble you, and thereby* ***many be defiled****;*

It must be pointed out again for emphasis, that if these traits are of such paramount importance in these last days, it is inevitable but that many indeed would be corrupted and defiled in heart and mind at this very time. Where might one find these *corrupt* and *defiled minds* to be employed at this moment? One can certainly see that they are involved in many carnally and spiritually perverse mischiefs in our day, but would those corrupt and defiled minds also be found in exercising their intellects, judgments and reasoning within areas of theology, biblical scholarship, research, textual criticism and translation?

Reprobate. We must not forget the terrible sequence that the Lord revealed in Romans, chapter 1, regarding the minds of men.

> *21 Because that, when they knew God, they glorified him not as God, neither were thankful; but became* ***vain in their imaginations****, and their*

foolish heart was darkened.
22 *Professing themselves* ***to be wise****, they became fools,*
23 *And changed the glory of the uncorruptible God into an image made like to corruptible man, and to birds, and fourfooted beasts, and creeping things.*
24 ***Wherefore God also gave them up to uncleanness*** *through* ***the lusts of their own hearts****, to dishonour their own bodies between themselves:*
25 *Who* ***changed the truth of God into a lie****, and* ***worshipped and served*** *the creature more than the Creator, who is blessed for ever. Amen.*
26 ***For this cause God gave them up unto vile affections****: for even their women did change the natural use into that which is against nature:*
27 *And likewise also the men, leaving the natural use of the woman,* ***burned in their lust*** *one toward another; men with men working that which is unseemly, and receiving in themselves that recompence of their error which was meet.*
28 *And even as they* ***did not like to retain God in their knowledge****,* ***God gave them over to a reprobate mind****, to do those things which are not convenient;* (Rom. 1:21-28)

There are profound depths of truth and revelation in the passage that must be foregone in order to remain on point. However, do please note that there are three stages in which God relinquishes certain "ground" to the sinner, and presumably, Satan.

1) *God also gave them up to uncleanness* (24)
2) *God gave them up unto vile affections* (26)
3) *God gave them over to a reprobate mind* (28)

Notice at each stage, the interaction with mind and heart:

1) *vain in their imaginations* (21)
2) foolish heart was darkened (21)
3) Professing themselves to be wise (22)
4) *through the lusts of their own hearts* (24)
5) changed the truth of God into a lie (25)
6) *worshipped and served* (25)
7) *burned in their lust* (27)
8) did not like to retain God in their knowledge (28)

How might a *reprobate mind* function? It would not only be influenced by the homosexual passions, but it would also be inclined to think and reason in an unholy and unsanctified manner.

Delusion. Another terrible truth God reveals to us about the workings of the mind of man, and the potential disaster that awaits the unapprised and careless, revolves around the idea of *delusion.* The context of 2 Thessalonians 2:11-12, is manifestly the revelation of the Antichrist in the Great Tribulation, so in direct prophecy, it has little to do with the body of Christ directly. It does, however, tell us a great deal about the workings of the human mind and its susceptibilities.

> *And for this cause God shall send them* ***strong delusion****, that they should* ***believe a lie****: That they all might be damned* ***who believed not the truth, but had pleasure in unrighteousness.***

Note once again the ominous connection between the dysfunction of heart and mind with a distant and adversarial relationship with ***the truth***. Webster provides us a dictionary definition which coincides with the scriptures' testimony:

> *1. The act of deluding; deception;* ***a misleading of the mind….***

2. ***Error or mistake proceeding from false views.***[99]

Isaiah 66:3-4 provides us with further witness regarding how a man comes to a deluded state of mind. In the context of idolatry and God's judgment upon the idolaters, the verses read *Yea, they have chosen their own ways, and their soul delighteth in their abominations. I also will choose* ***their delusions****, and will bring their fears upon them...*

It is likely at this point that some readers are greatly troubled by the testimony above, and the idea that God in some way is responsible for some of the deception and delusion. It must be added that God will only walk so far beside an unreasonable and hard man. A method that is certain to assure a person's eventual deception is to ignore on a regular basis the precepts and statutes of truth found in the word of God. Notice:

> *26 I also will laugh at your calamity; I will mock when your fear cometh;*
> *27 When your fear cometh as desolation, and your destruction cometh as a whirlwind; when distress and anguish cometh upon you.*
> *28 Then shall they call upon me, but I will not answer; they shall seek me early, but they shall not find me:*
> *29* ***For that they hated knowledge****, and* ***did not choose the fear of the LORD:***
> *30 They would* ***none of my counsel****: they* ***despised all my reproof.***
> *31 Therefore shall they* ***eat of the fruit of their own way, and be filled with their own devices.*** (Prov. 1:26-31)

---

99 *Webster's 1828 Dictionary*. Christian Technologies, Inc. version 2 (Build 20040406), 2004.

Consider this hypothetical picture for the purpose of focus. A theologian - a Bible scholar - has been taught, and has adopted a good deal of false doctrine in various areas, and to these doctrines he resolutely clings. He has either been resistant, negligent, or uncaring enough to change his position and he refuses to stand corrected. Further, he has been taught the various precepts of his academic specialty either by or from the works of unregenerate men who stand or stood quite opposed to much of what the Bible testifies in the scriptures. The scholar has been exposed to, and has proven to be scholastically invested in, some of those unfaithful principles. Why should we in any way trust that he is able to point us to the truth of the scriptures? Why would we trust that he has the authoritative word on interpretation, translation or meaning? Why does anyone pay him to train future pastors and missionaries? If he has been "misled" and "proceeds from false views," that means he is *deluded,* and has no corner whatever upon the truth. It may also mean that God had a hand in *deluding* him, and is using him to *delude* others who have no real love for the Bible or the words of God.

Brutish and Confounded. Another word used to describe the state of ungodly men's minds is the word *brutish.* Obviously, it is not a very cherished description by those who think their great exercises of religious and secular learning have placed them well outside a portraiture insinuating something base and beastly, not to mention untaught and stupid.[100]

Notice that Jeremiah includes certain pastors among the *brutish, For the pastors are become* ***brutish****, and have not sought the LORD: therefore they shall not prosper, and all their flocks shall be scattered* (Jer. 10:21). The accompanying traits

[100] *Webster's 1828 Dictionary.* Christian Technologies, Inc. version 2 (Build 20040406), 2004.

of this diagnosis revolve around these men not seeking God and their flocks being scattered. As for seeking God, we are told by Isaiah in most emphatic terms what that involves:

> *6 Seek ye the LORD while he may be found, call ye upon him while he is near:*
> *7 Let the wicked* ***forsake his way****, and* ***the unrighteous man his thoughts****: and let him return unto the LORD, and he will have mercy upon him; and to our God, for he will abundantly pardon.*
> *8* ***For my thoughts are not your thoughts, neither are your ways my ways, saith the LORD.***
> *9 For as the heavens are higher than the earth, so are my ways higher than your ways, and* ***my thoughts than your thoughts.***
> *10 For as the rain cometh down, and the snow from heaven, and returneth not thither, but watereth the earth, and maketh it bring forth and bud, that it may give seed to the sower, and bread to the eater:*
> *11* ***So shall my word be*** *that goeth forth out of my mouth: it shall not return unto me void, but it shall accomplish that which I please, and it shall prosper in the thing whereto I sent it.*
>
> (Isa. 55:6-11)

Seeking God involves forsaking man's way (*the traditions of men, the rudiments of the world, philosophy,* and *science* falsely-called) and man's own thoughts. Verse 11 reveals where one would find God's thoughts. Brother, a man not exercising himself in God's words is asking for mental trouble!

Backtracking to the issue of brutishness, notice that Jeremiah has yet more to add, *Every man is* ***brutish in his knowledge****: every founder is* ***confounded*** *by the graven image: for his molten image is falsehood, and there is no breath in them* (Jer. 10:14). It must be noted that a man who pursues *brutish knowledge*, whether it be blatant idolatry or otherwise, must face the risk of being ***confounded***. The idea of being ***confounded*** is quite a concept. May God help us never forget one of God's least appreciated purposes for man in this mortal domain: *But God hath chosen the* ***foolish things*** *of the world* ***to confound the wise****; and God hath chosen the* ***weak things*** *of the world* ***to confound the things which are mighty*** (1 Cor. 1:27). A man *confounded*, confused and blind in things relating to wisdom and power is *confounded* due to his source of knowledge, his brutish relationship with God, and his lack of esteem for the thoughts and words of God.

A *brutish man* has faulty knowledge and is misaligned with the thoughts and works of God. *O LORD, how great are* ***thy works****! and* ***thy thoughts*** *are very deep. A* ***brutish man knoweth not; neither doth a fool understand this*** (Ps. 92:5-6). Nor does he much care to be exposed: *Whoso loveth instruction loveth knowledge: but he that hateth reproof is brutish* (Prov. 12:1). There are those who are habitually resistant to reproof, seem to have lost the vision of the magnitude and glory of God's works, and have a dismissive or disdainful attitude about God's thoughts represented in words. Such men may only be said to be ***brutish men***.

Do you know someone whose "mastery" and "calling" is in the ministry or biblically related academics whose spirit matches the same spirit as the brutish man? Is he a sound conduit for the very words of God? Is he truly a faithful *ambassador for Christ* (2 Cor. 5:20)? Pastor, is he the man to whom you can safely entrust the education of your ministerial candidate? When he condescendingly disparages the Old Book and the people who are merely standing fast on the plain promises provided, should we just board his ship, forsaking our own?

Blindness. It would be remiss to leave undocumented what the Lord says regarding the blindness that occurs to the hearts and minds of men. Even though this chapter proves to be less than brief, please consider that we are still leaving vast expanses of the subject matter at hand unexplored, and many avenues that branch from this theme are bypassed for no other reason than brevity.

As has been so often repeated in this work, the piercing serpent (Is. 27:1) has an express interest and affect upon the minds of mankind. *In whom the god of this world hath **blinded the minds** of them which believe not, lest the light of the glorious gospel of Christ, who is the image of God, should shine unto them* (2 Cor. 4:4). In Revelation 12:9, he *deceiveth the whole world.* As this portion of this study relates to the compromised function and reliability of minds insinuated by the knowledge and wisdom of this world, let us allow the scriptures to paint a true picture.

The Jews suffered blinded minds in the reading of the Law and, indeed, still do; *But their **minds were blinded**: for until this day remaineth the same vail untaken away in the reading of the old testament; which vail is done away in Christ* (2 Cor. 3:14). In Ephesians 4:18, we learn that such is what the Gentiles in general still do suffer. *Having the **understanding darkened**, being alienated from the life of God through the **ignorance** that is in them, because of the **blindness of their heart**.*

A Christian should be careful to grow and progress in the traits and attributes of Christian maturity. Failing to do this can lead to *blindness*. *For if these things be in you, and abound, they make you that ye shall neither be barren nor unfruitful in the* ***knowledge*** *of our Lord Jesus Christ. But he that lacketh these things* ***is blind****, and* ***cannot see*** *afar off, and hath forgotten that he was purged from his old sins* (2 Pet. 1:8-9). Further, he should watch lest his passions get the better of him: *But he that hateth his brother is* ***in darkness****, and* ***walketh in darkness****, and* ***knoweth not*** *whither he goeth, because that* ***darkness hath blinded his eyes****.* (I Jn. 2:11)

With eyes, heart and mind *blinded* and *darkened*, what might be the state of such a one's thoughts and judgments pertaining to family, friends and spiritual matters? In Matthew 13:15, the people are unable to see or understand. *For this people's heart is waxed gross, and their ears are dull of hearing, and their* ***eyes they have closed****; lest at any time they should* ***see with their eyes****, and hear with their ears, and* ***should understand with their heart****, and should be converted, and I should heal them.* They cannot understand, but then, **they do not want to**! Within a context of idolatry, the Lord further testifies of the following: *They have* ***not known nor understood****: for* ***he hath shut their eyes, that they cannot see; and their hearts, that they cannot understand*** (Isa. 44:18). The defining sentiment of the Laodicean church age does not reflect the reality: *Because thou sayest, I am rich, and increased with goods, and have need of nothing; and* ***knowest not*** *that thou art wretched, and miserable, and poor,* ***and blind****, and naked* (Rev. 3:17).

It should be emphasized here that there are three main contributors to men's blindness of heart. First, the devil gets credit for blinding the minds of men in 2 Corinthians 4:4. Secondly, man must accept his own responsibility, for in Matthew 13:15 he closes his own eyes. Thirdly, the Lord steps in the picture at some critical juncture of judgment and recompense, and takes both action and responsibility for the dysfunction of men's hearts and minds. ***The LORD shall smite***

thee with madness, and blindness, and astonishment of heart (Deut. 28:28).

Isaiah 29:10-12 shows that the deep sleep and blindness of the eyes has to do with the fact that the prophets and seers of the day were no longer speaking the word of God.

> *For the LORD hath poured out upon you the* ***spirit of deep sleep****, and hath* ***closed your eyes****:* ***the prophets and your rulers, the seers hath he covered.*** *And the vision of all is become unto you as the words of a book that is sealed, which men deliver to one that is learned, saying, Read this, I pray thee: and he saith, I cannot; for it is sealed: And the book is delivered to him that is not learned, saying, Read this, I pray thee: and he saith, I am not learned.*

The prophets, seers and rulers were the eyes of Israel. We have the Bible today, not seers, but if the devil can succeed in obscuring the word of God, or if our "prophets" are busy displaying their lack of confidence in the Bible, then there is no doubt that Christianity will be blind just as Israel was and still is.

In another blow to the bellies of the ministers of our land who disparage the virtues of the Book God gave us, and to the wanton "watchmen" of the Faith who seem to have lost their focus,

> *All ye beasts of the field, come to devour, yea, all ye beasts in the forest.* ***His watchmen are blind****: they are all* ***ignorant,*** *they are all* ***dumb dogs,*** *they cannot bark; sleeping, lying down, loving to slumber. Yea, they are greedy dogs which can never have enough, and they are* ***shepherds that***

> ***cannot understand****: they all look to their own way, every one for his gain, from his quarter. Come ye, say they, I will fetch wine, and we will fill ourselves with strong drink; and to morrow shall be as this day, and much more abundant.*
> (Isa. 56:9-12)

Madness. Madness is another very strong term associated with what can go wrong in a man's head. Such terms are often subject to caricature and exaggeration in one's conceptions, and though one may presume to understand such terms, one is often simply entertaining prior conceived notions.

In the lord's promise to judge Israel in the day she departed from Him, God affirms that *The LORD shall smite thee with* ***madness, and blindness, and astonishment of heart*** (Deut. 28:28). Think of that. *Madness*! Israel reached such an hour of apostasy that God testified to her that *the prophet is a fool,* ***the spiritual man is mad****, for the multitude of thine iniquity* (Hos. 9:7).

Notice, though, that when it comes to the message of the gospel (the word of God), Paul diagnosed himself in retrospect. *And I punished them oft in every synagogue, and compelled them to blaspheme; and* ***being exceedingly mad against them****, I persecuted them even unto strange cities* (Acts 26:11). Granted, Paul was lost at the time. Nevertheless, if he diagnosed himself as being *mad*, not merely angry or enflamed, must that not reflect the spirit of the devil that worked within him? That spirit of illogic, unreason and blindness was the result of the hatred Satan had for Christ and the word of Christ. Might one who flirts with disdainfulness for that very same word be open to a bit of *madness* all his own?

Madmen are crazed lunatics, are they not? Well, not exactly…

> *MAD'NESS, n. [from mad.] Distraction; a **state of disordered reason or intellect**, in which the patient raves or is furious.*
> *1. Extreme folly; **headstrong passion and rashness that act in opposition to reason**; as the madness of a mob.*
> *2. Wildness of passion; fury; rage; as the madness of despair.*[101]

Brethren, madmen are those that are in "a state of disordered reason or intellect" or who possess a "headstrong passion and rashness that act in opposition to reason". The minds and thoughts of these individuals have been affected and disarranged.

This applies to those who were infuriated by the manner in which Christ did things – and when. *And they were **filled with madness;** and communed one with another what they might do to Jesus* (Lk. 6:11). It also applies to a man who was weak but ambitious, and utterly set in his intention to arrive at a big payday for himself. *But[Balaam] was rebuked for his iniquity: the dumb ass speaking with man's voice forbad the **madness of the prophet*** (2 Pet 2:16). That prophet was *mad* in ignoring the details - the specific and detailed words - of God's instruction.

Fables. This survey is by no means complete or exhaustive, as the volume of the Bible itself is completely overflowing with references to the function and dysfunction of the mind, heart and thoughts of man. The Bible is very literally saturated with the subject. One should find it instructive that in a day of incessant psychobabble, that man would, with such scrupulous care, overlook such a vast resource as God's word.

---

[101] *Webster's 1828 Dictionary.* Christian Technologies, Inc. version 2 (Build 20040406), 2004.

The survey would be much less complete did we not acknowledge where common men and Bible scholars alike are headed when they do not take proper account of the true words of the Lord.

> *3 For the time will come when they will not endure* ***sound doctrine;*** *but after their* ***own lusts*** *shall they* ***heap to themselves teachers, having itching ears;***
> *4 And they shall turn away their ears* ***from the truth****, and shall be* ***turned unto fables****.*
> (2 Tim. 4:3-4)

Bible and textual scholars have a need and obligation to be exercised unto *sound doctrine* just like all Christians. Make no mistake, what the Bible says about the inspiration, preservation and translation of *itself* is certainly doctrine, just as much as is the deity of Christ or the virgin birth. So the scholars too, just like us, have *their own lusts* to mortify and put down. Ambitions are just as likely to lead them to *heap to themselves* other unsound men who agree with them. At this very hour, there are men sitting on academic boards relating to the Bible or biblical education that have indeed turned their ears from the truth (or significant portions of it) and have been ***turned unto fables.***

What Not To Do	**How?**
1Tim.1:3-4 *Neither give heed to* ***fables*** (4)	*teach no other doctrine* (3)
1Tim.4:5-7 *refuse... old wives'* ***fables*** (7)	*nourished up in the words of faith* (6) *...and of good doctrine* (6)
2Pet. 1:16-20 *not followed*	*a more sure word*

cunningly devised ***fables*** (16)	*of prophecy* (19) *prophecy of the scripture* (20)

Furthermore, Paul writes this in Titus 1:14-16:

> *Not giving heed to **Jewish fables,** and **commandments of men,** that **turn from the truth.** Unto the pure all things are pure: but unto them that are defiled and unbelieving is nothing pure; but even their **mind and conscience is defiled.** They profess that they **know God;** but in works they deny him, being abominable, and disobedient, and...*

Brethren, the *fables* of verse 14 are connected with one of the great "schools" of thought and brainwashing that the devil uses in this world, the *commandments of men.* They are further connected with both a *defiled mind and conscience.* These men's minds do not work right, and their consciences are no better. They are *unto every good work reprobate.* Is not the work of teaching, preaching and translating the Bible a good work? If so, then might it be suggested that the men that labor in those areas ought to be held accountable in adhering to true Biblical principles and precepts in doctrine, but also in their faith in the words of God? Their foundations ought not to be laid on apostate men's works and upon the *fables* which the devil has inspired.

Loose Ends on Blinded Minds

Truly, much is being left unsaid and untouched in this work with regard to the mind of man. It is important because, obviously, the minds and hearts are the resources by which men apprehend God and the things of God. Therefore, if the devil has been unsuccessful at snaring a man's soul, he is yet gleeful and victorious if he can deceive that man's heart and mind. It is no game. The common Christian is absolutely susceptible if he is unwary, but the halls of biblical academia are by no means a battlement or haven from the insidious work of blinding minds.

Besides those categories which have been summarized at greater length, the reader should be aware that the Lord categorizes other frames of mind at which sinners can become ensnared. It should be pondered that each category describes a mind that is operating outside of its intended function. It is a mind that is compromised in integrity and, in one measure or another, dysfunctional.

In the scriptures, besides what has here been covered at greater length, there is the:

- *wicked mind* (Prov. 21:27)
- *despiteful minds* (Ezek. 36:5)
- *mind hardened* (Dan. 5:20)
- *doubtful mind* (Luke 12:29)
- *evil affected* minds (Acts 14:2)
- *changed* minds (Acts 28:6)
- *carnal mind* (Rom. 8:7)
- *earthly* mind (Phil. 3:19)
- *fleshly mind* (Col. 2:18)
- *shaken* mind (2 Thes. 2:2)
- *double minded man* (James 1:8)

For a born-again Christian, the devil's guns and efforts are all positioned to the end that he might compromise, defile and corrupt the mind and heart. Though the passions and sentiments – what a person loves and longs for – are a ready and predictable target, Satan wants very much to effect how one thinks and reasons, what one thinks about, and what one meditates upon. Satan desires to alter the foundational principles of thought and reason. If he can pervert the thoughts and reasoning at their roots, he can grossly affect the outcome and fruits of those thoughts. What God builds in knowledge, *precept upon precept; line upon line* (Isa. 28:10), the serpent wishes to replace with his own lines and precepts.

There is no class or species of Christian that is immune from this onslaught. There are no vaccinations, no fortified bunkers. Each Christian must individually *fight the good fight* (1 Tim. 6:12). If a man's scholastic calling in life is to relay the words and thoughts of the Lord to God's people - *The counsel of the LORD standeth for ever, the thoughts of his heart to all generations* (Ps.33:11) – that man must ***first*** begin his course by being dutifully dedicated to basic foundational doctrines of the Bible. It goes without saying that he should not be an infidel when it comes to the Bible itself. This seemingly rudimentary and sensible tenet has been grievously and ridiculously overrun by a disgracefully long list of "learned men" and scholars of the Bible. It would be difficult, of course, to find a scholar with whom one agrees on every point, nevertheless there must be a doctrinal tilting point at some juncture. If a man shows no fruit of conversion whatsoever, and is unorthodox and unscriptural in his view of the Godhead and the Deity of Christ, for what reason should a Bible-believer trust his judgment in the fine points of textual fidelity, translation and Biblical insight?

Secondly, a scholar needs to know that he is in for the fight of his life. He has not been placed in some backwater section of the war on God's saints. The battle for the Bible is not the rear echelon, it is the spear-point. Men that go leisurely and obliviously cavorting down the halls of Biblical and textual learning are bunnies in the lion's den. Many such academics lend the impression that they would not know a spiritual fight if it occurred atop their office desk. Too large a number of these peepers and mutterers (Is. 8:19) do not even believe there is a spiritual battle for the word of God. If there is one thing the

Bible bears testimony to, it is the fact that the devil uses whatever he can to destroy and pervert the words of the living God. The average grammarian or translator/scholar of new versions is the absolute farthest thing possible from a warrior for Christ, girded for battle. In fact, the word picture may even lead one to snicker involuntarily.

The reality is that there is no class of "Christian" (term used loosely) more likely to more quickly meet the lion than someone who traffics in the word of God. The devil certainly loves to defeat a pastor or a missionary over his *pulpit,* but if the prince of darkness can defeat a scholar or translator at his *desk,* then he has already ruined the pastor's pulpit, all the students that the academic matriculates through his classroom, as well as the common man, who is unfortunate enough to fall into reading the academic's polluted tripe.

Every Christian is called to exercise himself to attain the mind of Christ. Every Christian is called to develop an intimate familiarity with the words of the Holy One. If the average, Bible reading Christian is called to utmost vigilance – and he is – the pastor, evangelist, missionary, professor, scholar and translator had better check the girding of his armor, batten down the hatches and keep the powder dry, because there is one storming across the plank who is interested in far more than a little bit of theological and philosophical swordsmanship. He is coming to run you through, defile your innermost sanctum, and make you like it. He is interested in twisting your mind, commandeering your heart and corrupting your stream of thought. He is coming to beguile you into mutiny against your Master. He is interested in perverting you, wresting your loyalties, and turning you into a traitor. He wants you to blithely and blindly surrender to him the sacred stewardship, the eternal precious treasure. He wants you to hand it to him and thank him for the honor of trading for Esau's pottage. He wants your ***mind*** and his success rate is staggering!

The vast majority of Christians in history have not been scholars or academics but common, everyday folks. Be it known that God did not entrust the keeping of the faith to scholars, but to the regenerate body of Jesus Christ, the Church of the living God. Fishermen, carpenters and farmers are the watchmen and the defenders of the Book alongside those of high scholastic achievements. In the translation and propagation of the word of God, it is necessary that scholarliness be involved, and there are those that must labor a lifetime therein. There are truly admirable and great heroes of faith who were most excellent academically: Tyndale, Wycliffe, Erasmus, Bois, Reynolds, etc. Nevertheless, it must be made clear that scholars are not the masters of the body of Christ, but rather the Spirit of Christ (1 Pet. 1:11) is the master. The necessary knowledge and wisdom of academics is a most fertile breeding ground for haughtiness and highminded condescension. God delivered the scriptures first to Israel and then to the Church via the pens and mouths of tax collectors, shepherds, fishermen and fruit gatherers. Do not mistakenly think that God's method has since changed, and that He now has come to appoint only heady, proud pinheads as scripture keepers. Matthew 7:18-20 is a passage well worth remembering: *A good tree cannot bring forth evil fruit, neither can a corrupt tree bring forth good fruit. Every tree that bringeth not forth good fruit is hewn down, and cast into the fire. Wherefore by their fruits ye shall know them.* Let the Bible-believer beware lest the scholars commandeer responsibilities that belong to every Christian! All too often in history, the scholars have oft fallen short of their wordy professions and have instead proven themselves a sequestered priest-class, peddlers of half-true tripe and nonsense, men yoked and chained to their own hothouse theories and sanctimonious unscriptural traditions. May the Christian soldier beware lest they exploit their presumptuous, hijacked authority and their academic notoriety to intimidate the sentry into relinquishing the post which God ordained. We all have a stewardship and a heritage from God, which we are called to defend. *Cease ye from man, whose breath is in his nostrils: for wherein is he to be accounted of* (Isa. 2:22)?

The Sanctity of the Scriptures

By this point, near the close of this chapter, one should be well-attuned to the devil's horrible strategy of wresting the minds of men, even if he fails to steal their souls. It is hoped that this might have shed some light, as well, on man's participatory role in Satan's ultimate plans for a deceived world. John said *the whole world lieth in wickedness* (I Jn. 5:19), and for those with opened eyes, the corruption and defilement that carnal man (and ultimately Satan) hath wrought is evident for all to see. Babes are only innocent in a measure, for the seed of Adam's sin resides with devastating potential even in the tenderest breast. Even the much exalted things of nature groan and travail in pain (Rom. 8:22), and *yea, the heavens are not clean in his sight* (Job 15:15). What man has touched, he has defiled, and left to himself, all that is entrusted to him quickly deteriorates under his hand.

This has led more than a few men to adopt a naturalistic and humanistic view of the preservation of the scriptures. What God gave at the first in perfection, was at that very juncture subjected to the degrading qualities of man's nature, in their view. From that moment the natural laws of deterioration and corruption took hold of the sacred oracles, and thus in some measure, all we now have is some shadow, some residual remnant, of the very inerrant words of Almighty God. The issue concerning the proportion of the inspired and divine residue of the true Bible left to us is a matter hotly contested by the scholars. The fraction of the scriptures which a scholar believes remains reliable to the original transmission by God is almost always a matter of degree - that degree depending upon the scholar's particular brand of academic training and his own prejudices. With rarest exception, the scholars and linguists are all unanimous in agreement that *no translation* of the scriptures ever was, or ever could be, a perfect and inerrant reflection of what God originally gave unto man. (No living man in many centuries has ever seen an actual original autograph, but today's wise men are most all utterly assured and adamant that no translation anywhere can, could or would be perfectly aligned with what God originally said.)

That leaves the still wide and variant school of thought that goes like this: what absolute truth doth yet remain in the scriptures after man defiled and touched them, would be contained in the thousands of fragments of Greek and Hebrew copies of those original writings. They hold that as the originals are indeed gone, long ago burned, buried, lost or deteriorated to dust. Thus, to them, these copies of copies of copies of Greek and Hebrew manuscripts contain in often teensy fragments the ultimate truths of God. So, men pile (collect) all these fragments in a heap, and sort through them to decide which of the many fragments of the many verses actually contain the truth of the scriptures. These men, themselves sinners and subject to error, then by various scholar-approved processes of tradition, prejudice, philosophy, science, hypothesis and high-brow guesswork put together (collate) like a jigsaw puzzle what they *think* is the best representation of what the original writings must have said. Some of these representations are manuscript monstrosities plagued by deletions, omissions, insertions and the general debauched prejudice of the unconverted yet pompous fools who put them together. Other forms are of a more respectful and reverent nature, the scholars having a more sanctified appreciation for the fact that what God inspired, He would also preserve. Thus, their collations of manuscripts in Hebrew and Greek are systematic, reverent and conservative with respect to God's words. All being said, and giving all due credit, these men too often still hold that there is a portion and proportion of God's words that are in question due to certain variances in the manuscripts, and thus they could never be committed to saying that we have every one of God's words, perfectly *preserved and known* in Greek and Hebrew. Nor do they hold that if we did have every Greek and Hebrew word, that every word could be perfectly translated and reflected in a translation of our own language. Even these hold that since man touched and handled the Bible, the sacred oracles are only sacred and perfectly true in a measure. A high measure, mind you, but a measure nonetheless. Thus summarized is the varying but unfaithful position that dominates "Christian" biblical scholarship.

It is true that one must always be wary of the corruptive influences of sinful man. Without outside influence, man ruins what he meddles with. It is true that a great deal of the biblical evidence and writings that man set his grimy hands to were indeed defiled and debauched. The entire scope of this chapter has to do with the fleshy and demonic influences infecting and seeding with falsehood and deceit all that is true and right. Nowhere is this nefarious degeneracy more evident than in the history and genealogy of the Holy Scriptures. Oft the worst of men and the most bastardized of intellects were drawn to the writings of the Bible just as vultures and buzzards are drawn to fresh kill. Much of the body of textual evidence has been grossly compromised by the pernicious hands of wicked men.

Be that as it may, the faith declared in the scriptures says that the scriptures are the provision of God, not men, and that those words of the scripture are not only inspired, but preserved, providentially - not humanistically. True enough, by natural course, man defiles all that he touches. This matter, however, is not governed by natural course, but by God whose words these are!

> *The words of the LORD are pure words: as silver tried in a furnace of earth, purified seven times. Thou shalt keep them, O LORD, thou shalt preserve them from this generation for ever.* (Ps. 12:6-7)

> *Every word of God is pure: he is a shield unto them that put their trust in him.*
> (Prov. 30:5)

The word which the Father gave us is not like any other word written on any other page anywhere in history. This is not merely due to its Author, its scope or its sublime language and insight. It is like no other book because it is *alive.*

> *For the word of God is* ***quick****, and powerful, and sharper than any twoedged sword, piercing even to the dividing asunder of soul and spirit, and of the joints and marrow, and* ***is a discerner of the thoughts and intents of the heart.***
> (Heb. 4:12)

> *For this cause also thank we God without ceasing, because, when ye received the word of God which ye heard of us, ye received it not as the word of men, but as it is in truth, the word of God, which* ***effectually worketh*** *also in you that believe.*
> (1 Thes. 2:13)

Let not the naïve Christian be bamboozled into believing less than is plainly written. God fully intended that we have each and every word of God.

But he answered and said, It is written, Man shall not live by bread alone, but by ***every word*** *that proceedeth out of the mouth of God.*

(Matt. 4:4)

My son, ***attend to my words****; incline thine ear unto my sayings.* ***Let them not depart from thine eyes****; keep them in the midst of thine heart. For they are life unto those that find them, and health to all their flesh.*

(Prov. 4:20-22)

One could quickly be lured off-point by the multitude of the glorious, eternal attributes of God's word and by the volume of the proofs for those attributes. The point here is that God Himself is the Author and Defender of each of His words. Man may corrupt all he touches by course of nature, but in God's word, man is not dealing with something after the course of nature. We cannot help but be reminded in Jeremiah 36 how Jeremiah, by the word of the Lord, had Baruch write in a book at Jeremiah's mouth all that Jeremiah had previously said to Israel through the years. The king upon hearing the words read, promptly cut up the manuscript and burned it. Ah, yes - man at his best! It would seem that the devil and wicked man managed in a small way to counter the effects of God's word in this case. Imagine an original manuscript lost! (Incidentally, it would have been an original manuscript recording words originally spoken at a previous time, but not necessarily recorded until that time.) But then, the Lord went beyond the bounds of man's capacity of desecration, for…

Then took Jeremiah another roll, and gave it to Baruch the scribe, the son of Neriah; who ***wrote therein from the mouth of Jeremiah all the words of the book which Jehoiakim king of Judah had burned in the fire: and there were***

> ***added besides unto them many like words.***
> (Jer. 36:32)

The bottom line is that God seems to allow man and the devil certain limited victories against the words of God. Clement of Alexandria and Adamantius Origen were allotted great latitude to pervert the scriptures, and the perversions that we see today are largely the product of their hands. The Catholic Church, throughout history, has been a veritable fountain of corruption with regard to the Bible. Holy Mother Church did much to obliterate the light of the scriptures to the vast majority of the population of Europe, North Africa and the near East for over 1000 years. Many apostate scholars wielding profound academic influence have given their lives and souls to do Satan's bidding and destroy the Bible. However, no matter what they accomplish, and no matter how it may seem that they have undermined God's foundations, ***God always overrules man and the devil!*** The scripture is the *Lord's* word! He is its sovereign Protector! If it came down to it, God could have recommissioned and reinspired the writings just exactly as He did in Jeremiah's day. Let not some haughty, naysaying scholar say God could not, and would not do so, for God DID do so in Jeremiah 36!

If one believes the Book, he learns that God holds His word in esteem above His own name, *for thou hast magnified thy word above all thy name* (Ps. 138:2). The ramifications are beyond the scope of this work, but a man or woman is a fool to believe that God allowed the potency and light of His words to somehow grow old, dilapidated and mildewed. Imagine the Word of God (Christ) allowing the perfection and purity of the words of God to be permanently overcome by man, *whose breath is in his nostrils* (Isa. 2:22). What He supernaturally inspired, He allowed to fade and wane into oblivion? Why? Because He did not realize what would happen? It caught Him unawares? He forgot His promise to preserve every pure word?

Or is it that what light He did inspire, He allowed to fade to a bare, almost indiscernible flicker, which sat on dusty shelves in musty unused languages until such a time that the New Testament priest-class of gnostic nobility known as *scholars* came along to dispense to the commoners and peons what fragments of truth they felt the unschooled might be able to digest? Such incompetence and failure do not belong either unto Christ or His Father.

In conclusion, man in his wisdom, thinks that he has God in a box. Man thinks he knows how God does or does not do things. Of course, man assumes this in the face of a fluorescent warning sign: *For as the heavens are higher than the earth, so are my ways higher than your ways, and my thoughts than your thoughts* (Isa. 55:9). Man thinks he knows what God can and cannot do, will and will not do. Man thinks this because man has certain ways he would or would not do things if *HE* were God. *These things hast thou done, and I kept silence; thou thoughtest that I was altogether such an one as thyself: but I will reprove thee, and set them in order before thine eyes* (Ps. 50:21). Man forgets or disbelieves that God made an ass talk (Num. 22:28) and the sun to stand still (Josh. 10:13). Five loaves and two fishes fed 5000 and supplied 12 baskets of leftovers (Matt. 14), and *the barrel of meal wasted not, neither did the cruse of oil fail* (1 Kings 17:16). The dead were raised, the lepers were cleansed and Israel walked through the sea on dry land. Man forgets that God is a God of miracles.

So man says, the original autographs were lost, mistakes entered, men fatally desecrated the inerrancy of scripture, and God does not guide translation. If God led Jeremiah to write again ***all the words of the book which Jehoiakim king of Judah had burned in the fire: and there were added besides unto them many like words*** (Jer. 36:32), how is it the scholars are so haughty and hasty to say how the Lord might accomplish something?

Perhaps such who reason thus have been sorely deceived, and having forsaken real and true biblical examples, they have been bereft *of a pure heart, and of a good conscience, and of faith unfeigned: From which some having swerved* ***have turned aside unto vain jangling*** (1 Tim. 1:5-6). Perhaps their mental and spiritual resources have been grossly compromised so that the information they process comes out more resembling the devil's reasoning than the Lord's. Should we think that being so careless with the words of Christ, they would be more careful of their own consecration and spiritual attainments, or of their own minds and consciences?

All a Christian knows is what he was told. The scriptures say *Let no man deceive you by any means* (2 Thes. 2:3), and *Wherefore by their fruits ye shall know them* (Matt. 7:20). If the scholars speak, reason and write like the devil spoke and reasoned, then their minds and hearts must have been compromised by the Lord's enemy. Judge not by men's professed sincerity or by the evident devotion of their labors. Judge them by their fruits – *what they say* (Matt .7:15-16). The issue is not eloquence, learning or persuasive powers. The issue is ***what they say***! *To the law and to the testimony: if they speak not according to this word, it is because there is no light in them* (Isa. 8:20). If their attitude and faith resemble the deportment and reasoning of Jesus Christ, Paul and Jeremiah, we can then conclude that they are of God, but if their attitude and faith resemble not Christ's attitude and faith, there is only one other conclusion that can be drawn.

Chapter 9

Ensamples Are Not Examples

> *But with many of them God was not well pleased: for they were overthrown in the wilderness. Now these things were our* ***examples****, to the intent we should not lust after evil things, as they also lusted. Neither be ye idolaters, as were some of them; as it is written, The people sat down to eat and drink, and rose up to play. Neither let us commit fornication, as some of them committed, and fell in one day three and twenty thousand. Neither let us tempt Christ, as some of them also tempted, and were destroyed of serpents. Neither murmur ye, as some of them also murmured, and were destroyed of the destroyer. Now all these things happened unto them for* ***ensamples****: and they are written for our admonition, upon whom the ends of the world are come. Wherefore let him that thinketh he standeth take heed lest he fall.*
>
> (1 Cor. 10:5-12)

For all who are even remotely aware that the language of the King James Bible is an issue of import in Christianity, it has become a routine yet hypnotic mantra that the AV contains obsolete and outdated words. This all too naturally insinuates and implies to irreverent men that those "obsolete" words need be updated. As usual, there is a wide range of heat and fever concerning the matter. There are those who hate everything about the King James anyway, so the verb endings, the pronoun forms, and the "outdated language" of the Holy Bible (as opposed to the unholy ones) to them serve as gasoline on an open flame, and helps them build a great inferno of rhetoric and bombast. There is no real substance to the momentary conflagration but the high, hot flames impress the bystanders.

Somewhere near the other end of the spectrum of the fevered criticism for the language of the Old Book are the people who actually do a fair, or even good, job in its defense. They know that the King James Bible has no equivalent in the English language in its translational accuracy, its superiority of text, or in its power and authority. This crowd though, is still plagued by specters and haunts which they just cannot shake. To them, as with their more liberal scholarly counterparts, there is no Bible on earth that is untouchable because they have bought into the first principle of apostasy, namely that there is no perfection here on earth when it comes to an actual material copy of the Holy Scriptures in any language. This is not a scriptural precept, mind you. It is a scholastically imposed one. Now remember, these folks are in the King James camp, make a sound enough defense of it, and stand by the KJV as the Bible in English. Unfortunately, they are either intimidated by scholarship, or they fawn after it with tongues lolled out, as the adoring and subservient admirers they are. Often adoration and intimidation are confusedly intermingled, but such is the nature of man. These are scared to death to illicit the wrath and disparagement of that elite and all-wise band of gnostic gods called scholars. Oh, they will reject and denounce certain of the heretic scholars who are not in accord with their particular clique, but they each have a scholar guru, or failing that, they have an exclusive little knitting-circle society of admired scholars, and the society or guru needs only to thunder forth from the mount of their academic chairs and the sycophants will acquiesce and yield. This is followed by the adoring payment of homage to the wisdom and pioneering work of the scholar-gods. In the end, it is nothing more than the fear of man (Pro.29:25), and the avoidance of the child-scholar's dreaded and ultimate hell: ***being mocked and laughed at by recognized scholarship***. Brethren, the fear of man is universal and only the utmost discipline and steadfast faith stands before it. It is just as easy for a scholar that favors the Textus Receptus to dread the repercussions of disdain and disrespect should he depart from the party line, as it is for utterly apostate pantywaist scholars to do the same.

No, this latter group does not thunder forth against the antiquated language of the AV as do the bonfire builders, but they cannot ignore the strident and insistent voices of their scholar masters either. The pressure is often too incessant for them. They simply feel that they have to yield somewhat to the ceaseless volume and cacophony of voices that insists that the King James' language is…*insufficient.* See Chapter 1, where many of those unreservedly committed to the King James Bible weigh in with less than enthralling and inspirational sentiments in this matter. They simply do not carry with them utter *confidence* and *trust* for every word of the Holy Scriptures – and it shows.

It is often then, that the Bible-believer and the non-believer alike hear the tale told and the accusation made of the sad and dilapidated condition of varying proportions of the language in the AV 1611. The scholars say "Tsk tsk" with their lips, but there is often a good deal of glee in their hearts, for this opens all sorts of opportunity for them.

I, personally, am wholly and 100% against any process that would change any words or word forms in our King James Bible. By 1769, and the publication of the so-called "Immaculate Text,"[102] there were no legitimate changes left to

---

[102] McClure, A.W. *Translators Revived,* Maranatha Publications Worthington, Pa – reprint p.224

be made in the King James Bible. Do not allow this last sentence to shake you. When the first editions of the AV were published in 1611 and later, printing itself was still an extremely awkward and excessively detailed process and it was utterly unavoidable that there would be printing errors. Any reader today can find errors in modern printing, and that with computers and publication software. There were various editions of the AV 1611 that had misprints and mistakes after that fashion. Obviously, the nature of these issues is not the same as errors of translation or transmission. Further, what we would call "font" today was then a fancy Gothic type of print that made it difficult on the eyes to read. This print type was changed in time to be easier on the eyes, all the while, these made no changes in the words of God except to font. The AV's worst critics today desperately claim this action to have been a "revision" of the King James – a change in the Bible. This is nonsense and exploitative "misdefinition" on their part. Finally, when the AV was translated, the spelling of English words was not as uniform as it is today, so there were quite a number of times that the same word in the Bible was spelled in different ways in different places. By 1769, the uniformity of spelling, punctuation, and the printing errors themselves were ironed out[103]. McClure testifies that there was only *one erratum* detected in the 1769 ***edition*** (not ***revision***) of the King James.[104]

To repeat, I personally am expressly against the infernal and unending process of critiquing the wording of the King James Bible. I am equally, and as fervently, against leaving the door of possibility open for some future changes to be made. Nothing needs to be changed. The AV does not need changing because it is perfect and inerrant as it is. Furthermore, though

---

[103] Gipp, Samuel C., *The Answer Book* Bible & Literature Missionary Foundation, Shelbyville, TN, 1989, p.18.
[104] McClure, A.W. *Translators Revived,* Maranatha Publications Worthington, Pa – reprint p.224

the scholastic vultures come along and pick at the language of the AV as if it were some road-killed carcass, I have never known it to fail that where a Bible-believer makes a sincere, patient and diligent inquiry into whatever "obsolete" rendering in the AV troubles him, he invariably comes away edified and enlightened, and realizes that there is actually method, design, accuracy and greater sanctification to the wording, vocabulary and grammar of the Holy Book - exactly as it is written.

This characteristic found in the "outdated language" of the King James has already been demonstrated in earlier chapters, and it is another similar case that now takes center stage.

It has been noted through the years that most all of us – even we genuine King James "fanatics" – can be a little quick on the trigger in saying that a certain word in the King James is outdated or unused today. The next obvious step is to update it – even if only in our minds. We "King James people" are not going to change a word in our Bibles, ***but we will just remember what it "really means" today***, right? Such ground is dangerous ground, for somewhere along the way a bunch of people decided that ***charity*** in the Bible, really means ***love***, and so not only do new versions change it, but King James Bible believers ***think*** it. As shown in Chapter 3, *charity* carries its own distinct meaning for Christians, and while it does involve *love*, *charity* is still separate and sanctified in its own right. There certainly are a number of words in the AV that are obvious synonyms of others, and there are also old-fashioned manners of speech that can be said and understood accurately in another form in daily life. Consider what follows before becoming flippant or dismissive in saying, "Oh, that's just an old fashioned way of saying…" or "That's just the old word for ______ that we don't use anymore."

Perhaps you *should* use it. Perhaps God left something in the meaning of that old word that He intended you to *understand* that another word does not quite convey.

Substance, Synonym or Senility?

In 1 Corinthians 10:6-12, there are two words in English used something like bookends in the passage. In the first case, as one can see, the Lord uses the word *examples* (vs.6), and in the second, He uses the word *ensamples* (vs.11). This testimony of the scripture regards the children of Israel while wandering in the wilderness and being judged by God for their various infidelities and transgressions. Note the included transliteration for the root Greek word from which each was translated and the Strong's number related to it.

> *6 Now these things were our* **examples (tupos – 5179),** *to the intent we should not lust after evil things, as they also lusted.*
> *7 Neither be ye idolaters, as were some of them; as it is written, The people sat down to eat and drink, and rose up to play.*
> *8 Neither let us commit fornication, as some of them committed, and fell in one day three and twenty thousand.*
> *9 Neither let us tempt Christ, as some of them also tempted, and were destroyed of serpents.*
> *10 Neither murmur ye, as some of them also murmured, and were destroyed of the destroyer.*
> *11 Now all these things happened unto them for* **ensamples (tupos – 5179)***: and they are written for our admonition, upon whom the ends of the world are come.*
> *12 Wherefore let him that thinketh he standeth take heed lest he fall.*

The first thing to note is that both English words have the look of being related to each other, and it would take a careful ear and a careful tongue to distinguish the two words in common speech. Next, both words are from the same root Greek word. This fact alone settles the matter for the Greek-centric scholars and all the new versions that this writer checked followed suit in translating both of the occurrences in the passage as ***example(s).***

Barnes notes ring in accord with the sentiments of a majority of all scholars.

> 1 Corinthians 10:11
> [For ensamples] Greek: "types" [tupoi (grk 5179)]. The same word which is used in <1 Cor. 10:6>. ***This verse is a repetition of the admonition contained in that verse***, in order to impress it more deeply on the memory; see the note at verse 6.[105]

Naturally, no one seems concerned that the AV 1611 translators do not seem to be in harmony with the rest of the boys' club, as they translated the term in two separate ways in English; but then, Bois, Reynolds and Co. were discounted long ago. Note that Barnes is careful to say that verse 11 is a mere ***"repetition"*** of the admonition in verse 6. Though the words in English differ, Barnes says it is ***"repetition".***

Once again, we have run headlong into the crux of the matter. The English words differ, but the Greek words are the same – or at least have the same root. The English says one thing, the Greek another. What is the scholars' final authority?

---

[105] Barnes, Albert. *Barnes' Notes* (1997) P C Study Bible (Version 2.11) [Computer Software]. Seattle, WA: Biblesoft.

No contest! The English of the King James Bible is "blown off" and disregarded. There is no evidence found that suggests that anyone even gave the matter a second thought. To most all the scholars, the Greek is the holy oracle – the only consideration. The King James Bible is a red-headed stepchild which must be acknowledged down a long, haughty nose at times, but mostly, given a choice, it is dismissed with a snort and ignored.

We shall see in a bit that there are some other times where the Bible uses both *example* and *ensample* that are well worth examining. For now, just to concentrate on 1 Corinthians 10, please consider just a few things that will place the matter in the open before all.

One possibility is that there is some sort of legitimate and **substantive** difference between the two words as the Lord uses them. They are obviously used in close proximity one to another, and being different words, the Bible student just might do well to consider that there is some slight and subtle distinction that the Lord wanted to make between the two particular portions of the passage. Rest assured that the main body of biblical scholarship will give no heed to such a suggestion, for they have been long programmed to immediately dismiss the English of the AV. In this case, as pointed out above, the two different English words are derived from one common Greek root word. This, to them, is a slam dunk, since the same Greek word should be rendered the same way, and the idea of some distinction made in English is preposterous and akin to heresy. The idea of a **substantive** distinction in English where there is no distinction in Greek is to be spurned forthwith and never entertained again. So a student that considers this possibility may as well resign himself to being considered a quack – or worse. The main issue, though, should be the truth, and a question worth asking and investigating is: is it possible that there is some **substantive** and **genuine** distinction made between the two English words?

Another perfectly reasonable consideration would be that the two slightly different English words are indeed **synonyms**. Throughout the King James Bible, the Lord uses two or more words in close proximity, in parallel contexts and statements, in order to convey that the two words are **synonyms**, and do indeed mean the same thing. The Lord's method of teaching knowledge of the Bible is by *comparing spiritual things with spiritual* (1 Cor. 2:13). Often those spiritual things sitting side by side with one another establish links in the reader's mind and heart that show similar or same meaning. On the other hand, the Lord also often places two contrasting or antagonistic ideas side by side so as to show the difference or disparity between the two.[106] That *ensamples* and *examples* might be the same in meaning is a distinct possibility, theoretically, and should be approached with that idea in mind. Nevertheless, that they are different words in our language from 1611 until now, should not escape the attention of the student. If God can make a distinction between a *jot* and a *tittle* (Matt.5:18) in Hebrew, a couple of letters difference between two English words may just indicate that the words are not the same. It should here be noted that the only way to know whether the words are **synonyms** or not, similar in meaning or distinct in meaning, is by studying the scriptures and their contexts.

The student and reader should also note that such Bible study mentioned above is disreputable and unadvised if the scholars are asked. The Greek has spoken. The scholars agree that there can be no way that God would (or could) make

---

[106] See the extraordinary evidence of this displayed at great length in two fine works by Gail Riplinger, *The Language of the King James Bible* and *In Awe of Thy Word.* Both may be found at A.V. Publications Corp., PO Box 280, Ararat, VA 24053.

distinctions or implications of meaning in English where the Greek did not indicate such. After all, God inspired the Greek, but English is a (imagine a *snort* and an *eye-roll* at this juncture) "mere translation." Scholarship's Rule #1: God would never, *ever* intervene in any way to direct the wording of a translation.

Examine and see.

As the two English words abide within five verses of one another, one other possible explanation would be that the AV translators were smitten with some weird form of **senility**...something that affected their acuity and sharpness of mind. Here are two words similar yet different, within five verses of one another, and these extremely scrupulous and detail-oriented giants of scholarship in their own right, simply let it get past them. Further, this mysterious affliction, affected the entire company of roughly 50 scholars uniformly, as they all reviewed each passage 14 separate times in committee[107], not including the post publication scrutiny the AV went through all the way until 1769, at which point all the spelling errors and misprints were eliminated. What a monumental mystery! It is not just one deskbound genius that might have "flipped out" for a while. All these profound academics, *as one*, effectively passed on making a simple correction to the spelling of the word *ensamples*! Their reverence for God's word being what it was, I am sure such mysterious affliction of mental acuity and intellectual capacity of the King James translators has caused modern scholars many hours of contemplation and inner reflection.

In summary, there is a **substantive** difference between the two words, the two words are **synonyms** and mean the same thing, or the entirety of the King James translation committee

---

[107] Sargent, Robert J., *Landmarks of English Bible: Manuscript Evidence,* Bible Baptist Church Publications, Oak Harbor, Washington, 1989, p.216.

went a bit crack-brained and **senile** all at once. Plainly, one will be forced to make a decision between the first two matters before knowing whether the AV translators were on the ball or absent from school.

To assist in comprehending how controversial and bitter is the battle over such wording of the Bible, briefly consider an article called *Is 17th-Century British English Holy?,* written by David Cloud of the Fundamental Baptist Information Service in Port Huron, Michigan on August 12, 2010. Cloud, an ardent defender of the King James Bible at least insofar as its Greek and Hebrew texts go, goes way out on an ill-advised limb in saying,

> *The only difference between "ensample" and "example" is that one is 17th-century spelling and the other is 20th-century.* ***The words are the same.***[108]

Cloud cites other instances of such words which he believes are mere updates, and some of the number of the examples he cites indeed appear to be nothing more than spelling changes. That one would carelessly and mistakenly offer this opinion about *examples* and *ensamples* is easily enough understood, but Cloud, a reputed AV 1611 defender, also yields his mind and pen to a vituperative acrimony that disparages every honest-hearted Bible believer when he thunders forth from his high and lofty perch of accusation,

> *My friends, this is* ***pure nutcase Ruckmanism/Riplingerism.*** *It is* ***nonsensical***

---

[108] Cloud, David. *Is 17th-Century British English Holy?* Fundamental Baptist Information Service, P.O. Box 610368, Port Huron, MI 48061, 866-295-4143, fbns@wayoflife.org Aug.12, 2010

> *and makes all King James Bible defenders look **ridiculous.***[109]

If the two words represent only synonyms in alternately archaic and modern form, then perhaps a case can be made for an obstinate Bible believer being afflicted with *"pure nutcase Ruckmanism/Riplingerism."* If, however, the differences prove to be substantive, there is at least one "scholar" who owes some of his brethren an apology and who obviously fears "looking ridiculous" more than he fears denouncing the wording of the Bible he purports to defend.

Substance It Is[110]

A few facts may help one get his mind around this matter.

> - *Example(s)* and *ensample(s)* show up a total of 15 times in the scriptures.
> - The word *example(s)* occurs 9 times.
> - The word *ensample(s)* occurs 6 times.

As for the Greek, all occurrences of the two words are in the New Testament and are thereby translated from Greek.

> - 7 of the 15 times the words occur, they are derivatives of *δεῖγμα (deigma).* Of the 7 times, 6 are translated *example(s),* yet one is translated *ensample.*

---

[109] Ibid.

[110] Credit where credit is due. The key to the distinction between the two words were unraveled by a young man in our church who requested to remain unnamed. Once he presented the material to me, I immediately agreed with him on his assessment. I may be unaware of some other author, preacher or scholar who saw the light behind the matter, but it remains a marvel and a blessing to me what a student who simply loves the words of God can uncover in the King James Bible!

- 7 of the 15 times, they are derivatives of *τύπος (tupos).* Of the 7 times, 5 are translated *ensample(s),* and 2 times *example(s).*
- 1 time *example* is translated from the root *γράφω (grapho),* which often means *to write* or *to engrave.*

What is important for the Bible-believer to recognize is that in the 14 total occurrences of *deigma* and *topos* in Greek, each word was at one time or other translated as **both *example* and *ensample*.** That is, with the same Greek words before them, the AV translators translated **both Greek words two different ways.** Further, through all the consultations and throughout that minimum number of 14 times the AV translators reviewed each other's work, and through all the post-publication scrutiny that the AV has undergone, the two separate English words have still been retained. So what is it? Is it design? Accident? Oversight? Senility? Stupidity?

The true way to tell if there is rhyme or reason for this is to study the Bible as opposed to being dependent upon scholars who prove to be adversarial to the Bible. The sooner a Christian learns that the scholars' union is enabled by the body of Christ's ultra-dependency upon the scholars for the truth, the sooner that Christian will realize that this is a subtle form of bondage not designed by the God of either testament, but of man.

Example(s)

Let us first evaluate the general usage of the word *example(s)* as it is used in the King James Bible. The following are all the cases where the word appears in the King James Bible.

> *Then Joseph her husband, being a just man, and not willing to make her a publick **example**, was minded to put her away privily.*
>
> (Matt. 1:19)

For I have given you an ***example****, that ye should do as I have done to you.* *(John 13:15)*

Now these things were our ***examples,*** *to the intent we should not lust after evil things, as they also lusted.* (1 Cor. 10:6)

Let no man despise thy youth; but be thou an ***example*** *of the believers, in word, in conversation, in charity, in spirit, in faith, in purity.* (1 Tim. 4:12)

Let us labour therefore to enter into that rest, lest any man fall after the same ***example*** *of unbelief.* (Heb. 4:11)

Who serve unto the ***example*** *and shadow of heavenly things, as Moses was admonished of God when he was about to make the tabernacle: for, See, saith he, that thou make all things according to the pattern shewed to thee in the mount.* (Heb. 8:5)

Take, my brethren, the prophets, who have spoken in the name of the Lord, for an ***example*** *of suffering affliction, and of patience.*
(James 5:10)

For even hereunto were ye called: because Christ also suffered for us, leaving us an ***example****, that ye should follow his steps:*
(1 Pet. 2:21)

Even as Sodom and Gomorrha, and the cities about them in like manner, giving themselves over to fornication, and going after strange

> *flesh, are set forth for an* ***example****, suffering the vengeance of eternal fire.* (Jude 1:7)

In Matthew 1:19, Joseph avoided making Mary, Jesus' mother, a public *example*. Had he done so, she would have been terribly disgraced, and since men of the day would have had no reason to believe her pregnant by any method other than adultery, her punishment would have been a warning – an *example* – of what would happen to others who did what the men of the day mistakenly thought she had done.

In John 13:15, Jesus gave His disciples an *example* that they should do as He had done. Jesus had just washed His disciples' feet. Personally, I have never had my feet washed by another in a Christian setting, and I have been saved for over 40 years. Though certain sparsely scattered churches practice foot-washing, as a rule, this is simply not done on anything like a universal basis in Christianity. It is not a scriptural ordinance of the church like the Lord's Supper and Believer's Baptism. Why do we not wash each other's feet? A wide range of things could be mentioned, and we could make a thesis out of the discussion of why or why not, but foot washing is not the theme here, so we will cut to the chase. Jesus Christ never intended for believers to wash one another's feet. He left an *example* of humble servitude one to another that extends far beyond foot-washing. He did not intend Christians to understand that living in the 21st century, we would have to go to church and peel out of our shoes and socks. He intended the saints to get the idea that Christians should serve one another in a range of things that goes well beyond a singular practice, and perhaps in some things that are even more humbling than washing another's feet!

An *example* is a pattern of behavior that is not necessarily intended to be exactly mimicked or emulated or precisely repeated, but a lesson to be drawn from and even extended to apply to other unrelated exercises. If you ever have to clean the bedpan of a fellow Christian, you will be following Christ's *example* of John 13:15, though you have never washed feet. If Joseph had gone public with Mary's condition, that act would have served as an *example* that one should not do what they thought she had done.

Next from the list of *examples*, in 1 Corinthians 10:6, the things the children of Israel went through in their wilderness wanderings and wilderness judgments are said to be our *examples.* Our walk as Christians, having been delivered from sin and the world, were foreshadowed by Israel's travails in the wilderness. Their lives and experiences there were *types* of many of our experiences in the Christian life. However, saved saints are not literally wandering as they did. We are not literally fed with manna. We do not physically drink water from a rock. We do not see the daily form of miracles and signs as did Israel. We are not literally plagued by serpents, nor do we die by the droves in quite the same way as those folks in the wilderness did. *Spiritually* and *devotionally*, we partake of some of the essence of their trials without being in their exact situation. We should not lust, murmur, fornicate or commit idolatry as they did, and if we do, God will punish us! It is doubtful that we will be swallowed alive by the earth (Num.16:33), be bitten by a pestilential brood of snakes (Num.21:6), or die dramatically en masse by the terrible judgments of God. Those things that overtook Israel in the wilderness are our *examples*, but they are not likely to be duplicated in literal detail. That is what an *example* is.

Next, in 1Timothy 4:12, Timothy is admonished to be *an* ***example*** *of the believers* in various respects. Now, as a young pastor, and in accord with the spirit of 1 Peter 5:3, there is no question that Timothy needed to be an ***example*** ***to*** the believers and to his flock (more on that later), but that is not what the scriptures said. He was to be *an* ***example*** ***of*** *the believers!* Again, though all in Timothy's position should be *examples* ***to*** the flock, let the reader consider that the specific wording of verse 12 is *an* ***example of*** *the believers.* Timothy was admonished to be an example **to unbelieving and lost people.** This is important because lost people are unregenerate and must be born again to receive the new nature as Timothy had. If this seems confusing, consider what most consider an equivalent statement in 1 Peter 5:1-3, only notice a critical difference: the wording!

> *1 The elders which are among you I exhort, who am also an elder, and a witness of the sufferings of Christ, and also a partaker of the glory that shall be revealed:*
> *2 Feed the flock of God which is among you, taking the oversight thereof, not by constraint, but willingly; not for filthy lucre, but of a ready mind;*
> *3 Neither as being lords over God's heritage, but being* ***ensamples*** *to the flock.*
> (1 Pet 5:1-3)

Although the discussion of *ensample(s)* is yet to be dealt with in detail, this passage is inserted because each passage is from an elder's frame of reference (An elder is a pastor). In 1 Peter, the pastor is not said to be an *example* to the flock, but an *ensample!* The flock is a congregation of converted Christians. The pastor is to be an *ensample* to them. They should be able to watch him live, and then follow, emulate and pattern their lives and behavior after his. Timothy, while his life would also be a pattern for his converted flock to emulate and copy (an *ensample)*, he is specifically told to also be an *example of the believers*… but to whom? Timothy, despite his youth, is to be *an example of the believers* to lost people. He and Peter would be *ensamples* to their own regenerate flocks, but *examples* of Christians to lost folk round about!

An *example* is a pattern, behavior or occurrence that is to be learned from, and lessons drawn from, but not necessarily copied or reproduced, because, in this case, until a person becomes a Christian, no amount of mimicry or emulation can supply that person a new birth. The English Bible does indeed make a definite distinction between *examples* and *ensamples*!

Peter's *ensample* will soon be revisited, but to continue the survey of *example(s)*, note that the next case, Hebrews 4:11, warns against falling *after the same* ***example*** *of unbelief* as Israel in the wilderness. The context is Hebrews 3:8 & 15, where the specific reference is the day of provocation when Israel refused to enter into the land when and how they were instructed to do so by God. Again, here, the word used is *example*, for while we are to believe God, which most of Israel did not, we will not be asked to believe and execute exactly the same things as the Israelites were supposed to. We do not exactly emulate their steps or their material circumstances, but we learn plain lessons from the *examples* of their failures.

The next case is Hebrews 8:5, which plainly states in the context that the holy things of the wilderness tabernacle were mere *shadow(s) of heavenly things* (8:5). Obviously, the real thing is in Heaven. The holy things of the tabernacle here on earth are mere types and patterns of the true things which are in heaven. So the priesthood of the Old Testament that ministered in those things, served *unto the* ***example*** *and shadow of heavenly things.* They did not serve unto the real things, but the mere *examples!*

Examine the next two together:

> *Take, my brethren, the prophets, who have spoken in the name of the Lord, for an* ***example*** *of suffering affliction, and of patience.*
>
> (James 5:10)

> *For even hereunto were ye called: because Christ also suffered for us, leaving us an **example**, that ye should follow his steps:*
> (1 Pet 2:21)

Do saints suffer the exact same sufferings of either the old prophets or of Christ? We are certainly called to suffer for Christ, but we will never, and could never, suffer all the same sufferings as He quite literally experienced. It is doubtful that any of us will be crucified, and I have yet to be whipped to ribbons. Though I do not suffer all the same sufferings as Christ, He is my *example* of strength, fortitude, faithfulness and courage. Nor do we suffer the extent of all the sufferings of the prophets of old. By some small degree we do and should, but if they were our *ensamples,* we would be going through the exact material and literal things that they did. We do not, so they are our *examples.* We learn from them and are inspired by them, though our circumstances are not identical. That is what an *example* is.

As our last *example, Sodom and Gomorrha* are mentioned in Jude 1:7. The scripture says that in ... *giving themselves over to fornication, and going after strange flesh,* (they) *are set forth for an **example**, suffering the vengeance of eternal fire.* Now we recognize prophetically that the Lord returns in flaming fire at the Second Coming, and unquestionably, many cities will burn. It is, however, doubtful that every city overrun and infested with sodomites will be individually destroyed in exactly the same manner as Sodom before that day. San Francisco may drop off in the Pacific, in which case *Sodom and Gomorrha* would have served as an *example* of God's judgment though their city did not burn. Of course, the individuals would still suffer the eternal fires of Hell. Key West, a sodomite haven, may well be obliterated by hurricanes one day. If this happens, though the destruction would be by waves and wind, *Sodom and Gomorrha* would still have served as an *example* to her- not an *ensample*, but an *example.*

In the King James Bible, an *example* serves as a warning or a pattern for those who are not in the exact same predicament or scenario. An *example* is a pattern of behavior that is not necessarily intended to be exactly mimicked or emulated or precisely repeated, but a lesson to be drawn from and even extended to apply to other unrelated exercises. An *example* is a pattern, behavior or occurrence that is to be learned from, and lessons drawn from, but not necessarily identically copied or reproduced. Lessons are to be drawn and applied to one's individual situation, though the situation does not match the *example* exactly.

Ensample(s)

Now look at the word *ensample(s).* It should be plain at this point in the evaluation that there is something "up" with the way these two words are used in the King's English. Keep in mind that an *example* is something that cannot be, or should not be, exactly emulated or copied. Certain lessons from Israel in the wilderness have to be applied in measure, for our circumstances are in some ways not literally comparable to theirs. They are our *examples.* Jesus washed the disciples' feet. We do not, and are not required to. You or I may one day be required to minister intimately to a bedridden saint, or to serve in a much more humbling or humiliating capacity than we care to. Though we may never wash another's feet, Christ would still be our *example* as set forth in John 13.

An *ensample*, though related to an *example*, is not the same.

In Philippians 3:17 Paul says, *Brethren, be followers together of me, and mark them which walk so as ye have us for an* ***ensample.*** In a day today where Christians are often taught that they should not follow a man, Paul admonishes and implores that the saints follow him. They are further to *mark them* which so follow Paul, because Paul served as an *ensample* of how a Christian should walk. Before continuing, note the two verses that precede this one:

> *15 Let us therefore, as many as be perfect, be thus minded: and if in any thing ye be otherwise minded, God shall reveal even this unto you.*
> *16 Nevertheless, whereto we have already attained, let us walk by the same rule, let us mind the same thing.* (Phil. 3:15-16)

The reader should take the initiative to go to Phil. 3 and read the passage to assure himself that the author is not in some way defying the context. Just note, in the two verses above, the admonition to all to be *thus minded* (15), is the correction implied for being *otherwise minded* (15). Notice the exhortation to *walk by the same rule, let us mind the same thing* (16). Brethren, Paul is urging the Philippians to be like him and to follow him to the extent that they think like him as well. This is more than a loosely fitted *example* from a different time and different circumstances from which these folks are to learn some lessons. This is a man who is walking before them, facing the same things in the same circumstances as they, and he is their ***ensample.***

An *ensample*, defined by biblical precept, is a person that one can pattern oneself after in every way, if possible, because he is precisely what one is supposed to be. Paul, under the inspiration of the Holy Spirit, told the Philippians that they should follow and emulate people who conducted themselves in the ministry like Paul and he urged them to think and be completely like-minded as Paul was. He was their *ensample.*

In 1 Thessalonians 1:6-7, Paul says to the Thessalonian Christians, *And ye became followers of us, and of the Lord, having received the word in much affliction, with joy of the Holy Ghost: So that ye were* ***ensamples*** *to all that believe in Macedonia and Achaia.* The Thessalonians followed Paul, and due to their excellent deportment as Christians "under fire" they were ***ensamples*** *to all that believe in Macedonia and Achaia.* They exhibited exactly the traits the Lord hopes all Christians will exhibit when faced with much affliction. A Christian could (should) follow their pattern to the extent that he become just like them. Their behavior was so noble and spiritual that it was not only *exemplary* – to be learned from if possible. They were exact *ensamples* of how it should be done.

Next, in 2 Thessalonians 3:9, in the context of orderly versus disorderly conduct among Christians, Paul, surrounded by busybodies, the slothful and troublemakers, reminds the Thessalonians of his behavior as an orderly, disciplined and hard-working Christian that was not merely a reflection of his status as an apostle. He says that he did not have to work, but did anyway. Why? *Not because we have not power, but to make ourselves an* ***ensample*** *unto you to follow us.* In this respect, Paul wanted these Christians to follow his pattern exactly. He was their *ensample.*

1 Peter 5:3 has already been referenced above, in conjunction with 1 Timothy 4:12 and Timothy's being an ***example*** *of the believers.* In Peter's admonition in 1 Peter 5:3, we read again, *Neither as being lords over God's heritage, but being* ***ensamples*** *to the flock.* Timothy was to be an *example* of what a *believer* should be to the lost world. Undoubtedly he was to be an *ensample* to his own flock, but unbelievers had to be born again before they could ever pattern precisely their lives after the young pastor. To unbelievers, he was to be an *example.* To believers, he was an *ensample*, for they could indeed follow, emulate and pattern their lives after his. Peter's exhortation to

the elders was worded as precisely as the rest of the word of God is. The elders were to be ***ensamples*** *to the flock.* Without question, they were also to be *examples of the believers* to lost men round about them, as well.

Examples in the scriptures are loosely fitted lessons, warnings and applications. They cannot be copied or emulated precisely due to certain boundaries or constraints of circumstance. *Ensamples* are to be followed as precisely and as exactingly as possible. They are literally the *samples* of how we should live, respond or act.

2 Peter 2:6, like Jude 7 above, raises again the issue of *Sodom and Gomorrha.* Those two cities appear to be both *examples* and *ensamples.* Peter says, *And turning the cities of Sodom and Gomorrha into ashes condemned them with an overthrow, making them an* **ensample** *unto those that after should live ungodly.* Jude 7 uses the other term: *Even as Sodom and Gomorrha, and the cities about them in like manner, giving themselves over to fornication, and going after strange flesh, are set forth for an* **example**, *suffering the vengeance of eternal fire.* Clear and precise distinctions have been drawn and shown in the rest of the cases to this point. It is consistent to say that the two sodomite cities are both *examples* and *ensamples*, for they are *examples* in the respect that it is unlikely that all sodomite cities will be destroyed in the exact same way (brimstone). If a sodomite city today is destroyed by earthquake, *Sodom and Gomorrha* would still serve as *examples,* for they will suffer the *vengeance* of God, though by earth, not fire; and their inhabitants, despite the method of mortal destruction, will suffer *eternal fire*. In that very way, the two cities are ***ensamples*** *unto those that after should live ungodly*, as well. The *ungodly* of 2 Pet.2:6 will be *condemned... with an overthrow* just as Sodom and Gomorrha, and they will also go off into *eternal fire*. There can be certain dissimilarities that make Sodom and Gomorrha *examples*, but

there are also similarities and a replication of certain details that also make them *ensamples* to the men of our day.

Having covered all the occurrences of both *example(s)* and *ensample(s)*, we return to the case where we first began, to see our last *ensample.*

> *4 And did all drink the same spiritual drink: for they drank of that spiritual Rock that followed them: and that Rock was Christ.*
> *5 But with many of them God was not well pleased: for they were overthrown in the wilderness.*
> *6 Now these things were our* ***examples,*** *to the intent we should not lust after evil things, as they also lusted.*
> *7 Neither be ye idolaters, as were some of them; as it is written, The people sat down to eat and drink, and rose up to play.*
> *8 Neither let us commit fornication, as some of them committed, and fell in one day three and twenty thousand.*
> *9 Neither let us tempt Christ, as some of them also tempted, and were destroyed of serpents.*
> *10 Neither murmur ye, as some of them also murmured, and were destroyed of the destroyer.*
> *11 Now all these things happened unto them for* ***ensamples****: and they are written for our admonition, upon whom the ends of the world are come.*
> *12 Wherefore let him that thinketh he standeth take heed lest he fall.*
>
> (1 Cor. 10:4-12)

To repeat again, the children of Israel were our ***examples*** in verse 6, since their circumstances and judgments are different in detail and in measure. Nevertheless, we are quite assured that while we may not be swallowed by the earth or bitten by snakes, God will still certainly judge New Testament Christians for their lusts (vs.6), idols (vs.7), fornication (vs.8), for tempting God (vs.9), and for murmuring (vs.10). Obviously, vs.11 uses the word ***ensamples***. Notice how the verse is worded. *(A)ll these things happened* ***unto them*** *for* ***ensamples***. Think about it and consider all that has been exposited in this matter. The Israelites in the wilderness are *examples* ***to us***. In verse 11, we are admonished by these things, but they are not our *ensamples. (T)hese things happened* ***unto them*** *for* ***ensamples***. Israel in the wilderness, and even in the Old Testament, was plagued many different times by exotic, and obviously providentially imposed, methods of death. From plagues while they ate (Num.11), to being swallowed by the earth (Num.16), to death by *fiery serpents* (Num. 21), huge proportions of the children of Israel died in truly imaginative and supernatural fashions. Considering the history of Israel after deliverance from Egypt, it happened many times. An exotic and unnatural death in the wilderness was truly an ***ensample*** to the rest of the Israelites of just how they themselves might die if they pushed God past the limits of His mercy! Nadab and Abihu experienced this in the matter of their *strange fire* in Leviticus.10, and Uzza learned the hard way in 1 Chronicles 13. Occasionally, a Christian dies in a somewhat unusual way, and the Lord is perfectly justified in anything that He does, but the proportion of Christian deaths by the judgment of God are not usually so dramatic and theatrical as in Israel's Old Testament times when they were justified in looking for signs from heaven and the miraculous. *(T)hese things happened* ***unto them*** *for* ***ensamples***. They were ***ensamples*** for the rest of Israel. They are indeed *written for* ***our admonition***, but *these things were our* ***examples***. We are not Israelites. Christians in New Testament times do not thrive on signs and wonders (1

Cor.1:22). The likelihood today of one being consumed by fire from heaven or swallowed *quick into the pit* is small. Nevertheless, we will be judged and chastened.

There is a profound and genuinely substantial difference between *example(s)* and *ensample(s)* in the AV 1611 King James Bible. Though the words are similar, they are not identical. Though they are plainly akin one to the other, they are not the same. There are distinct and discernable characteristics between them that are manifest in the King James Bible. Nobody is going to Hell because they confuse, or do not discern the differences between the two words, but let the saint take warning: the Lord is more exacting and precise in His verbiage and wording than is one's favorite scholar! A mortal scholar, who may be saved and sincere, will chase grammatical butterflies into left field somewhere along the way. He will become so preoccupied by tenses and obscure declensions that he forgets that he is dealing with the living words of the Living God. It is the Lord that preserves and delivers His word. Sometimes God uses a route or mode of delivery that men do not appreciate or acknowledge.

But, What about the Greek?

Oh, yeah…about that.

As outlined earlier,

- 7 of the 15 times the words occur, they are derivatives of *δεῖγμα (deigma)*. Of the 7 times, 6 are translated *example(s),* yet 1 is translated *ensample.*
- 7 of the 15 times, the words are derivatives of *τύπος (tupos).* Of the 7 times, 5 are translated *ensample(s)*, and 2 times *example(s).*
- For the record, 1 time *example* is translated from the root *γράφω (grapho)*, which often means *to write* or *to engrave.*

There is direct conflict between the usage of the words in Greek, and the way those words were differentiated when they were translated into English by the AV translators.

- In 1 Corinthians 10:6 & 11, from the same Greek word ***tupos***, comes first, *examples* in verse 6, and *ensamples* in verse 11.
- ***Tupos*** is translated as *ensample(s)* 5 of its 7 occurrences in the New Testament, but is translated *example(s)* in 1 Corinthians 10:6 and 1 Timothy 4:12.
- ***Deigma*** is 6 of 7 times translated *example(s),* but in 2 Peter 2:6 *ensample.* The interesting thing about this is that Jude 7 also contains *deigma.* That is, in the two passages about Sodom and Gomorrha, both passages have the Greek word *deigma*, but the word was translated *ensample* in one, and *example* in the other.

The issue is laid bare to the bone here. The Greek does not make the distinction of meanings between the two words that the King James Bible makes plain. The King James translators, flying in the face of what most today consider the final authority (the Greek), inconsistently translate the same Greek word (*tupos)* into two different words in English, and then repeat that practice again for *deigma.* To be blunt, one must make up his mind at this juncture which of the two he believes is the final appeal: the Greek or the AV 1611. It cannot be both. If one says, "The AV, as long as it translates the Greek correctly or uniformly," then such a one has chosen the Greek (a language it is unlikely that he reads or speaks) as his final authority, because the KJV conflicts with the Greek in the way it processes the two words.

If one does not choose the English, then such a one is rejecting clear and consistent light, instruction and distinction that is found in the King James English alone – not in the Greek and not in any other English version. What did James say? *But the **wisdom that is from above** is first pure, then peaceable, gentle, and easy to be intreated, full of mercy and good fruits, without partiality, and without hypocrisy* (James 3:17). What are YOU going to do?

If one chooses the Greek, it will be necessary to reject the King James English. If the Greek, as the scholars view it, is right, then the King James Bible is wrong. After all, we cannot have translators taking Greek words and just translating them willy-nilly!

If one chooses the English, such a one is in big trouble with the scholars' union, because he has chosen something that essentially overthrows the Greek texts that the scholars study, as well as a great deal of their grammatical and linguistic infrastructure that they have so piously drummed into the heads of their high-paying students. In this respect, is it not once again appropriate to raise the point of the monumental excellence of the King James translators' academic credentials and intellectual achievements? Why would such true and acknowledged scholastic giants allow such *inconsistency* to pass through their finely tuned committee process? The differences between *example* and *ensample* have proven to be substantive. Was the substance the design of the mortal men's minds, mere chance, or was it the intervention of God?

Too Quick On the Trigger

As previously stated, the "archaic argument" has been set forth so often with respect to the King James Bible, that it is now the *"go to"* excuse for just about everyone, just about every time, in just about every circumstance. Sadly, depending on whom one believes and one's "reading level," one might have to learn from 40-100 words which are not normally used in day to day life in order to comprehend the AV 1611. Scattered over one thousand pages or more, is this too monumental a task for the modern English speaker? In a world filled with specialized trade language, computer language, "texting," continuing education, medical specialization, and daily technological advancements, a Christian who loves the Lord "with all his heart" cannot learn 100 new vocabulary words, most of which have meanings that are immediately discernable from context? **The Bible does not have a *language* problem! Man has a *lazy* problem!**

Though there are bountiful places where a plentiful number of authors have gone out of their way to exposit and place on exhibition the superior advantages and accuracies of the King James Bible's "outdated" pronoun forms and verb endings, it is still by no means uncommon to hear the incessant whining and blubbering of alleged "scholars" about the difficulty of the matter. One might draw the conclusion that the issue for them is not really an issue of accuracy or clarity, as they bluster, but rather an opportunity to exploit their thinly veiled purpose: to alter the word of the Lord. Though reading levels of the King James are shown to be easier than the rest of even the new versions,[111] the whimpering and fit-throwing of the intellectually slothful usually overrides any empirical evidence. Though somewhat variant lists of 50 100 words from the AV that are purportedly "archaic" have been published for years, along with helpful definitions, the pink little feet of despoiled Christianity are fitfully stamped as though there were some never-ending, ever-flowing stream of archaic words that simply is too great a burden to bear.

It is a profoundly disastrous development that modern Christians now come to the Bible from the inflexible perspective that the living word of the Living God is

---

[111] Riplinger, G.A., *New Age Bible Versions,* AV Publications, Munroe Falls, Oh 44262, 1993, pp.195-196.

subservient to the language in which it is written. To Christians today, carefully trained and genuinely brainwashed by their scholar-masters, the truth and power of the Bible is both ***limited by*** and ***subject to*** the language in which it is written. In this case the language being considered is English. In their eyes, the English language is the obstacle the truth of the Lord must overcome. English is the problem. English is the issue. The English changes, they tell the saints, so the Bible must in effect change with the language lest "you lose the people". Tragic for naïve, English-speaking Christians is the fact that most have their facts seriously turned around. The devil has managed to invert the facts. ***The King James Bible, following its earlier English Bible predecessors, very much laid the foundations, and formed the streambed for our English language.*** If a potential critic has no time to read the exhaustive research that supports this statement found (as in other places) in *In Awe of Thy Word*, by Gail Riplinger, let him simply refrain from his disputation. The fact is that our native English language was very much sired by the pure English bibles that came before the AV, but the KJV had the profoundest impact upon English after its publication, as well. In many respects, ***the Bible gave us English. We do not alter or throw out the Bible because, in man's corruption, man has changed the English.***

Incidentally, it is reasonable to say that neither the Greek language, nor the Latin can make the kind of claims for origination as can be thus made for English. Neither German, Russian, Spanish, Polish nor any other language can as rightly claim the Bible as their sire, as can the English Bible. ***The English language of our day, or any day, does not set the standard for the Bible. The Bible – the King James Bible – sets the standard for our language!***

With this in mind, and with the generational degradation of our language occurring daily before our very eyes, men have become increasingly comfortable with simply declaring some particular form of a word in the KJV "archaic." They are equally quick to conclude or presume that an "outdated" form of a particular word used in the King James simply is a synonym to another word we are all familiar with. Undoubtedly, there are cases where this very thing is true. However, it is absolutely not true as often as careless scholars would claim.

The case of *ensample(s)* not being the same as *example(s)*, though all the new versions and scholars make them so, has been clearly demonstrated in this chapter. Even Webster, in his English dictionary masterpiece of 1828, makes the two words essentially equivalent:

> ***ENSAM'PLE**, n. [L. exemplum.]* ***An example;*** *a pattern or model for imitation.*[112]

Laurence Vance is a King James Bible defender in every respect, and does not fall into the category of those who would alter the AV in any way. In his edifying work on the so-called "archaic" words in the AV, he too essentially equates and defines *ensample* as an *example.*[113] Again, there is no question that some forms of words in the King James are less used or more "outdated" forms of words which we know and are familiar with in other forms today. For example, it can be said with some certainty that the 10 times the word *wot* is found in the AV equate to the more common form, the word *know* that is used today. This is verified contextually and linguistically. I would never, under any circumstance advocate changing the word *wot* in the KJV to *know,* but I have not *discovered* that understanding the word *wot,* as meaning *know,* in any way defies the sense of the verse or does any disservice to what the

---

[112] *Webster's 1828 Dictionary.* Christian Technologies, Inc. version 2 (Build 20040406), 2004.

[113] Vance, Laurence M., *Archaic Words and the Authorized Version,* Vance Publications, Pensacola, Fl., 32524. 1996, 1999. pp.120-121.

Lord was trying to convey. I remain ready and open to the idea that the Lord may show me or some other in the future, that His use of the word *wot* distinguishes or "flags" some truth or subtlety of meaning that we have not yet comprehended.

In a day where astounding flippancy has replaced profound reverence for the words of God, it must be advocated that the Lord's method is to communicate with us in words (1 Cor.2:13, Ps.12:6) - specific words. We walk by faith and *faith cometh by hearing, and hearing by the word of God* (Rom. 10:17). It is our brand of simple faith that apprehends and takes to heart the tenet that when the Lord uses different words, it is often because He is trying to signify and convey different things. Now, it is without a doubt true that God uses synonyms – two different words that mean the same thing - but the Lord also "flags" and "marks" subtle shades and distinctions of meaning by subtle changes and distinctions in wording, as well. Jesus Christ is the Incarnate Word of God. It is utterly preposterous, irreverent, and perhaps even blasphemous, ***to dictate to Him*** what He can or cannot do – would or would not do – with His word in any language. A novel concept might be to study objectively what He ***actually did do*** with a language, as opposed to trying to overthrow Him as Lord and Master of His own word!

It is left to the reader to discern and judge whether the case that has been made in this chapter is legitimate or not. I believe the evidence is compelling. I also believe that there still await vast treasures of knowledge in the scriptures for those who truly revere and love all the words of God. We are students, not editors; the corrected, not correctors. Before God, we are all students, not judges or gatekeepers of knowledge. We must not, as some, infer or inject meaning or distinction into the word where God has not. We must not in zeal, or for novelty's sake, become Athenian (Acts 17:21) in our quests or studies. *Itching ears* (2 Tim.4:3) is a serious and far-reaching ailment if mishandled. *Diverse and strange doctrines* (Heb.13:9) result when ulterior motives overcome the discipline of study that the scriptures lay out in pattern for us. There certainly can be an overbalance on one side of the pivot point of knowledge and doctrine as well as the other. Nevertheless, consider that the trend of the last days is not too much belief and zeal for the word of God, but a pandemic of doubt, criticism, irreverence and defiance. We are not living in a great *falling away* today because people took the literalness and fervor for all the words of God too far, but rather because people neglected to take them far enough.

All this is to say that King James Bible believers can, without being desirous of changing the Bible, fall into the habit of being too quick to replace in our mental dictionaries a Bible word with another word, or a hasty definition that is not accurate. It would have been (has been) all too easy to say that *ensample* means *example*, but it does not, in truth, hold the exact same meaning. Riplinger has set forth the case that ***bewray*** does not mean ***betray***, ***ensue*** does not mean ***pursue***, ***broided*** does not mean ***braided***, *and* ***alway*** does not mean ***always***.[114] And the case of ***ensample(s)*** versus ***example(s)*** is much the same.

God gave man the Bible to aspire to. The Scripture is a summit of knowledge and understanding to be scaled and labored over for a lifetime. Mountaineers do not set explosive charges on the ascents of Everest in order to make the mountain more accessible to climbers. They dream, plan, train and risk their lives to climb that vast summit as it is. To dynamite a path would ruin the entirety of the labor. There are parts of the Bible one may struggle to understand because God wants that Christian to labor and pray to gain understanding. There will be parts that are obscure because *...my thoughts are not your*

---

[114] Riplinger, Gail, *The Language of the King James Bible,* AV Publications, Ararat, VA. 24053. 1998. pp.80-84.

thoughts, neither are your ways my ways, saith the LORD. For as the heavens are higher than the earth, so are my ways higher than your ways, and my thoughts than your thoughts (Isa. 55:8-9). There will be words that one will have to learn and relearn because his native language is in a state of degradation and God does not use it like some street punk. It is morally wrong to dismiss any of the words of the English Bible as outdated and irrelevant. Learn the words! Do not dismiss and replace the words!

Furthermore, it is folly for the Bible-believer to automatically categorize, or too quickly categorize as a synonym a word that differs from another. It is advisable that one not be too quick on the trigger.

Thorny Observations and Conclusions

There is a clear demarcation and distinction made in the KJV between *ensample(s)* and *example(s).* This is not rocket science, as they say, and there is no necessity of academic degrees to be able to see that as a stand-alone study, the AV 1611 distinguishes between the two words. There is light and clarity in what the English Bible teaches about the two terms. The conclusions drawn are profitable, edifying, and are sown in the good faith promises of God's word. Scholars have not seen the distinction because they do not lovingly and believingly study what the English Bible says. They are quick to play the "archaic word" card, and they do not believe the King James to speak in authoritative voice. Their authority is the Greek. Their prejudice condemns them to blindness.

The Greek makes no such distinction. Let us face facts: Either there is a bumbling in the translation of the King James Bible, or else the Greek scholars missed something that was not missed in the AV. The two languages set forth different revelation of knowledge that is not mutually consistent. What is revealed in the two languages conflicts, even though, thankfully, no one is going to miss salvation over this matter. But then, salvation is not all that matters, is it, dear Christian? *I will make known my words unto you* (Prov. 1:23). *My son, if thou wilt receive my words...*(Prov. 2:1). *Let thine heart retain my words* (Prov. 4:4). *My son, attend to my words; incline thine ear unto my sayings. Let them not depart from thine eyes; keep them in the midst of thine heart* (Prov. 4:20-21). It cannot be both ways in the cases mentioned in this book. The AV translators were fools and blind, insightful geniuses, or vessels the Holy Ghost used to give us His word. The Greek scholars, who never discerned this matter of *ensamples* and *examples,* are either right about the finality of their understanding and views of the Greek behind these words and others, or they are wrong, and their entire infrastructure of scholarship and linguistic condescension is built upon eroding sand. No middle ground – the Greek is the final authority and the AV is precipitous, or else the AV reveals, manifests and instructs beyond the Greek.

The fruit of understanding in this particular case, as well as the ones that have previously been discussed in earlier chapters and will yet be discussed in later chapters, is indeed good fruit (Matt.7:20). Discerning that in accord with James 3:17, *the wisdom that is from above is first pure, then peaceable, gentle, and easy to be intreated, full of mercy and good fruits, without partiality, and without hypocrisy,* and considering the evidence showing the Old English Bible furnishes us *throughly* (2 Tim.3:17) that we *May be able to comprehend with all saints what is the breadth, and length, and depth, and height...*(Eph. 3:18), it seems necessary to point out a salient fact: **Where the Greek is ambiguous, the King James Bible delineates and clarifies what the Greek does not.** Frankly, it must be said that the Greek does not distinguish what the King James English differentiates. We have long been subjected to rambling discourses on the treasures of the Greek by that language's most reputed scholars, but in this case, as in others, the haughty would have done well to have believed, loved and studied the words that the Holy Ghost gave them in their native tongue!

Question: in what way does the English fall short of being superior to the Greek the scholars are working from? I, among many others, have been profitably instructed from the English in a manner that is godly and consistent, and that instruction will help me understand better my role as a Christian and a pastor, not merely as an *example,* but an *ensample.* These scholars of the Greek language do not comprehend the lesson in either Greek or English! Bible-believers are often held in acrimony and contempt for the pedestal upon which we place the King James Bible. Many defenders of the AV flee the battle and yield the ground when they sense their Alexandrian detractors are about to accuse them of holding the KJV as superior to the original languages contained in the texts that we have now. **How is the English anything less than superior?!**

Question: is not the English in this case an advance in knowledge and understanding, when compared to the Greek? The apoplectic scholar, so ready to crown the King James Bible believer with the dunce's hat, and denounce him with imaginative and vitriolic names, should consider the question. How is the nourishment, instruction, and admonition drawn from the KJV by devoted and attentive study anything less than an advance on what these scholars obviously do not know and did not garner from their Greek? How is it that a faithful, young student of the King's English can apprehend and discern the key to understanding the difference between the two words, while the lessons seem lost on entire generations of lofty minds which esteem other sources of light and so quickly dismiss as authoritative the treasure of the AV 1611?

Dual authority equals darkness. As of this writing, no scholar has been found who has spent any discernible time at all trying to unravel the mystery of two English words, so similar yet different, translated differently in such close proximity to one another. Did any Christian scholar or academic actually pray over the words of their English Bible? Did they pray with confidence and faith in God to deliver His word to them in their own language? One cannot tell. What seems evident from the commentaries both old and new, modernist and Fundamentalist alike, is that these men hit a snag when both *example(s)* and *ensample(s)* appeared in the AV, and with no answer readily apparent, they, as is their habit, resorted and fled to their Greek lexicons and dictionaries. Many give lip-service to the King James Bible and defend it to a point. Their defense of it is thankworthy and some of the work done has been profitable to all subsequent generations. The fact is, though, that for a goodly number of such men, when faced with an obstacle or conundrum in English, it takes them all of about three nanoseconds to hightail it to the Greek or Hebrew. They say the King James is the Bible in English, and will fight a modernist over it, but in a pinch they do not get in much praying, meditation or inquiry in those precious nanoseconds. They run to the "original languages" because ***those*** are their final authority. Ultimately they believe that the King James English translation is not worth praying over and meditating upon. In their minds, it is a lesser form of the word of God. They view it as a secondary source of truth, not one that is primary. It is for "lay people" – the unknowing. For the "true scholar", the ultimate truth lies to be found in the Greek and Hebrew, the lexicons and dictionaries, and naturally in the minds and commentaries of the learned gurus. Thus, they waste neither time, prayer, nor effort in laboring over the English words and the precepts set forth in English. All clarity will be in Greek or Hebrew! Their reward for doing so is the darkness that has been demonstrated in these examples to this point.

The million dollar question: Who is responsible for the distinction between the two words as translated in the King James Bible? Again, if the usage of *ensample(s)* and *example(s)* in the AV 1611 is a work of randomness and lack of design, how is it that the King James scholars were really so absent minded that they allowed such inconsistency to get past them? The proximity of some of the occurrences so nigh unto others and the translators' painstaking review and rechecking of the translation work seem to rule against the idea that they were merely unaware of their usage of the two words. So then, if the appearances of the two words were not random, then it only follows that this all must have been by design. If by the design of those 17th century translators, they must have had reason for translating them thus. They must have seen a distinction between the two concepts and those fifty-or-so men must have translated the King James Bible to reflect those distinctions. If that be the case, we should allow the work of those translators to stand unquestioned and unassailed since its manifold superiority is so lofty that modern scholars do not even apprehend what was done or the distinction that was made!

On the other hand, what if the responsibility for the actual translation of those two distinct terms as outlined does not reside merely in the academic excellence and the mortal scholarship of the translators? What if the translators did not cognitively grasp the full depth of the implications of all they translated? What if the Lord actually oversaw the details of the work in a way that the scholars of this hour consider preposterous and heretical? What if God directed the thoughts and meditations and choices of those men in such a way that the translation was not merely the devoted work of spiritual yet intellectual men? Do we not ask God to guide us in our lives? Do we not acknowledge that while many facets of wisdom and knowledge must be attained by discipline and exercise, that there is still a supernatural unction and anointing that exceeds the mere application of ourselves? Do we not ask that God guide our thoughts and hearts in our sermonizing and work for Him? Do we not plead for Him to grant us wisdom in counsel? Do we not seek providential intervention in times when our own measures fail us and our best intentions are insufficient? Do we not beg Him to fill our vessels, and *to do exceeding abundantly above all that we ask or think, according to the power that worketh in us*…(Eph. 3:20)? We plead for discernment from Him. We give Him praise when we consider that He has done such for us, but then it is considered quackery to suggest that God intervened in a special way in a translation committee?

I believe that the Lord is undeniably responsible for the manifold fruit that came out of the King James translation committee. The fingerprints of God seem to mark these places where other explanation falls short. Contrary to the hue and cry, there is no tenet or precept in all the word of God that would forbid God from taking an active role in the various translations of His words. Indeed by biblical example, one would have to conclude it extremely likely that He would indeed so participate. One can be certain from the fruit that there are many translations that He did not lead and involve Himself in, but the Christian must discern these as he does all other things.

To anticipate the predictable accusation, what has been described here is not ***double inspiration***. That particular topic will be addressed in a later chapter, but a Bible-believer must discipline himself not to yield ground and flinch every time the scorners fling an ugly name. God did not have to inspire the Bible over and over again. God did lead and direct men at many points in the Bible's journey through the last 6000 years. He led the Body of Christ to canonize the 66 books of the Bible. Without question, the Lord directed men individually and corporately to preserve and propagate the Bible throughout the Roman persecutions and the Dark Ages. God providentially guided Erasmus, Wycliffe, Tyndale, Luther, and many of the other laborers who passed God's words down through the ages. How is it that God might guide the minds and hands of so many of these men, and yet when it comes to the King James translators, if God directed them in an intimate and detailed way, that must be considered ***double inspiration,*** and heresy to boot?

Chapter 10

Given...For A Covering – Or Not

But I would have you know, that the head of every man is Christ; and the head of the woman is the man; and the head of Christ is God. Every man praying or prophesying, having his head ***covered****, dishonoureth his head. But every woman that prayeth or prophesieth with her head* ***uncovered*** *dishonoureth her head: for that is even all one as if she were shaven. For if the woman be not* ***covered****, let her also be shorn: but if it be a shame for a woman to be shorn or shaven, let her be* ***covered.*** *For a man indeed ought not to* ***cover*** *his head, forasmuch as he is the image and glory of God: but the woman is the glory of the man. For the man is not of the woman; but the woman of the man. Neither was the man created for the woman; but the woman for the man. For this cause ought the woman to have power on her head because of the angels. Nevertheless neither is the man without the woman, neither the woman without the man, in the Lord. For as the woman is of the man, even so is the man also by the woman; but all things of God. Judge in yourselves: is it comely that a woman pray unto God* ***uncovered****? Doth not even nature itself teach you, that, if a man have long hair, it is a shame unto him? But if a woman have long hair, it is a glory to her: for her hair is given her for a* ***covering.***

(1 Cor. 11:3-15)

The passage from 1 Corinthians 11 above is one that elicits rather strong responses from folks in 21st century America – and America is by no means alone in its sensibilities. Truly one of the most offensive attributes that God exercises, besides His continuing intrusion into the morality and spirituality of individuals is His judgment upon various aspects of man's society and culture. Often, it is sufficient for the Lord to merely mention how things should be, and that declaration is more than enough to send a fair proportion of the population right over the edge. To so many today, God is welcomed into their circles of fellowship and interaction so long as He keeps His nose out of personal failures in morality, and as long as He keeps His opinions to Himself regarding societal and cultural ins and outs.

It is no longer apropos in many circles that *(m)arriage is honourable in all, and the bed undefiled: but whoremongers and adulterers God will judge* (Heb. 13:4). In fact, the topic is a real conversation killer at a cocktail party. As the deterioration continues in society, the Lord is pretty much forbidden (at least as much as sinners can limit God) from any negative elucidations on the "gay lifestyle," more aptly described in the scriptures as *sodomy*. Much of what occurred in political and cultural life throughout the 20th century has left mankind at complete adversity with the Lord, and His input is no longer welcome for it is so contrary, negative, and unacceptable to man's agenda.

In many respects, this is true not only of the unconverted portion of the world which desires to give God an occasional wave time to time, but it is also true of a large segment of Christianity, whom the naïve might think would be more accepting of heavenly guidance in their lifestyles and cultural views. In many things, this is not the case at all, and certain chapters of the scriptures – like 1 Corinthians 11 – quickly pierce the thin skins of progressive "Christians."

1 Corinthians 11:1-16 is quick to offend any and all who for any number of reasons and motivations do not hold that the man in a marriage is more than just a "co-equal partner." Ladies in American society have been the targeted spoil of the devil for a long time, and it is quite uncommon to find a lady who has not at one time or other had her mind and heart compromised in regard to the notions of victimization, repression, and subjugation that the world has set forth. It should be clearly stated that it is an absolute certainty that the male gender has failed before the Lord in leadership, spirituality, morality, strength and love. Satan did not snipe at one of the sexes and ignore the other. Certainly, the results have been what the devil wanted: Legislation, ERA, burnt bras, haughty usurpation, resentment of paternalistic notions, oversensitivity to slights and inequities, denial of both the Bible and natural order, and in many cases, undeserved abhorrence of most anything male. Many are the homes that have fallen victim to the tumultuous revolution. Many is the 21st century male who is not one third the man his grandfather was, and one does not have to walk too far down many streets in America to see that bull-dykes and male fairies abound.

In the passage above, in conjunction with other New Testament passages, is set forth God's pattern for man and woman, husband and wife. Incidentally, the Lord's pattern is not the least bit "oppressive," but there is an authoritative and reverential order to the relationship. The marital relationship is supposed to be reflective of the headship and leadership of the Lord Jesus Christ. It is not expedient here to expound all the doctrinal import and implication in 1 Cor. 11, but a great deal is discussed and there are many connections to many other scriptures. Even *the angels* (vs.10) are brought into the whole affair, forewarning that how the man and woman relate to one another plays a pivotal role in the influences of other principalities and powers within the lives of husband and wife.

Tying the passage together from verses 3-15 is the concept of what the AV translators translated as *the covering*. In total, one form or other of the word occurs 7 separate times during the course of the passage. Note below the Bible's text and the insertion of the transliteration of the corresponding Greek word, along with the number for the word found in *Strong's Exhaustive Concordance*: and the *Greek Dictionary* found in the back of *Strong's.*

> *3 But I would have you know, that the head of every man is Christ; and the head of the woman is the man; and the head of Christ is God.*
>
> *4 Every man praying or prophesying, having his head* ***covered (kata – 2596)****, dishonoureth his head.*
>
> *5 But every woman that prayeth or prophesieth with her head* ***uncovered (akatakaluptoo – 177)*** *dishonoureth her head: for that is even all one as if she were shaven.*
>
> *6 For if the woman be not* ***covered (katakaluptetai – 2619)****, let her also be shorn: but if it be a shame for a woman to be shorn or shaven, let her be* ***covered (katakaluptesthoo – 2619)****.*
>
> *7 For a man indeed ought not to* ***cover (katakaluptesthai – 2619)*** *his head, forasmuch as he is the image and glory of God: but the woman is the glory of the man.*
>
> *8 For the man is not of the woman; but the woman of the man.*
>
> *9 Neither was the man created for the woman; but the woman for the man.*
>
> *10 For this cause ought the woman to have power on her head because of the angels.*

11 Nevertheless neither is the man without the woman, neither the woman without the man, in the Lord.
12 For as the woman is of the man, even so is the man also by the woman; but all things of God.
13 Judge in yourselves: is it comely that a woman pray unto God ***uncovered (akatakalupton – 177)****?*
14 Doth not even nature itself teach you, that, if a man have long hair, it is a shame unto him?
15 But if a woman have long hair, it is a glory to her: for her hair is given her for a ***covering (peribolaiou – 4018)****.*

(1 Cor. 11:3-15)

Consider acquainting yourself just for a moment with the words used. Notice in verses 5, 6, 7, and 13, the five occurrences of the boldfaced words. It is easy to see that ***kalupto*** is the root form of each of the words. The various endings represent the different verb endings. The ***kata*** portion of the words is a preposition denoting in these cases *down, down over, down upon.*[115] From hence originates the idea of a covering over something. In the case of verses 5 and 13, the ***a*** preceding the longer word is a negative particle which corresponds to the ***un-*** of ***uncovered***.

Notice that in verse 4, the preposition ***kata*** stands alone representing the word ***covered*** in English. This is consistent since the rest of the *kata's* are connected to the root word for *covering* throughout the rest of the passage.

---

[115] Moulton, Harold K. ed, *The Analytical Greek Lexicon Revised,* Zondervan Publishing House, Grand Rapids, Michigan, 1977,p 213.

Finally, and of special interest, is the fact that the final ***covering*** in the passage in verse 15, is translated from a Greek word that has not been seen thus far in the passage: ***peribolaiou.***

A Brief Synopsis From The AV's English

As stated before, there are plenty of landmines in 1 Corinthians 11 for the modern, socially sensitive soul. Opportunities abound for those who have been culturally programmed in college, in orientations sponsored by helpful employers, or by the news media to get their undies in a bunch. Various punji pits of disputation await the soul who dares broach one of the verboten subjects contained therein.

For the time being, the expository lessons of Christian womanhood and manhood, as well as the proper and honorable subjection to authority must be ignored. So much is contained here and in related passages regarding the sanctified relationship of husband and wife, and there is further the matter of spiritual influences and Spirit influences that should be of prime concern to all who want all the meat and instruction of the passage, but they will not here be expounded. Instead, let the focus be placed on the *coverings* of the passage.

> *3 But I would have you know, that the head of every man is Christ; and the head of the woman is the man; and the head of Christ is God.*
> *4 Every man praying or prophesying, having his head* ***covered****, dishonoureth his head.*
> *5 But every woman that prayeth or prophesieth with her head* ***uncovered*** *dishonoureth her head: for that is even all one as if she were shaven.* (1 Cor. 11:3-5)

Plainly, the *covering* is representative of authority and submission. The reason for the *covering* or lack thereof is explained in a subsequent verse. Suffice to say, it is evident, at this point, that a man praying or prophesying should be *uncovered.* Presumably, at this juncture in the passage, that means with his hat or head-covering off. A woman praying or prophesying should have her head *covered.*

> *6 For if the woman be not* ***covered****, let her also be shorn: but if it be a shame for a woman to be shorn or shaven, let her be* ***covered****.*
> *7 For a man indeed ought not to* ***cover*** *his head, forasmuch as he is the image and glory of God: but the woman is the glory of the man.*
> (1 Cor 11:6-7)

If the woman be not *covered*, she may as well have her hair shorn off or shaved. One thing that should begin to dawn, even at this point in the passage, is that the *covering* has now been connected with the hair in verse 5 and 6.

> *8 For the man is not of the woman; but the woman of the man.*
> *9 Neither was the man created for the woman; but the woman for the man.*
> *10 For this cause ought the woman to have power on her head because of the angels.*
> *11 Nevertheless neither is the man without the woman, neither the woman without the man, in the Lord.*
> *12 For as the woman is of the man, even so is the man also by the woman; but all things of God.*
> *13 Judge in yourselves: is it comely that a woman pray unto God* ***uncovered****?*

> *14 Doth not even nature itself teach you, that, if a man have long hair, it is a shame unto him?*
> *15 But if a woman have long hair, it is a glory to her: for her hair is given her for a* ***covering****.* (1 Cor. 11:8-15)

Verses 8 and 9 are a potent reminder that Genesis 1-3 is not the fable or parable that so many have come to depend upon it being. Every word of it is true, down to God making woman from Adam's rib. Verse 10 is an ominous exhortation relating all the way back to the Angel of light in Genesis 3, the defilement of womankind with God's fallen sons in Genesis 6, and deep prophetic and spiritual import in this very hour. Verses 11-12 trim the man's sails just a bit since tyranny is not an attribute beyond his base nature.

Verse 13 addresses the woman's *covering* yet again, and then in conjunction with that topic, brings the hair back into the equation again in verses 14 and 15. It is a shame for a man to have long hair, but long hair is a glory to the woman.

Verse 15 gets down to the crux of the matter that is most crucial to our concerns. The woman's *hair is given her for a* ***covering****.* At this juncture, there is no reason or room for debate. The woman's long hair is her *covering*, and that is why the Lord kept tying the *covering* to the hair as far back as verses 5 and 6. That is why the man's hair is to be short and distinctly different than a woman's hair.

Considering the cultural times when the passage was written, one should not necessarily stand in doubt that the first mentions of the *covering* in the passage was intended to bring to mind the head-coverings that men and women of the day wore. What covered the head, and when that covering should be applied, would certainly have been a concern, and the important linkage between *the covering* and the proper authoritative symbolism is obvious. Also, it is still true today that as an act of respect and reverence men should remove their hats for prayer and prophesying. Indeed, even as the man's hair is supposed to be short and is part of his *uncovering* before God, it would still be a scriptural mandate for him to remove his hat for prayer and preaching. To have short hair, but to still have his hat on for the specified exercises would be a contradiction, symbolically. On the other hand, women of the past, even in American culture, were much more likely to wear bonnets, scarves or hats than they are today. It simply seems to be not so much in vogue now, though some do argue the woman's *covering* should be understood to be headwear along the lines of bonnets, veils, scarves, etc. Nevertheless, as the wording stands in the AV, it is hard to engineer or wrest in the mind that the scriptures teach anything other than that it is the woman's hair that is her covering (vs.15) as the Lord sees it. The woman in history certainly had occasion to be covered otherwise, and she would still have the liberty to be covered in addition to her hair today, but the fact remains that the covering mandated of God, as she prays or prophesies, is her long hair.

There is no need here to debate all the ins and outs of the passage regarding the specific length of hair ("How long is long"), the changing culture ("That was then; this is now"), or any of the other things that can, and have, been debated through the years in 1 Corinthians 11. The focus here is singular – the *covering* - and by the time the Lord's judgment is rendered on the matter in verse 15, the concept of the hair and the *covering* being linked and connected has been affirmed twice in the passage, in verses 5-7 and 14-15. In all, those things which pertain specifically to hair are mentioned 7 distinct times in the passage. The great lesson regarding the *covering* in these scriptures is, *But if a woman have long hair, it is a glory to her: for her hair is given her for a* ***covering*** (1 Cor.11:15).

Bonnets, Veils, Scarves or Doilies?

Not unexpectedly, there are those who are not in agreement with the previously presented understanding of the final lesson of the passage. Any internet search on "headcoverings" will open a world of articles, sermons, writings and websites that are sometimes wholly dedicated to, at other times merely inclusive of, the subject of ladies' headcoverings. While there are, naturally, the supply outlets for the habits of the Roman Catholic nunnery, there are also many Mennonite and Amish based sites propagating the headcovering in one form or another. You will find these coverings are a concern to some of the old-fashioned Anabaptist movements, and also to many who still consider themselves related to the Reformed doctrines from the Protestant Reformation.

There is some debate and some degree of controversy from group to group regarding just what manner of headcovering is acceptable or ideal. Bonnets, hats, veils and scarves are all discussed, and their virtues or shortcomings commented upon. There is also the concern about length of the covering and what the limits of the head, neck and face that it is actually supposed to cover.

A few years ago, a family visited the church which I pastor on a Sunday morning. I learned later, in a personal meeting with him, that the husband was a Bible College graduate and had something of a preoccupation with the New Testament Greek, and presumably the Old Testament Hebrew. The fact that he revealed himself to be quite a determined Calvinist does not say much for either his ability to draw the truth from Greek, nor to reason with a great deal of clarity from the scriptures in general. During the morning service, as we were about to collectively bow our heads for prayer, I could not fail to notice that his wife would place a piece of cloth on her head. From my perspective, it looked somewhat like a handkerchief, but also something like a small doily. (Men, if you don't know what a doily is, you are probably to be commended. Unfortunately, I do. It is a mark upon my character.)

Allow me to say, at this point, that I appreciate anyone who is separated and courageous enough to *(s)tand... in the ways, and see, and ask for the old paths* (Jer. 6:16). It is not my desire to deprecate any of these groups who are willing to be marked peculiarly as Christians for the sake of the Savior. In a day when "Christians" seem more interested in conforming to the world rather than being transformed away from it, I appreciate someone motivated by godly and chaste ambitions. Myself, my family, and a goodly proportion of our church members have borne the *marks of the Lord Jesus* (Gal. 6:17) enough to have experienced the sharp criticisms of family and friends, as well as the open disdain of the public for some of our non-conformity to the world. The fact is that there is virtually an entire subculture that adheres to the notion of headcoverings for ladies can be considered a blessing to a point. I applaud Christians with guts and convictions. I hold no disdain for the family I described who attended our church. I believe, in many respects, that the young man had been misled in his doctrine and in certain aspects of his deportment. I hope that as a mark of maturity that he is able to recover from some of these things.

It should here be set forth that not every conviction is good or godly, and not every standard that a Christian sets for himself or herself is necessarily edifying or expedient. If one is a vegetarian by conviction, it is a weakness, not a strength (Rom.14:1). It is something that needs to be grown *past.* The real question revolves around whether the Christian standard one sets for oneself is indeed wise, godly, and ordained by God, or whether it is a product of false conviction, misapprehended scripture, or even careless and poor doctrine.

Now, it does the Savior's cause no damage whatsoever that a Christian lady wears a scarf, a hat, or a bonnet when praying, witnessing, or tending her vegetable garden. However, it turns out that this matter does fall directly into the purview of the study here being conducted, along with the concerns for why exactly we come to believe what we do from the scriptures.

What is the Christian's authority, ultimately, for believing what he or she believes about, say, the woman's proper *covering*?

It's In the Greek

As it turns out, one of the initial forks in the road where Mennonite, Anabaptistic and Reformed groups got off the track, pertains to the New Testament Greek, as testified in the following by R.J. Vogel.

> Many today, in mimicking what they've heard, say that the woman's hair is her covering, as it ***seems to imply in verse 15***. Such statements are ***not at all original or honest.*** Besides, the ***Greek word used for 'covering'*** in 1 Corinthians 11:15 ("for her hair is given her for a covering") is ***completely different from the one translated 'covered'*** prior to this in Chapter 11. ***This Greek word (peribolaion), here in verse 15, means*** to 'wrap around'. Hence the meaning would be ... "for her hair is given her for 'to be wrapped around'". ***There is no clear idea here, nor from any early Church writer, that the 'hair' is the women's 'covering'***. Furthermore, it would seem to be negating what Paul had just spent 13 verses on prior to this in chapter 11. ***The words translated "covering", "covered" or "cover"***

> prior to verse 15 in Chapter 11 use an ***entirely different Greek word (katakalupto). This one means to 'veil or cover up oneself'.***[116]

In the excerpt above, it is not hard to see that Vogel's mode of operation was to "go to the Greek." Again, this is the exact same mindset as that of so much of the rest of "Christian scholarship." To them, the Greek holds the New Testament answers. The true treasures, ultimate verification and final authority reside in Greek and overthrow what the AV 1611 says. Notice the opening sentence of the excerpt: *"Many today, in mimicking what they've heard, say that the woman's hair is her covering, as it seems to imply in verse 15.* Well, folks, it is not "mimicking" what one has "heard" to quote 1 Corinthians 11:15 of the King James Bible! That scripture more than "implies" that the woman's hair was given for a covering. It states it directly!

Vogel then directly cites that the Greek word for *covering* in verse 15 is entirely different than the prior words translated *covered* or *uncovered* in the rest of the passage. In this case, the Greek is either this author's ultimate weapon, for from it he gathers the truth he esteems is unavailable in the King James Bible; or, it is his snare and stumbling-block, for from the Greek he rejects the clear statements made in the Holy Bible. An insight into the mindset of this person and his fellow explorers of the "original Greek" is in the middle of the excerpt above: *"There is no clear idea here, nor from any early Church writer, that the 'hair' is the women's 'covering.'"* Well, the KJV clearly states that the hair is the woman's covering. It seems a

---

116 Is the Headcovering Really an Issue? A Serious and Indepth Study (2nd. Edition-revised 1997, 1999 R.J. Vogel) http://www.montanasat.net/rickv/Headcovering_Veiling.html

clear statement and "idea," and why would a real Bible-believer care what an early church writer's idea was or was not?

Thus, we see that in the mind of the author, the Greek trumps everything. To R. J. Vogel, the key is the different Greek word used for *covering* in verse 15. This denotes that the *covering* of the woman is NOT her hair, though that is exactly what the Bible says in plain English.

Another author, expanding on the headcovering issue, sallies forth on the matter of 1 Corinthians 11:15 in this way:

> Much unnecessary confusion has originated in this verse, in that ***some conclude that this must mean the long hair is given instead of a veiling.*** However, the confusion ends when one goes to ***the original text***. The ***Greek word here for 'covering' is peribolaion,*** which literally means 'something cast or thrown around'. The only other place this word is used in the N.T. is in Heb. 1:12, where it says, *"like a cloak (peribolaion) You will fold them up...* . The verb form of the word (periballo), found about 23 times, almost always refers to being covered with a robe cast around oneself. ***This is a completely different word than katakalupto. which is the 'veiling' mentioned in verses 5, 6, 7, & 13,*** and which again means 'something covering completely and hanging down'. The word translated 'for' in the KJV, NKJV, etc. in the phrase 'for a covering' is the Greek word 'anti', which has a range of meanings. but the context clarifies its definition to be 'in behalf of

or 'to serve as' - ***this is verified by the best lexical authorities.*** [117]

Not unlike the previous writer, this author sings pretty much the same song to the same tune. Notice that the "original text" is cited as the ultimate authority in this case. This author does not hold the original text in hand, one can be assured of that! It could be that he actually thinks some of the naïve souls that read him will not know the difference. He is undoubtedly correct in this thinking. More likely though, is that he is mimicking others whom he has heard spout such jargon. That is trade talk, complete with secretive winks, among the scholars, and those aspiring to belong to their club often parrot their verbiage. Notwithstanding this deceitful misdirection, the crucial fact is that this headcovering proponent has to go to the Greek to prove his point.

In the literature of these ladies' headcovering advocates, most of the same arguments are set forth over and over again. After all, it is just one passage, and I suppose there is only so much one can say and still be original. Most strain at various gnats in the passage, and build the same straw men over and over again for the sake of argument. They discard with a sniff the idea of the woman's hair fulfilling the necessary requirements for the *covering* as stated in verse 15. Their reasoning is that the man would then have to shave his head to be truly *uncovered.* Generally speaking, this overlooks two things: 1) the woman's long hair is her covering, and thus a man with short hair *actually is uncovered*, especially if he has no hat on. 2) None of them seem to recognize the progressive nature of the revelation through the passage. When Paul at first

[117] "...Let her Be Veiled." *An in-depth study of 1 Corinthians 11:1-16* edited by Tom Shank, Torch Publications, Kootenai Christian Fellowship, Eureka, MT
http://truthinheart.com/EarlyOberlinCD/CD/Doctrine/BeVeiled.htm#Chapter%201

mentioned the *covering*, it is quite likely that the association in the minds of his readers had to do with headcoverings such as hats or veils. However, Paul then links the *covering* with the hair when he mentioned being *shaven* or *shorn* in verses 5-7. The hair is then again mentioned in verses 14-15, and again linked with the *covering.* The bottom line is that the Lord through Paul gave the Corinthians – and us – a new level of knowledge and revelation in the passage. He took his readers from headcoverings to hair, and then showed in progression that the woman's *hair is given her for a* ***covering***.

Whether or not some have been led to this conclusion advocating the necessity of headcoverings without the aid of the Greek, one cannot really say. Many of the writers are simply synopsizing again what so many others before them have written and argued. Many quote sources all the way back beyond Calvin to Chrysostom and Augustine. This does serve as a reminder that there are two very insidious tools used to teach false doctrine all too often, and these folks have gone for the bait.

First, there is the tradition of men. Christ certainly had His say about this practice in Mark 7:9 and 13. *And he said unto them, Full well ye reject the commandment of God, that ye may keep your own tradition... Making the word of God of none effect through your tradition, which ye have delivered: and many such like things do ye.* It is certainly all too easy to fall back upon the works and teachings of the "great and godly men" of the past. To many, it is often more than sufficient to hear what Dr. So-and-so said or what Brother Somebody wrote about a particular matter. There are plenty of examples of even Independent Baptists, who in practice care a great deal more about what great Baptists of the past wrote than what the Bible actually teaches. The headcovering advocates are quick to quote what their brand and preference of spiritual luminaries said about the matter.

Secondly, there is the Greek and Hebrew. This is not stated merely to "blow the top off" or open a breech that cannot be closed. It is absolutely a fact that most of the cults in this world exploit misapplied and wrested scriptures. The Jehovah's Witnesses, among others, have proven themselves quite adept at playing the Greek game with doctrine so as to make the Bible say what they please, or else to avoid what they do not want to face. For every year that goes by, there are more and more "Christian" people, young and old, who feel perfectly at ease in retranslating the word of God after their own image and prejudices. The "original languages," along with an auxiliary library of reference material, prove to be the perfect instruments - inexact, flexible, dynamic, moldable, and esoteric - by which the foolish student and scholar may, in his own self-delusion, shape and lay the snare that will, in time, trap him.

The fact does remain that most of the arguments these folks set forth for their brand of doctrine, revolve around the salient point that ***peribolaion***, the *covering* of verse 15, is a different word in Greek than ***katakalupto***, the root verb form used for *covered, cover,* and *uncovered* throughout the rest of the passage. Those who argue strictly from the English text for the headcovering as a necessity for Christian women, have precious little force of reason or doctrine that weighs in their favor. The fact is that the strongest argument that they have is the reasoning that the final conclusive covering in the passage is a different Greek word than in any of the previous mentions. The obvious conclusion to draw from this is that if God places as much weight on the Greek as scholars say He does (a big "if" indeed), then having used an entirely different word in Greek for the final *covering* in the passage, the Lord intended us to understand that the woman's hair was a different and distinct *covering (peribolaion)* from the veil or shroud *(katakalupto).* Therefore, a woman's hair is not her only covering. She is supposed to have both an artificial covering upon her head, as well as long hair.

How is one supposed to know that? Well, it is in the Greek!

No, It's In The King James English

It does not make a lot of sense that the Lord would introduce the different concepts of the artificial covering and the hair together, link the two ideas together twice in the short passage, conclude the passage by saying that the woman's *hair is given her for a covering* (1 Cor. 11:15b), only to establish that a woman has to wear both long hair and veil. The fact is that if we exposited our Bibles in everything as these folks exposit theirs in 1 Corinthians 11, we would be in a much different place overall, doctrinally speaking, than we are today. The lessons and meanings of the ordinances of both Communion and Believer's Baptism are to be understood, not by the first places in the scripture that they were introduced, but by the continuing revelation and insight that the Lord gave chronologically throughout the scriptures. There is more conclusive understanding to be had of baptism in 1 Corinthians 1:17 than any Cambellite understands in Acts 2:38. 2 Timothy 4:20 is a much more complete and conclusive commentary on the role of the miracle signs of healing today than Mark 16:17-18. The perspective of the Old Testament law in our lives is better understood by grasping Colossians 2:14, than by remaining stuck in Exodus 32!

The fact is that the headcovering proponents shot themselves in the foot. The Lord's conclusion in 1 Corinthians 11:15 should be final and produce rejoicing. It makes no sense to conclude the matter by remaining stuck in verses 4-6. But then, the King James English is not the problem. The problem is that someone went to the Greek and found what they felt to be a disparity, or they found something to support their predetermination. The Lord's doctrine and conclusion about the matter was perfectly clear in English. There is no necessity or reason to seek elucidation from the Greek.

This brings to light several cogent lessons.

There is a danger that exists in going to the Greek. Acknowledging this danger is nigh unto blasphemy to the bible scholars and the Christian academic powers that be. Going to the Greek today is elevated to something of a sacred pilgrimage or sanctified act of holiness. It is the distinct message of "Christendom" - most seminaries, churches, and radio broadcasts - that nothing could be more spiritual than making that hallowed journey. Congratulations on your success, oh wise ones! Now anyone (with or without a seminary education) who owns bible software is given to believe that he may routinely wrest the scriptures *unto* his *own destruction* (2 Pet. 3:16). The propaganda blitz by the apostates has been so successful that nearly everybody ***just knows*** the original languages are the final authority, and further, they ***truly believe*** that *they* are capable of making the necessary linguistic adjustments to God's Holy Word.

Is there no reason for caution and circumspection, some blood-chilling sixth sense that communicates that trespass is imminent upon unfathomably holy ground? Would to God that the rattlesnake's rattle would animate the previously unwary; that the deafening siren of conscience would overwhelm the senses and drive out the intruder! One should realize that in theory, almost every word of the New Testament Greek text could be translated in some other form than it is presently. Once one commences to make judgments about which word choice is correct versus which one is debatable, where will such a one draw the line? Oh ye who enter here, are you prepared to truly discern God's mind with respect to changes you wish to make in these words? Did God call you to recast the face and form of the scriptures? Are you authorized to do it, and will He bless you for doing it?

By regressing to one's (or someone else's) own understanding of the Greek, one may blatantly affect and wrest an already perfectly clear doctrine or reading in the Holy Bible. Is this something that God will reward at judgment? Can one be so sure that he is credible and knowledgeable enough to overthrow what 47 men at a spiritual and providential crossroad in history accomplished? Is such a one certain – utterly certain – that he has been elected and chosen by God to overthrow the translators work at so critical a juncture in time as this? Can one be so deathly sure that he is unerringly led to renovate that form of words and doctrine that God has blessed for nearly 400 years; that he is called to set his judgment on par with the AV translators? Actually, such a one is presuming to overthrow the judgment of the AV translators with his own where he sees fit. Art thou such an one? Thy favorite "godly" scholar is he whom God hath so anointed, is he?

My personal testimony is that I have never reverted to the Greek or Hebrew in pursuit of clarity, explanation, or treasure. When I do study it, I find much evidence that God's hand did proactively lead in the choices of words in my native English. Yes, understand that to mean that I believe God involved himself, at times, in the translation process. A creationist sees God's handiwork in every single element in nature. As a Bible-believer, I see God's hand in every word, at the turn of every phrase, in the King James Bible. The fact is that I have observed that this preoccupation with the Greek and Hebrew is in many cases the same as playing chicken with the devil. I have never known someone who, in constantly referring to the Greek, did not at one point or another find themselves stumped as to why one thing or other was translated in the King James Bible in its chosen wording. There is no translation that can be utterly consistent in every case, but the angel of light will not point that out. No, Satan will make your old English Bible look like some poetic but careless anomaly. Satan is revealed to be *more subtil than any beast of the field* (Gen.3:1), *wiser than Daniel* (Ezek.28:3), and his first onslaught on man's mind and soul was in regard to what God said.

Yes, the Greek and Hebrew is a road where often men and the formerly anointed cherub play chicken. There, on that isolated, dark, country road (a road a man might best have avoided), in a game he best had avoided, the man plunges headlong into a confrontation which he understands less than he knows. The "boys" all do it, and assure him there are great thrills and much profit in playing. The road is lined with participles, prepositions, tenses, particles and declensions - and experts! The byway is stacked three-deep with expert advisors and counselors in the original languages. He races into the vision-obscuring dust and fog of languages unfamiliar, finds the experience more disorienting than he expected, and comes face-to-face with circumstances the "boys" had not prepared him for. He suddenly confronts eternally weighted matters and everlastingly profound precepts. All of men's souls, all their victories and all their defeats, rest on the power and intricacies of the words that he is playing games with. He is toying around on a battlefield where the eternally *holy* and the unfathomably *sinister* have waged their warfare. He is an intruder; a small, vain, ill-equipped child. He thinks he might yet come out of the experience unaffected, but about that time, he hears a voice that whispers, "*Yea, hath God said?*"

A game of chicken with the devil may seem an overly dramatic representation to some, but that haughty, presumptuous man will come face to face with a linguistic conundrum in the word of God that he is not prepared for. The devil will see to it that he does.

Why did they translate this in this fashion when they did it in that fashion in another place? Why did they render this here and that there? Gesenius says this about this phrase and Kittle says this about that one. Why didn't they honor the tense of the verb here? Thayer presents us with a clearer alternative here. Why did they respect the Vulgate reading there but not here? This is unfortunately archaic and does not communicate the proper sense. Is it not so much clearer to be translated like this? Scholars have long held that this particular portion was unfortunately translated. Dr. So-and-so researched this particular form for his doctoral thesis and concluded...

That man will be caught in a weak moment, with a question for which he has no answer. Or, he may be stunned by the fact that in Greek, the final word in a sequence is different than the other 5-6 in the sequence. He may view this as a failure scholastically or an oversight by the AV translators. A slick scholar with a gift of eloquence and an academic reputation that intimidates many may buttonhole the Bible-believer, who may not feel he has the tools to resist the master. There will be ten thousand decisions made by the AV translators that he could conceivably bring under review. If he is wise, he will determine that he is unequipped to overthrow their work, and if he feels he is equipped, he should at least have the humility to realize that he is not called to do so. If he does decide to enter the revision business, will he stop with one? If so, which one? The likelihood is that he will not cease with one. Bible correction is a heady and addicting racket. Will he stop with one dozen corrections? One hundred? One thousand?

Perhaps, he will be wiser than most and hunker down where certain scholars have settled and will just say that there are places that *could* be changed, but that he doesn't want to commit to saying that they *should* be changed. Strategically, this will advantage him because he will not have to put himself on the line as to what exactly should or could be changed, but it would also keep him out of truly defending each and every word of God as revealed to us in the King James English Bible. Add to that, he might thus avoid being called a Ruckmanite, which is secretly what he fears more than anything. Nevertheless, the Lord *who trieth the hearts* (Ps.7:9), would still know of his reservations, and where his faith ends. Because he has played *The Greek Game,* he now has reservations, although he is still a King James Bible defender. Will the Lord reward this sort of faith in His words more than a faith that unwaveringly trusts the Author of the Book? Will the faith of he who wavers due to the scholarly opinions of the day be blessed above him who considers each and every promise of God inviolable, unerring, unchangeable and precious; not something to be linguistically dissected, dismantled and scrutinized under the microscope of the wisdom of man?

A man who plays poker must absolutely be prepared to lose money. A man who plays *the Greek Game* all but guarantees that he will lose something as well. The devil has played "Chicken" for a long time with man and knows how to win. The devil wins if he causes a man to flinch. If... *faith cometh by hearing, and hearing by the word of God* (Rom. 10:17) - and it does - and if the absoluteness of what the word of God ***is*** or ***says*** is undermined by linguistic games, then a man who plays the game will lose a critical part of his faith if not all of it. The initial and most damaging loss to a child of God playing the Greek Game is his unabashed and steadfast ***certainty***. From that point, it is merely an issue of how much of his faith he will lose.

The real light in this passage in 1 Corinthians 11 is in English, not Greek. The *covering* of verse 15 is perfectly consistent and in harmony with the concept of being *covered* and *uncovered* in the rest of the passage. There is no disconnect, discord, or confusion. Whatever a *covering* had been considered before, by verse 15 all is plain: The woman's *hair is given her for a* ***covering***! The English is perfectly uniform and clear throughout.

On the other hand, the Greek introduces ambiguity and confusion. A student is suddenly faced with two words reflecting a *covering*, where in the English there is only one. **That student is face to face with the monster: two authorities**. More exactly, in the King James he has what he essentially considers a lesser authority anyway. On the other hand, he has the much-vaunted authority of scholarship: the Greek, an authority that presents two concepts instead of one; two ideals; two different words. Are these to be considered disparate and distinct ideals, or were they intended to reflect essentially the same thing? Is the Lord talking about two separate things or merely using two words to teach about one thing? No light or depth of understanding whatever has been attained by going to the Greek in this matter, only confusion. "Going to the Greek" has thrust the student into a decision that has to be made, a judgment that must be passed.

The decision was already made long ago. Someone already made the decision about how to translate two diverse words for *covering* and *covered* from the Greek to English. It should be considered that all this was hashed out some 400 years ago in the AV translation committee. It should at least be considered by the kindergarten quality Greek scholars of our day, that an assembly of men of unsurpassed scholarship considered this matter between 1604 and 1611 and settled it *THEN*! Interestingly, the King James Bible does not even stand alone against the incursions of the overactive Greek correctors in this case. Almost all the new versions actually translate ***peribolaion*** in verse 15, ***covering***. It is a rare occurrence, but even the new versions are relatively clear on the matter, and someone would do better attending to even *them* in this particular instance than in going to Greek.

Once again, the reader should contemplate the idea that it was not merely the excellence of the translators that led them to decisively simplify two possibly distinct words and concepts into the intended reading in English. Perhaps God Himself affected the decision. Whether one considers it the work of man or the work of God directly, there seems one undeniable conclusion: there are ambiguities in Greek that the King James English settles and clarifies.

Again, one must note that reverting back to the Greek is quite literally going "backwards." It is essentially the same as unraveling what God wove, undoing what God did. Perhaps to the Greeks of the day, the uses of the Greek words as God used them, were not the least confusing. Those uses have certainly proven confusing to the men of our day. That is why the Lord said what He said, the way He said it, in the translation of the King James Bible. In this particular case, even many of the new versions are right about it. Generally, men think it an idiotic idea to go backwards technologically or medically, in communications, in transportation, or in matters of convenience in our society. Why then would men think it an advancement to regress to Greek ambiguity when the Lord has given perfect clarity in English?

It can then be said without fear of error that **the English translation of this passage in the King James Bible is manifestly superior to its Greek roots!** The English translation of 1611 is an advancement in simplicity, clarity and understanding as compared to the original language. The English does indeed ***correct*** any misunderstandings, misapprehensions, or misgivings that may have arisen due to uncertainty about the Greek meaning.

Chapter 11

"Synagogues'" Strange Setting

(Psalms 74:8)
They said in their hearts, Let us destroy them together: they have burned up all the ***synagogues*** *of God in the land.*
(AV 1611)

It seems almost insultingly elemental to have to specify that the word of God is a Book that is composed of and inclusive of all the words from God that He intended for us to have. By faith, the Bible-believer understands that the "word of God" certainly encompasses all the words of God, that it is not polluted by insidious words originating from some other source. That same faith instills within the Bible-believer the belief that the mighty power and majestic integrity of God has overseen the acts of inspiration, preservation, interpretation and even translation. It is a holy and simple guilelessness in childlike faith and trust that understands that our pure God would inspire, preserve and deliver to us pure words in the pure word of God. *Every word of God is pure: he is a shield unto them that put their trust in him* (Prov. 30:5).

Bible-believers are not offset by the fact that the Lord used fallen and mortal vessels to deliver His words in utterly pure form. It is no more remarkable that God would use fleshy vessels to deliver a perfect and inerrant product than it is that Satan would use fleshy vessels to insert and promulgate vile pollutions and corruptions. In the former case, *The words of the*

LORD are pure words: as silver tried in a furnace of earth, purified seven times. Thou shalt keep them, O LORD, thou shalt preserve them from this generation for ever (Ps 12:6-7). In the latter case and in the same context, *The wicked walk on every side, when the vilest men are exalted* (Ps 12:8).

It is amazing, but profoundly insightful scripturally, to apprehend just how few "Christians" there are today who in childlike simplicity and trust believe the actual attributes and characteristics that God promised regarding the nature and excellence of His word. Great wonderment indeed should accompany the realization that those great swaths of scholars who have "given their lives" to the study of matters related to the Bible, are the very ones who have fomented infidelity and undermined Christian confidence in the very scriptures they profess to so love and adore.

This great departure *from the faith* (1 Tim.4:1) often strikes far closer to home than is imagined. There are several internet lists of "King James Bible-believing churches" designed to assist Bible-believers in finding churches when relocation is contemplated, when a friend in a far-off city is seeking a church, or a vacation is imminent. Many has been the disappointed soul whose expectation was that he would find a body of genuine like-minded King James people, but who found little more than a body of Neo-Alexandrians who merely made a show of fidelity to the Old Book in order to be legitimized. This is not a criticism of online lists, which have several obstacles in the way of discovering the true nature of certain churches. It is a criticism and an indictment of the type of Christian who knows they owe allegiance to the acknowledged word of God, but wish to get by with lip-service and an occasional salute thrown in the direction of the "old King Jimmy." Many is the Fundamental, Baptist, King James Bible-waving pulpiteer who still fancies that he is being true to the KJV and the Lord by his attempts to embellish and refine his

Bible with the Greek. He proceeds in this endeavor without understanding that he is not only undermining confidence in the words of the Bible, but that he is also undercutting the truth, short-circuiting his power and starving the Lord's sheep. Many is the higher-profile pastor, radio preacher or Fundamentalist educator that, having jump-started some young Christian's spiritual life, must be largely forsaken in time as it gradually dawns on the young Christian that the teacher is not the defender of the faith or the Bible-believer he professes to be. Further, it is a bitter, sad awakening for many to learn that Textus Receptus-brand King James defenders can often be as vitriolic and condemning of real King James Bible believers as can full-blown Alexandrian bible promoters.

For all the legitimate research and study that can be invested in the whole King James Bible issue; for all the years, strength and energy that can be poured into it; for all the books that, thankfully, have been written; for all the debates that have ensued over the issue; and for all the books and sermons that should be received and digested about it – there still remains the fact that the whole issue still devolves down to a gloriously simplistic principle. It is this: ***a guileless and child-like faith in the God who delivered His words to us, His saints.***

Again, it seems almost insultingly plain to say that words individually communicate very specific and individualized meaning to the heart and mind. Lawyers, diplomats, doctors, mechanics, computer programmers and chemists would never suffer one to browse through their documents, research papers and technical manuals and replace or substitute words and terms willy-nilly. How is it that the meanings of certain words are immutable and inviolable to those of the legal or medical profession, as those words hold such crucial and critical distinctions of meaning, yet Christians now suffer any *Joe Six-pack* who knows the Greek alphabet to change the words of the Living God?

It was God that chose the words He designed to use. God - Jesus Christ - is the incarnate Word of God. The words He uses and chooses all carry with them distinctions in meaning and tone. They come across with various degrees of force, inference, insinuation and dogma. The King James Bible molded the form and meanings of the English language that we know in a way that few modern, 21st century CNN addicts comprehend. Our English language does not dictate meaning to the Bible. The AV 1611 has, instead, dictated and defined the meanings of the English language that is our historical tongue. Most importantly, the words God uses form chains and links of meaning one with another, so a vast interconnected web and network forms in the heart and mind of the man who immerses himself and delights himself in God's word. The Lord marks certain truths by sanctifying certain words for usage specific to those certain truths. The words *deacon* and *charity* mean something very specific in the English Bible, and those specific meanings are not necessarily carried in Greek or in the secular and degraded brand of English spoken today. The Lord highlights, illuminates and earmarks specific truths by the words that He has chosen and led men of God to write and translate. An out-of-place or unwieldy translation in a lexicographer's "opinion" is often a key or a landmark for which the Lord is responsible, and it is placed there to attract the attention of the Bible-believer and to open the truth of a passage.

An example of just such a case is found in Psalms where the word *synagogues* is used.

> *They said in their hearts, Let us destroy them together: they have burned up all the* ***synagogues*** *of God in the land.*
>
> (Ps.74:8)

Synagogues - In Psalms?

The usage of the word *synagogues,* as found in this passage, is not much unlike tossing a skunk into the midst of a gathering of *Mary Kay* enthusiasts. A great deal of confusion proceeds from that one element that is discordant with the theme and surroundings.

First, in the entirety of the Old Testament, this is the lone occasion where the word *synagogue(s)* is found. With this exception, there simply are no *synagogues* found in the Old Testament. Biblically a New Testament concept, the term *synagogue(s)* is routinely found some 70 plus times in the New Testament.

Secondly, the scholars are forced to try to isolate the exact time of the origin of the synagogue in Jewish history and do not have a great deal of success. Adam Clarke acknowledges that their origins must be "supposed."

> It is ***supposed*** that there were no synagogues in the land until after the Babylonian captivity.[118]

The Zondervan Pictorial Encyclopedia likewise postulates:

> The later lit. always connects the origin of the synagogue with the period of Babylonian captivity and return under Ezra and Nehemiah.
>
> …the term has traditionally been applied to the Jewish communities in the Diaspora.

[118] Clarke, Adam. *Clarke's Commentary.* (1998) P C Study Bible (Version 2.11) [Computer Software]. Seattle, WA: Biblesoft.

> …the historical aspects which led to the formation of the synagogue can be ascertained from the society which existed under Pers. (Persian) and later Hel. (Hellenistic; Greek) rule.[119]

The bottom line is that nobody is exactly sure when the actual concept and construction of the synagogues arose. Any Bible-believer can figure out that once Israel and Judah were led into captivity by Assyria and Babylon, respectively, that the curtailment of the duties of the priesthood and the temple worship itself being ended, some other form of Jewish religious gathering and institution would form. This too is acknowledged by *The Zondervan Pictorial Encyclopedia.*[120]

The commentators and scholars are forced to speculate. In speculating, Matthew Henry presumes that the synagogues were equal to the schools of the prophets.

> He complains of the desolations of the synagogues, or ***schools of the prophets***, which, before the captivity, were in use, though much more afterwards. There God's word was read and expounded, and his name praised and called upon, without altars or sacrifices.[121]

…And, of course, with their speculations come Hebrew lessons:

---

[119] Tenney, Merrill C., ed, *The Zondervan Pictorial Encyclopedia of the Bible* (Grand Rapids, Michigan: Zondervan Publishing House, 1975, 1976) Vol.5, p.555

[120] Ibid. pg.555.

[121] Henry, Matthew. *Matthew Henry's Commentary on the Whole Bible.* (1998) P C Study Bible (Version 2.11) [Computer Software]. Seattle, WA: Biblesoft.

> The word ***mow`adeey*** (heb 4150), ***which we translate synagogues***, may be taken in a more general sense, and mean ***any places where religious assemblies were held***: and that such places and assemblies did exist long before the Babylonian captivity, is pretty evident from different parts of Scripture. It appears that ***Elisha kept such at his house*** on the sabbaths and new moons. See <2 Kings 4:23>. And ***perhaps to such James may refer***, <Acts 15:23>, a species of synagogues, where the law was read of old, in every city of the land. And it appears that ***such religious meetings were held at the house of the Prophet Ezekiel,*** <Ezek. 33:31>. And perhaps every prophet's house was such. This is the only place in the Old Testament where we have the word synagogue. Indeed, ***wherever there was a place in which God met with patriarch or prophet, and any memorial of it was preserved, there was a mo`ed (heb 4150), or place of religious meeting***...[122]

This chapter is not intended to document all the speculations of scholars or to track down every arcane historical detail that Bible encyclopedia writers are so adept at recording. Anyone who has ever researched anything through Bible dictionaries and encyclopedias knows that a researcher can just about go blind reading all the trivia and minutiae contained therein. Furthermore, such details do not always contribute to any real or edifying knowledge of the matter being researched. The prior information has been included to show that the one-time Old Testament word *synagogues* in Psalm 74:8 caused a stirring and a restlessness among the scholars. They had to

---

[122] Clarke, Adam. *Clarke's Commentary.* (1998) P C Study Bible (Version 2.11) [Computer Software]. Seattle, WA: Biblesoft.

figure out why it showed up in Psalm 74 once only, for it does not appear anywhere else in the Old Testament. They had to speculate that the "schools of the prophets" were "synagogues" all along. They had to speculate about exactly when the synagogues got started, as they must have had some beginning before the time of the New Testament, which contains so many references to them. The scholars had to resort to Hebrew for light, and perhaps the judge is still out on the nature of the "light" they did get.

In the end, the scholars treat the word *synagogues* in Psalm 74:8 like the proverbial red-headed stepchild. New versions, including the NKJV, do not venture to follow the King James by translating the troubling term ***synagogues.*** Most all of them opt for the non-commitment of the term **"meeting places."** The majority of the commentators immediately made assumptions about what the *synagogues* ***really were*** instead of accepting that the Lord just may have meant *synagogues* in the Old Testament just the same as He meant it in the New.

About Those *Synagogues*...

The reader would do well to stop and consider that the word from which *synagogues* is translated in Psalm 74, is the Hebrew word ***moed*** *(mo-ade').* The interesting thing is that according to the Englishman's Concordance, ***moed*** is translated over 230 times in the Old Testament as something other than *synagogues.* In fact of 230-plus times, it is only translated *synagogues* one time. The rest of the time it is most usually translated as *congregation,* but sometimes *solemn feasts, solemnities* and a few other terms. Think of it - a singular Old Testament occurrence of a word in English which was translated some 230 other times as something else. A spiritual minded man who was *certain* God had given him His very words might be inclined to think that the Lord was actually trying to point out something from such an occurrence!

Naturally (as in the *naturally* of 1 Cor. 2:14) the average scholar's perspective is that *synagogues* is one of those nasty loose ends, translationally speaking, that slipped through the scholarly cracks, and that it was seemingly translated outside of conformity with the rest of the occurrences of ***moed***. In their minds, the poor suckers who read the King James need to employ some editorial penmanship in the margins of their Bibles beside *synagogues* in Psalms 74:8. The scholars *tisk-tisk* those King James translators and think it is such a shame how they misled folks so badly by their "constant scholarly misfires."

So, there you have it. The word *synagogues* sticks out like a red Bee Farmall tractor in a field of green corn. It is likely that somebody either fouled up, linguistically speaking, or that God is alive and chose to translate the word thus so as to attract attention and teach something to His children who believe the Book. Which do you think it is?

For a Bible-believer the intrigue deepens just a bit upon the realization that there is another occurrence of the Hebrew word ***moed*** in the same passage. Notice verse 4 as well as verse 8:

> *Thine enemies roar in the midst of thy* ***congregations (moed)****; they set up their ensigns for signs.* (Ps 74:4)
>
> *They said in their hearts, Let us destroy them together: they have burned up all the* ***synagogues (moed)*** *of God in the land.*
> (Ps 74:8)

Whether one ultimately considers the Lord or the King James translators in control of what was ultimately passed on to us in the KJV, one has to admit that either of those two entities had to have realized that He/they had just translated ***moed*** in verse 4 as *congregations*. It seems unlikely that either of the two would blindly translate the same word four verses later as *synagogues* without being aware of it. This is a particularly salient consideration when one again ponders that this is the solitary occurrence of *synagogue(s)* in the Old Testament. Just taking as a given that the Lord had His hand in the translating controversy here, one must ask a question. What exactly is it that He was flagging and marking for us that we might give it our attention and be able to understand?

About Those *Synagogues'* History

A Bible-believer who is well grounded in dispensational truth and in *rightly dividing the word of truth* (2 Tim. 2:15) may have made an observation when reading classic Bible commentators and expositors. He may have noticed that there is a wrestling with the application of the text at hand.

Now it should be understood that there are commentators who do not believe the Bible to be historically factual at all. These particular commentators think the Bible is virtually useless as a history book. These liberals, when they do use the Bible, basically devotionalize and spiritualize everything in sight. Classic conservative commentators battled this movement by recognizing the truth, which is that the Bible, as an inspired Book, is also an inspired history Book. The fact is that God focused and centered His perspective of history geographically in a place where the world's historians do not: Israel. The Lord also focused on people and events within that geographical region that worldly historians have no knowledge of and little concern for. Without the Bible, the world's historians would have entirely overlooked the insignificant nomad named Abraham and an anointed shepherd boy named David. Even with the Bible, most of them consider the majority of events contained in the Bible as superfluous, at best. Thus, most of the popular, recognized, conservative commentaries focus on finding the historical place and setting for the events recorded in the Bible. This is a good exercise and is vastly superior to spiritualizing almost everything in the Bible and divorcing it from its historicity.

So it is that *The Zondervan Pictorial Encyclopedia* readily, and perhaps rightly, says that Psalms 74, along with a few other Psalms, *...were produced by Asaphites and Korahites who apparently survived the destruction of Jerusalem in 586 B.C.*[123] This date would place the historical application of the Psalm at the destruction of Jerusalem under Nebuchadnezzar with the subsequent Babylonian Captivity following.

This application is fine, but it assumes that there were synagogues in the land before the captivity. When exactly did the synagogues come into vogue? Nobody is quite sure. Before the Babylonian Captivity? After the Babylonian Captivity? If they were not in fashion until after the Captivity, then when and by whom was the 74th Psalm written? Considering that *synagogues* went unmentioned in the Old Testament except in Psalm 74, why try to jam the synagogues in and make for awkward and uncertain application? To locate the synagogues prior to the destruction of the first temple in 586 B.C. is difficult at best, since they are never mentioned and even the commentators have to "suppose."

---

[123] Tenney, Merrill C., ed, *The Zondervan Pictorial Encyclopedia of the Bible* (Grand Rapids, Michigan: Zondervan Publishing House, 1975, 1976) Vol.4, p.928.

The Lord placed *synagogues* in Psalm 74:8 to show us *a more excellent way* (1 Cor.12:31).

Those *Synagogues* are Prophetic

One of the remarkable traits that mark the writings of modern commentators, exegetes and scholars is their unending propensity for presuming that God was never able to communicate exactly what He meant in language that we all understand. It seems that the way God said things is never sufficient, accurate or best in the eyes of these scholars, and one of the first lines of approach is to correct God or help Him say it better. In combination with man having diagnosed the Lord as being *language challenged* is the scholar's inclination to look for different and deeper linguistic meanings than that which the Lord plainly set forth in His Book.

There is virtually no end to the audacity and temerity of fallen mortals.

In this particular case, no one seems to consider allowing the *synagogues* of Psalm 74:8 to stand exactly as written and to be understood in the common way with which men are familiar. The new bibles must alter the translation across the board. The commentators and dictionaries must leap into the chasm of misunderstanding to help us grasp that the Lord really meant and intended us to apprehend that he was speaking of the "schools of the prophets" and other similar assemblies that they "suppose" were contemporary with the times surrounding the Babylonian Captivity.

But wait…

What if the Lord intended Christians to think of the *synagogues* of Psalm 74 just as we think of them today? What if the *synagogues* He spake of were literally the synagogues of our day, which the Antichrist will cast down in his ardent abhorrence for the Jews? Besides that, what if there is a dual prophetic application, referring to the destruction of the second temple (70 AD) by Titus along with all the subsequent Jewish persecutions that arose at that time? Were any synagogues burned in 70-100 AD? Will not many synagogues be destroyed when the Antichrist turns the full force of his wrath upon the nation of Israel and Judaism during the prophetic time of the Great Tribulation?

The Lord is a God of words, Christ being the Word of God Himself. The scholars fly right past *synagogues* in Psalm 74:8 due to their presumptions, their irreverence and their unbelief. Nevertheless, the word *synagogues* is the key, for it stands out like a sore thumb in the Old Testament scriptures – which is exactly what the Lord intended! He intended the singular occurrence of the word to be a marker and an eye-opener for someone that took Him at His word. The solitary occurrence of the word is a flare sent up above the wide plains of scripture in the blackness of night. It is supposed to attract attention, not be explained away. This is in no way presented to disprove or disavow any application of the Psalm to 586 B.C. or thereabouts. It is simply intended to elucidate the reading as found in the AV 1611 (*synagogues*) as being correct, accurate and revelatory, and to take the mask off the folly which meets every oddity or conundrum in the scriptures with a blasphemer's eraser and pen.

1) Applying the Psalm to the destruction of Jerusalem and the *synagogues* at the time of the Babylon Captivity is awkward, for one first has to explain why *synagogues* were not mentioned prior to the captivity, or at any other time in the Old Testament. To explain this, one has to make assumptions and suppositions about the nature of those *synagogues*. This, naturally, gives the scholars both excuse and opportunity to

twist and wrest scripture, to dig deeply into secret word meanings, and to generally tear up the Bible as it is written, while tailoring their own speculations to their precious prejudices and opinions. All in all, the proposition that *synagogues* were burned up in 586 BC is possible, but there are better explanations that are *eas(ier) to be intreated* (Jas. 3:17) and more praiseworthy as far as God's record of the event is concerned.

2) The *synagogues* of Psalm 74:8, marking a prophecy regarding the destruction of the temple and the persecutions of the Jews under Rome and Titus in 70 AD and beyond, are in complete concord with the passage. The synagogues were certainly in fashion and were common in everyday life in Israel in those days. Nobody would need to go to either Greek or Hebrew to apprehend any meaning whatever. What is remarkable is that God would seed the Old Testament passage in Psalms with the word *synagogues* to point directly to at least one time-frame to which He was referring. This breaks entirely from His habitual translation of the Hebrew word ***moen***. One must understand that this would mean that God planted a key to meaning in the English translation of the Authorized King James Bible that is found nowhere else at all.

3) *(S)ynagogues* in Psalm 74 also points to an even more distant (for the Psalmist) prophetic peak – the destruction of the future temple and *synagogues* during the reign of the Antichrist in the time of the Tribulation. As long as we understand that the application is virtually current in time for us, no one should have a problem understanding what is meant by the word *synagogues*! Again, the salient and profound point in this scenario is that the prophetic applications which most readily are suited to Psalm 74 are marked by the English word, *synagogues*. Most earth shaking to a biblical scholar is that the truth of the matter is pointed out in the Old Book in a way that utterly exceeds the capabilities of biblical Hebrew and the mere

linguistic excellence of the certified and acknowledged expert in Hebrew. Without believing the English of the King James Bible and accepting *synagogues* as the correct and faithful translation in Psalm 74, neither the Hebrew nor any linguistic expertise can shed a ray of light. The truest and most seamless applications of the Psalm are specified in the ***translation of the English***, not in the Hebrew original. ***Somebody*** provided the key to understanding when the scriptures were ***translated into English.***

Exploring the passage a bit more affirms the legitimacy of the later time applications of the Psalm. Again, the three possible time frames center basically around 586 B.C., (the Babylonian Captivity), 70A.D., (the persecutions of the Jews under Titus and Rome), and the yet future desolations prophesied of and engineered by the Antichrist in the Great Tribulation.

The Synagogues. Already much discussed in this chapter, they are the flag that earmarks the passage in Psalm 74 as being primarily applicable in prophecy to the times of the New Testament – either 70 A.D., 2011 and beyond, or both. Interestingly, on the date that I wrote this particular paragraph, a simple Google search of "synagogue destroyed" revealed three synagogues in Israel destroyed since 2008, but that was only on the first page of the search results. As a foretaste of the "big event", Psalm 74 is being fulfilled in part right now.

The Sanctuary. Notice that consistent with the three possible time-frames is the mention of the Lord's *sanctuary*, which is understood to mean the *sanctuary* of the Lord's temple in Jerusalem.

> *Lift up thy feet unto the perpetual desolations; even all that the enemy hath done wickedly in* ***the sanctuary***. (Ps. 74:3)

> *They have cast fire into **thy sanctuary**, they have defiled by casting down the **dwelling place** of thy name to the ground.* (Ps. 74:7)

The *sanctuary* is *the dwelling place of thy name* (vs.7). It is the temple. The temple was destroyed in Nebuchadnezzar's day (586 B.C.). After being rebuilt under Ezra, it was destroyed again in the turmoil after the death, burial and resurrection of Christ (70 A.D.). The temple site, presently commandeered by the Mosque of Omar and administrated by the Philistines, will soon once again be occupied by the Lord's house! The full complement of ritual Jewish worship and sacrifice will again be instituted and exercised until the Antichrist, in the fullness of his power, *shall cause the sacrifice and the oblation to cease* (Dan. 9:27) in the middle of the Great Tribulation. The *sanctuary* will yet again be *defiled* (Ps.74:7) during that time which is yet future.

In Bible history – *Bible history*, now – since no *synagogues* were mentioned but in New Testament times, it is reasonable to consider that the *sanctuary* also mentioned in the Psalm would also refer to the ones in New Testament times: The one of Christ's day and the one of the Antichrist's day.

The Signs. Take note that the psalmist complains about the *signs* which are absent for Israel at the time referred to in his prophecy:

> ***We see not our signs**: there is no more any prophet: neither is there among us any that knoweth how long.* (Ps. 74:9)

The *signs* are very important landmarks for Israel and they are very important concepts to be understood by Christians who have hopes of digesting the meat and vegetables of Bible doctrine. Israel is the particular and principal repository for the

Lord's signs and wonders. Charismatic and Pentecostal craziness notwithstanding, it is certainly true that God can and does work miracles in people's lives. Nevertheless, the Bible facts remain that God established the nature of His dealing with Israel as a nation upon supernatural signs and wonders from the very start. In Exodus 4:8, Moses was given *signs* for the first time to prove his absolute authenticity as a deliverer unto Israel. Throughout the entirety of Israel's Old Testament history, their prophets exhibited miraculous signs and God Himself supplied them with signs from both heaven and earth. Jesus Christ came as the Jewish Messiah bearing great signs and miracles, but it is not often appreciated these days that those signs were not for the Gentiles round about, but for the Jews for whom He came first and foremost. *Go not into the way of the Gentiles* (Matt 10:5), He said to the apostles at the first, and even Romans verifies who was first in line: *to the Jew first* (Rom. 1:16). The Jews were thus the primary and intended recipients who were to profit by the *signs*. Early in the Church Age Paul established the nature of God's dealings with Jews versus Gentiles: *For the Jews require a sign, and the Greeks seek after wisdom* (1 Cor. 1:22). The signs that God and the Apostles worked in early New Testament times, and the sign gifts given, were primarily for the benefit of the Jews whom God had always favored with signs. Thus, *tongues are for a sign* in 1 Corinthians 14:22. As the Book of Acts records, when the Jews increasingly rejected the Gospel, God increasingly opened the Gospel doors unto the Gentiles (Acts 13:46, 18:6 & 28:28). So, by the end of his ministry, sometime in the 60's A.D., Paul, the man who worked miracles even with *handkerchiefs* which he had touched (Acts 19:12), left a fellow-laborer *sick* (2 Tim. 4:20), prescribed medication for illness (1 Tim. 5:23), and traveled with his own physician (2 Tim. 4:11).

An understanding of all this reveals that the primary prophetic application for Psalm 74, may well belong primarily to the yet future Tribulation period, for the Jews of 70 A.D. had enjoyed a vast richness of *signs* and miracles from God during both Christ's ministry on earth and the subsequent supernatural ministries of the Apostles. Paul is said to have died in the 60's A.D., but John did not die until 90 A.D. or so. A Jew bemoaning the destruction of the temple and the *synagogues* in 70 A.D. would have had to be delusive, blind or forgetful to say, *We see not our signs.* The Jews of that day were probably all three (blind, delusive and forgetful), and thus the passage does have application to New Testament times past. However, the statement of Psalm 74:9 fits the future even better.

Today, one does of course see *the signs of the times* (Matt. 16:3) and one does see the latter day prophecies coming to pass in the incremental fashion which the Lord promised. However, with open disdain for the Benny Hinns and the other Crazy-matics of the world, there are no longer to be seen the type of signs and miracles ministry from God today as the people of 30-50 A.D. witnessed! These signs are no longer prevalent because the gospel is now primarily directed towards the Gentiles, and in this dispensation *we walk by faith, not by sight* (2 Cor. 5:7). More importantly, ***ISRAEL is not seeing signs as in days of old either.*** As things stand at this very hour, Israel can testify that *We see not our signs!* As prophetic times and events march onward, the body of Christ, the Church, will soon be raptured. That dispensation ended, the Lord will once again begin His primary dealings with Israel in accord with *the time of Jacob's trouble* in Jeremiah 30:7. Most of Israel, along with the rest of the world, will be deceived and deluded by the Antichrist. He will arrive on the scene *with all power and signs and lying wonders* (II Thess. 2:9) and the vast majority of Jews will likely believe they are in the very shadow of their long-awaited Messiah. One day though, the Son of Perdition, *that Wicked* (2 Thess.2:8), will defile the Jewish temple yet again, and place *the abomination of desolation, spoken of by Daniel the prophet... in the holy place* (Matt 24:15). There will indeed be a small remnant of Jews that escape. These will be the ones that take heed to the ***scriptures*** and recall the Lord Jesus' admonition, *(whoso readeth, let him understand:) Then let them which be in Judaea flee into the mountains* (Matt. 24:15-16). This remnant will be treated to great signs indeed for they will not only see God (Christ) face to face as in Exodus, but they will be provisioned supernaturally as well (Micah 7:14; Hos. 2:14-15).

> *And I will bring you into the wilderness of the people, and there will I* ***plead with you face to face****. Like* ***as I pleaded with your fathers in the wilderness of the land of Egypt****, so will I plead with you, saith the Lord GOD.*
>
> (Ezek. 20:35-36)

> ***Feed thy people*** *with thy rod, the flock of thine heritage, which dwell solitarily in the wood, in the midst of Carmel****: let them feed*** *in Bashan and Gilead,* ***as in the days of old. According to the days of thy coming out of the land of Egypt will I shew unto him marvellous things.***
>
> (Micah 7:14-15)

In the midst of their national tragedy and Great Tribulation, the tiny fragment of believing Israel will once again enjoy the light in the face of their God. THEY will see their signs, but the majority of Jews that amalgamated with the rest of the nations in being subtly seduced by the Man of Sin will not see those signs. Having killed their own Messiah and received the Devil's anointed one, having rejected the miracles of God and Christ and having fallen for the Devil's deceitful power, lost and unbelieving Israel will be utterly without rudder, light, revelation, priest or *signs*!

The Seers. Another detail of note in the passage is with respect to the prophets. Notice what the psalmist further complains of:

> *We see not our signs:* ***there is no more any prophet****: neither is there among us any that knoweth how long.* (Ps. 74:9)

It should be noted that there certainly was a prophet in the days of the destruction of Jerusalem. His name was Jeremiah. Further, Daniel, once in Babylon was prophet to Israel for many decades.

Further still, it is a bit hard to view the psalmist-prophet's complaint as accurate in 70 A.D. or thereabouts. John Baptist was haranguing Jews and Romans by around 30 A.D. His light was naturally overwhelmed by the luminescence of *that Prophet*, the Lord Jesus Christ. In 34 A.D., even after Christ ascended to the right hand of the Father, the world was turned *upside down* (Acts 17:6) by the thunderous ministries of the apostles and New Testament prophets. The Jews may have chosen blindness and rejected their prophets, but it is certainly not accurate for a Christ-rejecting Jew in 70 A.D. to say, *there is no more any prophet.*

It is pertinent to point out that Israel is at this hour sans prophet, at least any prophet that is prophesying anything to them besides that already written for the past 2000 years. Israel will not always be without, for Malachi 4:5 clearly states that Elijah will precede Christ at His coming. From Revelation 11, it is also evident that Moses also will minister alongside Elijah before the *great and dreadful day of the LORD.* These *two witnesses* (Rev.11:3) will be overcome by the Beast, and mankind, presumably including deceived Israel, will be ecstatic and jubilant at their deaths! *And they that dwell upon the earth shall rejoice over them, and make merry, and shall send gifts one to another; because these two prophets tormented them that dwelt on the earth* (Rev. 11:10).

Again, the remnant of believing and faithful Israel will rediscover their God out in the wilderness and will sit at the feet of the *Prophet...like unto* Moses (Deut.18:15). But it is also quite plain that the majority of Israel will remain sightless and blind (Rom.11:25), and quite without a legitimate prophet since they reject every authentic one God sends their way.

So, the complaint of the psalmist that there is no more any prophet, can logically be seen to apply to a time that is yet future even more than it applies in the first century after Christ's death.

The Signposts. There are a few other significant scriptural landmarks to be found in Psalm 74 that help us to locate ourselves with respect to the time the psalmist indicates:

- Psalm 74:3 states, *Lift up thy feet unto the perpetual* ***desolations****; even all that the enemy hath done wickedly in the sanctuary.* Considering the context and the proposed time setting in the midst of the Great Tribulation, we cannot help but wonder if the word ***desolations*** is but supposed to make connection in the Bible-believer's mind and heart with the *abomination of desolation* of Matthew 24:15. Obviously this would support time placement in Daniel's 70th week.
- Psalm 74:10 says, *O God, how long shall the adversary reproach? shall the enemy* ***blaspheme thy name*** *for ever?* Blasphemy will be no new thing for the last days before Christ's advent, nevertheless, it is difficult once the connection is made to the Great Tribulation to overlook the Antichrist's blasphemies in Revelation 13:5-6, and the blasphemies of men in general during that time in Revelation 16:9, 11 & 21.

- Though it proposes an astonishing explanation for the miraculous source of the food believing Israel will benefit from in the wilderness according to Micah 7:14-15, Psalms 74:14 establishes that *Thou brakest the heads of leviathan in pieces, and gavest him to be* ***meat to the people inhabiting the wilderness****.* Leaving the extraordinary explanation to stand on its own, what we cannot bypass is that the miraculous provision of Israel, herein prophesied, is unequivocally during the future Tribulation period.
- Psalm 74:15 specifies, *Thou didst cleave the fountain and the flood:* **thou driedst up mighty rivers.** Is this not a sister verse to Revelation 16:12: *And the sixth angel poured out his vial upon the great river Euphrates; and the* ***water thereof was dried up****, that the way of the kings of the east might be prepared*?
- While ***the covenant*** of Psalm 74:20 (*Have respect unto* ***the covenant****: for the dark places of the earth are full of the habitations of cruelty)* could apply to various aspects of various of the covenants God made with Israel, in light of all the evidence which has mounted for a primarily future Tribulation fulfillment, it would be an oversight to ignore God's evident Tribulation vow to Israel in Ezekiel 20:35-37:

  And I will bring you into the wilderness of the people, and there will I plead with you face to face. Like as I pleaded with your fathers in the wilderness of the land of Egypt, so will I plead with you, saith the Lord GOD. And I will cause you to pass under the rod, and ***I will bring you into the bond of the covenant****:*

The *synagogues* of Psalm74:8 are prophetic, looking primarily to the yet future Great Tribulation. The psalmist that authored the psalm was a prophet who not only recorded and prophesied events which we can now see occurred, in part, around 586 B.C. and 70 A.D., but also events which have proven to be another 2000 years beyond, and will prove to be the ultimate fulfillment of the passage. The almost fluorescent marker in the passage is the word ***synagogues***, the sole and singular occurrence of the English word in all the Old Testament. The word from whence it was translated, ***moed***, occurs over 230 times in Hebrew, but is translated by the AV translators only one time as *synagogues*. Those *synagogues* are uniquely New Testament concepts except in Psalm 74. No one can definitively show that there were ever *synagogues* as we today know them in existence during Old Testament times. It is plain then, that the translators either truly botched the translation for some inexplicable reason in the one place, or there was a method to their madness, or a Mastermind to their method. It was either a mistake or the Lord inserted a translation into the Old Testament scriptures that would key an attuned, Bible-believing, spiritual mind to the fact that the ultimate fulfillment of the prophetic events would be very deep in the New Testament. The new versions and scholars, in general, consider it a mistake to have translated the word as *synagogues*. Nevertheless, it remains that it is specifically and exclusively the King James' *synagogues* which functions as a cue and unmistakably directs the English-reading Bible-believer to the primary Tribulation application of the passage.

What Those *Synagogues* Settle

A study of the Psalm 74:8 term *synagogues* reaffirms the observations previously explored throughout earlier chapters in this book. This study also illustrates the all sufficiency of God's true English scriptures. Should this come as a surprise? *According as his divine power hath given unto us* ***all things that pertain unto life and godliness***... (2 Pet. 1:3). *All scripture is given by inspiration of God... That the man of God may be perfect,* ***throughly furnished*** *unto all good works* (2 Tim. 3:16-

17). Through the years, and unto this day, there are many who wish to salute the AV 1611 with one hand while slapping it away with the other. Some, though, hold that God hath delivered to man in plain English the entirety of His promises regarding His word, instead of some war torn fragment, pilfered by apostate vultures, and then marketed as whole by spin doctors. For their simple and guileless faith in a volume containing God's perfect words, scorn, derision, name-calling and demands for answers have been heaped upon the believers of the Old Book. According to the liberal, mainstream and Fundamentalist Christian scholars who disparage our assessments of the virtues of our King James Bible, we:

- Believe that the English *corrects* the originals.
- Believe that the English is *superior* to the Greek and Hebrew.
- Disdain the study of Greek and Hebrew as authoritative in finality.
- Think that God *inspired* the King James Bible.
- Believe the AV translators were *inspired.*
- Are mere unscholarly, unreasonable rabble-rousers worthy of little but dismissal.

Critics and sincere searchers alike, ought to review the assessments and the *reason of the hope that is in* us (1 Pet. 3:15) in this chapter along with previous ones. The Lord God never ordained that man should be subservient or acquiescent to the conclusions of mainline or Fundamentalist scholarship just because scholars "say so." *(W)e are ambassadors for Christ* (2 Cor. 5:20), *stewards of the mysteries of God* (1 Cor. 4:1), and are called to know *the certainty of the words of truth* (Prov. 22:21). It is a priesthood of believers that God ordained, **not a *priesthood of scholars!*** The Father gave the rest of the saints access to the mind of Christ right alongside the academic, and He calls us all to Him to *reason together* (Isa. 1:18). The conclusions here presented regarding the intricacy of God's handiwork and involvement in the outcome of the King James Bible do not mesh with mainline Christian scholarship, and those conclusions extend a fair way past where Fundamentalist scholars are willing to go. The truth lies not merely in the conclusions, but in the evidence and the process of the reasons.

The study of the *synagogues* of this chapter, and the examples found in other chapters of this book, should reasonably settle certain specific and general lessons in the mind of an honest child of God.

Settled: the original languages are not the ultimate keys to understanding the scriptures. The Hebrew word, ***moen***, was singularly unhelpful in unraveling the truth of Psalm 74:8. It could have been translated any number of ways should its previous and succeeding occurrences be taken into account. It certainly should not have been translated *synagogues* if the previous and succeeding occurrences set the standard. Virtually all the published translations, scholars and commentaries agree to this.

The fact remains that it is the English of the Authorized Version that yielded spiritual light in its translation of the term as *synagogues*, and all the rest of the prophetic luminance found in the chapter flowed through the window that the English translation alone opened. The Hebrew itself yielded no light on the passage whatever.

Settled: the original languages are obscure and ambiguous in their own right. Left with the Hebrew alone, one would still be stuck translating ***moen*** as "meeting places" or "congregation" or some such thing. Perhaps it should be settled here that all languages are by percentages ambiguous and obscure when it comes to translating intricacies and details. Hebrew and Greek are simply not at all the exceptions in this rule. In something as stupendously and eternally indispensable as *the engrafted word, which is able to save your souls* (James 1:21), is it not rational that in every step of inspiration, preservation *and translation* that it would be necessary for God to have an intimate and minutely involved part?

Given the evidence that the original languages of the Bible are ambiguous in their own right, it would be well to here emphasize a point that is well understood by scholars, but which is often particularly poorly emphasized. Nobody anywhere has the original Old or New Testament documents! Even when a man is dealing with the original languages, he never sets eyes on the original documents. We do take by faith that God preserved His word in both Hebrew and Greek, but it is important for the reader to realize that no scholar from either the most liberal or conservative viewpoint could ***prove*** he deals with the very word that God had the original writer write down. First, then, consider that when that scholar refers to the Greek or Hebrew, he is not only unable to say unequivocally that he is in communion with the very words from God's mouth, but further, he seldom advertises that in dabbling in Greek and Hebrew meanings and translational alternatives, he is ultimately only citing another man's opinion written in a Greek or Hebrew lexicon, dictionary, or grammar work. He tells you that he is going to the Greek or Hebrew…but, ***no, he is not! He is going to a list of words and meanings that another man claims are the meanings of the Greek or Hebrew!***

Settled: the Greek and Hebrew are *NOBODY'S* final authority! What men wrote in lexicons and dictionaries are "the Greek and the Hebrew" to which the scholars who wish to decimate your Bible most often refer. Further, lexicons were often authored by men whose judgment and discernment have oft proven notoriously faulty. Lexicons and dictionaries certainly do occupy a useful place, ***however the usurpation of God's word is most assuredly not their place.***

The King James Bible believer has adversaries to his position about every word of the KJV being true in most every imaginable scholarly circle. Bible-believers are almost universally derided and accused of believing that the mortal translators of the King James Bible were "inspired" or "re-inspired" in their work. Such terminology will receive further explanation later, but it is little appreciated that the One whom we trust for His word is God, and whom He used is His business, though we certainly profess to see His evident handiwork in the result that those 17th century scholars produced. It is critical to understand that the Bible correcting scholars wish to lend the impression that they have a more certain and exalted authority than the mere men of a translating committee. They have the Greek and Hebrew. They claim to have the root from whence the Bible came. *They* have the source, but *we* have only a faulted offshoot of the true and glorious BIBLE –which in their minds is the Greek and Hebrew. It is indispensable to understand that the Greek or Hebrew hold no magical or mystical meaning. It is indispensable to understand that scholars do not open the Hebrew Old Testament or Greek New Testament and say, "Ah-ha, there is the true and real meaning undisclosed in Bible translations." Those scholars open other reference books, written by other fallen men, and then they parrot what *those* men opine. The original languages do not have an authoritative voice for these scholars. Fellow scholars are their authoritative voice.

It is important to take note that where the scholars accuse true Bible-believers of putting their faith in the fallible men of the AV translation committee, such detractors themselves place their faith in the reference works of demonstrably fallible, and often, apostate men.

Dear Christian, is your final authority the Bible? The scholars' authority is not the Bible. Their final authority is what some man said a word in the Bible meant.

> *Thus saith the LORD; Cursed be the man that trusteth in man, and maketh flesh his arm, and whose heart departeth from the LORD.*
> (Jer. 17:5).

> *For it is written, I will destroy the wisdom of the wise, and will bring to nothing the understanding of the prudent. Where is the wise? where is the scribe? where is the disputer of this world? hath not God made foolish the wisdom of this world? For after that in the wisdom of God the world by wisdom knew not God, it pleased God by the foolishness of preaching to save them that believe.* (1 Cor. 1:19-21)

Settled: the English of the Authorized Version clarifies the Hebrew and resolves the obscurities of the original language. When the King James translators translated the word ***moen*** as *synagogues*, while breaking from habitual translation of the word, they settled that the passage's primary application would belong in New Testament times, for *synagogues* is not only a New Testament word, it is a New Testament concept. This primary application is verified by the prophetic components in the rest of the Psalm. The scriptures of the passage itself concur that the proper translation would be *synagogues*. Thus, the English clarifies what is unclear and undefined in the Hebrew. The English corrects false translations, false translators, commentators and scholars, and it also corrects and redirects false interpretations of the passage.

Settled: the English is superior to the Hebrew. If one thinks not, then such a one must answer this question: ***how is it***

not superior to the Hebrew in this case? The Hebrew left the reader high and dry when it came both to meaning and to prophecy. The Hebrew is obscure and indeterminate with regard to the specific meaning and light needed in this passage. No new version and no lexicon is any legitimate help in this case. God gave light in the English of the AV which is inaccessible elsewhere. The AV 1611 broke from the usual translation of ***moen***, but it was demonstrably correct in doing so. Therefore, the English of the King James is superior to the Hebrew of Psalm 74:8.

Settled: the habit of referring back to the "original language" is to revert backwards into darkness and to devolve downward into confusion. "If it ain't broke, don't fix it," goes the saying. The habit spoken of has the effect of undoing the work of God that has already been accomplished in the King James Bible. It is quite literally following along behind God and tearing up what He has already accomplished. Tell me, brethren, are we *labourers together with God* (1 Cor. 3:9), or do we *fight against God* (Acts 23:9)?

Settled: the scholars whose first resort is to linguistic references and extra-biblical sources receive pitifully little light on the obstacles they encounter in the scriptures. In both of these options so oft the resort of the scholars, it should be insightful to the Bible-believer that each of those paths will leave its traveler at the footstool of man's opinions. *Cease ye from man, whose breath is in his nostrils: for wherein is he to be accounted of* (Isa. 2:22)? *Cursed be the man that trusteth in man, and maketh flesh his arm, and whose heart departeth from the LORD* (Jer. 17:5).

As mentioned earlier, the lexicons and linguistic aids are notorious for their errors, and their authors are very seldom the species of "Christian" that are worthy of repute, if they were even Christians at all. The actual perverseness and influences of the lexical writers will be made plain in a later chapter. The fact is that most Fundamental, separated Christians would not be caught anywhere near the same pew, and oft not at the same dinner table (1 Cor.5:11), as some of these debauched men. Nevertheless, they are on people's bookshelves where they oft bear the distinguished role of correcting the Holy Bible.

When one resorts to the Bible dictionaries and encyclopedias to resolve nagging matters of the scriptures, that person is usually deluged with a landslide of presumed facts regarding customs, history, facts, figures, geography, archaeology, ancient writings, literature and speculation by great bodies of ensconced experts. It is often the experience that one leaves his hour of research glutted with information which he presumes has informed and enlightened him, only to later realize that he received no answer to his Bible question. Welcome to the world of scholarship! *Neither give heed to fables and endless genealogies, which minister questions, rather than godly edifying which is in faith* (1 Tim. 1:4). A man that receives no light, has none to give.

Settled: "Someone" is responsible for the enlightening translation found in the Authorized Version. Someone is responsible for translating *synagogues* where there was no precedent for it, and in doing so providing thc kcy to the entire passage. That the average new version scholar is incapable of discerning the design and intention is to their discredit. The critical question is: who was responsible? This presents a very discomfiting quandary for even Fundamental King James people, for they have been taught to disdain and dismiss instantly the idea that God inserts Himself so profoundly into the processes of the translation of the King James. But they have also been programmed to be uncomfortable with the idea that the King James translators had such profound prophetic insight so as to affect such providential wisdom exhibited here. To them the translators were very gifted men who did the best they could with what they had, but who still made mistakes and rendered the translation in unfortunate terms at times. In their eyes, the King James is the best we have, but obviously it is less than perfect.

Well, all that can be said is that *someone* is responsible for the intentional and inspired reading of Psalm 74:8. Either God did it through the translators or the translators did it on their own. In either case, the Fundamentalist scholar is left in a philosophical swamp, for he has no answers for how such a key and pivotal translation could come from the Hebrew supplied in the manuscripts.

Is it not wonderful and glorious to have a God that is bigger than man's investigations or explanations?

Chapter 12

From God's Heart and Mind to Man: The Scriptures vs. Semantics, Traditions, and Fables

*And they have built the high places of Tophet, which is in the valley of the son of Hinnom, to burn their sons and their daughters in the fire; which I commanded them not, **neither came it into my heart**.* (Jer. 7:31)

*And they built the high places of Baal, which are in the valley of the son of Hinnom, to cause their sons and their daughters to pass through the fire unto Molech; which I commanded them not, **neither came it into my mind**, that they should do this abomination, to cause Judah to sin.* (Jer. 32:35)

*For as the heavens are higher than the earth, so are my ways higher than your ways, and **my thoughts than your thoughts**. For as the rain cometh down, and the snow from heaven, and returneth not thither, but watereth the earth, and maketh it bring forth and bud, that it may give seed to the sower, and bread to the eater: **So shall my word be that goeth forth out of my mouth: it shall not return unto me void, but it***

> ***shall accomplish that which I please, and it shall prosper in the thing whereto I sent it.***
> (Isa. 55:9-11)

Man's Mind and His Alienation from God

Two passages bring to remembrance Israel's gross proclivity to idols and false gods, Jeremiah 7:31 and 32:35, and both bear witness to what was manifestly *not* on the Lord's mind and heart. The two passages are exploited and forced by some to teach that God is not prescient - that He does not foreknow everything. The purpose here is not to exposit the very correct Bible doctrine of the omniscience of God. Nevertheless, while God does, in fact, know everything, it is very plain that He did not conceive and initiate all of the wretchedness that man has involved himself in through the millennia. The Bible bears witness to another entity, *the god of this world*, who *hath blinded the minds of them which believe not* (2 Cor. 4:4) and who has shown himself a malevolently successful corrupter of the minds of men. However, man cannot justifiably point the accusatory finger at the devil as sole cause for man's debauchery: *And GOD saw that the wickedness of man was great in the earth, and that every imagination of the thoughts of his heart was only evil continually* (Gen. 6:5). In the New Testament, the Apostle Paul chimes in with a dark yet brief evaluation on the thoughts and heart of man,

> *This I say therefore, and testify in the Lord, that ye henceforth walk not as other Gentiles walk, in the vanity of their mind, Having the understanding darkened, being alienated from the life of God through the ignorance that is in them, because of the blindness of their heart:*
> (Eph. 4:17-18)

The deadly combination of man's fallen nature and Satan's subtlety are the source of every species of woe that man knows in this world.

Jeremiah 7:31 and 32:35 surely attest to the fact that things enter the minds and hearts of man which are not conceived or ordained of God. Man's mind does not work like God's mind, and Proverbs 21:8 testifies to the fact that *(t)he way of man is froward and strange.* The thoughts of man's heart, in their natural and uncontested course, are divergent from the Lord's thoughts.

God's Mind and His Communication with Man

While the verses above are witness to the verity that men think and conceive things foreign and froward to God's thoughts and ways, they leave unspoken the idea that the Lord would communicate His heart and thoughts to us. That the Father would communicate those things to us is witnessed by hundreds of verses and promises which are meat to those familiar with the Bible version issue. Wallowing in such debauched degeneracy, man would not be expected to intuitively know the Lord's mind. Neither did it turn out that mental telepathy would be the means God would choose to arrest man's serpentine slide. First pronouncing to us that *...as the heavens are higher than the earth, so are my ways higher than your ways, and my thoughts than your thoughts* (Isa.55:9), the Lord continues, *So shall my word be that goeth forth out of my mouth: it shall not return unto me void, but it shall accomplish that which I please, and it shall prosper in the thing whereto I sent it* (Isa. 55:11). We do learn from Psalm 33:11, that *The counsel of the LORD standeth for ever, the thoughts of his heart to all generations,* but God formulates His thoughts into His word which *goeth forth out of (His) mouth* (Isa. 55:11). Hundreds of verses embody the extensive set of vows and promises which affirm and assure that He has made His mind and heart available to us. Those thoughts of God are communicated to us by very specific and meaning-bearing words. Specific thoughts that are without the equally specific medium of well-chosen words do not equal the word of God. *(W)e have the mind of Christ*, says 1 Corinthians 2:16, and a little diligence in reading will lead one to conclude that the mind of Christ is not some mystic presence in the brain pan of a Christian, but rather *in the words...which the Holy Ghost teacheth* (1 Cor. 2:13). Those words are the words of the Bible.

Taken as a whole, the verses which directly state the pledges and promises of God to supply His very words, statutes, and precepts to us - in addition to the verses which proclaim that He did so - certainly number in the hundreds, if not thousands. There is not a drum beaten more oft in the scriptures than the subject and theme of the word and words of the Lord. *Word* and *words* appear more than two thousand times in the King James Bible, with the majority of these referring the Lord's word(s). This number is independent of the number of times the Lord's statutes, commandments, ordinances and precepts are mentioned. The number further does not tally the times God *spake* or *said* something to a man, prophet or otherwise. There is virtually nothing easier to illustrate from the Bible than that God spake directly and definitively to man, and that man has been required to act upon the Lord's communication to him with detailed exactitude. Adam, Cain, Abel, Noah, Abraham, Isaac, Jacob, Joseph - it is more difficult to find a major Bible character with whom God did not explicitly communicate than to readily find 25 with whom He did. The fact is that virtually every page of the scriptures is a testament to the fact that our Father hath communicated His thoughts, passions, wishes, precepts, commandments and ordinances to man in precise, detailed and exacting terms.

Despite the overwhelming number of times the Lord testified that He both did and would supply man with the very words of God, this is the sacred ground upon which the battle is joined. God has thoughts and desires that He communicates to man via words. Conceptually, He could have accomplished this through some sort of mind-meld by which thoughts flow from Him to us in some mystic communication stream. This is a moot point, for this is not the method He chose to the great disappointment of the Charismatic pretenders. No, God placed His thoughts and verities into words in order to communicate, just as man communicates through the use of words. The scriptures testify that *In the beginning was the Word, and the Word was with God, and the Word was God* (John 1:1). Jesus Christ, who is God, is not named the "Thoughts of God" or the "General Ideas of God". ***(H)is name is called The Word of God*** (Rev. 19:13). The idea that Christ, though named in the collective sense *the Word of God*, would communicate His truths to us via some indistinct, corporate conglomerate message called *the word of God*, without distinctive and exacting words, is the type of philosophical nonsense that Satan has propagated for 6000 years now. The nonsense notwithstanding, the old dragon has found the ground fertile and initiated many disciples into this system of esoteric religious babble.

Meddling Mortals' Disdain for God's Medium

Man in general is ever irritated and huffy over how the Lord providentially designs to do things. If there is one eternal truth that stands out in the relations between the eternal and omniscient God and his fallen and haughty creatures, it is the fact that man always thinks he has a better idea. It may be a function of man's "god complex" (Gen.3:5) that he feels he must critique and largely dismiss God's methods.

It is a strange, sovereign twist of irony that when man fell from his proper relation with the Father by taking to himself license with the words the Lord had spoken, that God, in turn, ordained men as the medium by which He would communicate His words to the rest of mankind. The failed steward, so subtly seduced by the serpent, would nevertheless be the medium by which mortal man would receive holy and unerring communication from the Father. God's life-giving thoughts in words would still be delivered to the understanding of corrupt men by the pens, tongues and labors of other fallen men. Whether man likes it or not, the Lord has designed His affairs in such a way that the ominous presence of man's tainted nature must come into contact with God's pure words, with the product of this unlikely union still being a pure and godly one. The words of the Lord have always been the confluent point of conflict in this spiritual fight, and it is by God's design that those words are still the crux and crossroad of the matter. In Genesis 3, Eve was forced to obey or disobey the word of the Lord which she had not heard with her own ears, but which was delivered unto her by a middle-man, Adam (Gen.2:16-17). So it has ever been with God's people since. God ordained that man would be the vessel by which He would deliver His very words, words which man either chooses to believe or to disbelieve, words by which man will either live or die. Men must choose to either delight in those words or disdain them.

Back in 1999, a book was released called *From the Mind of God to the Mind of Man: A Layman's Guide to How We Got our Bible.* The book was written by a consort of Bob Jones University faculty and graduates with Dr. James B. Williams as General Editor. At the formal book launch at the World Congress of Fundamentalism in 1999, Dr. Williams made a presentation of the book to Dr. Bob Jones III, at which point,

> Dr. Bob held up the book and called it "the most significant book for Fundamentalism in this decade, no, in this century..."[124]

At a distance, *From the Mind of God* sounds like a gangbuster of a book and a banner around which to gather the troops. It is, in truth, merely a pathetic façade thrown up by the spin-masters of a fallen former bastion of Christian truth. It is a book which kisses the King James Bible at the same time that it betrays it, all the while elevating and defending Westcott and Hort and their demoniac scholastic brood as orthodox and misrepresented.[125] Williams whines about the militancy of the "King James Only group" which believe the KJV to be "inspired and inerrant," and naturally he also is repulsed, as is Dr. Waite, the reviewer of the book, by the "most extreme" group – one that "contends that the KJV contains new revelation from God."[126] One gets a bit of the feel for the palpable scholastic haughtiness and condescension of this particular scholars' union when Dr. Williams puts the unlearned hicks in their place.

> These problems have increased because of the mass of misinformation that has been proclaimed from the pulpits and spread in print by those who because of ***their lack of theological understanding and biblical language training are not qualified to speak to the issues.***[127]

---

[124] Waite, Donald A., *Fundamentalist Mis-Information on Bible Versions,*(The Bible For Today Press, Collingswood, New Jersey 08108, 2000) p.4
[125] Ibid. p.34-36
[126] Ibid. p.29-30
[127] Ibid. p.31

As can be seen from the quote above, Bible-believers are the ones who *have...troubled Israel* (I Kings 18:17-18), and not Ahab's house! We are the bumpkins as far as "theological understanding and biblical language training" is concerned. We simply are not "qualified to speak to the issues."

These men wrote a book called *From the Mind of God to the Mind of Man*, and the tenet of the book is that the mind of God currently resides in fragmented and uncertain form, contained in shattered and scattered pieces of the Critical Greek Text of Westcott and Hort, which came to us by way of Clement's and Origen's labors in Alexandria, Egypt. In truth, to these men the real Bible actually was only the original manuscripts, once inspired by God, but now long lost - and that presumably by God! Now, what Christians are supposed to do, according to these ensconced scholars, is to read their Bibles (any good version will do) and having read their favorite new bibles, they can rest assured that they can always turn to the scholarship of Bob Jones University and other likeminded Fundamentalists to learn what God really said or meant.

Yes, these wrote a book called *From the Mind of God to the Mind of Man,* and they do not believe that God transmitted and communicated anything in perfect certitude to man today. This very sort of mindset has become regular fare when it comes to dealing with the location and perfection of the words of the Living God. It has been through the most disgraceful tangle of semantics, duplicity and double-speak that the truth seeking Christian has had to fight to get a simple and unvarnished answer to the most rudimentary truth about God's word. It seems that most Fundamentalist scholars require space and time for long circuitous dissertations in order to answer a simple question about bible versions or the state of inerrancy of the word of God. Most Bible-believing pastors and Christians can answer the same question in a brief and decisive sentence, without the avalanche of convulsive verbiage. Many of my own congregation faced just this sort of stonewalling when they were lost in the Catholic or Lutheran church and began to seek answers. They did not get anything but roundabout evasion and doubletalk because their sources were in fact bereft of the water of life. Brethren, if Fundamentalists had disseminated the gospel as they have disseminated the truth about where to find God's words, seven eighths of the people sitting in Independent Baptist churches this day would be on their way to Hell. It is time to dismiss the crippled and misdirected scholarship of Fundamental orthodoxy when it comes to the Bible just as so many Catholics had to dismiss the illegitimate authoritative claims of the priesthood when the issue boiled down to the matters of the eternal soul.

In this chapter, as the topic of how God communicated His mind and thoughts to man is explored, there are no coveys of cooing, dovish scholars masquerading behind facades of militant and God-pleasing Fundamentalism. While they *by good words and fair speeches deceive the hearts of the simple* (Rom. 16:18), they also must use one thousand words to say something in a way that will mask what they actually believe. The form of communication which man has in common with God is the recorded and written word! Not only is He the ***Word*** *of God* (Rev.19:13), but He upholds *all things by the* ***word*** *of his power* (Heb. 1:3). This is more deeply affirmed to us by the fact that *The entrance of thy* ***words*** *giveth light* (Ps. 119:130), and in the **words** of Christ Himself: *It is written, Man shall not live by bread alone, but by every* ***word*** *that proceedeth out of the mouth of God* (Matt. 4:4). *Let them not depart from thine eyes,* says the wise writer of Proverbs (Prov. 4:21). Within the creation and above the brute beasts, man has the unique capacity for thought, wisdom, understanding, intellectual progression and reason of which the rest of God's creatures are comparatively bereft. Though, *Thou (God) madest him a little lower than the angels* (Heb. 2:6-7), all of man's unique and superlative spiritual and intellectual capacity would be of no real effect whatsoever if man had no means by which to communicate the specific and exacting details of his thoughts with his fellow man, and more importantly, to receive just such communication from his God.

So much of what man ***is*** revolves around his capacity for words. All of man's brilliance and ingenuity would be of comparatively little effect were he unable to communicate the specifics of his thoughts with words that bear exclusive and definitive meaning. And if man truly is a manifestation of God's special creative powers above the beasts, and if it was, and is, God's eternal intention to have communion and fellowship with man in a way that He does not commune with lions, giraffes and gophers, then it is utterly imperative that God the **Word** would communicate to us in words that are not only ***profoundly specific***, but also ***routinely accessible***.

It is no exaggeration to say that on the whole, modern scholars utterly abhor even the suggestion that God may have used sinful men (even though such men would have been of the same vocation as they) to deliver perfectly pure and eternal words to men in our own language. They are violently repulsed by even the prospect of this possibility. It is, of course, good that many scholars have rightly discerned the proper form of Greek and Hebrew text, and because they recognize the correct textual genealogy, they support and defend the AV 1611. It is a fact, however, that many such men still remain militantly opposed to even the concept or possibility of a perfect translation into our common language. It has become absolute and foundational orthodoxy to even Fundamentalists that God did not, would not, and could not fully bridge the communication chasm between the mind of God and the minds of men. They will concede that God was able to get as far as the originally inspired languages of the Bible by "***breathing***" the Hebrew and Greek words into fallen men. This concept is acceptable to them. In their estimation, He was also able to overcome the fallen nature of man in using man to ***preserve***, even in man's weakness, the word of God in copies of the original languages. But in their view, it was at this particular juncture that God's power and providence met with insurmountable obstacles. The crossing of the barrier from one language to another proved to be a chasm too wide and a mountain too high. It was there that God no longer even pursued inerrancy and the utter accuracy of His "pure" words, if we are to believe the scholar's union. There, God gave up the fight. There, the words of the Lord, inspired of God, preserved by the power of God and propagated in the gospel of God faltered and were thwarted by the insurmountable obstacle of translation into other languages. There – according to them - perfection ended! Never again, since the original languages, has the word of God been extant in utterly pure form. One cannot help but wonder how these intelligent and reportedly spiritual men might reckon that the Lord could achieve the following:

> *So shall my word be that goeth forth out of my mouth: it shall not return unto me void, but it shall accomplish that which I please, and it shall prosper in the thing whereto I sent it.*
> (Isa. 55:11)

If the claims of the scholars are to be believed, how does one obey the admonition of Proverbs 4:20-22?

> *My son, **attend to my words**; incline thine ear unto my sayings. **Let them not depart from thine eyes**; keep them in the midst of thine heart. For they are life unto those that find them, and health to all their flesh.* (Prov. 4:20-22)

There stymied and frustrated in what God said His mission was, we are to accept, apparently, that God suddenly and inexplicably resigned Himself to a half-done job, that mere scholars were to become His appointed arbiters of truth, and that He became satisfied that His words should be merely "accurate and reliable" in a generalized sense. It is an interesting observation that the profound and excellent work of the mortal men, who were the members of the King James translation committee, is routinely criticized and denigrated as a matter of course today. At the same time, we are plainly encouraged to accept the work of the modern scholars, who are mortals just as the AV translators. The modern scholars do not believe that perfect translation work can be done. Why would the Lord cease to use mortal men to transmit His words to other sinners? He used men in His acts of ***inspiration***. Most all accept that He used men in His work of ***preservation***. Pray tell, where is it written, or even implied, that the Lord would cease His *perfect* (Ps.19:7), *pure* (Prov.30:5) and *excellent* (Is.28:29) working with respect to His words prior to the indispensable act of ***translation***? Is He, or is He not, *able to do exceeding abundantly above all that we ask or think* (Eph. 3:20)? Perhaps such who adhere to modern scholarship's claims for the scriptures should consider *thinking* more highly of the Bible and the God of the Bible, as well.

Never are modern scholars brief or particularly forthcoming in explaining their peculiar opinion of how or why the Father halted in His mission of delivering the pure and perfect scriptures to latter day man. This is indeed what they believe though it takes brutal cross examination to get them to actually verbalize it, and they do profoundly resent being forced to admit to their position in simple and stylistically unadorned terms. Nevertheless, make no mistake: to the scholars the treasure of the pure and perfect truth is locked and sealed away exclusively in the languages in which the Bible was originally written. Oh, but we are treated to sweeping descriptives and poetic oratory! Through all the sweet smelling flowers of rhetoric, we are assured and reassured of "faithful translations," "accurate renderings," "godly devoted scholarship," "godly devoted scholars," "scientific and scholarly excellence," and of course, the Lord's great pleasure in their heroic labors for Him. Make no mistake about it though – in the eyes of the scholars, one can never hold the perfect words of the living God in the English language. The perfect words are locked away in the obscurity of Greek and Hebrew. All other language translations are second rate and inferior. Both the livelihood and the reputations of these men are the booty and spoil if their theories and philosophies prove to be untrue, and they have no intention that such should ever be the case.

Thus with all the ferocity of self-preservation, the intellectuals scholastically slash and snarl at all who venture within their presumed academic territory. To question their stone-graven conclusions about the process of the propagation of the scriptures through time, texts and languages is to be instantly marginalized intellectually and branded as a theologically detestable sample of Christianity, worthy of little more than being cast out. All of this, though, is carefully couched in polite terms and smooth words. It drips with the so called "love of Christ." All the correct biblical elements and terms are exposited. The scholars all – well, most of them – believe in the ***inspiration*** and ***preservation*** of the scriptures. They all believe in ***"the scriptures."*** They all are effusive in discussing the elements involved in ***translation*** and ***interpretation***. They all speak in dogmatic terms about principles and boundaries for each of these terms. They resolutely and adamantly exposit to all what did happen with each of these elements, what was possible and impossible, how things happened and how they cannot have happened. One would think that the Lord must have whispered into these fellows ears about the limitations and possibilities under which

He labored in delivering the word to man. Plainly, in each of their armories of personal theology and dogma, each Fundamental scholar has fitted all the separate elements of God's having delivered the scriptures to man into its particular niche. For them, all is in place, and it guarantees near violent trauma to the tranquil haven of their personal theologies to ask searching questions.

The Mind of God and Men's Misuse of Words

It is peculiar that while Fundamentalist scholars usually profess that the Bible is their final authority (this usually refers to a Bible one cannot hold in his hand), they are oft-times quite superficial and shallow in the scriptures they do use to justify their positions. They will cite general Bible references and qualities of the Bible with which everyone agrees in order to establish that God's word is eternal and wonderful, that God inspired it and promised to preserve it; that we are to love it and that it is to be our life and all the fodder of our meditations. Having thus established their unshakeable orthodoxy and their undying devotion to the "Word," they then proceed to the real heart of the matter, give an always necessary salute to the King James Bible, after which they exposit that no vernacular translation of the Bible could ever really be a pure and perfect Bible. According to these scholars, the real treasure of the scriptures lies in the Greek or Hebrew. It is questionable how many people notice that very little actual Biblical material is presented to actually establish the scriptural validity of their positions. It is utterly predictable that these lofty intellectuals must cite the Greek behind 2 Timothy 3:16 to justify themselves, but it shall soon be seen that they do not think about it too much or too well, as 2 Timothy 3:16 has become marked by scholastic preconceptions to which all men are expected to genuflect. Broad and sweeping statements are made about what ***inspiration, preservation*** and ***translation*** involved, but sweeping statements are not the same as examining the particulars or the scriptures.

The fact is that at this very juncture where *the Lord gave the word* (Ps.68:11) according to His promise and integrity, Satan still enters the fray today just as he did in Genesis 3. The critical seam where Satan doth always attack is at the point where man is called upon to apprehend and grasp the very words of God. *Ye shall not eat of every tree of the garden?* (Gen 3:1) and *Ye shall not surely die.* (Gen 3:4) were Satan's thrusts at Eve. The first thrust, a question, was designed as a direct challenge to what the Lord had definitively commanded. The second, in Genesis 3:4, was a disdainful denial of fact that was intended to impress upon Eve the idea that she did not know the whole truth of the matter. At that critical intersection where man conceptualizes and understands what God said, ***Eve was told that she needed an intermediary, a third party, to inform her what was the real truth behind God's words.*** Understand that Eve needed nothing besides what she already knew, but Satan convinced her that she did need something more. Eve understood all that she ever needed to and she was fully equipped in knowledge to overcome and have victory. Yet the devil impressed upon her that she needed him. She was treated as being too inept, too shallow and ox-dumb to trust in her own understanding of what "*thou shalt not*" truly meant. And she fell for it. One must always remember and never forget just who that intermediary and third party was: ***Satan***.

So, today, most Fundamental scholars are all too happy to expand and magnify the wonders of the ***inspiration*** and ***preservation*** of God's word. For the vast majority of them conceptually, the glowing and magnanimous verbiage still leaves the words of God imprisoned in the original Greek and Hebrew languages. Oh, it is utterly glorious how God inspired and preserved His word, but to these scholars, the meanings and treasures of that word sits on a shelf too high for men of blue-collar academic credentials like you and me. The words of God were ***inspired*** and ***preserved in perfection***, however the scholars believe those words just cannot be delivered to ordinary people in perfection. The word of God is truly perfect and glorious, but according to the claims of Fundamental scholars, the common man cannot read it in perfection and glory because at the critical seam where he would apprehend it (that is, by ***translation*** into his native tongue), the word of God IS NOT perfect. Since they say no ***translation*** can wholly capture all the meaning of God, then unscholarly individuals, as Eve, have been left with the short end of the stick. At that profound transitional juncture where man receives the full apprehension of what God meant and said, ***we are routinely informed today that we still require a third party to inform us of what God really meant and said.*** Now it is true that God does use men for light and insight (Acts 8:31). He has certainly ordained *pastors and teachers* (Eph.4:11). We must have the Holy Spirit illuminate us (1 Cor.2:14) and *guide... into all truth* (John 16:13). God did use men in the entire process of inspiration (2 Pet.1:21), preservation and the publication of His word (Ps.68:11). Notwithstanding all of that, if God's word is perfect, but it is not transmitted to us in utterly certain language that we can understand, then inerrancy and perfection is virtual nonsense in practice. The third party and the intermediary that *murdered Eve and all her seed* was Satan. Who is it then, today, that attacks that critical point where one must understand exactly what God says?

Much attention has here been devoted to exposing how much Satan and the scholars are agreed and are of one mind in their hatred for the precept and promise that God would deliver, and has delivered, to common people His word in the complete, pure and perfect sense that He vowed He would. Let the readers of this work all stop and soberly consider the existence and implication of this very sordid agreement. *Can two walk together, except they be agreed* (Amos 3:3)?

Furthermore, the decisive and vital point of concentrated attack is not so much where God ***inspired*** or ***preserved*** the scriptures, though those issues are certainly attacked by infidels and liberal scholars. The bitterest point of battle is at the crucial interface where God's word crosses the barrier of man's language, so that man can apprehend what the Lord hath said. In concord with Satan's propaganda and tactics in Genesis 3, even the main body of Fundamentalist scholars attack with vitriolic fervor all who profess that God has delivered perfect words to us in our English language. Condescension is heaped upon such rustic crackpots who hold in high confidence those words which the Lord hath delivered to them, and not one of the scholars seems to discern their own cooperation with the Serpent in the practical application of Genesis 3.

Now, Satan is subtle (Gen.3:1), and Satan has ministers (2 Cor.11:13-15). Therefore, Satan's ministers will be subtle. Satan is a liar (John 8:44), and therefore so will be his earthly ambassadors. A liar must be good with words, and Satan has certainly proved to be that! In fact, this entire debate revolves around the perversion, wresting and interchange of words. Thus, Satan and his witting or unwitting servants will major in twisting words and constructing deceitful, cunning and guileful arguments, justifications, and assurances. The subtitle of this chapter is *The Scriptures vs. Semantics, Traditions and Fables.* The chapter bears this subtitle because this battle is fought over words and with words. Men may use words to argue and convince us of certain things when behind the curtain it is the old *god of this world* (2 Cor.4:4) who is the puppeteer pulling the strings on the tongues of those who speak. It is for that very reason that Bible-believers are to assess the words which men speak and write in the following manner:

> ***To the law and to the testimony: if they speak not according to this word,*** *it is because there is no light in them.* (Isa. 8:20)

> *Which things also* ***we speak****, not in the* ***words*** *which man's wisdom teacheth, but which the Holy Ghost teacheth;* ***comparing spiritual things with spiritual.*** (1 Cor. 2:13)

Of all the places in this world where deceitful and beguiling words run rampant, it is the battle for the Bible, where the devil will employ his most artful ingenuity and most convincing masquerade. It is critical to understand how words, so profoundly crucial to a scriptural understanding of the matters herein discussed, have been largely wrested from their Biblical usage and their meanings commandeered by men to mean what men want them to mean. An all too familiar fact is that the cults have kidnapped certain scriptural terms critical to salvation and spiritual life and reformed them into meanings not consistent with the scriptures. Catholics have now become more comfortable with the term "born-again" because they have been spoon-fed a wholly new definition contrary to the scriptures. Jehovah's Witnesses and Mormons are quick to confess that Jesus Christ is the Son of God, but they do not mean what a Bible-believer means when he accepts the term. Since Christ is the Word of God and Satan is the great imitator of Christ, Satan's expertise will be in manipulating words and wresting meanings of words. There is no place where man should more expect the cunning and deceitful employment of words and argument as in the battle for the Bible.

One should expect a great battle of **Rhetoric**, the art of speaking with propriety, elegance and force. Rhetoric involves the power of persuasion or attraction, that which allures or charms. Be reminded, when it comes to such matters, of the

Bible writers' repeated warnings, of which the following are in no way exhaustive:

> *For they that are such serve not our Lord Jesus Christ, but their own belly; and by **good words and fair speeches** deceive the hearts of the simple.* (Rom. 16:18)

> *And my speech and my preaching was not with **enticing words of man's wisdom**, but in demonstration of the Spirit and of power:* (1 Cor. 2:4)

> *And this I say, lest any man should **beguile you with enticing words**.* (Col. 2:4)

> *The words of his mouth were **smoother than butter**, but **war was in his heart:** his words were **softer than oil**, yet were **they drawn swords**.* (Ps. 55:21)

> *And through covetousness shall they with **feigned words make merchandise** of you...* (2 Pet. 2:3)

One of the words mentioned in this chapter's subtitle is the word **Semantics**, which deals with the meanings of words and the study of the subtle changes of those meanings. For example, a Mormon and a Bible-believer may both be extravagant in their enthusiasm for Jesus Christ as the "Son of God", but the Mormon's definition of the term will not include Christ being *God manifest in the flesh*, which is the scriptural definition, graven in iron. This is an exercise in *semantics*. Former President Clinton disgraced his office and his manhood when he resorted to *semantics* with regard to the word "is". His tactics were far more than "lawyerly." They were *satanic.* Through the prism of *semantics*, two individuals may agree that the Bible is truly God's word, yet one may refer to the Book in his hand and the other may refer to an esoteric and mystical book that no longer even exists on paper in the real world. *Semantically*, those two individuals may quote the same scriptures about the perfection, eternality, inspiration and preservation of the scriptures, but in today's world, one could still be embracing a depraved version of the scriptures. Both defend, exalt and embrace the King James Bible as God's word in English *semantically*, but when the matter is boiled down one may hold that it needs (or conceivably could use) some improvements. Semantically, the two may have an honest misunderstanding between them, but often the disparity in understanding is the product of cunning, craft and premeditated deceit.

Tradition is another word mentioned in the subtitle to this chapter. It is a tenet that has already been discussed in chapter 9. It deserves to be reiterated that *tradition* is a more terrible vortex in which to be caught than its name implies. The Lord Jesus Himself rebuked the religiously orthodox of His day with what should have been an alarming judgment: *Thus have ye made the commandment of God of none effect by **your tradition*** (Matt. 15:6). Paul cited tradition as a spoiler of Biblical Christianity: *Beware lest any man spoil you through philosophy and vain deceit, **after the tradition of men**, after the rudiments of the world, and not after Christ* (Col. 2:8). The reason the Lord gave us the Bible is so the Bible itself could be the guide and rule of all truth. The Lord gave his scriptures to man so that man would never have to rely on mere habitual practices, rituals, or stories passed from generation to generation. It was God's intention that we would have the truth itself in hand. If any *tradition* was to be held, it would be the Bible *tradition* itself, self-contained and clearly defined within the scriptures. Despite this providential safeguard and treasure, men not only now regularly argue what "Christian" and religious traditions are to be kept (and how), but men also debate what scholarly tradition(s) they should adopt regarding the Bible itself. These scholarly and theological traditions prove to imprison men behind strong and narrowly spaced iron bars, in tight and powerful shackles. Scholarly traditions are intimidating to many because often they have been established by extremely intelligent and gifted men. Extremely intelligent and gifted men have no more of a corner on the truth of God than do the souls of modest intellect and few gifts. In fact, the pride of men of such gifts has proven to cause error where humility and faith would have led them aright. Nevertheless, men hate to be thought less than intelligent. Intelligent men despise few things more than being intellectually disrespected. They fear condescension more than Hell or the wrath of God. They are terrified of being laughed at or marginalized academically by their peers or their superiors. Through time, brilliant men have studied, learned, memorialized, and adopted the works and ideas of other brilliant men. The fact is that many of those very brilliant men were unconverted, infidels and apostates. Ah, but they were brilliant, and so many of their ideas and tenets are embraced, because to reject their ideas and to object loudly would open one up to the criticism of the intelligentsia, which could well lead to censure and even open scorn.

We see this very evil today when scholars, schools and seminaries so often mirror one another in their scholarly traditions regarding the Bible. Pastors, too, often fall into the deep rut of tradition for fear that a stand other than the position officially sanctioned by their particular fellowship or circle of preachers would lead to bearing the cross of disdain. They do not want to be considered liberal, New Evangelical, Alexandrian or compromisers (Bible correctors), but neither can they allow themselves to be categorized with rubes, rednecks, rustics and Ruckmanites who believe the King James Bible is perfect. The scorn, the loss of scholarly respect and the academic ostracism of such labels would be too much to bear! Christianity now labors under the massive weight of hundreds of years of accumulated scholarly tradition regarding the Bible, when the Lord gave man the Bible to avoid that very extremity of nonsense and imprisonment.

If one is to access the mind of the Lord through His very words, then he must fully comprehend that which is aligned against him. All the power of twisted and wrested words will be brought to bear. All the **Rhetoric**, the **Semantics** and the falsified **Traditions** that Satan can align against the word of God will be employed. An interesting word the Bible uses in contexts like this is the word **Fables** (2 Tim. 4:4). Would it not be a sight if Christians should get to judgment, only to learn that a fair fraction of what men have accepted as "gospel truth" with regard to biblical textual and linguistic scholarship and theory is a fable? Much of what Westcott and Hort believed about the Bible were figments of their own wretched imaginations. At this point a long synopsis of biographical summaries of men who have been grossly wrong in their views and theories about the Bible's text and transmission could be inserted. Graf, Wellhausen, Wettstein, Griesbach, Lachmann, Liddell, Schaff, Thayer, Moulton, Tischendorf, Driver, Briggs and Nestle all are just a line or two of a much longer list of men deserving long chapters in Church History's hall of shame for their despicable attitudes and false labors in the word of God. But usually, men are not 100% wrong about everything in which they believe and labor. It is likely that none of the men listed above were 100% wrong about every aspect of the Bible which they labored to pervert. That means that a certain percentage of their work could be accepted as genuine. Indeed a number of those listed above wrote reference works that are regularly visited by many "Bible-believing" pastors today. Are such pastors aware of the satanic work that many of those men accomplished? If they are, can they be certain that they have culled out absolutely all the falsehood and debauched theories that these men were responsible for? Can a pastor certainly know if a lexicographer's work is wrong when referencing him in the study? Does the pastor discern all the corrupt handiwork of these men (and all the others not listed) that the pastor's seminary or Bible school was culpable in trying to pass on to him in his training? What might his brilliant and respected Bible college professor have passed on to him that was really some small (or large) remnant of apostasy and falsehood that one of these infidels engendered? Are all his conceptions involving **inspiration, preservation, translation** and **the scriptures** 100% correct and wholly biblical? One would know this only if he had incrementally checked the details of what he has been taught in school and through affiliations, fellowships, and books as compared to what the Bible says of these matters. Ought not our Bible teachers and preachers to be aligned 100% with the Bible on what it says about the scripture's **inspiration, preservation and translation**?

The question is asked because some of the great latter day warnings of the scriptures involve **fables**. Notice how in 1 Timothy 1:3-4, that *other doctrine* is the issue, and that *fables minister* more *questions* than genuine answers! Does your doctrine of Bible transmission, preservation or translation rear more questions or more resolved answers?

> *As I besought thee to abide still at Ephesus, when I went into Macedonia, that thou mightest charge some that they teach* ***no other doctrine****, Neither give heed* ***to fables*** *and* ***endless genealogies, which minister questions, rather than godly edifying which is in faith****: so do.*

Why do many King James defenders still double-talk about the certainty of final authority and the exact words of God? Is not the continuing quest for final authority an *endless genealog(y)*? Since *faith cometh by hearing and hearing by the word of God* (Rom.10:17), how is an uncertain final authority *godly edifying...in faith*? How is the notion that our Heavenly Father cannot keep His specific promises regarding His words supposed to be *edifying*?

1 Timothy 4:6-7 says,

> *If thou put the brethren in remembrance of these things, thou shalt be a good minister of Jesus Christ, nourished up in the* ***words of faith*** *and of* ***good doctrine****, whereunto thou hast attained.* ***But refuse profane and old wives' fables****, and exercise thyself rather unto godliness.*

Does the reader think some of those *profane and old wives' fables* might just pertain to *the words of faith* and even the sound and *good doctrine* concerning those words of faith? This is an epistle written by the Apostle to the Gentiles regarding Gentile times in the latter times (1 Tim. 4:1). An omniscient God just might have seen this very dilemma regarding His *words of faith* in this hour, and He further might have just rung the bell back in 60AD or so regarding the great dual between the very words of God and the fables that seek to offset and overthrow those very words. Should we not carefully consider and scrutinize a scholar, preacher or teacher who is in authority or position of influence over our souls, spiritual well-being or our children's education, when he spouts some theory – whether well accepted or not – that actually is inconsistent with *the words of faith and of good doctrine, whereunto thou hast attained*? If what he propounds is not good doctrine, then what is it? It is a fable!

2 Timothy 4:3-4 says quite a mouthful with a great efficiency of words. These two verses provide dozens of hours of preaching material. For the purposes of this chapter, briefly take note of the departure from *sound* Bible *doctrine* due to fallen *lusts* and *itching ears*. Doctrines are communicated in words, the same medium of communication that ears, itching or not, hear.

> *For the time will come when they will not endure* ***sound doctrine****; but after their* ***own lusts*** *shall they heap to themselves* ***teachers****, having* ***itching ears****; And they* ***shall turn away their ears from the truth, and shall be turned unto fables.***

The verses further delineate that these lusts and these ear problems are falsely remedied by *teachers*. These *teachers'* end work is to have given their students and disciples fables for fodder instead of the truth, the words of God. The doctrines of concern are not just limited to the doctrines of Christ's deity, blood atonement, separation or Pre-millennialism. The god of this world strikes at the very root of the matter today, just as he did in Genesis 3. His simple method is to turn the ears of the people to fables concerning the nature of the transmission of God's word.

Titus 1:12-15 bears witness in this way:

> *One of themselves, even a prophet of their own, said, The Cretians are alway liars, evil beasts, slow bellies. This witness is true. Wherefore rebuke them sharply, that they may be sound in the faith; Not giving heed to* ***Jewish fables****, and* ***commandments of men, that turn from the truth****. Unto the pure all things are pure: but* ***unto them that are defiled and unbelieving is***

> ***nothing pure; but even their mind and conscience is defiled.***

The *Jewish fables* and *commandments of men* are given equal pairing in the passage for their capability of turning *from the truth.* Christ said, *Sanctify them through* ***thy truth: thy word is truth*** (John 17:17). Undoubtedly, while the application of *the truth* in these verses must be broader than only the word of God itself, these admonitions must apply first to the word of God! Note the *unbelief* to which the verses testify. Today, many men who "defend" the Bible do not even *believe* the Bible, insofar as crediting God with being able to deliver His words to us in His own way with His own quality controls. These men cannot explain or fathom how God did or could deliver perfect words in the common language; therefore, they do not believe He did. This is (duh) ***unbelief***! Where, according to the passage, does that leave *their mind and conscience*?

Simon Peter, in 2 Peter 1:16-18, makes certain to clarify that what he experienced on what is now known as the Mount of Transfiguration was no fable.

> *For we have not followed* ***cunningly devised fables****, when we made known unto you the power and coming of our Lord Jesus Christ, but were eyewitnesses of his majesty. For he received from God the Father honour and glory, when there came such a voice to him from the excellent glory, This is my beloved Son, in whom I am well pleased. And this voice which came from heaven we heard, when we were with him in the holy mount.*

Peter then follows on to establish, amazingly enough, that there is something far better than a genuine experience in hearing the very voice of God Himself! The *more sure word of prophecy* winds up being the *prophecy of the scripture.*

> *We have also a* ***more sure word of prophecy****; whereunto ye do well that ye take heed, as unto a light that shineth in a dark place, until the day dawn, and the day star arise in your hearts: Knowing this first, that no* ***prophecy of the scripture*** *is of any private interpretation. For the prophecy came not in old time by the will of man: but holy men of God spake as they were moved by the Holy Ghost.* (2 Pet. 1:19-21)

Having said what he said about his eye-witness experience of the glory of the Lord being no fable, and then having stated that the scripture is an even surer word, could one just imagine, for a moment were he here, Peter's reaction to what these born-again, soul-winning, Fundamentalist scholars (some preachers!) are actually saying when they proclaim that God did not deliver the *more sure word of prophecy* to the saints at all? To the man who heard God's voice in his ear and who pointed to the Bible as the superior of the two means of communication, some would actually say that God left the *more sure word of prophecy* inaccessible in its perfection except to scholars? How could one claim in the face of Simon Peter that perfect scriptures delivered to common men is for all practical purposes a fable?

The point is that, Biblically speaking, the men who hold to many accepted theories of what is now considered Fundamental biblical orthodoxy are playing in an entirely different arena than in the Bible itself. They are playing their own game, by their own rules, by their own definitions, and are adorning much of what they believe with Bible verses hung hither and yonder for no other reason than to lend an aura of biblical authenticity to what is essentially a charade. It should be recognized, also, that it is all too possible to be wholly biblical about certain cardinal doctrines – salvation, soul-winning, separation, creation, Christ's deity – while at the same time having adopted false or unbiblical views regarding certain aspects of biblical transmission – inspiration, preservation, translation. These scholars referred to have basically defined or redefined the processes of Bible transmission after their own conceptions and preconceptions. In many respects Bible words and precepts no longer have Bible definitions or usages. Bible means and methods are subjugated to committees of scholars who determine whether or not "it could even happen that way." In the thousands of miracles of the Bible, the Lord defied all natural laws and scientific explanations to accomplish His ends, but Bible scholars have come to require that what God accomplished in the transmission of the scriptures across the generations be explainable in method and scientific in process. God, not only the Author of the Book, but *the author and finisher of our faith* (Heb. 12:2), is edited and corrected like some junior journalist in a biweekly community newspaper.

Following is a very brief and inexhaustive collection of scripture that comments upon the nature of those who insist upon speaking with forked-tongue and deceitful hearts:

> *And through covetousness shall they with feigned words make merchandise of you...*
> (2 Pet. 2:3)

> *And my speech and my preaching was not with enticing words of man's wisdom…*
> (1 Cor. 2:4)

> *And this I say, lest any man should beguile you with enticing words.* (Col. 2:4)

For neither at any time used we flattering words, as ye know, nor a cloke of covetousness; God is witness: (1Thes. 2:5)

If any man teach otherwise, and consent not to wholesome words, even the words of our Lord Jesus Christ, He is proud, knowing nothing, but doting about questions and strifes of words... (1 Tim.6:3-4)

For when they speak great swelling words of vanity, they allure... (2 Pet. 2:18)

...prating against us with malicious words... (3 Jn. 1:10)

These are murmurers, complainers, walking after their own lusts; and their mouth speaketh great swelling words, having men's persons in admiration because of advantage (Jude 1:16)

He that is of God heareth God's words; ye therefore hear them not, because ye are not of God. (John 8:47)

With her much fair speech she caused him to yield, with the flattering of her lips she forced him. (Prov. 7:21)

...by good words and fair speeches deceive the hearts of the simple. (Rom. 16:18)

But I will come to you shortly, if the Lord will, and will know, not the speech of them which are puffed up, but the power. (1 Cor. 4:19)

Seeing then that we have such hope, we use great plainness of speech: (2 Cor. 3:12)

Sound speech, that cannot be condemned... (Titus 2:8)

Nevertheless they did flatter him with their mouth, and they lied unto him with their tongues. (Ps.78:36)

To deliver thee from the strange woman, even from the stranger which flattereth with her words; (Prov. 2:16)

A lying tongue hateth those that are afflicted by it; and a flattering mouth worketh ruin. (Prov.26:28)

And such as do wickedly against the covenant shall he corrupt by flatteries (Dan .11:32)

The words of his mouth were smoother than butter, but war was in his heart: his words were softer than oil, yet were they drawn swords. (Ps. 55:21)

For the lips of a strange woman drop as an honeycomb, and her mouth is smoother than oil: (Prov. 5:3)

Behold, they belch out with their mouth: swords are in their lips: for who, say they, doth hear? (Ps.59:7)

The lips of the righteous know what is acceptable: but the mouth of the wicked speaketh frowardness. (Prov. 10:32)

The tongue of the wise useth knowledge aright: but the mouth of fools poureth out foolishness. (Prov. 15:2)

The heart of him that hath understanding seeketh knowledge: but the mouth of fools feedeth on foolishness. (Prov. 15:14)

The heart of the righteous studieth to answer: but the mouth of the wicked poureth out evil things. (Prov. 15:28)

Out of the same mouth proceedeth blessing and cursing. My brethren, these things ought not so to be. (James 3:10)

He that hideth hatred with lying lips, and he that uttereth a slander, is a fool. (Prov. 10:18)

Lying lips are abomination to the LORD: but they that deal truly are his delight. (Prov. 12:22)

An ungodly man diggeth up evil: and in his lips there is as a burning fire. A froward man soweth strife: and a whisperer separateth chief friends. (Prov. 16:27-28)

> *For their heart studieth destruction, and their lips talk of mischief.* (Prov. 24:2)

> *Burning lips and a wicked heart are like a potsherd covered with silver dross.* (Prov. 26:23)

> *He that hateth dissembleth with his lips, and layeth up deceit within him;* (Prov. 26:24)

> *Their throat is an open sepulchre; with their tongues they have used deceit; the poison of asps is under their lips:* (Rom. 3:13)

> *He answered and said unto them, Well hath Esaias prophesied of you hypocrites, as it is written, This people honoureth me with their lips, but their heart is far from me.* (Mark 7:6)

So, when it comes to what the Bible actually reveals about the processes of the transmission of the words of God from the Lord's heart and mind to ours, we get quite a different view than that presented by Fundamental scholarship today.

The Lord's Means for Delivering His Mind and Heart to Man

2 Timothy 3:16 – *Theopneustos*

The first stop on the way to observing how the Lord delivered His mind and heart to man, as well as exposing how men have misused, exploited and misapprehended God's usage of words, is a port of call at a very popular spot called *theopneustos*. *Theopneustos* is the Greek word that the King

James translators translated as ***is given by inspiration of God*** in 2 Timothy 3:16. This is a tremendous verse for the Bible-believer, deserving of further examination at a later point, but is here important because the Greek word *theopneustos* has become practically the Holy Grail at which most all scholars stop and genuflect. This includes scholars that fall well within the liberal Critical Text camp of Westcott and Hort and their friends, as well as within the very conservative camp of Textus Receptus scholars that at least marginally defend the King James Bible. Nothing is quite as predictable as the verity that most every species of Greek Bible scholar, when asked or challenged about the accuracy or infallibility of God's word, will immediately fly to 2 Timothy 3:16. Now, using 2 Timothy 3:16 as first resort with respect to God's word is perfectly legitimate and no better verse exists to begin a defense of the scripture. The problem is that these scholars, conservative and liberal alike, do not just go to the verse, quote it, and apply it. They do not quote the verse as an authoritative and definitive statement of finality from the Lord. They exploit it to escape to the Greek! It is virtually an automatic and utterly predictable response that they only refer to 2 Timothy 3:16 in order that they may take the inquirer to *theopneustos*.

In fact, what a scholar says next is altogether and equally predictable. Again, a very large majority of Textus Receptus-brand of King James defenders and Alexandrian Origen admirers say the same thing next, as if programmed as automatons. Almost with no exceptions, they proceed to tell the reader or seeker that *theopneustos* means ***God-breathed***. Importantly, they almost universally downplay or overlook altogether what the English Bible actually says: *all scripture* ***is given by inspiration of God***. Plainly, the final appeal for these men is not the AV 1611 KJV, but the Greek, and many of them are quick to assent to that very fact. Nevertheless, the fact remains that the phrase ***all scripture is given by inspiration of***

God is almost uniformly dismissed in favor of informing us of what our Bibles "really should say," instead of what they do say. Plainly, for the scholars, the glittering and luminescent gem from the Greek is that *theopneustos* means ***God-breathed.*** It is important to understand how widely and uniformly this singular "tenet" is held among scholars and Christians of all stripes and kinds.

Dr. John R. Rice can lead off:

> We are told that the Scriptures are *theopneustos* (God-breathed).[128]
>
> But the word "inspiration" here means a great deal more than the English term usually would imply... But the meaning in the original Greek, *theopneustos*, is much more definite. It is literally *God-breathed.*[129]

Rice further cites Edward J. Young, who says regarding *theopneustos*, "...and we should properly translate, 'breathed of God'."[130]

He also quotes B. B. Warfield thus, "What is Theopneustos is 'God-breathed.'"[131]

Harold Lindsell agrees,

> The Greek word for "inspired" is *theopneustos*. Literally this word means "God-'spirated'" or "God-breathed-out."[132]

---

[128] Rice, John R., *Our God-Breathed Book – The Bible* (Sword of the Lord Publishers, Murfreesboro, TN., 1969) p.69

[129] Ibid. p.49.

[130] Ibid. p.50.

[131] Ibid. 51.

[132] Lindsell, Harold, *The Battle For the Bible,* (Zondervan Publishing House, Grand Rapids, MI 49506, 1976) p.

David Sorenson weighs in,

> The word inspiration, as found in 2 Tim.3:16, literally means "God-breathed."[133]

J.J. Ray, a well-known defender of the King James Bible, even says it means "God-breathed."

> Inspiration is from the Greek word THEO-PNEUSTOS… This is how we arrive at the statement: "All Scripture is GOD-BREATHED."[134]

David Otis Fuller says,

> The Bible…claims to be "Theopneustos," "God-breathed."[135]

Dr. D.A. Waite adds,

> I don't like to use the word "inerrant" of any English (or other language) translation of the Bible because the word "inerrant" is implied from the Greek Word, *theopneustos* (2 Timothy 3:16) which means literally, "God-Breathed."[136]

The *Wycliffe Commentary*:

> Paul then gives the reason for this efficacy of Scripture: it is of divine origin. 16. Inspiration of

---

[133] Sorenson, David H., *Touch Not The Unclean Thing* (Northstar Baptist Ministries, Duluth, MN 55811, 2001) p.6

[134] Ray, Jasper James, *God Wrote Only One Bible* (The Eye Opener Publishers, Eugene, OR 97401, 1955,1970,1983), p.118.

[135] Fuller, David Otis, *Which Bible* (Grand Rapids International Publications, Grand Rapids, MI 49501,1981), p.5

[136] Waite, D.A., *Defending The King James Bible A Fourfold Superiority* (The Bible For Today Press, Collingswood, N.J., 1992) p.239-240

> God is a simple word, meaning, [God-breathed].[137]

Robertson's Word Pictures in the New Testament is aboard,

> [Inspired of God] [theopneustos (grk 2315)]. "God-breathed." A late word (Plutarch)[138]

Vincent agrees,

> [Is given by inspiration of God] [Theopneustos (grk 2315)]. Occurs only here in the New Testament. Not occurring in the Septuagint. From [Theos] (grk 2316) "God" and [pnein] (grk 4154), "to breathe." "God-breathed." [139]

The *International Standard Bible Encyclopedia* appears awfully certain in the judgments that it hands down,

> For the Greek word in this passage--theopneustos-- **very distinctly does not mean "inspired of God."...** The Greek word **does not even mean, as the King James Version translates it, "given by inspiration of God,"** although that rendering…has at least to say for itself that it is a somewhat clumsy, perhaps, but not misleading, paraphrase of the Greek term in the theological language of the day. The Greek term has, however, nothing to say of inspiring or of inspiration: it speaks only of a "spiring" or "spiration." What it says of Scripture is, not that it is "breathed into by God" or is the product of the Divine "inbreathing" into its human authors, but that it is breathed out by God, "God-breathed," the product of the creative breath of

---

[137] Wycliffe Commentary, 2 Tim.3:16.

[138] Robertsons Word Pictures in the New Testament, 2 Tim.3:16

[139] Vincent's Word Studies of the New Testament, 2 Tim.3:16.

> God. In a word, what is declared by this fundamental passage is simply that the Scriptures are a Divine product, without any indication of how God has operated in producing them.[140]

James Strong, in his Greek Dictionary in the back of his concordance says that *theopneustos* means "divinely breathed in."[141]

The *New International Version reads,* "All Scripture is God-breathed and is useful for teaching, rebuking, correcting and training in righteousness… (2 Tim 3:16)

Zondervan's writers concede the same,

> "All (every) scripture is inspired by God (*theopneustos* – God-breathed) and profitable for teaching…The Greek word *theopneustos* is a compound of *theos* (God) and *pneustos* (breathed)… "breathed of God," i.e., "that which is breathed out by God."[142]

John MacArthur has a sermon series on *Our God-Breathed Bible.*[143]

---

[140] International Standard Bible Encylopaedia, Electronic Database Copyright (C) 1996 by Biblesoft)

[141] Strong, James, (*The Exhaustive Concordance of the Bible*, Holman Bible Publishers, Nashville, TN,) p.36

[142] Tenney, Merrill C.ed., (*The Zondervan Pictoral Encyclopedia of the Bible*, Regency Reference Library, Grand Rapids, MI 49506, 1976) Vol.3, pg.290.

[143] MacArthur, John. *By the Way*. "Our God-Breathed Bible." *Bible Bulletin Board*. Web. 11 Dec. 2010. http://www.biblebb.com/files/mac/55-17.htm>.

A simple Google search of "God-breathed", a subject you would consider to be limited fairly closely to the issue which we discuss here, returned 2,420,000 "hits." Someone, for example, named Hugo McCord, in a piece entitled (what else) *God-Breathed Scriptures,* said,

> In the creation of the Bible, "every Scripture" was "God breathed" (theopneustos, 2 Timothy 3:16) into selected authors "guided by the Holy Spirit" (2 Peter 1:21) to write "words taught by the Spirit" (1 Corinthians 2:13). The Greek word theopneustos, "God breathed,"...[144]

In his own right, a man by the name of Steve Zeisler wrote, *God-Breathed Scripture Series: Great Truths Reconsidered.*[145] *Entirely God-Breathed* was placed online by the Reverend Bryn MacPhail.[146] Someone named Paul White proclaims of 2 Timothy 3:16, "The Greek structure of verse 16 says, 'All scripture is God-breathed.'"[147]

This goes to show that easily thousands and thousands of people – devotional writers, bloggers, teachers, preachers, ministry help writers, internet warriors, etc. – have taken the phrase "God-breathed," made it a doctrine and run with it. Some are friendly to the idea of "God-breathed" going hand-in-hand with *given by inspiration.* Others consider that "God-

---

[144] McCord, Hugo. "God-Breathed Scriptures." *TheBible.net.* Web. 11 Dec. 2010. http://www.thebible.net/modules.php?name=Read&itemid=99&cat=3.

[145] "God-Breathed Scripture." *PBC.* Web. 11 Dec. 2010. <http://www.pbc.org/files/messages/7727/4606.html>.

[146] "Entirely God-Breathed." *The Reflections of Bryn MacPhail.* Web. 11 Dec. 2010.<http://www.reformedtheology.ca/2tim3bb.htm>.

[147] By Sight. "Scripture Is 'God-Breathed'." *Abundant Grace Daily Devotional.* Web. 11 Dec. 2010. <http://paulwhiteministries.blogspot.com/2009/08/scripture-is-god-breathed.html>.

breathed" essentially corrects and alters the understanding of *given by inspiration.* Somewhat humorously, there are those who think it means that "God breathed in" and others that "God breathed out." Even the scholars go back and forth with regard to that particular detail, but just about everybody is aboard with the fact that "God-breathed" fundamentally trumps *given by inspiration* of the old King James.

To reiterate the point, from non-denominational and New Evangelical ministers and scholars who openly embrace new versions, to ardent defenders and fellow-soldiers in the cause of the King James Bible, to reference materials that most pastors have in their libraries, when it comes to *theopneustos* and 2 Timothy 3:16, everybody seems to agree that "God-breathed" is the real key to the matter. The fact is that even most new versions (except the NIV) do not read that way. The King James Bible certainly does not read that way. Importantly, a great and preponderant segment of scholars, writers, teachers and ministers ***have been programmed to mentally default*** to "God-breathed" as soon as 2 Timothy 3:16 crosses their intellectual radar.

Here is the question: **Does *theopneustos* really mean "God-breathed?"** If it does, then in reality it would be necessary to ignore the 400 year old standard in English, and to default to a meaning not clearly stated in the Bible. If it does not mean "God-breathed," just how is it that every Tom, Dick and Harry from one end of the theological spectrum to the other automatically prostrate themselves on prayer mats before that meaning?

Does *theopneustos* really mean "God-breathed? *Theopneustos* is indeed a compound Greek word that is composed of *theos* and *pneustos.* (I am uncertain why, but I suddenly feel compelled to say, "Man! That's deep!") Anyway,

theos is Strong's word #2316 in his Greek dictionary and means "God." No big revelation there. ***Pneustos*** is not as clear-cut as the scholars' union would have you believe. It is generally recognized as being derived from Strong's word #4154, *pneo*. D.A.Waite and H.D. Williams, both of the Dean Burgon Society, are adamant in their jointly written preface of Kirk DiVietro's *Cleaning Up Hazardous Materials,* that, the second half of the Greek compound word, comes from *pneo*, meaning "to breathe,"[148] but most often translated in the AV as "to blow." They are adamant that *pneustos is* unrelated to *pneuma*, a similar appearing Greek word meaning *spirit.* (The reason for mentioning the issue of *pneuma* will become evident shortly.) This assessment is repeated by the book's author, Dr. DiVietro, in his evaluation, as well.[149] Greek lexicons and Strong all seem to agree to this assessment of the ***pneustos*** part of *theopneustos* meaning ***"breathe."***

If *theopneustos* really does mean "God-breathed" so absolutely and finally, and given what has already been shown in this book to be the extraordinary character of the work of the AV translators, and given the well-attested scholarly excellence of King James' committeemen, it should be asked why those translators did not translate *theopneustos*, "God-breathed" instead of *is given by inspiration of God.* For that matter, **why did William Tyndale translate *all scripture geve by inspiracion of god*[150] instead of "God-breathed"?** Tyndale was "so skilled in seven languages, Hebrew, Greek, Latin, Italian, Spanish, English, French, that whichever he spoke you would suppose it his native tongue."[151] Why would we dismiss

---

[148] DiVietro, Kirk,*Cleaning-Up Hazardous Materials: A Refutation of Gail Riplinger's Hazardous Materials,*The Dean Burgon Soiety, Collingswood, NJ 08108,2010, pg.iv.
[149] Ibid. pg.2-3
[150] *The Wesley Center Online: Home.* Web. 11 Dec. 2010. <http://wesley.nnu.edu/biblical_studies/tyndale/2ti.txt>.
[151] Moorman, Jack, *Forever Settled.* The Dean Burgeon Society Press, Collingswood, New Jersey 08108), 1999, p.212.

the expertise of one so skilled in Greek? **Wycliffe too,** was more nigh unto the AV1611 translation than to the cacophony of squawking, subversive scholars of today: ***al scripture inspirid of God is profitable***...[152] Granted, neither Tyndale nor Wycliffe exactly match the statement of the AV, but at least they use the same word structures, and "God- breathed" is not to be found! A form of the AV word *inspiration* is given in both Tyndale and Wycliffe's translation work.

If *theopneustos* really does mean "God-breathed" so absolutely and finally, why did not Tyndale, Wycliffe, Lancelot Andrews, John Overall, John Reynolds, and John Bois come to ready agreement with our modern scholars? Bois was "so familiar with the Greek Testament, that he could, at any time, turn to any word that it contained."[153] Andrews learned a new language every year during his month long vacation.[154]

Are we to believe that these true giants of scholarship, who were truly used of God, were themselves unacquainted with the same linguistic and grammatical "issues" that have led the consort of today's "scholars," listed earlier in this chapter, to embrace "God-breathed" as the true meaning *of theopneustos,* as opposed to *is given by inspiration of God*?

If theopneustos so incontrovertibly and indisputably means "God-breathed," then why did not the AV Translators (50-plus of them), Tyndale and Wycliffe translate it so? For what reason exactly should I, or any other Bible-believer, choose the scholarship of John Rice, Harold Lindsell, David Sorenson, D.A. Waite, Kirk DiVietro or John McArthur over

---

152 *The Wesley Center Online*: *Home*. Web. 11 Dec. 2010. <http://wesley.nnu.edu/biblical_studies/wycliffe/2ti.txt>.

153 McClure, Alexander, *Translators Revived,*Maranatha Publications, Worthington, PA 16262, pg.206

154 Ibid. pg. 78

that of Bois, Reynolds, Overall, Andrews, Saravia, Bedwell, Chaderton, Tyndale and Wycliffe?

In the end, a King James Bible-believer's Bible - his final authority - says *All scripture is given by inspiration of God,* but modern scholarship - even AV 1611 defenders – has for so long repeated with hypnotic regularity that *theopneustos* means "God-breathed," that men dismiss and largely ignore what their Bible actually ***says.*** The observation and lesson that is not to be missed in this scenario is that there has been a virtually uniform and universal **superimposition of "God-breathed" over *is given by inspiration of God.*** What the Bible of Englishmen since 1611 says has been subjugated, subverted and overthrown by even some of its defenders. The meaning of the verse has been supplanted and replaced in men's minds by "what it really means." Just as men are certain that *charity* can be replaced by *love*, and that *ensamples* and *examples* are the same thing, so by the work of the pens and tongues of scholars *All scripture is given by inspiration of God* now is understood to mean "God-breathed."

Shell Games and Meaning Shifts

Certainly, most readers understand what a shell game is, an old sleight of hand trick at carnival booths manned by shysters. The victim is to keep his eye on the ball, coin, or other object while the trickster moves clam shells around on the tabletop. The guy who is about to lose his money is to keep up with which shell the object is under. Needless to say, the jackleg proprietor is quick and slick with his hands, and the ball or coin is never under the shell to which the sucker points.

Satan distracted Eve from the true meaning of God's prohibition of the tree of knowledge and hijacked her attention over to a different, more obscure, and convoluted meaning. She may arguably be credited with wanting the knowledge of God, but she had her eye on the wrong shell.

Men today are misled and have their eyes on the wrong shell in seeking meaning from God's words. This is true universally and on a broad scale with respect to the King James Bible versus the Greek or Hebrew. This book has shown that the treasures of meaning in the Bible are found in the AV, not the original languages. It goes without saying that the allure and deception of the idea of deeper meaning and truth in the originals is masterminded by a malevolent and insidiously devious creature. Consider the specific case of the meaning of *theopneustos* as an explicit and influential example of this deception.

As noted earlier, biblical scholars have well-succeeded in imparting a new meaning to 2 Timothy 3:16 as opposed to that which is actually written. They have achieved the impressive feat of virtual unanimity among themselves regarding their chosen meaning of the word *theopneustos*. This remarkable feat is the more striking for the fact that they not only are unified in opinion about the meaning of the verse, but that they almost wholly ignore what their much acclaimed King James Bible actually does say in 2 Timothy 3:16. To them, it means "God-breathed" - nothing more and nothing less, and the AV's *All scripture is given by inspiration of* God is largely ignored and its legitimacy is dismissed as it is written.

The devil has accomplished with almost an entire body of biblical scholars of all types what he only had to accomplish with one woman in Genesis 3. He has the entire body looking under the wrong shell (the Greek) for the treasured meaning, while that meaning has resided in perfect clarity in our native language for nearly 400 years – more than that if one counts Tyndale and Wycliffe's translational work.

Interestingly ***pneo***, Strong's word #4154, which the scholars insist means "breathe," is only translated in its various forms as *blew, blow, bloweth, wind, choked or strangled* in the King James' New Testament, with the exception of Acts 17:25 which says that God *giveth to all...**breath** and all things.* That is, the only time ***pneo*** is translated according to the meaning the scholars propound, is where the Spirit simply states that God gives all living things *breath.* ***Importantly,*** at no time in the New Testament is the breath of the Lord connected directly to the scriptures. The following verse is the only verse in the Bible where God's breath is definitively connected to His words.

> *By the **word** of the LORD were the heavens made; and all the host of them by the **breath of his mouth.*** (Ps. 33:6)

This verse, of course, is an Old Testament verse, so the Greek would not apply.

Importantly, the Greek scholars are fervent and insistent about the intimate and inseparable connection between God's word and God's breath. It is certainly true that both God and Christ spoke, and that speaking is accomplished in part with breath. The Lord's breath is oft spoken of in the AV scriptures. In Genesis 1, God spake the worlds we know into existence. Yes, we know that His word *goeth forth out of (His) mouth* (Isa 55:11). Certainly, in speaking of Adam, the Lord *breathed into his nostrils the breath of life* in Genesis 2:7, and a bit more mysteriously, Christ *breathed on them, and saith unto them, Receive ye the Holy Ghost* in John 20:22. Of Israel in the beginning of the Millennium it is spoken that *So I prophesied as he commanded me, and the breath came into them, and they lived, and stood up upon their feet, an exceeding great army* (Ezek. 37:10). At the Second Coming of Christ *with the breath of his lips shall he slay the wicked* (Isa.11:4). Thus it is evident that God's breath is an important theme in the scriptures. For these reasons, there is no reason to object to a Christian praying that God would "*breathe*" upon a ministry, a spiritual undertaking, or a man's work and labors.

The disturbing fact remains that the infallible and inerrant English scriptures of the AV 1611 do not emphasize the relation of God's breath with His word with the same heat and fervor of the Greek-foraging scholars. Again, there is no arguing the physics and physiology involved in speaking, and it is a blessing that God hath spoken. There is certainly no denying the importance of God's breath. It is, however, important to note that the emphasis in the English scriptures is different than the emphasis of Greek scholars.

Perhaps it is acceptable to pause at this moment for the sake of perspective:

> *The counsel of the LORD standeth for ever, the thoughts of his heart to all generations.*
> (Ps. 33:11)

> *But God hath revealed them unto us by his Spirit: for the Spirit searcheth all things, yea, the deep things of God.* (1 Cor. 2:10)

> *Let this mind be in you, which was also in Christ Jesus:* (Phil. 2:5)

It is the highest calling for a Christian that he grows to be so much like Christ that he actually thinks and acts like Him. God's word was given us that we might know His mind (1 Cor. 2:14-16) and His thoughts (Ps.33:11); that we might mold ourselves to His precepts and judgments, and hold to His views of things. Our decisions and thought processes ought to grow to reflect His own. That is His purpose for communicating the details of His mind to us through His word.

The Lord's emphasis then should become ours – whether it be holiness, souls, Jesus Christ or His word. Pointedly, God did not emphasize His **breath** in connection with His **word** so much as He emphasized something else. Rather than God's **breath** being emphasized as the scholars so uniformly set forth, it is found instead that in His word God's **Spirit** is emphasized in the context of God's words.

> *It is the **spirit** that quickeneth; the flesh profiteth nothing: the **words** that I speak unto you, they are **spirit**, and they are life.* (Jn. 6:63)

In John 6:63, who can deny the intimate interrelation between the words Christ spake and their very spiritual nature? The Lord Jesus Christ Himself said that ***the words**…**are spirit***! They are ***not breath,*** then. They ***are spirit***. They are ***spir**itual*. It is certain that Christ breathed across His vocal cords when He spake, but this is not what the Lord desired to draw attention to when He gave 2 Timothy 3:16 as a testament to the nature of His word. Those words are ***spirit***, and they are ***life*** as well. One cannot help but wonder then whether the Lord might have fully intended the English Bible-believer to inexorably connect ***spir**it* with *in**spir**ation*, rather than connecting the unrelated *breath* with *in**spir**ation*. Remember, it was the AV translators, as well as Wycliffe and Tyndale that used the word *inspiration.* The Greek scholars of much of the past and today have functionally rejected the word that careful English readers would connect with "spirit." Considering that only the Greek treasure hunters insist that *theopneustos* must absolutely connect God's breathing with His words, we find instead that the words in the English Holy Bible indicate that *Breath* is not the trait or characteristic He desired to have coupled with the concept of *in**spir**ation.* It is the ***Spirit*** or ***spirit*** that is connected to that concept! Furthermore, according to John 6:63, the ***words*** are not only ***spirit***, but they are also ***life***! We know from the rest of the Bible that it is the spiritual nature of those words that makes them *quick* (Heb.4:12) - that is, alive - and it is for that reason that the word of the Lord is *not bound* (2 Tim.2:9). So, the true nature of the words of the Lord is not only ***spirit***, but also ***life***. If the spiritual nature of those words is obscured, at what point are those words no longer life? How much of the essence of ***spirit*** can be compromised before ***life*** is no longer imparted? Men that are nigh but still adversarial to the Bible-believing camp are, wittingly or unwittingly, misdirecting men to a pseudo-definition that is not substantiated in the very Bible they claim to advocate. It is the spiritual nature of the words that impart life, not God breathing, as such. If the crucial spiritual coupling of ***spirit*** and ***life*** is broken by the insidious pilfering of foolish and presumptuous man, at what point are those words no longer ***life***?

2 Samuel 23:2 is another verse that verifies the foundational idea of God's emphasis being ***spirit*** (*inspiration*) as opposed to the *breathing* which the lexicographers and scholars emphasize. The prophet, David, says, *The* ***Spirit*** *of the LORD spake by me, and his* ***word*** *was in my tongue.* The Spirit's word was what David spake when he prophesied. When David spake the words of the Lord, what came from his mouth was not merely vocalized vibrations physically caused by his *breath*. What came from his mouth and pen were words that were not merely endued with the *breath of the Lord*, but they were words that were the Spirit's words, and the spiritual essence and potency of those words did not cease after they were breathed. They are still potent and *quick* (Heb.4:12) today, because they ***are spirit***!

Notice again the virtue of the words of God in Proverbs 1:23, where the pouring out of His spirit is inexorably linked to the Lord making His words known! *Turn you at my reproof: behold, I will pour out* ***my spirit*** *unto you, I will make known* ***my words*** *unto you.* Brethren, the words of God are eternally enlivened and animated by His Spirit, *not His breath.* Those words *are* spirit!

If one has any doubts remaining about this, consider Zechariah 7:12, which states,

> *Yea, they made their hearts as an adamant stone, lest they should hear the law,* ***and the words which the LORD of hosts hath sent in his spirit*** *by the former prophets: therefore came a great wrath from the LORD of hosts.*

The Lord *sent...****the words****...in* ***his spirit*** *by the... prophets.* Again, notice the profound connection of spirit, His Spirit in this case, to the words of God. To reiterate, God does breathe, and He breathes into and upon both men and things. It is a presumptuous error, however, to substitute the effects of His breath in place of the effects of His Spirit in 2 Timothy 3:16. If the Lord wanted to emphasize His breath in relation to His words, He would have done so. He did not do so. He clearly did not desire to do so. Instead He cued us in to His purpose, by the phonetic rendering of the word *in**spir**ation.* Beyond even that, He granted light and illumination in His discriptives of the words of God in verses like John 6:63 and 2 Samuel 23:2, as well as the others we have surveyed here.

It is best not to ignore that Christ *breathed on them, and saith unto them, Receive ye the Holy Ghost* in John 20:22. The only sensible way to exposit the verse is to say that this was plainly a messianic blessing bestowed upon the apostles, presumably in anticipation of the day in Acts 2 when the apostles and disciple did genuinely receive the Holy Ghost (Acts 2:4). That they did not receive the Holy Ghost in John 20 is obvious by John 7:39b: *for the Holy Ghost* ***was not yet given; because that Jesus was not yet glorified***. Interestingly, when they did receive the Holy Ghost in Acts 2, the singular manifestation of the Spirit upon them was that they began to speak words by the Spirit.

> *... they were all filled with the Holy Ghost, and* ***began to speak with other tongues, as the Spirit gave them utterance.*** (Acts 2:4)

The Bible, as written, does not magnify God's breath in relation to His words, but rather His Spirit. Notice the connection again regarding the Son of God:

> *For he whom God hath sent* ***speaketh the words of God****: for God giveth not the* ***Spirit*** *by measure unto him.* (John 3:34)

Using the Greek definition of *theopneustos* (God-breathed) is merely a vertical shaft dug downward that culminates as the bottom of a hole, whereas, trusting the God appointed method of that *which the Holy Ghost teacheth; comparing spiritual things with spiritual* (1 Cor. 2:13), leads to true treasures and God's true emphasis by allowing the Spirit to speak through the scriptures. The truths shown by this method are expansive, definitive and unforced. The Bible in this way comments upon and defines itself. Such an end should be carefully compared to that which must import a forced and foreign definition upon which the Lord doth not further expand.

> *But the wisdom that is from above is first pure, then peaceable, gentle, and easy to be intreated, full of mercy and good fruits, without partiality, and without hypocrisy.* (Jas. 3:17)

It may be ventured at this point that perhaps the reason the AV translators, along with Wycliffe and Tyndale, did not translate *theopneustos* as *"God-breathed,"* was due to the fact that the emphasis implied by *"God-breathed"* is not in accord with the emphasis that the rest of the scriptures place upon the "Spirit" as related to God's words. In other words, perhaps they realized that the inferences drawn by the translation *"God-breathed"* would be in conflict with the actual definitive commentary of the entire body of scripture.

More insidious is the verity that ***they who emphasize God's breath as integral to* God's word *in place of God's Spirit, do so for the purpose of limitation upon God's word.*** Again, while not dishonoring the Biblical implications of God's breath, it must be noted that when the main body of scholars resort to the old party line of *theopneustos* meaning *God-breathed,* they define it in that way out of the explicit determination that the divine nature of the words of God is confined to the original languages. The entire idea of using that definition is one of ***limitation***. That is, for most all scholars who cite the *God-breathed* definition, that meaning is their justification and reason for saying that no Bible or translation has ever been entirely perfect since the originals were first *"God-breathed."* The false definition either allows them to justify what they falsely teach about the words of God, or else the definition misled them to the false position which they hold. Either scenario is disastrous. Again, this cuts fairly close to home, because certain classic defenders of the King James Bible have been caught up in the rhetoric and in the presumed definition.

> I don't like to use the word "inerrant" of any English (or other language) translation of the Bible because the word "inerrant" is implied

> from the Greek Word, *theopneustos* (2 Timothy 3:16) which means literally, "God-Breathed."[155]
>
> Dr. D.A. Waite

> All this GRAPHE [scripture] has been once and for all THEOPNEUSTOS (God-breathed) never will God repeat this miracle "breathing out" in any form or in any way. This verse teaches clearly that God "breathed out" all of His original Hebrew, Aramaic, and Greek Words. God did not "breathe out" or "inspire any other words in any language of the world.[156]
>
> Dr. Kirk DiVietro

> Inspiration is from the Greek word THEO-PNEUSTOS... This is how we arrive at the statement: "All Scripture is GOD-BREATHED."[157]
>
> J.J. Ray

> The Bible...claims to be "Theopneustos," "God-breathed."[158]
>
> David Otis Fuller

There may be some cases where men have fallen prey to the usage of the definition without grasping the ramifications of

---

[155] Waite, D.A., *Defending The King James Bible A Fourfold Superiority* (The Bible For Today Press, Collingswood, N.J., 1992) p.239-240

[156] DiVietro, Kirk,*Cleaning-Up Hazardous Materials: A Refutation of Gail Riplinger's Hazardous Materials,*The Dean Burgon Soiety, Collingswood, NJ 08108,2010. pg. 3.

[157] Ray, Jasper James, *God Wrote Only One Bible* (The Eye Opener Publishers, Eugene, OR 97401, 1955,1970,1983), p.118.

[158] Fuller, David Otis, *Which Bible* (Grand Rapids International Publications, Grand Rapids, MI 49501,1981), p.5

retooling the terminology or without intending to blatantly undermine God's word. It is important though that the reader and the Bible-believer make no mistake that the vast proportion of scholars fully intend to communicate that *God-breathed* means that ***what God actually breathed (the originals) was the true, perfect and inspired word of God. According to them, whatever form of the Bible we have had since then (manuscript copies, vernacular translations, quotations in history) is not divine, is not perfect and is not truly inspired, for God did not breathe it!*** If the *breath of God* is the key to the divine nature of the scriptures, then whatever God did not actually breathe cannot be categorized as divine. For that reason, to them, no copy of an original manuscript, no translation and no vernacular Bible could then be inspired, because the definition of inspiration has been hijacked to mean *God-breathed*, instead of *given by inspiration of God* with the emphasis being on *Spirit,* not *breathe.* For this reason, these guys believe that the only word that is *settled*, is that *in heaven* (Ps. 119:89), and the only words ever inspired or divine down here were the ones *God breathed.* Those words (the originals) are lost and gone to dust. Many believe that what we have left are only representations of the originals that vary in accuracy, depending upon one's school of thought. Some do hold that the Greek and Hebrew words of the Received Text and Masoretic Text are perfectly preserved, and that is why they do not believe that we can hold a perfect translation in our own language. This is the result of defining *theopneustos* as *God-breathed*, instead of acquiescing to the AV translators and the King James Bible: *All scripture is given by inspiration of God.*

2 Timothy 3:16 – *All Scripture…*

Men of most recent centuries have seemed to ignore the scriptures' own definition of what the scriptures are. Remember, the theme here is the idea that men have long since departed from the Bible and its clear and concise definitions, and have instead resorted to fanciful fables and smooth, slick semantics. They have twisted meanings. They have fallen back on historic positions, the traditions of infidels, and they have been more infected by rationalism than they even know.

If ***All scripture is given by inspiration of God*** (2 Tim. 3:16), it would seem that someone would ask the question, "What is scripture, then?" Since ***All scripture*** *is given by inspiration of God*, the first question **is not**, "What does *theopneustos* mean," but rather,"**What is scripture?"** After all, according to this Bible verse, if what one has is *scripture*...well, it *is given by inspiration of God*! Wherever it is that one finds *scripture*, one can know that that *scripture is given by inspiration of God.*

Perhaps it would be best to begin with proximity. In the verse before the great 2 Timothy 3:16 is a glorious insight. In 2 Timothy 3:15, it is clear that Paul did not consider the original *God-breathed* manuscripts the only scripture!

> *And that from a child* ***thou hast known the holy scriptures****, which are able to make thee wise unto salvation through faith which is in Christ Jesus.*
>
> (2 Tim. 3:15)

Folks, Timothy did not have any more access to the original writings that *God breathed* than YOU do! Yet Paul, who could say right along with David, *The* ***Spirit*** *of the LORD spake by me* (2 Sam.23:12), called what Timothy read and knew, ***holy scriptures***, and then followed that statement with the immediate declaration that ***All scripture is given by inspiration of God***. It should be of tremendous importance to the Bible-believer that there are no Bible characters – prophets, apostles or Christ Himself – who ever spake or emphasized what modern scholars and commentators magnify. What Timothy had were holy scriptures that were *given by inspiration of God*. These scriptures were not the originals.

There are 53 occurrences of the word *scripture(s)* in the King James Bible and none of these occasions refer to anything but what men had in their hands, which they read and studied, and what they heard in their ears, which was read to them. The Bible's *scriptures* are/were not limited to originals, though the originals were no doubt holy scriptures. Often what the Bible calls scriptures were copies of copies of copies, and incidentally, no one could prove that some of those scriptures referred to were not translations of the originals as well as copies of them in the original languages.

For instance, when the Bible says,

> *For* ***the scripture saith*** *unto Pharaoh, Even for this same purpose have I raised thee up, that I might shew my power in thee, and that my name might be declared throughout all the earth.*
> (Rom. 9:17)

The quote is from Exodus 9:16, in which Moses would have translated the Hebrew into Egyptian so Pharaoh could understand. The scripture Pharaoh heard was a translation.

You see, the key question is, "What is scripture?" If it is scripture, it was given by inspiration of God. Preacher, do not wave a leather-bound book in the pulpit and call it "scripture," and then turn around and say that no translation is inspired!

Incidentally, in this light, if the scholars were to consider the matter more carefully, they would realize that they have a problem with their unending citation of *"God-breathed"* in place of *is given by inspiration of God.* You see, if one calls the Bible he holds "scripture," by definition it is "inspired," for *All scripture is given by inspiration of God.* If a scholar replaces *is given by inspiration of God*, with *"God-breathed,"* he is still entrapped by what his Bible says, for if he ever refers to the translation in his hand as "scripture," he must in consistency declare from his pseudo-definition that those "scriptures" are *"God-breathed"!* After all, his rendition of the verse is in effect *"all scripture is God-breathed."* Whatever he calls "scripture," he also declares to have been *"God-breathed"!* This, of course, is heart attack material for scholars, because they believe only the originals to have been *"God-breathed."*

The biblical evaluation of these scholars' self-applied conundrum would be, *For it is written, **He taketh the wise in their own craftiness*** (1 Cor. 3:19).

2 Timothy 3:16 – *Is Given…*

Again, it must be emphasized how little actual care is given to the specific wording of the Bible, and the implications of that wording as it affects what men assume and presume to be true. It seems that one of the most insidious dangers to the *faith of God* (Rom.3:3) is man's tendency for preconceptions. Christ's condemnation of the religious zealots of His day was that they made *the word of God of none effect through (their) tradition* (Mark 7:13). Entrenched in the fervor and carelessness of their traditions, they had powerful inclinations toward preconceptions about God and the Messiah that, in the end, led to the most awful national tragedy of all time: Israel's rejection and murder of their Messiah and King!

Today men (some of them brilliant men) approach the Bible with their minds saturated in preconceptions:

- •Only the *God-breathed* originals were perfect.
- •Inspiration can only be an action of the past.
- •It is a heresy to say that anything but the originals *were* inspired
- •The only place the "Word" is perfect is in Heaven.
- •God used man in inspiring the perfect originals, but any actions of man since have been of a corruptive nature.
- • All translations are imperfect and fallible.
- •The work of lexicographers and scholars is honorable, objective, and scientific even when they were/are lost.
- •The language of the Bible constantly needs updating.
- • Scholars are constantly uncovering new evidence that legitimately changes the Bible.
- •Scholars and academics are invested with the responsibility of keeping the scriptures.
- •Training in Biblical languages is needed to really be equipped to understand or teach the Bible.

These preconceptions are the product of propaganda, programming and rhetoric. Men acquiesce to traditions taught to them by other men whom they admire and whom they disdain to ever contradict or question. They accept cunning twists and convolutions of meaning. In so doing, they become well-exercised and accustomed to the mental calisthenics required of semantic subtleties. Often, even in Bible schools, students are not so much taught the Bible, as they are taught things about the Bible. They are taught what men say the Bible teaches. They are taught what other men say about particular passages. They are taught what they should teach about the Bible. They are often well equipped with convincing phrases and verbiage that are intended to authenticate to their hearers their orthodox standing with respect to the Bible. They are not, however, really taught the Bible. They are not exercised in believing and dissecting each word of the scriptures and rejecting the foreign intrusion of concepts from outside the scriptures. The reason they are not taught to do this is because neither they, nor their teachers, actually believe that the words they read and study are so accurate and concise as to justify believing in them in this way.

No place is this better illustrated than in 2 Timothy 3:16:

> *All scripture is given by inspiration of God, and is profitable for doctrine, for reproof, for correction, for instruction in righteousness:*

The verse says that *All scripture* ***is given***... It ***is given.*** Not, ***was given***! The whole implication of the concept of *God-breathed*, as previously noted, is to limit God's action of inspiring and supernaturally giving the Bible to the past tense and to the one-time action when He actually *breathed* the originals into His chosen writers. By the continual recitation of the mantra of the *God-breathed* doctrine, in combination with the incessant repetition of the *perfection-is-only-in-the-originals or original-languages* theories, men – scholars, students, Christians – approach 2 Timothy 3:16 without really evaluating what it actually *says.* After all, they have already been thoroughly taught what it *means.* In this way, to them, it does not even matter what it *says.* Nevertheless, the fact remains that what it does say is that *All scripture* ***is given*** *by inspiration of God*!

Interestingly, in the main the new versions mostly agree, at least with respect to the present tense of the verb.

> All Scripture **is** inspired by God and profitable...
> (NAS)

> All Scripture **is** God-breathed and **is** useful…
> (NIV)

> All scripture **is** inspired by God and profitable…
> (RSV)

As one might suspect, no real confidence can be placed in the modern Bible corruptions, especially since they expectedly butcher the remainder of the verse in question. It is, however, worthy of note, that even in the modern perverse translations, translated by men who drank Westcott and Hort's fruit punch, that even they felt compelled by the rules of Greek grammar to translate the English verb in the present tense: ***is***. In fact, in the AV, note ***is given*** and ***is profitable*** in the same half-sentence. The new perversions mess up the words, which they erroneously consider synonyms, but in all cases they even translate ***is inspired (God-breathed)*** and ***is useful,*** or imply, ***is profitable***. These all use present tense verbs! For the most part, even the new versions do not make the argument that the translation should read, ***was given***, and they would be truly stupid to translate ***was profitable***.

The point is that even the false bibles do not place or limit the effects of inspiration to the realm of the past only. At least with respect to the tense of the verb (*is*), though not the remainder of the wording, even they agree that the "inspiration" belongs in the present tense. Why is it, then, that "all scholars agree" that ***inspiration*** was an action set in effect by God that is wholly locked and confined **to the past, and the past alone**? Why would it be a heresy to retain the inspiration of God, as it applies to the scriptures, as an effectual issue of the present? The point is that men have been propagandized and pre-programmed concerning the things of the Bible to the extent that they *know* and are *certain* that inspiration applies only to the original manuscripts. In the meanwhile, even the false

Bibles, along with the King James, testify that inspiration is a present matter.

All scripture ***is given*** *by inspiration of God, and* ***is profitable***... The ***is given*** of 2 Timothy 3:16 is a very real and very present promise which matches the fact that many things ***are*** still very much ***given*** to us by the Lord. A list of these things includes *frost* (Job.37:10), *wisdom* (Mark 6:2), *the Holy Ghost* (Rom.5:5), *grace* (1 Cor.1:4), the woman's *hair* (1 Cor.11:15), and the commission for *suffering* (Phil.1:29). The plain and incontrovertible statement of the verse is that the inspiration of the scriptures continues at this hour. How else could the scriptures truly be alive and *quick* (Heb.4:12) if all God's "action" rested in the past? How is the word of God *not bound* (2 Tim.2:9) if what the scholars say is true? Why in the world would the Lord supernaturally "give" the scriptures "*by inspiration*" and then retire into passivity?

With an air of dismissal and a certain species of conceit, DiVietro, in expositing his final authority, the TR Greek, says,

> The word "IS," is implied, even though not stated.[159]

I believe that he intends for us to infer from that statement that he holds that the present tense (*is*) is a translation lacking real authority and is worthy of dismissal from the mind even if not the scriptures. Since he is critiquing Riplinger's *Hazardous Materials*, he is referring to that author when he says,

---

[159] DiVietro, Kirk, *Cleaning-Up Hazardous Materials: A Refutation of Gail Riplinger's Hazardous Materials,* The Dean Burgon Soiety, Collingswood, NJ 08108,2010. pg.3.

> There is nothing to justify her translation of "are being given" which is necessary if this verse applies to translations.[160]

It is nowhere evident in Riplinger's work that DiVietro cites that Riplinger has ever advocated a translation of the scriptures that should read "are being given" in 2 Timothy 3:16. However, this does reveal the mindset of the classic Textus Receptus scholar. They think that leaving the AV reading as it stands ***(is given)*** means that a Bible-believer must then be an adherent to some theory that new, inspired revelatory scripture is still being given as in prophetic and apostolic days of the past. Thus Bible-believers who adamantly stand on what the King James Bible actually states are branded as crackpots and are misrepresented as believing things as represented above.

Examining the statement *All scripture **is given** by inspiration of God, and **is profitable**,* it is reasonable to ask how it is that *All scripture **is given** by inspiration of God.* The Lord is certainly no longer granting revelation to men today other than that revelation that has been recorded in the canon of scripture: the sixty six books of the Bible. The canon of scripture is clearly closed. In contrast to the prior prophetic, and even apostolic, times since the Lord finished speaking to John on the isle of Patmos around 90 A.D., the rule of our day (the Church Age) is that *we walk by faith, not by sight* (2 Cor. 5:7). We are no longer led by signs, wonders or miracles. Further, the mystical and esoteric "leading of the Spirit" that some practice is a fine way to wind up in *the ditch* (Matt. 15:14), or worse. No, *we walk by faith, not by sight*, and the source of our faith could not be more plain or pronounced: *So then faith cometh by hearing, and hearing by the word of God* (Rom. 10:17).

---

[160] Ibid. pg. 3.

How is it then that *All scripture is given by inspiration of God…?* It *is given* in the same sense that it *is profitable*. The action and viability of what God did in first giving the scriptures still remains in the present. The scriptures are still inspired and the effectual nature of that inspiration is still as much in application today as in 60-70A.D. It is not merely a finalized completion of the past. That the word of God is inspired is just as much a reality today as it was that day when the Father last spake to John on Patmos. Contrary to what liberal scholars have taught since at least the 1800's, the Bible is a living document, not merely an historic one! That which is scripture still receives the action of the inspiration by which that scripture was first given. That which is scripture is still *inspired scripture*! Scripture did not cease to be inspired after it was given at the first. *THAT* is the travesty that has been sold to Christians and preachers by scholars. *THAT* is the vortex one enters when he accepts that the inspiration, and the so-called "*God-breathed*" act of God is merely a matter of past history, a one-time effect that has no ramifications for what we hold in our laps today. The fact is that if what a man holds in his hand is scripture, then it is inspired, for *All scripture is given by inspiration of God*. The scripture that we believe and love is certainly preserved scripture (Ps. 12), but it is inspired, as well. Nothing has had to be ***re-inspired***, as the accusers charge. ***No King James Bible believer I am acquainted with believes the AV to be re-inspired. That is an accusation based on sophistry and rhetoric.*** If what one holds in his hand is *scripture*, it is inspired, for *All scripture is given by inspiration of God.*

Look at it this way. A blinded unbeliever approaches a Bible-believer. The unbeliever seeks "light" on what to do about his sin or his particular dilemma. What is the best thing the Bible-believer can do? What should the Bible-believer do, given that he is properly equipped? ***Give him* the scripture!** When one tells an unbeliever that he needs to repent, get right, be born again, believe, or otherwise follow the scripture, what does the sinner then receive? Now, be reminded that *we are ambassadors for Christ, as though God did beseech you by us: we pray you in Christ's stead, be ye reconciled to God* (2 Cor. 5:20). The Bible-believing witness speaks to him by the scriptures, and presumably by the Spirit, *in Christ's stead.* A mortal man having been told by another mortal what Christ said according to His word, may as well acquiesce to the fact that he may as well have been spoken to by Christ Himself! What was it that such a sinner has received? Well, brethren, he has been on the receiving end of *All scripture* ***is given*** *by inspiration of God*! Scripture inspired by God is still given. Scripture given by inspiration of God is still inspired when it is given. Inspiration is not limited to a one-time act of God breathing.

Further, consider that in this late hour of the *far spent* night (Rom. 13:12) of the Church Age, a missionary is called to go to a tribe in a still very dark corner of the world. It is a place where there are no scriptures. In the process of time, he learns the language and endeavors to deliver to these backward people the Bible in their language. By God's grace, he is successful in mastering the language and translating the Bible for them. We will presume that his work linguistically is excellent and accurate. This people now have the Bible in their native tongue. **Is their Bible *scripture*? If yes, then, *All scripture is given by inspiration of God and is profitable…*** If it is scripture, it is given by inspiration. If it is scripture then it is inspired. Note that the key question is, "What is scripture?", for if what those backward people have is scripture, then it is given by inspiration. If it is not scripture, then what is it?

One may say, "Well, the missionary did a fair job of translating their Bible, but there were problems he ran into and he had to go back over and over and make corrections and improvements." If that be the case, then what he translated accurately and concisely was scripture, and that which he bungled at the time was not. In that case, *All **scripture is*** (still) ***given** by inspiration of God*! If it is scripture, it *is given by inspiration of God.*

We will deal more with inspiration in the next section, but the evidence remains that our King James Bible is utterly 100% pure scripture. Every word of it is scripture, and *All scripture **is given** by inspiration of God*! Notice that in the situation described regarding the "hypothetical" missionary above, the admission that where he bungled part of the translation and that part was wrong, that *THAT* part was not scripture. Is that not a fair analysis of the situation in which we find ourselves today with the multiplicity of new versions? While some say that no one can get saved out of a new version, I actually am not acquainted with very many King James Bible believers that believe this to be the case. In reality a great number of Christians have been manifestly saved out of new versions. Make no mistake, the new versions are perversions and they have corrupted and polluted the pure word of God into an admixture that disgraces the name of the Bible. This is abominable before the Lord. While the AV 1611 is 100% scripture, wholly unadulterated and pure, is it nevertheless consistent to say that whatever percentage of the translation of the new versions is right, is also scripture? In comparing the AV to new versions, there are certain verses to be found in the new bibles that are left largely intact. Make no mistake, it is wretched to have a bible that has tens of thousands of omissions, additions, and adulterations in its New Testament alone, but apparently there is still enough scripture in the new versions to grant enough light and power to impart the new birth. Just as the hypothetical missionary had "mistakes" in his Bible that were not scripture, the new versions have a satanically high percentage of verses that are perverse and corrupted. Again, when we have a 100% pure Bible in our language, there is no excuse. However, is it not true that whatever scripture is contained in the new versions, it too ***is given** by inspiration of God*? It is for this reason that people can still get saved out of the new versions, though it is the vague equivalent of taking your meal from the dumpster. While one can survive out of the dumpster, it is not what the Lord intended!

Inspiration

Plainly, there is much controversy that revolves around the proper definition, and the limits of this act of God called ***inspiration.*** Other elements of 2 Timothy 3:16 have been dealt with in detail which have been the subject of man's prejudice, rhetoric and semantics. The spotlight now turns again to the crux of the verse and the cause of all the heartburn for the scholars. Again,

> *All scripture is given by **inspiration** of God, and is profitable for doctrine, for reproof, for correction, for instruction in righteousness: That the man of God may be perfect, throughly furnished unto all good works.*
> (2 Tim. 3:16-17)

For what would appear to be a straightforward statement, there has been a remarkable amount of fancy linguistic maneuvering that has accompanied attempted explanations and definitions. We have already seen the approach which goes back to Greek, redefines it, and in some cases, retranslates it to read and mean, *God-breathed*. This is falsifying the definition as outlined earlier in this chapter. Instead of apprehending from the AV English that the ***-spir-*** part of *in**spir**ation* better relates scripturally to ***spir**it*, they have tried to relate it to God *breathing*, that is, re***spir***ing. There is a "disconnect" of reasoning if this be the case. Respiring, that is, breathing includes the dual acts of inhaling and exhaling. If we thrust *inspiration* into this context of meaning, ***inspire*** would presumably relate to ***in****haling*. Webster's 1828 English dictionary does define the word inspire thus: "To draw in breath; to inhale air into the lungs; opposed to expire."[161] *Expiring* would relate to *exhaling*. Not only does this particular word game produce the alarming association of the expiring of *breath* with the expiring of *death*, the direction of God's breathing seems to be confused. Presumably, by their theory, if God *breathed* the scriptures, He would be breathing them ***out***. How then can *God-breathing* be called ***in****spiration*, if God was *breathing* ***out***? That would be called ***ex****piration!* Furthermore, it cannot be consistently argued by those who alter the words and meaning of the verse that inspiration is man breathing ***in*** what God breathed ***out***. If their *God-breathed* "doctrine" is right, then it must absolutely be God doing the breathing, and if God is doing the breathing, then He is breathing out the scriptures. It would be moronic to call that inspiration for He would have been exhaling, i.e. expiring!

In the end, and in accord with the theme of this chapter, men have approached the issue of inspiration with a bushel basket full of preconceptions and prejudices. Their misapprehensions and precious scholarly traditions have mired them in the swamp of inconsistency and prejudicial opinion.

The Bible Usage of the Word Inspiration. The Bible word, *inspiration*, is used only twice in the entire Bible, once in the Old Testament and once in the New Testament. Rather than making the Bible use of the word the foundation for meaning, the scholars often ignore the Bible's use, fly to the Greek or Hebrew, and go off on their own lexicon-led tangent. The basis

---

161 *Webster's 1828 Dictionary.* Christian Technologies, Inc. version 2 (Build 20040406), 2004.

for this action, of course, is that they hold the English usage of the word in tragically low esteem, since the Greek and Hebrew is their actual final authority. Their lexicons and the words of men are their final arbiters of meaning, certainly not the old English Bible. It has been shown, however, that the King James Bible a more dependable and consistent arbiter of meaning than these other sources and exercises which the scholars follow. These fellows decry the outdated language and verbiage of the AV, while the very fruits of their labors in Greek and Hebrew have proven to be the height of obscurity, confusion and inconsistency.

The occurrence of *inspiration* in the English of the KJV's 2 Timothy 3:16 is immediately carried back to Greek, and scholars come up with a definition that most all seem to accept, but obviously, few care to examine in clear light. What about the other occurrence? Think ye not that there might be profit in examining ***the only other occurrence of the word*** in the entirety of the Book?

> *But there is a spirit in man: and the* ***inspiration*** *of the Almighty giveth them understanding.*
> (Job 32:8)

It takes less than a nanosecond for the one-track minded scholars to fly again to the original language – Hebrew this time. This time the root word *neshamah* or *nesham* is the scholars' blunder and blinder. They insist that it means *breath*, and so all the new versions translate that the *breath of the Lord gives understanding*. Naturally, they do not mention that Job 26:4 and Proverbs 20:27 both translate *neshamah* as *spirit*! Nor are they given pause by the fact that Isaiah 57:16 translates the word as *souls*. The Hebrew word is indeed rightfully translated *breath* several times in the Old Testament, but God does not grant understanding by breathing! Again, it should take no genius to be able to relate the ***spir****it in man* of the first portion of the verse, to the *in**spir**ation of the Almighty* of the latter half. For some reason, obsessed with *the breathing of God* in both testaments, the heady "Biblicists" cannot seem to connect *in**spir**ation* with ***spir**it* as is plainly written. It is a sobering and important observation that to them the great treasures of knowledge in the Bible revolve more around what **is not written** as opposed to what **is written**.

But there is a spirit in man: and the inspiration of the Almighty giveth them understanding.

Christian brethren, we may devotionally speak of being desirous of the breath and blessing of God upon our lives and work. There is no question that God has breath. *By the breath of God frost is given* (Job 37:10). The breath of God is real. *The Spirit of God hath made me, and the breath of the Almighty hath given me life* (Job 33:4). The breath of God is of sobering import for the future Day of the Lord. *For Tophet is ordained of old; yea, for the king it is prepared; he hath made it deep and large: the pile thereof is fire and much wood; the breath of the LORD, like a stream of brimstone, doth kindle it* (Isa. 30:33).

That said, the Lord does not grant *understanding* by breathing! *(T)he **inspiration** of the Almighty giveth them understanding.* Breathing would be a notably sorry definition for inspiration, since the understanding spoken of plainly involves far more than breath. God imparts understanding by His Spirit.

9 But as it is written, Eye hath not seen, nor ear heard, neither have entered into the heart of man, the things which God hath prepared for them that love him.

> *10 But God hath revealed them unto us* ***by his Spirit****: for* ***the Spirit searcheth*** *all things, yea, the deep things of God.*
> *11 For what man knoweth the things of a man, save the spirit of man which is in him? even so the things of God knoweth no man, but* ***the Spirit of God.*** (1 Cor. 2:9-11)

To say that God breathes understanding would be, and is, a great mistake. The fact that in the rudiments of the Greek and Hebrew languages there exist a fragile linguistic connection insinuated between breathing and *inspiration*, does not overturn the profound scriptural connections between the *(S)pirit* and *inspiration.* Notice how many times *(S)pirit* occurs in the passage of 1 Corinthians 2 given above. In this passage, the theme is God revealing the things of God to man so that man will know them. It cannot be emphasized enough that the ***-spir-*** in ***inspiration*** is linked to the ***-spir-*** in ***spirit*** not the ***-spir-*** in ***respire***! Importantly, in 1 Corinthians 2:13, it is further emphasized that the Holy Ghost (the Spirit) teaches in words: ...*we speak, not in the words which man's wisdom teacheth, but which the Holy Ghost teacheth...* The Spirit of God gives man understanding. It all begins with words that He chooses and uses, not words man chooses and uses, and the Lord then spiritually imparts understanding to man. This spiritual impartation is what the book of Job refers to as inspiration - *the inspiration of the Almighty giveth them understanding.* It does not have anything to do with breathing. It has to do with the inward work of the Spirit helping man grasp what God means.

Job 32:8 provides very important spiritual light because the scriptures themselves are the best commentary upon the scriptures. It is elementary that when the AV 1611 uses the word inspiration only two times, that the light those two occurrences shed upon each other should not be ignored. Nevertheless, ignoring Job 32:8 is exactly what Christian scholars have done, and by this method have both limited what inspiration *is* and made it into something that it *is not,* all at the same time. Job 32:8 shows that inspiration is not a one-time act of breathing by God, limited in action to the past only. It is a continuing work of the Spirit, within the spirits of men by which they attain an understanding of the things of God. Truly, the Lord did inspire men at one juncture to speak and pen His words, and those words eventually became the canon of scripture, which we know and embrace today. No, He is not revealing newly inspired words today. The canon of scripture is closed and finished. Nevertheless, *inspiration* is not limited to just the divine "giving" of the scriptures, for *inspiration* does also include the impartation of an understanding of the scriptures. It should be obvious to the Bible-believer and reader that the two aspects of *inspiration* go hand in hand.

Now most all scholars – certainly Fundamentalists – would say that the Spirit of God does indeed impart understanding to men today that they might be saved first, and then *grow in grace, and in the knowledge of our Lord and Saviour Jesus Christ* (2 Pet. 3:18). No soul conscious Christian would deny this truth. This work of thc Spirit makes it possible for the average man to receive understanding in the intimate and deep things of the Lord. It is in this way that *the inspiration of the Almighty giveth them understanding*. Though a vast majority of Fundamentalists would be in perfect agreement with this necessary and orthodox view of how the Spirit enlightens man's spirit, they would most all, in this day in time, be aghast and repulsed by the proposal that this particular work which Job 32:8 calls inspiration be an extension and an integral part of the inspiration of the Holy Scriptures themselves. The two aspects are disassociated in their minds, and have for too long been essentially divorced from one another by the academics who have approached the entire matter with their preconceptions and prejudices at the ready.

Dictionary Definitions and the Inspiration of the Bible. It is little appreciated these days that all dictionary definitions cited for particular words are not to be perceived as interchangeable in every context. Just because a dictionary offers several citations for what a word means, does not mean that the definitions are not context sensitive. This, by the way, is true of lexicon definitions of words, as well. In this case, for instance, Webster, in his 1828 English dictionary, acknowledges the definition of inspire that relates to respiration, that is inhaling. However in the context of the scriptures, here is his definition:

> **The infusion of ideas into the mind by the Holy Spirit; the conveying into the minds of men, ideas, notices or monitions** by extraordinary or supernatural influence; or the **communication of the divine will to the understanding by suggestions or impressions on the mind, which leave no room to doubt the reality of their supernatural origin.** All Scripture is given by inspiration of God. 2 Tim. 3.[162]

The *Random House College Dictionary* says that in theological contexts, inspiration means **"a divine influence directly and immediately exerted upon the mind or soul of man."**[163] *The American Heritage Dictionary* defines inspiration thus: "Divine guidance or influence exerted directly on the mind and soul of humankind."[164] One of the definitions

[162] *Webster's 1828 Dictionary.* Christian Technologies, Inc. version 2 (Build 20040406), 2004.
[163] *The Random House College Dictionary, Revised Edition* Random House, Inc., New York, NY 10022. 1975.
[164] *The American Heritage® Dictionary of the English Language,* Fourth Edition copyright ©2000 by Houghton Mifflin Company. Updated in 2009. Published by Houghton Mifflin Company.

found for inspiration in the *Compact Oxford English Dictionary* is **"a special immediate action or influence of the Spirit of God… upon the human mind or soul;** said esp. of that divine influence under which the books of Scripture are held to have been written."[165] While the *Compact OED* does acknowledge the idea of "breathing" in its theological definition of *inspiration*, note the remainder of its definition given: "a breathing or **infusion into the mind or soul**." Under the *Compact OED*'s theological definitions for *inspire*, note the verbs it uses to define the word:

> "**to infuse** some thought or feeling into (a person, etc.) as if by breathing. **To animate** or **actuate by some mental or spiritual influence**; **to impart, communicate or suggest by special divine or supernatural agency; to kindle, arouse or awaken in mind or heart**."[166]

While Bible scholars have done their best to limit the definition of the word *inspiration* strictly to *God breathing* the scriptures in their original form, the Bible itself negates this faulty conception by its use of the word inspiration in Job 26:4. Apparently, before the propaganda campaign by deceptive scholars took full effect, there were men who were more careful and observant of the usage of words. Webster's spiritual and scriptural definition of inspiration in his work of 1828 is the exact match which covers the concept of the word found in its two places in the AV scriptures. The other dictionaries cited show that Webster was not alone in his assessment of the biblical meaning of *inspiration.* In both of the cases of *inspiration* in the King James Bible, men's minds were infused

---

[165] *The Compact Oxford English Dictionary,* Second Edition. Oxford University Press, 1989 (reprint 1999) p.857.
[166] *Ibid.*

with lofty ideas and concepts from God. These ideas were conveyed to men's minds and were the communications of the divine will. The Father imparted and conveyed these ideas into the minds of those who wrote down those original scriptures, but that same inspiration infuses the minds of men who read those words with understanding through the scriptures. Once again this shows that inspiration is a very cogent and effectual reality today as men try to apprehend the things of God. Yes, all scripture **was** given by inspiration, but inspiration is in effect at this very moment! The scriptures are alive (Heb. 4:12), and when they are disseminated, preached, taught, published, spoken, written and translated, they are still inspired. *All scripture* ***is*** *given by inspiration of God.* ***Inspiration is not breathing. It is God infusing, imparting and conveying His heart and mind to men by both the inspired word and by the supernatural effects of the Holy Spirit upon men's perceptions and understanding.***

.

Semantics and the Inspiration of the Bible. Much of the controversy about Bible inspiration really revolves around scholars' disputation with King James Bible believers (and vice versa) over the concept of what exactly can be called "inspired scripture." Were only the original manuscripts truly inspired? This question only leads to another sequence of questions: What about direct copies from those originals? What about subsequent generations of copies? One then must try to frame in words what exact relationship vernacular translations of the Bible have to do with the concept of inspiration. There is no surer way to assure that the fur will hit the fan than to ask this simple question: ***can the AV 1611 King James Bible be called "inspired?"***

The reason for the fracas that follows this question has to do with the fact that Bible scholars have here run into a group of people who will yield no ground. The insidious effects of pseudo-scholarship have infected most every nook and cranny of Christianity. In Church History, Catholics never had a Bible to which they were in subjection. The Anglicans yielded themselves readily enough to unscriptural concepts regarding the holy words of the Bible (Even the highly regarded Dean Burgeon did not believe every word of the AV.) The line where the sacred inviolability of the scriptures is drawn has moved over and over again through the years for all branches of Protestantism. The old Anabaptists, who were not "Protestants" and who in time became Baptists, were not much behind the mainline Protestants when it came to yielding to the scholarly enemy the holy ground of scripture. By the time Fundamentalism was born as a movement, most of the leaders of that movement did not hold the individual words of the King James Bible resolutely sacred. They simply had sense enough to know that God's people needed one standard, so they took their stand on the King James being "good enough." The fact is that every nominal grouping of God's people through time has crumpled under haughty scholarship's onslaught, and has given up its birthright of a perfect Bible.

The one group that is the exception to this surrender is the true King James Bible believers. Nobody else even professes to have a perfect Bible. Scholarship's (read that *Satan's*) victory has been complete, but for the King James Bible believers. They alone have refused to be bluffed out of the bulwarks of their fortifications by the bullying and bellowing of academia and intellectualism. No Methodists, Presbyterians, Episcopalians, Evangelical Free, Covenant churches, non-denominational churches or mega-churches care one iota what bible is used in their congregations. The AV 1611 is the only Bible that makes them nervous. Most seminaries and Bible schools either do not care or only profess to care. There is no contest or conflict between the rest of the bibles and their scholarly yoke-masters, so the only crowd that brings scholars' blood to a boil is the category of so-called "Ruckmanites" and the "KJV-Only" crowd. In that arena, all one has to do is ask the question, ***"Is the AV 1611 King James Bible inspired?"*** *or even,* ***"Is it possible that any translation of the Bible is inspired?"*** and the fireworks begin! One can always tell those who have come under the bewitching influences of pseudo-scholarship, for it only takes a fraction of a second for them to grow indignant and irate when any form of these rudimentary questions is asked – regardless of what they profess in their statements of faith.

By an insidious wresting of word meanings and a remolding of what the Bible actually teaches regarding the matter of how God transmitted His word from His mind to ours, the devil has managed to recast the entire issue of final authority for the body of Jesus Christ. By definition, this is an exercise in **semantics**. In some circles it is called "reprogramming." In others it is dubbed "brainwashing." It is accomplished with incessant propaganda. It is accompanied by piles and streams of mind-numbing rhetoric. It replaces the authority of the word of God with scholarly "traditions" (Mark 7:13). It replaces verities and certain, eternal precepts and promises with the falsehood of the ***fables*** (2 Tim.4:4) of which Paul so ardently warned.

Inspiration - What is Scripture? The question, "Is the AV 1611 King James Bible inspired?" sends the scholars into virtual cardiac arrhythmia. But, hold on. Here is the more important question: ***"What is scripture?"*** That is the more fundamental question because,

> *All* ***scripture*** *is given by inspiration of God, and is profitable for doctrine, for reproof, for correction, for instruction in righteousness:*
> (2 Tim. 3:16)

If it is true that *All scripture is given by inspiration of God*, then those *scriptures* can be said to be "inspired." After all, *All scripture is given by inspiration.* If it is scripture, then it was *given by inspiration,* and must be thus labeled as ***inspired scripture***. This applies to (a)*ll scripture.* Whatever is truly scripture *is given by inspiration of God.* Given this, the verse preceding verse 16 plainly states that Timothy knew the *holy scriptures* from his childhood!

> *And that from a child thou hast known the* ***holy scriptures****, which are able to make thee wise unto salvation through faith which is in Christ Jesus.*
> (2 Tim 3:15)

The Holy Spirit, in calling what Timothy read *the holy scriptures*, said that what Timothy read was inspired. What Timothy read were not the originals of the Hebrew Old Testament, nor is it the least bit likely that Timothy had physically read the originals of any of the New Testament writers except what Paul was writing to him at the moment. Timothy was an inhabitant of Derbe and Lystra, and in checking the New Testament index, no epistle is found written to either of those places by name. Timothy did not live in a town where he would have access to those particular originals addressed to his local church. The scriptures that Timothy knew, excepting those that were directly addressed to him, would have been quotations from original epistles or gospels, or copies of epistles or gospels, or even (perish the thought!) translations of epistles or gospels! They were not only scriptures, they were holy scriptures. And *All* ***scripture is given by inspiration of God****, and is profitable for doctrine, for reproof, for correction, for instruction in righteousness.*

The real question is, "What is scripture?" The scriptures Timothy held, though not the originals, were called *holy scriptures* and thus had to have been *given by inspiration.* Whenever a man holds up a bible and calls what he holds "the scriptures," biblically speaking, he is ascribing inspiration to the bible in his hand. He might be wrong in even categorizing what he holds as "scripture," but if he calls it "scripture," he is wittingly or unwittingly attributing inspiration to that set of writings that he holds. Whenever scholars carelessly categorize one thing or another as scripture, whether they realize it or not, they are ascribing inspiration to that which they are referring. If they do not believe that anything on earth today is inspired, then they should not make the mistake of calling anything here "the scriptures."

Is anything on earth today inspired? The scholars say no, but it is expedient that the Bible-believer realize the semantics of the game being played. If something is given by inspiration, it is only fair to say that it is inspired. If the scriptures that you hold in your hand today are indeed the scriptures, and descended to you from the stream of those first scriptures *given by inspiration of God*, then the scriptures you hold are inspired. By their *God-breathed* doctrine, where only the originals were inspired and where "God's breathing" only occurred once in the past, these scholars have semantically and philosophically denied the existence of the *holy scriptures* to anyone today. In fact, by their intellectual bumbling, they have denied that anyone except a painfully small handful of men has ever held the New Testament scriptures for the last 19 centuries.

Inspiration - What is 100% Scripture? If it has been settled that *All scripture is given by inspiration of God*, and has further been established that *All scripture* that *is given by inspiration of God* is ***inspired***, then the next critical question is, ***"What is 100% scripture?"*** There is no way to avoid the fact that the standard of our faith, the Bible, unwaveringly requires the existence of scriptures with 100% of God's words in them. Nowhere have the scholars more blatantly and disgracefully denied the plain promises of the Lord Himself than in this particular matter. If the following simple and clear passages are true as they stand, then the scholars know that a sizable percentage of their work and labor has not only been in vain, but it has been tragically and profoundly wrong.

> *Every word of God is pure: he is a shield unto them that put their trust in him. Add thou not unto his words, lest he reprove thee, and thou be found a liar.* (Prov. 30:5-6)

> *The words of the LORD are pure words: as silver tried in a furnace of earth, purified seven times. Thou shalt keep them, O LORD, thou shalt preserve them from this generation for ever.* (Ps. 12:6-7)

> *My son, attend to my words; incline thine ear unto my sayings. Let them not depart from thine eyes; keep them in the midst of thine heart. For they are life unto those that find them, and health to all their flesh.* (Prov.4:20-22)

> *But he answered and said, It is written, Man shall not live by bread alone, but by every word that proceedeth out of the mouth of God.* (Matt. 4:4)

> *Ye shall not add unto the word which I command you, neither shall ye diminish ought from it, that ye may keep the commandments of the LORD your God which I command you.* (Deut. 4:2)

This means that the vocations of such men have been built on falsehoods, and their reputations and writings rest on vanity. It is simply too great a disaster for them to contemplate that they have been wrong while the common Bible-believing

Christian has been right, so they have buried even the possibility of God having perfectly delivered His mind and heart to the average man beneath an avalanche of vituperative rhetoric. All their efforts notwithstanding, still *all flesh is as grass, and all the glory of man as the flower of grass. The grass withereth, and the flower thereof falleth away: But the word of the Lord endureth for ever* (1 Pet. 1:24-25). *Thy words were found, and I did eat them; and thy word was unto me the joy and rejoicing of mine heart* (Jer. 15:16).

Pushed to the wall, the scholars as a whole do not believe that even the existing Hebrew Old Testament texts or the various Greek New Testament texts are inspired. They believe these texts to represent some varying and debatable percentage of reliability. They believe these texts to be all that remains of the "inspired originals," however, even the New Testament Textus Receptus scholars (a group which comes closest to the KJV Bible-believing position) acknowledge variances in the different species of Textus Receptus editions. These Textus Receptus scholars too, roundly and loudly object to any notion that the text which they champion is "inspired." They think it represents with a high degree of accuracy what they call the "inspired text," meaning the original "God-breathed" manuscripts. Even they do not, as a whole, proclaim that the Textus Receptus is 100% scripture. The Critical Text scholars, who all keep Westcott and Hort's fruit punch nigh at hand, certainly do not believe their text represents the scripture with 100% accuracy. Nobody that reads an NIV, NASV or New King James Version believes that he holds in his hand 100% scripture, and if any naïve soul thought so, all he would have to do is ask his favorite scholar who would be most happy to straighten him out.

Many of us who are King James Bible believers, hold that what we have in the King James Bible is 100% scripture. Some King James men hold that since it is the KJV that is the pure word of God, that salvation is not possible out of the new and vilely corrupt versions. I certainly do hold that the new versions are vilely corrupt, but it seems to follow more with reasoning from the scriptures that the new versions do contain a percentage of scripture, polluted and diluted as they are. The actual scripture that they do contain must be considered inspired, since *All scripture is given by inspiration of God.* The problem is that the amount of scripture they do contain has been much diminished, and it is impregnated with falsehoods that men have wittingly or unwittingly inserted. Further, much of the truth of these scriptures have been transformed and altered by man's scholarly pilfering. Therefore, the new versions must be considered dangerously corrupt, and no one knows the point where truth altered loses altogether its effectualness and viability. That being said, it is evident to most Bible-believers that many folks have been saved out of new versions and some Christians have even grown and profited, up to a point, from being instructed out of them. This is by no means an endorsement of new versions, but it is a marvelous thing that God's scriptures are so powerful, that even when polluted, they are still able to impart faith and power.

That being said, one can find 100% scripture in the King James Bible. *All scripture is given by inspiration of God.* Yes, it is inspired, for all scripture is inspired. Yes, it is 100% inspired for it is 100% scripture.

I was accused once of claiming from the pulpit that Christians saved and still reading the new versions are "second class Christians." As happens so often with such accusations, these actually were not my exact words, however, if *faith cometh by hearing and hearing by the word of God,* what kind of faith is imparted by grossly polluted scripture? I am not aware that God groups types of faith into "classes," but it is very plain that a "new version Christian" will have a faith weakened and undermined by the corrupt bibles that he reads and from which he is taught. He will certainly be limited in his growth, and his confidence in God's promises to him will be undermined because he will be continually told that he cannot know exactly what God said unless he knows Greek and Hebrew. He certainly may love the Lord and he may be a fine man and Christian, but how much better a man and a Christian could he be if he had 100% of the inspired scriptures, and full confidence in them?

What of the Accusation of Re-Inspiration or Double Inspiration? One of the criticisms for which AV 1611 Bible believers come under fire is the idea that they are said to believe in ***re-inspiration*** or ***double inspiration***. In the mind of the critic this means that the true King James man holds that the King James translators were "inspired" in the exact same way as the men who first penned the originals. They claim that we hold that the originals were first inspired, and then some 1500+ years later, the King James translators came along and after 15 centuries, God ***re-inspired*** the scriptures in the King James. Thus – ***double inspiration***. This representation of the King James Bible believers' position is a straw dummy erected by critics who do not really want to deal with the issues at hand. I personally do not know anyone who believes such nonsense and I have administered the words of the KJV since 1987.

It should first be stated that the critics who represent Bible-believers in such light are hopelessly mired in the idea that the originals were "God-breathed," and they believe that any functional activity of inspiration itself stopped then and there. It is further obvious that they have not considered any other facet of inspiration as described in the Bible.

It seems appropriate at this time to both emphasize and summarize that the Bible describes two somewhat separate aspects of what it calls inspiration, even if Fundamental Bible scholars do not recognize both. **First,** *All scripture is given by inspiration of God* (2 Tim. 3:16). Therefore the scriptures are inspired scriptures. Most conservative Bible scholars hold forth that the scriptures receive the action of the inspiration. I believe, since the giving of the scriptures was by inspiration, it is fair to say that the writers were inspired to whom the scriptures were given, and that the scriptures that were given were inspired, as well. It seems fair to say that God inspired men who wrote inspired scriptures. *(H)oly men of God spake as they were moved by the Holy Ghost* (2 Pet. 1:21). In this way, both men and scriptures were inspired. Importantly, the men of God were moved at one time by inspiration in 2 Timothy 3:16, but the scriptures' attribute of inspiration did not cease because they were once spoken. That is why the word of God is still *quick* (alive) and *powerful*, and that is also why the word of God is attributed the anthropomorphic trait and quality of being a *discerner of the thoughts and intents of the heart* (Heb. 4:12). So, the scriptures are inspired still.

Secondly, one cannot help but consider Job 32:8, *But there is a spirit in man: and the inspiration of the Almighty giveth them understanding*. In this case, it is men who receive the action of inspiration. If it is certain that the scriptures are inspired, as were the writers of the originals, it is equally certain, as far as the word of God is concerned, that men, by an action the scriptures call inspiration, are infused with understanding from the Lord's Spirit. Notice that Job 32:8 does not say that those men receive a new revelation from God, but it does say that they are given understanding.

In this way, there is a two-way street in the matter of inspiration. The scriptures were/are inspired by the Lord, but by the same token, men are inspired to understand. Man is given understanding by inspiration in the meaning of the scriptures God gave him. Should not one also consider that

God *giveth them understanding* as related to bringing the scriptures' truths to men in their own languages? Did God give understanding to Origen, Clement of Alexandria, Westcott and Hort? Did *the inspiration of the Almighty* give them understanding? No. Wycliffe, Erasmus, Luther, and Tyndale are all lauded for their excellent and courageous contributions to the cause of the Bible in contrast to the pollutions of the former list of men. Did God give them understanding? If so, by what means did He give them understanding? If God gave them understanding, Job 32:8 says it was *by inspiration of God*! Textus Receptus scholars, and even some Critical Text scholars, laud the profound contributions of these men and others who were so indispensably influential in the cause of the Bible. Scholarship needs to sincerely take reckoning of what it has held or rejected as truth, for it is not stretching the scriptures, but the earnest and studied application of them, that attributes the fruitfulness of these man's work to *the inspiration of the Almighty giv(ing) them understanding.*

While heaping praise and exulting in the accomplishments and the scriptural categorization of the work of such men as Wycliffe and Tyndale, perhaps one should tell why this same wreath of honor may not be laid at the remembrance of fifty-odd of the very greatest scholars who ever sat down to one work together. Did the Almighty give any of these men understanding at the critical junctures between 1605 and 1611? If the Almighty did just that, one would have little choice but to ascribe the giving of such understanding to what the Bible calls *the inspiration of the Almighty.*

Was the King James Bible an act of "re-inspiration" as some are accused of believing? **No.** The scriptures are given by inspiration, period. The scriptures are thus inspired. The scripture in the King James Bible is inspired, according to the scriptures themselves. Then, in spite of Satan's best efforts through Origen, Jerome and Roman Catholicism to utterly vilify the scriptures, God reared up men – men with faces set as a flint. In conjunction with their scholarly excellence, God took Erasmus, Wycliffe, Luther, Tyndale, Coverdale and company, and He imparted the understanding of the issues to their spirits by His own Spirit. This is called *inspiration* in Job. There is no reason whatsoever that one should not view the magnificent and unmatched work of the King James translators as the very same work of God. ***The scriptures were never re-inspired. The scriptures did not need re-inspiring.*** The KJV committee was not re-inspired. *(T)here is a spirit in man: and the inspiration of the Almighty giveth them understanding.*

In the end, the difference between Origen, Westcott, Hort and their crack-brained cronies when compared to Wycliffe, Tyndale, Reynolds, Bedwell, Smith and their noble fellow-laborers had to do with the burning desire for the truth and love for the words of the Lord. The former group was composed of profound infidels, blinded by Satan and adversarial to the ultimate authority of the words of God. The latter group was made up of men who had a profound, heartfelt burden for the truth and an incessant love and devotion for God's word. To which group might God inspire understanding?

Closing Thoughts on Inspiration. It is hoped that the reader has been convinced that what men often come to believe about the Bible and its doctrines is often more the product of tradition, presumption and exclusive preconception than it is the end of a personal quest for biblical truth. If it is important to know the length of a thing, it is best to measure for oneself rather than trusting the reported measurement of another. President Ronald Reagan once said, "Trust, but verify." This is altogether good advice for the Bible-believer and nowhere is it more indispensable than with respect to what the Bible actually says about the nature of the scriptures themselves. Men have dehydrated, shrink-wrapped, and prepackaged definitions and bylines concerning the nature of the inspiration of the Bible. As demonstrated, these neatly wrapped little predigested packets do not stand up well under real scrutiny.

As Dr. Sam Gipp is careful to point out, "It isn't that easy!"[167] He points out that Jesus, in John 4:37, cites a saying written nowhere in scripture previous to His quotation. Was it inspired when it was said prior to Christ, or did it only receive its inspiration when Christ cited it? Similarly, both Paul (Acts 17:28 and Titus 1:12) and David (1 Samuel 24:13) quote unsaved poets and otherwise unrecorded proverbs as scripture. When exactly did inspiration occur for those words? Among other examples, Dr. Gipp also points out that Caiaphas spoke inspired and prophetic words in John 11:48-51, but Caiaphas actually meant it in another way than that in which it was fulfilled! Paul gave his opinion in 1 Corinthians 7:12, but that opinion wound up, in fact, being inspired scripture.[168] It is tough trying to stuff God into a pre-formed theological mold, and just because a theological seminary says something is so, does not mean that it is truly so.

Dr. Gipp really ties the rag on the bush for the prefabricated inspiration position in the example of Jeremiah. In Jeremiah 36:1-2, an original scripture is given to Jeremiah, but in 36:23, the inspired original is burned! ***End original #1.*** Yet in Jeremiah 36:28 & 32, that scripture is rewritten with additional words! This particular writing is contained in the King James Bible in Jeremiah chapters 45-51, which fact is evidenced by comparing Jeremiah 36:1 with Jeremiah 45:1. Yet, if one reads Jeremiah 51:59-63 in the King James Bible today, one will find that the original roll of this writing (original #2) was cast into the Euphrates. ***End original #2.*** It is profound to note, though, that every bible contains those pages

---

[167] Gipp, Sam. *Is Our English Bible Inspired?* (Daystar Publishing, Miamitown, Ohio 45041, 2004), pg.8.

[168] Ibid, pg.8-10.

of scripture in Jeremiah 45-51. From whence did those chapters come? They did not come from original #1 or original #2, for the first of those was burned and the second was thrown in the river! What we have today in Jeremiah 45-51 then, must have come from a copy of one of those writings! Dare we call that copy ***original #3***?[169] Whatever one calls it, it shows that the scholars, for all their grammatical and linguistic gnat-straining, are not very careful with their Bibles, and they are far more interested in getting Christians to conform themselves to the preconceived scholastic position than in actually apprehending the true biblical position.

The truth seems to be well represented in a simple statement Dennis Corle ascribes to Pastor Rick Sowell of Toledo, Ohio. The preacher said, "Inspiration is more of a process than a singular act."[170]

Preservation

Preservation and the Clear Statement of Scripture. In order for God's mind to be made known to man, it is obvious that certain steps were (and are) required besides just the initial inspiration of the words of God. As discussed earlier, the Bible is still inspired today and that inspiration is a continuing and active component in both the propagation of the scriptures and the apprehension of their meaning by men wherever the bread of life is broken. However, it is plain that the scriptures had (and have) to be more than just inspired. The Bible gives guidance in this for it resolutely establishes that the words of the Lord are also **preserved**. As Dr. Gipp accurately declares,

---

[169] Ibid, pg.28-31.

[170] Corle, Dennis. *God's Inspired Book – The Bible.* (Revival Fires! Publishing, Claysburg, Pennsylvania, 2009) p.12

"Inspiration without preservation is a 'Divine waste of time.'"[171] Dr. Dennis Corle sums it up nicely, as well: "What good is inspiration without preservation? Who cares if there ever was an inspired Bible if we don't have it today? The whole point of inspiration is defeated without God supernaturally preserving the Book."[172]

> *The words of the LORD are pure words: as silver tried in a furnace of earth, purified seven times. Thou shalt keep them, O LORD, thou shalt* ***preserve them*** *from this generation for ever.* (Ps. 12:6-7)

Though preservation of God's word is accredited in theory among scholars, with the exception of the rankest of liberals, it has proven to be a controversial topic among even the most conservative Fundamentalists. There are those that have exercised the wretched ploy of trying to deny that it was the *words of the Lord,* of Psalm 12, verse 6, which God promised to preserve. Naturally, these who say such attempt to intimidate others by their use of the "original Hebrew," but said critics have been answered from the Hebrew on many occasions, and as the King James English indicates, it is indeed the *words of the Lord* to which the promise of preservation belongs. Further, it must be carefully emphasized that the passage promises that it will be the Lord Himself who is the active Agent in the preservation of the words. It should at least give the hasty pause to realize that preservation is the Lord's direct handiwork and labor. One might prove prudent by not plunging headlong into criticism of the scriptures he has just because some academic pied piper plays a pretty tune. Just as inspiration is a supernatural act of God, so it is that preservation

---

[171]Gipp, Sam. *Is Our English Bible Inspired?* (Daystar Publishing, Miamitown, Ohio 45041, 2004), pg.16.
[172]Corle, Dennis. *God's Inspired Book – The Bible.* (Revival Fires! Publishing, Claysburg, Pennsylvania, 2009) p.9.

too is a manifold function of the supernatural activity of the same Lord.

The Extent of Preservation. The controversy over preservation, within the context here, mostly revolves around how extensive the preservation is. The mainline "Christian" Evangelical scholarship of this day may profess the word of God has been preserved, but they speak of the word of God as an entity only. In their minds the word of God is not so much made up of individual words, but is represented only in its overall message. To them, the Alexandrian Greek Text of Origen, Westcott, Hort and Tischendorf is the preserved word of God in Greek. It preserves the basic message and the general gist of "God's Word," but in their view, never since the original words of the Greek were written have individual words that make up scripture been viable as far as peoples' New Testaments are concerned. This makes God's promised action of preserving His words slipshod at very best. Dost thou have a slipshod God?

As one can imagine, there is a continuum of positions that vary in degree one from another regarding the extent of the preservation of God's words. Addressing those who abide a little closer to our position, the conservative Fundamental, Textus Receptus scholar says that God's word and words are preserved in the Greek of the Textus Receptus - the Greek behind the Latin Waldensian Bibles, Luther's German, the Syrian Peshitto and, of course, the English of the AV 1611. Importantly, these, who often are advocates and defenders of the King James Bible, also can be profoundly dogmatic in their position that the supernatural aspects of preservation can only extend to the original languages, and never, ever, ever to such a vernacular translation as the KJV. While they may allow that the Old Latin or even the Latin Vulgate may have played some role in the "restoration" of the text (like God lost it!), it is virtually blasphemy to them to say that the King James Bible or any other general vernacular translation be the very preserved words of God.

In the end, what liberal Greek and Hebrew scholars and conservative, Fundamentalist Greek and Hebrew scholars have in common is not necessarily the texts they endorse, but the fact that they uniformly agree that the true power of God in preservation resides only in the Greek and Hebrew. To them, the virtue of the King James Bible, or for that matter the NIV or RSV, lies in how accurately men translated those versions from the Greek and Hebrew texts. In other words, God is credited for supernaturally preserving the Greek, but it was there that His work in the preservation of the Bible stopped. For these scholars, God had nothing to do with the translation of the preserved text into the English language. To them, that part of the equation was utterly humanistic and mortal in its working. Just as God ceased His work of inspiration in the originals, and inspiration as a force is effectually dead, so His action in the preservation of His words ended with the original language texts.

Was this God's grand plan for communicating His heart and mind to mortal men? He inspired His word in the originals, and then labored against all the devices of Satan to preserve those words, yet His work of preservation ceased with Greek and Hebrew? He admonishes us that, *Man shall not live by bread alone, but by every word that proceedeth out of the mouth of God* (Matt. 4:4), and He thrills our heart with the battle cry of Job, *Neither have I gone back from the commandment of his lips; I have esteemed the words of his mouth more than my necessary food* (Job 23:12). In addition our God commands, *My son, attend to my words; incline thine ear unto my sayings. Let them not depart from thine eyes; keep them in the midst of thine heart* (Prov. 4:20-21). Having said to us these things, are we to then accept, at the word of heady scholarship that God Himself failed to get His words out of the launch stage of the original languages?

Dear brethren, it is not God that has failed. As it has always gone, so it goes in this matter. It is man that has failed miserably, as he always has. It is sad that so many good and sound men are compromised by the predictable failures of deceived and deluded men. Citing Dr. James Sightler, Riplinger records,

> It has been stated by Sandeen that the Princeton Theologians Archibald Alexander Hodge and Benjamin Breckinridge Warfield, in 1881, were the first to **claim inspiration for the original autographs only** and **to exchange the doctrine of providential preservation for the restoration of the texts by critics.** This shift was accompanied by a change from reliance on internal verification of the scripture by the witness of the Spirit and the structural integrity of the entire Bible to reliance on external evidences.[173]

In 1876, Warfield made the mistake of studying for a year in Leipzig, Germany, in the company of, and under the influence of, higher critics who denied that God gave the Bible to man. As a result of these pressures, Warfield tried to merge his previous beliefs with the rank apostasy of those scholars he found in Germany. As usual, apostasy successfully dragged Warfield down with it. According to Riplinger:

---

[173] Riplinger, G.A., *Hazardous Materials: Greek & Hebrew Study Dangers* (A.V. Publications, Corp., Ararat, VA 24053, 2008) p.1154.

> He invented a plan whereby he could retain the creed that stated the Bible was inspired. He redefined the word "Bible" for seminary students. **He moved the locus of inspiration from the Holy Bible to the lost originals.**[174]

Riplinger continues,

> "Warfield's invention has darkened the sense and spread a faltering faith to even good Christians such as John Burgon, Edward Hills, and their modern day proponents, some of whom have cowered and acquiesced to alleged spots of conceivable future updates or improvements to the KJB. These men have become rationalists, naturalists and modernists in practice **by exalting man's role in the transmission of the Bible and denying the miraculous intervention of God.**"[175]

Preservation and "Double-talk." Regardless of what Fundamentalist heralds say about "historic positions," it is Corle that hits the reeling Textus Receptus scholars where they live:

> Recently a new theological discussion has surfaced. It is based on the false idea that the King James Bible is preserved but it is not inspired. My question is very simple. ***If we begin with something inspired, and we preserve it, how do we lose inspiration in the process of***

---

[174] Ibid. p.1152.
[175] Ibid. p.1156

preservation? This is theological double-talk.[176]

Dr. Corle continues, "...if you take the breath or the inspiration out of the Scriptures, it is a dead book. If our Bible is not inspired, then it is equivalent to an embalmed Bible. The form is still there, but the life is gone."[177]

"Theological double-talk" is the term used by Corle, and it is in this very way that the scholarly powers-that-be have obscured God's handiwork, not only of inspiration, but of preservation, as well. Semantics, rhetoric, fables and tradition all provide a diseased swamp of festering falsehood. In this way, many who even defend the King James Bible have been, in a measure, compromised in their principles. Just as the divine effectualness of inspiration cannot be restricted to one singular fleeting occurrence in the past, neither can the equally divine process of preservation be confined to manuscripts written only in the original tongues.

Seeing that inspiration is still as effectually active and viable today as in ages past, and as God's work of preservation is unceasingly in effect *from this generation for ever* (Ps. 12:7), it simply follows that there must be another component involved in the preservation of the words of God. Mere preservation of the words of God in the language of the time does not deliver in fact the thoughts and heart of God to the multitudes of the nations God is trying to reach.

.[176] Corle, Dennis. *God's Inspired Book – The Bible.* (Revival Fires! Publishing, Claysburg, Pennsylvania, 2009) p.11.

[177] Ibid. p.13.

Translation

Translation: An Indispensable Gateway to the Mind of God. It is extraordinarily distasteful to the scholastic intelligentsia to even hear the possibility that translation must play an intimate role in God's plan to transmit His words out into the world. Let the student be warned that the brainwashing of "Christian" academia extends to the point that it is, to many, virtual blasphemy and literal heresy to imply that God actually played an active and involved role in the translation of the scriptures into languages other than the original tongues of Greek and Hebrew. It has become the inflexible "industry standard" among Bible scholars that the Lord simply did not involve Himself intricately in the Bible transmission process beyond "breathing" the originals and preserving His words in the Greek and Hebrew manuscripts. Such sentiment extends well into the King James Bible defenders' camp, and for one to verbalize a position to the contrary will result in that individual being called ugly names and dis-fellowshipped. One cannot help but be reminded of the verse in Ps 78:41, *Yea, they turned back and tempted God,* ***and limited the Holy One of Israel.***

Again, the thesis in this chapter is that men tend to depart from the Bible whether or not they know or admit it. This departure occurs even in the middle of "defending the Bible." What replaces the Bible for such folks are "historic positions," "scholarly traditions" and statements of faith that are rife with theological double-talk, rhetoric, semantics, and the *fables* and *traditions* to which Christ and the epistle writers referred with such vigilance and fervor. "Positions" and "traditions" do not deliver the words of the Lord into the hands of man in a manner by which he is able to ingest and be nourished by them. Translation is a variable that the Lord would have had to make central in His blueprint and pattern for the Bible. Translation is the practical gateway that God fully knew men would have to pass through to understand His words.

Why would inspiration and preservation halt ***outside*** the gate? Is the ***"No Translation Can Be Inspired"*** doctrine scriptural, or in any way exemplified in the scriptures? In erecting and protecting their "orthodox positions," it is enlightening to see how much scripture the linguistic and theological experts ignore and remold.

Translation in the Bible, Minus the Fables. Just take Romans 16:26 for example. In the context of the *revelation of the mystery, which was kept secret since the world began* (25), Paul goes on to say that the mystery is,

> *...now... made manifest, and by the* ***scriptures of the prophets...made known to all nations*** *for the obedience of faith:*

As stated in the verse, *by the* ***scriptures of the prophets*** it is ***made known to all nations***. When the scriptures of the prophets are made known to all nations, are we to believe that the mystery is not made known to the nations in their own languages? Did the Lord really intend for us to conclude that the scriptures of the prophets madc known to all nations were only in Hebrew and Greek? If God did carry out a plan to deliver His ***scriptures*** to ***all nations***, how could preservation be limited only to the original languages? Is this the biblical model?

In Acts 2:8-11, the promise of the coming of the Holy Spirit was fulfilled, and at that initial fulfillment the apostles preached to the people, and the following scene ensued.

> 7 *And they were all amazed and marvelled, saying one to another, Behold, are not all these which speak Galilaeans?*

> 8 *And how* ***hear we every man in our own tongue, wherein we were born****?*
> 9 *Parthians, and Medes, and Elamites, and the dwellers in Mesopotamia, and in Judaea, and Cappadocia, in Pontus, and Asia,*
> 10 *Phrygia, and Pamphylia, in Egypt, and in the parts of Libya about Cyrene, and stangers of Rome, Jews and proselytes,*
> 11 *Cretes and Arabians,* ***we do hear them speak in our tongues*** *the wonderful works of God.*
> (Acts 2:7-11)

Over a dozen separate groups of people heard the Spirit-filled disciples preaching, and the scriptures specify that they all heard in their own tongues. It is interesting to consider whether the disciples actually preached in all the separate languages or whether each group only heard in their own language. ***(Wouldn't THAT be something?)*** Nevertheless, that they heard the words in their own ***tongues*** is certain. Either the disciples spake in languages they had not previously understood, or the men of the nations heard them in their separate languages although the disciples were not actually speaking those languages. In either case, translation is inherent and integral to the process - either from the tongues of the disciples or into the ears of the hearers. Whichever the case may have been, God's Spirit moderated and initiated the translations. Furthermore, is it so impossible to consider that some, or all, of the men of those nations would have taken the time to write down the things they had heard? If any one of them did so, let the reader realize that the words he wrote down would be the original, and that writing would not have been written down in Hebrew or Greek.

Is it not strange how adamant and vociferous has become the orthodox and scholarly position that God in no way, and certainly not *supernaturally* or in an *intimate way*, had any part in actually translating the Bible? Is it not *strange* that men would conclude that God would disengage and remove Himself utterly from the critical exercise of translating His words into the languages of the heathen? *God so loved the world* (John 3:16) that in His glorious and divine plan, He gave the heathen (like us) inspired originals and preserved Greek manuscripts, but stepped back and let men loot, pilfer and pervert the words of the Bible beyond that? What could lead men to think that the Lord would leave translation of the Bible as a purely human and mortal literary exercise after supernaturally inspiring and preserving it?

In Genesis 11:7-9, the Lord confounded the language of men at the Tower of Babel. In an instant in time, He established some uncertain number of languages from whence all our multitude of modern languages came. In that instant, and all at once, He both imparted and restricted human comprehension of various languages. Thousands of years later, in Acts 2, the Lord saw fit that instantly a conglomerate of men of different nations should receive the words of God in their own diverse languages, with complete understanding. These biblical facts notwithstanding, Bible scholars and their accompanying institutions act as if the transmission of God's own words from one language to another over the last 1900 years represents some terribly complex and impassable obstacle for the Lord. They are repelled and appalled at the idea that God could and did overcome this obstacle. The truth is that He both created and bridged all the intricacies and complexities of the language gap between the nations in singular and simple moments in time in Genesis11 and Acts 2. Why would Bible translation prove *too hard for the LORD* (Gen.18:14)?

Granted, try as he might, man has been unsuccessful in tracking and documenting each minute stage of Bible transmission through Church History. Through the immolating fires, persecutions and destruction to men, documents and facts, it has proven impossible to track and find absolutely certain evidence for ***every*** solitary movement of God in the last 2000 years. Rome exacted her satanically inspired devices upon both her subjects and her enemies. Catholicism, with her incessant, truth-burning infernos ruled Europe and the Biblical lands for 1000 years, casting men into a darkness from which many nations have never recovered. Islam arose, and with bloody scimitar, cast the birthplace of Christianity and the Bible into light-obscuring disarray from the 700's AD to this very day. The Barbarian Invasions and a multitude of bloody religious and political wars must not be forgotten, along with the smaller-scale and lesser-known variables which on the grand scale were conspiracies against God's truth and the gospel. For these reasons it is not easy – likely impossible – to document in complete exactitude how God, at a word by word level, overcame all the fires, all the blood and each pointedly direct assault upon His words by the world and the devil. There are spaces of time and sequences of events where the trail of God's precise movements in history and Bible transmission is untraceable. There cannot always be a "smoking gun" produced for just how He did what He did and how He accomplished His designs, ***but that is why we have His promises!*** That is why *we walk by faith and not by sight* (2 Cor.5:7). See, ***we have a God we can trust, not a God whom we must hold accountable for each move that He makes.*** In this way, just as the Lord, in an instant, gave understanding of languages at Babel and in Acts 2, so He supernaturally and providentially oversaw, transmitted and delivered His word to man through the ravages of history whether men can track it all or not. Why? Because He is God, and because He is trustworthy.

Scholars generally say that God was uninvolved and disconnected from the process by which the Bible was quite necessarily translated for the nations. Those who say this are often the first to declare that the Bible is to be our "final authority in all matters of faith and practice." Is the scholars' and educators' firmly held doctrine of God's limitation (Ps.78:41) truly biblical?

• In Genesis 11:9, God confounds the languages of the nations in a moment of time. Therefore, He is equally able to unravel them.

• In Genesis 42:23, Joseph speaks to his brethren in the Egyptian language by way of an interpreter, yet, the scholars tell us that the originals were recorded in Hebrew. If the originals were recorded in Hebrew, then a translation had already occurred from the Egyptian language before the originals (or as the originals) were written. *GOD* was the active force behind that translation, and all honest scholars would have to say that He endorsed it!

• This type of instance is repeated throughout Moses' recorded dialogues with Pharaoh in Exodus. Not a word of their conversations in Egyptian was recorded in the original manuscripts that we know of. The Egyptian language they spake was recorded in the Hebrew tongue, *already translated from Egyptian.*

• In Ezra 4:7-16, the Jews are thwarted for a time in rebuilding the temple by a letter written to King Artaxerxes by various of the Lord's enemies in the land. This letter was written in the Syrian tongue (Ezra 4:7), but recorded in Hebrew in Ezra 4:11-16. The words were written in the God-inspired originals already translated from Syrian. Does God involve Himself in the translation process?

• Isaiah 28:11 specifies that *with stammering lips and another tongue will he speak to this people.* With what other tongue will God speak to Israel? Some say, "In Greek," and He did speak to them in Greek later in their history, but is that all? Not only did God use the Egyptian, Syrian, and Babylonian languages, as Israel fell under their respective influences, but in the Jewish dispersion after 70AD, the Jews were scattered to every land! In most all those lands there was the testimony of the gospel of Christ and the word of God. According to the Bible, ***God spake*** to those Jews in Polish, German, Latin, French and all the various other languages of the lands where the Jews have been. Is not God somewhere in those translations?

• Why in Mark 16:17 were the apostles given the gift of *new tongues*? They were given this gift that they might communicate to the nations and diverse peoples. While the gift of tongues, in the apostolic sense, passed with the apostolic age, there is plainly the manifold need recorded through the last 1900 years for the Bible to have been written in the tongues of the nations. Translation was an integral, God-inspired process during the window of time that God used this particular gift.

• In Acts 1:19, God *interpreted* - that is ***translated*** - an Aramaic word into Greek. Is God involved in translation? God interpreted from one language to another in Matthew 1:23, Mark 5:41, Mark 15:22, Mark 15:34, John 1:38, 41 & 42 and John 9:7. This is by no means an exhaustive list of ***Bible examples where God did translate languages!*** So, is God ever involved in translating languages? By what authority does one say that God interpreted languages in the Bible, but now wholly disengages Himself from involvement in translating since the originals were given?

• In Acts 21:40 and 22:2, Paul spoke to the men of Jerusalem in Hebrew, yet the account was recorded in the inspired originals in Greek. Obviously translation occurred from the Hebrew language Paul spake into the Greek language in which his words were recorded on paper. Every Bible scholar in just about every Bible camp would declare that the Greek original of Acts 21:40 and 22:2 was inspired and perfect. Most of the same scholars would also say that God does not "inspire" translations. In this case, by the time the original was written down, a translation had occurred! God did that!

• In Acts 26:14, Jesus Christ spoke to Paul in the Hebrew tongue, but the God-inspired originals record the event in Greek. According to the Bible, one must conclude that God is involved in translation, and if one should still claim that God is not involved in that process, then it must be asked, "On what scriptural grounds does one make that judgment?"

• In Luke 23:37, the superscription upon Christ's cross was written in three languages, and Bible readers are given the translation of those languages written in the "original Greek." Who is responsible for that translation?

These examples are not an exhaustive catalogue of such occurrences. The goal is not to comb the Bible and catalogue and comment upon them all. The goal is to call to account those who claim to build their beliefs and precepts upon the Bible. They recite the creed loudly and blow the trumpet well, but in the end, they are mere manipulators of information who brainwash and deceive God's admittedly lazy and naïve people. If one intends to box in God, then he had best know what he is talking about! So many scholars say that God does not take part or inspire translations, yet anyone who is saved and reads his Bible can see, at least, that such a scholar does not take any care at all to align himself with the Book of which he speaks.

The Great Precept of "Translation" in the Scriptures. Men today are nearly 2000 years removed from the close of the canon and the past narratives of the scriptures. Those 2000 years have magnified man's propensity and inclination to carelessness and corruption. Being two millennia removed from the first giving of the scriptures has opened wide the door for misconstruing and misusing words. What man is particularly bad about (the scholars have not helped) is exchanging the sanctified and exclusive meanings of Bible words with degraded and misrepresented meanings of the now demeaned language. The *gay clothing* of James 2:3 must be defined from the sanctified context of the scripture, or by our standards today the meaning is twisted. The *hope* of the scriptures is an *expectation* (Phil. 1:20), not the, "Oh, I hope so!" of the religious reprobate trying to get a soul-winner off his front steps. *Charity* in the New Testament does not have anything to do with the Red Cross or the United Way. *Naughty* things in the word of God are not indicative of deliciously sinister-but-acceptable sins committed by impish little boys and feisty old men. *Naughty* things in the word of God are utterly rotten to the core! Hundreds of other examples exist but have been pooh-poohed away, as men reconstruct the Bible after their own image.

More than anything else, the Bible itself defines what a word should mean, along with that word's parameters. Even Bible-believers have grown accustomed to letting the dictionary determine what a word from the Bible means. This often works well enough, especially with the right English dictionary, for the old-fashioned dictionaries tended to define so many of our words by scriptural mandates and contexts. It is for this reason that writers who truly know languages say that the King James Bible and its English predecessors did more to mold the English language than the reverse.

The word, "translation," in current 21st century circumstances, carries with it barnacles of meaning and innuendo that are more the product of brainwashing than genuine substance. By the same token, it has lost certain indispensable shades and inflections of meaning, as man has ever strayed from the Bible but has still used the word. ***Translation*** in the worldly mind is only a process of converting the meaning of things to another language. The world says,

- It is a function of intimate familiarity with languages.
- It is an exercise of a man's academic expertise and devoted scholarship.
- It is an inexact science. There is a flexibility and an artful element to translating.
- It is an imperfect science. There is always room for improvement or "tweaking."
- Bible translation (to entrenched modern scholarship) always results in an inferior product as compared to the God-inspired originals. After all, God inspired those and they were perfect, but man cannot translate "perfectly" what God inspired perfectly.
- God never, ever, ever (*ever*) inspired, perfectly guided or administered a translation of the Bible. He never *did*. He never *would*… ever.

The first four of these points are true enough when dealing with the world's literary, technical, or everyday languages. However, the last two points mark the trespass of the world's mindset into territory for which it is unfit and unequipped. The translation of God's Book does not track with the translation of Shakespeare, medical journals or common compositions of man. God wrote the Bible. It is His Book. ***Translation*** is a word and a concept from His Book. Here are the foundations and parameters *He* lays out for the word, ***translation***. Here are the standards *He* sets in His own Book:

1) The kingdom is translated to the right house. Saul was the first king in Israel, but he was a king God never intended, though at Israel's request, He allowed him. The day came that David, the progenitor of the Lord Jesus Christ, should take the kingdom. Abner's mission, according to his own testimony, was,

> *To* ***translate*** *the kingdom from the house of Saul, and to set up the throne of David over Israel and over Judah, from Dan even to Beersheba.*
> (2 Sam. 3:10)

The most important observation to make is that there can be no question that the kingdom was better for having been ***translated*** to the house of David. It was certainly more in concord with God's original plan than during the time that Saul reigned in the mere permissive will of God, devil possessed though he was. ***Israel was made better by the translation of the kingdom!***

2) A Christian is translated into the right kingdom.

> *Giving thanks unto the Father, which hath made us meet to be partakers of the inheritance of the saints in light: Who hath delivered us from the power of darkness, and hath* ***translated*** *us into the kingdom of his dear Son:*
> (Col. 1:12-13)

A man, before Christ, is dead in his sins (Eph. 2:1), a child of the devil (Jn. 8:44), without Christ, hope, or God (Eph. 2:12), and under the power of darkness. At the instant of the new birth, that man is regenerated (Tit. 3:5), redeemed (Col. 1:14), sealed (Eph. 4:30), circumcised (Col. 2:11), baptized by the Holy Spirit (1 Cor. 2:13) and quickened (Col. 2:13). He receives the atonement (Rom. 5:11) and he is made to sit in heavenly places in Christ (Eph. 2:6). Yet by no means last, is that man *delivered... from the power of darkness, and...* ***translated****... into the kingdom of* Jesus Christ (Col. 1:12-13)! This ***translation***:

- is a supernatural act of God.
- is inexplicable in terms of man's understanding.
- is unobservable in process.
- is a vast improvement upon a man's destiny and circumstances.
- is an act by God that makes a man perfect.

3) Enoch is translated to Heaven.

> *By faith Enoch* ***was translated*** *that he should not see death; and was not found, because God had* ***translated*** *him: for before his* ***translation*** *he had this testimony, that he pleased God.*
>
> (Heb. 11:5)

Elijah was caught up to heaven by whirlwind and a chariot of fire (2 Kings 2:11). Moses did have a mortal death (Deut. 34:7), but Michael and Satan had a disputation over the body (Jude 9). Since Moses is one of the two witnesses in Rev.11, it is plain that Michael "won" the dispute. Unlike Moses, who died once, and will yet die again by execution in the Tribulation, and unlike Elijah, who was caught up without dying, but will also die during the Tribulation, Enoch was ***translated*** without dying and never, ever shall die! He is the great type of the body of Christ in that regard.

The ***translation*** of Enoch was a small-scale occurrence of what will happen to the Lord's body, the Church (Col. 1:18). This pre-tribulation event is commonly referred to as *the rapture*, but it might more correctly be called ***the translation.*** Again, the observations worth noting are that the ***translation***,

- is a supernatural act of God.
- is inexplicable in terms of man's understanding.
- is defiant of natural laws and processes.
- is a vast improvement upon man's circumstances.
- is an act by God that results in perfection.

It is with a magnificent display of avoidance that all the new bibles disdain to categorize anything as a ***translation***. New versions do not contain the word ***translate*** in any form. Men and kingdoms are "transferred," "conveyed," "taken up" or "taken away," but nothing in a new bible is ***translated***. Thus, applying practically the King James Bible's own definition of the word, the new versions being bereft of the concept, one can conclude the following: The NASV, the NIV and all the rest of their perverse, inbred siblings:

- do not exist by supernatural power.
- are explicable and their corrupt processes are most observable.
- are a degradation of God's word rather than an improvement.
- are the handiwork of Satan and his many mortal little minions.
- are a byproduct of perversion instead of perfection.

In the end, the Christian is confronted with whether he will accept the Bible meaning of words and concepts, or whether he will allow the encroachment of men's preconceptions, prejudices and representations of meanings.

Eve presumed to inject her own sour insertion into the scriptures (Gen. 3:3), while Satan presumed to deny the plain statements of scripture (Gen. 3:4) and to further deceive by slandering God's motives (Gen. 3:5). To conclude that this very battle is not still raging in the realm of Bible scholarship is the height of naiveté.

For years now, conservative scholars have had to battle against liberal ideas regarding the inspiration and the preservation of the scriptures. Much of that battle has been to defend the precept that God's work in the preservation of the scriptures is as much a potent and supernatural accomplishment of the Lord as is the inspiration of those same scriptures. Both biblical evidence and precept point to the fact that the intervention of ***the hand of God is likewise as necessary in the translation of the scriptures as in inspiration and preservation***.

The Role of Translations in the Preservation of the Bible. Modern scholars' narrow and stilted opinions about Bible origination and transmission have taken several severe and decimating blows. These blows have been delivered by Bible-believing authors, scholars and preachers who have dared to apply the scriptures and superior research to the modern scholars' ill-thought positions.

Among these literary bombs, and others to his credit, Dr. Sam Gipp simply demonstrates that according to the scriptures, God, the Author of the Bible, in no way values the original writings of the scriptures as highly as does the obsessive and compulsive scholarship of our day. Gipp concludes, "Since we have the text of the Originals preserved in the King James Bible, we have no need of the Originals themselves."[178] His incisive, applied analysis from the scriptures forces upon scholars the point that God "had plans" for the inspiration of His scriptures continuing in and through the process of translation into the languages of the heathen.

Another severe drubbing is administered when Riplinger points out in her writings, "The Acts 2 'Scriptures in tongues,' as Wycliffe called them, were created directly by the Holy Ghost and were not man-made *translations* from 'the' Greek."[179] She goes on to point out that since the scriptures dictate that in Matthew 4:24, *his fame went throughout all Syria*, and that considering the missionary center of Christianity became Antioch, Syria (Acts 11), an "immediate Syriac translation" would have been "mandatory."[180]

When Riplinger cites H.C. Hoskier, an acknowledged textual scholar, as holding that not all the NT originals were written in Greek, and that vernacular language translations were concurrent and coexistent with the originals, it threatens to bring the walls down around the traditional scholars' ears. Hoskier's basic conclusion was that "the originals were created immediately in multiple languages,"[181] and that there were "Graeco (Greek)-Syriac bilingual MSS. of different parts of the N.T." which were current among the Christians at Antioch.[182] It is further plain from his statements that he believed the same to be true of the Latin. He held that the "oldest Latin translations" were "practically contemporary with the Greek originals." He said, "In other words, as regards the Gospels, Latin and Syriac were made at the same time, or Latin and

---

[178] Gipp, Sam. *Is Our English Bible Inspired?* (Daystar Publishing, Miamitown, Ohio 45041, 2004), pg.27-31.

[179] Riplinger, G.A., *Hazardous Materials: Greek & Hebrew Study Dangers* (A.V. Publications, Corp., Ararat, VA 24053, 2008) p.1095.

[180] Ibid. p.1096.

[181] Ibid. p.1097.

[182] Ibid. p.1099.

Greek from a Syriac original; or Latin from a Graeco-Syriac original."[183]

This is a terrible blast against the theoretical house of textual cards erected by these latter day "orthodox" Greek scholars. It means that Gipp is right, and that God never endued the physical original manuscripts with the same idol-like glory as have the academics of our day. Furthermore, it means that the Bible has always been a living and dynamic entity that has never allowed itself to be imprisoned in one or two languages for prideful and presumptuous peacocks to exploit for the purposes of their own exaltation.

Riplinger concludes:

> The Bible cannot clearly be made to give any other impression than that its books were made available immediately and concurrently in multiple languages. No primacy and exclusivity of the Greek language is afforded by Acts 2.[184]

Riplinger further states that Hoskier, in his book, *Concerning the Genesis of the Versions of the N.T.,* "gives hundreds of pages of examples demonstrating his conclusion that even Greek manuscripts, used to establish the current text, were taken from vernacular editions."[185] In other words, the Greek texts that we have today – even the right ones – have been established in part by translating other vernacular texts back to Greek! Since the 1500's, editors of printed Greek text editions have used Bible portions in other languages to create their own particular flavor of Greek text. [186] It would be

---

[183] Ibid. p.1101.
[184] Ibid. p.1101.
[185] Ibid. p.1101.
[186] Ibid. p.1102.

profitable to anyone who reads the materials of Bible scholars making statements about "the Greek text" or "So-and-so's Greek text," to realize that anybody's and everybody's Greek text (whatever it may be) is a compilation of a complex multitude of scripture fragments that have been drawn from the four corners of the earth, and puzzle-pieced together in whatever manner the compiler believed to be best. These Greek texts are often by necessity helped along using a Latin or Syriac (or other) reading to tell what the Greek reading ought to say!

One of the most prominent of such cases is Beza's highly respected Greek New Testament, which was consulted and used by the King James translators and made use of the Syriac Peshitta, as well as of a Latin translation of the Peshitta.[187]

For Bible-believers, the bottom line is that God has used translation and translations with great liberality through time, without any regard for whether the scholars approve or disapprove. The scholars hold that He did not do so, and they apparently believe that He could not do so, but the Bible, as well as much manuscript evidence, indicates that He could, and indeed that He did.

Earlier Christians' Attitude about Translation. It is also worthwhile to briefly note that many true heroes of the faith did not share the cynical and condescending views of translation as do the modern academic offspring.

John Wycliffe said, "The clergy cry aloud that it is heresy to speak of the ***Holy Scriptures in English***, and so they would ***condemn the Holy Ghost, who gave tongues*** to the

---

[187] Ibid. p.1103.

Apostles of Christ ***to speak the word of God in all languages under heaven***."[188]

Wycliffe considered the scriptures to be holy in English, first of all. Secondly, he said that the clergy of his day had an issue with the Holy Ghost who gave "tongues to speak the word of God in all languages under heaven." That he considered the Holy Ghost the active agent in the translation of the scriptures into English is evidenced in the following:

> You say it is heresy to speak of the ***Holy Scriptures in English***. You call me a heretic because I have translated the Bible into the common tongue of the people. Do you know ***whom you blaspheme***? Did not the Holy Ghost give the word of God at first in the mother-tongue of the nations to whom it was addressed? Why do you ***speak against the Holy Ghost***?
>
> I am astonished, therefore, that some of our own people would slander those who say that they ***possess the Holy Spirit speaking to them in this way***.[189]

It is apparent that Wycliffe did not hold the same views as modern scholars who limit the Lord to the mere realm of inspiration and/or preservation, but not translation.

Desiderius Erasmus said, "Heresy does not arise among the laity who have the ***scriptures in the vernacular***, but among the doctors."[190] His commendation of "the vernacular" would

---

[188] Riplinger, G.A., *In Awe of Thy Word, Understanding the King James Bible,* (A.V. Publications, Ararat, VA 24053, 2003) p. 757.

[189] Ibid. p. 758-759.

[190] Ibid. p.996.

not have met the approval of scholars in our day any more than it met the approval of the Catholic priests with whom he did battle in his day. ***Is it not profound that Catholicism forbade the vernacular scriptures to its poor, blinded subjects in the Dark Ages, while today it is the enlightened scholars (some of them "King James Only") who deny that the vernacular translations could be pure and perfect?***

Erasmus further stated that, "***The Spirit teaches***, not Aristotle; grace, not reasoning; ***inspiration***, not the syllogism."[191] Furthermore, he expresses this:

> "I would have the weakest woman read the Gospels and the Epistles of St. Paul…I would have ***those words translated into all languages***… These ***sacred words*** give you ***the very image of Christ speaking, healing, dying, rising again***, and ***make him so present, that were he before your very eyes you would not more truly see him***."[192]

Interestingly, ***The Columbia Encyclopedia*** states that the English scriptures were first given to Caedmon (c.600), and this "by ***divine inspiration***…Linguistic evidence proves that they are not of Caedmon's region."[193] It is virtually certain that the compilers of the *Columbia Encyclopedia* did not personally hold this view, but it is fascinating that they used the particular phraseology that they did. Also fascinating is the fact that ***Bede*** (c. 600's) wrote of Caedmon saying that, "the sublime gift was bestowed upon him ***by inspiration…***"[194] This sounds like an application of Job 32:8. These accounts only illustrate the fact that men today have rather successfully button-holed and

---

[191] Ibid. p.997.

[192] Ibid. p.998

[193] Ibid. p.997

[194] Ibid. p.997

limited the meanings of certain words and principles in ways that were not shared, either by the scriptures, or by writers and Christians from earlier times.

According to ***Miles Coverdale***,

> …pondering also mine own insufficiency therein, and how weak I am to perform the office of ***a translator***…Yea we ought rather to give God thanks therefore, ***which through his spirit stirreth up men's minds***, ***so to exercise themselves therein***…[W]e have great occasion to give thanks unto God, that he hath opened unto his church the ***gift of interpretation*** and of printing…"[195]

Coverdale's "gift of interpretation" would of necessity be understood to mean that of translating the Bible into English! Coverdale believed that God "stirreth up men's minds" just like Job.32:8 says. That is, unlike the modern robbers of God's glory, Coverdale believed that God was involved in the work of interpretation and translation. Coverdale would have been called bitter and ugly names if he lived in our day, for he said, ***"No, the Holy Ghost is as much the author of it in Hebrew, Greek, French, Dutch, and English, as in Latin."***[196]

Cutting to the Quick: From God's Mind to Ours.

The King James Bible believer should understand this: The pilferers and scholastic scavengers will never ever cease in

---

[195] Ibid. p.845

[196] Connolly, W. Kenneth, *The Indestructable Book,* (Baker Books, Grand Rapids, MI., 1996) p.148.

their work of digging, undermining and condemning what God hath wrought with respect to the Bible. They will never cease to speak evil of that which is good. It is plain that cynicism, skepticism and criticism have become ingrained and integral attributes of most Bible scholars' makeup and training. Even men who oppose the blatant evils of what is known as "Higher Criticism," are themselves critical and vitriolic against the concept that the word of God's perfection extends past the original manuscripts, or beyond a certain brand of Greek or Hebrew original language text. The dedication of some of these very men, who, within limits, have done yeoman's labor in bringing to light great truths with respect to the Bible is greatly appreciated. Nevertheless, it must be forcefully pointed out that Satan never could and never has "left well enough alone" in anything. His minions never shall either. Sometimes Satan uses good, sound men who get slightly off-track in some way. Sometimes good, sound men are trained wrong, or simply accept the wrong conclusions of other men.

From God's creation to both advents of His Anointed One; from His salvation to His judgment; from His mighty handiwork to His merciful blessing; from Heaven itself to a fiery Hell – all these have been attacked unrelentingly and unceasingly by His own creatures. The Bible does declare that *He is the Rock, **his work is perfect*** (Deut. 32:4) and *As for God, his **way is perfect**: the word of the LORD is tried: he is a buckler to all those that trust in him* (Ps. 18:30). It also makes evident that *The LORD will **perfect that which concerneth me*** (Ps. 138:8). Though those faithful tenets are manifestly obvious in the scriptures, His fallen creatures – even most of His saved ones – do not agree with the Holy One's assessments.

The gloriousness of God's pure word is too high a standard, too wondrous an accomplishment, too inexplicable a marvel to be left unmolested. Just as Israel, God's chosen and peculiar people, cannot escape the bitter hatred of the nations round about, so His perfect and peculiar words, all bound in one volume, cannot escape the notice, the animus, and the cruel attacks of those same nations. In accord with the prophesied *depart[ure] from the faith* (I Tim. 4:1), the words of God which impart that faith do not even escape the pillaging of those actually redeemed by the blood of the Lamb.

For those of us who are convinced that the promises of God exceed beyond what man can discover by his scientific methods and fully comprehend by his academic exploits, we have chosen to stand by the assurances and guarantees of the God of the Book. If His thoughts and ways, as He says, are truly so much higher than our thoughts and ways (Isa. 55:8-9), then we must to trust our God's power and integrity for those gaps in our knowledge for which we have no explanation. Make no mistake; the scholars union would rather have everyone trust their machinations than the promises of God Himself. That we do not trust man as they say we ought earns us the role of scholastic outcasts and heretics. Nevertheless, we have *know(n) them by their fruits* (Matt. 7:16), and taken the measure of the words that God has delivered to us. In the case of the unbelieving and semi-believing scholars, as with Belshazzar's lot, we have *weighed* them *in the balances*, and found them *wanting* (Dan. 5:27). As for the King James Bible, by all the abundance of the fruit gathered, and by the excellent balm it has been to our souls, we find evidence that in it the Lord has fulfilled the expectations of Paul, who said, *Now unto him that is able to do exceeding abundantly above all that we ask or think, according to the power that worketh in us...* (Eph. 3:20)

Since it is a given that the pure words of God will always be attacked, right along with every pure act and every perfect attribute of God, the Bible-believer must settle it in his heart that what he holds most dear will always be under barrage. He should cease to be fretted by each objection and he should learn to dismiss out of hand the unceasing propaganda that proceeds from foes, but also from some of those who purport to be friends. A sound goal might be stated in this way: *That we henceforth be no more children, tossed to and fro, and carried about with every wind of doctrine, by the sleight of men, and cunning craftiness, whereby they lie in wait to deceive* (Eph. 4:14). In the end, as far as our King James Bible is concerned, the evidence of its excellence in every respect is overwhelming. Even some foes concede this much. We should be comforted that the Lord has not betrayed our trust in Him. We do not have to answer to man for what the Lord decided to do (or not do) with all His jots and tittles. Our God told us to trust Him and He would take care of ***perfect(ing) that which concerneth me*** (Ps. 138:8).

In the end, Dr. Sam Gipp may sum up best what our attitude as Bible-believers ought to be. The simplicity of it should be most satisfactory to the trusting heart, but one may be well assured that it will be a terrible abomination in the eyes of the scholars' union. Speaking of the AV 1611, Bro. Gipp said, ***"The final word on what words are inspired and what words are not is simple: <u>if it's in the Bible, it's inspired.</u>"***[197]

To some men it falls that they should research, scour, debate, contend, strive and sally forth to battle over the King James Bible issue and all its ramifications. Yet even for those men and women, one indispensable thing must yet be embraced nigh unto the bosom: ***Nothing substitutes for simple, child-like faith in the promises of God!*** In the end, it all boils down to trusting in the God that promised.

---

[197] Gipp, Sam. *Is Our English Bible Inspired?* (Daystar Publishing, Miamitown, Ohio 45041,
2004), pg. 12.

Chapter 13

Hijacking the New Covenant

*But now hath he obtained a more excellent ministry, by how much also he is the mediator of a **better covenant**, which was established upon better promises. For if that **first covenant** had been faultless, then should no place have been sought for the second. For finding fault with them, he saith, Behold, the days come, saith the Lord, when I will make a **new covenant** with the house of Israel and with the house of Judah: Not according to the **covenant** that I made with their fathers in the day when I took them by the hand to lead them out of the land of Egypt; because they continued not in my **covenant**, and I regarded them not, saith the Lord. For this is the **covenant** that I will make with the house of Israel after those days, saith the Lord; I will put my laws into their mind, and write them in their hearts: and I will be to them a God, and they shall be to me a people: And they shall not teach every man his neighbour, and every man his brother, saying, Know the Lord: for all shall know me, from the least to the greatest. For I will be merciful to their unrighteousness, and their sins and their iniquities will I remember no more. In that he saith, A **new covenant**, he hath made the first old. Now that which decayeth and waxeth old is ready to vanish away.*

(Heb. 8:6-13)

Indifference and careless negligence are not traits that the Lord looks upon with favor. Uzza certainly found the Lord's fuse to be short when it came to laying hands on the ark of the covenant in 1 Chronicles 13:10. David had the advantage of standing far enough off on that day not to be smitten with Uzza, for the mistake was his as much as Uzza's. As a man of tender conscience, one can assume that David relived, in his memory, that terrible scene often and with smitten heart. Nadab and Abihu (Lev.10) quite fatally learned a lesson about what kind of fire was to be built in the tabernacle, and King Uzziah discovered that there were repercussions for stepping beyond his bounds of office (2 Chron. 26:16).

Uzza was only trying to help. Nadab and Abihu leave the impression of being flippant and slipshod. King Uzziah was presumptuous. Moses' anger propelled him to cross the line (Num. 20:10). Samson played adulterous games with his vows and his calling one too many times (Jgs. 16:17). Korah and his cohorts pushed all the wrong buttons, not imagining the consequences (Num. 16:32), and Herod never dreamed of the price to be paid for his grand oratory to an over-enthused audience (Acts. 12:22).

The world we live in today is a dirty and derelict place and the times are such that men have virtually no concept of the holy and sanctified ground around a burning bush. Joseph well understood the hallowed nature of holy matrimony (Gen.39:9), but the men of Bethshemesh thought they had open season to peer like curious cats into the ark of God. They were wrong (1 Sam. 6:19). The brutish may, for a time, get away with keeping their shoes on at the burning bush, and while most all men have long ago lost their trepidation at being *thrust through with a dart* (Heb. 12:20), the Judgment Seat of Christ draws nearer by the hour for every Christian, and it brings with it the *terror* (2 Cor.5:10-11) of accountability in detail and depth that no mega-church pastor has given thought to in years. Indeed, the time is well nigh when men of all walks and persuasions will once again learn the hard lessons that await trespassers in holy things.

Men's slipshod and indifferent mishandling of the scripture and the treasures which it contains has and will yet cost many more their eternal souls. The shoddy and slapdash manufacture and distribution of careless and heedless doctrine may well cost a staggering number of saints the better part of their inheritance. It is a disgrace and a travesty how little Christians seem to care about the vast treasure of doctrine (read that *Truth*) that is laid up in the scriptures by our loving Father. It seems to slip past the attention these days that believers have been appointed stewards of the treasures found in the Book of God. *Let a man so account of us, as of the ministers of Christ, and stewards of the mysteries of God. Moreover it is required in stewards, that a man be found faithful* (1 Cor. 4:1-2).

There is one explanation for this blithe indifference that sticks out among several others. It is fair to conclude that a God whose ways and thoughts are higher than ours (Isa. 55:8-9), would in communicating these high, lofty, intricate and detailed concepts, require that the use of words and language be precise and exact. God Himself would need to say exactly what He meant, expressing it with exactitude, simplicity and thoroughness. It is reasonable to conclude that since the Word of God ***was*** God (John 1:1), that this would present no real obstacle to the Lord. Another requirement would be that man would have to receive on his end those words with the same exactness and precision by which they left the Lord's mind and mouth. It is not difficult for the honest man to see that God would have envisioned how the infinitely precise meaning by words would have had to leap the chasm from one language to another. It makes virtually no sense to hold with the idea that God did never, and would never, involve Himself in the translation of His words from one language to another. If God said exactly what He meant in Greek and Hebrew through prophets, apostles and scribes (inspiration), and promised to keep those words and meanings in spite of all influences (preservation), there is still a vast and logically preposterous disconnect in the plan if the Lord did not address how to bridge the gap from the original languages to the rest of the tongues of the world (translation).

Most Bible scholars are fanatically zealous about the concept that God inspired and preserved the scriptures (the originals), and then left the translating to men's fallible abilities. Hence, no perfect translation could ever exist. This view, as popular as it is, envisions the Lord supernaturally delivering the Bible to man (which He did), promising by His glorious power to pass it on preserved to succeeding generations (which He did), but then, in the final leg of the journey, forsaking His means of supernaturally over-riding the corruptive work of men and Satan, and turning over those perfect words to be translated by degenerate men without any absolute guidance from above! This is the equivalent of inventing and developing an entirely new generation of jet engine which operates perfectly and revolutionizes the industry, but then leaving it unattached to the airplane, thus rendering the new engine useless. To hold that God inspires and preserves the scripture, and yet stands distant and aloof altogether from the translation of His perfect word is not only unscriptural, it is illogical and quite stupid when placed under scrutiny.

Bible-believers often find that the feast of truth and doctrine (*the mysteries of God* – 1 Cor. 4:1) contained in the scriptures is barely even conceptualized by Christians today, for they have come to view the bounty of doctrine and truth as a table of a few interesting morsels, but mostly they have experienced doctrine as a conglomerate of controversial obscurities, entangled and confusing arguments, and dead, dry concepts that numb all interest. They have experienced little doctrine indeed that is sweet to the taste; that enlivens the appetite, brings joy to the heart, and draws a man into a zealous and hungry quest to know more of his God and Savior.

God communicates exact, detailed and lofty truths by words that must themselves be exact, detailed and lofty. Many scribes and scholars have been careless, unfaithful and indifferent with these words. These scholars have schooled themselves and others into believing that the eternal truths written in our Bibles are not holy ground. To them they are not sacred, for God did not involve Himself directly in delivering them to us in our native language. ***This is the reason they are slipshod and indifferent.*** They all imagine that in Moses' place, they too would have fallen unshod upon holy ground and would have earnestly rendered the Lord His due. They imagine themselves as Peter, face down in the bottom of the fishing boat, crying from the soul, *Depart from me; for I am a sinful man, O Lord* (Luke 5:8). The brutal truth is that they all have been brought to the holy ground at the foot of the burning bush, and far from loosing their shoes and falling prostrate, they have treated the holy ground as their own scholastic playground. They have been *weighed in the balances* and are *found wanting* (Dan. 5:27).

These academics will have to face judgment for that. The result of their profligacy, though, is that the common man now views those words from God as inexact, flexible, ill-defined, variable and interchangeable. The resultant, popular view now is that nothing written to men from God communicates exactly what God intended. The Bible, in their judgment, is an amorphous mass of ill-communicated, poorly conceptualized truths obscured by inept translators, evolving languages, clashing cultures and the passage of far too much time. The Bible, to them, does not say or mean what God said and meant. Therefore – and who can blame them – men, as a whole, are not interested. Respectfully speaking, they are justifiable in this attitude if the scholars are right. ***Why should***

men give careful heed or thought to the words of a God who only communicates by garbled, convoluted and misshapen messages, translated by a bunch of bumbling, corrupt degenerates?

By very definition, God's words must be exact, precise and definitive. To the disdain of the naysayers, many of them orthodox, Fundamentalist scholars, Bible-believers are blessedly assured that the word of God is *quick* (alive), *powerful*, *sharp*, *piercing*, and, itself, *discerning* (Heb. 4:12). The Bible's attributes are those of an animated and living entity. Its words must be able to communicate the broad sweep of universal truth, while at the same time conveying and imparting to the mind the intricate weave and elaborate detail of complex and artful verity. And they do! God accomplished what He set out to do.

It is with this in mind that the next masterpiece of God's handiwork is presented as well as the butchered remains of sound doctrine left by the hatchet men.

The Precise Meaning of the *New Covenant*

Jeremiah 31:31-34 is the OT reference for the passage quoted in the beginning of this chapter from Hebrews 8. Jeremiah prophesies thus:

> *31 Behold, the days come, saith the LORD, that I will make a* ***new covenant*** *with the* ***house of Israel****, and with the* ***house of Judah****:*
> *32 Not according to the covenant that I made with their fathers in the day that I took them by the hand to bring them out of the land of Egypt; which my covenant they brake, although I was an husband unto them, saith the LORD:*

> 33 *But this shall be the covenant that I will make with the house of Israel; After those days, saith the LORD,* ***I will put my law in their inward parts, and write it in their hearts****; and will be their God, and they shall be my people.*
> 34 ***And they shall teach no more every man his neighbour, and every man his brother, saying, Know the LORD****: for they shall all know me, from the least of them unto the greatest of them, saith the LORD:* ***for I will forgive their iniquity, and I will remember their sin no more.***

It should be mentioned that the *new covenant* is mentioned by name in the scriptures of the AV 1611 only a total of four times. Jeremiah 31:31 is the first, and it is quite definite and unmistakable to a careful reader. Several obvious and salient points are to be noted.

1) The ***new covenant*** is made specifically with *the house of Israel* and *the house of Judah* (31:31).
2) ***After those days*** (31:33) specifies a certain period of time, and the passage makes obvious that the time of this prophecy will be after the Great Tribulation, early in the Millennium, during the 1000 year reign of Christ.
3) The law of God is at that time written in the hearts and minds of the children of Israel (31:33). It is not memorized or learned. It is imparted there by the Lord Himself.
4) In that day, none of Israel is taught about the Lord or about doctrine (31:34). That knowledge of God will be spiritually written in the hearts of Israel. After all, Jesus the King will be living among them and reigning from His throne in Jerusalem.
5) At that time, the nation of Israel as an ethnic people will corporately have their sins removed and forgiven (31:34). Acts 3:19 and Romans 11:26 are commentaries upon this occurrence.

New Testament scholars who have labored in the doctrines of the Church Age for the last 2000 years have become notorious in their own right for commandeering all doctrine anywhere in the scriptures and subjugating it forcibly to the Church Age plan and promises of salvation. All of the details of all salvation anywhere in the Old Testament, or even that of the Great Tribulation, Millennium, and New Heavens and New Earth, are devotionalized, trimmed and fitted by scholars and writers to fit what is clearly and correctly understood to be salvation doctrine today.

Square pegs are fitted into the round holes of doctrine by hacking off the edges.

This notwithstanding, observe in the above passage that both houses of Israel are specified. Notice too, that the law is not to be taught or learned, but rather, God imparts it supernaturally into the minds of Israel. I have been born-again as a child of God (John.3:3). I am a new creature in Christ (2 Cor.5:17), and I have been thus converted for over 40 years as of this writing. Though I can testify to a quickened conscience and an inner spiritual witness of the Holy Spirit, to this hour, I have never had the law and doctrine of God supernaturally implanted into my mind and heart in any kind of detail. No Christian of my acquaintance has had this experience either. Jeremiah 31:34 plainly says that the Bible will have no need to be taught in that day. We, on the other hand, are admonished to read (1 Tim. 4:13) and study (2 Tim. 2:15) the Bible with great diligence that we *may grow thereby* (1 Pet. 2:2). We are commanded in our Great Commission to *Go ye therefore, and* ***teach*** *all nations* (Matt. 28:19)! What is this aspect of scripture about not teaching *every man his neighbour* in Jeremiah 31? We are commanded to teach all nations.

The blunt fact is that Jeremiah 31 is not specifically concern you and me, doctrinally speaking. It is not about born-again, Church Age Christians. It is not describing our salvation, though the forgiveness of iniquities and new relation with the law and the Bible are comparative issues that we have in common. In Jeremiah 31, God is describing a day after the Church has been raptured, after the Judgment Seat of Christ, after the marriage of the Lamb, after the Second Coming of Christ at Armageddon, at which time the Lord will redeem Israel as a nation. He will then restore them, become their visible, physical King, and He will pour out His Spirit *upon all flesh; and your sons and your daughters shall prophesy, your old men shall dream dreams, your young men shall see visions* (Joel 2:28).

Specifically, the ***New Covenant,*** as named and prophesied by the Lord, is the event by which Israel as a nation is truly reborn at the beginning of the Millennium, and by which they have the law of God literally *put* and *written* in their *inward parts* and in their *minds*.

This is the scriptural definition of the ***New Covenant***.

Before delving further, it is important to acknowledge that it is fully realized that there is a dual nature to the *new covenant* and that we born-again, Church Age Christians do, in fact, partake and share with redeemed Israel certain blessings and characteristics of the *new covenant*. A comparison of Hebrews 8:8-13 and Hebrews 10:14-17 will reveal that God specifies *the house of Israel and... the house of Judah* in Hebrews 8:8, but allows for a much less specific application in Hebrews 10:16 where it says only *them*. The Lord leaves the application more generic in Hebrews 10 because Church Age Christians also partake in the forgiveness of sins due to the fact that *by one offering he hath perfected for ever them that are sanctified* (Heb. 10:14). There is no question that certain *new covenant* attributes and blessings are applicable to the Church.

However, as Walker states in *the Bible Believer's Guide to Dispensationalism,*

> The fact that the New Covenant relates *primarily* to Israel is unmistakable.[198]

Referring to *The Dictionary of Premillennial Theology,* Walker says, "It also points out that 'the full realization of the covenant remains future.'"[199]

While born-again Christians share with future Israel certain aspects of the *new covenant,* it nevertheless remains a doctrinal verity that the New Testament gospel promises to Church Age believers **are not** equivalent to the ***New Covenant*** promises to Israel. To reiterate, such believers certainly have "realized" a new relation with God by the new birth and new nature, but as stated above, when considering the intricate details of the doctrine, "the full realization of the covenant remains future." One may be assured that millennial Israel and the Bride of Christ will be two entirely distinct entities during the thousand year reign of Christ, and the promises they each "realize" will be distinct from one another while bearing certain common blessings. They are distinct now, and they will be distinct then.

The precise ***new covenant*** promises to Israel in Jeremiah 31 are repeated virtually word for word in Hebrews 8:8-13. The theme of Hebrews 8 is God's millennial ***new covenant*** with Israel. The applications of Jeremiah 31 and Hebrews 8 are exactly and precisely the same. God said exactly what He meant, and He used language in the King James Bible that made the unity and unanimity of the two passages inseparable except to the spiritually blind.

---

[198] Walker, David E., *The Bible Believer's Guide to Dispensationalism* (Daystar Publishing, Miamitown, OH 45041, 2005) p.280.
[199] Ibid. p.280.

This exposition may prove somewhat disorienting to some who have been nurtured in the Christian life by Christian radio and devotional writings, and who have come under the influence of mainstream Bible commentators and the loose-as-a-goose doctrine of many church ministries. More explanation is forthcoming. For now, please make allowance that the language of the King James Bible, which uses the term only four times, definitively designates that the ***new covenant*** detailed in Jeremiah 31 and Hebrews 8 is millennial doctrine for Israel. Christians have realized certain of its blessings that are shared with Israel, but it is not Christian doctrine for the Church Age. The somewhat generic address of the promises quoted in Hebrews 10 allows the Body of Christ to see our common ground with Israel, and we are grateful for the instruction in our own lives which we can carry away from the passage. It is critical, though, to realize that certain elements of even Hebrews 10 are in discord with a born-again, Church Age Christian's relation with the things of God. In Hebrews 10:25, while all should fervently accept the admonition, *Not forsaking the assembling of ourselves together, as the manner of some is,* it must be recognized that the verse following sets forth dire warning that is in unmistakable discord with the clear doctrines of eternal security for those in the Church Age Body of Christ. The next verse says, *For if we sin wilfully after that we have received the knowledge of the truth, there remaineth no more sacrifice for sins* (Heb. 10:26). The *day approaching* of verse 25 is plainly the day of *fiery indignation* (vs. 27) at Christ's advent, not at the earlier Church Rapture, which *deliver(s) us from the wrath to* come (1 Thes. 1:10). Those being specifically addressed in Hebrews are not only *Hebrews*, but they are Hebrews living in the middle of the Great Tribulation, awaiting not the pre-tribulation Church Age Rapture, but the post-tribulation rapture and the Second Advent of Christ! Hebrews 2:5 specifically designates the fact that the author of Hebrews is looking forward to and addressing, *the world to come, whereof we speak.* That is, the millennial world! This is the exact application of passages like Matthew 24:13, *But he that shall endure unto the end, the same shall be saved.* It is doctrinal suicide to wrest these scriptures from their contexts or to fly to the Greek to try to mollify one's preconceptions and prejudices. The people being addressed in these passages, which have been so briefly and cursorily discussed here, are people dwelling in the time of the great Tribulation and they are anxiously anticipating the day of the lord and the millennial reign.

The point of this doctrinal explanation is to highlight the fact that no Christian has ever experienced in its fullness what is described in Jeremiah 31, Hebrews 8, and for that matter, Hebrews 10. The full realization of the promises of those passages belongs to a future time (the Millennium) and is specified to Israel, although we will share in part with their blessings and inheritance.

To make sure the nail has been set firmly, the ***new covenant*** is not what many consider a New Testament Christian's covenant. It is not the equivalent of the gospel which has saved the Christian today. It is administered to Israel in the Millennium. The administration of each individual's salvation since Pentecost to this hour is far different in several matters of detail than the administration of the ***new covenant*** to Israel. Yet again, believers do have the forgiveness of sins in common with those addressed in Jeremiah 31 and Hebrews 8, thank God, but no Christian since 34 A.D. has ever experienced in fullness what is described in either of those two passages. Church Age Christians have not experienced it, because it is not for the Body of Christ to experience. The ***new covenant*** in its fullness is exclusively for Israel!

As the ***New Covenant*** and the ***New Testament*** have been demonstrated to be somewhat contrasting entities, let there be no time wasted in addressing what the ***New Testament*** is.

The *New Testament* as Distinct From the *New Covenant.*

Most "Christians" who adhere to the Bible – actually there are fewer and fewer as time progresses – know that there is an obvious division between the book of Malachi and Matthew that marks the dividing line between the Old Testament and the New Testament. This is a division that is taken for granted more than it is understood. Most have never explored much of the real meaning of the names of the two testaments and have precious little concept of the nuances contained within each. To most, it is sufficient to know that the Old Testament occurred prior to Christ's mortal birth and work here on earth, and that the New Testament is simply the dispensation after His birth. This is true enough, but there is a great deal more information to be apprehended.

Many, for instance, fail to appreciate that most of the first portions of the four gospels (Matthew, Mark, Luke and John) are technically still Old Testament narratives. No, no one advocates moving them to the Old Testament, but in Matthew 26:28, it was Christ that said in presenting the cup, *For this is my blood of the **new testament**, which is shed for many for the remission of sins.* This should help the reader to see that Christ was actually born under the Old Testament, and lived virtually all His mortal life under it. It was in the very final days of His 33 earthly years that He instituted the ***new testament***!

The following passage should be a great help in understanding this.

> *14 How much more shall the blood of Christ, who through the eternal Spirit offered himself without spot to God, purge your conscience from dead works to serve the living God?*

15 And for this cause he is the mediator of the ***new testament****, that by means of death, for the redemption of the transgressions that were under the* ***first testament****, they which are called might receive the promise of eternal inheritance.*
16 ***For where a testament is, there must also of necessity be the death of the testator.***
17 ***For a testament is of force after men are dead: otherwise it is of no strength at all while the testator liveth.***
18 Whereupon neither the ***first testament*** *was dedicated without blood.*

(Heb. 9:14-18)

While Jesus Christ was unquestionably a monumental influence and force in the lives of His family, His apostles, His disciples and the people in His immediate vicinity in the years prior to His death, plainly from the passage above it can be seen that the broad sweep of the power and promises of the New Testament could not have been in effect, as a rule, until at least Christ had died! Notice below that while they suggest further nuances and textures of the New Testament landscape, the texts plainly show that Christ's death, resurrection and ascension were indispensable requirements before New Testament salvation as we know it could be imparted.

John 7:38-39
38 He that believeth on me, as the scripture hath said, out of his belly shall flow rivers of living water.
39 (But this spake he of the Spirit, which they that believe on him should receive: ***for the Holy Ghost was not yet given; because that Jesus was not yet glorified.****)*

Colossians 1:20
20 And, having made peace through the ***blood of his cross****, by him to reconcile all things unto himself; by him, I say, whether they be things in earth, or things in heaven.*

Hebrews 9:22
22 And almost all things are by the law purged with blood; and ***without shedding of blood is no remission.***

It is critical to recognize then that the term ***New Testament*** encompasses all of the sweeping doctrines and changes that the death, burial, resurrection and ascension of Christ wrought. Equally critical is the recognition that all of the ***New Testament*** is not one seamless and uniform dispensation. Within the ***New Testament*** is included not only the **Church Age**, ruled by the tenet that *...we walk by faith, not by sight* (2 Cor. 5:7), but also the **Millennium**, in which Christ ruling for 1000 years as King, administrates the Spirit and the law to Israel as never seen before. In the Millennium, He also will rule the nations with *a rod of iron* (Rev. 19:15). Christ will be *seen* in the Millennium by Israel and all nations and will further require of the nations that they appear at Jerusalem yearly for the Feast of Tabernacles or else drought and plagues will overtake their crops and land (Zech. 14:17-18). This brings to light the doctrinal fact that is uncomfortable for many New Testament scholars, which fact is that the Mosaic Law becomes an intricate foundation of life to mortal men that live on Earth during the 1000 year reign of Christ. The return of the Law is a doctrinal pillar often treated in the most superficial and dismissive of manners by the scholars. Deserving of more detailed treatment, for the purposes of this work the following texts will have to suffice for commentary and proof on this matter: Colossians 2:17, Ezekiel 45:17, Matthew 24:20; Isaiah 66:23.

Yet another distinct time frame in the ***New Testament*** will be the eventual **New Heavens and New Earth** which will come after the Millennial reign of Christ (2 Pet. 3:13; Rev. 21:1). Plainly, in this time, after the great meltdown of the elements and the remaking of the heavens and earth, and with the vast city of New Jerusalem having descended from heaven, the things of God will be administrated in a much different manner than they are these days.

To state the matter in brief, the ***New Testament*** encompasses all the dispensational, administrative and doctrinal variations after the death of Christ, including the Church Age, the Tribulation, the Millennium, and the New Heaven and New Earth. The ***New Covenant***, on the other hand, is merely one phase of the ***New Testament***. It is restricted to Christ's particular covenant with Israel commencing in the Millennium at which time He says,

> *I will put my law in their inward parts, and write it in their hearts; and will be their God, and they shall be my people. And they shall teach no more every man his neighbour, and every man his brother, saying, Know the LORD... for I will forgive their iniquity, and I will remember their sin no more.* (Jer.31:33-34)

Again, it is recognized that there are certain elements of the *new covenant* which Church Age Christians share with Israel, and certain likenesses of our relationship with God can be seen in the promises He has made to millennial Israel. Still, it is plainly evident that a pre-millennial Christian is not a complete partaker with Israel of all the intricacies of the millennial *new covenant*.

If this sounds strange to the Laodicean Christian's ear, the Christian might first consider objectively just *what kind* and just *how much* true Bible doctrine he has or has not been taught. Secondly, he might consider that the ***Old Testament***, as known today, is composed of a number of different covenants: The Adamic Covenant, the Abrahamic, the Noahic, the Mosaic and the Davidic covenant. These covenants do not actually represent precise frames of time. They overlap and coincide one with another, most of them carrying shades of prior covenants with them into the next covenant, and each carrying its ramifications and all the power of God's promises forward unto the day when all these things are fulfilled. This acknowledged, it still remains that no one can deny the distinctiveness of each covenant. Each covenant was a pact made by God with each of these individuals and groups. They each had a distinct beginning, and will yet be independently fulfilled in their time. Each covenant before Christ was independently a part of the greater whole – the ***Old Testament***.

In the grand and most simplistic biblical scheme of things, God's testament to man may be divided into the time prior to the coming of the Messiah and Savior, and the time after that Savior's work at Calvary was culminated. That would be the ***Old Testament*** and the ***New Testament***. For scholars not to recognize that there are other divisions of doctrine (2 Tim. 2:15) within those two testaments demonstrates profound ignorance with a train load of slothfulness intermingled in the mix. Just as the Davidic Covenant and the Noahic Covenant are subcategories and mere parts of the ***Old Testament***, so is the ***New Covenant*** an independent dispensation and subcategory of the ***New Testament***. The death, burial, resurrection and ascension of Jesus Christ made the fulfillment of this Israelite ***New Covenant*** possible, just as it made the salvation and promises enjoyed by the Bride of Christ possible, nevertheless each of those things are independently and separately encapsulated within the larger ***New Testament.***

Without further exegesis or detailed analysis of these verities, the goal at this point is to communicate something very simple indeed: the ***New Testament*** and the ***New Covenant*** are scripturally very different things! To make them the same is to make the truth found in the King James Bible a travesty.

The Scholars, the New Versions and the *New Covenant*

The Scholars and Commentators

The Lord Jesus Christ and His eventual work for mankind at Calvary and beyond are foreseen, foreshadowed and typified on almost every page of the ***Old Testament***. What He fulfilled in the ***New Testament*** cast all the plans and patterns God had laid in the ***Old Testament*** in glorious and magnificent light. Thus it is that one can read the ***Old Testament*** through eyes that know the truth of the ***New Testament*** and see our Savior, our gospel and our salvation all on wonderful display. This is a marvelous thing indeed!

The snare for the unaware lies in the fact that no matter what patterns and figures of things are foreshadowed or pre-typified in the Old Testament, Israel is never, ever the Church. The Law is not Grace, and the Old Testament is not the New Testament. The kingdom that God did materially establish in Israel in the days of the kings (and which He will again establish in the Millennium) is not the kingdom which He has established in converted saints and believers in the Church Age (Lk. 17:21). As stated earlier in the chapter, those who have labored in study, writing and commentating upon the great doctrines of grace, redemption and free salvation in the New Testament often have a bit of an Achilles heel. It comes from the great emphasis that must be justifiably laid upon Jesus having fulfilled all things in the ***Old Testament;*** that man might perceive and receive the gift and the inheritance that is his in the ***New Testament***, freely. The snag comes because Bible students have a tendency to subjugate all doctrine anywhere in the Bible to that of their own time. Sometimes in the labor to edify and magnify Christ, it has been shown to be easy to gently wrest the principal truth of a passage so it will fit better with doctrines in the New Testament.

For instance, in Romans 4:12, we are, in faith, the children of our father Abraham though we are not circumcised. Wonderful! Circumcision no longer matters to God. Nevertheless, one must remember that Abraham's children did indeed *then* have to be circumcised or else they were not in God's covenant (Gen. 17:10-16). We know Noah's ark represented Christ Himself and all inside were safe. Nonetheless, Noah himself did have the backbreaking and lonely labor of building that gargantuan boat before he knew true safety. The Sabbath, representing God's day of rest, which is to be fulfilled in the Millennium, has very few real doctrinal ramifications in the average Christian's life today, however, in Numbers 15:32-36 getting lax in the matter *in that day* got an otherwise good man executed!

So it is that such commentators come to Jeremiah 31 and Hebrews 8. They see the ***New Covenant***. They see the pardoning of iniquities. They know that Jesus Christ is the ultimate fulfillment of these things, and so they shave off all the edges that do not fit the doctrinal hole just right, and they devotionalize and spiritualize the things in the passage so that it all becomes simple ***New Testament***, Church Age salvation. To them, it becomes the very same gospel as the one that saved each Church Age Christian, even though the two do not match in details. The details that do not fit their preconceptions are simply dropped, devotionalized, or deformed so that they do fit. It plainly is not the gospel that saved you and me, for we have experienced what is described in Jeremiah 31 only in a measure.

Jeremiah 31 represents Israelite Millennial salvation! Church Age saints actually will get to stand in rank behind Jesus Christ and watch Him administer this salvation upon Israel.

On Jeremiah 31:31, Adam Clarke does not comment at length, but it is plain what he believes:

> [A new covenant] ***The Christian dispensation.***[200]

In Jeremiah 31:34, Clarke's comments are baffling, and it is plain that he had preset his opinions on the matter without particular reference to what the passage said. Though the Bible says people are not to be taught, he insists that they *are* taught:

> [And they shall teach no more] It shall be a time of universal light and knowledge; all shall know God in Christ, from the least to the greatest; the ***children shall be taught to read the New Covenant***, and to understand the terms of their salvation.[201]

In his continuing comments on verse 34, Clarke is plainly reading the passage through New Testament gospel and Church Age-tinted glasses. He thinks that the places where people go for instruction in the Church Age fulfill the tenet of Jeremiah 31:34 that no man will be taught.

> [I will forgive their iniquity] It shall be a time of GENERAL PARDON; multitudes shall be daily in the Christian church receiving the witness of God's Spirit, and in their life and conversation

---

[200] Clarke, Adam. *Clarke's Commentary*. (1998) P C Study Bible (Version 2.11) [Computer Software]. Seattle, WA: Biblesoft.
[201] Ibid

> witnessing a good confession. How wonderfully is this prophecy fulfilled in the age of Bibles, Sunday schools, and village preaching.[202]

The Wycliffe Commentary sees, in spite of its context, the ***New Covenant*** as being fulfilled in the creation of a new heart in New Testament Christians, and the institution of the Lord's Supper. The commentators plainly ignore the defining application to the houses of Israel and Judah and insist upon "back-reading" devotional details in the New Testament to the passage that are not contained in the passage in question. Make no mistake, it is a blessing to be able to see salvation spiritualized in the Old Testament, but it would be preferable if Bible scholars would actually expound the Bible in its undefiled doctrinal context as well as presenting a devotional application.

> The concept of the new covenant is Jeremiah's most important contribution to Biblical thought. The OT frequently mentions the covenant God made with Israel (<Exo 19:3-8; 24:3-8; Deut 29:1-29>), which covenant was the foundation of the Israelites' national and religious life. God makes clear, through Jeremiah, that Israel has failed to keep this covenant (<Jer 7:21-26; 11:1-13>) and predicts that He will make a new one with His people. ***The new covenant*** will not be a new law (the old law was still good), but it ***will produce a new "heart"*** —i. e., it will confer a new motivation to obey the law of God. Jesus, ***while instituting the Lord's Supper,*** declared, "This cup is the ***new covenant*** in my blood" (ASV, <1 Cor 11:25>; cf. <Lk 22:20>). The Hebrews epistle teaches that Christ brought in the new covenant by his perfect and final

---

[202] Ibid

> sacrifice for sin (<Heb 7:22; 8:7-13; 10:15-22>; cf. <2 Cor 3:5-14>).[203]

As stated before, the Hebrews 8 context matches the Jeremiah 31 context exactly. Matthew Henry, in his comments on Hebrews 8, makes sweeping application by including the Lord's Supper and baptism, which are found nowhere in the context, while again ignoring details that are given that do not match what he is saying.

> The articles of this covenant are very extraordinary, which are **sealed between God and his people by baptism and the Lord's supper;** whereby they bind themselves to their part, and God assures them he will do his part; and his is the main and principal part, on which his people depend for grace and strength to do theirs.[204]

Henry feels free to retool and remold what God said about putting His law into Israel's hearts and **minds**.

> (1.) God articles with his people that he will put his laws into their minds and write them in their hearts, v. 10. He once wrote his laws to them, now he will write his laws in them; that is, ***he will give them understanding to know and to believe his law; he will give them memories to retain them; he will give them hearts to love them and consciences to recognize them; he will give them courage to profess them and***

---

[203]Pfeiffer, Charles and Harrison, Everett, ed. *The Wycliffe Bible Commen* (1962) Moody Press. P C Study Bible (Version 2.11) [Computer Software Seattle, WA: Biblesoft.

[204]Henry, Matthew. *Matthew Henry's Commentary on the Whole Bible.* (1 P C Study Bible (Version 2.11) [Computer Software]. Seattle, WA: Bibles

> ***power to put them in practice; the whole habit and frame of their souls shall be a table and transcript of the law of God.*** This is the foundation of the covenant; and, when this is laid, duty will be done wisely, sincerely, readily, easily, resolutely, constantly, and comfortably.

Regarding Hebrews 8:10, Adam Clarke again shows his predisposition to take great latitudes with context and application.

> [This is the covenant] This is the nature of that glorious system of religion which I shall publish among them after those days, i. e., ***in the times of the Gospel.***
> [I will put my laws into their mind] ***I will influence them with the principles of law, truth, holiness, etc.; and their understandings shall be fully enlightened to comprehend them.***
> [And write them in their hearts] ***All their affections, passions, and appetites, shall be purified and filled with holiness and love to God and man; so that they shall willingly obey, and feel that love is the fulfilling of the law***: instead of being written on tables of stone, they shall be written on the fleshly tables of their hearts.[205]

Concerning Hebrews 8:9, Barnes makes the entire application a matter of conscience in the Christian, rather than allowing what the Bible says to dictate the meaning. He applies the passage to the "times of the Messiah," apparently meaning something other than the actual Millennium, and makes the application to the "new dispensation," in his mind, the age in

---

[205] Clarke, Adam. *Clarke's Commentary.* (1998) P C Study Bible (Version 2.11) [Computer Software]. Seattle, WA: Biblesoft.

which we live. He equates the message of Hebrews 8 with our gospel. Certainly his evaluation of external rites and Christian conscience is a fine application for our day and is worthy of note. However, it has little indeed to do with the passage in question, doctrinally.

> [I will put my laws into their mind] that is, in that subsequent period, called in Scripture "the after times," "the last days," "the ages to come," meaning the last dispensation of the world. Thus interpreted, the sense is, that ***this would be done in the times of the Messiah***. "I will put my laws into their mind." Margin, "Give." The word "give" in Hebrew is often used in the sense of "put." The meaning here is, that they would not be mere external observances, but ***would affect the conscience and the heart.*** The laws of the Hebrews pertained mainly to external rites and ceremonies; ***the laws of the new dispensation would relate particularly to the inner man, and be designed to control the heart. The grand uniqueness of the Christian system is, that it regulates the conscience and the principles of the soul rather than external matters***. It prescribes few external rites, and those are exceedingly simple, and are merely the proper expressions of the pious feelings supposed to be in the heart; and all attempts either to increase the number of these rites, or to make them imposing by their gorgeousness, have done just so much to mar the simplicity of ***the gospel***, and to corrupt religion.[206]

[206] Barnes, Albert. *Barnes' Notes* (1997) P C Study Bible (Version 2.11) [Computer Software]. Seattle, WA: Biblesoft.

As in all things of faith, spirit and the scriptures, the Christian scholar and student, as a matter of conscience has to determine whether the comments of mere commentators and writers really coincide with what the Bible actually says. In these latter days, God's people have become very accustomed to having the scriptures loosely applied, and they have adapted their taste to devotional pap. One theoretically may be nourished to some shadow of physical adulthood by feeding on nothing but high fructose milk, but that is not to say that he *should be*. While the need for *some man to guide* (Acts 8:31) is still an indispensable precept in our day, there is also a profound necessity that what men say, write, preach and teach be compared for authenticity and verity to the word of God! *To the law and to the testimony: if they speak not according to this word, it is because there is no light in them* (Isa. 8:20). The reader must realize that he, and he alone, must determine whether what he hears or reads coincides with the word of the Lord. *I have esteemed the words of his mouth more than my necessary food* (Job 23:12). Being teachable does not have to mean being vulnerable to doctrinal victimization, predation and the ignorance of other men.

We have seen what the exegetical scholars and Bible commentators do to the ***New Covenant***. No evaluation would be complete without seeing how the new versions have treated this precious doctrine of the scriptures.

The *Per*versions

The title of this chapter is *Hijacking the New Covenant*. The King James Bible specifically distinguishes the ***New Covenant*** four times, while using the word *covenant* in other contexts many other times. The new versions, generally speaking, also retain the usage of the term *new covenant*, but there is more than one way to corrupt the scriptures! What the new versions have done has been to eliminate altogether the use of the word ***testament.*** Excepting the New KJV, which does retain *testament* three times (do not pin a star on it for heroism just yet), the rest of the major new versions (NASV, NASU, NIV, RSV, etc.) uniformly and completely remove *testament* from the Bible and replace it with the word *covenant.* Thus eliminated are the 14 times that a ***testament*** of any kind is distinguished from a ***covenant*** in the KJV. The word *testament* does not occur in the text of the NASV, RSV, or NIV at all. If one reads the NASV or the NIV, he will never see the word *testament* in what is supposed to represent the text of the scripture itself!

This means then that the difference and distinction between the *testament(s)* and the various *covenant(s)* established in God's true word are obliterated and destroyed in the new versions and the doctrinal understanding clearly imparted by the demarcation of those differences is confused and obscured. The *testament(s)* and the *covenant(s)* of the King James are all lumped together into one indistinguishable mass designated in the new versions as *covenant(s)* alone. Further, if the teachings of the mainstream writers and commentators are any indication, there is virtually no doctrinal grasp of any of the contrasts, dissimilarities, or implications that mark the two concepts.

There are therefore profound ramifications for this atrocious miscarriage of what is called biblical scholarship and translation.

1) By translating Christ's institution of ***the new testament in my blood*** in 1 Corinthians 11:25 in the AV as the "new covenant in my blood" in the NIV and others, the perverse translation equates the *new covenant* with the *new testament,* and thus makes the Millennial *new covenant* with Israel the same as the broader *new testament* of which saved Gentiles are

also partakers. This very doctrinal miscarriage can be heard at almost any hour on Christian radio these days, and wends its way into almost every biblical devotional writing and commentary. It is inexcusable confusion of which God is not the author (1 Cor. 14:33).

2) Further disservice is done by the confusion, for there are now entire "Christian" denominations that flirt with cultism for they believe that Church Age Christians are in a "covenant relationship" with God. These have it that since the Old Testament *covenant* was entered **by circumcision** (Abraham – Gen.17) the New Testament covenant is entered **by baptism**. They believe that baptism replaced circumcision and thus the "Christian life" is properly commenced at baptism. This is old, moldy and dangerous Reformation nonsense and it is bad doctrine to boot, but the battlements of false doctrine have been strengthened greatly in this case by the historic satanic method: altering the Bible.

3) Thus perverted, the new versions make saved people "competent as ministers of a new covenant" (2 Cor. 3:6) (NIV) instead of ***able ministers of the new testament*** (KJV). The Great Commission thus corrupted, ambassadors for Christ are to minister a *new covenant* where no one is to be taught and instructed (Jer. 31 & Heb. 8). Obviously this is in disruptive conflict with what our Savior definitively commissioned: *Go ye therefore, and **teach** all nations, baptizing them in the name of the Father, and of the Son, and of the Holy Ghost* (Matt 28:19). Christians are not ministers of a ***new covenant***. We are *able ministers of the **New Testament***!

4) The new versions paint themselves into a convoluted and contradictory corner, for Hebrews 9:17 in the KJV resolutely states: *For a **testament** is of force after men are dead: otherwise it is of no strength at all while the testator liveth.* Nothing could be plainer. Christ had to die before His ***New***

Testament could be of force. Ridiculously, the new versions have eliminated the word ***testament*** in their peculiar species of "scripture" and most all coincide with the NAS: "For a ***covenant*** is valid {only} when men are dead, for it is never in force while the one who made it lives." Stated thus, they proclaim that a ***covenant*** is invalid until he who makes it dies. Were the Adamic, Abrahamic, Noahic and Davidic *covenants* *in force* in the Old Testament? Did the One who made those *covenants* die in the Old Testament before they were *in force*? What nonsense! Yes, the *Old Testament covenants* were *in force*. No, obviously, God did not die in the Old Testament to put those *Old Testament covenants in force*! That is why the King James Bible did not make the mistake of calling the *testament* of Hebrews 9:17 a *covenant*. If it had stated, as the new versions do, that a *covenant* is of no force until the death of the one who makes it, then it would have been necessary that God would have had to die before the *covenants* of the Old Testament were in force![207] This is manifestly not true. Over 250 times in the Old Testament is the term *covenant(s)* used. *Testament(s)* is never used in the Old Testament. Plainly the Old Testament *covenants* were in force.

---

[207]It is necessary to address the question that since Hebrews 9:17 says that ... *a testament is of force after men are dead,* who then died in the OT to put the Old Testament in force? Obviously God did not. The answer is that the sacrificial animals died to put it in force. However since ...*it is not possible that the blood of bulls and of goats should take away sins* (Heb. 10:4), the Old Testament was limited in force. Sin could not be properly addressed until Christ came and died, for sins could not be cleared and redeemed. See Exodus 34:7, Romans 3:25 and Hebrews 9:15. Importantly, it still remains a mistake to replace *testament* with covenant. God's covenant promises to various men and Israel were in force without anyone's death. A *testament* is what requires the death of a testator, and while the Old Testament moderated by the blood of bulls and goats was only a band-aid, the matter was fully addressed by the death of the Lamb of God. The *testament* requires death. The *covenant* does not.

The scholars, translators and commentators continually shoot themselves in the foot (and perhaps higher) due to the frighteningly lax and flippant ease which they feel in subjecting the word of God to their incessant editing. They think nothing of changing and interchanging words. There exists no more finely attuned and precisely worded piece of literature in the world than the King James Bible. I indeed hold that its precision is perfect. The process of this intricate accuracy involved hundreds of years of purification and refinement beginning with the earliest English versions (and even prior to that). To change the weight and timber of one word is to affect the meticulously fine balance of some other truth interlinked with it. The fact is that there is no reason to believe that anyone but God Himself is responsible for the elaborate complexity of that balance of truth and wording in the AV 1611. Due to the philosophical misconceptions imparted by the education they have received, and due to the massive inertial weight of the scholastic propaganda to which they are subjected, most all mainline scholars, commentators and translators have three characteristics inbred within their own hearts which make them unfit and unqualified to be heeded. Those three characteristics are ***disbelief, irreverence and carelessness***. They no longer even ***believe*** the holy words of God are accessible and communicable in exactness, and because of this ***unbelief***, they largely proceed without the kind of ***reverence*** and humility that is prerequisite for dealing with God's holy things. Naturally, pious ***reverence*** is given a great deal of lip service at appropriate times, but there is little sense of the holy in the destruction and reconstruction that these academics foist upon the word of God. With the death of ***reverence*** quickly follows the funeral of ***carefulness***. Holy things are soon juggled and tossed about the room for they are no longer truly holy to their handlers. ***Carelessness*** in doctrine and flippancy in handling and altering the words of God is one of the true earmarks of apostasy.

Apparently without even a whimper of conscience or whisper from better judgment, these scholars and commentators have determined that the word *testament* no longer belongs in the Bible, that *covenant* is a word that is all-sufficient, and thus they have rammed recklessly together all the distinctive and separate shades of meaning and truth into one indiscernible conglomerate. They have hijacked the *New Covenant* and cast into confusion both *Old* and *New Testaments* as well as all the rest of the biblical *covenants*. All of this is done under the auspices of accuracy, clarity, and excellent scholarship.

Greek: The Perpetrators' Justification

In the day when plane hijackings were all the rage, the perpetrators always had some grand and glorious cause which justified the theft of time and resources, the disruption of society, and the threats upon the lives of innocent people. Terrorists, Jihadists, animal activists and radical environmentalists, anti-Semites and femi-nazis have always had profound and monumental causes that have animated and inspired them to perpetrate idiocy and disruption upon people with more important things to do in life than try to disrupt everyone else.

All Bible-believing Christians have a bucket-full of trouble as it is in battling to keep things in the proper order and priority. True Christians are in a spiritual fight and are on the front line in battle every day. They fight against the wickedness of their own hearts (flesh), the encroaching aggression of the realm in which they live (world), and then there is the ever-present chess master (the devil). With the *cares of the world, the deceitfulness of riches, the lusts of other things* (Mk. 4:19) and *the pleasures of this life* (Lk. 8:14) always lurking, Bible-believers are in an hourly fight to keep the word of God and the tenets of inspired truth first in their lives. While these soldiers sweat, fight, fail and rise again to the end that they might remain viable and faithful *stewards of the mysteries of God* (1 Cor. 4:1) and be found *good soldiers of Jesus Christ* (2 Tim. 2:3), misdirected but sincere little men peck away at the very foundations of the truth delivered to the children of God. In their grand cause of altering the words of Lord, they seek to undermine the saints' armory (Eph. 6:14-17), their provisions (Job 23:12), their guide (Ps. 119:105), and their anchor (Jer. 15:16).

Why do they do it?

It is invariable that these scholars, when called to account, will wave the banner of the original languages – the Greek and the Hebrew. It is their glorious cause. It is a cause fraught with many potential disasters to the truth of the scriptures. Many are misled and choose the wrong Greek. The pride of scholarship and "knowing" what the common man does not know is a well-documented propensity of corrupt human nature. The academic enclaves of scholars that populate around the study of Biblical languages are, and have been, inhabited by many confirmed egotists and heretics for a very long time indeed. Many is the scholar that has been instructed and trained by an utter apostate. What might such a student have learned, and how might his judgments have been altered by such instruction? A truly devastating snare is the precept that the Greek or Hebrew scholar becomes the final authority for what the Bible says – not the Bible itself. Should man's fallen opinions be considered eternally final? Finally, even for the most conscientious and faithful of heart, there is the inexactness and imprecision of timber, tone and meaning when studying a biblical language and translating it to another language. Many word forms and grammatical constructs have no exact parallel in the next language. No matter how faithful and true is the devotion of the scholar; he will find himself over-matched by the task, though he may well not admit it or even recognize it.

The scholar and translator must again be haunted by the verity that without God Himself being personally invested in both understanding the scriptures and the work of translation, the work will always invariably wind up corrupt and impure.

In the case outlined in this chapter, it is necessary to expose the foibles and fallacies produced by the scholars, commentators and translators when they came to this matter of the ***new covenant*** and the ***new testament.*** May the reader please remind himself that the *new covenant* is decisively and concisely defined in the English of the AV 1611? It is the *covenant* God will make with Israel at the start of Christ's millennial reign here on earth. The Israelites, by this covenant, will have the law and statutes of God imparted supernaturally into their minds and hearts, and this to the extent that they are not to be taught the Bible in the Millennium at all. There will be no need to teach them.

The *new testament*, as revealed in the Old Book, is a much broader term. Christ's death was necessary to institute it, and as such, all biblical ages after the death and resurrection of Christ are to be understood as being contained in the *new testament*. This includes the brief Apostolic Age, the 2000 year Church Age, The Tribulation, the Millennium and, finally, the Eternal Age – the New Heavens and the New Earth.

It is imperative to see that the *new covenant* is contained within the *new testament*. The *new covenant* is a subcategory – a dispensation – within the much more inclusive *new testament*. Importantly, in God's word, contained in the King James Bible, these truths are manifestly evident, clearly delineated, plainly distinct from one another, and providentially set at the table for our consumption and nourishment.

This is all recast and scrambled into confusion by the new bibles and most commentators. There is no word "testament" in the texts of most of the new bibles. (Outside of the scripture texts themselves, they do still contain the headings and titles "New Testament" and "Old Testament," but the word is not contained within what they consider the scripture texts themselves.) All distinction between *covenants* and *testaments* has been erased almost uniformly across the board by the scholars' and translators' fateful decision to use the word *covenant(s)* only. Everything in the new versions is a *covenant.* In so doing they have entangled the terms and concepts, and have obscured to the eyes of most every Christian any difference between the two ideas. So much for *rightly dividing the word of truth* (2 Tim. 2:15). This is accomplished by eliminating the differences in concept and meaning by ***obliterating*** the differences in words.

These scholars do this for what reason? Why, because of the Greek, of course!

Though the doctrine involves the Old Testament passage in Jer.31, the real damage is done via the New Testament Greek. The words *covenant(s), testament,* and *testator* occur a total of 39 times in the King James New Testament. Of these times:

Covenant(s) **occurs 23 times**
Testament **occurs 14 times**
Testator **occurs 2 times**

In every one of the cases above, the translation comes from the Greek word ***diatheke*** or a derivative thereof. Strong, not surprisingly, gives the Greek word the definition of *covenant* or *testament.*[208] Thus revealed is the reason the scholars erased the word *testament* from the texts of the new versions and obliterated any distinctions in their commentaries. The AV 1611 distinguishes distinctly between the concepts of *covenant* and *testament,* but since "the Greek" presents only one

---

[208]Strong, James. Strongs Analytical Concordance

root word form, the scholars dismissively overrule the King James, eradicate the separate concept of *testament,* and fatally mingle the two ideas as if they were one.

Thus is the body of Christ so sacrificially and wondrously served and edified by the learned men. They rejected the work of more excellent scholars than they (AV translators), eliminated distinguishing verbiage from God's holy word (*testament*), co-mingled and conjoined concepts God intended to be understood separately, and unraveled and undid plain doctrine which the Lord had providentially settled in the translation of the King James Bible.

The *New Testament,* the *New Covenant* and the King James Bible

Having touched somewhat on the far-reaching consequences of the misjudgments in this chapter, and having visited related ramifications in prior chapters, it is important to inventory once again, not only the honor and glory of the Lord's work (Ps. 111:3), but the disgraceful and destructive labors of precipitous and foolhardy men.

Neither the new versions nor modern scholarship provide the clarity that they claim. The King James Bible is perfectly clear and precise about what the *new covenant* is, and its foresight in distinguishing the contrast between the *new covenant* and the *new testament* reveals not only the masterful design of the Author, but the living nature of the word of God (Heb. 4:12). Once the reader is alerted and understands all of the differences that those distinct terms communicate, the clarity of the AV in this case, as in others, is stark.

The devil and his little helpers must be given their due. The manipulation of human nature at large is a mighty accomplishment. Publishers and proponents of the new versions have succeeded in unifying the masses in a reverberating, and near-to-universal, chant: "The King James is hard to understand. The new versions are clearer." The masses not only chant it, apparently they also believe it. Nevertheless, the evidence presented in this work is to the contrary. The new versions do not clarify the truth. They obscure it. In this case - and this case is far from unusual - mainstream Christian scholarship, and a great segment of Fundamental scholarship, are a far cry from providing a true witness and from being faithful stewards and ambassadors for the truth of Jesus Christ. In the ritual and stylized dance of the scholars with their traditions, their philosophies, the reverence of their academic predecessors, their fear of man, their preconceptions, their pride and their prejudices, they have only succeeded in raising dust, trampling truth under foot and bumbling into and kicking over the Lamp that lights the feet of the saints.

The light and clarity they so arrogantly proclaim as such victories for modern scholarship, only turns out to be obscurity and darkness misnamed. *Woe unto them that call evil good, and good evil;* ***that put darkness for light, and light for darkness****; that put bitter for sweet, and sweet for bitter* (Isa. 5:20).

The Greek was not helpful in any respect. The usual tactic by the scholars, no matter what may seem vague or unclear in the scriptures, is to seek immediate answers and light from the Greek or Hebrew. These are the true final authorities for these men and women, and they are advertised as the exclusive treasure trove of higher knowledge and the exclusive portals into true spiritual understanding. Ideologically, this sounds lofty and noble in a pamphlet or in a classroom filled with the naïve. The product proves to fall short of expectations and predictions, in actuality.

For the umpteenth time, in the case of the *covenants* and *testaments* of this chapter, there was no disharmony or obscurity in the doctrine and words of the AV 1611. It presented a perfectly defined word picture of the limits, boundaries and details of the relation of the *new covenant* and the *new testament.* The scholars apparently fled to the Greek before even trying to grasp the English, and in doing so they overlooked that the King's English made the defining distinctions between the two concepts, and that running back to the Greek yielded nothing in the way of understanding or light. The Greek obscured the differences between the two concepts, and the truth as well, because the Greek only presents one singular word form. The Greek used one word. The English translators used two. Those who prejudicially adopted the Greek as their final authority and dismissed the King James' English, were thus left with no grounds to differentiate between what the Holy Spirit revealed as two distinctly separate ideals.

There is meaning and truth in the King James' English not found in the Greek. This is a most repulsive and disreputable statement to make as far as mainline, orthodox scholarship is concerned. It will be the cause for great disdain and disgust for most of biblical academia, and will predictably end in the author being called disparaging names by reviewers and critics. These spiritual expletives *(Ruckmanite, King James Only, unscholarly, non-intellectual, Heretic*, etc.) are designed and intended to drive one into ostracized silence and they execute an expulsion from the circles of any possible academic respect.

This certain and assured response, nonetheless, does not answer the evidence presented in this chapter. How is one to answer the fact that the King James English sets forward clear, edifying and consistent doctrine and truth that the Greek does not? The AV distinguishes by words and plain terms ***what the Greek does not distinguish at all!*** The English provides light that the Greek only obscures. Light and spiritual understanding is found in the Elizabethan English scriptures, and a Greek student, limiting himself to the study of the Greek would not receive that light!

The English provides distinctness and clarity where the Greek is ambiguous. A Christian is greatly benefited by adhering to the King James English and is helped in no way whatsoever in retreating to the Greek. Returning to the "original" Greek as the primary appeal causes a great deal of trouble, and undermines clarity and sound doctrine.

The subtitle for this book is *How the King James Bible Resolves the Ambiguity of the Original Languages.* As distasteful as this entire concept is to traditional biblical scholars, it seems rather evident that by whatever means, the ambiguous and more general singular term found in the Greek, ***diatheke***, is rendered as two separate terms in English to clearly define the difference between the *new covenant* and the *new testament,* among other things. This very quality of the AV has been repeatedly demonstrated in this work, and outperforms the Greek or Hebrew in this respect. At some juncture, evidence presented should tip a balance to the extent that acknowledgment be given to evident truth.

It has been exclaimed for very long that all the treasures of the Bible actually reside in the original language texts. Is biblical academia sincere and honest enough to acknowledge that at least sometimes the sword cuts in the other direction? Bible-believers for many years now have been subjected to the propaganda of the scholar's union. This has habitually proven itself to be a band of men and women who have a studied and well developed condescension toward the biblical knowledge and intellectual capabilities of the common Christian. The scholars believe they hold the keys to knowledge that no man with a common Bible can apprehend. It may as well be faced that these academics have largely conducted themselves as those who have an absolute monopoly on their product, and for far too long the actual priesthood of believers has sickeningly acquiesced to what has become in fact a ***bully's mentality***. It is indispensable to realize that what these scholars have dictated all these years has been merely a species of rhetoric and propaganda that has disarmed the average Christian and wholly enabled the academic mafia. Generally, men are intimidated by other men with greater knowledge or training. Too many Christians have rolled over and shut their mouths about the treasure of God in the King James Bible because the scholars know Greek, the average Christian does not. Even the Bible-believing saint does not cherish the idea of looking stupid, and so it is natural to avoid getting in a sword fight with someone the saint secretly fears has knowledge that the saint does not have. Thus scholarship has succeeded in stealing the Bible because the scholars have controlled the propaganda and brainwashed the students that Bible-believing parents and pastors have sent to their godly institutions. Those same ill-deserving scholars have largely convinced the entire body of Christ that they are the arbiters of all truth.

Think about it this way, though: the scholars know Greek and Hebrew, but it has been proven that they do not know the Bible. Their carelessness and irreverence, their notoriously poor doctrine and spiritually impotent preaching and teaching reveals that there is something dreadfully missing in their lives' works. They know Greek and Hebrew but they have done precious little to advance true biblical knowledge and power. They know Greek and Hebrew and by that knowledge alone they have advanced themselves to a lordly authority above those they treat as peons and peasants, intellectually.

A Bible-believing saint, attending a true Bible-believing church, on the other hand, may not know Greek, but does he know the Bible? Obviously, no one knows the Bible as they should, but if one understands, for instance, the distinction between the ***new covenant*** and the ***new testament,*** that same one grasps more of the Bible than Matthew Henry, Adam Clarke, the Wycliffe commentators and all the editors, translators and scholars of every one of the rancid new versions! In actuality, who knows more – the well instructed Bible-believing saint or the scholars? Who is it that has more useful and fruitful knowledge? What is the knowledge to be preferred, the knowledge that largely has profited the scholars nothing, or the true and potent knowledge of the Old Book that inspires holiness, feeds men's souls, calls men to preach, wins the lost to Christ and sets the spirit of a sinner alight?

The English expands on what is in the Greek. Contrary to that material contained in scholarly and institutional propaganda, it is the English text of the King James that elucidates, expands and explains what is contained in the Greek. According to them, it is supposed to be the other way around. It is Greek which is supposed to illuminate the inferior English. Once again, in this case that is certainly not the case! There is no discernible differentiation made between the *new testament* and the *new covenant* in Greek. Except by context, the reader would never know that there was a difference. It is the King James English, held in such disrepute by the scholars and their traveling "amen section," that makes the issue clear to the Bible-believer.

In the case outlined in this chapter, does this not make the English of the King James Bible superior to the Greek? Though rank blasphemy to most seminary chairs and classrooms, how can an objective observer but conclude that the English of the AV 1611 is superior to its Greek mother-texts in this particular instance? The KJV gives light, instruction and revelation in plain and clear words, none of which is contained in the Greek or in the new versions and commentators which flee to the Greek. Phrased another way: **how isn't the English**

superior to the Greek? Would one expect vigilant and informed Bible-believers to deny the plain words delivered unto them? Should scholarship expect Bible-loving saints to deny what their English translation says that the saints might nurture the scholars little man-made doctrine of universal translational inferiority? Apparently the scholars fully expect Bible-believers to subjugate themselves to preconceptions which not only protect the scholars' delusive livelihood, but which also supports the scholarly practice of filtering and limiting the light that the saints are to receive from the Bible God delivered to them. In Paul's words, *God forbid* (Rom. 9:14). Conclusion: a Christian that reads and studies the AV 1611 English is better equipped as a Christian, in this case, than a mere student of the original language. Here is a verifiable instance, among others, where the English is demonstrably superior to the original language texts used by the scholars.

To lean upon the Greek as a final authority, in this instance, is to retreat again into more obscure and less distinct knowledge and, in fact, darkness. Via all of the almost universal anti-King James propaganda, we have all been thoroughly remonstrated with regarding the harmonious bliss found in the Greek texts and the sadly inferior nature of the old "King Jimmy." Nevertheless, the demonstrable facts and fruit of the matter do not seem to coincide with the cacophony of rhetoric.

Substantive evidence has been presented here validating that what was accomplished for the Lord *by* and *through* the King James translators (taking into account the vast and sacrificial labors of their predecessors) was a ground-breaking, superior and unmatched product in comparison to anything since. Also presented is evidence that the finished work of the AV demonstrably exceeds the limits and bounds of even the best preserved original language texts in practicality, light, revelation and detail. To hold to Greek as a final authority in this case is to disdain and disavow what God accomplished in the translation of the King James English.

Who is responsible for this clarity and superiority found in the AV? This question has been asked before, and it will be asked yet again. As the King James' superiority and clarity has been demonstrated and discussed with respect to the specifics of this chapter, someone must be given the credit for it.

By those who love the AV and defend it, the translators are vociferously defended for their Christian characters and scholarly impeccability. This defense is largely undeniable and objections to the contrary mostly come from those who are entirely set to reproach the King James Bible regardless of any evidence whatsoever. All KJV defenders read and studied stand in awe of the intellectual and Christian qualities of these men and the astounding product that was the result of their labors. That notwithstanding, many pro-King James men become instantly offended and *offensive* at the suggestion that the AV translators were providentially led and guided in their work. The possibility that there was a profound and intimate supernatural guidance and leading in the details of the translation is often cause for an explosive negative response by even some of the most erstwhile AV defenders, and the suggestion of such is likely to lead to that old, well-worn option of calling he who suggested the possibility ugly names.

However, if the AV translators went beyond the details revealed in the Greek to make the type of distinctions between the *new testament* and the *new covenant* that are undeniably found in the King James English, who is responsible? To whom should credit be given? Would modern day scholars truly praise the 1611 translators for extending themselves beyond the bounds of the Greek texts? In short, for those who appreciate the grandness and superiority of the work, they are perfectly happy to give God praise for the strictly human decisions and academic excellence that led to the Bible we now hold in our hands. That is, if it is merely mortal man's academic excellence that delivered the King James Bible to us, most Bible-believers are satisfied to abide by the KJV translators' product in contrast to those of our present day who seem so giddy to abide by the scholastic fruit of much lessor men, semi-apostates and infirm compromisers. If the saints must lay their loyalty at the feet of mortal men and trust explicitly their work as men, Bible-believers will happily be subject to the AV translators' judgments and understanding rather than yield ourselves to the alternative crowd.

In the end, it does not seem reasonable that the King James translators should get the glory for the excellence of their work. They would not have accepted the glory for it. The difficulty and complexity of their labors would be burdensome and all-consuming enough. How would they humanly have managed to organize and agree on the intricacy, minute order and detail of the end product as mere committeemen? How would they ever have managed all the delicate distinctions, the uniformity, the balance, and the precision?

Brothers and sisters in Christ, it is not a heresy to hold and embrace the idea that God meticulously led the King James translators in that committee, any more than it is a heresy to believe that God led Wycliffe and Tyndale in their works. These were pious, praying Christian men and spiritual warriors. They loved God and were born in a window of time in which the Lord brought them to a critical crossroad. Great Britain was rising and would be the world superpower for many years and would spread her language to the ends of the earth and even unto the last days. The Catholic Church had been kicked in the slats by Bible-believing street preachers and witnesses, and while she was rolling on the ground for a time, the Lord needed to culminate a great work with respect to His word. He had opportunity to bring the Bible out of two disparate Biblical languages that were largely dead, into a singular language which would prove to be the universal language of the last days. Far to the west, across the sea, was a vast land which would speak that language, become the beacon of liberty, refuge and the gospel for the remainder of the 2nd millennium AD.

It is certain that these men prayed, fasted and pled for God's guidance. Many have prayed for that very thing, and those prayers have been answered. Is the idea that the Lord guided those translators in specific and even minute fashion really such an outlandish idea? This author holds that the patterns, plan and design in the King James Bible mark the very fingerprints and handiwork of God. I believe there is every reason to credit the Author of the Book with the intricacies and details found within the Book. God gets the glory for the inspiration and preservation of His word, but it does not end there, though many scholars wish that it did. The Lord gets the credit for His counsel, leadership, guidance and oversight in the translation of His holy word, as well.

Chapter 14

Death in the Pot

> *So they poured out for the men to eat. And it came to pass, as they were eating of the pottage, that they cried out, and said, O thou man of God,* ***there is death in the pot****. And they could not eat thereof.* (2 Kings 4:40)

The narrative of the story that provides the backdrop for the incident in the verse above, alerts the reader to the fact that there was a dearth in the land in those days. Even in dearth, men need the necessities of life – including food. So, in the gathering of the food to feed the sons of the prophets, at the behest of the man of God, one among them gathered a lap full of gourds, which when shredded into the stew served only to poison the entire batch. Understandably, the alarmed response to this development was the despairing cry, *O thou man of God, there is* ***death in the pot.***

The *dearth*, in verse 38 of the passage, cannot but remind the Bible-believer of that prophesied by Amos 8:11, *I will send a famine in the land, not a famine of bread, nor a thirst for water, but of hearing the words of the LORD.* One is to recall that, as in dearth when men must still eat, famine does not alter the fact that *Man shall not live by bread alone, but by every word that proceedeth out of the mouth of God* (Matt. 4:4). Even in famine though, with the necessity and indispensability of food more emphasized for its scarcity, the dangers of poison and death cannot be overlooked. A careless gathering and shredding of the wrong ingredient means that there can be ***death in the pot.***

If Amos 8:11 is applicable to the spiritual condition of today's Laodicean Christianity, and if the famine is a reality today, quite interesting is the form which that famine takes. If this famine is a reality (it is), one must acknowledge that it is for no lack of "bibles." Christian households usually contain multiple bibles, different versions though they are, and even many homes of lost men and women contain bibles sitting on shelves and coffee tables. The fact is that the Bible is still interwoven in American culture, although this is less and less so as the days go by. Political candidates exploit passages and wrest certain sentiments from the Bible, perverse though the applications be. Certain, though usually distorted and scorned, aspects of biblical culture find their way into movies and entertainment. The cameras for NFL football games still find John 3:16 signs placed strategically for viewing by the spectators across TV-land. I recall that a certain permanently placed trash bin located on the public sidewalk in downtown Minneapolis was actually left for several years by city workers reading in spray-painted glory, "Jesus Saves"!

Nor can the great drought be for lack of churches. Churches abound in great numbers everywhere, and many of them show evidence of being very well attended. The mega-church movement has yielded way to what are now giga-churches, that is, churches even more monstrous in size. Great numbers of worshipers now flock in droves to vast auditoriums where they are treated to a concert atmosphere, live bands, worship teams, and slick new philosophies of how to minister the word of God to "our culture."

While these things are indeed a reality in modern Christianity, it is still the lamentation of discerning and biblically oriented Christians that both the Bible and Christ seem to have less and less potency and impact in lives today. Somehow the familiarity many Americans have with the scriptures, the only medium they have for knowing God, seems to be of the unholy, unsanctified and irreverent variety. Though so many are blessed to be so familiar with certain tenets and concepts from the Book, these precepts seem to wield little more potency in their lives than does Monopoly money in the United States' economy. Certain Bible commentators, in discussing the plethora of bible versions and Bible reference tools available to students, have called this condition an "embarrassment of riches." If this assessment is really true, the trends in American "Christianity" are interesting, though tragic, because as mega-churches and giga-churches grow, as the "Emerging Church" *emerges*, and as the "Purpose Driven Church" proceeds with its *purpose*, men continue to meander further and further away from the Bible, and the revealed attributes of God's character, as their churches emphasize the scriptures less and less.

No description of this sad Laodicean situation can do justice to the profound tragedy of the matter. That Christianity in general should lack potency is catastrophic, not only because, in such condition, it cannot affect the salvation and transformation of the unsaved world, but because it also means that Christians have frittered away the responsibility and the glorious privilege of their great commission and stewardship of the mysteries of God (1 Cor. 4:1). Christ said

> ***All power is given unto me in heaven and in earth. Go ye therefore****, and teach all nations, baptizing them in the name of the Father, and of the Son, and of the Holy Ghost: Teaching them to observe all things whatsoever I have commanded you:* ***and, lo, I am with you alway, even unto the end of the world.*** *Amen.* (Matt. 28:18-20)

If *all power is given* to Him, and it is He that commissioned Christians, how is it that Christianity seems cursed with such desultory powerlessness? If Christ gave power to men, commissioned men, and then promised His presence to those very men, how is it that those men now have to resort to rock bands, fog machines, carnal side-shows and gimmicks to affect the lives of men?

The answers to these questions are not as difficult or as complicated as one might imagine. The simple fact is that the mighty river of God's power and efficacy flows along a certain stream bed. If one desires to stand upon the banks of the ponderous trek of the Mississippi River, such a one should not travel to New Hampshire or Arizona, for the Mississippi does not flow through either of those places. Christ did not promise that His power would be accessible to man at every whimsical juncture. Man seems to be of the polluted opinion that God and Christ are committed to using most anything or everything that man may devise. The name of Christ is not a magic incantation by which all fleshy or stupid innovations or methods are cleansed, purified and made useful. He saved sinners to change man, not to change for man. The power of God does not necessarily flow to Christians wherever they may be, especially when they are in a place that is repulsive to Him. The saints are to migrate spiritually to the banks of the river through which the power of God flows, and stay there.

The Dissemination of Power

The power of God must have a source and a fount from which it flows. Christians know the source is God, but it is essential to understand just how it is that the power is dispensed and disseminated to men. Does it come via prayer beads, the sacraments or the prayers of Benny Hinn? It is understood that by nature there are things inexplicable and unpredictable about the power of God. It is necessary to grasp that the power of God is not dispensed as from a candy machine, where one may put in money and receive his choice of items at his own whim and pleasure. It is also understood that there are precepts and principles which rule many of the things that God will and will not bless, and many of those ordinances also apply to where and how He will bestow His power.

> 2 *Grace and peace be multiplied unto you* ***through the knowledge of God,*** *and of Jesus our Lord,*
> 3 *According as* **his divine power** *hath given unto us all things that pertain unto life and godliness,* ***through the knowledge of him*** *that hath called us to glory and virtue:*
> 4 *Whereby are given unto us* ***exceeding great and precious promises****: that by these ye might be partakers of the divine nature, having escaped the corruption that is in the world through lust.* (2 Pet. 1:2-4)

In 2 Peter 1:3, the apostle testifies that what ***his divine power*** has given us, was accessed ***through the knowledge of him*** *that hath called us to glory and virtue.* The plain witness of the verse is that the treasures and riches of God's power are accessed through his knowledge. That knowledge is irrevocably connected to God's *exceeding great and precious promises* (vs.4). Those *promises* can be no other than the words of God.

> 5 *Having a form of godliness, but* ***denying the power thereof:*** *from such turn away.*
> 6 *For of this sort are they which creep into houses, and lead captive silly women laden with sins, led away with divers lusts,*
> 7 *Ever learning, and never able to come to* ***the knowledge of the truth.*** (2 Tim. 3:5-7)

From 2 Timothy 3:5, it is clearly seen that there is a power in true godliness. Further clarified in the passage is a firm diagnosis regarding those with the mere form of godliness but who lack the power thereof. The problem is that they are *never able to come to* ***the knowledge of the truth*** (vs.7). In this way, the power of God is once again linked to *the knowledge of the truth.* No Bible-believer has a moment's confusion as to what that truth is. *Sanctify them through thy truth:* ***thy word is truth*** (Jn. 17:17).

> *Who being the brightness of his glory, and the express image of his person, and upholding all things* ***by the word of his power****, when he had by himself purged our sins, sat down on the right hand of the Majesty on high;*
> (Heb. 1:3)

Christ, who is God, the Creator and Upholder of the universe and all of its elements, clearly carries out this vast and unimaginable accomplishment ***by the word of His power***. The Faithful Witness once again legitimizes the Lord's clear position that the word of God is the access point to the power of God.

Obviously, the word of God's power was given to man that he might have power in his own life. The natural progression of this potency is that men might then minister the gospel of Christ and the words of God to other men, hence, the Great Commission, which was mentioned earlier. It is through the ministry of the word that the power of God is passed on and on. This is the purpose of Bibles and churches. This may seem elementary knowledge to some, but it is the forsaking of the elemental and rudimentary things in Christianity that has led the body of Christ to this present *falling away* (2 Thes. 2:3). Elementally, then, a powerful Christianity, and a potent ministry, requires a powerful Bible and a powerful means of ministering the word of God. It is for this reason that Paul says,

> *For the* ***preaching of the cross*** *is to them that perish foolishness; but unto us which are saved* ***it is the power of God.*** (1 Cor. 1:18)

Paul further testifies that,

> *4 And my speech and my preaching was not with enticing words of man's wisdom,* ***but in demonstration of the Spirit and of power:***
> *5 That your faith should not stand in the wisdom of men, but in the* ***power of God.***
> (1 Cor. 2:4-5)

God did empower the men of the Bible to speak in His behalf. This authority was often accompanied with signs and wonders in the days of Israel's emergence and greatness, and during the times of Christ's ministry. The more specific empowerment spoken of at this point was given at the Pentecost feast in Acts 2, when men received the Holy Ghost in a way they had not known before. The great lesson of all this is that while men today are often on a great, vague and winding quest for the power of the Holy Spirit, and while prayer, fasting and personal holiness have a great deal to do with the realization of this power, men also often ignore the actual contact point where access to the power of God is attained – the words of the living God. Men are quick to sing that "faith is the victory," but they are terribly slow, and nowadays often altogether delinquent in acknowledging whence that faith comes.

The great mystery of the powerlessness of both ministries and the lives of men has to do with men's unbelief and lack of faith in the word of God and the church's infidelity in believing it and preaching it.

The Demise of Potency

It has been the observation of the perceptive that men often have complexes about their shortcomings. The famous *Napoleonic Complex* is related to the preoccupation of short men with the projection of power and successful conquest in comparison to the more sizable specimens of their gender. Often, the preoccupation with his perceived shortcoming overwhelms the discernment of the individual and the results appear either silly or even demented to other men, depending upon the severity of the case. Some men are so compulsively sensitive about hair loss that they resort to comb-overs that take on the appearance of birds' nests, or in the case of high winds, a partial scalping. Some "big-boned" ladies flee from horizontal stripes on a garment as from marauding Mongols.

A little levity notwithstanding, it has been observed that much of Christianity is compulsively obsessed with genuine power. The Fundamentalist movement that endeavored to draw great crowds and did succeed in building huge churches, seemed to be forever reciting and salivating over the numbers of people saved and the number of saints baptized at Pentecost. They longed for, and in some cases, lusted for and sought the same successes as in Acts 2 to such a degree as to employ gimmickry to get the great crowds to services. This resulted at times in unabashed crowd manipulation during the invitation, and out-and-out misrepresentation of attendance and "soul-winning" counts. This movement continues at this hour, and many lives have been changed under the portions of these ministries that do administer the real power of God through the word. There does still exist, though, an element of many Fundamental ministries that instead of reliance upon the professed power of God, they overemphasize loyalty to "the man of God" for manipulative purposes. Guilt, easy-believism, quick-prayerism, promotion, marketing, emotionalism and other elements, have all too often been the fires built that have kept ministries going rather than reliance upon the power of God through the ministry of the word.

The Charismatics and Pentecostals are famous for their unending claims of ongoing miracles, tongues and signs after the manner of the apostles. Personally known are ministers who claim that the dead could be raised, though they are still batting exactly .000. Talking in tongues and "miracle-working" are the main entrees in the Charismatic menu. Then again, how might the authenticity of tongues be verified when it is claimed that the tongue spoken is a "heavenly prayer language"? Crutches and wheelchairs may be discarded, but then again, perhaps they were never needed. It may be testified that great pains and agonies were miraculously removed, but the results are difficult to authenticate. That which may be authenticated is avoided. No Pentecostal drinks poison as set forth in Mark 16, nor does it seem to dawn upon any of the healers with international reputations what an opportunity for the display of their power exists in cancer wards and hospice centers throughout the world. Is it not funny how the deathly ill are expected to make their way to stadiums which healers lease for their "campaigns," rather than the healers making their way to the places where the dying and infirmed lie?

It seems further strange that mainline evangelical and non-denominational Christianity boasts and exults in the life-changing and transforming power of Jesus Christ, when, truth be told, there is pitifully little evidence of transformation or evident changes in so many of the lives of such Christians. The immediate objection to such a statement is, naturally, that it is judgmental and overtly hypercritical. It is certainly understood that the immediate transformation that results from the new birth is inward. A new Christian has been Born-again, washed in the blood, and sealed by the Spirit (Eph. 4:30) inwardly. Instantaneous outward manifestations of the new creature (2 Cor. 5:17) are often tenuous, sometimes disingenuous, and can be misleading. It is further understood that beginning at salvation, God *worketh in you* (Phil. 2:13), and that works must then exercise its way outward from the heart, and the evidence and fruit of redemption is seen on the outside only after both time and effort (Phil. 2:12). Nevertheless, a criticism borne out of both observation and scripture does not revolve around the immediate manifestations of a brand new creature in Christ. It revolves around the verity that many mainline "Christians" who are well into the Christian life time-wise, claim the transformational potency of Christianity without much evidence for it. They are "powerfully transformed," yet what are the fruits*?*

> *16 **Ye shall know them by their fruits**. Do men gather grapes of thorns, or figs of thistles?*
> *17 Even so every good tree bringeth forth good fruit; but a corrupt tree bringeth forth evil fruit.*
> *18 A good tree cannot bring forth evil fruit, neither can a corrupt tree bring forth good fruit.*
> *19 Every tree that bringeth not forth good fruit is hewn down, and cast into the fire.*
> *20 **Wherefore by their fruits ye shall know them**.* (Matt. 7:16-20)

Blunt admonitions – they seem even *brutal* to the thin-skinned, seeker-friendly Christians of today - adorn all the writings of the New Testament scriptures, demanding separation from the world and the ungodly. Idols, fornication, adultery, habits that gain *power* over us (1 Cor. 6:12), the works of darkness, ungodly friendships, immodesty, immoderation, intemperance, doctrinal and moral compromise, the love of money, lusts, wicked imaginations – in the Bible, all these transgressions and more are carefully and tediously documented and rebuked as being oppositional and unbefitting a genuine Christian. Yes, genuine Christians may fall over some of these sins, but we also know that many movements that have grown out of mainline evangelical Christianity have repudiated the separation from these sinful things as being pharisaical. Any rebuke of immoderate and sinful behavior is denounced as judgmental, critical and adversarial to the grace of Christ.

The result of this departure from sound doctrine is that now there are vast numbers and movements of "Christians" who profess the powerful transformation of their inner spiritual lives, and yet their visible testimonies still sport fruits that include adulterous relationships, smoking, drinking, homosexuality, party lifestyles, forbidden friendships, the world's music, immodesty and a hundred other things that remain as marks and tattoos of ungodliness in their lives. Entire churches and church movements are built upon the precept that almost all outward standards of behavior and deportment are legalistic and hypocritical in nature. They are preoccupied with the power that changes lives, but the observable potency and pure fruit of their Christianity is often far from evident on any kind of practical basis. The question we mull, is not so much whether they are Christians, though some would consider this a justifiable consideration, but rather, where is the glorious and promised power behind their profession?

> *Having a form of godliness, but denying the power thereof: from such turn away.*
>
> (2 Tim. 3:5)

The still-fallen, corrupt nature of even saved people – the *old man* of Romans 6:6, Ephesians 4:22 and Colossians 3:9 – guarantees that there will be a proportion of genuinely regenerate Christians *who walk... after the flesh* (Rom 8:1). The power of the gospel and of the word of God certainly relies in part upon man to consciously and willingly *mortify the deeds of the body* (Rom. 8:13), and to *put on the new man* (Col. 3:10). In this way, the power of Christ in the lives of men is certainly often undercut by nothing more than man's own flesh.

There is, however, something else that grossly undermines the work and power of God in the lives of the regenerate. Ever since God began speaking to man by His word, Satan (Gen. 3:1) has tirelessly and unceasingly conspired to sow distrust in man's heart for the very thing that gives man power to overcome the world, the flesh and the devil: the words of God. From Eve's tragic encounter with the Serpent in Genesis 3, to Christ's final warning at the close of the canon of scripture (Rev. 22:18-19), Satan's greatest conspiratorial work has been to entice man to distrust Holy Scripture.

Final authority is the ultimate philosophical issue for man. Who gets to determine and pronounce in finality what is so? What word, what statute, what court is the place of final and ultimate appeal? For Adam and Eve, it was *But of the tree of the knowledge of good and evil, thou shalt not eat of it: for in the day that thou eatest thereof thou shalt surely die* (Gen. 2:17), and that is very exactly how it turned out. God's pronouncement was final! However, Satan convinced Eve that such was not so. So it has been from that time until now. Cain, Noah, Abraham, Isaac, Jacob, Moses, David, every prophet, every king, every apostle - and finally, you and I – all have been given *the word of His power* (Heb. 1:3), yet Satan has set himself to break our confidence in that word, and we are either empowered by keeping it or we are weakened and broken by discounting or altering it.

Long before so-called "Fundamentalists" opted to set their church-building reliance upon marketing and promotional gimmicks as well as crowd manipulation, the power of their message was gutted and drained of its life-blood in the halls of academia, in the sacred name of scholarship. The Charismatics and Pentecostals, with their predisposed weakness for walking by sight and for miracles, were still the more compromised by the Satanic and scholarly precept that the words of the Bible, which they read, might have alternate variations of meaning. Why should one trouble one's self to learn to *rightly divide the word of truth* with respect to signs and miracles, when the words which are to be divided rightly are variable, depending upon which translation one uses, or depending on which scholar to which one appeals? By the 20th century, when Evangelicalism arose, men grew to question and alter the word of God as a matter of course. New versions were published and printed with almost mechanized precision. Every man who cared to try was given permission by proxy to investigate and question the accuracy of the Bible he read. Every man routinely heard the Bible's words wrested and corrected. Every man was given license by scholarship's sordid claims and practices to basically believe what parts of the Bible he should choose, and to reject that which he thought, or had heard, was inaccurate. In this manner, Evangelicalism departed from several central doctrines of the Bible: separation, negativism, distinction from the world, non-compromise in preceptual matters, and non-dialogue with heathen ideals. So, Evangelicalism lost its power, as did the Pentecostals, the Protestants and the Fundamentalists. They lost their power, for they forsook their power: the word of God: the final authority: the court of final appeal.

An alien and strange interloper became "Christianity's" final appeal. This trespasser, this intruder, was accepted as the ultimate authority in spite of the Father's blunt, bone-breaking bludgeon of a warning:

> *For it is written, **I will destroy the wisdom of the wise**, and will **bring to nothing the understanding of the prudent**. Where is the wise? where is the scribe? where is the disputer of this world? **hath not God made foolish the wisdom of this world?*** (1 Cor. 1:19-20)

And,

> ***For the wisdom of this world is foolishness with God.*** *For it is written,* ***He taketh the wise in their own craftiness*** (1 Cor. 3:19).

Indeed, the very wisdom God promised to destroy became the standard by which men in seeking to know the Bible rejected its sublime truths and disconnected themselves from its power. Lowly, unbelieving, bastardized scholarship became their final appeal, but rather than singular and final answers, scholarship only provided men with a multiplicity of possibilities, a Bible full of uncertainties, and doctoral degrees in the ministry of questions.

> *Neither give heed to fables and endless genealogies,* ***which minister questions, rather than godly edifying which is in faith****: so do.* (1 Tim. 1:4)

In this way the words of Phinehas' wife insinuate themselves across the ages like the slender, accusing fingers of a creeping, haunting fog: *The glory is departed* (1 Sam 4:21). And with the *glory* went the *power.*

The Disguise of Pretense

In Genesis 25:31-34, Esau sold Jacob his birthright. It was a great loss and Esau was unable to hide from the fact that the birthright was gone, sold into the hands of another. In 1 Samuel 4:21-22, Israel, in stupidity, allowed the Philistines to capture the ark. The aforementioned, heart-broken mother declared Israel *Ichabod...the glory is departed* (4:21). Plainly the ark was gone. There was no hiding the fact that the Hamites possessed it. No amount of pretense could change the facts. A birthright was sold and the lifeblood of a nation was captured: the ark of God.

The departure of the power of Christianity is a good deal more subtle. Samson had been an unholy terror to the Philistines in the days in which he was judge in Israel, but after a nap in the lap of a traitorous hag, Samson arose again to do battle with his foes with this particular lack of understanding: *And he wist not that the LORD was departed from him* (Judg. 16:20). To the church in Sardis, the Lord declares, *I know thy works, that thou hast a name that thou livest,* ***and art dead*** (Rev. 3:1), and the Laodiceans He promises to spew, *Because thou sayest, I am rich, and increased with goods, and have need of nothing;* ***and knowest not*** *that thou art wretched, and miserable, and poor, and blind, and naked* (Rev. 3:17). It is reasonable to conclude that Sardis did not know how dead she was and the divine judgment is that the church of Laodicea knows not the depths of her tragedy, either.

So, what do folks do when they find a power outage in their religion or their Christianity? When the ark was gone from Israel, there was no disguising that it was gone. When Jesus' earthly parents lost track of Him in Luke 2 when He was twelve years old, there was simply no denying or misrepresenting the fact that He had been lost. Jesus was plainly gone. But, the power of God and the presence of Christ spiritually are a great deal more subtle than those examples. Neither of those things is present in a material and physical way. Each of those things defies the physical senses, quite unlike the actual ark and the twelve year old mortal presence of the Lord. *For we walk by faith, not by sight* (2 Cor. 5:7). So much of what is known as the reality and presence of God in our lives is defiant almost entirely of our physical senses. Thus, when asking, "What do people do when they find the power of God missing from their lives, works and ministries?" the answer is not at all difficult. The answer is, ***they pretend***. They simply… *pretend.*

The fact that their god, Baal, did in no wise speak or answer, did not curb the efforts or the zeal of the 850 prophets of 1 Kings 18. They went right on doing their pagan, Elvis impersonations, all the while scourging and flagellating themselves like a flock of Franciscans. Jereboam's two idols are not recorded to have wielded any power or worked any miracles, but that did not stop the ten northern tribes of Israel from serving them lustily and faithfully. They simply *pretended* their gods were real, just as the Philistines had pretended that Dagon's power was real, and just as the Muslims pretend that Allah is a potent force. There is no question that often Satan himself (or some other dark principality or power) animates certain pagan religious routines with his presence, and gives the glazed-eyed heathen a bit of a demonic show of fireworks in order to assure their interest. This acknowledged, the fact remains that the Hindus still have to pretend that their 325,000,000 gods' (no exaggeration) powers are real. Buddhists pretend about Buddha, just as the American Indians pretended about the powers of their Great Spirit.

Pretenders have abounded and do still abound. Roman Catholicism has built perhaps the most elaborate system of pretense possible, yet it is bereft and vacant of any real power whatsoever. All of the wealth and intricacy of her immense golden cathedrals, her lavish rituals, her devoted clergy, her much-lauded traditions and her vast infrastructure is only a corrupt façade, a complex and ornate shell that is a house to no uncorrupted spiritual substance whatever. She is not only a *Great Whore*, but she is the Queen of all Pretenders. She departed from the word of God, the source of spiritual power, and was self-exiled into a system of hypocrisy and pretense. So it is with all that turn away from the real power of the words of the Lord. They lose their power. They have no authority.

Ambitions, however, are not lost. Nor do the substructures of their various entities necessarily cave in upon themselves. Saul may have lost the Spirit of the Lord and the blessing of God, but he was still king, and he was willing do anything to retain the throne. It seems certain that the blessing of God waned in Solomon's life long before his one-thousandth wife took residence, but he was on a roll, so he kept collecting princesses and concubines, and he continued his clinical studies in pagan philosophy and partying all the while (Ecc. 7:25). No, the loss of the power of God's blessing and commendation so often does not mean the dissolution of a once-blessed man or ministry. All too often it only means that the man or the ministry finds something to substitute for the blessing of God.

When the Fundamentalists, having adopted a biblical authority which no one could study, hold or see (the original manuscripts), found that the power of their movement had waxed weak, they pretended that it was not so. They *pretended* the power was still upon them, and *substituted* various things for that power. They substituted promotional gimmicks and marketing. They substituted crowd manipulation for conviction and developed "hard-selling" invitations to replace results lost when the Holy Ghost left. They replaced real power with hyper-authoritarian pastoral "leadership," and they created egotists and cult personalities to replace the true men of God. The declining power of their pulpits, and the spectacle of starving sheep, was masked by the numbers posted on the attendance board and by the acreage covered by their bricks and their asphalt. These things were their pretense.

The Protestants – never great Bible students to start with – walked away from what truth from the Bible they had embraced, and simply found the easiest replacement for the power was the slightly modified ritualism and ecclesiastical bondage of the Roman Catholicism which they once protested. Their once loud protestations now amount to little more than sycophantic whining.

The Pentecostals, and all their religious cousins, simply ignore right Bible doctrine and 2000 years of the Church's history, which utterly defies their pipe dream of continuing Messianic miracles and healings as in the days of the apostles. Unwilling to yield an inch dispensationally, they mostly just pretend that their yammering is spiritually substantive, and that the circus sideshows which mark them are the same things that were the works of the Lord Jesus' hands. Sometimes pretending can become delusional (Isa. 66:4).

The New Evangelical movement is filled with genuine Christians, many of whom love the Lord, but they have little concept of the stock from whence they came or the nature of the birthright which their forebears sold out from under them. Water chooses the path of least resistance in its downhill travels. Human nature is ever vulnerable to ways that do not cause pain or thwart "progress." When the Evangelicals walked away from the old English Bible, they conveniently discarded Jeremiah 6:16 and all the rest of the old things along with it. They discarded the old ways of separation from the world, doctrinal distinction, negative truth, and the singular identification of Bible Christianity being unpopular with the populous. Evangelicals think that Dr. Dobson and John MacArthur are right-wingers and doctrinal heavyweights. The folks in New Evangelical and non-denominational churches like to think that their psychobabble, laser light shows, Purpose Driven drivel, hip and tattooed pastors, and in-house rock concerts place them in the same "dynamic" with Elijah, the Lord and the apostles. This is delusive pretense.

The "heroes" of the faith that in large part made all these wondrous developments possible, were the sacred and holy minds which devised academic methods by which the Bible's plainly stated facts and precepts could be subjected to scholastic scrutiny and then subjugated to change and alteration. Biblical "critic" is a badge and title worn proudly amongst its practitioners. "Higher Criticism," "Lower Criticism," and "Critical Scholarship" are considered to be honorific and scientific among the elite club members. They seem not to grasp that the verbal impression left upon the minds of common, Bible-believing folk, which justifiably link "criticizing" the Bible with infidelity and apostasy, to actually be the reality. They haughtily and condescendingly define these titles and their fields of study for the sake of the hicks and hill-billies, apparently without grasping that the hicks' conception of "criticizing the Bible" is quite exactly what the scholars have done, inspiring the last several generations of impotent "Christians" to do the same.

These high-minded academics, too, are pretenders. Yet these are they that have been the devil's elite Special Forces, for they have attacked the life and power of Christianity at its taproot. The groups of Christians discussed heretofore have lost their power, but then have sought to replace the manifestation and fruit of that power. In so many cases, the Fundamentalists, the Charismatics and the New Evangelicals substituted something else for the fruit of God's blessing and power. These scholars, however, have done something far more insidious and sinister. They have assaulted the source of the Christian's power, the authority for all he is and all he is commissioned by God to do. They have impugned the word of God. Unforgivably, they have then substituted something altogether alien and foreign in place of that rightful source of power. They will not admit it, for after years of exposure, they yet hide behind their rhetoric. In place of the word of God, they have substituted a truly sorry surrogate. ***Scholarship has taken the place of the word of God itself***. *Good words and fair speeches* (Rom. 16:18) notwithstanding, these are the salient facts that represent their position:

- The Bible Christians hold in their hands is not the source of power, for it is a mere translation.

•The original manuscripts, though the professed source of power, cannot be that source, for the originals have perished.
• There are different schools of thought as to which text type in existence today best represents the original manuscripts. Whichever is deemed best is actually relative, for translating from the originals to another language yields many different variations of readings.
• In this way, no Bible or text is the final authority, nor are either of the two the source of power. Neither Bible nor text dictates God's tenets to man. Scholarship is the final arbiter, and the highest court of appeal.

By this method, the unwary Christian's focus is removed from the Bible itself and reoriented upon that which "brilliant" men say that the Bible says. The scholars' pretense is their breathless and sacrificial love and devotion to "the word of God." Under the guise of being God's emissaries and His most dedicated servants, scholars have successfully turned men's hearts away from the Bible, which they have supplanted with their own profane and corrupt opinions. These pretend that they hold the keys to understanding, yet that is not the fruit observed in today's Christianity, nor is it what the sincere Bible student finds when he opens the Old Book. These pretend that they hold the solitary commission of the Lord to keep the word and dispense its treasures, yet it is easily found in the scriptures that this commission was given to churches made up of very common men. The imposters pretend that scholarship equips men with privy and secret knowledge from God. These pretend that they themselves have the latitude and license to forge again what God hath already forged by fire and blood. ***That*** is where the power of Christianity has gone!

Do be careful, brother. ***There is death in the pot.***

The *Death in the Pot*

The young man that gathered the wild gourds which he shredded into the pottage (2 Kings 4:39-40) had no idea that he would be poisoning the entire company. For a time, neither the gatherer, the cook, nor the partakers had a clue of the toxic nature of the mixture. Without question, everything else in the stew that day was probably perfectly nutritious and healthful.

So it is today with mainline Christianity's disseminators of the word of God. Undoubtedly, most do not detect the poison; much less do they understand how it came about. Much of the Bible that is taught is nutritious and healthful enough. There is, however, a certain shredded ingredient that is killing the Christianity of our forefathers.

Scholarship *Approved* of God (2 Tim. 2:15)

Few in good conscience would or could declare that all scholarship is bad. This is certainly not the contention of this book. *Study to shew thyself approved unto God, a workman that needeth not to be ashamed, rightly dividing the word of truth* (2 Tim. 2:15). I believe 2 Timothy 2:15 to contextually apply to the scriptures, however, it is certain that Paul was bilingual and probably multilingual (Acts 21:40; 1 Cor. 14:18). Solomon was a writer and a scholar (Ecc. 12:12; 1 Kings 4:32), and David was a prolific student of music as well as the Bible. Daniel and his brethren were rather profound students (Dan. 1:4), and every indication is that God appointed them so.

The great conflict between God and Satan often reveals itself in the two-sided duality of good and bad, right and wrong. There is God's knowledge, then there is the devil's (Gen.3). There is the wisdom of God, then there is the wisdom of this world (1 Cor.1:20-21). There is the fear of God, and then the fear that this world imparts (2 Tim. 1:7). Further, whether it be music, religion, joy, hope or even "christs," God has His own, but so does the devil.

Many have concluded after long consideration that what is generally known as "biblical scholarship" today is tremendously tainted and polluted by falsehood and unbelief. It is well to remember that we live in the latter days and the *perilous times* (2 Tim. 3:1) are most certainly upon us. It is necessary to reveal how most all of today's biblical scholarship has been infected by the poison, but in the meantime it is well to remember that there is a scholarship that is to be celebrated. One must not forget that John Wycliffe was a scholar, and as such, he became the "Morning Star of the Reformation." Wycliffe, in complete contrast to the corporate "Christianity" of his day, had a profound faith in the all-sufficiency and verity of the words of God. This marks his scholarship as a distinct and different species from that scholarship which has become the rule, even in Baptistic and Fundamentalist circles.

Desiderius Erasmus was also a scholar of a different bloodline from the mainstream today. Like Wycliffe, a Catholic (great fodder for his critics), Erasmus nevertheless departed severely from most everything Catholicism stood for, including its only occasionally veiled hatred for the Bible. Sargent refers to Erasmus as "the greatest Renaissance scholar" and "**the** giant intellect of the Reformation-eve."[209] Erasmus' entire lifetime was given to the study, research, gathering and collation of Bible manuscripts. He was offered high positions in royal courts in England, France and the Netherlands. He was offered professorships by the emperor of Germany. The Pope tried to bestow a Cardinal's cap upon him in order to shut him up.[210] All of these were rejected by Erasmus whose genuine

---

[209] Sargent, Robert, *Landmarks of English Bible: Manuscript Evidence.* (Bible Baptist Church Publications, Oak Harbor, WA 98277) 1989, 2001, p.159.
[210] Ibid, p.159.

scholarship remains a landmark that disgraces those whose hearts have succumbed to the scholarship of the other variety.

William Tyndale, a true scholar, was a student and admirer of Erasmus. In fact, he was "so skilled in seven languages, Hebrew, Greek, Latin, Italian, Spanish, English, French, that whichever he spoke you would suppose it his native tongue."[211] Moorman further states that "[o]ne man stands out silhouetted against the horizon above all others, as having stamped *his genius* upon English thought and upon English language. That man is William Tyndale."[212] Those who succeeded Tyndale were said to have "worked with him and were under the spell of his genius."[213] Grady states that 90% of the wording of Tyndale was left in place by the King James translators.[214]

The King James translators are also a great body of genuine scholars that do the title true justice. The literary and linguistic accomplishments of so many of these men have been well-rehearsed often by those who defend the King James Bible. The unsurpassed scholarship and spiritual devotion of men such as Lancelot Andrews, John Reynolds, John Overall, William Bedwell, Edward Lively, Lawrence Chaderton, John Bois, Thomas Holland and Miles Smith are freely assailed today by far lesser men, that assault made easy now, for obviously the AV translators are dead. It is certain that their gifts and accomplishments have not been equaled, and arguably, cannot be equaled.

---

[211] Moorman, Jack, *Forever Settled.* The Dean Burgeon Society Press, Collingswood, New Jersey 08108), 1999, p.212.
[212] Ibid, p.211-212.
[213] Ibid, p.213.
[214] Grady, William, *Final Authority; The Christian's Guide to the King James Bible.* (Grady Publications, Schererville, IN 46375), 1993, p.161.

In this way, it is certain that there is a scholarship and a discipline of study and learning that is godly, commendable and necessary. What might be the attributes of such a scholarship, and what would mark the difference between itself and the wisdom of the world (1 Cor. 3:19), philosophy (Col. 2:8), and vain deceit (Col. 2:8)?

1) Genuine scholarship would itself be in subjection to the precepts and tenets of God's word. *To the law and to the testimony: if they speak not according to this word, it is because there is no light in them* (Isa. 8:20). It would never pervert, twist or wrest obvious and plain truth that is stated in God's word in any language.

2) It would revere the words of God and would mirror the wonderment demanded by the Eternal God having communicated with man in words. It would fully grasp that it is the word of God that is holy, not scholarship. A genuine scholar needs to hold the words of God in the same light as the Lord Himself both did and does. *The words of the LORD are pure words* (Ps. 12:6), *Every word of God is pure* (Prov. 30:5), *It is written, Man shall not live by bread alone, but by every word that proceedeth out of the mouth of God* (Matt.4:4). A man who believes that God does not deal singularly with individual words fails the qualifications of a "godly" and faithful scholarship, for the Bible is altogether plain with regard to the matter.

3) A genuine scholar must be regenerate. *But the natural man receiveth not the things of the Spirit of God: for they are foolishness unto him: neither can he know them, because they are spiritually discerned* (1 Cor. 2:14). It is complete folly to have lost men laboring to discern the meaning of the things of God.

4) Genuine scholarship would have the necessity of exhibiting a reasonable amount of fidelity to sound doctrine and spiritual discrimination. While it is to be expected that every scholar would not exhibit 100% doctrinal agreement with us, it is also to be expected that should such a scholar depart from sound doctrine to a significant degree, that he would lose a Bible-believer's confidence in his processes of thought and logic. Why would a Christian be expected to honor the conclusions of a man's scholarship in translation or interpretation, when he proves himself incapable of rightly discerning the Deity of Christ, the Trinity, the basic tenets of soteriology or a reasonable timeline of eschatology? If an individual proves that he does not know where or how to insert the car key in the door lock or the ignition, why would I conclude that he should be entrusted to *drive* my car? Everyone differs at some fractional level from one another, and there is no reason to have a different expectation for scholars and theologians. However, should that scholar misapprehend basic doctrine and prove to embrace theological nonsense, there is no cause whatever to believe that the rest of his scholarship is particularly trustworthy.

5) A godly scholar would grasp that the battle for the words of God is the foremost issue in all eternal and temporal issues. As such, he would apprehend that keeping his own mind and heart pure from the pollutions and corruptions (2 Cor. 11:3) of falsehood and philosophy (Col. 2:8) would be an absolute necessity. He would, in prudence, seek to avoid the snare of the fool *who having separated himself, seeketh and intermeddleth with all wisdom* (Prov. 18:1), and he would know, in his wisdom, that *evil communications corrupt good manners* (1 Cor. 15:33), especially when those communications involved the writings and influences of apostates and infidels.

6) Genuine scholarship would not only admit, but would proceed in its exercises in the authentic knowledge that

biblical translation is not a science. More an art form than a science, true scholarship would remind itself and its readers of this fact – often. This would immensely reduce the innate haughtiness and condescension of scholars toward the common Bible-believer that is so prevalent. This would not only improve relations between scholars and common folk, it might just remove God's curse and condemnation of prideful scholarship's labors. *Thou hast rebuked the proud that are cursed* (Ps. 119:21); *Though the LORD be high, yet hath he respect unto the lowly: but the proud he knoweth afar off* (Ps. 138:6); *God resisteth the proud, but giveth grace unto the humble* (Jas. 4:6).

7) Genuine scholars would plead and beseech God for His involvement, guidance, leadership and blessing in their work. If such scholars truly believed God's promises about His word, they would hope to see His hand revealed within the work, instead of bitterly and profusely denying that He would do so – or ever had. Should not a scholar translating the Bible into some language without the scriptures implore the Lord to guide the scholar's mind and thoughts and bless the work?

8) Genuine scholarship has always sought to deliver the Bible into the hands of the common folk. Christian men and women serving Jesus Christ attempt to deliver the words of God to other men, not to withhold them. This was the great burden for Wycliffe, Erasmus, Tyndale and Luther. The sentiments of modern scholarship, and to some degree Fundamental King James-defending scholarship, incline themselves toward the ministry of doubts and the impartation of distrust in God's very words. God's scholars would seek to bolster the faith of the unscholarly, not to leave that faith crippled and dependent upon the scholars.

Scholarship's Hypocrisy: *Two Masters* (Lk.16:13)

There is *death in the pot*, and the need to carefully identify the poisonous weed should be obvious. Just as God's wisdom has been duplicated by the subtle but diabolical brand of wisdom all Satan's own, so it is with scholarship. Truthfully, scholarship could be said to be a branch of wisdom and knowledge, either of the godly or ungodly variety. In looking at the attributes of a godly scholarship just outlined, it is not hard to see how modern Evangelical and mainstream "Christian" scholars, new version translators and Christian college professors have fallen far short. Indeed, it is evident that they seem to have fallen into a far lower and far different category.

Importantly, it is not just mainline Evangelical or liberal scholarship that has suffered the breach of godly integrity and verity. Truly, conservative biblical scholarship has also allowed itself to be infected with the scabbed-over mange of uncertainty and indefiniteness in doctrine and scriptural authority. Even King James Bible-waving Independent Baptists have suffered an oft-documented double-mindedness with respect to the authority and true reliability of what they still call their "grand old Book." It is true that many publicly defend it with both enthusiasm and power, but many of the same are also deferential, and even acquiescent, to scholarship's doubts and misgivings about its accuracy and perfection in private. While Fundamentalism's public stance is usually adamant and wholly devoted to the KJV as "the word of God in the English language," and while words including "perfection," "inspiration," "preservation," "infallibility," and "inerrancy" are so often used in the gush of orthodox and reverent prose, the Fundamentalists are so often a great deal less effusive and more reserved when not beating the drum from a pulpit or rallying students for the beginning of a new school year. What was enthusiastically, and even tearfully, extolled as the pure word of God and the perfect Bible in the pulpit, is embraced with far more reservation and clinical detachment in the relative privacy of an office or a classroom.

A great many Christians have experienced this dual face in authors, speakers and leaders who have beaten the drum for "old time religion" and "revival." A great many students have observed it in their own professors. Closer to home, and more tragically, many have been disturbed and disillusioned to observe it in their own pastors. Truth be told, many is the pastor that has earnestly and zealously raved and pounded the pulpit in support of the tenet of the necessity for and the inerrancy of every word of the Bible he holds in hand. That same pastor has so often found himself in a terrible quandary, for by faith he knows his pulpit position must be the correct position; meanwhile, there awaits in his study the words and works of "brilliant minds" that tell him that what he has said in the pulpit cannot be true. The pastor soars in the pulpit, but he gets kicked in the stomach in his office. The reason for the two different faces, the hypocrisy, the inconsistency and this disturbing brand of double-mindedness, is due to the adversity and opposition that exists between true, Christian, scriptural faith versus the doubting, subversive, and unchristian nature of the pseudo-scholarship now prevalent.

In the pulpit and behind the podium, the preacher/scholar is able to exult in the simple and plain truths regarding the Bible. He gladly sets forth the glorious and miraculous nature of the Bible that he holds in his hand in the enthusiasm of his public preaching, in his edification of the saints and in his exhortation of sinners. He knows the people need the power of which the Bible testifies, and he revels and glories in being a vessel used to carry forth the authoritative voice of God. In his pulpit, he can be an uncompromising and faithful firebrand.

In his office, however, there awaits a mistress.

He descends from the podium and crosses the threshold of his study flushed and alight with having been the faithful ambassador for Christ. There, he is met by a hard-faced and even harder-hearted brawler of a woman. She is an unfaithful and defiled hag. She is a Jezebel and an Athaliah rolled into one. She is a "battle-axe." She stands for unbelief, unfaithfulness, infidelity and corruption. She is a polluter of minds and hearts and men are afraid of her in ways, and for reasons, that they will never admit. So there, in the sanctity of the pastor's study, this froward and perverse woman confronts, subjugates and dominates the preacher in a way which he never would allow his wife, or anyone else for that matter. She rails upon him, castigates and shames him. She condescendingly berates him and puts him in his place. He is to serve *her*, and in his pulpit, he has just pledged his loyalty to another, whom she despises! She cuts his legs from under him. She cites page numbers of reference materials, the works of "brilliant and dedicated men," which contradict and contravene what he just said in his own delivery from his own God-commissioned pulpit. She challenges, criticizes and contradicts his public statements and calls upon the likes of Thayer, Machen, Robertson, Strong, Wuest, Vincent and others to witness against him. She dares him to think himself wise enough to challenge her oft-apostate academicians. She screams and spits, slams down her hands upon his desk, shouts into his face, rants, raves and intimidates. She reminds him of the ostracism and exclusion that might ensue should his fellow-ministers and his alma mater get the idea that he has flirted with *King James Only-ism.* She disdains him and humiliates him for he allows her to do so.

He is in conflict due to double-mindedness, for he longs for the power of "old-time Christianity," but he has yielded to her sway intellectually and academically. He fears being thought unscholarly – being called a rube or a hick. He is trapped between two oppositional positions. He wants to stand for God and the Book, but he is convinced that he needs his wretched mistress. How can he ignore the voices of the much acclaimed and venerated ghosts of the academics that shout to him from his own bookshelves? In this way, his true zeal and ardor for the Book is subdued, and the power derived from his faith and his steadfastness (1 Cor. 15:58) is suppressed. The brawling woman is a fearsome presence and her name is ***Biblical Scholarship***. She reduces the courageous lion in the pulpit to a whipped dog in the study.

The Poison vs. The Profit

Some might assume that this book advocates discarding scholarship altogether. This is not the case. Much of what is treasured and defended here has been delivered to the body of Christ by the hand of true scholars that loved the Lord, the truth and the word. A total revocation of scholars and scholarship is neither desirable nor needful. The young man who gathered of the ingredients for the pot in 2 Kings 4:40 needed not reject *all* the herbs and ingredients that went into the stew on that day. He certainly *did* need to identify and discard that which poisoned the whole batch. As discussed earlier, Church History is filled with the names of men whose scholarship bore all the fruits of faith and belief, and whose work God has plainly used and blessed. To group and categorize the work of modern scholarship in the same class with Wycliffe, Tyndale and the King James translators, though, would be a charade. After Wycliffe, Tyndale and the AV translators were done, someone introduced some ingredient into the pot that poisoned it. Much of Christianity is now sick and dying, but hardly realizes it.

One must keep in mind that all of God's regenerate people wrestle with a corrupt nature. The old man - the old nature - is a swamp that breeds all manner of pestilence. A saved man or woman, elder or child, pastor, deacon, husband, wife, mother, father, sister or brother – each lives day to day in the swamp. ***Vigilance*** is the quality required for overcoming the disease found in that quagmire, but somehow such a singular word does disservice to the ponderous and all-consuming duty that it entails. A regenerate new man must still fight off the unregenerate old man at every turn.

Many are the pitfalls for all categories of saints, and the scholar is in no way excluded from this pestilential bog of fallen human nature. Indeed, a discerning Bible reader might conclude that as the Bible scholar carries out the daily responsibilities of his calling, that he, of all men, would be the most targeted by the devil for the simple fact that he traffics in that which Satan hates worst and attacks first: the words of God: the final authority in heaven and earth. Personal pride and haughtiness, ambition and a love for recognition, are true and deadly traps. So is carelessness bred of the familiarity of dealing with holy things. Moreover, there is the adaptation to which Hophni and Phinehas fell prey (1 Sam. 2:22). *Knowledge puffeth up* (1 Cor. 8:1), and with that possibility also resides the very real menace of adopting a knowledge and wisdom not of God, but of this world. The desire for personal security, professional respect and honor is a malady that often walks hand in hand with the manipulation and exploitation that comes with the fear of man. There is the heady accomplishment of achieving entry into the exclusive guild of scholars. There is the delusion of spiritual and professional safety in acquiescing to esteemed colleagues' preponderant judgments upon the Bible. There is the specter of agonizing professional repercussions should one dissent from the opinions of the guild of exalted scholars. There is ever the delusive personal precipice where one concludes that he is the arbiter of truth, that he is God's anointed editor and personally approved censor of the eternal word.

There certainly is a *study* (2 Tim. 2:15), and therefore a "scholarship," that is both "godly" and "of God." But there is a scholarship that is not of God, as well, and discerning the two has proven quite the conundrum in Christianity. In fact, many are unaware that there exists a scholarship "not of God." Where ungodly scholarship is acknowledged, it is very likely that great heated debate could ensue in trying to define distinctly where the threshold between the two is located. All the shades and shadows of godly vs. ungodly scholarship would be contested. All along the continuum would the various schools of scholarship harangue one with another over which was which. Just as the Renaissance scholars, known as *Schoolmen,* debated endlessly about infinitesimal points of Catholic doctrine (which was mostly false and heretical anyway), so could Christianity seemingly endlessly debate each miniscule point. The fact is that Christianity – from lost liberals to right-wing King James Only people – has debated this matter for over 100 years now. Each of these miniscule points has been fought and bled over already, and still remain unsettled. The truth is that the scholars will continue the debate unabated until Jesus comes again.

Since these linguistic and grammatical "specialists" cannot bring the matter to a conclusion, is there a way for the average, blue-collar, Bible believing "non-scholar" to readily grasp where exactly "scholarship" became a poison to Christianity, and exactly which scholarship is which? There certainly is a way.

Written for all to see (scholar and non-scholar alike), the scriptures testify of themselves plainly and concisely:

> ***Every word of God is pure…Add thou not unto his words,*** *lest he reprove thee, and thou be found a liar.* (Prov. 30:5-6)

> ***The words of the LORD are pure words****: as silver tried in a furnace of earth, purified seven times.* ***Thou shalt keep them****, O LORD,* ***thou shalt preserve them*** *from this generation for ever.* (Ps. 12:6-7)

> ***Ye shall not add unto the word*** *which I command you,* ***neither shall ye diminish ought from it…*** (Deut. 4:2)

> *My son,* ***attend to my words…Let them not depart from thine eyes; keep them in the midst of thine heart.*** *For* ***they are life*** *unto those that find them, and health to all their flesh.* (Prov. 4:20-22)

> *For I testify unto every man that heareth* ***the words of the prophecy of this book****, If* ***any man shall add*** *unto these things, God shall add unto him the plagues that are written in this book: And* ***if any man shall take away from the words of the book of this prophecy****, God shall take away his part out of the book of life, and out of the holy city, and from the things which are written in this book.* (Rev. 22:18-19)

There is no cause whatever for any ensuing debate over the nature or content of the verses above. Many other verses could be added to this list. Any honest-hearted saint understands full well the implications of the verses:

1) All of God's words are pure.
2) No one is permitted to add to them or take from them.
3) It is God, through His power, that keeps them; and it is His handiwork and responsibility to give them

to man.
4) Man's part is to attend them and keep them.

There is a school of thought that does immediately snatch these plain promises from the hands of a Bible-believing saint, and straight away begins to qualify and gainsay the statements and promises. One cannot but recall that the *fowls of the air* (Mk. 4:4), which devour the seed sown are said to be *Satan*, which *cometh immediately* (Mk. 4:15) to take away the word of God. The trick of unbelief and infidelity is to place unsubstantiated limitations upon the clear statements and contexts. The deceit lies in resisting plain tenets and in refuting most anything imaginable. The devil was quick to enter into disputation with Eve about that which was stated by God with utter clarity. Even many Fundamental Baptist scholars feel the need to restrict the plain meanings above with qualifiers and limitations.

Since *All scripture is given by inspiration of God, and* ***is profitable*** (2 Tim. 3:16), and the Christian is admonished to ***(s)tudy*** *to shew thyself approved unto God* (2 Tim. 2:15), clearly there is a Bible scholarship that is profitable. What identifies the profitable scholarship from the poisonous kind? It may clearly be stated that the distinction between the two may be summated in the following simple and repeated precept:

Bible Scholarship is poisonous when it supplants the word of God with itself.

In Genesis 27:36, Esau translated Jacob's name for us. Jacob was a *supplanter*. Esau was not as innocent as he would have the reader believe, for while Jacob was buying the birthright, at the same time Esau was selling. That notwithstanding, Jacob does go down in history as a supplanter and a sneak. Jacob will dress himself in goatskins and cook a dish with substitute ingredients in order to deceive a blind and doddering old man – in this case, his father! Isaac thought Jake was Esau and Jacob knew it. He wittingly disguised himself and substituted himself into the place of Esau. In this respect, he did supplant Esau.

This seems to be the actual pivotal point where scholarship's legitimacy and profitability morphs into satanic deception and the poison of asps. Neither John Wycliffe nor William Tyndale were usurpers or supplanters as far as the word of God is concerned. Wycliffe said, "The clergy cry aloud that it is heresy to speak of the ***Holy Scriptures in English***, and ***so they would condemn the Holy Ghost, who gave the tongues to the apostles of Christ to speak the word of God in all languages under heaven***."[215] Tyndale said, "For I call God to record against the day we shall appear before our Lord Jesus, to give a reckoning of our doings, ***that I never altered one syllable of God's Word against my conscience.***"[216] Their burning desires were to use their scholarly gifts to establish the word of God in the language of their own people. They each did want to "supplant" the fables and traditions of the damning religions of the Pope and the king of England, and give to the people that which is truly profitable: the word of God.

Erasmus' scholarship was not used to replace or usurp the word of God, but rather to establish it. Neither Miles Coverdale, John Rogers nor Richard Taverner used their scholarship to undermine or supersede God's word, but rather to embed and anchor it all the more deeply into the universal language of the latter days. None of the King James translators misused their unsurpassed academic attainments to thwart or supplant the words of God. Instead, they used their gifts to impart the words of God ever more deeply into the hearts and

---

[215] Riplinger, Gail. *In Awe of Thy Word,* (A.V. Publications Corp., Ararat, VA 24053) 2003, p.757.
[216] McClure, Alexander W., *The Translators Revived,* (Maranatha Publications, Worthington, Pa. 16262. p.26.

minds of all English speakers. Far from exploiting their scholarship to unseat and undermine the Bible, they engraved each word into granite with an iron pen. The result of their scholarship was a form of language and prose that became the cornerstone of entire cultures and even nations! What Christian person could objectively look upon the work of those mentioned, and call the results a usurpation? The English Bible that resulted from the progressive work of Wycliffe through the AV translators influenced every single country and province that ever knew Great Britain's presence on their shores. However distasteful the British imperialism of yesteryear is to modern historians, that very imperialism brought with it a Book of unsurpassed influence and in many cases it transformed societies and forever affected cultures. Largely, America is here today because of the English Bible, and it will fall because it has departed from it. To this very hour, English is the universal language of commerce and travel. Not too many Americans undertake to learn to speak Chinese, Farsi or Hindi. How is it then, that they of India and China will break a leg to learn English?

Bible Scholarship is poisonous when it supplants the word of God with itself.

Many are the laborers alongside Wycliffe, Erasmus and Tyndale whose ceaseless labors were exercised in holy reverence to holy words in God's holy Book. For an alarming and educational contrast, merely take a snapshot of scholarship at its work in this modern era. Consider that which is heard daily on "Christian" broadcasts, from pulpits across America, and in seminary classrooms. An entirely different species of scholarship is secreted and now oozes from materials in Christian bookstores, and it is entirely common that "Christian" bunglers with Bible study programs essentially make their own translations and alter their own Bibles as they go blithely along.

A subtle yet monumental change has occurred in the heart of men who still claim the Bible as their Book. Now, no Bible translated in any language is a holy Bible. No final authority in a vernacular language exists in the modern Christian scholars' minds. Much lip service is given to the original manuscripts, but those admittedly exist nowhere on earth. Even Greek and Hebrew texts are conglomerations and collations of many multiple sources, and few even hold forth that such texts are ultimate in the finality of their authority and witness. In the main, in modern scholarship's opinion, there is no Bible – in any language – on earth wherein lies indisputable finality in authority or perfection.

In all these cases in the mainstream of Christianity, ***it is the scholarship itself that has become the final and absolute arbiter of God's truth!*** It is impossible to overemphasize the colossal and epic usurpation that this represents. ***The Holy Bible, to both scholars and simple Bible-believers, used to be the ultimate truth and final authority.*** For most of Christianity, this is no longer so. ***Scholarship hath supplanted the word of God as final authority.*** "Christian scholarship" has replaced the Bible itself as holy. In most "Christians'" minds, the Bible has been unseated. Scholarship no longer renders service to the Holy Scriptures. It has subjugated and superseded them. Men no longer study what the Bible says, for they now study what scholarship says the Bible says.

Hardly any even profess to hold Holy Scriptures in hand. Scripture that is holy only exists esoterically and philosophically. For most, no words written anywhere on physical paper are holy words. Those words written down may be either erased or replaced on the actual paper on which they are written or, in the obscure and esoteric ethereal recesses of scholarship, those words that are written down in Greek and Hebrew texts are endlessly elastic in the flexibility and the non-finality of their translations and meanings. The range of contorted meanings of those words has been debated and contested for centuries now. More specifically, scholars debate them. One thing is evident: scholars and scholarship, in general, will always debate the meanings of those words. Scholarship will never settle for adamant and conclusively final meaning for the words of the Bible. Scholarship will always reserve the license to change, alter and embellish the words of the Bible.

400 years ago, the King James translators, excepting the subsequent but expected printing errors and mere changes in spelling, completed their "scholarly" work: the Authorized Version of 1611: the King James Bible. They finished it. Their work was done. Never revised, only reprinted in various editions that changed printing font, standardized spelling, and corrected printing errors, the King James Bible is the same Bible today as it was in 1611. ***The scholarship of the translators, in service to God, translated His words, and then put down their pens.*** With respect to further consequential alterations of words and meanings, ***they also shut their mouths.*** That kind of scholarship is a reverential tribute to the Bible, and has done both God and mankind great service.

Modern scholarship is not nigh so honorable. Modern scholarship will not bring to finality its work of alteration and modification of the Bible. It will never be done. The labor "twill ne'er be complete." Until Jesus Christ returns, bastardized scholarship will never cease its work. It will not cease its never-ending revision and correction of the scriptures themselves because it has no vision whatever of delivering to people the word of God in final form. That would be delivering to the people a final authority. Mainline scholarship will never do that, for ***"scholarship" has become the final authority!***

Bible Scholarship is deadly when it replaces the word of God with itself.

Even among King James defenders, the King James Bible is defended as the best English translation, and yet in standing for the verity of this position, the defenders proceed in their well-rehearsed defenses with an eye more to the Masoretic and Received Texts for finality than to their native English Bible. As documented in Chapter 1, so many of these fine men cannot bring themselves to relinquish authoritative finality and perfection to the testimony of the AV 1611 as written. The King James is simply the best English translation of the Greek and Hebrew – nothing more. Their *speech bewrayeth* them (Matt. 26:73). However, neither are the Greek and Hebrew texts, for them, the final authority, word for critical word, because there is a certain variability of readings among the manuscripts, and there is also certain dissent among scholars as to exactly how the Greek and Hebrew words of the proper texts should be translated. In the end, scholarship is their final authority, as well. That is why the men documented will not concede that the AV translation is "perfect" in its translation. To them it still is not a perfectly pure Bible.

When one wishes to know what a Bible-believer's final word is on a particular matter, the Bible-believer takes the inquirer to the King James' scriptures. There is no higher appeal. When one goes to a Textus Receptus (TR) scholar with the same question, he may read something from the King James Bible, but for finality the scholar turns to his Greek Text. However, that does not end the matter, for the Greek word or phrase can be rendered in certain various forms, and this is proven by all of the Greek reference works that may be dragged off the TR scholar's bookshelves. Once these reference materials are opened, there are numerous ways in which the word or phrase may be rendered. Which one is right? On that, there is no end to scholarly debate, and the inquirer simply has to choose which ***scholar*** to believe. One scholar prefers this particular reading, but this reference writer makes a strong case for another way, and yet another lexicographer makes a defensible case for still another. Though the man with his Greek Textus Receptus open may usually acquiesce to the AV English's words of choice, where he does not do so, he is flirting with that earlier described mistress again. He is considering, at least in some cases, allowing scholarship to dictate what the word of God "really says."

Bible Scholarship is certain death when it unseats the word of God and declares itself the final arbiter.

In this way, the scholarship that endeavors to translate the word of God into the pioneer languages of the mission field is an honorable and godly branch of study. In these cases, academic gifts and talents for languages, as well as the disciplined linguistic and grammar skills of the scholar are the work of the Lord Himself. In such a case, no one is trying to unseat and replace a powerful and pure Bible of the people.

Often, missionaries on fields where languages are more common, find themselves in difficult circumstances with respect to the Bible. They often "inherit" a historic translation of the Bible, which comes from corrupted texts or is poorly translated. This is always a difficult situation and such missionaries should be allowed to write and to propose how best to handle such circumstances. It can confidently be said that this too is an obvious place for the labors of a faithful linguist and scholar potentially to shine through. Such a scholarship that labors to bridge or repair such an obvious breech is not to be rejected or declared satanic. Again, this would be a case, barring foolish judgment, where no one is seeking to usurp and overthrow the word of God in its purity.

Neither of these examples is the reality of what has transpired between scholarship and the King James Bible in the modern era. Those who believe that the King James Bible needs intensive, wholesale changes have been philosophically and spiritually compromised, and simply choose to reject or ignore the many works which document the vast superiority of its texts, translators, history, language, fruit and power. They simply drank the tainted fruit punch. They are to the Bible issue what evolutionists are to creationism. They are irreconcilable, unreasonable and unteachable. Any legitimate scholar that has written on the matter, even when he designs to tear down the AV, must pay homage to the accuracy of its translation, to the excellence of its translators, to the power of its language and phrasing, to its long history and to its manifest power. There simply are no glaring breeches in the King James Bible. There is no shortcoming. There is no failed attempt at excellence. Any shortfall or deficit perceived in the AV is most usually the work of the presuppositions of a prejudicial mind, careless reading and study, an unregenerate spirit, gross ignorance, or the aforementioned soul who is philosophically subjugated to polluted doctrine and low expectations of his God.

Now 400 years old, the King James Bible is the gold standard in Bibles. All new versions compete and compare themselves with it – not each other. The Authorized Version both *is*, and *has been*, ***the Bible*** for the English-speaking world for four centuries. So far in this book, the endeavor has been to try to place on exhibition how this old Book bears every single mark of inspiration, preservation, purity, perfection, life (Heb. 4:12) and power. It is the Bible. The brand of scholarship which comes rooting around the King James Bible like a mud-caked sow is a usurper and a supplanter. It finds a Bible that is not only excellent, but perfect after God's own standard, and scholarship simply wants to **replace the AV with *itself!***

Bible Scholarship is satanic when it supplants the word of God with itself.

It is in no way deemed necessary that all scholarly reference works should be discarded and rejected. It would seem that the critical and decisive point would be where the reference work sought or seeks to supersede the Bible and unseat the authority of its words.

For example, there is no need to reject or dismiss all commentaries, commentators or expositors. Commentaries are man's exegesis and explanation of his understanding (or lack of it) of the Bible. The labor, study and scholarship that went into many of the multi-volume commentaries are astounding. As with direct preaching from the pulpit or teaching from the podium, one looks to commentaries to grasp and ruminate on what God showed another man. It cannot be forgotten that God did choose men to be the teachers of men. All saints and sinners have need that *some man should guide* them (Acts 8:31). Let it also be remembered that one's subjection to another man's teachings are limited by biblical mandate:

> *To the law and to the testimony*: ***if they speak not according to this word****, it is because there is no light in them.* (Isa. 8:20)
>
> *If there arise among you a prophet, or a dreamer of dreams, and giveth thee a sign or a wonder, And the sign or the wonder come to pass, whereof he spake unto thee, saying, Let us go after other gods, which thou hast not known, and let us serve them;* ***Thou shalt not hearken unto the words of that prophet, or that dreamer of dreams****: for the LORD your God proveth you, to know whether ye love the LORD your God with all your heart and with all your soul.*
> (Deut. 13:1-3)

Should the scholarship of commentators press to the point of teaching contrary to the Bible, or if in trying to teach the Bible, they are willing to change, wrest or alter the word of

God – then that scholar's comments are obviously to be dismissed, regardless of his qualifications. Furthermore, the scholarship that led him to diminish, add or change the words of the King is exposed for what it is: ***poison.***

The old Scofield Reference Bible has long been highly recommended for its notes and cross references. There are times that Scofield hedges on sound doctrine and tends to yield to some of the burgeoning scholarly influences of his day. There is no need to burn the old Scofield Bibles, but where Scofield's scholarship attempts to supplant what the King James' text says, his scholarship is to be rejected.

Strong's Analytical Concordance remains one of the most important books ever printed and bound. Behind the Bible itself, it might be the very next most indispensable book a Bible student might own. James Strong burnt his eyes out for nearly 35 years, accounting for every word in the Bible, alphabetically, and where each one occurs. The scholarship he and his assistants poured into the book, without the assistance of computers, is an almost unfathomable achievement to a 21st century Christian wallowing in technological conveniences. All in all, it is perhaps the most useful Bible tool ever put into print. This kind of scholarship is to be celebrated.

Importantly, that is only part of the equation as far as James Strong's scholarship is concerned. The main body of the book is the concordance. In the concordance is found a species of scholarship that wholly honors the word of God in making those words all the more accessible to anyone who can use the English alphabet.[217] The scholarship in the concordance does not intrude or insert itself into what the Bible itself says. What is in the Hebrew and Greek dictionaries found in the back of the

---

[217] The reader should note that some of the later editions of Strong's produced in these latter years have seen an increase of changes by different publishers.

volume is another matter. The dictionaries not only define words, but essentially provide the basis for the use of alternative readings for the words that are used in the King James Bible. Depending on the word chosen and in what language, a student/scholar may be given anywhere from five to twenty alternate words that "could have been used" instead of the one that the AV translators (and God) *did use.*

First, it is a temptation to substitute Strong's definition of a word as a final and authoritative meaning. Neither Strong nor any other man is the God-ordained definer of words. The actual meaning of God's words are learned by man in the process of *comparing spiritual things with spiritual* (1 Cor. 2:13), that is, defining Bible words by the Bible. We have seen how this works, for instance, in the case of *charity* in the King James Bible. Man is ready, and has tried, to discard the Biblical use of *charity* altogether, but God distinguishes and defines it specifically by its usage in the Bible itself. In this light, it is also important to say that as Englishmen, neither do we trust English dictionaries to render authoritative and exclusive definitions of Bible words. Once again, the Bible defines its own words, and often uses them in sanctified and select ways in which dictionaries fail. It is important that we place the scholarship that assembled English dictionaries in the same category as that which has assembled Greek and Hebrew dictionaries. Where such scholarship is consistent with the Bible's use of the word, fine: however, the devil is subtle, and one should be cautioned to put his labors into the Bible and not to lean too heavily on dictionaries. Where such scholarship interposes itself or seeks to commandeer or supersede the Bible itself, such scholarship is poison. It kills.

Secondly, for the student/scholar there is a terrible temptation with Strong's dictionaries, as with all Bible lexicons and dictionaries, to substitute one of Strong's alternative words into the Bible itself. Since he and others say that *charity* actually is "love," people have grown to think nothing of replacing the Bible word *charity* with "love." This is a regular exercise of scholars, and men now think nothing whatever of substituting a lexicon or dictionary word into the ***very text*** of the scripture itself! Men have bought so deeply into the philosophy of scholarship being the final authority that they unthinkingly and casually insert one of the several word choices given in Strong, Nelson or Unger without a twinge of conscience. A scholarship that flirts with changes in wording, and encourages one to think after words that men propose to use instead of the words that God chose to use is poison.

Bible Scholarship is blasphemous when it inserts and interposes itself over the word of God.

Scholarship Falsely So-Called

Hopefully having relieved any anxiety that the proposal is being made to throw away all reference materials written by scholars, and that all should cease to acknowledge any scholarship as a viable entity, the nature of the beast may actually be confronted. The proposal is that scholarship be judged (Phil. 1:9) and proven (1 Thes. 5:21) by the same standard as the Christian is to judge everything else in this world: by the words of God, the Holy Scriptures.

As for the nature of the beast - the beast being mainline biblical scholarship - this section will demonstrate that scholarship is an altogether loathsome and unworthy ***replacement*** for the Bible. As with science and scientists, scholarship and scholars have long luxuriated in oft-undeserved respect and honor. *(H)onour is not seemly for a fool* (Prov. 26:1). As men tend to think all doctors are good, so they also tend to think the work of scientists and scholars is always honorable and profitable to all. The fact that the common man is intimidated by doctoral degrees, professorships and arcane terminology and studies, has helped secure "Bible scholars" a shroud behind which they may work evil as well as good.

As detailed earlier, biblical scholarship has managed to insert itself in an authoritative position of finality over the word of God itself. So much of scholarship now judges the Bible instead of the opposite being true. Mainline Christians do not register that there has been an actual inversion of authoritative entities, but experience has shown that most "Christians" readily and unwittingly accept the atrocious circumstance of scholarship having exalted itself to a place between the saints and the scriptures. What manner of master have they allowed to be thus enthroned? As when Israel insisted upon a king when the LORD was their King (1 Sam. 12:12), so it is with the saints and their scholarship. The Lord told Samuel to *shew them the manner of the king that shall reign over them* (1 Sam. 8:9). Is scholarship a more worthy arbiter of truth than the Bible?

Christianity's Exposure to Poison

The pure scriptures God delivered to the first New Testament Christians, and the untainted doctrines and ideals with which the apostles were entrusted in the first century, were both born into a filthy and dirty world. The innocence and purity of both Bible and doctrine were to undergo immediate and enduring onslaughts to spoil, soil and pollute Christianity by the world and its *god* (2 Cor. 4:4). This was more than an attack or assault. It was a sky-darkening blitz by all the demons of Hell.

Christianity was "born" under the rulership of the Roman Empire. A vast heathen amalgamation of religions, Rome found Christianity an illicit and illegal religion, for she attempted to convert people from other religions and she reflected the negative views of the God of the Bible with respect to man's nature. It did not take long for both official and unofficial persecutions to begin.

It was prophetic that Paul admonished the Colossians to *Beware lest any man spoil you through philosophy* (Col. 2:8), for newborn Christianity was cast amongst pagan Philosophy virtually from the allegorical womb. The Platonic and Gnostic philosophers immediately scrambled to make a nest for Christianity among all their ideological idols. To this hour, the Gnostic pollutions introduced into Christianity and her Bible and doctrine by men such as Clement of Alexandria and Origin, are viewed by many as heaven sent innovation.

In the fourth century, Constantine the Great decided that embracing "Christianity" instead of exterminating it was an expedient way to undergird his empire and his popularity. In a nifty propaganda move, he proclaimed his empire "Christian," and made it a requirement by law to be a "Christian." Naturally, few of the national population's new "Christians" were actually Christians at all, but they signed the forms, jumped through the hoops, and got sprinkled. In the end, it turned out that the true Christians – the ones prior to Constantine's decree – were still the enemies of the state since their Bible and their Savior left them still at adversity with their deadly "Christian" emperor.

Out of Constantine's political savvy and vision, the Mother of Harlots (Rev. 17:5) got her auspicious start and began her sordid "ministrations" to all the nations of the earth. The Roman Catholic Church as known today is acknowledged by most historians to have had her administrative beginnings around 500 A.D. In truth, she existed long, long before in Mesopotamia, Babylon, and in the various other pagan sorceries that infested the hearts of the heathen round about.

In this way, Christianity enjoyed beginning its existence by fighting for its life against secular Romanism, Gnosticism, the paganized "Christianity" of Constantine, and the extraordinary whoredoms of what would become the Roman Catholic Church.

All of this occurred before the lights went out. Around 500 A.D., the Dark Ages began, and historians do not acknowledge the end until around 1000 years later. During that 1000 year period, the devil's church ruled Europe, and the very top priorities of the Pope were to 1) affect the death of all true Christians, 2) destroy all the Bibles, and 3) replace all of God's divine authority in the lives of men with his own diabolical and depraved brand of delusive tyranny.

As dark and horrific as was society, politics and life in general during those now romanticized Middle Ages, spiritual life was a devastating blackness for the average citizen. Unequivocal and unrelenting ignorance and bondage was life under the "Vicar of Christ" and his satanic religious realm. Mere elemental standards of cleanliness that sprinkle page after page of scripture were unknown to medieval man. Not only did the Pope's idols cause the devastating Black Death to fall on his kingdom, but the ignorance of simple sanitation and the proper disposal of the dead helped to multiply the effects of the plague. After the 1000 years allotted the Dark Ages, faint light began to illuminate the eastern horizon. Wycliffe, "The Morning Star of the Reformation," Gutenberg, the Lollards, the Waldensians, and the Albigenses helped pull the veil back from off the lamp of the word of God. Erasmus, Luther, Tyndale, Huss, Knox, Jerome of Prague were soon casting blinding light into the gloomy and sinister recesses of the Old Whore's kingdom. The Protestant Reformation spoiled the Popes' sick, perverse celebration of damnation, and though it ended up a sadly failed reformation instead of an out-and-out rejection of Catholicism, there were limited victories at the time, and one ever-enduring accomplishment: the AV 1611 King James Bible!

The landmark accomplishment of the Reformation being the KJV, not Lutheranism or Calvinism, assured from the start that the devil would have a potent countermove. By 1572 A.D. the Protestant Reformation had reached its limits territorially, as beyond this date no other countries defected from Catholicism to become Protestant.[218] The Pope had begun to strike back vengefully by this time, as he had already sanctioned and removed all restrictions from the newly formed Jesuit Order, conceptualized by Ignatius Loyola in 1534. By the time of the death of Loyola in 1556, the Jesuits had already had great successes in instigating uprisings and infiltrating colleges and universities.[219] The insidious Jesuit influence, in combination with the movement called the Enlightenment or Age of Reason was a masterful counterattack by the devil. The Enlightenment gave way to a philosophical spin-off called Rationalism, which was a revolt against the bondage of Catholic tradition and abuses. Rationalism basically held that truth could only be justifiably based on reason, observation and experiment. This was a blatant denial of faith as defined in the Bible, and it severely wounded the concept of the supernatural in the minds of far too many.[220]

Arguably, those most influenced by the philosophy of Rationalism were the intelligentsia and academics of the time. Having never been introduced to true biblical faith, for these men Colossians 2:8, 1 Corinthians 1:19 & 1 Corinthians 3:19 became the choking, deadly snares and pits of that day. It was German Rationalism in the late 18th century that gave rise to the spiritual plagues of unbelief or part-belief that poison

---

[218] Sargent, Robert, *Landmarks of Church History,* Bible Baptist Church Publications, Oak Harbor, WA 98277, Vol.II, pg 307
[219] Ibid. pg 309
[220] Ibid. pg 339.

Christianity to this hour. Preceded in biblical criticism by two French Roman Catholics, Richard Simon and Jean Astruc, J.S. Semler, in the late 1700's became the "Father of German Rationalism." Helping him carry the banner of unbelief were such notable apostates and infidels as Gotthold Lessing, Johann Eichhorn, H.E.G. Paulus, Fredrick Schleiermacher, Ferdinand Baur, David Strauss, Julius Wellhausen and Karl Graf. There is no better way to summarize the work of these men than to say that they and their cohorts made doubt and denial of Bible truth pathetically and blasphemously systematic and routine.

The Poison Becomes Prevalent

That the effects of the philosophy of Rationalism have become a widespread and systemic poison is not difficult to observe firsthand today. It is both amazing and revealing how many "orthodox," and even Fundamental Christians today hold a less than reverent opinion of the miracles in the Bible as well as the miracle *of the Bible*. The nature of the Red Sea crossing, Christ walking on the water, the manna, the healings, the plagues, the historicity of basic Bible accounts, the death and resurrection of Christ is now, and has been, held in open question for many years. The legitimacy of eternal Hellfire and torment are questions that even the much-touted Billy Graham holds in question. Needless to say, Graham should have stuck by the Book! One theological casualty of this damnable philosophical battle is the very supernatural nature of the Bible as the Book of God, containing all the words of God. The Bible has almost become like the holy grail, a mythological thing – once real – but which is now relegated to shrouds of mystery and almost mystical scholastic experience.

New Evangelicals, Emerging Church people, Purpose Driven Christians and "mega-churches" do not have a Bible they believe is God's Book. They have ethereal and rather esoterically variable communications and messages from the Lord. The liberal baloney upon which they subsist oozed from the pits of Hell via German Rationalism. At a certain level, even the defenders of the AV 1611, which gird their loins in the Textus Receptus and Masoretic Text camps of Fundamentalism are quick and ardent about limiting the Holy One of Israel (Ps. 78:41) in what they will concede that He could or could not have done with His words. They find scriptural excuses for their quasi-unbelief, and effusively spout rhetoric *under colour* (Acts 27:30) as if complete biblical orthodoxy abides in the traditions which they hold (Mk. 7:8). They do ignore a great deal of biblical exposition and are lightning fast in consigning simple, Bible-believing faith into the categories of *Ruckmanism* and *heresy*, which they presume will torment and humiliate the recalcitrant.

> *But this I confess unto thee, that* ***after the way which they call heresy, so worship I the God of my fathers, believing all things which are written in the law and in the prophets:***
> (Acts 24:14)

Part of the prevalent nature of this scholarly poison is the verity that many of the unfaithful Rationalists and scholars are responsible for biblical reference works such as dictionaries and lexicons commonly found on pastoral bookshelves. In his book, *The Modern Version Hall of Shame*, David Cloud bears testament to the names of many men, such as Henry Liddell, Joseph Henry Thayer, Francis Brown, Charles Briggs, Samuel Driver, the Kittels, A. T. Robertson, and the Moulton family who, among others, have so often provided the modern scholar with foundational reference works, and the much- treasured academic mandate to alter the Bible.

Many scholars will vociferously protest that the scholarly works by these men are only tools, and cannot be viewed as precipitating alteration of the scriptures. Such sentiment is propaganda-based and is akin to saying that the modern news media is not left-leaning. The life works of most of these men were philosophically rationalistic and critical of the testimony of the Bible. Further, their very views and practices are what have led to the present hour where prep school children and knuckleheaded bible study "leaders" consider it their place to take latitude to alter the Bible at their whim and pleasure.

The Bible, despite the protestation, states *Be not deceived: evil communications corrupt good manners* (1 Cor. 15:33), and the foolhardy and rebellious spirits of these men do indeed animate and insinuate themselves into their works. The very influential Joseph Thayer was rebuked by the publishers of the lexicon that bears his name in this way:

> "A word of caution is necessary. Thayer was a Unitarian and the errors of this sect occasionally come through in the explanatory notes. The reader should be alert for both subtle and blatant denials of such doctrines as the Trinity (Thayer regarded Christ as a mere man and the Holy Spirit as an impersonal force emanating from God), the inherent and total depravity of fallen human nature, the eternal punishment of the wicked, and Biblical inerrancy."[221]

James Strong of *Strongs Exhaustive Concordance of the Bible* fame, was a member of the English *Revised Version* committee as well as the *American Standard Version* committee. Rudolf and Gerhard Kittel were modernists with respect to the Bible and anti-Semites to top it off. Gerhard was

---

[221] Cloud, David *The Modern Version Hall of Shame*(wAy of Life Literature, Port Huron, MI 48601,2005p.122-123

a Nazi in Hitler's Germany. Three generations of Moultons were modernists and Bible critics, yet exercised their scholarship in lexicography, the discipline of formulating a dictionary, a vocabulary or book containing an alphabetical arrangement of the words in a language, with the definition of each, or an explanation of its meaning. In other words, a lexicon tells you what God's words mean. How much can one trust unbelieving minds to correctly communicate what God's words mean? Most people know that Westcott and Hort were grossly compromised spiritually, and it has been documented that Henry Liddell, also a lexicographer, was nefariously involved in sin that shall not be detailed here.[222]

Upon reading the preceding, many scholars will virtually scream that scholarly reference works are neutral tools and that it is unacceptable to judge scholarly material by the moral or spiritual failings of said scholars in their lives. Emphasis has been made, and the reader should be reminded, that it has already been stated plainly that there is no advocacy here made for the out and out rejection of biblical reference materials written by those who hold a different position. ***Remember, the point at issue is whether scholarship supplants and replaces the scriptures themselves as the final authority***. It should be disgusting and repulsive to any Christian should even the most fundamentally sound and orthodox scholar imaginable usurp the final authority of the Bible with his most excellent and orthodox scholarship. In this light, how much more abominable is it that the Body of Christ would so blithely allow doctrinally perverse, or even morally bankrupt men to kidnap the authority of the Holy Scriptures by their septic scholarship? For instance, it is not necessary to reject James Strong's concordance because of his affiliation with the *Revised Version* of 1881, or with the *American Standard Version* of 1901, for there is much profit to be found in that remarkable work, but every user of his

---

[222] Riplinger, G. A.,*Hazardous Materials*: *Greek & Hebrew Study Dangers*(A.V. Publications, Ararat, VA 24053, 2008, pg.276-327.

concordance must heed the warning regarding his *proclivities* and *inclinations* and steer clear of his dictionary entries that would mislead as to the meanings of Bible words. An excellent example of this is the aforementioned King James word, *charity*. Strong and his fellow dictionary writers and lexicographers have provided entire generations of Christians with a misperceived scholarly mandate to change *charity* to "love." Granted, the student is responsible for using reference works with care, and he changes the Bible at his own risk regardless of what any scholar says, but one must judge it far from precipitous to ramp up his vigilance and caution when he knows full well the heretical or modernist tendencies of certain writers. ***Again, it is specified that the issue in any case is whether scholarship is allowed to depose the Bible itself as the final authority***. No dictionary – even Webster's English of 1828 - is ever to be allowed to overthrow or distort how the Lord uses a word in His Book. Again, in the case of *charity*, Webster fails to do the actual Biblical definition justice. The scholarship found in commentaries, sermons, devotionals, lexicons, encyclopedias and Bible dictionaries is ever subject to the Bible itself – never vice versa!

It is at this critical juncture where matters really come to a boil in the camp of King James defenders. Many love the AV and defend it, but their point of reference is purely from the Hebrew Masoretic Text and the Greek Textus Receptus position. That is, they hold that the KJV is the right Bible in English entirely due to its textual superiority, and the arguable – and much argued – correct translation of its Greek and Hebrew texts. Superficially, this seems to be a fine enough position to take but for the fact that many of these men still wish to debate what is the correct translation. Some feel that certain passages in the AV are translated incorrectly, while others simply feel that they have a mandate to excavate from Greek and Hebrew whatever color or sense they feel is missing from the translation supplied by the translators in the King's English. Generally, these fellows are zealous to acknowledge God's providential guidance in supplying the King James Bible, but they are utterly repulsed and indignant that such providence should extend to the Lord's participatory influence in the individual English words themselves. Because they hold that the real mysteries of the Bible still reside in the original languages, and still have to be mined via Greek and Hebrew scholarship, many such men, when pressed, feel a great compunction to defend many of the machinations of modern scholarship and its rationalistic reference writers. For a student or preacher to hold that the AV might need updating or correcting, or for that matter to believe that the real keys to the scriptures lie exclusively in the Greek and Hebrew texts, leaves open the proverbial door for the proverbial camel. In so doing, they are still at great risk of acquiescing to the beguiling influences (2 Cor. 11:3) of the scholarship we have discussed, and of allowing it to displace the Bible itself as the final authority in spiritual things.

There has long been friction between Bible-believers that hold the AV to be the perfect word of God, and those who defend it only as an extension of the Textus Receptus and the Masoretic texts. The defenders of the texts decry what they call *ad hominem* attacks (attacks against the person of a man as opposed to his position), which King James Bible believers have at times been guilty of. Nevertheless, the pot, in this case, calls the kettle "black," because so many of the TR defenders are absolutely instantaneous in bitterly labeling anyone who holds to the perfection of God's words in English a *Ruckmanite*, or other presumably derogatory names intended to demean and humiliate the simple Bible-believer into ostracized and disgraced silence. In accord with the theme of this chapter, and to illustrate the narrow view of the modus operandi of the mere defenders of the original language texts of the AV 1611, the following is presented.

Dr. Kirk DiVietro, in a recently published book very well represents the TR and Masoretic text position on the King James Bible. The book is published by Dr. D.A. Waite's Dean Burgon Society, long a stronghold of the King James being the English Bible that best translates what they consider the *real* Bible – the OT Hebrew Masoretic text and the NT Greek Textus Receptus. Waite and the Society have long repudiated and disdained the entire idea of a perfect, God-given Bible in any language other than Greek and Hebrew. DiVietro's book, *Cleaning Up Hazardous Materials: A Refutation of Gail Riplinger's Hazardous Materials*, is written to be a point by point rebuttal of Riplinger's 1200 page book called, *Hazardous Materials: Greek and Hebrew Study Dangers: The Voice of Strangers,* published in 2008 by A.V. Publications, Corp. The purpose in addressing this matter in *this* book is not to refute a refutation, but to clearly exemplify that the scholarly mindset can indeed be a more intrusive, beguiling and insidious thing than its ardent defenders even recognize. It turns out that it does not take much scholarly pride to catalyze a deception that deposes the Holy Scriptures and elevates bastardized scholarship as the final authority of God.

DiVietro, in his 375 page (including the Appendix) rebuttal of Riplinger's *Hazardous Materials,* feels compelled on several occasions to remind his readers of his long experience with, and much use of, Greek, Hebrew and scholarly tools.[223] In fact, on page 49, he says that he avails himself of lexicons daily. Plainly comfortable and experienced in the "original languages" setting, and even setting guidelines and instructions for Bible preachers to follow in referring to the original languages, DiVietro refers to himself in the third person when he states,

---

[223] DiVietro, Kirk,*Cleaning-Up Hazardous Materials: A Refutation of Gail Riplinger's Hazardous Materials,*The Dean Burgon Soiety, Collingswood, NJ 08108,2010,ppg.49,79,89,110,123.

> "He [DiVietro] freely uses Bible study aids. In 30+ years of ministry as a pastor and part-time college professor ***he has NEVER once corrected the King James Bible. He has never once invited anyone to question its meaning or authority."***[224]

This is a curious statement, in light of the fact that on pg. 94, that author has just stated that,

> In preaching on "Jesus wept." ***The words "and stirred himself" in John 11:33*** is in the middle active form of *εμβριμαομαι.*[225]

The critical issue with respect to this quotation is the fact that the AV 1611 does not contain the words "and stirred himself" in John 11:33. This is something that DiVietro digs out of Greek and then cites as if that is what the Bible actually says. Make no mistake; he does openly believe the Greek text to be the actual authoritative and preserved word of God. Interestingly, he cites the words "and stirred himself" as authoritative and essentially superimposes them over what the KJV does say in John 11:33! In his refutation of Riplinger, DiVietro continually revisits his contention that lexicons and scholarly works do not alter or correct the Bible. Though it has been stated plainly that burning all the lexicons and dictionaries is not advisable, it cannot be ignored that it seems to make no impression upon DiVietro that men have become enraptured by the polluted process of altering the Bible to suit their own fancy, and that lexicons, dictionaries and commentaries are the ready tools that men use - or misuse - to do so. Presumably, Dr. DiVietro queried one of his "daily" used lexicons before he superimposed this alleged treasure from the Greek over what his "NEVER once corrected King James Bible (see quote above)"

---

[224] Ibid. pg.110
[225] Ibid.pg.94

says. How is it that this does not "invite" someone to question the authority or meaning of the AV 1611 he so ardently defends?

This is the very species of scholarly rubbish that King James Bible believers have put up with and, often, now dismiss as Biblical infidelity. In the end, this brand of Bible correction (and *THAT is* exactly what it is) is viewed as the same kind of breach as a corrector who uses the Critical Text. It all winds up the same! It seems the Bible-believers must always listen to men pledge their lives, hearts and ministries to the King James Bible with the most syrup-sodden sincerity, only to have them pull this very kind of scholarly stunt. Specifically, this is the very reason why the Textus Receptus position is without real credibility to so many Bible-believers. Preachers and teachers claim they would never ever correct or circumvent the KJV – but then they do so in the very shadow of their professed and acclaimed fidelity. Most of these vows turn out to be smoke and "spin" in practicality. DiVietro's claim of 30+ years of utter fidelity to the AV is found in his book 16 pages ***after*** having already breached his faithfulness to the King James Bible! By the time he professed that he had NEVER (his emphasis) once corrected it, ***he already had done so!*** Evidently, he does not even realize that he has already crossed the threshold of usurpation! He does not recognize it for what it is.

Bro. DiVietro insists that the Greek *εμβριμαομαι* in Jn.11:33 means that Christ stirred himself in anger, or in the doctor's words in a "furious rage."[226] According to him, ***"the whole story hinges on this situation,"*** and is ***"central to the message."*** Returning to this matter a few pages later, DiVietro makes certain that we understand that the lesson from the Greek in John 11 is ***"priceless and does not appear in the King James Bible."*** So, to be very clear: one is to accept the premise that in

[226] Ibid.pg.94

the AV 1611, the "hinge" and the "priceless" lesson of the passage is missed. Just as the devil convinced Eve that her source of knowledge, the word of God, did her disservice in its incompleteness, so DiVietro plainly states that the AV does not contain the precious information that is needed in John 11.

On the other hand, the believer might consider that DiVietro may have been foolhardy in second-guessing the AV translators, for in focusing on superimposing his translation of the verse (remember, he has "NEVER once corrected King James Bible"!) he overlooked that Christ groaned in His Spirit both in verse 33 AND 38, and sandwiched between the two occurrences, *Jesus wept* (36). The "furious rage" DiVietro insists upon, is misconstrued and apparently is not at all consistent with the Holy Ghost's narrative.

This is not Dr. DiVietro's only misstep when his practice and his profession are compared. Though, in reference to the KJV, he claims he has "never once invited anyone to question its meaning or authority," He states that Romans 5:15 is a sentence that is ***'"impossible" in English.'*** He continues, ***"The only way to fully exegete it is to refer to the Greek grammar."***[227] Odd, as a Bible-believing pastor who is committed to teaching the Bible to the flock the Lord has entrusted me with, I have habitually taught the Bible verse by verse for over 20 years and I have repeatedly exposited Romans 5:15 to the saints without consulting Greek grammar one single time.

The purpose here is not to examine all the missteps of a particular author, ***but to point out that a supplanting and poisonous brand of destructive scholarship is a creeping and deceptive thing. It insinuates itself into men's minds.*** A KJV-defending Fundamentalist who believes that he has never overturned anything in the AV1611 is presented here, yet his

[227] Ibid. pg.91

scholarship has led him to superimpose that scholarship over the very Book he believes he defends. This is a common affliction among "TR men." He does not even recognize what he has done.

Just one other example of this species of scholarship will suffice. DiVietro claims that the word *propitiation* of Romans 3:25 and 1 John 2:2 and 4:10 is a word unable to be understood without a lexicon.[228] Importantly, one of his consistent diatribes throughout *Cleaning-Up Hazardous Materials* is his utter disdain and denigration of Riplinger's and others' contention that the King James Bible is self-definitive. This position is in no way unique to Gail Riplinger, as I and many others have read, taught and comprehended Bible meanings in just this fashion for years and years. DiVietro becomes increasingly acerbic toward this idea as the book goes along,[229] though 1 Corinthians 2:13 has always been a plain precept to me since I have been a Bible-believer. Because the lexicons connect the Greek word for *propitiation* with a Hebrew root out of the Septuagint (says he) which is connected to the Mercy Seat and the place of the sacrifice made on the OT Hebrews' day of atonement, readers are informed that only via lexicography could we apprehend the depths of *propitiation* being the place where the **"justice of God is completely satisfied so that he can forgive men without being inconsistent with his own nature."**[230] Oddly Bible-believers find the very concepts DiVietro uses to define the word within the very contexts where the AV uses the word, though he dismisses such a practice.

Please note the emboldened words below, noting first ***propitiation*** in verse 25.

---

[228] Ibid.pg.108-109
[229] Ibid. pg.181
[230] Ibid. pg.109

> *21 But now* ***the righteousness of God without the law is manifested****, being witnessed by the law and the prophets;*
> *22 Even* ***the righteousness of God*** *which is by faith of Jesus Christ unto all and upon all them that believe: for there is no difference:*
> *23 For all have sinned, and come short of the glory of God;*
> *24* ***Being justified freely*** *by his grace through the redemption that is in Christ Jesus:*
> *25 Whom God hath set forth to be* ***a propitiation*** *through faith in his blood****, to declare his righteousness*** *for the remission of sins that are past, through the forbearance of God;*
> *26* ***To declare, I say, at this time his righteousness****: that* he might be just, and the ***justifier*** of him which believeth in Jesus.
>
> (Romans 3:21-26)

In verses 24 & 26, the Bible-believer finds the idea of the "justice" ***(justified; justifier)*** of God being satisfied, though DiVietro said we couldn't find the concept in English.[231] Furthermore, the declaration of and imputation of *the righteousness of God* (vss. 21, 22, 25, & 26) in place of the sins of man would pretty much cover the concept of God being "completely satisfied."

It can only be said that despite his claims, I and the flock I pastor have known the definition of *propitiation* for a long time, and none of us acquired our knowledge by anything other than the King's English.

Plainly the Dean Burgon Society and its adherents provide an "amen section" for Dr. DeVietro's detractions from the AV and his glorification of the preserved original language

---

[231] Ibid.pg.109

text position. He does, by his example, magnify scholastic excursions to Greek and Hebrew, which continue to bear the fruit of overthrowing the authority of the scriptures in our own language. This is, in actuality, sadly pathetic, for it has been shown that the same scholarship which seeks to replace the authority of the word of God with itself animates some of the King James "defenders" as well as modernist scholars.

When it comes to Biblical scholarship, beware, brother. There is ***death in the pot.*** It will blind thee.

Chapter 15

The Great Greek Dilemma: Believing or Obeying?

John 3:36
*He that **believeth** on the Son hath everlasting life: and he that **believeth not** the Son shall not see life; but the wrath of God abideth on him.*
(King James Authorized Version)

For most Bible-believers who take seriously Christ's commission to be witnesses and fishers of men, there are a few soul winners' tools that are necessary to have ready at hand. It does not take even a weekend carpenter too long to figure out which hand tools he needs strapped to his person lest he make many an exhausting and wasteful trip up and down a ladder: Hammer, measuring tape, speed square, pencil, utility knife, nails, screws, screwdriver and chalk-line. Some things migrate from tool belt to tool box alternately, depending on the job, but a man on a ladder without what he needs is not getting the "honey-do" list finished anytime soon.

So it is with a witness for Jesus Christ. A great deal of John 3 needs to be ready at hand at all times. A lot in Romans 3, 4, 5, 6 and 10 needs to have been well-digested and stashed where it can be easily accessed, as well as 2 Corinthians 5:17, Hebrews 9:27, Hebrews 7:25 and Ephesians 2:8-10. John 14:6 and 1 Timothy 2:5 are indispensable. It is necessary for sinners to be thoroughly convinced that they are "bad and lost" before they can get "good and saved," so a good volume of scripture needs to be ready at hand out of Exodus 20, Matthew 5:28 and 12:36, 1 John 3:15, Ecclesiastes 7:20 and Psalms 53:3. That the witness may show the unregenerate where damnation lands them, Revelation 20 and Luke 16 contain material necessary for memory and mastery.

Many a self-justifying sinner brings a slight twist to certain subjects, so eventually one will wind up with a really large toolbox with a lot of specialty compartments, nooks and crannies in it. After a few years of dealing with people, the Bible-believer will find that the entirety of the Bible is useful in reasoning with the lost and with wayward sheep.

That being said, it remains that certain verses are bread and butter. Some verses have a real sharp edge, cut to the chase and put the truth right across the plate waist high. John 3:36 has always been one of those bread and butter verses for *fishers of men. He that* ***believeth*** *on the Son hath everlasting life: and he that* ***believeth not*** *the Son shall not see life; but the wrath of God abideth on him.* Obviously, if someone knows nothing spiritually whatsoever, there is an abundance of other necessary supporting scripture that needs to be brought in to help fill the knowledge gaps; nevertheless, John 3:36 is a straight-from-the-shoulder, down-to-the-bone type of verse that will ricochet through a convicted sinner's conscience in the wee hours of the morning on a sweat-soaked bed. "If you do believe, here is what you get. If you do not believe, here is what you got," is a blue-collar synopsis of the subject matter contained in the verse. If the sinner does not get saved immediately at the presentation of the gospel, then it is desirous that he have simple, soul-piercing truths reverberating through his mind that the Holy Spirit can use to produce discomfort and spiritual stress. John 3:36 is just such a verse among others. It is a concentrated blessing to the saint, but an ominous, looming verity to a sinner, depending on the relation of that sinner's faith - or lack of it – to the Lord Jesus Christ.

John 3:36 sums things up quickly and nicely. It can be quoted to close a testimony, it has a rhythm and cadence to it that sticks to the walls of the mind, and it is short enough to verbally insert through the crack of a closing door as the unconverted resorts to flight. It sets the two contrasting mindsets up nicely: *He that believeth* and *he that believeth not.* It is concentrated light and darkness, conversion and non-conversion, all side-by-side – no frills, no excess information, no poetry and no unnecessary rhetoric.

This is true, that is, as long as the witness for Christ wielding a King James Bible. If one is hauling around and quoting an NASV or an RSV, he is left with a truly clumsy mess which is awkward to quote, contains contradictory messages, and rather than concisely summing up the matter, it leaves the sinner confused and requiring a lot of explanation. Chances are that the sinner receiving such a convoluted witness will smirk, roll his eyes, and the Holy Spirit will have a great deal less to work with in the middle of the night. Please take a moment to compare the sublime and sound truth the King James so succinctly and simply imparts with the confusion and tomfoolery of the gems of modern scholarship.

John 3:36
He that ***believeth*** *on the Son hath everlasting life: and he that* ***believeth not*** *the Son shall not see life; but the wrath of God abideth on him.*
(King James Version)

John 3:36
"He who **believes** in the Son has eternal life; but he who **does not obey** the Son shall not see life, but the wrath of God abides on him."
(New American Standard)

John 3:36
"He who **believes** in the Son has eternal life; but he who **does not obey** the Son will not see life, but the wrath of God abides on him."
(New American Update)

John 3:36
He who **believes** in the Son has eternal life; he who **does not obey** the Son shall not see life, but the wrath of God rests upon him.
(Revised Standard Version)

It does not take theological prodigy to see that the new versions quoted above place two entirely contradicting ideals in head-to-head conflict one with another in the very same verse. Tyndale's ploughboy[232] certainly has no trouble seeing the confusing shadow that obscures the gospel light by the unseemly co-mingling of ***believing*** and ***obeying*** in the new versions' renditions of the verses. Indeed, it likely takes an education of a higher order to be able to perform the kind of semantical gymnastics necessary to assuage the conscience and

232 Farris, Michael. *From Tyndale to Madison*, B&H Publishing Group, Nashville, TN 2007, pg.3-4. In 1522, while tutoring the children of John Walsh, William Tyndale fell into a dispute with a traveling priest. The priest, flustered by Tyndale's fierce reasoning from the scriptures, declared with a good deal of heat and ignominy, "We were better to be without God's laws than the pope's!" Tyndale's reply has reverberated through history: "If God spare my life many years, I will cause a boy that driveth the plough to know more of Scripture than you do."

reason into accepting the dissonant mismatch. For contenders of *the faith which was once delivered unto the saints* (Jude 1:3), it is not an uncommon scenario to have to repel and fight off those who ever attempt to inject works and labor into the simplicity and purity of grace and faith. That is exactly what now has to be done as the usurpers have replaced ***believeth** **not the Son*** (KJV) with ***does not obey the Son*** (NASV, RSV). The rebuke and reproof that answers such nonsense and heresy comes readily to mind for those set to defend the nature of Church Age salvation. Sadly, the answers are so elementary that one wonders at the stunted spiritual maturity and theological tunnel vision of the scholars that would countenance such an evident contradiction.

> *For by grace are ye saved through faith; and that not of yourselves: it is the gift of God:* ***Not of works****, lest any man should boast.*
> (Eph. 2:8-9)

> ***Not by works of righteousness*** *which we have done, but according to his mercy he saved us, by the washing of regeneration, and renewing of the Holy Ghost;* (Titus 3:5)

> *But to him that* ***worketh not, but believeth*** *on him that justifieth the ungodly, his faith is counted for righteousness.* (Rom. 4:5)

Yes, it is certainly understood that "a faith that saves is a faith that works." Yes, it is known that the kind of profound belief and faith which the Lord seeks to impart is a faith that results in certain outward manifestations and fruit. Surely, the *obedience of faith* of which Paul speaks in Romans 1:5 and Romans 16:26 is known, practiced and endlessly promoted. And yes, we are very aware of the clash of faith and works in James 2 – a theological clash for which there are sound and scriptural explanations. Neither the fact that faith should produce certain action, nor the difficulties of James 2, justifies the deplorable admixture of faith and works in a passage where the Lord Jesus Christ Himself highlighted the plain, clear and unmixed simplicity of salvation by ***belief*** and ***faith***. The admixture is, in its effect, a desecration of the words of scripture. In fact, if one has graduated in knowledge as far as Galatians in the Bible, he learns that such an admixture brings upon its proponent a **curse** (Gal. 1:8-9)!

The book of John is written that *ye might believe* (Jn. 20:31), and if there is one thing the New Testament scriptures make plain, it is that Church Age salvation is a heartfelt transaction of faith and trust between a Savior that died and rose for sinners and those individual sinners themselves. Truly, a Christian is *his workmanship, created in Christ Jesus unto good works* (Eph. 2:10), but those works are a result and a fruit of grace and salvation, and to insert a confusion between faith and works in a salvation passage is utterly inexcusable. A translation that does so is polluted and corrupt, and that likely says something profound about the scholars and translators who are so whimsical and unconsecrated doctrinally as to lend their hand to such a piece of work. A man is saved from his sins, and the punishment of those sins in Hell, ***by faith and faith alone***. Nowhere is the truth and verity of this gospel so well stated and so ardently protected and preserved as in the King James Bible. This is a trait that cannot be attributed to the new versions.

The New Versions: A Further Infusion of *Works* Instead of *Faith*

Though their translators and proponents insist with ardent ferocity that the new versions change no essential doctrine in the word of God, anyone who spends any time actually reading through the Bible and comparing what differences actually exist between the versions knows better. The marketers and professorial front-men are able to sell this rhetoric only because their target audience is not a Bible reading or Bible studying audience. Their audience, though it may be "Christian," is much more interested in reading books about the Bible and hearing teachings about the Bible than it is in reading and studying the Bible itself. These folks are even less likely to compare two different versions side-by-side at length. As of this date, in 40 years as a Christian and 24 years in the pastorate, I have not known very many blue-collar proponents of a new version that actually discovered the vast disparity of the new versions on his own, or who challenged the claims of the marketers of the new versions that state that there are no differences that exist between the various species of bibles. This is because the average Christian does not read and truly study his Bible. I have known many who have been challenged by Bible-believers about the issue, and having had the disparities shown to them, have taken up the banner and dug deeper into the matter on their own, but the point is that the hawkers of the corrupt versions victimize a market which prefer darkness to light and ignorance to wisdom (Isa. 30:10).

In spite of the evident laxity of Laodicean "bible study," there are no dispensable doctrines in the word of God, else God would have dispensed with them. They are all precious and blood-washed Christians are appointed *stewards* of them (1 Cor. 4:1). Surely though, anyone should see that when the attack involves the very nature and soul of salvation itself, that alarm must be raised. It should be expected that the devil would despise and abhor such doctrine. Should not expectations be higher for the professed "godly, Christian translators"? Perhaps the issue is only that, once again, Christians have grown so distant from their bibles (any bible), they no longer have an awareness of what details their bibles contain (or no longer contain).

There are many aspects of the doctrine of salvation that are attacked in the new versions. The deity of Christ is one of the most insidious, for if Christ was not *God manifest in the flesh*, all of this is a moot point. The blood of Christ is removed in some cases and undermined in others. The name of the Lord Jesus Christ, by which salvation is attained (Acts 4:12) is routinely and habitually edited and altered in the versions that come from the Alexandrian influences. Jesus' lordship is removed in places, and His ascension from this earth is omitted in Luke 24:51. The prerequisite for baptism is removed or placed in brackets ("*the verse really doesn't belong there*," the brackets hiss) in Acts 8:37. A book could be written on the new versions' aggression against the many aspects of the pure doctrines of salvation, but for the purpose at hand, how and why the new versions undermine the salvation of the soul by replacing ***belief*** with ***obedience*** will be dealt with.

The damage done to John 3:36 has been seen. As one might expect, there is more. Notice the changes made in Acts 19:9.

> *But when divers were hardened, and **believed not**, but spake evil of that way before the multitude, he departed from them, and separated the disciples, disputing daily in the school of one Tyrannus.* (KJV)

> But when some were becoming hardened and ***disobedient***, speaking evil of the Way before the multitude, he withdrew from them and took away the disciples, reasoning daily in the school of Tyrannus. (NAS)

> But when some were becoming hardened and ***disobedient***, speaking evil of the Way before the people, he withdrew from them and took away

the disciples, reasoning daily in the school of Tyrannus. (NAU)

If the change made above doesn't set off any alarms, see the spectacle made in Romans 11:30-32. The context relates how the Jews are enemies *as concerning the gospel*, and then it specifies in verses 30-32 why both Jews and Gentiles have been at enmity with the Lord through the centuries:

> 28 *As concerning the gospel, they are enemies for your sakes: but as touching the election, they are beloved for the fathers' sakes.*
> 29 *For the gifts and calling of God are without repentance.*
> 30 *For as ye in times past have **not believed** God, yet have now obtained mercy through their **unbelief:***
> 31 *Even so have these also now **not believed**, that through your mercy they also may obtain mercy.*
> 32 *For God hath concluded them all in **unbelief,** that he might have mercy upon all.*
> 33 *O the depth of the riches both of the wisdom and knowledge of God! how unsearchable are his judgments, and his ways past finding out!* (KJV)

Notice how the New American Standard renders the key portion of verses 30-32:

> 30 For just as you once were ***disobedient*** to God, but now have been shown mercy because of their ***disobedience***,
> 31 so these also now have been ***disobedient***, in order that because of the mercy shown to you they also may now be shown mercy.

32 For God has shut up all in ***disobedience*** that He might show mercy to all.

(NAS)

Goodness! In verse 32 of the AV 1611, God *concluded them all in **unbelief***, but in the NAS, He "has shut up all in ***disobedience***"! The Lord "shut them up in disobedience"? The NKJV says He "committed" them and the RSV says He "consigned" them. This is quite a theological determination in itself, but the main object is to see that the new versions all agree that the issue was not ***unbelief***, but ***disobedience***. And, thus do the new versions, including the New King James, chime in. The entirety of the verses has not been presented for brevity's sake:

30 … ***disobedient*** …***disobedience***…
31 …***disobedient*** …
32 …***disobedience***…

(NIV)

30 …***disobedient*** …***disobedience***…
31 …***disobedient*** …
32 …***disobedience***…

(NKJV)

30 …***disobedient*** …***disobedience***,
31 …***disobedient***…
32 …***disobedience***…

(RSV)

Consider that it is quite a profound alteration, of course, that the King James Bible has declared now for 400 years that the issue with Israel and amongst the Gentiles through the millennia has been ***unbelief***, yet now at this late time in history, from all the depths and wonders of modern scholarship, it is learned instead that the issue is actually ***disobedience***!

But one cannot simply stop here, for Romans 15:31 says,

> *30 Now I beseech you, brethren, for the Lord Jesus Christ's sake, and for the love of the Spirit, that ye strive together with me in your prayers to God for me;*
> *31 That I may be delivered from* ***them that do not believe*** *in Judaea; and that my service which I have for Jerusalem may be accepted of the saints;* (KJV)

Though most new versions previously surveyed also use the term ***believe*** in this case, the NAS does not concur.

> 31 that I may be delivered from ***those who are disobedient*** in Judea, and {that} my service for Jerusalem may prove acceptable to the saints; (NAS)

Hebrews 3:18-19 is another passage that is butchered by the new versions in such a fashion that it is no wonder that folks cannot make hide nor hair of the meaning of scripture. The King James Bible presents the situation in its usual concise and consistent manner.

> *18 And to whom sware he that they should not enter into his rest, but* ***to them that believed not****?*
> *19 So we see that they could not enter in because of* ***unbelief.*** (KJV)

As anyone can see below, the new versions are agreed in contradicting the King James Bible's readings.

> 18 And to whom did He swear that they should not enter His rest, but to those ***who were disobedient***?
> 19 And {so} we see that they were not able to enter because of ***unbelief.*** (NAS)

> 18 And to whom did God swear that they would never enter his rest if not to ***those who disobeyed***?
> 19 So we see that they were not able to enter, because of their ***unbelief.***
> (NIV)

> 18 And to whom did He swear that they would not enter His rest, but to ***those who did not obey***?
> 19 So we see that they could not enter in because of ***unbelief***. (NKJV)

> 18 And to whom did he swear that they should never enter his rest, but to ***those who were disobedient***?
> 19 So we see that they were unable to enter because of ***unbelief.*** (RSV)

Brethren, there are many passages that are hard to be understood in the word of God, even as testified by the apostle in 2 Peter 3:16. No one is making the case that every single thing written in the King James Bible is perfectly and clearly understood. Somewhere, though, a line must be drawn between that which would be "hardly understood" for the simple fact that it is deeply doctrinal material that men struggle to assimilate, as opposed to that which is understandable, but which is obscured and confused by sinful and fallible men tinkering around and editing to their deceived hearts' desire. The fine balance of words in the holy scriptures is providential and infinitely coordinated. It is wicked and a manifest evil that men would consider themselves called to muddle that which is perfectly plain. In the AV 1611, the issue is ***unbelief***, period. In the new versions, it is ***disobedience*** first, and then it is the contradictory idea of ***unbelief***.

Similar damage is done to a nearby passage: Hebrews 4:6 & 11.

> Heb. 4:6 & 11
> *6 Seeing therefore it remaineth that some must enter therein, and they to whom it was first preached entered not in* ***because of unbelief****:*
> *11 Let us labour therefore to enter into that rest, lest any man fall after the same* ***example of unbelief****.* (KJV)

> Heb. 4:6 & 11
> 6 Since therefore it remains for some to enter it, and those who formerly had good news preached to them failed to enter ***because of disobedience,***
> 11 Let us therefore be diligent to enter that rest, lest anyone fall through {following} the same ***example of disobedience***.
> (NAS)

> Heb. 4:6 & 11
> 6 …***because of their disobedience.***
> 11 …***example of disobedience***.
> (NIV)

Heb. 4:6 & 11
6 ...***because of disobedience***,
11 ...***example of disobedience***.
(NKJV)

Heb. 4:6
6 ...***because of disobedience***,
11 ...***same sort of disobedience***.
(RSV)

In this way, the new bibles turn the whole cloth of the verses in question on their ear. The KJV plainly established the issue as ***unbelief***. The modern versions alter that issue to one of ***disobedience***. No matter what arguments can be set forward to justify this wholesale change, the fact remains that words mean things and entirely different words carry entirely different connotations and meanings with them. If the last sentence has no meaning to a Bible-believer, and if the game of semantics of meaning is the game that defines such a one's Bible education, that person may just as well forsake the Bible altogether and run after the spiritual phantoms and feelings of his own mind and heart. If the sum of the labors of Bible scholars and translators is to present to the body of Jesus Christ two such profoundly conflicting ideas as ***unbelief*** and ***disobedience*** in their sadly disparate "versions" of God's word, expecting believers to see clarity instead of disparity and conflict, then it is long past the time to draw the line on those who can only be compared to Nebuchadnezzar's *magicians, astrologers* and *sorcerers* (Dan. 2:1-10). To anyone who suggests that the new versions change no doctrine in the Bible whatsoever, one has to look no deeper than any single one of the examples given here. ***Unbelief*** and ***disobedience*** are not the same thing. They never have been, and obviously never will be.

As a last example before broader analysis, one can turn to – this is most ironic – what is known as the "faith chapter" in the word of the Lord. Hebrews 11:31 in the King James states explicitly and simplistically,

> *By faith the harlot Rahab perished not with them that* ***believed not****, when she had received the spies with peace.* (KJV)

Once again, as seen previously, ***believing*** is not allowed to stand by the scholars of the new versions in these examples we have set forward. While the double-minded New King James rejoins ranks with the AV on this one, the rest of the bible perversions, in the main, do not.

> By faith Rahab the harlot did not perish along with those who were ***disobedient***, after she had welcomed the spies in peace. (NAS)

> By faith the prostitute Rahab, because she welcomed the spies, was not killed with those who were ***disobedient***. (NIV)

> By faith Rahab the harlot did not perish with those who were ***disobedient***, because she had given friendly welcome to the spies. (RSV)

The King's English plainly sets forth the oppositional contrast between Rahab who ***by faith…perished not***, and the remainder of the people of Jericho who ***believed not*** and who did indeed perish. The *faith* and the *belief* in the verse are match mates, and theirs is a relationship long established in the New Testament scriptures. Again, it is clearly recognized that a belief and faith that is genuine *should* indeed obey and bear outward fruit. Nevertheless, by inserting the word ***disobedient*** into the verse in place of ***believed not*** is to, first, do violence to what God said Jericho's problem was. Secondly, it breaks the comparison and dichotomy between the believing Rahab's faith and the unbelieving city's lack of faith. The issue for the men of Jericho was their ***unbelief,*** not their ***disobedience*** as stated in the new versions.

A Few Greek Tools

To grasp the whole of the issue outlined here, and to understand the decisions that translators and scholars of every New Testament era have faced, just a brief acquaintance with a few facts about the Greek is necessary. It is high time that the Lord's Bible-believing children be willing to hold accountable those who have for so long operated behind the curtain of Greek and Hebrew. As stated before, these oft philosophically Gnostic academics have trusted that peoples' innate laziness, paired with their basic trepidation of dealing with a foreign language, would provide said scholars with largely impenetrable "cover" to do as they please and rescue them from genuine and detailed accountability to the body of Christ.

That an intimate knowledge of language is needed to actually translate from one language to another is inarguably a given. However, the fact is that it does not take an intimate familiarity with Greek or Hebrew to hold scholars accountable, and to, in fact, unveil what is often their trail of infidelity with respect to the word of God. With basic reference tools – and caution is required, for many of those tools were written by infidels and virtual infidels - a student desiring to hold the scholar class accountable may do so with little more than an inquisitive mind, patience, and a Strong's concordance. Numbers are provided beside entries of biblical words in

Strong's. Those numbers are indexed to the corresponding words in both the Greek and Hebrew dictionary in the back of the concordance. Now, Strong's dictionaries are notorious for inaccuracy and for being a major route of infiltration for the illegitimate readings of liberal, apostate scholarship. Nevertheless, a reasonable and thinking student can by this means read the sign and follow the trail of the spiritual thieves and wresters of the truth. In this way, the student does not actually have to even know the Greek or Hebrew alphabet in order to track words. With the listing of what words were used and where, and by comparing what various versions do with those words, many of the careless and shallow lies that biblical scholarship has told about the Bible are often swiftly uncovered. This is accomplished by using their own toolset! Add to Strong's, a stack of new versions and a Greek Lexicon (which will lead the student wrong if he looks to it as an arbiter of the truth, but will allow him to uncover apostates twisted track), and a prudent saint is equipped to behold the inconsistencies, the carelessness and much of the nonsense that scholars have gotten away with for well over a century.

In this case, the disparities between the right Bible and the wrong bibles have been shown with respect to several isolated cases involving the basic scriptural concepts of ***belief*** and ***obedience.***

It should be helpful to know a little of the Greek behind the various forms being dealt with in this section.

* ***Believe*** – **πιστευω - pisteuo** – verb form
* ***Belief*** – **πιστιs - pistis** – noun form
πιστοs - pistos – noun form
* ***Faith*** – almost always from **πιστιs** or **pistis**, as well
* When α- is added as a prefix to the word form, it thus becomes some form of ***believing not,***

believeth not or ***unbelief.*** Think atheist – *a* (no), *theist* (God); or *agnostic* – *a* (not), *gnostic* (knowing).

* The vast majority of the occurrences of the various forms of ***believe*** or ***belief*** in the New Testament, are from one of the Greek roots above beginning with πιστ- or **pist-**.

There is another word form that is less often used, and it has much to do with all of the aforementioned controversy over ***belief*** versus ***obedience.***

* **πειθω - peitho** – root form meaning ***to persuade, be confident of, to put trust***, and importantly ***to believe*** or ***to obey.***

* Once again, When **α-** is added as a prefix to the word form, it becomes, for our purposes some form of ***unbelief, unbelieving, believing not*** or ***disobedient, disobedience.***

* Again, **peitho** and its forms are much less seldom used when compared to **pisteuo.**

* **Peitho** in all versions is rather alternately translated both ***believe*** and ***obey***.

* **Apeitho** in all versions is alternately translated both ***disbelieve*** and ***disobey***.

Please do not allow thy head to swim! In the main, what matters is that **pisteuo**'s word forms are almost always rendered ***believe.*** Another Greek word used occasionally to express both ***belief*** and ***obedience*** is the word form **peitho.**

One other fact that will play into later analysis is that Strong[233], Moulton[234] and Perschbacher,[235] all recognized

---

233 Strong, Strongs Concordance, A Concise Dictionary pg.58

234 Moulton, Harold K., The Analytical Greek Lexicon Revised, pg.326

distinguished lexicographers, agree that even **pisteuo** in all its forms is traced back to the Greek word **peitho.**

Having summarized all of that, if one reads the Greek New Testament, he would find that translated into English, the word **pisteuo** would almost always be translated as some form of the word ***believe***, and that the different forms of **peitho** would be translated alternately as the different forms of either ***believe*** or ***obey.*** For the purposes outlined in this discussion, that is all a Bible-believer really needs to keep straight.

The AV 1611 and *Peitho (Apeitho)*

In the ***believe*** vs. ***obey,*** and the ***unbelief*** vs. ***disobedience*** controversies outlined earlier in the chapter, it is the translation of the word **peitho (apeitho)** that causes all the upheaval. While it would not seem that one word in Greek would be translated as a form of ***believe*** in one place, and as a form of ***obey*** in the next, this is indeed the case in all English versions, including the AV 1611.

Remembering that **peitho** can be translated ***believe*** or ***obey***, and remembering that **apeitho** can be translated ***unbelieving*** or ***disobey***, here is how the King James Bible renders the verses where the words are contained.

Peitho / Apeitho (AV 1611)

Reference	**Translation**
Lk.1:17	*disobedient*

[235] Perschbacher, Wesley J., The New Analytical Greek Lexicon, pg.329

Jn.3:36	*believeth not*
Acts 5:36	*obeyed*
Acts 5:37	*obeyed*
Acts 14:2	*unbelieving*
Acts 17:4	*believed*
Acts 19:9	*believed not*
Acts 26:19	*disobedient*
Acts 27:11	*believed*
Acts 28:24	*believed*
Rom.1:30	*disobedient*
Rom.2:8a	*do not obey*
Rom. 2:8b	*obey*
Rom.10:21	*disobedient*
Rom.11:30a	*have not believed*
Rom.11:30b	*unbelief*
Rom.11:31	*not believed*
Rom.11:32	*unbelief*
Rom.15:31	*do not believe*
Gal.5:7	*not obey*
Eph.2:2	*disobedience*
Eph.5:6	*disobedience*
Col. 3:6	*disobedience*
2 Tim.3:2	*disobedient*
Tit.1:16	*disobedient*
Tit.3:3	*disobedient*
Heb.3:18	*believed not*
Heb.4:6	*unbelief*
Heb.4:11	*unbelief*
Heb.11:31	*believed not*
Heb.13:17	*obey*
Jas.3:3	*obey*
1 Pet.2:8	*disobedient*
1 Pet.3:1	*obey not*
1 Pet.3:20	*disobedient*
1 Pet.4:17	*obey not*

Plainly, when it comes to the translation of this Greek word form, the King James translators did not translate it consistently one way. Expectedly, criticism is often leveled – which criticism is often just the product of hearsay – that the AV translators were not "consistent" in their various methods of translating the AV into English. Looking at what has thus far been presented, the superficial observation would seem to be that the men of the KJV committee indeed were not consistent.

It should be stated that the reader and the critics alike might contemplate that there may well have been other considerations that contributed to the translators judgment besides that to which we have just been introduced. On the heels of that meditation, it should be swiftly established that what criticism is good for the goose, is also good for the gander. The scholarly maestros of the new versions are not consistent either, and it shall later be seen what it was that contributed to their discordant judgments on how **peitho** should be translated. For now, let us summarize how the new versions rendered the Greek.

The New Versions and *Peitho (Apeitho)*

* See Appendix I (pg.811)

As anyone can see who actually scans Appendix I, none of the versions of the Bible in English translate the Greek in one solitary and consistent way, even limiting consideration mostly to the issues of ***believing*** and ***obeying***. Any charge that the King James is inconsistent in translation in this case must be disregarded, for all of the versions are inconsistent.

While none of the versions translate **peitho** in any singular uniform way, there are some observations to be made.

One cannot help but notice that the new versions lean more toward translating forms of the word **peitho** as some form of ***obedience*** (or ***disobedience*** as the case may be) as opposed to ***believing*** or ***disbelieving***.

In the tally of the 36 cases above for each version:
* The AV translates the various forms of ***obey*** 21 times and the various forms of ***believe*** 15 times.
* The NAS – **obey** – 29 times; **believe** – 1 time. The NAS translated "followed" 2 times, "persuaded" 3 times, and did not translate the word in Col.3:6.
* The NIV - **obey** – 23 times; **believe** – 4 times. The NIV translates it "reject" 2 times, "follow" 4 times, "persuaded" 1 time, "convinced" 1 time and does not translate it in Col.3:6.
* The NKJV – **obey** – 29 times; **believe** – 4 times. The NKJV translates it "persuaded" 3 times.
* The RSV – **obey** – 27 times; **believe** – 3 times. The RSV translates "followed" 2 times, "persuaded" 1 time, "paid more attention" 1 time, "convinced" 1 time and did not translate the word in Col.3:6.

Certainly, where the new versions translate **peitho** as **persuade** or **convince**, the argument could be made that those words represent some essence of ***believing***. While such sentiment can be understood, neither of those words is the same word as ***believe***, and this marks a dangerous trend toward the inexact word-switching of the new versions discussed at length before. Whatever else is the case, please note that the tallies above show a significant shift toward **obey** in the new versions. This shift, then, is a significant shift towards ***works*** as opposed to ***faith***.

Obey / Disobey

* KJV – 21 times; NAS – 29 times; NIV – 23 times; NKJV – 29 times; RSV – 27 times

If the trend towards ***works*** is significant – notice that the NKJV tallies as the worst along with the NAS – the shift and transition away from the crystal-clear concept of ***believing*** in the new versions is downright radical!

Believe / Disbelieve

* KJV – 15 times; NAS – 1 time; NIV – 4 times; NKJV – 4 times; RSV – 3 times.

Thus far, examination shows a Greek word form, **peitho**, which in no English translation is rendered in only one way. Even the King James translators translated it ***obey*** at times. **So the Greek shows itself, in this case, to be quite inexact when it comes to meaning.** This is contrary to what has been held forth by Greek scholars of all stripes, though the lexicons, dictionaries and reference materials all allow a plurality of meanings. For the purpose of consideration here, a diligent Christian knows that there is still a monstrous conflict across the denominations and among the unconverted that revolves around the controversy of faith and works – in this case ***believing*** and ***obeying***. A sincere and honest scholar knows full well the chasm that lies between the concepts of ***believing*** and ***obeying***. If the Greek does not provide certainty as to the meaning of **apietho** and **peitho** in any given case, and if it can be either *unbelief* or *disobedience, believing or obeying,* why is it, then, that the new versions radically shift and slide toward a more works and labor-oriented emphasis with respect to the truth of God? If, somehow, the choice between ***believing*** and ***obeying*** scholastically were a toss-up due to the lack of clarity in the Greek, why would the whole of modern scholarship and biblical academia begin to load the scales on the ***works*** and ***obeying*** side of things?

This seems particularly odd when considering the fact that the scholars concede that the word **peitho** is actually the root of the words **pisteuo**, **pistis** and **pistos** which words are almost universally translated as ***belief, believe, believing*** or ***faith***. If Greek were the ultimate authority, why would one lean toward translating a word *away* from the meaning of its Greek roots? Why would the scholarly scales not tip back toward the ***faith*** and ***belief*** of the Greek root word?

For the purposes of ecumenical harmony, one might give the scholars of the new versions the benefit of the doubt. After all, they have such reputations for "godliness" and their professions abound with cherished commitment to the blessed word of God. Instead of regard for mere profession and reputation, let the Christian look upon the bald, unmitigated, written proof of their work. Given the grammatical and linguistic ambiguity of the Greek alone in this case (some would call it latitude or uncertainty), why would there be such a radical shift away from ***faith*** and towards ***works*** in modern translations and scholarly materials? Why would there be such a shift away from the admitted classic English Bible, now 400 years old, and for no demonstrable grammatical reason? Further, why would there be such a general and uniform witness among the new bibles for just such a translational shift? Why is there such unanimity of opinion among the academics in this matter when there is no evidence or material reason presented for such a theologically directional shift in readings?

Consideration of the reality of academic collaboration among the scholars must certainly be weighed. One work is influenced by another. Scholars train scholars, build upon common reference works and adopt mutual academic opinions. Collaboration cannot, in itself, be considered conspiratorial since the King James translators themselves collaborated amongst themselves. Pastors collaborate and cooperate among themselves, as do missionaries and other ministers. *Hear counsel, and receive instruction, that thou mayest be wise in thy latter end*, says Proverbs 19:20, therefore the convening and agreement of translators together cannot be made a conspiracy all by itself. Nevertheless, people are left with the troubling, printed, and copyrighted evidence of a dramatic shift in supposedly objective bibles from ***faith*** toward ***works***, and this when the Greek is ambiguous and neutral with respect to clarity and meaning. It should be alarming to *Greek-is-the-final-authority people* because they ought to be quite surprised by how inexact Greek can be at times, despite what they have been told. It should truly alert any Bible reading Christian who ought to be able to recognize a hijacking of gospel and scriptural precepts when he sees one!

No, even those who would desire to grant benefit of the doubt must admit there is something afoot here that goes beyond the beneficial collaboration of colleagues, just as it certainly goes beyond the objective "science" of linguistics and grammar. The only possibility that seems reasonable is the conclusion that the translators of the new versions are predisposed more toward works than faith in their opinions and prejudices. Truly, they may not deny ***faith*** or ***belief*** in a verse where the language and grammar are inarguably clear. No, they do not mess up John 3:16 or Ephesians 2:8-9. For this, rejoice, but what happens when the Greek is slightly more ambiguous and is not so distinctively narrow in its meaning? What happens when the Greek is not absolutely definite? What happens when the translator has to fall back on his judgment and discretion, rather than on grammatical rule? This much is known: when possibilities for meaning are as far apart as ***believe*** and ***obey*** (in many respects, this is 180 degrees apart), and the Greek does not specify meaning, ***one does learn a great deal about a translator's predispositions, proclivities and prejudices!*** All quantifiable evidence in the new versions with respect to the handling of **peitho** and **apeitho,** points to nothing other than the markedly opinionated and preferential choice and a propagation of works over faith!

Chapter 8 of this work is an essay that biblically documents and analyzes some of the means by which Satan, *the god of this world* (2 Cor. 4:4), blinds *the minds of them that believe not*, and succeeds ultimately in deceiving *the whole world* (Rev. 12:9). Just such a sliver of this demonic phenomenon is right before the very eyes of the reader in the case of **peitho** and **apeitho**. With no rule or grammatical law by which to justifiably digress from the English tradition of the King James Bible, the scholars have with astounding uniformity and unity migrated theologically to the works side of the scale. Consider this question: who was it that succeeded in alluring the entire corporate mind of academia, as found in the new versions, into a uniform departure from ***believing***?

A Word About the Relation of *Believing* and *Obeying*

As it has been set forth above, the general fact is that *believing* and *obeying*, and thus by proxy, *disbelieving* and *disobeying*, are oppositional concepts theologically. When speaking of salvation, *believing* equals *faith* and *obeying* generally equals *works*. In the passages listed and which will be henceforth discussed, the illegitimate and unfounded transition by scholars and translators from the issue of *believing* to the issue of *obeying*, presents a truly confusing and confounding intermingling of faith and works at critical doctrinal crossroads where the Lord is obviously laboring to establish the preeminence of *faith* and *belief*.

That being said, it certainly is important to acknowledge that in the scriptures there is an *obedience* that is related to *faith*:

> *25 Now to him that is of power to stablish you according to my gospel, and the preaching of Jesus Christ, according to the revelation of the mystery, which was kept secret since the world began,*
> *26 But now is made manifest, and by the scriptures of the prophets, according to the commandment of the everlasting God, made known to all nations* ***for the obedience of faith****:*
> *27 To God only wise, be glory through Jesus Christ for ever. Amen.* (Rom. 16:25-27)

Obviously, the nations are to act *in obedience* to the preaching of the gospel and to the admonitions of the scriptures *by believing*. In other words, in this context *believing* the gospel is *obeying* it. Another example of this relationship is Romans 10:14-17,

> *14 How then shall they call on him in whom they have* ***not believed****? and how shall they* ***believe in him*** *of whom they have not heard? and how shall they hear without a preacher?*
> *15 And how shall they preach, except they be sent? as it is written, How beautiful are the feet of them that preach the gospel of peace, and bring glad tidings of good things!*
> *16 But they have* ***not all obeyed the gospel****. For Esaias saith, Lord,* ***who hath believed our report****?*
> *17 So then* ***faith*** *cometh by hearing, and hearing by the word of God.*

Again, in a passage which theme is *belief* and *faith*, there is inserted the concept of *obeying the gospel.* (Incidentally, the Greek behind this passage's cases of not *obeying the gospel* is not the word ***apeitho*** which is the issue in this chapter). Once again, *obey(ing) the gospel* in this case is manifestly defined as *believ(ing) our report* in verse 16.

The point is that there is an *obedience* that is connected with hearing the gospel truth and, hence, *believing*. In this regard, *believing* is an act of *obedience*, yet in the same respect is no manner of works whatsoever.

It is also true that the right kind of *faith* and *belief* leads to *obedience* and work for the Lord. An example of this is found in the faith chapter of Hebrews 11:8:

> ***By faith*** *Abraham, when he was called to go out into a place which he should after receive for an inheritance,* ***obeyed****; and he went out, not knowing whither he went.*

Again, this *obedience* is translated from a word unrelated to the ***apeitho*** being critiqued in this chapter. Here Abraham *obeyed...by faith.* Obviously, his faith led him to do something; to go somewhere.

The reason for this brief section is to clearly acknowledge that there are tenets and times in the scripture where and when *faith* and *obedience* are not polar opposites and where they follow and are related to one another. However, it is also important to note that the two concepts are many times adversarial and oppositional to one another, as well. They often represent opposite ends of the spectrum in certain theological contexts. In the cases which are highlighted in this chapter, the insertion of the concept of *obedience* into passages devoted to and expanding upon the nature and precepts of *faith* and *belief*, introduces discord, confusion and blatant contradiction. In the proper context, there is a relation between the two, but these are two attributes that are not be tossed together and interchanged willy-nilly in most passages of scripture. As "willy-nilly" appears to be the controlling factor for quite a lot of the translation decisions observed in the new versions, it is no surprise that the collective doctrine of mainline Christianity is such the train wreck as is seen today.

The AV 1611: The Correct Translation of *Peitho (Apeitho)*

The masquerading and strutting *science* of this world, which is *falsely so called* (1 Tim. 6:20), has enjoyed enormous success at establishing itself in the world's collective mind as the ultimate authority. No matter how illogical, ridiculous or cartoonish the tenet set forth today, if it can be declared *scientific*, it is received with virtually a religious reverence. Evolution may be an absolute debacle to the rational mind, but it is *science*, so virtually none consider making a loud objection. Psychiatry and psychology have long been the roosts of genuine quacks (Spock) and truly vulgar and perverse thinkers and practitioners (Freud and Freeman), but since both are now categorized as *science*, the saints who are now *sitting, and clothed, and in (their) right mind(s)* (Mk. 5:15), may all be put away in a rubber room at the word of one of these fruitcake doctors. After all, they are scientists!

In the theological realm, the scholars have an almost obsessive fixation on making critical scholarship and translation a *science*. Just as an evolutionary microbiologist authoritatively states some nonsense using $14 words and referring to some fictional event 350 million years ago, the biblical scholars are well known for castigating a particular translation or phrasing, pompously stating as fact what the original said, expanding voraciously on the intricate "in's and out's" of his intellectual excellence. In both cases the purpose is the same: to shut people up in the presence of such a superior authority. Sadly, far from being *science*, evolution is fiction, and modern biblical scholarship has always been a haven of, and a magnet for, charlatans and prideful egos (Isa. 14:12-14).

Bible-believers are glad to have been delivered a Bible that can be known, studied and loved in their own language. They are Bible students, endeavoring to know God's word and hoping to achieve a scholarship by which they may know God and the mind of Jesus Christ in depth. For those who have been called to scholarly labors in the Biblical languages, the track is truly a treacherous one. It is often not appreciated that a simplistic idea in one language may be profoundly difficult to translate exactly into another. How much more so when ideas and concepts are complex, inter-related, built one upon another, and men's souls do well hang upon the product of the work? Verb forms, noun forms, specific adjectives, word order, phrasing, pace and rhythm can present baffling puzzles to translation. Transparency in meaning, synonyms, antonyms, similitudes, comparative language, poetic meter – all of these are the linguistic tangle that a translator concerned with exact meaning must face. At this juncture it should be stated that while scholarship is the realm of many truly learned and profound minds, and while there are laws and rules aplenty that bound and limit the world of the scholar, Biblical scholarship is every bit as much an art form as it is a science.

John 3:36 – The AV 1611 Reading Justified

As a reminder, here is how John 3:36 looks with the transliteration of the words in question supplied:

> *He that **believeth (pisteuo)** on the Son hath everlasting life: and he that **believeth not (apeitho)** the Son shall not see life; but the wrath of God abideth on him.* (KJV)

To repeat, ***pisteuo*** is almost always translated in the New Testament as some form of *believing* or *faith.* **Peitho,** for the purposes being deliberated, is alternately translated *believe* or *obey* and ***apeitho*** as *disbelieving* or *disobeying.* As we considered before, the new versions tend toward translating ***apeitho*** as *disobeying* more than *disbelieving*, and in John 3:36 ***apeitho*** is, in the new versions generally, rendered *does not obey.*

Anyone can see the contradictory nature of the declaration that, on one hand, *He that **believeth (pisteuo)** on the Son hath everlasting life,* but on the other hand, *he that **does not obey (apeitho)** shall not see life.* The exalters of the Greek stridently proclaim that Greek is the ultimate authority biblically. Yet the Greek alone helps little or none when trying to determine what the translation of ***apeitho*** should be. The lexicons and dictionaries themselves offer both of the two significant possibilities in this case, *believeth not* and *does not obey*, with utterly no direction whatever as to which translation is absolutely correct. How is the Greek the final authority? How is it not instead the enabler that empowers the translators' personal opinions, prejudices and predisposed theological bent? How is the Greek not rather the stick with which the translator or scholar is allowed to flog the naïve and unwary into subservience to the scholar's own private interpretations?

The fact is that the Greek in this case carries within itself neither the direction nor the authority for a final determination of how ***apeitho*** should be translated and understood. Wherein, then, is the authority? Where does the determining factor lie? Very simple. As novel as the idea sounds to the Christian ear today, ***final authority lies within the context of the scriptures themselves***. First, in the context of the English of the King James Bible, to translate and insert *not obeying* into the passage of John 3 is a clanging, clashing discordant note in a passage entirely dedicated to believing and faith. The fact is that John chapter 3 alone has *believe* in its various forms showing up 9 times. In the entirety of the book of John the word *obey* or *obedience* does not show up one singular time. All forms of the word believe and faith show up around 100 times in the Book of John in the King James Bible. The only time ***peitho*** or ***apeitho***, which according to lexicographers *could* be translated *obey* or *disobey*, is used in the Greek in the book of John, it is in John 3:36, the very passage being considered. With the unanimous voices of over 100 scriptures proclaiming the unwavering theme of ***belief*** and ***faith*** in the book of John, the translators of the new versions translate the single lonely occurrence of *apeitho* as "***does not obey"***! With all the weight of the scriptural testimony against them, as well as the declarative thesis of John, clearly stated in John 20:31 (*But these are written, **that ye might believe** that Jesus is the Christ, the Son of God; and that **believing** ye might have life through his name*), the scholars brutishly forge right ahead and translate John 3:36b as "he that **does not obey (apeitho)** shall not see life."

Even if the lexicons and dictionaries allow that *apeitho* could be translated "obey not" as well as "believe not," how could a man, in the name of the Lord, justify translating it "obey not" when literally all the testimony of all the scripture throughout all the book of John attests to believing and faith? What deficiency of judgment and equity would lead a translator to try to redirect or mar the utterly uniform attestation of the scriptures from belief to obedience, and that against all witnesses?

The profound and sublime lesson is simply this: The Greek is neither the final appeal nor the final authority for matters of truth and doctrine in the New Testament! A translator simply cannot, and in the case of the AV translators, did not, merely open a Bible dictionary or lexicon and be directed to the profound truth of the scriptures. In this case, the context of the surrounding scriptures dictated that the Bible read "*believeth not*," and it is most important to note that the AV English scriptures supplied both the proper context and the proper translation of the singular word. It is easier to determine the absolute truth of faith and belief in the King James Bible than it is to determine it in the Greek, for the Greek leads confused minds into yet more confusion.

Acts 19:9 – The AV 1611 Reading Justified

This reading, discussed earlier in the chapter, is another perfect example of the AV English always leading the Bible-believer right, while the Greek believer is left in confusion and without clarity. The King James translates thus:

*But when divers were hardened, and **believed not (apeitho)**...*

The NAS and the NAU translators scuttle and slither to their lexicons and feel that on the authority of what they find therein, they have the latitude to translate ***apeitho*** differently than the AV, and in doing so, they change the entire complexion of the issue in the minds of their readers and countless numbers of eternal souls:

> But when some were becoming hardened and ***disobedient***... (NAS)

But when some were becoming hardened and *disobedient*... (NAU)

Fleeing to Strong's dictionary or the plethora of lexicons only convinces the researcher and scholar that autonomy and leeway is granted to translate it "*disobedient*" just as justifiably as *believed not*. No scholar has the latitude or liberty to blithely choose between "disobedience" and "disbelief" when it comes to the words of the living God. Such latitude, left to the mere discretion of corrupt sinner-scholars, would allow the truth to be commandeered and then be turned 180 degrees from faith to works. And in the New American Standard and its sister update, it is just that. No better example exists of merely one of the species of quandary in which a translator may find himself, as a word in the Greek New Testament, which could by virtue of the information provided in the lexicons, literally be translated either of two ways - and those two ways are diametrically opposed to one another doctrinally. What is one to do, flip a coin? ***No, you are going to defer to man's opinion, aren't you, Mr. Scholarman?*** You will defer to your own opinion, somebody else's opinion, or some combination of the two. ***You are going to place preference and prejudice above the words of the Holy God***, and then you are going to try to sell the execrable result to the body of Christ under the auspices of scholarship and godly academia.

Is the final authority for the reading of the Bible in Acts 19:9 the Greek? Obviously, it is not, for obviously it cannot be. The Greek alone does not contain the necessary information or direction to make the determination. It cannot alone provide the necessary light needed to make the crucial decision between believing not and disobeying. The Greek here does not contain the hidden treasure or the key necessary to provide 100% certainty to the reader or Bible-believer.

What does provide the certainty that would allow us to proceed forward in God's commission to us as mandated in Proverbs 22:21, *That I might make thee* ***know the certainty of the words of truth****; that thou mightest answer the words of truth to them that send unto thee*? Why, the text and context of the very scriptures that bear the handprints of God, given to an English-speaking Bible-believer in his very own language in 1611!

In Acts 19:9, the issue was stated thusly:

But when divers were hardened, and ***believed not (apeitho)****...*

Yet in the same passage, all the keys to understanding and certainty lie round about!

> *He said unto them, Have ye received the Holy Ghost since ye* ***believed (pisteuo)****?*
>
> (Acts 19:2)

> *Then said Paul, John verily baptized with the baptism of repentance, saying unto the people, that* ***they should believe (pisteuo)*** *on him which should come after him, that is, on Christ Jesus.*
>
> (Acts 19:4)

> *And many that* ***believed (pisteuo)*** *came, and confessed, and shewed their deeds.*
>
> (Acts 19:18)

Once again, the translation of the word in the verse in question (vs.9) is literally surrounded by the ridiculously apparent and unmistakable precept of *believing.* There are utterly no grounds for altering verse 9 to read *disobedient.* It is in complete defiance of context to do so.

Further, while Greek is not the final authority, the pertinent Greek words have been included above to show that ***apeitho*** in verse 9 (the scholars say it could be *believed not* or *disobeyed* - either one) is surrounded by ***pisteuo***, a Greek word uniformly understood to mean *believe,* as it is translated in the AV. If ***peitho*** can mean either *believe* or *obey*, and it is surrounded by a word, ***pisteuo***, uniformly translated *believe*, why in the world would an objective translator actually opt to translate ***apeitho*** as "*disobedient*" in opposition to *believed not*? The stream, flow and theme of the passage are the same in Greek as well as English. Where did "*disobeying*" come from? If those preoccupied and obsessed with the Greek are going to play the Greek game, why then would they not be consistent with the Greek word usage? We understand that they disparage and disrespect the King's English, but these hypocrites are not even faithful in the confines of the language that they promote and exalt as containing the vastly superior treasures of truth.

Romans 11:30-32 - The AV 1611 Reading Justified

Romans 11:30-32 from the KJV is presented once again with the pertinent Greek transliterations:

> *30 For as ye in times past have* ***not believed (apeitho)*** *God, yet have now obtained mercy through their* ***unbelief (apeitho):***
> *31 Even so have these also now* ***not believed (apietho)****, that through your mercy they also may obtain mercy.*
> *32 For God hath concluded them all in* ***unbelief (apietho)****, that he might have mercy upon all.* *(KJV)*

The false translation of the New American Standard is representative of the new versions pretty much across the board, including the NKJV:

> 30 *For just as you once were* ***disobedient*** *to God, but now have been shown mercy because of their* ***disobedience,***
> 31 *so these also now have been* ***disobedient,*** *in order that because of the mercy shown to you they also may now be shown mercy.*
> 32 *For God has shut up all in* ***disobedience*** *that He might show mercy to all.*
>
> *(NAS)*

There is the obvious wholesale departure preceptually from the issue of *unbelief* in the AV 1611, to the issue of *disobedience* in the new versions. The AV translators' time-tested work is flagrantly dismissed on what basis? The grand theme of *belief vs. unbelief* is set on the shelf in favor of the works-related theme of *obedience vs. disobedience* because ***apeitho*** is the Greek word in question, and ***apeitho*** is translated both *unbelief* and *disobedience* at times. Because the lexicographers allow *disobedient* as one of the meanings, Satan's little minions jump off the scriptural precipice in exercising their presumed prerogative to translate it so. The latitude they take is sacrilegious presumption and it is precipitous beyond measure, for they hijack the "faith" theme of the passage and make it a "works" theme. Someday their sin will find them out (Num. 32:23).

If the bare Greek reading does not provide true and inspired guidance for translation and understanding, something else must certainly do so. Once again the issue is settled by context. Aside from the fact that the previous chapter, Romans 10, is uniformly concerned with the faith and belief issue (faith and belief show up 10 times in Romans 10), the theme is extended into Romans 11 where the unbelieving nation of Israel is discussed thus:

> Romans 11:20-23
> *20 Well; because of* ***unbelief (apistos)*** *they were broken off, and thou standest by* ***faith (pistis)****. Be not highminded, but fear:*
> *21 For if God spared not the natural branches, take heed lest he also spare not thee.*
> *22 Behold therefore the goodness and severity of God: on them which fell, severity; but toward thee, goodness, if thou continue in his goodness: otherwise thou also shalt be cut off.*
> *23 And they also, if they abide not still in* ***unbelief (apistos)****, shall be graffed in: for God is able to graff them in again.* (KJV)

It is enough to see in the English of the AV that Romans 10 is the immediate foundation of Romans 11, which foundation is entirely of faith and belief. Following Chapter 10, Romans 11:20-23 clearly establishes the issue of belief and faith, which extends on to Romans 11:30-32. It is an exercise of wresting scripture and defying definite and clear contexts to insert the issue of obedience and disobedience into Romans 11:30-32.

To show again that the Greek itself is not – and cannot be - the final arbiter of truth, the Greek transliteration above shows ***apistos (unbelief)*** and ***pistis (faith)*** as being the distinct and clear precepts under discussion in verses 20-23. All scholars agree uniformly throughout the course of the entire New Testament that these two Greek words are words denoting and conveying the precepts of faith and belief. How is it that the theme to which all agree is faith and belief in verses 20-23, turns without preamble to obedience and works in verses 30-32? What on earth would lead one to think that the theme and principle of faith being discussed would contradictorily and inexplicably become disobedience seven verses later? The fact is that the naked Greek of verses 30-32 could be translated in either fashion, unbelief or disobedience, according to all the lexicographers. Therefore, it is obvious that the Greek itself is insufficient, ineffectual and confusing as a final authority. It is just not as simple as skipping off to a Greek dictionary and replacing one of the words of scripture with another alternate word that Strong, Perschbacher or Moulton might advocate. Often what a word can mean is divergent and contrary to one of its other meanings. Belief and obedience may follow and be contingent upon one another in certain contexts, but they are oppositional, and in many ways antonyms, when it comes to other contexts.

In this case, the context is as much the arbiter of how the verse should read as is the Greek grammar itself. The context dictates what the proper translation of ***apeitho*** should be. Most importantly, the King James Bible clarifies how the passage should read from the very start. As a Greek student, in order to get the intended meaning, one would have to grasp that God intended ***apeitho*** to be translated *not believed* instead of *disobedient*, since it could indeed be either translation if only the Greek word is taken in consideration. In order to get that right, a person would have to grasp the context first to realize that it dictates that the reading should be *unbelief.* The KJV resolves the elementary and intrinsic obscurities of the Greek language by translating the passage as it should be translated into English. That is a significant improvement upon the so-called "original Greek"! In this way, the King James English is truly superior to the Greek. It clears up the native ambiguities of both Hebrew and Greek.

Romans 15:31 – The AV 1611 Reading Justified

Romans 15:31 records Paul's prayer,

> *That I may be delivered from them that* ***do not believe (apeitho)*** *in Judaea; and that my service which I have for Jerusalem may be accepted of the saints.* (KJV)

Naturally, certain of the new bibles do not agree.

> (T)hat I may be delivered from those who are ***disobedient*** in Judea... (NAS)

> (T)hat I may be rescued from those who are ***disobedient*** in Judea... (NAU)

Romans 15:13 helps establish the context of 15:31. It says, *Now the God of hope fill you with all joy and peace in* ***believing (pisteuo)****, that ye may abound in hope, through the power of the Holy Ghost.* The issue in the passage is ***believing***. There are utterly no grounds in Greek to change the reading of Romans 15:31 to *disobedient,* or the timber of the passage to *disobedience*.

One is left with the distinct impression that the scholars of the new versions, as well as critical scholarship, are inclined to change the wording in the King James Bible for no better reason than that they *can.* One has to remember that no single translated word holds any sacred meaning to them, for all translations are faulted in their minds. Bible-believers' final authority, the AV 1611, has words in it that are sacred and unalterable to those Bible-believers whether they fully apprehend the meanings of them or not. Even those King James people, who are apprehensive about claiming perfection for the King James, are extremely reticent, in the main, about having the words in the blessed old Book changed. It is indispensable for the reader to realize that such reticence is nothing like the mindset of the scholars and their minions of whom this book is so critical. Their final authority is the original Greek, in the New Testament case. Their final authority is by no means final, for as has been repeatedly seen, they relish the latitude which is granted to them by their lexicons and dictionaries, to interchange and shuffle the word choices and meanings. Their final appeal and final authority for life and for all eternity grants to them a vast and great variety of choices and shades. By their standards as seen in this matter of ***apeitho***, they get to choose essentially whether the issue of life is *unbelief* or *disobedience*… whether it is *faith* or *works*! The variableness of their lexicons and dictionaries make possible for them to dictate what the Bible says or means. This is the polar opposite of God's intent for the word of God. The Bible dictates truth to man – not vice versa! These scholars allow themselves the temerity to choose what their Bible says, for indeed, they themselves are their own ultimate arbiters of truth.

Hebrews 3:18-19 - The AV 1611 Reading Justified

Hebrews 3:18-19 presents much the same translating scenario and mode of operation by the scholars which has been now repeatedly demonstrated. Apparently, the power of choice and alternative offered in Greek lexicons and dictionaries - which books often proceed from the fallible minds of demonstrably fallible scholars - so enamors and grips the spirit of the modern academic, that it completely blinds the mind and corrupts the judgment to the end that they are neither careful nor consistent.

As demonstrated before, the AV 1611's reading is thus (Root Greek words have been supplied for the English words in question):

18 And to whom sware he that they should not enter into his rest, but to them that ***believed not (apeitho)****?*
19 So we see that they could not enter in because of ***unbelief (apistos)****.*

The new versions – NASV, NAU, NIV, NKJV, RSV – are uniform in their departure from ***believed not*** in verse 18, rendering it ***disobeyed*** or ***disobedient***. They leave the ***unbelief*** of verse 19 unaltered, apparently not apprehending the ridiculous and contradictory conflict this presents to the passage. Are these men so profoundly blind that they cannot keep track of a context from one short sequential verse to the next? Is it blindness or carelessness? Is it utter sacrilegious unconcern, or is it monumental, condescending arrogance? Is this the collective action of simply lost and unconverted men uncomprehendingly making a mess, or is it intentional and conspiratorial vilification of the words of the Living God?

The theme of this chapter is that ***apeitho*** is in all Bibles, including the King James, translated ***believed not*** sometimes, and ***obeyed not*** or ***disobeyed*** sometimes. In verse 18, ***apeitho*** is *believed not* in the King James, well as it should be, since verse 19 follows with *unbelief*. The *unbelief* of verse 19 is matched by its Greek word ***apistos***, which is unquestionably *unbelief* even in the new versions, as it is throughout the New Testament. Brethren, the context between the two verses is one and united. The English of the AV bears testament to the uniform context between the two verses, and while in other contexts ***apeitho*** of verse 18 might be translated *disobeyed*, it certainly cannot be translated that way in verse 18, because verse 19, even in Greek, inflexibly establishes the issue as *unbelief*, not *disobedience*.

Again, the Greek forms of these words are not being presented to prove and supply authority to the truth and accuracy of the King James readings. They are being supplied to show that while the King James is right, that a bit of accounting in the Greek proves that the exalted scholars of the Greek are careless, inconsistent, contradictory and wholly unworthy of the mantle of respect and authority now granted them by their modern fawning and sycophantic followers.

As a further witness, Hebrews 3:12, six verses earlier, establishes the context of the passage by stating,

> *Take heed, brethren, lest there be in any of you an evil heart of **unbelief**, in departing from the living God.* (AV 1611)

Once again, the *unbelief* of verse 12 is translated from the root ***apistos*** and is uniformly translated *unbelieving* or *unbelief* in all the main body of the new versions cited in this work. Hence, all the versions agree the issue is *unbelief* in verses 12 and 19, yet only the AV renders ***apeitho*** of verse 18 as *believed not*. All others insert the contradictory idea of *disobedience*. The King James Bible rightly remains on track contextually and in consistency while the new versions make a sort of soiled and spoiled salvation sandwich of *disobedience* between two slices of *disbelief*.

Yes, Dorothy, the King James English is indeed superior to the Greek, for no one who believes the English of the AV ever even has to think twice about how ***apeitho*** should or could be translated. That unsettled issue in Greek is settled and affirmed in the King James Bible. It is also correct to say that the King James corrects the Greek where the Greek and its affiliated lexicons and dictionaries mislead people into thinking the issue is *disobedience* when the issue is *unbelief*. The AV 1611 corrects the new versions, it corrects the infiltrations of the false Greek texts and it corrects scholars' misjudgments and prejudices just as it corrects man's thoughts, heart and imaginations.

Hebrews 4:3, 6 & 11 - The AV 1611 Reading Justified

The scenario plays out in this example. Hebrews 4:3, 6 & 11 look like this in the King James, once again with the appropriate Greek root word supplied:

> *3 For we which have* ***believed (pisteuo)*** *do enter into rest, as he said, As I have sworn in my wrath, if they shall enter into my rest: although the works were finished from the foundation of the world.*
> *6 Seeing therefore it remaineth that some must enter therein, and they to whom it was first preached entered not in because of* ***unbelief (apeitho)****:*
> *11 Let us labour therefore to enter into that rest, lest any man fall after the same example of* ***unbelief (apeitho)****.* (KJV)

Uniformly, the NASV, NAU, NIV, NKJV and RSV all translate verse 3 as *believed*, but revert to their old ways and nature in verses 6 and 11, and translate it either *disobedience* or *disobey* across the board. Hence, the mantra once again: They opt to depart from context and consistency when it comes to translating ***apeitho*** in the two verses in question. With the options allotted them in their treasured lexicons, and with one option – *unbelief* – staring them in the face, they uniformly "preferred" the other option – *disobedience.* With the contextual standard bearer in verse 3 – ***pisteuo;*** *believed* –

defining the matter at hand, they opted for confusion and contradiction.

Is the KJV superior to the Greek, and does it establish what the Bible should say and correct any errant Greek ramblings or English perversion? Chalk it up! It sure is and it sure does!

Hebrews 11:31 - The AV 1611 Reading Justified

As the final example of the Holy Spirit's oversight and correct translation of the word ***apeitho*** into the King's English, we revisit Hebrews 11:31:

> *By faith the harlot Rahab perished not with them that **believed not (apeitho)**, when she had received the spies with peace.*

Most all of the same likely suspects show up for mug shots again, with mostly the same results and indictments. In this case, the NKJV double-mindedly decided to agree with its older, purer British namesake, but the rest of the coven of corrupt volumes predictably stayed true to their Luciferian nature, defied the context, changed God's word and translated ***apeitho*** as *disobedient.*

Faith in some form appears 25 times in Hebrews 11 alone. *Believe* ***(pisteuo)*** appears in 11:6, rendered by all versions as it should be: *believe.* One would think the remaining piece of the puzzle in 11:31 would not be too overwhelming to those with such profound and carefully groomed academic and spiritual reputations. Apparently, such gaudy reputations are oft ill deserved. There are no justifiable grounds whatever to translate ***apeitho*** in Hebrews 11:31 *disobedient.* The King James Bible never, ever leads a person wrong. The new perversions certainly do. The great lexicographers were sinners like you and me, and frankly, those who know the inner workings of such matters, attest to the fact that there were many in their ranks which were not merely unconverted apostates, but genuine demonic perverts and reprobates. The Greek of the New Testament will also lead one wrong, for, 1) No one can be utterly certain that the Greek word or phrase one *has in hand* is the Greek *God gave*. 2) The works which define Greek words were written by very fallible men indeed. Often, in Greek reference works, there are veins of scholastic degeneracy whose foundations for word meanings are laid in pagan literature, which then flowed through the unsanctified vessels of dishonor (scholars of liberal, unbelieving bent), whom mainline Christianity now falsely elevates to virtual academic deities.

Conclusions on *Apeitho*

It is not likely that a clearer series of examples could be presented that demarcate just how erroneous and prejudicial is the idea that the original language of the New Testament alone holds all the treasures and secrets of knowledge. When amateur or professional scholars correct or embellish the Bible with Greek, they do little more than fly to reference materials that intimidate those who are not so familiar with those tools. No matter how vast or how petty their working knowledge of Greek (or of Hebrew, for that matter), they still resort to Greek (or Hebrew) based reference lexicons or dictionaries. Their final authority is not really "the Greek." Their final authority is what some other man wrote about "the Greek." That man, in his reference work, simply gives the Bible-believer's scholar antagonist other options of what the Bible "could" say. The scholar then makes up his own mind about which option to choose. Ultimately, in this way, the scholar is his own final authority, but while he made the decision to change the English Bible, he gets to hide behind the sacred and hallowed "Greek."

It is for this reason that a growing number of true Bible-believers refer to this ridiculous and pompous parody as "the Greek game." It is little more than a shell game where half-truths and blatant falsehoods are dexterously shuffled under various scholastic shells to deceive the eyes and minds of Christian suckers. The performers deftly pull linguistic quarters from behind the ears of the naïve and pull grammatical bunnies from top-hats of apostasy and unbelief. The crowd is awed, but truth be known, the entire deceptive act has been practiced and promulgated for as long as the old deceiver and master sorcerer has been around (Gen. 3).

1) *Apeitho* can mean, and is translated as, both *disbelieve* and *disobey.* The Greek itself here discovers its limits, for left with only Greek, no modern scholar, lexicographer or student has the slightest idea which way to translate the word.

2) One is utterly forced to commit to one English translation of the word - either *disbelieve* or *disobey.* The scholars have no secret source of knowledge whatsoever. The average Christian's misconception is that scholars hold some master key, some fount of knowledge and insight, that is only accessible to species of men of their academic attainments and credentials. This is not true. They may well, and likely do, have possession or access to libraries of reference works which are often not of much interest to the average blue-collar Bible-believer. The shaggy and flea-ridden little secret, though, is that in the end, the high-profile scholars of exalted reputation also simply choose *disbelief* of *disobedience* from the choices given them in their lexicons. Their preferences – so often cited – and choices will then be most likely affected by their a) doctrinal predispositions, b) their prejudices for or against certain translations, language sources or readings, c) or their personal favor for certain other men's opinions of scholastic repute. Every scholar is made of the same flesh as the rest of mankind, and despite his degrees and working vocabulary; he is faced with the same basic sinful choices and spiritual discernments as anyone else. His expertise has oft been achieved by exposure to the works and "wisdom" of some of the worst infidels and most errant minds in history. Exposed to decades of mind-bending propaganda against the finality of the words of the Lord, whose judgment is better attuned to the mind of God, a simple Bible-believer's or the much-acclaimed scholar's?

3) The AV 1611 translators successfully translated the word in such a way that it is seamlessly in harmony with the context and theme of the various passages where it occurs. The AV translators were exponentially better translators than their successors. This is proven not only by their academic excellence and by the way the Holy Spirit has proven to have used their gifts, but also by their minds and hearts which were incisive and insightful enough theologically to recognize that the insertion of certain options in translation would have thrown entire passages into complete contradictory nonsense. The fruit of those particular options has been, of course, realized in the new versions of the Bible.

4) The new version translators – supposed masters of the Greek language - manifest themselves to be more interested in rejecting the AV readings than they are in getting at the truth of the passages. Contexts and thematic elements are almost universally ignored. Consistency is merely a paper tiger for them as they almost entirely dismiss any real consistency in translating or communicating the truth of a passage. Why exactly the scholars do what they do is really irrelevant. The end result is that they change the Bible and manifest themselves as Satan's tools and fools. *(T)he god of this world hath blinded the minds of them which believe not...*(2

Cor. 4:4). As such, it can be seen that they prove themselves ready and willing servants of the old serpent. They hate the King James Bible and they make changes petulantly and for no reason other than to set contrary words on paper. Safe inside the imagined scholarly security of their apostasy, *the spirit that now worketh in the children of disobedience* (Eph. 2:2) directs them by their academic pride and theological liberalism to change the Bible on a whim. Is it not interesting that they uniformly and universally unite to pen the very same whims?

5) It is the English of the KJV, then, that clearly distinguishes when *apeitho* means *disbelieve*, and when it means *disobey*. The 1611 English distinguishes the matter and the Greek languishes.

6) This means that the English of the AV is superior to the Greek. That means *any Greek* – Alexandrian or Textus Receptus. The AV translation makes clear to anyone who can read English what is not clear to anyone who can read Greek. In fact, once a Greek reader knows what the English says, he need henceforth have no question about how *apeitho* should be understood in his native Greek New Testament!

7) If this is not actually "correcting the Greek," it is, at the least, correcting any false conceptions that might have come out of Greek alone! It corrects false Greek texts. It corrects false conceptions and translations out of even the right Greek texts. It corrects the new versions. It *is a discerner of the thoughts and intents of the heart* (Heb. 4:12), which means that it corrects you and me and any scholars who might wish to pull the wool over the eyes of the Savior's sheep.

It is consistent with the theme of the subtitle of this book that states clearly that the King James Bible resolves what obscurities and ambiguities exist by natural state of affairs in the Greek and Hebrew languages. *Apeitho* is obscure and ambiguous because there is no method limited to the Greek that is able to determine in any singular case whether it is to be translated *disbelieve* or *disobey*. The AV 1611 resolves and settles the matter.

8) The Greek lexicons do not dictate what the Bible should say, but rather the King James Bible correctly finalizes and *authorizes* what is the correct reading from the reference materials. The AV is the final authority. It establishes and seals what the truth of the word of God is in English.

9) One may believe that these preceding statements are true for no other reason than that it was God Himself who added His hand to the labors of the AV 1611 translation committee.

Chapter 16

Short Samples

> *Hear; for I will speak of excellent things; and the opening of my lips shall be right things. For my mouth shall speak truth; and wickedness is an abomination to my lips. All the words of my mouth are in righteousness; there is nothing froward or perverse in them. They are all plain to him that understandeth, and right to them that find knowledge. Receive my instruction, and not silver; and knowledge rather than choice gold. For wisdom is better than rubies; and all the things that may be desired are not to be compared to it.* (Prov. 8:6-11)

In prior chapters, some of the fetid fruit that comes from "Bible" scholars' flippancy and careless dismissal of the long-honored text of the King James Bible has been exposed. A good number of their "orthodox" positions, exuding forth from the tenured safety of academic chairs and from behind the protective bulwarks of scholars' desks, have been unmasked as being fallacious in the real light of the scriptures themselves. If, for most of them, there ever were pricks of conscience over having altered the words of the Living God, these reminders from the Holy Ghost were soon quenched by the companionship of their fellow-cohorts in spiritual infidelity or the honorific auras of their institutions of employ. Sadly, the conscience of a twice or thrice festooned doctor of divinity is *defiled* (Tit. 1:15) and *seared* (1 Tim. 4:2) in every bit the same way as a gambler's or a pornographer's conscience. When a sinner partakes and imbibes often enough, he winds up callused and hard.

Also demonstrated have been the sound and solid examples of how the King's English plainly clarifies and resolves the ambiguities and obscurities of the Greek and Hebrew which all hear so much about. This flies in the face of all that the too-much-trusted scholars have made such a habit of telling naïve Christians. Translation from one language to another and the transmission of precise meaning through that process is uniformly acknowledged by all linguists to be a tremendous challenge. Insofar as Bible readers must lean upon the expertise of men, many Bible-believers have concluded that the giants of textual criticism and modern scholarship are fundamentally imposters and deceived children in comparison to the excellence of the gifts and labors of the AV 1611 translators. Quite simply, it takes more than brainpower for God to use a man. However, where reality necessitates reliance on men, King James Bible believers will choose the king's committeemen. Insofar as all realize that man always fails at one point or another, Bible-believers simply entrust all the machinations required to deliver to man the word of God unto the God of the word.

Here the believers in the AV 1611 make their stand. It is not difficult to judge the difference between the fruit of Origen, Jerome, Westcott and Hort, as compared to the fruit of Tyndale, Coverdale, Bois and Reynolds. It is only that the fruit is accompanied with the deafening cacophony of screeching scholarly fowls which influence and intimidate by the intensity and volume of their rhetoric rather than by spiritual fruit and power.

There is also in play the camp of certain Fundamentalist pro-King James scholars who exalt the Greek and Hebrew texts which lie behind the AV 1611. In so doing, the King James

Version is exalted and recommended in a measure, but when the pulpit-pounding is done and the somewhat disingenuous rallying cry to the King James is completed, the AV is still just a translation – albeit an excellent one - to this category of scholars. To them it "has its weaknesses," "it's not perfect," and there may even be a time and a circumstance under which it "might be improved." Ultimately, these fellows' final authority still resides in the original languages. Now, their final authority has uncertain bounds (there are still various and variable editions of the Textus Receptus recommended), and such a position still allows these men the latitude to alter God's words as they pass from Greek and Hebrew to English. Some do not do so often, some claim they would not do so at all, but others use this illicit license liberally. It is simply another variation of the age-old game: *Yea, hath God said…* (Gen. 3:1).

Having elaborated at quite some length in earlier examples on how the AV 1611 English, quite contrary to the scholars' byline, actually demonstrably brings clarity and distinction of meaning to the Bible that the Greek and Hebrew do not, in this chapter other examples follow, but with more brevity.

~~~~~~~~~~~~~~~~~~~~~~~~~~~~~~~~~~

Hell, Sheol, Gehenna, or Hades

Anyone possessing faith in what the Bible says and an ounce of spiritual foresight, understands immediately that a place where the everlasting wrath of God burns unendingly against the particular iniquities and the more general unregenerate nature of man – as well as fallen spiritual principalities – is going to come under philosophical, theological and rhetorical attack. Hell is too horrible a concept and a destiny for corrupt human nature to allow it to remain without renovation. One preacher aptly said that when they
~~~~~~~~~~~~~~~~~~~~~~~~~~~~~~~~~~

start air conditioning Hell, it is usually because they are getting ready to move in!

In any case, Hell has always been an unpalatable doctrine, and, as such, it has not escaped the attention of those who consider themselves qualified to edit the truth of the Bible. Jehovah's Witnesses are famous for having explained away Hell. Naturally, Greek and Hebrew are the tools they use.

Hell in the Old Testament Hebrew – *Sheol*

Hell shows up **31 times in the Old Testament of the AV 1611**, and each time it comes from the Hebrew word, ***Sheol***. The new versions are not fond of the word Hell, so it is most often rendered ***"Sheol," "realm of the dead," "the underworld," "death"*** or ***"grave"*** in the new versions.

However, it is also important to know that the word ***Sheol*** actually shows up in the OT Hebrew just over 65 times. As stated, 31 of those times it is translated ***Hell*** in the AV. But it is also translated ***grave*** around 30 times in the AV and it is also translated ***pit*** in the AV for the remainder of those times. As a side note, while it is unnecessary to track every occurrence of all these words for this study, it is also important to know that there are several other Hebrew words that are translated as both "grave" and "pit" in the AV 1611 King James Bible.

The new versions generally make a terrible and truth-obscuring debacle of the whole affair. For the sake of brevity, only the mutilation by the new versions of the prophetic passage regarding Christ's pre-resurrection journey into Hell in Psalm 16:10 will be pointed out.

> For thou wilt not leave my soul ***in hell***; neither wilt thou suffer thine Holy One to see corruption. (KJV)

> For Thou wilt not abandon my soul ***to Sheol***; neither wilt Thou allow Thy Holy One to undergo decay. (NAS)

> because you will not abandon me to ***the grave***, nor will you let your Holy One see decay. (NIV)

> For thou dost not give me up ***to Sheol***, or let thy godly one see the Pit. (RSV)

The new versions either cop-out and transliterate the word so as not to commit themselves to translating it, or they translate it "grave" as in the NIV. These types of changes are generally uniform and almost predictable wherever *Hell* is found in the AV's English.

The important thing to notice throughout the Old Testament is that the King James Bible translates "Sheol" 31 times as being distinctively *Hell*, while the other versions trend toward transliterating "Sheol," or otherwise translating it as some other, less offensive term. In so doing, the new versions basically obliterate *Hell*, as Bible reading Christians know it, and they thus dampen the Hell-consciousness that ought to animate all Christians as servants of God and soul-winners.

As has been asked so many times in previous chapters, who is responsible for translating Sheol as ***Hell*** in one place in the AV and as ***grave*** or ***pit*** in another? Is there a method behind the shifting translation? More importantly, is the AV right in translating it so?

Two immediate examples from the AV come to mind: Isaiah 14 and Ezekiel 31. Just as Jesus Christ addressed Satan through Peter in Matthew 16:18, so did God also address Satan through the King of Babylon in Isaiah 14 and through Pharaoh in Ezekiel 31. Both of these passages surrender invaluable information regarding Hell, and even the origination of Satan, as he is known today. For the purposes of this study, the passages also provide precious insight with respect to grammar, translation and word choices.

> 9 ***Hell*** *from beneath is moved for thee to meet thee at thy coming: it stirreth up the dead for thee, even all the chief ones of the earth; it hath raised up from their thrones all the kings of the nations.*
> 10 *All they shall speak and say unto thee, Art thou also become weak as we? art thou become like unto us?*
> 11 *Thy pomp is brought down to* ***the grave****, and the noise of thy viols: the worm is spread under thee, and the worms cover thee.*
> 12 *How art thou fallen from heaven,* ***O Lucifer****, son of the morning! how art thou cut down to the ground, which didst weaken the nations!*
> 13 *For thou hast said in thine heart, I will ascend into heaven, I will exalt my throne above the stars of God: I will sit also upon the mount of the congregation, in the sides of the north:*
> 14 *I will ascend above the heights of the clouds; I will be like the most High.*
> 15 *Yet thou shalt be brought down* ***to hell****, to the sides of the pit.* (Isa. 14:9-15)

All can see the reference to Lucifer in verse 12, and most Bible-believers are likely to be familiar with this being the origin of all the trouble with Satan from God's perspective. The passage holds many doctrinal treasures, but take note of the three underlined words:

- Hell (vs.9)
- grave (vs.11)
- hell (vs.15)

Importantly, the Hebrew behind all three words is Sheol. The NASV just transliterates ***Sheol*** in all three places. That is really insightful. The NIV translates Sheol as the ***grave*** in all three places, and the NKJV translates ***Hell*** in verse 9, and ***Sheol*** in verses 11 and 15.

In the previous examples in earlier chapters, the uncanny and manifest characteristic of the King James Bible has been shown to draw out doctrinal distinctions in English that are in no way observable in Greek and Hebrew, or in all the accompanying linguistic tools that seem to travel in troop with them. Much commentary could be written on Isaiah 14, but brevity is necessary. Let the reader insert "grave" into verse 9 and then let him ask whether the grave moves. In verse 15, insert "grave" and ask whether that is a better and clearer choice than *hell*. In verse 11, ask why *grave* is not perfectly acceptable seeing that it is sandwiched between *hell* in verses 9 and 15, and considering that people are brought down to the *grave* and from there the unregenerate proceed directly to *hell*.

It is also important to state here that as the reader now realizes that *Sheol* is the Hebrew behind every word that is questioned above; and as the new versions and their scholars have arbitrarily translated or transliterated with inconsistency and without direction, the reader is every bit as qualified to make a judgment about whether the AV 1611 is correct or whether the new versions are. The scholars here hold no special or sacred key of knowledge in this passage that specifically equips them more than the reader is equipped. Indeed, the reader may be better equipped, for he may well be more spiritual, prayerful and faithful to the Lord than these academics. The reader may be wiser in the scriptures and among *those who by reason of use have their senses exercised to discern both good and evil* (Heb. 5:14). In short, The King James Bible did it again. It made perfectly clear distinctions in English that are uncertain and confusing in Hebrew.

Ezekiel 31:15-18 provides a very similar example for Sheol.

> *15 Thus saith the Lord GOD; In the day when he went down to the **grave** I caused a mourning: I covered the deep for him, and I restrained the floods thereof, and the great waters were stayed: and I caused Lebanon to mourn for him, and all the trees of the field fainted for him.*
> *16 I made the nations to shake at the sound of his fall, when I cast him down to **hell** with them that descend into the pit: and all the trees of Eden, the choice and best of Lebanon, all that drink water, shall be comforted in the **nether parts of the earth**.*
> *17 They also went down into **hell** with him unto them that be slain with the sword; and they that were his arm, that dwelt under his shadow in the midst of the heathen.*
> *18 To whom art thou thus like in glory and in greatness among the trees of Eden? yet shalt thou be brought down with the trees of Eden unto the **nether parts of the earth**: thou shalt lie in the midst of the uncircumcised with them that be slain by the sword. This is Pharaoh and all his multitude, saith the Lord GOD.*

This passage flows along much the same lines as Isaiah 14. The bold-faced, underlined words above are all represented by Sheol in the Hebrew. The NAS opts again for the transliteration, "Sheol." The NIV goes with "grave". The NKJV, double-minded and inconsistent, translates all three as "hell", but in verse 15 has "it" going down to hell rather than "he." Hopefully, the NKJV translators and students are clear about what this means for it is doubtful that anyone else is.

In the end, it can be certainly known that when an unregenerate man goes down to the grave, the next and immediate step is down to Hell. There is no inconsistency or doctrinal discord that arises out of the AV's translation of Sheol. Simple, clear and precise distinctions and statements are made and understood by believing readers. The NAS leaves the reader in no man's land with its uncommitted transliteration, ***Sheol.*** The NIV misleads their readers and students into a bit of a foray into Jehovah's Witnesses' theology in making Hell the ***grave***!

The Lessons Learned From the AV 1611's Translation of *Sheol*:

- **There is no information to be gained in referring back to the Hebrew.**
- **Only confusion and the diminishment of the clear doctrine of Hell results from referencing the Hebrew.**
- **The King James Bible clearly distinguishes Hell and the grave in English.**
- **The King James Bible makes distinctions that the Hebrew does not.**
- **The new versions are forced to make distinctions or else compromise the doctrine of Hell. They botch their responsibility.**
- **In this way, the King James is not only superior to the new versions, but to the original**

Hebrew, for it delineates meaning where Hebrew does not do so.

- **In this way also, believing readers do get revelation in the English of the AV unavailable in the Hebrew or in the lexicons.**
- **Reverting to the Hebrew for light is to regress in knowledge and to return to darkness.**
- **Someone is responsible for the superior translation and the understanding imparted in the King James Authorized Version, either the translators or God. Who is the responsible party?**

Hell in the New Testament – *Gehenna, Hades & Tartaros*

Three words from Greek are translated *Hell* in the New Testament English of the King James Bible.

1) ***Gehenna*** – Occurs **12 times** and is translated *Hell* all twelve times.
2) ***Hades*** – Occurs **10 times** and is translated *Hell* all ten times.
3) ***Tartaros*** – Occurs only **once** in 2 Peter 2:4 and is translated *Hell.*

The new versions tend to all translate ***Gehenna,*** *Hell.* So, *Hell* does still exist in the new versions. However, most all of the new versions simply transliterate ***Hades*** wherever it occurs, so the versions wind up with ***Hades*** instead of *Hell* in 10 of the 23 places *Hell* occurs in the New Testament. Even the NKJV is complicit in its common use of the word Hades in place of the translation, *Hell.* ***Tartaros*** is generally translated *Hell* in the new versions.

In several particularly noteworthy cases does this wresting and pollution of scripture in the new versions prove to alter the entire complexion of the doctrine of Hell in the New Testament. While all is perfectly consistent in the King James Authorized Version, the new versions,

1) Turn the *gates of hell* in Matthew16:18 into the "gates of Hades."
2) Place the rich man of Luke 16:23 in "Hades."
3) Pervert and obscure the prophecy of the Lord Jesus' pre-resurrection work in Acts 2:27 and 31, by placing His soul in ***Hades*** instead of *Hell.* One should recall that the foolish and intermeddling scholars also corrupted the reference in the OT in Psalms 16:10 by transliterating ***Sheol*** or translating ***grave*** in place of Hell.
4) Give Christ the keys of Hades in place of the keys of Hell in Revelation 1:18.
5) Have "death and Hades," in Revelation 20:14, cast into the lake of fire in place of *death and hell.*

Again, there are 10 places in the New Testament where "Hades" is the word for Hell in Greek. In accord with the examples above, in none of those ten places would a Bible-believer be in any wise benefited by the alterations made by the new versions and justified by the scholars. The AV is perfectly consistent with its translation and doctrine with respect to Hell. It uniformly brings three Greek words across the translation barrier into English, rendering the words, *Hell.*

The new versions, and they who flirt with apostasy (commentators and scholars), insert the separate concept of Hades into the mix and regress to darkness and uncertainty by only transliterating the word, or else translating it falsely as "the grave." In this way, the Jehovah's Witnesses are given scholarly fodder for their nonsense, and wide-eyed and naïve students and Christians acquiesce to the poor judgment and polluted scholarship of those whom they consider experts.

Lessons Learned From the AV 1611's Translation of *Gehenna, Hades* and *Tartaros*:

- **There is no profit or enlightenment that comes from referring back to the Greek.**
- **Only confusion and the diminishment of the clear doctrine of Hell results from referencing the Greek.**
- **The King James Bible is perfectly clear with respect to Hell in English.**
- **The King James Bible takes 3 Greek words and simplifies and clarifies the doctrine they represent by the use of a single word: *Hell*.**
- **The new versions do not bring the concepts in Greek together in their English translations and thus compromise the doctrine of Hell. Their scholarship and clarity is inferior…again.**
- **In this way, the King James is not only superior to the new versions, but to the original Greek, for it coalesces meaning where the Greek does not.** It is worthwhile to point out at this juncture, that from the Hebrew, the AV took one Hebrew word (Sheol) and distinguished clearly multiple meanings, including *Hell*, *grave* and *pit* in English. From the Greek, the AV took multiple words (*Gehenna, Hades & Tartaros*) and clarified and simplified unnecessary complexity to one word in English, *Hell*.
- **In establishing the singular New Testament concept of Hell, as opposed to three words in Greek, the English of the AV provides information unavailable in the Greek or in the lexicons.**

- **Reverting to the Greek for light is to regress in knowledge and to complicate that which has already been correctly simplified.**
- **Is this remarkable attribute of the AV the mere product of the AV 1611 translators' profound scholarship, or did God involve Himself intimately in the mechanics of the translation process?**

~~~~~~~~~~~~~~~~~~~~~~~~~~~~~~~~~~~~

Baptism

Not only has the practice and mode of baptism long been a matter of controversy between the divisions and sects of what is known as "Christendom" (for long, dark generations Roman Catholicism regularly hunted, tortured and warred against those of contrary opinions), but the very translation of the word itself has been the source of quite a lot of steam and bickering. Though the new versions use the word "baptize" regularly in their translations, as does the King James Bible, there have been folks even in the King James camp who take umbrage that words such as *baptize, baptist* and *baptism* are even used. An oft-heard complaint is that the word is not even a translation but a transliteration of the word *baptizo*, in Greek. Thus, the AV translators are considered to have fallen down on the job, and our Bibles ought to be changed to read "immerse," or some say, "dip."

> Why is it that those who translated the Bible from Greek into English have, since the sixteenth century, chosen to transliterate *baptizo* rather than to translate it? It is a fact that "baptize" remains an untranslated word in our English
~~~~~~~~~~~~~~~~~~~~~~~~~~~~~~~~~~~~

Bibles even to this day. Since the word means "immerse," why not translate it as such?[236]

Paul Kirkpatrick answered this charge and others quite some time ago in a tract published by Tabernacle Baptist Church in Lubbock, Texas.[237] He showed that while the word "baptize" may have been transliterated, it already was in regular usage in 17th century England, and was understood to mean immersion. He further shows that the Church of England, of which most all of the translators were a part, practiced immersion baptism at the time. The bottom line is that, transliterated or not, any of the forms of the word *baptize* as found in the King James Bible belong there just as they are. Nobody I know would be too energetic about changing the name of their church to *Calvary Immersionist Church,* or *Blessed Hope Dipper Church.* Were such actions taken, John would be *John the Dipper* and some of the brethren would still have doctrinal problems which Bible-believers would be compelled to call *Immersionist Briderism.*

The fact is that there are still King James Bible defenders who believe that some words would be best reevaluated and retranslated for "accuracy's sake." Some of this camp would prefer that *baptizo* be translated "immerse" or "dip." If they aren't too dogmatic about the need to openly change the KJV, they at least are very quick to take a person back to the Greek in order to define by lexicon that *baptizo* truly means something beyond what the Bible actually says. In so doing, the implications and ramifications are plain: hidden treasures and necessary meaning reside only in Greek. What the Bible-believer has in hand is insufficient for complete

---

236 "Baptism's Practice | Articles | NTRF." Weblog post. *House Church | Relational Church | New Testament Church | Organic Church | NTRF*. Web. 13 Dec. 2010. <http://www.ntrf.org/articles/article_detail.php?PRKey=38.>.

237 Kirkpatrick, Paul, "*Baptism" In The King James Version* (Tabernacle Baptist Church, Lubbock, TX. 79410, Tract #218.

understanding. Where, oh where, would a Christian be without the Greek and its resident panel of scholarly experts which ultimately determine God's sayings and meanings?

In truth, in certain respects "baptizo" in Greek and *baptism* in English do not always mean "immerse" or "dip" in the word of God, and the KJV translators were demonstrably correct in bringing the family of "baptizo" words forth into English in its present form. Baptism in the Authorized Version of 1611 in its present form is superior to any change anybody could suggest. Here is why.

Differing Bible Baptisms

Because many scholars' confidence in the words of God is so profoundly compromised, their study of the actual word of God is compromised right along with it. They simply have no reason to study what the Bible actually says in their language and in the English of the AV. Greek (or Hebrew) is always the first option for "light" and "true meaning." Therefore what their English Bible actually says and differentiates is carelessly and habitually overlooked. If they see profound distinction in English, they still tend to deemphasize it in their own minds, for Greek is the ultimate repository for truth to them.

Here is what a Bible-believer learns when he allows the Bible doctrine of Baptism to stand as it is written in the King James Bible. Some groups stand in opposition or confusion regarding the distinct categories that follow, but an objective Bible student must be able to see the legitimacy of the following different baptisms in the word of God.

- John the Baptist's Baptism (Matt. 3:1-6)
- The Baptism of the Holy Ghost (Matt. 3:11)
- The Baptism of Fire (Matt. 3:11)
- Jesus Christ's Baptism of Suffering (Matt. 20:22-23)

- Believer's Baptism (Matt. 28:19)
- Israel's Reconciliatory Baptism (Acts 2:38-41)
- The Baptism Unto Moses (1 Cor.10:2)

These are listed in order of mention in the New Testament. It shall be seen soon that these may be grouped in other manners, but allow first a brief explanation of each:

1) John the Baptist's Baptism (Matt. 3:1-6). While this explanation must unfortunately fly in the face of the Baptist Briders' conception of the New Testament ordinance and its ramifications, the author is compelled to persist with holding fast *the form of sound words* (2 Tim. 1:13). While John's mode of immersion is unquestionably the same as New Testament believer's baptism, its meaning is quite different. For beginners, Mark 1:4 testifies that, *John did baptize in the wilderness, and preach the* ***baptism of repentance for the remission of sins.*** John 1:31 further quotes John Baptist in speaking of Jesus Christ, *And I knew him not: but* ***that he should be made manifest to Israel, therefore am I come baptizing with water.*** In those two brief statements, two glaring points are illuminated. First, John's baptism was a ***baptism of repentance for the remission of sins***, and was thus connected with sins being remitted. Secondly, what John did was done in order that Christ ***should be made manifest to Israel***. In those two things, it is easily seen that John's Baptism is absolutely not equivalent to believer's baptism. The emphasis of the mission of John had special relation to Israel, as is again seen in Acts 13:24, where Paul specifies that *John had first preached before his coming the baptism of repentance to all* ***the people of Israel.***

The profound importance of these distinctions is seen upon reading further how John's baptism was, in time, antiquated and ineffectual! Acts 18:25-26 reveals that by that juncture in time Apollos, who was preaching only John's baptism, needed an update.

> *This man was instructed in the way of the Lord; and being fervent in the spirit, he spake and taught diligently the things of the Lord,* ***knowing only the baptism of John****. And he began to speak boldly in the synagogue: whom when Aquila and Priscilla had heard, they took him unto them, and expounded unto him* ***the way of God more perfectly****.*

This is more particularly shown in the next chapter when men who were still "stuck" on John's Baptism, needed to be baptized again.

> *1 And it came to pass, that, while Apollos was at Corinth, Paul having passed through the upper coasts came to Ephesus: and finding certain disciples,*
> *2 He said unto them, Have ye received the Holy Ghost since ye believed? And they said unto him, We have not so much as heard whether there be any Holy Ghost.*
> *3 And he said unto them,* ***Unto what then were ye baptized? And they said, Unto John's baptism****.*
> *4 Then said Paul, John verily baptized with the baptism of repentance, saying unto the people, that they should believe on him which should come after him, that is, on Christ Jesus.*
> *5* ***When they heard this, they were baptized in the name of the Lord Jesus.***
> (Acts 19:1-5)

2) The Baptism of the Holy Ghost (Matt. 3:11). There truly is a baptism that **saves**, and this is it! It has nothing to do with water. As Luke testified in Acts 1:5, *For John truly* *baptized with water; but ye shall be baptized with the Holy Ghost not many days hence.* Furthermore, this baptism of Spirit, while misconstrued and wrested by many to signify water baptism, is the Holy Spirit's baptism that put all true believers into Jesus Christ: *For* ***by one Spirit*** *are we all baptized into one body, whether we be Jews or Gentiles, whether we be bond or free; and have been all made to* (1 Cor. 12:13). No Christian was "water-baptized" into Christ, nor did he literally, materially *drink into one Spirit*! These actions were spiritual, exercised by the Holy Spirit when the believer was converted. That is why Romans 6:3 reads as it does: *Know ye not, that so many of us as were* ***baptized into Jesus Christ*** *were baptized into his death?* Contrary to the Briders' wrested reasoning, when the believer got saved, he was baptized into Christ – His death, burial, resurrection (Rom. 6:4), and into His body, the Church (Col. 1:18). Then he was sealed by that same Spirit *unto the day of redemption* (Eph. 4:30).

3) The Baptism of Fire (Matt.3:11). Despite the Charismatic mumbo jumbo and the devotional pap, the Matthew 3:11 promise that Christ *shall baptize you with the Holy Ghost, and with fire*, is a promise regarding the two separate advents of Christ. He came the first time to save and *baptize you with the Holy Ghost*, and He will return the second time to baptize the unbelieving world *with fire*. This interpretation is only verified by reading the next verse: Matthew 3:12 - *Whose fan is in his hand, and he will throughly purge his floor, and gather his wheat into the garner; but* ***he will burn up the chaff with unquenchable fire.*** This is only difficult to see for those who have been inundated with bad doctrine. *...(T)he Lord Jesus shall be revealed from heaven with his mighty angels,* ***In flaming fire*** *taking vengeance on them that know not God, and that obey not the gospel of our Lord Jesus Christ* (II Thes. 1:7-8). Of Christ, and matching the description of Him in Revelation 1, Daniel 7:9-10 says, *I beheld till the thrones were cast down, and the Ancient of days did sit,* *whose garment was white as snow, and the hair of his head like the pure wool: his throne was like the fiery flame, and his wheels as burning fire.* ***A fiery stream issued and came forth from before him*** (Dan. 7:9-10).

4) Jesus Christ's Baptism of Suffering (Matt. 20:22-23). If one reads the passage, there can really be no argument that this refers to the Lord's trial of suffering before Pilate and Herod and at Calvary.

5) The Believer's Baptism (Matt. 28:19). This baptism is equally obvious. As the Ethiopian eunuch (Acts 8) and the Philippian jailor (Acts 16), believers in Jesus Christ need to obey the Lord and be baptized by immersion after they are born-again in accord with scriptural examples.

6) Israel's Reconciliatory Baptism (Acts 2:38-41). This passage has caused endless debate and hatched several different heretical sects. Much is explained by the fact that Acts is a transitional book which, sometimes confusingly, leads mankind from an Old Testament economy under Law, to a New Testament dispensation under Grace. It also documents a transition from God's 2000 year-old preoccupation with Israel, to His now 2000 year-old ministration to the Gentiles, primarily. In Acts 2, Peter reads Israelite rejecters of their Messiah the riot act. The following ensues.

> *37 Now when they heard this, they were pricked in their heart, and said unto Peter and to the rest of the apostles,* ***Men and brethren, what shall we do?***
> *38 Then Peter said unto them, Repent, and be baptized every one of you in the name of Jesus Christ* ***for the remission of sins****, and* ***ye shall receive the gift of the Holy Ghost.***

39 For the promise is unto ***you****, and to* ***your children****, and to all that are afar off, even as many as the Lord our God shall call.*
(Acts 2:37-39)

The Israelites' response is to address the ***Men and brethren*** (Israel) and to ask ***what shall we do?*** Importantly, once again, while the mode was immersion baptism, this baptism does not match a present day believer's purpose for baptism. For the Acts 2 baptism, there is once again the connection of ***remission of sins*** with the baptism, as well as the added stipulation that, ***ye shall receive the gift of the Holy Ghost.*** This is not the same fruit as the Church Age Christian's baptism which only symbolizes the death, burial and resurrection. Again, in verse 39 *…the promise is unto* ***you****, and to* ***your children***, with the immediate context limiting the application to Israelites who crucified their Messiah (Acts 2:36). No one else in the Bible was ever baptized under the same conditions and promises as in Acts 2. This is an isolated baptism offered to Israel one time.

7) The Baptism Unto Moses (1 Cor. 10:2). One is not told until 1 Corinthians 10 that there even was a baptism attributed unto Moses. It is unlikely that Moses even knew it at the time. While water was involved - *And were all baptized unto Moses in the cloud and in the sea-* it is noteworthy that this was not immersion baptism, but rather a baptism by aspersion if it is the water itself to which the scripture refers. In actuality, one of the great lessons of the passage is that this establishes that an indispensable aspect of baptism is the affiliation which it symbolizes. Israel by passing through the cloud and sea beneath the upraised rod of Moses and God, inexorably became affiliated with not only Moses, the man, but with the God of Israel.

Analyzing the Bible's Baptisms

1) John the Baptist's Baptism (Matt. 3:1-6)
2) The Baptism of the Holy Ghost (Matt. 3:11)
3) The Baptism of Fire (Matt. 3:11)
4) Jesus Christ's Baptism of Suffering (Matt. 20:22-23)
5) Believer's Baptism (Matt. 28:19)
6) Israel's Reconciliatory Baptism (Acts 2:38-41)
7) The Baptism Unto Moses (1 Cor. 10:2)

Many Bible readers and students of the scriptures have noted that false or ill-conceived doctrine tends to instill certain theological preoccupations. Jehovah's Witnesses are preoccupied with the false idea of there being no Hell. Calvinists read Calvinism into everything. Catholics see the "papacy" in Peter and "Catholicism" in every mention of the word *church* in the scriptures. Any of the forms of the word ***baptize*** tend to illicit and excite a preoccupation with water, and often that preoccupation extends to what is known to be the proper method of water baptism, immersion. Thus, there are branches of folks who think that ***baptism*** in the Bible ought to be replaced with "immersion" or "dip." Failing that, they wish to inundate everyone with what the Greek "really means" every time they cross the tripwire of ***baptize*** in the King James Bible. A little Bible analysis reveals a problem with that line of thinking.

Note the listing of the Bible's baptisms above, along with their corresponding numbers.

• **Only 4 of the 7 actually involve water - Numbers 1, 5, 6, & 7.** Let it suffice to say that it is important to take note that there are three baptisms in the word of God that have nothing whatsoever to do with water.

• **Of the 4 that involve water, one of them does not involve immersion – Number 7.** Again, the children of Israel did not go through an immersion into the Red Sea, but Pharaoh did - and died! Moses' baptism was by aspersion, not immersion. In this way, only 3 of the Bible's 7 baptisms have anything to do with immersion baptism.

• **One might say that the Spirit baptizing Christians *into one body* (1 Cor. 12:13) is an immersion, but it certainly is not water.** How understanding would be profited by reading immersion into this baptism by the Spirit is very questionable. It would certainly add confusion, for many of the brethren have already confounded understanding and wrested these scriptures to force them to mean water baptism.

• **The Baptism of Fire at Christ's Second Coming (#3) is not an immersion, but that of being engulfed by fire (Is. 30:27-28) from His mouth and lips.** Damnation will eventually lead a sinner to a lake of fire where he will, no doubt, be baptized in flame, but once again, the word "immersion" would lead to confusion.

• **Christ's Baptism of Suffering (#4) might be considered an immersion, but one must remember that Christ rose from both the dead and His suffering!** The actual definition of immersion does not necessarily include a withdrawal out of the medium of immersion. A plate that is immersed in the kitchen sink is soaking. A Christian that is immersed in water for more than a couple of minutes is …*dead*!

Prayerfully, the reader can see by these basic observations, that the word ***baptism*** actually is a far more inclusive term than just "immersion" or "dip." To replace the word with "immerse" or "dip" would not represent the same spectrum of ideas that ***baptize*** represents. Even in believer's baptism, the immersion part is really only half of baptism! The believer must be brought back up out of the water, just as Christ brought the sinner up spiritually out of judgment, damnation and death! There is also an affiliation in baptism that is not conceptualized in mere "immersion." John's baptism and Moses' baptism – besides the water part – had a role of connecting and affiliating those Jews with the baptizer. Baptism affiliates the believer with Christ, as well. These ideas are not conceptualized with the mere idea of "dipping."

In short, ***baptism*** is a concept that covers a greater array of understanding than the word "immerse" can impart. The fact is that part of the reason the concepts to be apprehended in the word ***baptism*** have been so ill-conceived by modern Christians, rests in the fact that the academics have come to rely on Greek to the extent that they no longer are willing to conceptualize and digest what their Bible says in said scholars' own language.

> *Let them alone: they be blind leaders of the blind. And if the blind lead the blind, both shall fall into the ditch.* (Matt. 15:14)

Conclusions on the Bible and Its Baptisms

Many scholars want to force believers back to the Greek of the New Testament that the idea of baptism might be properly "conceptualized." What is entirely plain in English, they seem intent upon obscuring by a wasteful and irrelevant exercise. Some are satisfied to play the Greek game, while others blatantly press to alter the wording of the English Bible.

There was a reason that the Lord led the translators to transliterate *baptize* instead of translating it. Translating the word would have placed undesirable restrictions upon the meaning of the Bible concepts that are available to the believing reader, and it would have led to the very misapprehensions that are seen reflected in those who lean so heavily on understanding from the Greek.

In this way, the Lord sanctified the forms of the word *baptize* to mean something that would have been lost in mere translation. *Baptize* is a sanctified and a

consecrated concept that the Lord left transliterated for a reason. To regress to Greek is to also regress to the oft-subjective, preconceived, and sometimes utterly secular definitions of the infidels and gross apostates who authored the Greek lexicons and dictionaries. Bible scholars who cite the Greek to impress or intimidate the average Christian are seldom ever actually going back to Greek! They are referring to lexicons and reference works that were authored and edited by some who were shockingly apostate and notorious for their infidelity. The unsuspecting reader does not know this because the authors are mostly long dead, and the reader's favorite Greek teacher did not inform him of the dubious scholastic lineage because he most likely doesn't know himself, since he went to school, was taught by men who accepted the "scholarly" reputations of other men, and thus, drank the "fruit punch."

They who lobby for "immerse" or "dip" actually prove that the preoccupation with Greek limits understanding. They never studied their Bibles carefully enough to recognize that "immerse" would be a limitation to doctrine, and destructive to Biblical knowledge.

In the case of *baptism*, the English is superior to what the Greek-obsessed scholars say. The fact is, in this instance, unlike other cases, *baptize* in the writings of the Greek texts yields the same contexts as English. That is, ***baptizo*** is almost always brought into the English Bible as ***baptize,*** or some form of the word thereof. At times, God seems to have over-ruled certain Greek words and ideas when the words were translated into English, and in so doing, He has imparted understanding otherwise unattainable. In this case, ***baptizo*** in Greek, is pretty much ***baptize*** in English. Why is that important? It is important because the Greek scholars cannot even find and differentiate evident truths in their Greek texts! So busy are they mining for Greek nuggets, that they miss the truths evident even in Greek, and many wish to actually dim the light in English by re-translating. How can they find deeper truths in Greek than are available in English, when they cannot even discern basic truth in Greek that is also available in English?

The English of the King James Bible always leads a Bible-believer to the truth that Greek scholars cannot grasp in their Greek. Over and over, this book has shown that the reader of the Bible, who believes the words he is reading, has no necessity whatsoever to *look back* into the Greek or Hebrew from whence the AV 1611 came. As repulsive an idea as this is to modern scholars, this is actually the practical and profound lesson that has been repeatedly demonstrated.

What is considered "archaic" wording by many is actually sanctified and consecrated language that has very specific meaning to God. Though many good Christians, including some fine scholars, think that certain updates and modernization of language is something to be considered for the AV 1611, openness to such changes marks a disturbing inclination to allow the word of God to be blatantly changed and altered. What is being discussed here is not the editing that took place up through 1769, when spelling was standardized and printing errors were rectified in the King James Bible. Make no mistake, the "updating" and "modernization of language" that men routinely discuss will turn out to be genuine ***change*** in the word of God. Remember, many of these fellows, have literally insisted for years that there is no significant "change" or "difference" between the KJV and the new versions. Disregarding for a moment their motive or purpose, whatever else may be true, these scholars have displayed a blindness and a delusion which does not even allow them to acknowledge ***change*** that has occurred. Because of their own unbelief and infidelity, they cannot be trusted as watch-keepers of the treasure, much less as the editors of it! Given liberty, they ***will*** add to, take from and pervert the words of the living

God, and this includes some that presently defend the AV 1611, but have gone on record as being "open" to certain undisclosed exercises of updating and modernizing it.

~~~~~~~~~~~~~~~~~~~~~~~~~~~~~~~~~~~~

Calvary

It has long been the author's contention that those who promote or tolerate the new versions, and who are resistant to acknowledging how profoundly the modern readings have affected what the Bible says, simply are too lazy and dismissive to set the different versions beside the King James and ***read them.*** Many who defend the King James Bible have10, 20, or 100 places they can quickly reference to show the atrocious omissions and butchered phrasings of the new versions. These certain places are usually high profile changes. Sometimes, even for Bible-believers, there is a vast and assorted array of changes that fly beneath the radar, simply because it is not a regular exercise to compare the different versions side-by-side and word-by-word as a habit. To read Proverbs word-by-word with the King James Bible, the NIV or the NASV side-by-side is to step back and forth between two very different oracles.

I have long showed skeptical new version readers the profound changes: the removal of the blood of Christ, the attack upon His deity and the incessant removal of parts of His name and title. I show them how Christ's singularity as *the bright and morning star* in Revelation 22:16, is suddenly invaded in Isaiah 14:12, and where Lucifer, the ***son** of the morning* in the AV is suddenly transformed into the ***star** of the morning* in the NASV, the NIV and others. Lucifer is given the same title as Jesus Christ in the new versions! Many other similar and profound changes are easily shown. Others are fairly easy to overlook if one is not aware of them.
~~~~~~~~~~~~~~~~~~~~~~~~~~~~~~~~~~~~

One of the most common and well-known details about Christ's crucifixion is that He was crucified on ***Calvary***. Our hymnbooks are filled with references to ***Calvary***. Pastors' sermons and teachers' lessons are replete with references to this famous place, where such an eternal transaction took place – the bearing of our sins by the Lamb of God!

It is likely though, that many readers may not have registered one profound thing: The place called ***Calvary*** is mentioned only in one singular passage in all the scriptures, and we know the word only in English since it is translated from *kranion* in Greek, the root word for "cranium" or "skull." ***Calvary*** is in only one verse in the entire Bible:

> *And when they were come to the place, which is called* ***Calvary****, there they crucified him, and the malefactors, one on the right hand, and the other on the left.* (Luke 23:33)

A Christian should be infuriated and indignant to learn that ***Calvary*** does not exist by name in the NASV, the NIV or the new versions in general. The exception to this is the NKJV, which nonetheless remains a corruption of the word of God.

The Flippancy of Man Regarding *Calvary*

The temptation and inclination of scholars is to become accustomed to that with which they labor. Eli's sons in 1 Samuel, and multiple generations of priests that followed, all become acclimated to handling holy things. In the typical fashion of sin, they became comfortable, dismissive and offhanded in their hearts and in their sanctification. It did not take long for open abominations to follow: adultery with the women in the gate, idols in the holy place, and sodomites just without the temple walls (2 Kings 23:7). As in the days when sodomy was the companionable neighbor to the temple next door and abominable idols filled the spaces of the most holy place, it now means absolutely nothing for scholars to flippantly and routinely dismiss, reject and replace a word in the Holy Bible for another word of their preference. One scholar prefers this alternative, another that. The alteration of the holy words of the Holy God is exercised with little more trepidation than choosing chocolate over strawberry at the local ice cream shop.

Though they roar in protest and indignantly defend their frivolity as solemn, noble and pious spirituality, in the end the scholars feel that they have every latitude and license to interchange or dismiss the words of the Bible at their whim. With the audacity of haughty and condescending royalty, they *take away the key of knowledge* (Lk. 11:52), *corrupt the word of God* (2 Cor. 2:17), and expect the unenlightened peons to subsist on that which they are allotted by the ruling intellectual elite.

These men long ago ceased to even wonder if they might be committing trespass or sacrilege. They have no practical sense of holy ground. They continually miss the reality of the great loss of power in the "Word" which they administer. The edge is dulled and tarnished. It pierces only superficially, and that in ragged tears rather than precise incisions. It leaves too much unsaid. It only delivers marginal victory – if that. The message is proclaimed, but the results are not profound or electric, but rather flat, wet and sticky. Auxiliary power is needed, so rock bands are supplied to assist the atmosphere, scruffy worship teams help excite the flesh, and the ever-available, humanistic, feel-good communicator-types leave people with the "fuzzies" rather than the power and truth of God. The faint and musty smell of death wafts down the corridors of the "bastions of the faith" for the professors and good doctors have busied themselves in ministering mummified remains rather than the quick, powerful and unbound word of God.

This is the scholarship that as only one example, simply dismissed ***Calvary*** from the English Bible. They went to the Greek, consulted a lexicon and sent ***Calvary*** packing.

The Power of the Word *Calvary*

One should ever wonder at just how certain things gain such a foothold and such notoriety in this world. Coke and Pepsi are almost elemental to American culture, but untold billions of dollars have been spent in advertising and marketing. Names of certain athletes, entertainers or celebrities rise to prominence by virtue of some vain accomplishment or success, and while most all the names fade from fame over a few years' time, some disappear quickly into oblivion. A line spoken in a movie may enjoy prominence in some peoples' consciousness for a time. A song or an album might outlive its originator. Yet, how many of this generation know immediately what AMC stood for in 1975? 8-track tapes and record players are now items for collectors rather than for routine use. The winners of the Super Bowls, the Word Series or the Indy 500 back in the '70's and '80's will only be recalled by sports buffs. Few people can even name the presidents in order from 1900 until the present. It may be that iPods and Macs will be the names of some dinosaur technology if the Lord were to tarry for another generation.

The point is that words that stick in our minds, in a culture, or in prominence for a period of time usually revolve around extraordinary accomplishment and marketing on an almost unimaginable scale. Even then, in perspective, the "power" and fame of such words actually wind up being short lived.

How is it, then, that a word mentioned one singular time in scripture could be utterly etched in the consciousness of fallen man for 2000 years? It is remarkable enough, and a testament to the supernatural work of the Holy Spirit that Jesus Christ, for all His glorious labor, would be remembered these two millennia after His work on earth. Not to be dismissive of Christ, consider the kind of "juice" that it takes to graft into the collective minds of sequential generations of people a word ***that is mentioned as a factual statement only one solitary time in the entire English Bible!*** Has one word, one concept, ever in the history of the world, so overwhelmed the collective conscience of man after one singular mention?

Calvary is an incessant theme in God honoring music, and is constantly mentioned, by sacred hymn writers and even contemporary "Christian" musicians. ***Calvary*** is always on the lips of ministers whose Bibles no longer even contain the word. Commentators seem almost oblivious to the fact that Calvary is a continuing theme in their commentaries though they so often support the brand of scholarship that does away with it in scripture. ***Calvary*** is so preeminent in the consciousness of many Americans that they seem preoccupied with it even when talking about a military troop of horsemen, ***the cavalry***! How often is heard someone discussing the ***cavalry***, mistakenly referring to it as the ***Calvary?*** How often is someone overheard to mention "calling in the ***Calvary***"? The speaker meant a troop of *horsemen*, but he actually referred to the place of Christ's crucifixion! How can it be that from a single book of "literature" (the Bible), with only one singular mention of the word (Luke 23:33), ***Calvary*** would hold such a prominent place in the minds and consciences of a people who are no longer even reading the Book whence the word came?

Such semi-conscious preoccupation with a word can only be explained by the promises of the scriptures, God's Book. Christ's promise of the Holy Spirit was given His disciples in this way: *And when he is come, he will reprove the world of sin, and of righteousness, and of judgment* (John 16:8).

It was the Holy Ghost that seized upon the English word ***Calvary***, and though it was written and translated only one solitary time in the AV, the Spirit of God has been flogging the consciences of wicked men, and fanning the flames of their guilt for hundreds of years with a single bombshell which testifies of the place where their debt of sin was paid. It is doubtful that the average Joe who happens to know what Calvary *is*, has the slightest clue of where it *came from*.

Concerning the Spirit, the Lord also added, *But when the Comforter is come, whom I will send unto you from the Father, even the Spirit of truth, which proceedeth from the Father, he shall testify of me* (John 15:26). So it is with one resounding blow, the Lord has smitten English speaking men with a word that rebounds and echoes in their collective heads and hearts, for it was at ***Calvary*** that everything that matters for man was settled by the Lamb of God (John 19:30).

The new versions and the scholars can deluge men with rhetoric and propaganda about the value of their own work, but it is God that uses what He chooses as well as whom He chooses. Paul aptly said, *For not he that commendeth himself is approved, but whom the Lord commendeth* (2 Cor. 10:18). The King James translators translated the Greek *kranion* as ***Calvary*** in Luke 23:33, as did Wycliffe[238] and Tyndale,[239] but it is the Lord Himself who has taken that English word and seared and engraved it into the semi-conscious minds of English speaking men and women in this wicked 21st century world.

In an age where the immensity and weight of electronic media is unfathomable and where images overwhelm and

---

238 *The Wesley Center Online*: *Home*. Web. 11 Dec. 2010. <http://wesley.nnu.edu/biblical_studies/wycliffe/2ti.txt>.

239 *The Wesley Center Online*: *Home*. Web. 11 Dec. 2010. <http://wesley.nnu.edu/biblical_studies/tyndale/2ti.txt>.

mesmerize the mind and imagination, God hath still managed to take a word mentioned in the AV 1611 ***one time*** and has made it relevant in America in 2010 and beyond. It is He who has made it a sharp pinprick even in the consciences and works of apostates who have sought to destroy the sanctified language of the Bible.

It is thy God, O Christian, that did that, and He did it with a King James Bible and its authentic predecessors. He did not use the new versions. The new versions have no record of God guiding and using their words in this way. The new version editors and scholars dismiss and reject the declarations of the King James Bible whenever they feel they can get away with it and still make sales. On the other hand, it is evident from this single sliver of historical evidence, that God has quite completely rejected and dismissed the new versions and the work of the men that are behind them. God does not need them to make sales.

> ***How do ye say, We are wise, and the law of the LORD is with us****? Lo, certainly in vain made he it; the pen of the scribes is in vain.* ***The wise men are ashamed, they are dismayed and taken: lo, they have rejected the word of the LORD; and what wisdom is in them?***
>
> (Jer. 8:8-9)

The Implications of the Translation, *Calvary*

Four times the Greek word *kranion* is found in the New Testament Greek texts. Three of those times – Matthew 27:33, Mark 15:22 and John 19:17 – it is translated ***skull***, or rather ***place of a skull*** in the King James Bible, as it is in the new versions. Yet, on a fourth time, when *kranion* appears, the AV translates it ***Calvary***. What faithful lessons might a faith-based people, serving a God who requires faith (Heb. 11:6), reading a

Book that imparts faith (Rom. 10:17), draw from what the cynical scholars see as inconsistency and ineptitude?

All should happily observe the power of the word, *Calvary*. Let the Bible-believer open his eyes and see what God did with the mention of *one word... once*! The word ***Calvary*** reverberates at this hour with a power that defies all the synonyms and definitions in the lexicons and dictionaries. God uses that word in a way that He never used the word ***skull***. God has blessed that word in history, in songs, in hymns, in tracts, in sermons and in evangelism in a way that can only be described as powerful.

All should be quick to ascribe God's providence to the word, *Calvary*. Why on earth would men, of themselves, translate *kranion* as ***place of a skull*** in three places, and then translate it ***Calvary*** in Luke 23:33? Each passage is a sister passage, a different narrative of the same event. One would think that men, left to themselves, would err on the side of consistency. Perhaps not. Perhaps the AV translators, out of their own ingenuity and insight, simply decided to translate Luke 23:33 a different way. Perhaps, then, it was a matter of God simply blessing what men did. If this is the case, then it behooves men to concede their adverse opinions to the discretion of the AV translators, since it is their work that God manifestly hath blessed.

While this is one possibility, distasteful in the extreme to mainline Bible scholars today, it is this writer's considered opinion that it was not the translators' gifts which God passively watched being exercised, and which He then blessed in the aftermath. It is held that God guided the judgment of the translators to the decision they made about that word, ***Calvary***. This is a possibility utterly abominable to the aforementioned scholars, but every tenet in the scriptures that pertain to the words of God, lead to the conclusion that God has been involved in the infinite intricacies of the transmission of His words from the beginning until this moment. This is inclusive of not only inspiration and preservation, but translation, as well.

In the end, the scholars sometimes seem to be merely snide and mean children. God blessed a certain line of manuscripts and a certain line of faithful scholars, and the other line of scholars, using the other line of manuscripts, or even the philosophy that pervades that line, have not been blessed or used of God in the same way as the first, and now they respond as reproved, rejected and spiteful juveniles. Good morning, Cain! There were prophets God used throughout the Bible and prophets He did not use or bless. There are preachers that God has blessed, and others that He has not. God simply does not bless the new versions or the proponents of their brand of scholarship the same way He blesses the textual line, the scholarly line, the translational line and the translation of the King James Bible! One does not get to choose what God blesses, but it is such a one's calling to find out what He blesses and get aboard! The doctors and professors of Bible and linguistics have the same options as Cain: "***Get right and get aboard, or... don't.***"

It is God that took this singular word, ***Calvary,*** from its native language, gave it birth in English, and then blessed and used it in the way that He has. Man is merely an observer. He did what He did and no man can stop Him. But then, many Bible-believers do not want to stop Him. We see what He did and we approve of it! Is that the reader's attitude?

All should see that God sanctified the word *Calvary* by the way that He translated and used it. By God's usage of the word, ***Calvary*** encompasses, as a concept, a lot more than merely a place, ***the place of a skull.*** ***Calvary*** is where the eternal transaction occurred where Christ took upon Himself the sins of the entire world (1 Jn. 2:2). There He *his own self bare* *our sins in his own body on the tree* (1 Pet. 2:24). There is where stood the cross in which saved men glory. The law is crucified there (Col. 2:14). I am crucified there (Gal. 2:20). There the world is crucified unto me, and I unto the world (Gal. 6:14). Calvary is a place, but it represents something far more - a transaction! There is no other transaction that really matters on the eternal scale. God *sanctified* ***Calvary.*** There is no other place or transaction like it. God *ordained* ***Calvary***. The word is a unique word. It was given birth to designate where Christ was crucified and what He there accomplished. To this author's knowledge, there is no other meaning or separate use of the word, apart from men confusing it with the *cavalry*. God *sanctified* ***Calvary***. This sanctification could only be accomplished by translating it differently than in its sister narratives. ***Skull*** brings forth all manner of mental connections for which ***Calvary*** does not stand, for though it was a place of death, a skull could never ever stand as a symbol of the benefits with which Christians are blessed.

Therefore, God sanctifies words and establishes associations in the English of the AV 1611 which are not evident in Greek. Whether one chooses to argue for the human element (the ingenuity of the AV translators) or the divine element (God's intimate involvement in the translation), such a one is still ensnared with the manifold majesty and superiority of the English over the Greek.

The AV's English is superior to the Greek. Simply put, God established and distinguished certain things in the King James English that were not manifest in Greek. One does indeed receive light and enlightenment in the AV that he does not from the "original language." Maybe it should be framed it this way: ***how isn't the English superior to Greek in this case?***

Reverting to Greek or a new version is a regression, not a progression. Going back to the Greek, *kranion*, or leaning on a new version is an act that essentially rejects what God did with the word ***Calvary*** in the AV. It is a journey backwards to a place of less light and revelation. We are taught by orthodoxy today that forays into the Greek are always enlightening and expansive to our spirituality and Christianity. This certainly is not the case. A Greek safari in this case narrows a student's horizons, regresses into less light and, perhaps most importantly, overthrows the Lord's intricate working in the details of the Holy Scriptures. Progress in knowledge and understanding was made when the Bible was translated into the English of Wycliffe, Tyndale and King James I of England! If the translation of the AV 1611 was not ***progress*** with respect to the word of God, why is it that the continuing rejection of it for the last 150 years has resulted in nothing but Christianity's down-spiral and retrogression into spiritual darkness?

All should be reminded of modern scholarship's handicaps. Scholarship, for scores of years now, has been unable or unwilling to see the attributes of the word of God, which have been clearly pointed out in this book. ***Calvary*** is but one example. Many scholars are saved men and women, but they have been taught to approach the word of God from an essentially unbelieving viewpoint. Modern scholarship – and that which is not so modern – is ***handicapped by a lack of faith.*** Well, *faith cometh by hearing, and hearing by the word of God* (Rom. 10:17), so if they begin by not having faith in God's word, the whole spiritual structure collapses from there. Scholars are predisposed by their institutional and educational preconditions and prejudices to come to an unfaithful view of God's words. In the face of all the evidence clearly stated in the scriptures themselves, even many King James defenders and scholars are still bound by Satan's humanistic philosophy that no translation could be the perfect handiwork of God. Their great problem resides in what they have chosen (or been taught) to accept by faith. They are thus further ***handicapped by a bias***

that is against that which is plainly promised in scriptures. Just as evolutionists are biased to view all evidence through the spectrum of natural selection, mutation and billions of years of incremental change, most biblical scholars today are preconditioned to banish all thought that God's word exists in perfection in any translation today. They are simply programmed to forbid the thought that the original languages, in the state in which they are possessed today, simply do not provide the light or the power that all the rhetoric promises. In this way, the end result is that the scholars are ***handicapped by blindness.*** They simply do not want to see, so they do not. Much of the blindness is willful, but much is imparted, or else is the natural, residual blindness of the fallen nature of man in general. This blindness is not mere accusatory mud-slinging on the part of frustrated Bible-believers, but is literal spiritual sightlessness that is demonstrable by the fact that all these attributes of the AV 1611 that are pointed out in this book have existed under the noses of Bible scholars and linguistic geniuses for many decades. By the thousands, there are men better equipped than this writer to intellectually decipher and bring these attributes to light. They do not, have not, and will not, because they are trained to have a predisposition to unbelief in certain areas. They are trained to be subverted by bias and they are resolutely educated to be blind. They are "ordained" and academically groomed to unbelief. A Bible-believer's advantage is his trust in God.

> *And Jesus said, For judgment I am come into this world, that they which see not might see; and that they which see might be made blind.*
> (John 9:39)

> *23 Turn you at my reproof: behold, I will pour out my spirit unto you,* ***I will make known my words unto you****.*

*24 Because I have called, and **ye refused;** I*
*have stretched out my hand, and **no man***
regarded;
*25 But ye have **set at nought** all my counsel,*
*and **would none of my reproof:***
26 I also will laugh at your calamity; I will
mock when your fear cometh;
27 When your fear cometh as desolation,
and your destruction cometh as a whirlwind;
when distress and anguish cometh upon you.
28 Then shall they call upon me, but I will
not answer; they shall seek me early, but they
shall not find me:
*29 **For that they hated knowledge, and did***
not choose the fear of the LORD:

(Prov. 1:23-29)

~~~~~~~~~~~~~~~~~~~~~~~~~~~~~~~~~~~

Science

In His omniscience, the Lord certainly foresaw and anticipated developments before they came to pass. Scores of examples could be cited from the scriptures. In fact, it is this kind of pre-knowledge that gives Christians one of their most sublime advantages over false religions: prophecy. This marvelous attribute of God allowed Him to make adjustments which were intended to be advantageous to us.

For example, has the bible reader noticed that the scriptures present the Lord Jesus Christ's dialogues and dealings with His mother in a rather stern, and by some standards, a discourteous light? Christ's response to Mom after being "lost" for three days was, *How is it that ye sought me? wist ye not that I must be about my Father's business?* (Luke 2:48-49) When Mary made a suggestion at the marriage in
~~~~~~~~~~~~~~~~~~~~~~~~~~~~~~~~~~~

Cana, *Jesus saith unto her, Woman, what have I to do with thee? mine hour is not yet come* (John 2:4). When she arrived for one of His preaching conferences, His response was, *Who is my mother? and who are my brethren* (Matt. 12:48)? Mangled and dying at Calvary, *he saith unto his mother, Woman, behold thy son!* (John 19:26)

The existence of a loving and warm relationship between Jesus and Mary is not in question, but foreseeing beforetime the Catholic idol-makers' agenda, the Lord God saw fit to present Christ in the scriptures in this light to the end that cuddly and warm intimacies might not be exploited and abused to support idolaters' Mary-worship.

Another thing that the Lord foresaw was the manufacture of one of the most egregious idols to ever exist. In the modern world, Science has become the totem by which sin is justified, lies are concocted and promoted, and every manner of excuse is made. Science is the anvil on which sinners hammer out the details for justifying and promoting evolution, homosexuality, drunkenness, adultery, dope-headedness, environmentalism, vegetarianism, Bible rejection, and every crackpot scheme or gimmick imaginable. If one can say, "It's scientific," he can sell and justify just about everything. People are petrified of the prospect of being accused of being "unscientific." Science may be Satan's master idol in these last, dark days.

Only two verses in the AV 1611 contain the word, ***science***. In Daniel 1:4, Nebuchadnezzar sought Hebrew children that had certain characteristics:

> *Children in whom was no blemish, but well favoured, and skilful in all wisdom, and cunning in knowledge, and understanding* ***science****, and such as had ability in them to stand in the king's*

> *palace, and whom they might teach the learning and the tongue of the Chaldeans.*

In the second example, Paul gives Timothy explicit admonition:

> *O Timothy, keep that which is committed to thy trust, avoiding profane and vain babblings, and oppositions of* ***science*** *falsely so called:*
> (1 Tim. 6:20)

Evident Lessons on *Science* from the AV 1611

Daniel 1:4 –

- **The Hebrew children's *Science* was good.** It was blessed by God and perhaps authored by Him, as well. In the end, their "scientific" understanding wound up being *ten times better* (Dan. 1:20) than that of the other "scientists" in Nebuchadnezzar's realm.
- **The Lord can use a certain kind of *Science*.** As the experience of Daniel and his friends progressed in the captivity, it is obvious that God used what they knew and further expanded their knowledge for His glory in the kingdom of Babylon. Again, this is "good ***science.***" This is the opposite of that mentioned in 1 Timothy 6:20, ***science*** *falsely so called.*
- ***Science* in the verse is distinguished from *knowledge* in the same verse.** The new versions do not make the distinction, as they tend to botch the passage by shuffling knowledge, understanding and wisdom as if the three were indiscriminately interchangeable. They are not! More information will follow, but for now, may the reader simply recognize that God differentiates between *knowledge* and ***science.***

1 Timothy 6:20 –

- **This *Science* is the polar opposite of Daniel's.** The Christian must then stand vigilant, for the Bible reveals that there is a ***Science*** that God will use, and a ***Science*** that He will not use and bless. Just as the Bible reveals two types of wisdom and knowledge, so there exists a duality of ***Science***; one, an enlightenment and one, a pollutant.
- **The *Science* in Timothy is oppositional.** This ***Science*** opposes the knowledge of God and is adversarial to *that which is committed to (our) trust.* In this way, this brand of ***Science*** is at enmity with a Christian and his walk with God.
- **It is to be avoided.** While the world, and even some of the household of faith, is preoccupied and mesmerized with it, a Bible-believer has but one commission: avoid the wrong kind of ***Science***!
- **It belongs in a category akin to *profane and vain babblings*.** This kind of ***Science*** is not Godly or holy. It is not noble or honorific. It is worthy of no pedestal, nor of any laurels. It is not even worthy of attention! It belongs in the same bin where a Christian would place cursing and profanity, as well as the nonsensical blather of the insane and fools. It belongs in the trash.
- **Its name is a lie.** It is ***Science*** *falsely so called.* It is misnamed by the world and the worldlings. It is not worthy of the name ***Science.*** It should be called "Foolishness."
- **The Lord does not use this kind of *Science* other than to lay a snare for those that are *wise in their own conceits.*** See 1 Corinthians 1:19 and 3:19.
- **The Lord designates by name, once again, one of the crucial spiritual issues of these present days.** As when He specified Philosophy and Tradition as "spoilers" in Colossians 2:8, so He calls by name here the plague of 20th and 21st century man: ***science.***

Indistinct Murkiness of the New Versions and the Greek

Science in the King James Bible comes from words in Hebrew and Greek that are almost universally translated "knowledge" in the rest of the cases in which they are used. The Hebrew word is *maadah*, otherwise translated in four places as "knowledge." The Greek word in the New Testament is *gnosis* and its root word is *ginosko.* 28 of 29 times, *gnosis* is translated *knowledge*, the exception being 1 Timothy 6:20. Hundreds of other times, *ginosko* is used and is most usually translated *to know*, and is less often translated *to perceive, to understand.*

The two passages that truly stick out are the two passages under discussion, for they alone, for "some" reason, use the word ***Science***, instead.

The new versions make quite the confounding jumble by intermingling and interchanging, seemingly at random, terms such as *knowledge, wisdom* and *understanding.* Any side-by-side comparison of versions in the book of Proverbs will reveal a truly astonishing rat's nest of inter-tangled terms. In general, it is safe to say that the new versions zealously discard the ***Science*** of the King James and opt for "knowledge" in its stead.

Obviously, the new version editors ran back to the Greek and Hebrew, discovered the original language roots, and decided that the King James translators went too far and unjustifiably translated ***Science*** in these two cases. The commentators, plagued by the same bias and blindness, dismiss the AV reading and take their readership back to "knowledge."

Enlightening Conclusions About *Science* in the English

Though modern scholarship takes umbrage and even offense at the King James Authorized Version's audacity at translating these cases as ***Science***, one should be reminded that the AV seems always to manage to "get the goat" of the sinners who resent the word of God's authority and intrusion into their particular playhouse. Here are some open and evident observations that do not surface in most mainline and Fundamental Bible College class settings.

By the use of the word *Science*, the AV draws and focuses attention on two verses that define the issue. In the Greek, the Hebrew, and in the new versions, the concept of *knowing* is massed into hundreds of different verses. By the strategic translation, ***Science,*** in these two verses of the KJV, the Lord focuses attention on verses that define the issue. "Running" the word ***Science*** in a concordance or Bible program elicits only two "hits," and in these two verses are found the major attributes of the two kinds of ***Science***, which characteristics were outlined earlier. To change the word ***Science*** is to break the linkage to the isolated information the two verses contain. To change the word ***Science*** is to make clear and plain light a good deal dimmer.

The King James Bible blatantly *names* the culprit. In Colossians 2:8 the Bible names two spoilers: Philosophy and Tradition. The AV does the same in 1 Timothy 6:20 in naming ***Science***; however, on this occasion all the new versions bail out on the translation. The world's ***Science*** is itself the problem, but it remains unnamed in the new versions and camouflages itself amidst the velvet of softer wording.

The translation, *Science,* foresaw several hundred years in advance an "institution" that has, in large part, become a lie. It may always be heard how the language of the

KJV is outdated and antiquated. Is it not odd that it is the old, outdated AV that identified the adversary by name 400 years ago? (Incidentally, Tyndale identified ***Science*** – *sciece*[240], in his translation – even before that!) Dear reader, the modern translations have not caught up to identifying the perpetrator even at this late hour. Apparently, if man must wait on them, he will just never know!

The King James Bible brings to light in English what is not seen in Greek or Hebrew. The AV makes distinctions in English that are not evident in either Greek or Hebrew. It distinguishes and differentiates truth that is not observable in either original Biblical language. It illuminates and highlights details that the original languages, as studied by scholars today anyway, leave in ambiguity and obscurity.

The AV is translated in sanctified language. Though there certainly is a sanctified and godly *knowledge* in the Bible, the King James further distinguishes details and categories of things. ***Science*** is a specialized and sanctified word that the Lord translated to represent specific and spotlighted truth to us all. ***Science*** is as specific a word as is *atonement, charity, inspiration,* or *Calvary.* It is so specific and sanctified that He used it only twice.

For these reasons, the AV 1611 translation is superior to the Greek and Hebrew out of which it came. As evidenced, this is really quite indisputable. The English distinguishes more truth, grants more light, discriminates more finely, and focuses and illuminates the understanding of the Bible-believer in a way that the Greek and Hebrew never did for those who have made a living by exploiting it.

---

[240] *The Wesley Center Online*: *Home*. Web. 11 Dec. 2010. <http://wesley.nnu.edu/biblical_studies/tyndale/2ti.txt>.

The AV wording in English also contains revelation not in evidence in the Greek and Hebrew. This has long been a bitter bone of controversy for Fundamentalists who do not wish to bear the reproach of the scholars. They *hate* being called by names that are associated with men who have borne the brunt of believing and defending every written word of the Book. Nevertheless, they *DO* have a problem.

The problem is that it was 400 to 500 years ago when the AV (and even Tyndale) named ***Science*** as the present day culprit. The word of God in the AV prophesied beforehand what the problem would be in a way that neither Greek nor Hebrew foresaw! The AV ***revealed*** certain facts and categories in ***advance***. In this way the King James Bible does demonstrably provide ***advanced revelation*** absolutely not contained in the Greek, the Hebrew, the new versions, or in the hearts and minds of scholars who abhor the concept.

To elaborate or retreat to the Greek and Hebrew, in this case, is once again a journey *backwards* into a darker and less enlightened place than in the old English Bible. Referring to the original languages here is not an act of progress. It is an act of regression. One goes backward. This might be even regarded as "backsliding."

Someone is responsible for the excellence of the grand old Book. Responsibility for such enlightening translation must either be ascribed to the humanly gifts and wisdom of the AV translators, or man must give God Himself the glory. Either possibility is despicable to the palate of the 21st century scholar. If the excellence is attributed to the translators, then the academic judgments of the modern, inferior scholar must simply step aside for manifestly superior gifts. If the glory is given to God for such brilliance and distinction, then they must admit that God must have had an integral part in the actual translation in question.

In this way, the irreverent scribes and scholars are in a box where they must either repent of their infidelity or else malign those who point out their untenable circumstances.

A man with a King James Bible, who actually believes that Bible, is better off in every respect than the man who exercises himself in all the linguistic tools available. None of the scholars with all those tools, or who authored and edited those tools, ever even acknowledged the existence of these things which are evident in simply believing the Book as God gave it to man.

~~~~~~~~~~~~~~~~~~~~~~~~~~~~~~~~

Excess

In case it has escaped the attention of anyone, one of the marks of latter day Christianity is a notable departure from the basic tenet that a Christian should live holy unto the Lord and that in doing so he should separate himself from the world (2 Cor. 6:14-17). While the precept is readily accepted that Christians must still live in the world, where they are salt, light and ambassadors, it remains true that Christians are not of the world and ought to labor to separate themselves from it as *becometh holiness* (Tit. 2:3). This principle is not the pattern by which the mega-churches and the modern religious kingdoms are built. One "succeeds" these days in drawing a crowd only when he tells folks that they can come as they are, stay as they are, and place no restrictions of behavior, morality or spirituality upon them. The more they are convinced that God is really quite like themselves (Ps. 50:21), and that He has no real "outward" or behavioral expectations for them (Rom. 12:2), the better people in general like it.

When the bands and cords (Ps. 2:3) of holiness and sanctification are removed, it doesn't take very long for the old
~~~~~~~~~~~~~~~~~~~~~~~~~~~~~~~~

nature of the unsanctified Christian, the old man, to assert himself with a force and a vengeance. Unseparated churches have become a hatchery for idolatries, adulteries, addictions, debauchery and drunkenness. They have convinced themselves that rock bands and a multitude of writhing, dancing, ill-dressed hooligans with upraised hands are the workmanship of a holy God. They are wrong.

Many things today are acceptable among Christians that anybody two generations ago would have discerned, judged and damned immediately. Adultery, bastardization, shacking up, cigarettes, petting, partying, profane humor, Rock & Roll, Country & Western, and even sodomy are often condoned at one level or another by those that are called "Christians." Even among good people who love the Lord, there is an increasing tendency to let slide some of the standards of behavior that not only illuminated Christian paths a generation or so ago, but also are established in the scriptures for the truth-loving Bible-believer.

Many are the areas where Christians simply are getting looser and looser, and one of these areas, to be forthright, is drinking… as in, booze and beer. It not the author's intent to undertake here a review of all that the Bible says about drinking alcohol, and it is well known that there are many ins and outs to the matter. For one, the Bible-believer has to consider the impact of both new wine (Is. 65:8 – grape juice) in the Bible versus alcoholic wine. Bible-believers find many admonitions and reasons in the scriptures to utterly abstain from alcohol. They who wish to keep the door open a crack, cite passages that relate to medicinal issues (1 Tim. 5:23), and those which some conclude allow for social drinking, but not drunkenness (1 Tim. 3:3, 3:8 & Tit. 1:7). These think that there is no genuine New Testament admonition to abstain. It is this issue which will be addressed and which contributes to this thesis on the superior clarity of the AV 1611.

The King James is Clear – The Wine is Excess

Those who hold that the New Testament does not condemn drinking booze in moderation seem to have not discerned a passage that makes the matter clear. There are a couple of passages that are actually often presumed to advocate social drinking, but closer examination will show that they do not. Note Ephesians 5:18, first of all, and then 1 Pet.4:3-4:

> *And be not drunk with wine,* ***wherein is excess;*** *but be filled with the Spirit;* (Eph. 5:18)

> *3 For the time past of our life may suffice us to have wrought the will of the Gentiles, when we walked in lasciviousness, lusts,* ***excess of wine****, revellings, banquetings, and abominable idolatries:*
> *4 Wherein they think it strange that ye run not with them to the same* ***excess of riot****, speaking evil of you:* (1 Pet. 4:3-4)

The Ephesians 5 passage is very often taken to mean that being drunk is *excess*, but that moderate drinking is perfectly fine. This may appear superficially to be the meaning, but readers are often careless with the breadth and depth of the words of God, and are sometimes presumptuous in thinking a tenet has been grasped when it actually has been misapprehended. Scripture comments upon scripture (1 Cor. 2:13), and one passage sheds light on another, which light often alters what was first thought.

For example, notice 1 Peter 4:3, which mentions again the ***excess of wine***. This seems to fortify what will turn out to be the *misconception* of drunken excess of Ephesians 5:18. These two companion passages have led some to say, "See… it is OK to drink wine, but just not to excess or drunkenness."

However, before a stop is made by the liquor store on the way home this Friday, take note of 1 Peter 4:4. It mentions ***excess of riot*** and commends Christians who do not take part.

Consider the phrase ***excess of riot***. The phrase construction is exactly the same as ***excess of wine*** in verse 3, except for the interchange of the one word. Since so many think a *little wine* is fine, is a *little riot* fine, as well? Imagine this: "Now, dear, when you go to the *riot* tonight, be careful that you don't go overboard and *riot* too much!" No. There is a marvelous thing revealed with the help of the Holy Spirit and a little common sense. The verse is not saying that *rioting too much* is *excessive*. It is saying that the ***riot is the excess***! The plain meaning of ***excess of riot*** means that the ***riot itself is excess!***

Again, the phrase construction of ***excess of riot*** and ***excess of wine*** is exactly the same grammatically, and that within two consecutive verses. Brethren, what the Lord revealed in the two verses is that since the ***riot*** of verse 4 is plainly the ***excess***, so it must be that the ***wine*** of verse 3 ***is the excess***, and not merely the excessive drinking of the wine. ***The wine itself is excess, not just drunkenness!*** This means that the presumed, superficial conclusion of Ephesians 5:18 has to be re-evaluated as well. Where Ephesians 5 says, *And be not drunk with wine,* ***wherein is excess***, the Bible isn't saying that being *drunk* is the *excess*, but that the *wine itself* is the *excess*. If one did not realize that the first time he read through Ephesians 5, he would have figured it out as he read 1 Peter 4:3-4 (if it was read carefully and believingly), and thought about the ramifications of the two grammatically identical phrases in two consecutive verses.

The King James Bible is clear. **The wine itself** ***is the excess, just like*** **the riot** ***is the excess***. A Christian should no more drink wine for preference or pleasure than he should join a violent mob of rowdies partying like animals and throwing bricks at the police!

Scholarship is not Clear – It Messes Up "Excess"

And be not drunk with wine, ***wherein is excess****; but be filled with the Spirit.* So reads Ephesians 5:18 in the AV 1611. The new versions generally replace *excess* with either "dissipation" or "debauchery." My, is that not so much easier to understand?

1 Peter 4:3-4 in the King James reads in part, *For the time past of our life may suffice... when we walked in...* ***excess of wine****...Wherein they think it strange that ye run not with them to the same* ***excess of riot****, speaking evil of you.* The butchery of the new versions is not for the faint of heart. They replace ***excess of wine*** with either "drunkenness" or, in one case, "drinking bouts." They further help us by substituting "excesses of dissipation" or "wild profligacy" in place of ***excess of riot***.

Importantly, when the new versions insert "drunkenness" in 1 Peter 4:3, in place of ***excess of wine*** in the King James Bible, they actually insert an **interpretation** instead of a translation, and **that interpretation is wrong**. They presumed that ***excess of wine*** was interchangeable with "drunkenness," but it is not. It is not, because, as seen above, the *wine* is the *excess*. We do not question that drunkenness is *excess*, for it is; but the KJV plainly reveals that the wine itself is *excess* before anybody gets drunk – and even if they do not get drunk.

As if obliterating and obscuring entirely the truth and the pure interpretation of the passage were not enough, the new versions also bless their readers with "dissipation," "debauchery," and "profligacy" - longer and more difficult words than the Lord used in the real Bible. Funny – Bible-believers are told that the King James is harder to read…

It should also be added that it is plain from the comments on the two passages by Matthew Henry, Adam Clarke and Jamieson, Fausset and Brown, that the ***excess*** is presumed and interpreted to be the *drunkenness,* and not the *wine*.

The Greek is Not Clear Either

The following shows the appropriate Greek words for the passages in question.

- **Eph. 5:18 – *excess* – asotia (Strong's #810)**
  ***wine* – oinos (Strong's #3631)**
- **1 Pet.4:3 – *excess of wine* – oinophlugia (Strong's #3632)**
  phluaros – excess (Strong's #5397)
  oinos – wine (Strong's #3631)
- **1 Pet.4:4 – *excess of riot***
  anachusis – excess (Strong's #401)
  asotia – riot (Strong's #810)

In particular, it is notable that three entirely separate Greek words are the basis for each of the times ***excess*** is translated in the AV. To restate in another way, three different terms are used in Greek for the one word, ***excess,*** in the King James Bible.

The Greek-focused Bible scholar or translator runs back to the Greek and finds three separate Greek words and is faced with how to translate or understand them. Most settle for "dissipation" or "debauchery" in Ephesians 5:18. In 1 Peter 4:3, most opt for "drunkenness", and in 1 Peter 4:4, "excesses of dissipation" and "wild profligacy" are found. The water surely does look muddy after they are through helping God out, and a Christian trying to decide whether to imbibe with boozers is left with an entirely different and more confusing picture than the evident exactness of the Authorized King James Bible.

The Greek leaves the issue in obscurity and ambiguity.

Lessons That *Are* Clear

The King James Bible makes very clear what "*excess*" is. *Excess* is not just the extreme of drunkenness, but the wine, as well. The AV is exact, precise and definitive where the Greek, the scholars and the new versions are not. It expresses very plainly what is acceptable for a Christian, where the other sources of "truth" leave a seeking soul without any accurate guide and the wayward imbiber a justification for his misbehavior.

The King James Bible simplifies the complexities of the Greek readings of the texts in question. It takes three rather disparate words in Greek and makes them one in English. In so doing, it removes all doubt as to the meaning. In other cases, the AV expands a singular Greek concept, as with *agape*, meaning both *love* and *charity*. These examples may be counted blessing for this means that God has granted King James Bible believers extra information not necessarily contained in Greek. In this case, He simplified information that was unnecessarily scattered, as He did when taking *phileo* and *agape* and translating them as the singular term, *love*. In the end, it is again found that a Bible-believer can trust God to both pare down unnecessary wording in the process of translation, and yet expand knowledge in cases where one Greek term is best represented by more than one English word.

The King James Bible clarifies the obscurities of the Greek text. It brings into focus the words and precepts in

English in a way that was not manifest (to today's scholars anyway) or understood in the "original language." The English is specific and distinct in these passages and in this precept in a way that the Greek is not.

The King James Bible provides very distinct and defined revelation in these passages that is unavailable in Greek. While other passages certainly teach abstinence, the scholars of Greek never grasped the definition of ***excess,*** which definition leads to the unwavering conclusion that a Christian should abstain from the hooch. It is in this way that the AV does, once again, advance the knowledge and revelation of the truth.

In these ways, the King James Bible is superior to any of the other versions, and the evidence points to superiority over the Greek, as well. If it is not superior, then why are the scholars still bumbling around in the passage, and why are they justifying Christian social drinking by proxy? Again, just how is it that the King James reading is *NOT* superior to the Greek reading?

Referring back to the Greek for light, in this case, is to essentially embrace the darkness. This is not a tremendous surprise, for men love *darkness rather than light, because their deeds (are) evil* (Jn. 3:19). Just because one is a scholar, does not mean that he loves the light or the truth. His scholarship may be little more than a fig leaf. Referring to the Greek in this case may also serve a double purpose, since man often also likes his liquor and beer. In either case, the light is in the AV English, and to revert to the Greek is to regress, and either deny or not recognize the progress and revelation the English provides. **There is no evident benefit in reverting to Greek and studying it in this case.**

A child of God is far better served and nourished with a King James Bible than with any new version or Greek text. He is a better Christian for having ***excess*** clearly defined, and for being able to discern God's mind with respect to drinking the sauce. He is advantaged, since the truth is not plainly evident otherwise. Though there are many areas of the Christian life that require sanctification, he will at least be a better Christian for knowing the truth and not drinking alcohol.

Someone deserves the credit for the clear definition of *excess* in the King James Bible, which was provided only by translation. To whom shall it be given? To the AV translators? If to them, then it behooves the cynics and critics who have berated the translators for all these years to shelve the criticism and recognize truly superior and unassailable scholarship at work. If the responsibility of the translation is to be given to God, then let the scornful scholar take his proper medicine. See, if God is given the glory for the excellence of the translation, then not only is the Bible in general a supernatural Book, but the magnificence of the King James Bible is due to supernatural and providential guidance. The very suggestion of this has been considered anathema to mainline scholarship. Such an idea has been an utter abomination to scholarship for a minimum of 150 years, and has been a concept roundly damned by even King James protagonists.

~~~~~~~~~~~~~~~~~~~~~~~~~~~~~~~~~~~

Easter

The translation ***Easter*** has long been a thorn in the side of scholarship. It occurs only one time in the AV 1611: Acts 12:4. The word does not occur in the new versions, and all the classic commentators either dismiss the AV's translation of the word, or simply bypass it.
~~~~~~~~~~~~~~~~~~~~~~~~~~~~~~~~~~~

A small taste of how irksome the King James can be to some is seen when considering the Jamieson, Fausset, and Brown comment upon the word *Easter*.

> *The word employed in our King James Version being an ecclesiastical term of later date, is* ***improperly used here.***[241]

The accusation of impropriety is bad enough, but Barnes takes things a good deal further than JFB:

> [Intending after Easter] ***There never was a more absurd or unhappy translation than this***.[242]

"Never…more absurd" is actually quite a claim. One gets the sense that Mr. Barnes sensibilities were insulted by Bois', Reynolds' and the Holy Spirit's choice of wording. Hopefully, he is not still in a huff.

The Source of Greek Scholarship's Snit

A man's final authority remains the singular most profound and far-reaching element in his life. Everything in life flows out of that one thing: Decisions, principles, morals, standards of behavior, vision of life and reasons for living. Most Christians say that the Bible is their final authority, but the devil, by his subtlety, has managed to open a contradictory and deeply divisive conundrum within "Christianity." What scholars say many Greek and Hebrew words mean often does not reflect what the Bible plainly says in a Christian's own

---

241 *Jamieson, Fausset, and Brown Commentary*. (1998) P C Study Bible (Version 2.11) [Computer Software]. Seattle, WA: Biblesoft.
242 Barnes, Albert. *Barnes' Notes* (1997) P C Study Bible (Version 2.11) [Computer Software]. Seattle, WA: Biblesoft.

native tongue. The scholars' union has devoutly declared that the keys of knowledge abide with said scholars, and only with them. These fellows resolutely overlook or ignore the scriptural precepts that illustrate God's effectual and supernatural working in the translation of His word from the original languages to the languages of the world. In this way, scholarship is not only disdainful and caustic toward the Bible that resides in the hands of the people, but it also insists in undoing what the Lord has already accomplished in revelation and knowledge. It is resolute in unraveling what God hath woven and in disassembling what the Lord hath engineered. The eternal and omniscient God's judgments and handiwork are not of high enough grade to escape second-guessing, pilfering and reconstruction by such eminent minds.

In this way, it is often a "no-brainer" to modern scholarship that a living, powerful, fruitful and enduring word or line of holy scripture can be altered and changed with impunity. Acts 12:4 is just such a case, and Mr. Barnes' haughty criticism, mentioned earlier, is the logical outcome of one pure final authority despised in place of another imposter.

A rather famous battleground of contention, Acts 12:1-4 says,

> *1 Now about that time Herod the king stretched forth his hands to vex certain of the church.*
> *2 And he killed James the brother of John with the sword.*
> *3 And because he saw it pleased the Jews, he proceeded further to take Peter also.* ***(Then were the days of unleavened bread.)***
> *4 And when he had apprehended him, he put him in prison, and delivered him to four*

> *quaternions of soldiers to keep him; intending* ***after Easter*** *to bring him forth to the people.*

The cause for the academic bile and scholarly ire revolves around the fact that the word ***Easter*** in the King James Bible is translated from the word ***pascha*** in Greek. ***Pascha*** occurs 29 times in the New Testament, and the King James uniformly translates it ***Passover*** except for the singular time in Acts 12:4, where it is obviously translated ***Easter.*** Since the Greek is the scholars' final authority, they have no qualms in either merely dismissing or roundly berating the King James translators' choice of ***Easter*** in this one place. Horror of horrors, they translated ***pascha, Passover*** 28 of 29 times, yet still allowed ***Easter*** to stand in Acts 12! What *impropriety* (Jamieson, Fausset and Brown)! What *absurdity* (Albert Barnes)!

The Reasons That the AV's English Translation is Right

Back in 1989 Dr. Sam Gipp wrote *The Answer Book* in which he repudiated the criticism of the scholars who wanted to revert back to ***pascha*** instead of the AV's ***Easter.***[243] As Gipp points out, should the passage have been translated in the real Bible as the scholars did in the modern frauds, a real and genuine conflict arises. Note the passage in Acts 12:3-4 again:

> *3 And because he saw it pleased the Jews, he proceeded further to take Peter also.* ***(Then were the days of unleavened bread.)***
> *4 And when he had apprehended him, he put him in prison, and delivered him to four quaternions of soldiers to keep him; intending* ***after Easter*** *to bring him forth to the people.*

---

[243] Gipp, Samuel C., *The Answer Book* (Bible & Literature Missionary Foundation, Shelbyville, TN 37160, 1989) p.3-8.

The real key to the passage lies in the parentheses of verse 3. ***Then were the days of unleavened bread*** are the words that reveal when Herod "took" Peter. The critical thing to understand about the Passover was that according to Exodus 12:13-18 the feast of unleavened bread was eaten from the 14th day of the first month to the 21st day of the month. Numbers 28:16-18 specifies that the actual Passover is the 14th day of the month and the feast of unleavened bread follows the Passover for seven days. **The key: the Passover is the 14th day of the month and the feast of unleavened bread <u>follows</u> for the next seven days** (Deut. 16:1-8; 2 Chron. 8:13; 2 Chron. 30:15, 21; Ezra 6:19, 22). **The Passover was first, and the feast of unleavened followed *<u>after</u>* the Passover.**

Since, according to Acts 12:3, Herod took Peter in the days of unleavened bread, therefore, it is evident that when Herod took Peter, ***the Passover was already past!*** No one actually thinks it likely that Herod was intending to hold Peter for another whole year!

While it may be argued that, in time, the entirety of the Passover and the feast that followed, became known generically as "The Passover," it should be pointed out that if the Holy Spirit distinguished with clarity the ***days of unleavened bread*** in verse 3, He fully intended us to distinguish the Passover, proper - a one night per year event preceding the feast of unleavened bread - as opposed to the generic meaning. If the AV translators had translated ***pascha, "Passover"*** (as did all the new versions), then they would have made the same mistake as did all the new version scholars. They would have been saying that Herod was going to hold Peter for another year, for *Passover* was already several days past, since Passover proceeded the days of unleavened bread!

Herod was not waiting until after the Jews "Passover" out of respect for the Jews. The Jews themselves had killed Jesus Christ during the times surrounding Passover (Matt. 26:17-19). Herod was waiting for the ancient pagan festival of Astarte, or Ishtar, the "queen of heaven" (Jer. 44:17-25). The debauched celebration was always held in the spring, representing the regeneration of the earth, when Astarte's *son/husband* (yes, you read that right) came back alive as the flowers and trees budded, and the animals began their spring mating sequences. This descends to the world today in ***Easter*** bunnies (very prolific little mammals), ***Easter*** eggs (symbolic of fertility) and Good Friday (a lie). Good Catholics only eat fish on Friday (fish lay millions of eggs) for Freya, the pagan goddess of fertility, another manifestation of the queen of heaven, might get upset of they eat red meat. Herod was waiting for his beloved ***Easter*** to kill Peter, because ***he had a record of killing prophets during celebrations*** (Matt. 14:6-11).

The AV translators, or else the God that guided them, saw that translating ***pascha*** as ***"Passover"*** would have been inaccurate, and would have invited all sorts of misunderstanding. William Tyndale was also apparently in tune with these facts and the mind of the Spirit in this matter, for he translated the word "***ester.***"[244]

In this, once again, the advantage of genuine familiarity and trust of the scriptures as they are written within the Bible is found, as opposed to being preoccupied (or even occupied) with whether the Bible actually means what it says.

The Lessons the *Learned* Have Not Learned

In 6000 years of men's history, the Lord has no record of having honored what men would consider the orthodox academic intelligentsia of any age. *Where is the wise? where is*

---

[244] http://wesley.nnu.edu/biblical_studies/tyndale/act.txt.

the scribe? where is the disputer of this world? hath not God made foolish the wisdom of this world (1 Cor. 1:20)? The Lord has always gotten along much more swimmingly with the down-to-earth. *And the common people heard him gladly. And he said unto them in his doctrine, Beware of the scribes, which love to go in long clothing, and love salutations in the marketplaces…*(Mk. 12:37b-38). The Lord has aggressive tendencies toward those brimming with presumption due to their intellectual attainments. *And Jesus said, For judgment I am come into this world, that they which see not might see; and that they which see might be made blind* (Jn. 9:39).

To open this segment on ***Easter***, it was shown that Dr. Albert Barnes forsook his reserve and revealed that he had his nose out of joint, saying of the AV's translation of Acts 12:4, ***"There never was a more absurd or unhappy translation than this."*** Barnes' failing is common with men and women of Bible letters. They labor in a field where Bible lessons flower all around them, yet they are only trained and acclimated by their scholastic conceptions to accept certain kinds of lessons. To them, ***Easter*** in the Bible really belongs among the discards and the rubbish. These are lessons they do not learn, perhaps, cannot learn…but, you can!

Easter* in the AV 1611 is a translation that is in concord with the rest of the scriptures.** To translate the word ***pascha as "Passover" in the passage would have been an exercise in contradiction. The feast of unleavened bread *followed* Passover! They were already in the days of unleavened bread. To translate the word ***Easter***, as did the King James Bible, presents a translation and concept entirely consistent with the rest of the facts of the holy scriptures.

There is more to pure Bible translation than Greek and Hebrew skills. As a boy, I worked constantly for a several years around Mexicans. In the process of becoming fairly adept in Spanish, I learned that words, phrases, contexts and constructions were not equivalent in Spanish as in English. It is not as simple as inserting a Spanish word for an English word in many contexts. Though ***pascha*** was *Passover* in the King James Bible 28 of 29 times, in Acts 12:4 it is ***Easter***... and it should be! Contrary to the impression left by some, translation is not a science. There are times that a word consistent and perfect in some contexts, simply does not suffice in others. In Acts 12:4, ***pascha*** simply does not mean *Passover.* It means ***Easter***, and ***Easter*** is consistent with the rest of what the scriptures reveal to a student of the word, but seems hidden to its critics.

The English of the AV, then, contains information not evident in Greek. This can be said with confidence, because all of the AV's critics with lofty linguistic credentials, missed the implications and intricacies just discussed.

The English of the AV clarifies this information clearly and plainly. Herod was going to celebrate Easter by executing Peter like he had done with John the Baptist at a birthday celebration. The Jews Passover was not an issue, for it was already the days of unleavened bread. What may have been (and has been) overlooked in Greek (the word ***pascha*** only), is boldly clarified in translating ***pascha*** as ***Easter*** one time in 29.

There is, then, revelation clearly manifest in English that is not clear at all in Greek. A careful Greek-speaking Bible-believer could see that ***pascha*** in Acts 12:4 must mean something other than the "Passover," for that understanding would be in conflict with the outlay for the Passover and the feast of unleavened bread in Exodus, Numbers and Deuteronomy. Thus, a Greek speaker could come to the correct conclusion. However, for the English-speaking Christian, the matter is laid out in pulsing black and white. ***Easter*** is not a wrong translation. It is a florescent, flashing marker highlighted with halogen lamps. The English reveals clearly what the Greek does not.

In this, the English of the King James is superior to the Greek. Perfectly understandable in 17th century English, are plain facts that Greek scholars, who have dedicated their lives to study, do not apprehend. Apparently, English speakers understand what modern, native-speaking Greeks do not understand. How exactly is it that the English of the King James Bible is not superior to the Greek in this instance?

Spiritual light was discovered, not in going back to Greek, but in going forward into English. Contrary to the claims made so obsessively by Greek scholars, little if any useful light is uncovered by going back to the original languages. Such an exercise is mostly tinsel, glitter and packaging. It is usually emphasis placed by man on often false and misleading details that God did not emphasize. The Greek casts no useful light upon the passage, but the King James translation distinguishes in English what was not evident in Greek.

A Bible-believer is better served reading, believing, learning, absorbing and meditating on the AV 1611 scriptures than seeking deeper truths in Greek or among Bible rejecting scholars. The King James Bible is the word of God and it brings to light and clarity the things God wants believers to see. Over and over again, it has been seen how these very things are obscured or withheld from the eyes of those preoccupied with the original languages. What genuine truth did the Greek scholars reveal that was not disclosed in the AV? What has been seen over and over is that digging into the Greek seems only to reveal currently dry wells that the AV translators already tapped into, or else a bankruptcy of knowledge and light altogether.

"Someone" is responsible for the excellent translation, *Easter*, in the King James Bible. Someone got it right while the rest of scholarship, even still, bumbles around, complaining about it and thinking it is wrong. Who is responsible and (W)ho gets the credit and glory: 1) The AV translators, or 2) God?

~~~~~~~~~~~~~~~~~~~~~~~~~~~~~~~~~~~

Replenish

> *And God blessed them, and God said unto them, Be fruitful, and multiply, and* ***replenish*** *the earth, and subdue it: and have dominion over the fish of the sea, and over the fowl of the air, and over every living thing that moveth upon the earth.*
> (Gen 1:28)

> *And God blessed Noah and his sons, and said unto them, Be fruitful, and multiply, and* ***replenish*** *the earth.* (Gen 9:1)

Honoring the specific wording of the King James Bible is what marks a true Bible-believer from someone whom I call "King James-kind-of." Either one accepts that the wording of the Bible is completely sanctified, or one does not. Either the words are sacred or one can alter them and pilfer them as he pleases. If the words are not sacred, then sinners will find opportunity to exercise their license. Academic qualifications or disqualifications have precious little to do with it in the end.

The words of the English Bible are in no way sacred to any group other than King James Bible Believers. They alone stand for its inviolability. The mainline academics, scholars and translators have proven themselves little more than intellectual
~~~~~~~~~~~~~~~~~~~~~~~~~~~~~~~~~~~

prostitutes, selling out the wording of any and every bible or pseudo-bible for the purpose of garnering new copyrights. Nothing is sacred to them except what they can *alter*. Speaking of prostitutes, Proverbs says this: *Lest thou shouldest ponder the path of life, her ways are* ***moveable****, that thou canst not know them* (Prov. 5:6). See, each new Bible has to differ enough from the last to justify issuing a new copyright for its printing. In the end, the Greek and Hebrew games played really devolve to money. *For the love of money is the root of all evil...* (1 Tim. 6:10). But the game is also about the more honorific element of respectability amongst fellow academics. There is an element of ambition involved, but there also is the very real and imposing shadow of the fear of man. *The fear of man bringeth a snare* (Prov. 29:25a). More than just about anything else, scholars fear the tarnishing of their reputations among their "peers," and they are, in many respects, slaves to the majority opinions of that which is considered orthodoxy by the majority. Christ Himself addressed this spiritual condition: *How can ye believe, which receive honour one of another, and seek not the honour that cometh from God only* (John 5:44)?

The branch of Christianity that is "King-James-kind-of" encompasses a very healthy portion of "Fundamentalism." These folks are very uncomfortable with new versions and the "neo" branches of Christianity. Yet they are also very, very itchy-footed about the sacredness of singular and separate English words of the King James Bible. The promises and the evidence are as available to them as to any, yet they know the stigma and the disreputable mark associated with embracing the manifold evidence and the manifest hand of God in the AV. They face being grouped with the "unscholarly." They fear academic marginalization. They shrivel from being called repugnant names. Therefore, they move to the center of the road. They disdain the liberal and unbelieving scholarship of the new versions and "neo-Christianity," but they also limit the promises of the propagation of the perfect word of God to the original languages. They restrict broad and sweeping promises of the scriptures (*Every word of God is pure* – Prov. 30:5) to narrow and unfounded strictures ("It only applies to Greek and Hebrew, and certainly not translations"). They then rationalize that such a position makes them the uncompromising and ardent defenders of the faith, the keepers of the *old paths* (Jer. 6:16), and the poster children for the "old-time religion." It is a carefully manufactured image and it is defended with a ferocity born of both desperation and insecurity, for in the end the highly reputed pastor or scholar who is "King James-kind-of" is still a man whose Bible is subject to vagaries and uncertainties. He will fudge the language and use adamant rhetoric, but in his study at night, he does not hold a complete and perfect Bible in his hand, and the original language texts that he truly leans on have substantive variations and translational complications that still leave him without a Bible with every word and thought of God perfectly contained therein.

Sacred and specific wording is how God communicates definitive and intricate truths. He either communicates in elaborate and precise fashion, or He does not. One either has God's specific words in accord with His promises, or one has a wordy mixture of nonspecific mush that might represent the message of God…maybe…perhaps.

God certainly knows the use of synonyms – different words that have the same meanings – but His use of differing words should not be received flippantly or with ready-made presumption. So often, there are profound and insightful lessons in His use of differing words.

Such is the case with the word ***replenish***, which, in all its forms, is used seven times in the KJV. With a rare exception here and there, the new versions avoid the word ***replenish*** like the Black Death.

The Implications of *Replenish*

As stated, ***replenish*** occurs seven times in the King James Bible, but its first two occurrences are what provide occasion for the fur to hit the fan. Again, a Christian is inevitably forced to choose whether he will sit up and take notice of God's use of specific wording or not.

In Genesis 9:1, *God blessed Noah and his sons, and said unto them, Be fruitful, and multiply, and* ***replenish*** *the earth.* ***Replenish*** never caused any heartburn in that passage, because an entire civilization had been destroyed in a biblically documented (and, for that matter, a scientifically documented) worldwide flood. The judgment of God fell on wicked man, and all that was left of animal and human life was harbored safe in a monstrous ark. The inhabitants of that haven, Noah, his wife, his three sons and their three wives, had a big job to do. They – eight people – had to ***replenish*** *the earth*! ***Replenish***, as in, "repopulate" or "refill." That is, they had to "plenish" the earth *again.* There had been a civilization there before and now it had to be redone, rebuilt, reconstituted and repopulated. When something is rewritten, reconstructed, reformed, revisited, revitalized, rebooted, rebound, rechristened, refurbished, regenerated, reengineered, redesigned, rejuvenated, recalibrated, relubricated, reviewed, republished, reprinted, resupplied, retried or rezipped, everyone knows exactly what it means. Each of those things is some action *done again.*

Noah and his family *plenished* the earth *again.* They ***replenished*** the earth. They refilled it again after the former population of wicked men was destroyed in the terrible wrath of God. This presents no problem to anyone's theology that believes the Bible at all, since Adam's progeny were in obvious and documented existence before Noah's flood.

The problem is not what the Bible said Noah's commission was in Genesis 9:1. The bee gets under a bunch of peoples' bonnets because of what *Adam's* commission was, as described in Genesis 1:28:

> *And God blessed them, and God said unto them, Be fruitful, and multiply, and* ***replenish*** *the earth, and subdue it: and have dominion over the fish of the sea, and over the fowl of the air, and over every living thing that moveth upon the earth.*

The problem is that Adam's commission was an earlier duplicate of Noah's commission, or vice versa. God told *both men* to do the *same thing:* ***replenish the earth***! Noah ***replenished*** that population which was destroyed while he was aboard the ark. What was it that Adam ***replenished?***

The "Gap" *Replenish* Indicates

The author holds that the "Gap Theory" is not a theory at all, but a doctrine. Thus, it is the "Gap Fact" or the "Gap Doctrine." Much pulling of the hair, protestation and misrepresentation accompanies the presentation of the Gap, but the issue is not something intentionally engineered to be divisive or insidious. It is merely one of hundreds of historical occurrences in the Bible that no one would know about had not God revealed it.

In the use of the word ***replenish***, in Adam's case, as in Noah's, is revealed the certitude of another population upon the earth <u>*before Adam*</u>. When might another population of beings have existed before Adam? The only reasonable possibility is between Genesis 1:1 and 1:2.

> *1 In the beginning God created the heaven and the earth.*

> 2 *And the earth was without form, and void; and darkness was upon the face of the deep. And the Spirit of God moved upon the face of the waters.* (Gen. 1:1-2)

Many "Gap Doctrine" proponents have pointed out that nowhere in the Bible is God particularly inclined to create something *without form, void*, or in *darkness*. God created Adam a full-grown man and Eve a full-grown woman. The commentators like to use the word "chaos" in their conception of what was going on in Genesis 1:1-2. Chaos is not something that is consistent with the testimony of all else that God created. Were the cherubim and seraphim, the sons of God, the angels, the animals or the heavens created in surroundings *without form* and *void?*

The indication is that after *God created the heaven and the earth* in Genesis 1:1, there was something that happened that caused God to cast the earth into the formlessness, voidness and darkness of which verse 2 testifies. If the judgment of God fell between those two verses, then there is introduced the idea of another population or civilization inhabiting the earth prior to this judgment.

The Corroboration for the Gap

It is natural for one to want to know if the Gap of Genesis hangs solely on the witness of a single word, and it does not.

The Witness of Peter

In the context of the very last days, and in a quite familiar passage, the Apostle Peter says some things in a way in which the Bible-believer should take note.

> 4 *And saying, Where is the promise of his coming? for since the fathers fell asleep, all things continue as they were from* ***the beginning of the creation.***
> 5 *For this they willingly are ignorant of, that by the word of God the* ***heavens were of old****, and the earth standing out of the water and in the water:*
> 6 *Whereby* ***the world that then was****, being overflowed with water, perished:*
> 7 ***But the heavens and the earth, which are now****, by the same word are kept in store, reserved unto fire against the day of judgment and perdition of ungodly men.*
>
> (2 Pet. 3:4-7)

(T)he beginning of the creation of verse 4 takes the reader back to the earliest verses of Genesis. The presumption in the passage is that the flood testified of is Noah's flood, and it would present no real problem if it were so. However, there is a certain aspect of the passage that rules against it being Noah's flood. Note in verse 6 that ***the world that then was*** could apply to Noah's flood, for that flood did destroy ***the world that then was***. However, note in verse 5 ***the heavens were of old***, but then again in verse7, ***But the heavens and the earth, which are now***. If the flood were Noah's, there would be (and there is) a different earth, but in verse7, also note **a different set of *heavens*** today, as well as ***earth***!

The earth was destroyed in Noah's flood, but the ***heavens*** were not destroyed. The flood that this passage is talking about destroyed the ***heavens*** as well as the ***earth***! When did that happen? It happened between Genesis 1:1 & 1:2.

Other Pieces that Fit the Puzzle

There are some other nagging and bothersome questions that are better answered by the existence of a pre-Adamic world followed by a wrathful destruction, a subsequent barren world and a recreation from Genesis 1:2 onward.

Satan's Fall. A theology that does not include the Gap has a problem. It does not account for a legitimate time frame for Satan's fall. Insight into his fall is given in Isaiah 14, but Isaiah 14 does not help with chronology or *when.* Without the Gap, God created everything, including Lucifer and the heavenly host, and then seamlessly in Genesis 3, Satan shows up as the subtle Serpent - already fallen. When did that happen?! With no more light, we just have to say that he fell somewhere between the creation and Genesis 3:1.

However, the Gap reveals a time for Satan's fall, and also an explanation for why the earth *was without form and void,* and why *darkness was upon the face of the deep* (Gen.1:2). The earth was in such a condition for God had judged it with another destruction, and that destruction was occasioned by Satan's rebellion and subsequent fall.

The Creation of the Heavenly Creatures. Oddly, Genesis 1-2 does not separately account for, or list in detail, the creation of Satan, the cherubim, the seraphim, the sons of God, and the angels.

Ezekiel 28:13-15 is another passage similar to Isaiah 14 that exposes the devil under the thin guise of the *king of Tyrus* (28:12). In verse 13, he is exposed as having been in *Eden the garden of God*, along with the revelation that he was a living musical instrument. That alone clearly enough marks him as Satan, but then in verse 14, he is more specifically revealed to be *the anointed cherub that covereth.* Importantly, verse 13 mentions *the day that thou wast created.* Satan, once a heavenly covering cherub, now the devil, was created!

Well, the rest of the cherubim and seraphim were created too. So were the heavenly sons of God (Job 38:7). Plainly, so were Michael and Gabriel. When were they created? Why does Genesis 1-2 not give us a hint as to when God populated Heaven with created beings?

Perhaps, it is because Genesis 1-2 is about the re-creation of the earth and the heavens, and as such, God details His creation of light, firmament, plants, fowls, fishes and animal life. He then details His creation of Man and Woman. Perhaps details regarding heavenly creatures are not included because they were already present from the prior creation – the one in which Satan was created. They got to see the upheaval that led to the judgment of the earth between Genesis 1:1 and 1:2, and sat and observed God's recreation of things anew.

The Dinosaurs. The dinosaurs have been a preoccupation of man for a long time. Evolutionary scientists try to browbeat Christians with their billions and billions of years, and they use dinosaurs to do so. Bible-believing Christians are faced with somehow trying to explain dinosaurs, since there seems to be precious little mention of anything that can be a dinosaur in the Bible. Creationist scientists place the dinosaurs on Noah's ark, though nothing like them is mentioned in the account, and I have personally heard certain scholars make Behemoth (Job 40:15) and Leviathan (Job 41) dinosaurs.

It is important to note that both Behemoth and Leviathan are primarily identified as Satan in Job.40:19 & 23, and Job 41:34. Many imaginative theories have been set forth for the dinosaurs having been a part of the creation that is accounted for in Genesis 1:2 onward, and that they would have therefore been represented on the ark of Noah. It seems very odd that the major animal groupings mentioned on the ark are still to be found in abundance but the "dinosaurs" are left with precious few representatives in today's world. (Evolutionists proclaim that crocodiles and Gila monsters are essentially dinosaurs.) Why did the alleged post-Noahic dinosaurs die out when cats, cattle, rabbits, gophers and sheep did not?

Considering the abundance of the evidence for dinosaurs, and if the scientists are correct about their size and numbers, it seems that the far better and more feasible explanation is that the dinosaurs were part of the pre-Adamic earth. This would have made them contemporaries with whatever was going on down here prior to Lucifer's fall and the subsequent judgment of the earth. Thus, all the dinosaur findings of paleontology are evidence not of dinosaurs in a post-Adamic age, but a pre-Adamic age.

God's Habit of Using Gaps. It is objectionable to some that God would skip right over such a profound and monumental event as a pre-Adamic judgment and destruction of the earth and heavens without more specific narration or detail. At first, this may seem a legitimate concern, but then one might be apt to notice just how often it is in the Bible that the Lord ordains gaps of time and details. A few will suffice.

- In Isaiah 61:1-2, a comma represents a 2000 year time frame known as the Church Age. Verse 1 is a plain reference to the first coming of Christ, but the comma in verse 2 that is situated between ***To proclaim the acceptable year of the LORD (,)*** and ***and the day of vengeance of our God***, represents a gap, a 2000 year long break in time, unaccounted for in the verse.
- After, the book of Malachi, there is a 400 year time frame, or gap, that marks God's complete severance of scriptural communication with man,

until the angel communicates God's intentions to John the Baptist's father in Luke 1:11.

- Genesis 5 represents a bridge between Adam's day and Noah's day encompassing over 1500 years. While Genesis 5 does provide a continuous genealogy of man over those thousands of years, there is a vast information shortage as far as details of their lives and generations are concerned.
- Another long, silent, gap is the time-frame from Babel in Genesis 11 to Abram's calling out in Genesis 12.
- Between Genesis 16:16 and 17:1 are 13 years of Abraham's life of which God records no narrative details at all.
- Only the barest of details are known of Moses' life, both between his infancy and flight from Egypt, and his time of dwelling in the land of Midian in exile from Pharaoh. These two 40 year segments represent 80 of Moses' 120 years.
- Of the Lord Jesus Christ's first thirty years on earth almost nothing is known with the exception of His being "lost" at the temple in Luke 2 during His 12th year.
- The book of Judges contains one incident after another of lost decades, and even half-centuries of time, that are unaccounted for with respect to details or narrative.
- In Daniel 9:26, Daniel's sixty-ninth week is finished with the Messiah being *cut off*. The prophet then continues his prophecy with respect to the seventieth week just as if Saturday became Sunday. However, there are 2000 years of chronological time between Daniel's 69th and 70th weeks!

In short, a Bible student, conscious of the written record of God's habits, must admit that gaps of time and detail that are not readily revealed without careful study are very common as far as the Lord's authorship is concerned. Grown, scholarly men have thrown hissy-fits over God having not explained His numbering of the generations of Jacob, His accounting of Ahaziah's age, His editing of genealogical listings and His counting of Solomon's chariots and horses. *It is the glory of God to conceal a thing: but the honour of kings is to search out a matter* (Prov. 25:2). It is a far cry from unusual that God would have concealed a pre-Adamic age within the folds and creases of scripture.

The Number of Generations of the Earth. While the following is not "proof" of a Gap between Genesis1:1 and 1:2, anyone who has studied numerology knows that the Lord Himself lays an extraordinary foundation of correlations between numbers in the Bible. He certainly gets to make exceptions in the times when He does not place a correlation with numbers and a Bible-believer should beware the presumption of inserting correlations where God does not. Many who have studied numerology, however, recognize the Lord's use of the number **seven**. Seven days of creation (recreation) are enumerated in Genesis 1-2, and Hebrews 4 reveals that God's plan for man's history revolves around seven millennia. Seven days of the week, seven whole notes on a piano, seven baptisms in the Bible, seven mysteries in the Bible, Daniel's 70 weeks of years, seven resurrections in the Bible... All these are mere superficial tidbits that are only indicators of the Bible's vast depths and its treasures of design.

In the end, the number **seven** in the scriptures communicates the idea of completeness. Just for novelty's sake, consider that if there is no gap in Genesis 1:1-2, there would be but **five** distinct generations of the earth, both past and future.

1) Edenic Earth
2) Pre-Noahic / Post-Adamic Earth
3) Present Earth
4) Millennial Earth
5) New Heavens and New Earth

On the other hand, notice what happens to the list of the generations of the earth if the Gap is taken into consideration.

1) Pre-Adamic Earth
2) Earth under judgment during the Gap (Gen.1:2)
3) Edenic Earth
4) Pre-Noahic / Post-Adamic Earth
5) Present Earth
6) Millennial Earth
7) New Heavens and New Earth

The Lord can do as He likes, and nothing forbids Him establishing only 5 generations of the earth, but in the scriptures, the number **five** tends to be associated with, variously, Death and Grace. Again, **seven** tends to be associated with completion.

Adam and Noah's Common Bonds. Several common elements in Adam's life and Noah's life are recorded by the Lord as important. Doubtless, hundreds of other separate characteristics could have been recorded, but were these recorded so that the reader would see that if commonality existed in these places, might not they have another abiding characteristic to share?

Note that Adam and Noah:

- Both had 3 sons by name
- Both had 1 debauched son who wound up cursed
- Both sinned in placing fruit in their mouths
- Both were given the exact same commission by the Lord

- Both fell into sin while naked
- Both were great types of Christ
- Both had sons in the lineage of Christ
- Both were sole possessors of the earth when they fell
- Both were given precisely the same, specific commission to *replenish the earth*
- *Is it possible that they both were preceded by a population destroyed by God's judgment and that a flood preceded both their identical commissions?*

The Heartburn Caused by *Replenish*

The so-called "Gap Theory," no matter the evidence cited above, sticks in the collective craw of many "Bible-believing Fundamentalists." There is a uniformity of indignation, argumentation and objection by those adverse to the Gap Doctrine.

One accusation is that Gap Fact adherents are attempting to accommodate evolutionary theory by "trying" to provide a time-frame for evolutionary ages. Answer: It is not known how much time might be indicated by the Gap, but for the entire time that I have been a Bible-believer, I have been continuously associated with men who see the Gap as a verity. In that time, I have never known a single Christian of that long association that was anything but a creationist, and I have never known a single one who sought to accommodate evolutionary ages.

They say that the Gap is a recent theological invention. There are actually indications in Church history that this accusation is not true at all. Let us pretend that it is. If it is so that the Gap has been relatively lately discovered in time, so what? If a definite and critical doctrine was discovered on this very day which had never been sorted out before by students of the Bible, is the doctrine still true? While the scenario is unlikely with respect to a theology that might totally redefine a major segment of sound Christianity, a Christian still needs to contemplate whether he/she is a Bible-believer or a mere adherent to some branch of traditionalistic theology. I know Independent Baptists whose final appeal is to historic Baptistic theology as opposed to the Bible itself. I am a Baptist for a reason, and generally, baptistic theology is Bible theology, but if one believes something simply because his favorite Baptist theologian believes it, he is really no better than a Pope-kissing Catholic.

They say that the word behind *replenish* in Hebrew and English means "to fill." Some King James Bible believers do not believe in the Gap, and they simply hold that ***replenish*** means nothing more than "to fill." There are several things that lead to the belief that there is more substance to this matter than the simple exchange of word meanings can resolve.

First, Webster's 1828 does cite one meaning of replenish as "To fill; to stock with numbers or abundance," but it also cites the following as a definition: "To recover former fullness."[245]

Second, God and the King James translators did use the word "fill" in Genesis 1:22, just six verses before the Lord told Adam to ***replenish*** *the earth.* Furthermore, the Hebrew word behind *fill* in verse 22 and *replenish* in verse 28 is the very same word in both cases: ***male***. Once again, Bible-believers are faced with the Lord using two distinct English words from a singular Hebrew word. The Bible reader and student is immediately, and once again, faced with "the dilemma." For now, suffice to say that God and the King James translators had the word "fill" as a part of their working vocabulary – even within the Genesis

---

[245] Webster, Noah. *Webster's 1828 Dictionary* (Christian Technologies, Inc. version 2, 2004, http://www.christiantech.com
.

1 passage. Why would God use the word ***replenish*** within six verses of having used ***fill***, if He indeed meant "to fill"?

Third, the word ***replenish*** unquestionably means "to fill," but that is not all it means. When I pull into a service station to "fill" my car with gas, I am also replenishing the tank to former fullness, unless it is literally the first time I am filling it. ***Replenish*** means to fill or plenish again. It does not mean only to fill. It means to fill again. I may replenish a glass with iced tea, a plate with food, or a living room with furnishings, but I wouldn't say I was replenishing these things if I were filling them for the first time. One is not renovating a house if he is building it the first time. One is not reprinting a book if he is printing it for the first time.

In Genesis1:21, *God created great whales, and every living creature that moveth, which the waters brought forth abundantly, after their kind, and every winged fowl after his kind: and God saw that it was good*, and in verse 22, the Bible says that He gave the commission to ***fill the waters in the seas***. Perhaps He used the word ***fill*** in verse 22 because the seas had not been filled with these particular creatures before, but He used the word ***replenish*** in verse 28 because the earth had been filled before, and had been emptied by judgment and needed ***replenishing***!

Finally, the word replenish in all its forms, is used seven times in the AV 1611. Besides Genesis 1:28 and 9:1, it is found in Isaiah 2:6, Isaiah 23:2, Jeremiah 31:25, Ezekiel 26:2 and Ezekiel 27:25. In each of these places, the meaning of "filling again" or "recovering former fullness" is contextually and manifestly obvious, unless one were intent on ramming their own preconceived meanings into the verses.

The Lessons Learned from *Replenish*

The Gap Doctrine does not rank on the level of the Trinity or the Deity of Christ as far as theological indispensability is concerned. Fellowship between Bible-believers need not be made or broken over the implications discussed here. If folks do not agree with this assessment of the scriptures, the definitions or the reasoning highlighted, there need not be any horrific ramifications as there would be if unable to agree that Christ is God.

It is, however, important to say that this matter does, again, go to the very heart of the controversy that does rip the body of Christ and the family of God to shreds. The Gap may not be utterly indispensable doctrine, but it does highlight the absolute inviolability and sanctity of the wording of God's own verbiage. God either said what He meant when He used the words He used, or He did not. That goes for Hebrew, Greek and English words, as well! Christ the Word is either master of English words, as well as Greek and Hebrew words, or He is not.

One may be certain that there are King James Bible defenders, who, having read this, absolutely believe that God did not, would not, could not make distinctions of meaning in English that are not found in Greek or Hebrew - the evidence notwithstanding. Let us, however, review what these observations indicate.

***Replenish* does not mean the same thing as "fill."** When replenishing something, you may "fill" it, but more importantly, you "refill" it.

***Replenish* comes from the same Hebrew word as *fill* of Genesis 1:22, but God made a distinction in English which He did not in Hebrew,**

This means that one gets clear and distinct information in the English of Genesis 1 and 9 that was not communicated in Hebrew.

This means that the English is, in this way, superior to the Hebrew.

This means that a person gets "revelation" in English that he does not necessarily get in Hebrew. This might be called "advanced revelation" by some. It should be added that it might be called this *correctly*.

This means that what truth might be obscure and ill-defined in the Hebrew, the English of the KJV drew out and highlighted plainly. Whatever God was willing, or is willing, to show a Hebrew-speaking truth seeker out of the Hebrew of Genesis 1:28 and 9:1, one cannot tell. It can be seen in clear evidence that God clarified truth in English that those preoccupied and infatuated with the original languages cannot draw from Hebrew.

This means that for an English speaker to go back to the Hebrew for clarity is to regress in light and knowledge.

This means that a Bible-believing student of the scriptures is hindered by focus being diverted to the Hebrew. On the other hand, the student who is single-mindedly devoted to the English scriptures God delivered to him, is greatly profited, progresses and *grow(s) in grace, and in the knowledge of our Lord and Saviour Jesus Christ* (2 Pet. 3:18).

This means that a student of the word of God can have utter and unwavering confidence in the English of the AV 1611. The same cannot necessarily be said of the Hebrew and Greek for repeated exhibition of the blindness and the incompetence of scholarship as it is practiced by double-minded and faithless scribes has been seen.

The King James Bible as a translation is something special – more special than mere flattering tongues will recognize. Either the King James translators or God Himself is responsible for the superiority and excellence of the AV 1611 as a translation. The choice to a Bible-believer is obvious, but the naysayers and the "King James-kind-of" people will have to take their medicine in either that they choose.

~~~~~~~~~~~~~~~~~~~~~~~~~~~~~~~~~~

Lucifer

Sadly for those afflicted by it, the blithe unawareness of the actual damage done in altering the Bible does not register due to the blindness of mind (2 Cor. 4:4) for which Satan is responsible. A great deal is heard about the ingenuity and profound spiritual devotion of the academics which have flooded the intellectual market with corrupt new versions, polluted Bible study "tools" and profoundly false information. While the Laodicean intelligentsia is preoccupied with what amounts to self-congratulation and self-glorification, it has escaped their attention that the principle mastermind of the entire debacle has not only covered his tracks, but has changed identities.

The opposite is true of simple Bible-believers, for they have been onto Satan for as long as they have read and believed their Bibles. King James people all have "favorite" stores of ammunition to pull out when it comes time to show how modern scholarship has changed and polluted the words of God. Many have both mental and physical lists prepared to show the profound changes made to the atonement, the Trinity, the Deity of Christ, the names and titles of the Lord, omissions, deletions and other alterations.
~~~~~~~~~~~~~~~~~~~~~~~~~~~~~~~~~~

To this writer's mind, the most blasphemous and profound alteration to the Bible has to do with Satan's identity. Bible readers all acknowledge his subtlety. Well known is the fact that he is *wiser than Daniel* (Ezek. 28:3) and that he *deceiveth the whole world* (Rev. 12:9). Nevertheless, a certain dread chill settles in the soul when it is realized that in a masterwork of delusive power, the devil, in the new bibles, has turned himself, identity-wise, into the person of our Redeemer, the Lord Jesus Christ!

The Deceitful Debacle

One of the final spiritual visions allotted to Christians by faith in the word of God is one of the Savior, Who will return in short order.

> *I Jesus have sent mine angel to testify unto you these things in the churches. I am the root and the offspring of David, and* ***the bright and morning star.*** (Rev. 22:16)

Even the new versions give Christ the glory of being the ***bright and morning star***, and some might hope that the canon of scripture even in the new versions might close on a high note, and without yet another spiritual atrocity. Sadly, the mastermind of deception saved one of his greatest heists of truth until the very last!

In the King James Bible, one of the definitive passages on the origin and work of Satan seems to be relatively unrelated to the closing vision of the glory of Jesus Christ in Revelation 22. In Isaiah 14, is given the information on how Satan got where he is today, and believers are told one of his names, which is recorded only in the AV as ***Lucifer***. The title ***son of the morning*** most likely relates to his exalted place on creation morn as *the anointed cherub that covereth* the throne of God (Ezek. 28:14). The critical juncture of concern, follows,

> *How art thou fallen from heaven,* ***O Lucifer, son of the morning****! how art thou cut down to the ground, which didst weaken the nations!*
>
> (Isa. 14:12)

No confusion exists in Isaiah 14:12 in the King James Bible. Lucifer is named and exposed for who he is, however, Satan is alive and well as yet, and has done a damnably profound amount of work since the publication of the King James Bible in 1611. Note the butchery of the scriptures and the blasphemy of the Savior that occurs in the new versions.

> How you have fallen from heaven, ***O star of the morning, son of the dawn***! You have been cut down to the earth, you who have weakened the nations! (NAS)

> How you have fallen from heaven, ***O morning star, son of the dawn***! You have been cast down to the earth, you who once laid low the nations!
>
> (NIV)

> How you are fallen from heaven, ***O Day Star, son of Dawn***! How you are cut down to the ground, you who laid the nations low!
>
> (RSV)

In a frighteningly deft and insidious display of cunning, Satan, through the medium of corrupt scriptures, brings off the abominable and the blasphemous. He obliterates the record of his name (***Lucifer***) and inserts in its place one of the singular titles of the Son of God, the Lord Jesus Christ (***morning star***)!

Identity theft has statistically become an increasing crime in society which people nowadays often have to deal with. Long before the age of computerization and peoples' identification by a numeric system, Satan had in place a plan by which he endeavored to steal the ultimate identity: Jesus Christ's! It is a disgraceful irony that by manipulating man's thoughts and philosophies, he accomplished the theft of identity by the exploitation and corruption of the Lord's own scriptures. They to whom was given the stewardship of the mysteries of God (1 Cor. 4:1), by their own clearly manifest apostasy, allowed Satan to name himself as Christ. The average new version reader has not a clue. Many of the much-esteemed Bible commentators do no better. Adam Clarke goes on record as the blind leading the blind...

> [O Lucifer, son of the morning] The Versions in general agree in this translation, and render heeyleel (heb 1966) as signifying ***Lucifer***, phosphoros, ***the morning star***, whether Jupiter or Venus; as these are both bringers of the morning light, or morning stars, annually in their turn. And although the context speaks explicitly concerning Nebuchadnezzar, yet ***this has been, I know not why, applied to the chief of the fallen angels, who is most incongruously denominated Lucifer***, (the bringer of light!) an epithet as common to him as those of Satan and Devil. ***That the Holy Spirit by his prophets should call this arch-enemy of God and man the light-bringer, would be strange indeed. But the truth is, the text speaks nothing at all concerning Satan nor his fall, nor the occasion of that fall, which many divines have with great confidence deduced from this text. O how necessary it is to understand the literal meaning of Scripture, that preposterous comments may be prevented!***

> Besides, ***I doubt much whether our translation be correct***. Heeyleel (heb 1966), which we translate Lucifer, comes from yaalal (heb 3213), yell, howl, or shriek, and should be translated, "Howl, son of the morning;"...[246]

Keil & Delitzsch fare no better in their attempt at shedding real light.

> ***Lucifer***, as a name given to the devil, ***was derived from this passage***, which the fathers (and lately Stier) interpreted, ***without any warrant whatever, as relating to the apostasy and punishment of the angelic leaders.***[247]

The bottom line is that, all the scholarly verbiage notwithstanding, Satan managed two things:

1) He expunged his name, ***Lucifer***, from the scriptural record in the new versions.
2) He replaced it with a title that is exclusively the Lord Jesus' title, ***the star of the morning***.

The Hebrew Behind the Heist

The word in question, which is translated ***Lucifer*** in the AV and "morning star" in the new versions, is ***heylel*** (Strong's word #1966). Strong reports that it comes from ***halal*** (#1984). ***Heylel*** occurs one singular time in the Hebrew OT (Is.14:12). Its root word, ***halal***, occurs nigh unto 200 times in the OT.

---

[246] Clarke, Adam. *Clarke's Commentary*. (1998) P C Study Bible (Version 2.11) [Computer Software]. Seattle, WA: Biblesoft.

[247] Keil, Carl Friedr., and Franz Delitzsch. *Biblischer Commentar Über Das Alte Testament: Carl Friedr..* Leipzig: Dörffling Und Franke, 1870. Electronic.

This is an excellent example to show just what kind of deathly intellectual quicksand is entered when one decides to play games with the "original Hebrew." Notice the following possibilities regarding meaning from both Strong's Dictionary...

> 1984 halal (haw-lal'); a primitive root; to be clear (orig. of sound, but usually of color); to shine; hence, to make a show, to boast; and thus to be (clamorously) foolish; to rave; causatively, to celebrate; also to stultify: [248]

...and another much respected source, Brown-Driver-Briggs,

> 1984 halal- 1) to shine
> a) (Qal) to shine (figurative of God's favor)
> b) (Hiphil) to flash forth light
> 2) to praise, to boast, to be boastful
> a) (Qal)
> 1) to be boastful
> 2) boastful ones, boasters (participle)
> b) (Piel)
> 1) to praise
> 2) to boast, to make a boast
> c) (Pual) to be praised, to be made praiseworthy, to be commended, to be worthy of praise
> d) (Hithpael) to boast, to glory, to make one's boast
> e) (Poel) to make a fool of, to make into a fool
> f) (Hithpoel) to act madly, to act like a madman[249]

---

[248] *Biblesoft's New Exhaustive Strong's Numbers and Concordance withExpanded Greek-Hebrew Dictionary*. 1994, 2003, 2006 Biblesoft, Inc. and International Bible Translators, Inc.

As the reader can see, there is a very broad spectrum of possible meanings, according to these men. Were they right? Maybe. Does the reader think that the list above grants any knothead the license to pick one of the definitions as an option and insert it into Isaiah 14:12? The reason this possibility is presented is because that is exactly what is happening across Christianity today. Naive Christians equipped with a library of Greek and Hebrew reference works, readily accessible via computer, with a few keystrokes find an abundance of alternatives to what the Bible says. They have been ardently taught that all the treasures of the knowledge of God lies, not in their Holy Bibles, but in the oft moth-eaten works of Greek and Hebrew scholars, now available online. All translations are mere superficial representations and shadows of the real truth, so they are urged to sally forth to battle in a war they do not understand, with the armament of fools and with the confidence and courage of the deluded. Satan takes them, exploits their simplicity, damns the next generation by their complicity, and then watches them die without light.

Meanwhile the faithful excellence of the scholarship, labors and decisions of the AV translators, Tyndale, Coverdale, Wycliffe, and a bevy of other men, who held the scriptures in profound sanctification, is excused and dismissed as if each new and subsequent generation is promised immunity from the encroaching apostasy promised continually by the prophets. Does one think that translating and handling the Holy Scriptures is comparable to applying the multiplication tables or the set laws of physics? Did such a one forget that the word of God ***lives*** and is ***not bound***? Does he really think that the mind and thoughts of God were ever "confined" within the limits, and never allowed to exceed the parameters, of one or two particular

---

[249] *The Online Bible Thayer's Greek Lexicon And Brown Driver & Briggs' Hebrew Lexicon.* 1993, Woodside Bible Fellowship, Ontario, Canada. Licensed from the Institute for Creation Research. First published in Canada by Online Bible.

languages? Does such a one really believe that the actual words that precisely communicate the thoughts of God died to the use of common men, and that they can only be brought out of their entombment by those that are compromised by the pride and haughtiness so inherent of scholarship, and so often on display at this very hour?

In the end, a Christian must decide. One must either believe in the integrity and power of the God that promised promises to the believer, or one must allow men to place doubt, work confusion and make alterations to what the Lord said He would do for man. No Christian was ever commissioned or admonished to exercise himself in all the semantical machinations of academia, and what has become known as "biblical scholarship." He was never charged to become mired in the complex web of philosophies, rhetoric, theories and presumptions. Indeed, man has been warned away from them (Col.2:8)! Many have lost their entire lives, souls and usefulness therein. Christians were commissioned to believe and embrace the words of the living God which He vowed and swore to deliver. Believers were charged to believe in His power and in His personal integrity. Bible readers were, ***and still are***, told to entrust that He brought and brings those promises to pass. We must either trust God and the men and processes that God chose to use, or we must trust other men who – most unknowingly – labor for another master. How will one know the difference? *Wherefore by their fruits ye shall know them* (Matt. 7:20). *To the law and to the testimony: if they speak not according to this word, it is because there is no light in them* (Isa. 8:20).

The Peaceable Fruit of Faith

If the devil is real (he is), then he must attack Jesus Christ, for He is the key to all that God has done and is doing. Satan could not defeat Christ either by sin, death or Hell.

Though Lucifer is a loser and Jesus Christ the winner, the dragon still is able to win a tactical victory until the culmination of all things by deceiving the sinners and saints for which Christ died, rose and makes intercession. He does this by corrupting man's conceptions of truth and faith. Since *faith cometh by hearing, and hearing by the word of God* (Rom. 10:17), the key for Satan is to pollute the fount of faith, the Bible.

He has done this very thing in thousands and thousands of places in the new, contaminated versions. Yet nowhere has he been more audacious and insidious than in successfully erasing his own identity (***Lucifer***), and appropriating to himself the blessed title of the Lord Jesus Christ (***morning star***)!

The King James Bible is the Bible that has not only remained true in this particular (a few other new versions like the NKJV retain Satan's true identity in Is. 14:12), but it has been the faithful and true witness of the truths of God's words throughout its pages. The following highlight the verity and fruit of reading and believing the AV 1611, and ignoring the compromised new versions and the scholarship of those who helped cast Christianity into its present sad state.

The AV 1611 calls the Devil by his name (*Lucifer*), while the new versions obscure and erase it. Complicity with Satan should be enough to discredit any new version guilty of it, as well as the brand of scholastic philosophy that inspired it.

The AV also sanctifies the name of Christ (*bright and morning star*), as it always does, while the new versions allow the dragon to commandeer Christ's name!

The KJV is manifestly superior to any reading that confuses Christ with Satan!

The decisive and definitive translation of *heylel* as *Lucifer* in the AV English clarifies and erases any obscurity that may have existed in Hebrew. Any compromise on that point gives the devil glory. The new versions and the proponents of such scholarship give the devil glory. This is contrary to scripture and to the work of the Holy Spirit. *Search the **scriptures**...and **they are they which testify of me*** (John 5:39). *But when the Comforter is come...even the **Spirit of truth**, which proceedeth from the Father, **he shall testify of me*** (John 15:26).

This means that the AV 1611 reading is superior to the reading of the Hebrew. Again, how isn't the English of the KJV superior to the Hebrew?

This means that there is revelation in the English not readily seen in the Hebrew. The English reveals Lucifer as Lucifer. The new versions hide his identity and instead give him the name of our Savior!

This means that there is no manifold benefit in going to the Hebrew in this case. Anyone who has reverted to the Hebrew has only managed to wreak havoc and tear down the most holy. Such practice has only undergirded doubt and thus supported Satan's entire agenda.

This means that the scholastic propaganda that the body of Christ has been fed by scholars for the last several generations is little more than smoke, mirrors and intimidation. It is also a usurpation of God's handiwork.

Someone is responsible for the Christ exalting reading of the King James Bible! Either an honest scholar has to renounce his historic criticism of the AV translators and give credit where credit is due, or he has to admit that there are things evident in the AV translation that exceed even the judgment and scholarship of the translators. Either way, the aforementioned scholar, if he has criticized the AV 1611, will either have to hush up and apologize to the memory of the AV translators, or else fall on his knees and apologize to God.

> *Then Job answered the LORD, and said, Behold, I am vile; what shall I answer thee? I will lay mine hand upon my mouth. Once have I spoken; but I will not answer: yea, twice; but I will proceed no further.* (Job 40:3-5)

Chapter 17

The Spark of Life

And the LORD God formed man of the dust of the ground, and breathed into his nostrils the breath of life; and man became a living soul.
(Gen. 2:7)

And he said unto me, Son of man, can these bones live? And I answered, O Lord GOD, thou knowest. Again he said unto me, Prophesy upon these bones, and say unto them, O ye dry bones, hear the word of the LORD. Thus saith the Lord GOD unto these bones; Behold, I will cause breath to enter into you, and ye shall live:
(Ezek. 37:3-5)

One of the enduring mysteries of God's creation and man's very own existence physically and spiritually is that of life itself. The mystery extends downward from human existence into the various kingdoms of animals, insects, plants, flora and fauna. Life animates fifty-ton whales and 300 foot Sequoias. While the massive forms of life, like elephants and great white sharks, tend to impress and astonish our immediate senses, it is the microscopic world where the abundance and preponderance of life flabbergasts and blows the mind. It is one thing to watch an elephant hulk around, but it is another to realize that each and every microscopic cell of the elephant's tonnage *lives.* I have stood awestricken at the foot of an utterly massive Great Sequoia, realizing that it was sprouted from a cone hardly larger than my thumb, which cone contained the genetic blueprint by which billions of individual plant cells replicated themselves to form a plant that was thirty full feet in diameter.

It is fortunate and a blessing that God made the attainment of eternal life… ***eternal*** life… so simple an achievement. Granted, the majority will not attain it for *wide is the gate, and broad is the way, that leadeth to destruction, and many there be which go in thereat* (Matt. 7:13). The fact remains that the majority of humanity will be condemned to a lake of fire, not because salvation is too hard, but because they reject the simple truth about themselves, their sins and their souls. Verily, it is a wondrous blessing that God gives eternal life on simple terms and without complicated conditions, for if man were to have as little success comprehending and understanding eternal spiritual life as he has had grasping mortal, biological life, he truly would be in trouble.

As a prodigal son and before I made my way again from the hog sty to the Father's door, my secular undergraduate coursework at the University of Texas at Arlington led me deeply into the hard sciences – Chemistry, Physics, Biology and Physiology. There, I received a thorough and expensive immersion into the finest evolutionary brainwashing that a public university could provide in the early 1980's. In time, my own spiritual poverty and misery overruled and outweighed the high-minded propaganda, and I decided that I needed the truth more than I needed a place to hide from my God and my sins. I learned by going the long and rocky way around that the Bible holds the real and satisfying answers to this life – all of them. In this way, I emerged from the darkness into *his marvellous light* (1 Pet. 2:9), but I had been in the enemy camp long enough to have observed some things.

Among other things, I learned that they – the "experts" in worldly wisdom - do not know ***what life is***. It is a given that they do not know or understand what spiritual life is, but I speak here of the life that they occupy themselves with continually – biological life. This is the *life* that they believe to have been extant for hundreds of millions of years. They have studied this ceaselessly and have built an entire false framework of lies and deceits around it. Nevertheless, it remains that man has never discovered the *spark* that makes living things ***live.***

Life is generally defined as the capability of certain life-forms to be able to do some specific things that non-living entities cannot do. Life is defined as the ability ***to respire***, that is, to take nutrients and life-giving sources from the environment and to be able to exploit those sources. To humans, that is eating, drinking and breathing. For a tree, it means taking water and minerals from the soil, along with sunlight and carbon-dioxide from the environment. Another characteristic of life is the capacity ***to reproduce*** and ***to replicate.*** Obviously, life would not last very long were it unable to replicate its cells and eventually reproduce offspring to carry on the species. Life also requires that the organism be able ***to react*** and ***to respond*** to external forces in the environment. Animals fight or take flight. They hibernate, migrate and take shelter. Trees are given certain attributes by God that they might be able to respond in measure to the seasons, drought, fire or flood.[250]

Vast amounts of information have been garnered in studying these few attributes of life. Entire lives and libraries have been devoted to mere, tiny segments of these categories. Furthermore, ponderous volumes of information and monstrous attainments of knowledge have been gained in these last years as Daniel so adeptly prophesied (Dan. 12:4). The living cell – the building-block of life – was once conceptualized in

---

[250] Wile, Jay L., Durnell, Marilyn F. *Exploring Creation With Biology.* Apologia Educational Ministries, Inc., Anderson, IN 46016, 1998, pg.1.

relatively simplistic terms. It turns out that singular cells are complicated beyond comprehension. In my undergraduate work, *Cell Biology* was a course that haunted every student's dreams, and was thoroughly dreaded for its difficulty. (I didn't have to take it. The disappointment was overwhelming...)

Cell membranes, ribosomes, mitochondria, lysosomes, nucleus, citrioles, Golgi Bodies, RNA and DNA are entities of the living cell whose functions are oft described in rudimentary terms in elementary biology. The complexity of their respective functions turns out to be mind-boggling and nigh incomprehensible. As man continues to "advance" in knowledge, he soon begins to trespass into territory that ought to be verboten. Man now is experimenting and "progressing" in genetic engineering and gene splicing. The genetic codes are contained within these areas and man is now dallying with that which blueprints and replicates our literal physical beings. Man has toyed for years in the laboratory with cloning and other frightening experimentations and developments that revolve around the cell's RNA and DNA. It is always easy to justify such exploration by envisioning all the good that may be done medically in improving the human condition, yet what is not so evident to all is the fact that there is a line easily crossed where man once again trespasses into territory that belongs to God alone.

Nevertheless, as far as man's profound advancement in knowledge goes, and as far as the new vistas of raw information he has made available to himself are explored, the profound mystery of life itself still remains. Man now explores scientific territory unthinkable to the early twentieth century mind. He is capable now of examining the complexities and functions of organic and biological structures that were mysteries to men mere decades ago. He understands the chemistry and physiology of organisms and organelles now that could only be guessed at in the still recent past. Man can, and does, now experimentally examine, dissect and isolate the makeup and function of infinitesimally tiny parts – molecules, compounds, and even atoms.

Given all that, it still remains that while man "understands" and "knows" certain details about the things in this world that live, he has yet to discover the actual spark that makes living things *live*. Man has broken living things down to their most rudimentary living entities and studied those entities. He has watched the functions of vacuoles in the cells. He has observed as the mitochondria convert nutrients to energy, as cell membranes transport necessary contents in and out, and as ribosomes synthesize proteins. He has documented the chemistry of the conversion of energy within the cells, and has watched as RNA and DNA dance at a sub-cellular level and assemble strands of complex nucleotides which replicate and become the organic blueprints of the profound processes of cell division and reproduction. He has managed to observe and deduce something of the infinite complexity of living things. Yet man has still not discovered the ***spark of life***. Once all the building blocks are pulled apart and the processes singularly understood, where among the component parts is life found? Man knows things live and he observes as things die. Cells that live can be distinguished from cells that are dead. Some of the causes and some of the chemistry of death may even be known. The processes of life and death can be documented. Nevertheless, for all that he knows, man cannot put his finger on that ***thing***, that esoteric ***spark***, that animates all things that live: ***life itself***. Man can put those component parts back together, but he has no capacity to either make them live or to understand *what it is* that makes them live.

This is the ultimate conundrum and the fatal snare for the evolutionist. In the end, he must believe that all things organic and biological - that all things that respire, reproduce and respond to stimuli - came from inorganic and non-living rocks and elements, coaxed to life only by the randomness of cosmic explosion, haphazard fire and indiscriminate chemistry. Whether the life forms he studies be "simplistic" single-celled organisms, or infinitely complex and intelligent mammals, he is left to believe that life sprang spontaneously out of that which was dead. From whence did the spark of life originate?

All of the theorizing, and all of the time he allots to the processes of randomness, cannot deliver the blind evolutionist from the precipice before which he stands. For him, in the end, life had to spontaneously spark from the dead, the inorganic and the inanimate. There he stands, and from there he must take a ridiculously long and tremendously dark leap of faith. Did life really, one day hundreds of billions of years ago, just spark and ignite? He believes so. He is a believer. His faith has found a resting place.

It is in this way that the Bible-believer is at great advantage over the believer of the *life-from-rocks theory* of evolution. The evolutionist has to grasp at a scientific and statistical impossibility, while the Christian simply sees that where there is a design, there must be a Designer, and that where there is life, there must be a Life-Giver. This is verified in the Book that the Christian's Creator supplied him. *And God said, Let the waters bring forth abundantly the moving creature that hath life* (Gen. 1:20), and *...the LORD God formed man of the dust of the ground, and breathed into his nostrils the breath of life; and man became a living soul* (Gen. 2:7).

Biologically, that great mystery which has troubled man as long as he has sought answers without acknowledging God is solved with the profoundest simplicity. ***God supplies the spark of life!*** This is not a statement supporting Pantheism. Pantheists, in seeing God in everything, desire to worship God in everything. In this way bugs, trees and the larger environment become sanctified and worship-worthy because

God indwells them. This, of course, is nonsense, pagan idolatry, and a fulfillment of Romans 1:25. Bible-believing Christians know from the scriptures that it is God that supplies life and animates all things that live. He, and He alone, is worship-worthy! Job puts it this way: *In whose hand is the soul of every living thing, and the breath of all mankind* (Job 12:10), and Paul, on Mars Hill, relates this: *For in him we live, and move, and have our being* (Acts 17:28). Biological life is supplied by the Lord at a level and in a way that none fully conceptualize. *I laid me down and slept; I awaked; for the LORD sustained me* (Ps. 3:5).

In this way, in the material biological world, the enduring and otherwise unanswerable mystery of the causation and source of life is answered with three simple letters and an exclamation point: ***God!*** Somehow, within the matrix of the microscopic molecular structures and complex organic compounds that make up living things, it is simply God, the Creator, that giveth *life.* He cannot be discovered. He reveals Himself. No one will ever succeed in disassembling all the mechanical parts, and therein find God. He is invisible. *For* ***the invisible things of him*** *from the creation of the world are clearly seen, being understood by the things that are made* (Rom. 1:20). In 1 Timothy 1:17, He is *eternal, immortal,* ***invisible****, the only wise God.* Life is not packaged in some organelle or in one specific place. It flows and emanates from God and His word. *(W)e understand that the worlds were framed by the word of God, so that things which are seen were not made of things which do appear* (Heb. 11:3).

Thus, the life source, biologically, is not discoverable by experimentation, observation, dissection or disassembly. No microscope can see it and no process can clinically isolate it. It comes from God.

With this in mind, it should be carefully noted that which the Holy Scripture states about its own nature:

> ***For the word of God is quick****, and powerful, and sharper than any twoedged sword, piercing even to the dividing asunder of soul and spirit, and of the joints and marrow, and is a discerner of the thoughts and intents of the heart*
>
> (Heb. 4:12)

The scriptures are very emphatic about the fact that the ***word of God is quick***. The word of God is ***alive!*** It ***lives!*** This has been the cornerstone of real Christian faith for as long as there have been real Christians. Christ was and is the Word of God, and man has the word of God. The word of God is *not bound* (2 Tim. 2:9). It *goeth forth* out of God's mouth, and it shall not *return...void* (Isa. 55:11). The scripture itself *foresees* the future in Galatians 3:8. In Hebrews 4:12, it is *powerful*, *piercing*, and is given the living, cognitive attribute of being a *discerner of the thoughts and intents of the heart*.

Simple, rudimentary, trusting, child-like faith completely accepts that the word of God is quick, alive and powerful. Such faith holds that the preaching and witness of that word unleashes a spiritual potency and supernatural influence that is not explicable by the enunciation of the mere words of man. These arc God's words that are a part of a larger entity, the word of God. This idea is not the same as the baloney propagated by various species of half-cracked, Charismatic TV evangelists. This revolves around the fact that God, Who by His word spake the universe into existence and still does *uphold all things by the word of his power* (Heb. 1:3), and also by His word invades the consciences of men, convicts them, permeates their thoughts, smites their hearts, and in the end, is able to save their souls (Jas. 1:21). Christ is the embodiment of that word, but God the Holy Spirit is the One who animates, invigorates and empowers it. By that word, the Holy Ghost *reprove(s) the world of sin, and of righteousness, and of judgment* (John 16:8). It is interesting and insightful that in John 5:39, Christ said that men should *Search the scriptures for... they are they which **testify of me***, and in John 15:26, in speaking of the Spirit, He said *But when the Comforter is come... he shall **testify of me***! Those are the only two entities said to ***testify of (Him)***! The living potency of God's words is essentially inseparable from the power and influence of the Holy Spirit of God.

A big deal is made out of this because man's fallen and corrupt ideas always seem to pervade and subjugate the more sublime. Just as man came to hold that the life of biological organisms arose spontaneously and without God's influence, so it is that the word of God has been subjected to the same blind and polluted train of thought. Paul testified that the sanct and holy authority of the word of God came under fire and attack almost as soon as it was given. *(B)ut there be some that trouble you, and would pervert the gospel of Christ* (Gal. 1:7), he said, and further, *For I know this, that after my departing shall grievous wolves enter in among you,... Also of your own selves shall men arise, speaking perverse things* (Acts 20:29-30). Elymas the sorcerer went about *pervert(ing) the right ways of the Lord* in the very presence of the apostle in Acts 13:10, and of Hymenaeus and Philetus, he said that ... *their word will eat as doth a canker* and *Who concerning the truth have erred* (2 Tim. 2:17-18). This was going on in the very days the holy scriptures were being originally penned!

There has never been a time that the word of God was not under attack by Satan and his minions. They who were known as the Church Fathers in the earliest days of the Church Age, specifically named men who polluted the scriptures. Some who were known as "Church Fathers" *were* polluters of the scriptures. There are many substances by which a well or fountain may be poisoned, but the word of God has been subjected to nothing so much as it has the utterly relentless assault upon its supernatural origin and propagation. Every heretic that ever undertook the task to change and profane it did so with the belief that it was not holy, inviolable and living, just as it stood. Each believed he had the latitude and license to alter it, for it was a faulted and non-living Book. Clement of Alexandria and Origen corrupted the Bible in order to align it more with Gnosticism. The Catholic popes and kings of the Dark Ages burned it, forbade it, and wrested it, all under the premise that its words were not truly living words from God. The Renaissance is viewed today as a good thing and is celebrated by many, but while in its art and music is revealed the then new-found expression of the human spirit, there is also in its humanism the seeds of philosophy which sought to explain away the supernatural attributes of the Bible. After the Protestant Reformation, Roman Catholicism counter-attacked in 1546 A.D. with the Council of Trent, and out of that arose what is known as the *Enlightenment* or the *Age of Reason*.

This may be more properly called the "age of unbelief," as Cloud puts it.[251] The Enlightenment swept across Christianity, and elevated *reason* above *revelation* and effectively placed *man* over *God*. Its fruits were *Deism* in England and the USA, *Skepticism* in France and *Rationalism* in Germany.[252] Many are the bastards and the disasters fathered by the *Age of Reason*, but they all revolved around there being naturalistic, rational, non-supernatural explanations for the things of the Bible and the Bible itself. Schools of liberal theology fed on this as vultures do carrion, and from this all sprang the "Higher Criticism" and "Lower Criticism" we hear

---

[251] Cloud, David W., *The Modern Bible Version Hall of Shame.* Way of Life Literature, Port Huron, MI., 48061. 2005, pg.13

[252] Sargent, Robert J., *Landmarks of English Bible: Manuscript Evidence.* Bible Baptist Church Publications, Oak Harbor, WA 98277. 1989, pg. 248-249.

so much about today. Many of Fundamentalism's most respected biblical reference book writers drank this vile potion and passed the poison of rationalistic unbelief about the Bible on to 21st century students of the Bible. Westcott and Hort were the "natural" outcome of this sequence of biblical apostasy, followed, of course, by the viral infection of new bibles.

Just as evolutionary scientists peer down between the compounds, molecules, functions and physiology that make up living things and cannot uncover the actual source and ***spark of life***, so have men done with the Bible. They have sought naturalistic explanations for its existence. They have pulled it apart, and dissected its every word down to its component parts. They have microscopically examined its Hebrew, its Aramaic and its Greek. They have gone over the nouns, verbs, and articles, along with all their assorted tenses, forms and declensions. The grammatical and linguistic makeup of the Bible has been endlessly scrutinized and disassembled. Sadly, for all the scrutiny and dissection to which the Bible has been subjected, scholarship has had no success in uncovering the actual life-giving spark – that isolated characteristic or quality – that makes the Bible quick and alive.

When a man, with painstaking care, disassembles a functional car engine piece by piece, and nut by nut, he is able to come to an understanding of what it is that makes the car "run." Fuel is supplied in a combustion chamber; spark supplies an ignition, and the ignition provides force against moving parts. This sequence occurs in multiple combustion chambers at once, usually, and the process simply continues until fuel or spark is no longer supplied. However, man has had no such success in observing, capturing, emulating or uncovering that elusive spark which gives organisms ***life***. He is able to come to some understanding of certain life functions and processes, but the causation of that life is ever elusive. Nor have scholars by their meticulousness and fastidiousness been successful in identifying or isolating that particular attribute that animates and enlivens the Bible. They pull apart all the grammatical cogs and washers, and separate all the linguistic gears and bolts, yet they do not discover the secret or the miracle of ***life itself***!

The reason that man does not discover that particular secret of life, resides in the fact that the very essence of life itself no more originates spiritually from the grammar forms and linguistics of the Bible than it does from tissues and organelles biologically. God Himself gives life to the organic and biological elements of His creation. Life emanates from those things and resides in those things, but God is the Originator of that life and it is elementally "undiscoverable" and its origins unobservable.

In this very way, brilliant but blind and faithless men have scrupulously torn down the Bible to its tiniest component parts, and having studied those parts, they have been unable to observe and demonstrate the ***spark***, the essence, the elemental origination of the life in the words thereof. Because they have disassembled it, and because they have not discovered the actual spark itself, they have come to quite the same tragic and debauched conclusion about the scriptures that evolutionists have come to about life biologically. They have concluded that God is not present in the process.

Each of the two categories of "unfaithful" and "unbelieving" men abide in a netherworld of denial, irony, discrepancy and pseudo-faith. Evolutionists desperately and vainly cling to the jaw-dropping myth of a "Big Bang," followed by hundreds of billions of years of statistical monstrosities, spontaneous generation and mutational gymnastics. Modern biblical scholars genuflect toward and worship the distant memory of original manuscripts, long ago perished – manuscripts supernaturally and potently supplied by a loving and self-sacrificial God, but lost forever, quite naturally, by bumbling and impotent men. Evolutionists live in both a microscopic and telescopic cosmos that screams of design – yet they are blind to the Designer. Christians, while worshipfully glorifying and crediting God for His word, do not actually believe it is wholly and unconditionally delivered to them. Evolutionists believe profoundly in a sequence of events that are mind bending in their abject arbitrariness. Christians trust their souls and eternities to a Savior, Whose promises they routinely and practically distrust as pertaining to the record of those promises. Evolutionists routinely ignore all evidence and reasoning that is oppositional to their godlessness. Christians now customarily deny what their professed holy scriptures plainly posit.

It is no puzzle or secret that men degenerately desire to walk by sight. They wish to see before they believe. For lost men, Science has become the all-pervading supplier of their seeing, so that they might believe. At every turn people are admonished that Science and scientists have proven *this, that* and *the other*. However, when their Science fails them, lost men fall back on hopelessly futile and desperate faith. Evolutionists cannot find or observe the "life-source" biologically (God), so they leap like lemmings into the abyss of faith in the spontaneous generation of all living things. Tragically and unfortunately, Christians secretly want to walk by sight as well, though this defies the great tenet of the New Testament: *For we walk by faith, not by sight* (2 Cor. 5:7). Christians want to see their Bible and their "faith" proven, so they have delved back into the history and lineage of the scriptures themselves to show scientific, visible evidence of the authenticity of the Bible. Archeological "finds" and discoveries are desperately clung to as if Christians are pre-weaned suckling pigs. Christians can, and many have, become virtually enslaved by the demonstrable, the traceable and the substantively verifiable. Led by their scholars, they have come to expect certain quantitative and material evidence of the faith with which they were entrusted by the God that *cannot lie* (Tit. 1:2). While having been graciously blessed with great mounds of evidence for the authenticity of the Bible, Greek and Hebrew scholars have sought the actual life of it in its linguistic makeup, down within the crevasses and textures of the words and letters themselves – ***and they have not found the essence, the spark of life***. They have found manuscripts, partial pieces of frayed papyrus, time-worn leather and stone engravings. No power or life, though, appears to emanate or pulse from these portions of old bibles. God's residence within them is not in evidence, tucked between and within tenses and declensions. So fallen men – fallen *Christian* men – do much like what lost men did when they sought something to see but were stranded sightless.

Some merely hold that the Bible, as it is known today, was written by men. In this way, man is left to the mysterious allegories and partial truths of a bible that is more a fireside legend than anything else. It may be viewed from a variety of philosophical slants, and man is left to follow his heart and the ever-elusive voice of God through church tradition, ritual liturgy, a touch of sorcery and good, old-fashioned, fleshly feelings. To these men, the Bible does not really ***live***, but it does sometimes serve as a *Ouija Board*.

For some others, life is not discovered in the Bible that is available today, but they are certain that there was once a Bible that truly lived! Once, when the original manuscripts existed here on earth, the Bible was truly alive. As evolutionists, who in not finding genuine answers in the present, obsess upon an imagined event in the past (the Big Bang), these *Christians*, believing the Bible today is merely dependable, are on a vain, never-ending and glassy-eyed pilgrimage back to the original manuscripts. Until they arrive at this un-promised shrine of dust and ashes, the journey allows them to treat the Bible which exists today somewhat like the potato-shaped children's toy. As the eyes, ears, mouth and nose of the toy can be variously interchanged in a wonderfully robust number of combinations, so these perpetuate the presumptuous substitution and swapping of words, phrases, prepositions, "better readings," "preferred readings," and good, old, down-home changes and perversions. Christians are told not to worry, though. Real life was only in the originals, so there is nothing truly holy about the Bibles commonly seen ravished today.

Gladly, there are yet others who are much friendlier to the precept of genuine holy scriptures for today. These hold that God preserved the words of the originals in the Greek and Hebrew texts, which have come to modern Christians through the sieve of history. To them, it is the King James Bible that ***represents*** the real truth of the originals in English as witnessed by these Masoretic Hebrew and Textus Receptus Greek manuscripts of the Old and New Testaments. This all appears so fine superficially, until one realizes that neither do these believe that there is a perfect Bible to actually be printed, purchased, possessed and clasped to the bosom. To them, life only resides in the King James Bible in a measure. The real living and final word resides in the TR and the Masoretic texts. That the living word might not fully exist in our native language is not the worst concern here. The worst concern is that none of this brand of believers can consistently point to one singular and particular edition of the Masoretic and Textus Receptus texts as completely and irrevocably authoritative and representative of God's living word. Their final authority is not much more a matter of eternal finality than the other categories of men discussed above. These too, sadly, fell for the idea that the true living words of God abide elsewhere than where one might routinely access *all of them in their perfection!*

The categories of men just discussed – though some are mostly friendly to the cause of the pure word of God, and have made valuable contribution – have been infected in one measure or other by an insidious element. At one level or another, they expect a naturalistic and demonstrable explanation for the miracle of the word of God. They are not brute evolutionists or true rationalists, but they expect substantive evidence of God's hand in the Bible. They require that they be allowed to walk by sight in this matter. They demand it. They expect to be able to trace and track the footprints and handiwork of a supernatural lineage. They consider that God is obliged to them to reveal the intricate workings of His hand. Though what makes the word of God alive is the breath of an utterly unobservable and invisible Being, they require that they be allowed to peer into the guts of the Bible and verify what is God's doing, and what is not. Where they do not observe or recognize His hand, they very often declare that it is not present. Where they find elements of the Bible that do not meet their presuppositions and that defy their linguistic standards and explanations, they are quick to pronounce these elements *unfortunate*, and the product of mere man. As the Pharisees required that Christ operate and abide in accord with their preset boundaries, so do these make compulsory that the Lord function according to their preconceived notions of words and language. Moreover, they refuse to accept as a practical article of faith that there is a perfect, wholly inspired and fully inerrant specimen in the world today.

Regarding certain false teachers of his day, Paul said the following: *To whom we gave place by subjection, no, not for an hour; that the truth of the gospel might continue with you* (Gal. 2:5). Nor do true Bible-believers find that they should give *place by subjection*, either. What makes the word of God alive is not measurable or observable. It cannot be clinically studied, as one would the anatomical structures in a dissection class. The processes of its *living* cannot even be observed in quite the same way as scientists would observe under microscope the metabolism and respiration of a living cell. The living nature of the words of God can only be attributed to one singular Entity –

God! Only He imparts life. Only He coaxes words to life. All of the processes are not explained to believers, but this we know: as God breathed into the first man's nostrils (Gen. 2:7) and Adam became a ***living*** *soul*, so too live God's words. As God shall make dead bones ***live*** (Ezek. 37), so does He animate and invigorate nouns, verbs, subjects, predicates, participles and prepositions.

It is certain that when God spake by the prophets and wrote by the hands of the apostles, that the resulting words were quick, alive and powerful. It is also scripturally certain that when the seventeen separate ethnicities mentioned in Acts 2:9-11 heard God's words in their own languages, that what they carried back to their lands were living words from God. It is utterly consistent with the devil's mode of operation that many pollutions and corruptions would be introduced to the words of God, but it is equally consistent that God the Holy Spirit would get the Syrian Christians (Acts 11) a living word in their language, along with those that spake Latin. A very long list could follow – Persians, Arabs, Africans, Mongols, Goths, Visigoths, Angles, Saxons, Franks and Teutons – these all were peoples to whom God promised living words.

If God sent living words to these peoples in their own tongues, then ***He*** was the spark of life that animated the Bible in their separate languages. This means that study-bound clinicians and academicians of seminaries and Christian colleges are quite wrong when they say that God would not (and perhaps, could not) involve himself in translations. They say that only because they have been brainwashed to hate the abiding and genuine example of the miraculous and wondrous handiwork of God in our day: the AV 1611 King James Bible. To them, almost all other truth and reasoning must be subjugated to the bondage of that one prejudicial tenet.

It is not man's place to understand exactly how or why. It is man's place to trust and believe. It is not man's place to dictate how God would or should propagate His word. It is man's place to find, discern and sanctify God's words from among the devil's perverse substitutions. The process is not a scientific application, but rather a vigilant and studious observation, *by their fruits ye shall know them* (Matt. 7:20). There is certainly a great deal of historical evidence for the Bible, and plenty of manuscript evidence pointing the saints to the correct Bible, but God has no intention that His children be allowed to walk by the light and sight of evidence. God has another species of evidence in mind by which we walk: *Now* ***faith*** *is the substance of things hoped for, the* **evidence** *of things not seen* (Heb. 11:1). That ***faith*** is the *evidence*, and we walk by that faith, *not by sight* (2 Cor. 5:7). And, again, *So then* ***faith*** *cometh by hearing, and hearing by the word of God* (Rom. 10:17). Christians do not believe because they see. They see because they believe. Central to that faith is the living word which, of necessity, is composed of individual living and powerful words.

God does not owe man a detailed inventory or history of each minute step of Biblical inspiration, preservation or propagation. There are gaps in the Bible-believer's knowledge of how God has done what He has done, and much of God's handiwork and guidance through the centuries abides hidden and undisclosed. He is not accountable to man or obligated to itemize and explain His every move and intervention. As He never, on the record, elucidated to Job the reasons for His actions in Job 1 and 2, so ambassadors for Christ are left to walk in the stewardship of His word, in faith and in trustful reliance. *(H)ow unsearchable are his judgments, and his ways past finding out* (Rom. 11:33).

As the spark which ignites the life of biological things will never be isolated because that spark is supplied supernaturally by the Creator, neither will the most dedicated and scholarly of men ever academically demonstrate that attribute which enervates and makes the words of God *quick*. God Himself supplies the element that actuates the power and animates the words and letters of the Bible. The reason there are "bibles" that are dead is because God is not in them and does not honor them. The reason that the King James Bible is potently living is because God wrote it and imparted life into it. Throughout history, the reason that certain Bibles in other languages have wrought mighty works and fruits is because God wrote them too. The secret, however, does not simply abide in the originals as opposed to all the generations of the manuscript copies and translations. The secret does not merely abide in the proper categorization and evaluation of original language texts. The treasure of life is not found by the mere mastery of biblical languages and the excellence of linguistic skill. Did God follow a pattern? Yes. Did He use certain manuscripts and reject others? Yes. Did He use men's mastery of language and grammar? Yes. Did He honor faithful and true copies of manuscripts and bibles as opposed to those that were polluted and corrupted? Yes. But none of those things imparted life to the scriptures. Should an actual Greek original of 2 Timothy 3:16 be uncovered, it would be no *quicker* or more *powerful* than 2 Timothy 3:16 in our King James Bible. God's Spirit imparted ***the life and spark*** to the scriptures, and that ***spark*** was passed on from generation to generation, from translation to translation, from mouths to ears, from lips to paper, from heart to heart and from Spirit to spirit. The life-spark does not abide in Greek or Hebrew. The issue is not comprehended within mere manuscript families, and its secrets do not abide behind the brilliant linguists desk.

The spark of life and the mysterious power of God's living words in the King James Bible come from the Living God Himself.

Appendix I

(Chapter 15 pg 672)

Peitho / Apeitho

Ref	KJV	NAS	NIV	NKJV	RSV
Lk.1:17	*disobedient*	disobedient	disobedient	disobedient	disobedient
Jn.3:36	*believeth not*	not obey	rejects	not believe	not obey
Acts 5:36	*obeyed*	followed	followers	obeyed	followed
Acts 5:37	*obeyed*	followed	followers	obeyed	followed
Acts 14:2	*unbelieving*	disbelieved	refused to believe	unbelieving	unbelieving
Acts 17:4	*believed*	persuaded	persuaded	persuaded	persuaded[253]
Acts 19:9	*believed not*	disobedient	refused to believe	not believe	disbelieved
Acts 26:19	*disobedient*	disobedient	disobedient	disobedient	disobedient
Acts 27:11	*believed*	persuaded	followed	persuaded	paid more attention
Acts 28:24	*believed*	persuaded	convinced	persuaded	convinced
Rom.1:30	*disobedient*	disobedient	disobey	disobedient	disobedient
Rom.2:8a	*do not obey*	do not obey	reject	do not obey	do not obey
Rom. 2:8b	*obey*	obey	follow	obey	obey
Rom.10:21	*disobedient*	disobedient	disobedient	disobedient	disobedient
Rom.11:30a	*not believed*	disobedient	disobedient	disobedient	disobedient
Rom.11:30b	*unbelief*	disobedience	disobedience	disobedience	disobedience
Rom.11:31	*not believed*	disobedient	disobedient	disobedient	disobedient
Rom.11:32	*unbelief*	disobedience	disobedience	disobedience	disobedience
Rom.15:31	*not believe*	disobedient	unbelievers	not obey	unbelievers
Gal.5:7	*not obey*	from obeying	from obeying	from obeying	from obeying
Eph.2:2	*disobedience*	disobedience	disobedient	disobedience	disobedience
Eph.5:6	*disobedience*	disobedience	disobedient	disobedience	disobedience
Col. 3:6	*disobedience*	-[254]	-	disobedience	-

---

[253] Recall that **peitho** is translated in more ways than just ***believe*** and ***obey.*** **To persuade, to trust, to have confidence** are other ways commonly seen. Our study relates to the conflict between ***believe*** and ***obey***.

[254] The author is aware that some editions of the *New American Standard* do translate "disobedience" into Col.3:6. The particular edition I habitually reference in this book does not translate "disobedience" into the verse.

2 Tim.3:2	*disobedient*	disobedient	disobedient	disobedient	disobedient
Tit.1:16	*disobedient*	disobedient	disobedient	disobedient	disobedient
Tit.3:3	*disobedient*	disobedient	disobedient	disobedient	disobedient
Heb.3:18	*believed not*	disobedient	disobeyed	not obey	disobedient
Heb.4:6	*unbelief*	disobedience	disobedience	disobedience	disobedience
Heb.4:11	*unbelief*	disobedience	disobedience	disobedience	disobedience
Heb.11:31	*believed not*	disobedient	disobedient	not believe	disobedient
Heb.13:17	*obey*	obey	obey	obey	obey
Jas.3:3	*obey*	obey	obey	obey	obey
1 Pet.2:8	*disobedient*	disobedient	disobey	disobedient	disobey
1 Pet.3:1	*obey not*	disobedient	not believe	not obey	not obey
1 Pet.3:20	*disobedient*	disobedient	disobeyed	disobedient	not obey
1 Pet.4:17	*obey not*	not obey	not obey	not obey	not obey

Bibliography

"Baptism's Practice | Articles | NTRF." Weblog post. *House Church | Relational Church | NewTestament Church | Organic Church | NTRF.* Web. 13 Dec. 2010. <http://www.ntrf.org/articles/article_detail.php?PRKey=38.>.

Barnes, Albert. *Barnes' Notes* (1997) P C Study Bible (Version 2.11) [Computer Software].
Seattle, WA: Biblesoft.

Biblesoft's New Exhaustive Strong's Numbers and Concordance with Expanded Greek-Hebrew Dictionary. 1994, 2003, 2006 Biblesoft, Inc. and International Bible Translators, Inc.

Bullinger, E.W. *The Companion Bible* (Humphrey Milford Oxford University Press, London, New York, Toronto & Melbourne).

By Sight. "Scripture Is 'God-Breathed'." *Abundant Grace Daily Devotional.* Web. 11 Dec. 2010. <http://paulwhiteministries.blogspot.com/2009/08/scripture-is-god-breathed.html>.

By the Way. "Orthodoxy's Liturgical Vestment Colors." *Al's Web Niche.* Web. 13 Dec. 2010. <http://aggreen.net/vestment/liturgical_colors.html>.

Cairns, Earl E. *Christianity Through The Centuries: A History of the Christian Church.*Zondervan Publishing House, Grand Rapids, MI. 1954, 1981.

"Catholic Encyclopedia: Vestments." *New Advent: Home.* Web. 2 Dec. 2010. <http://www.newadvent.org/cathen/15388a.htm>.

Clarke, Adam. *Clarke's Commentary.* (1998) P C Study Bible (Version 2.11) [Computer Software].Seattle, WA: Biblesoft.

Cloud, David. *Is 17th-Century British English Holy?* Fundamental Baptist Information Service, Port Huron, MI. Web 12 Aug, 2010. <fbns@wayoflife.org>

Cloud, David W. *Myths About The Modern Bible Versions.* Way of Life Literature. Oak Harbor, WA. 1999.

Cloud, David W. *The Glorious History of the King James Bible.* Way of Life Literature, Port Huron, MI. 2006.

Cloud, David W. *The Modern Bible Version Hall of Shame.* Way of Life Literature, Port Huron, MI. 2005.

Connolly, W. Kenneth. *The Indestructable Book.* Baker Books, Grand Rapids, MI. 1996

Corle, Dennis. *God's Inspired Book – The Bible.* Revival Fires! Publishing, Claysburg, PA. 2009.

Definition of Gesenius, Wilhelm in the Free Online Encyclopedia." *Encyclopedia.* Web. 11 Dec. 2010. <http://encyclopedia2.thefreedictionary.com/Gesenius, Wilhelm>.

DiVietro, Kirk. *Cleaning-Up Hazardous Materials: A Refutation of Gail Riplinger's HazardousMaterials.* The Dean Burgon Soiety, Collingswood, NJ. 2010.

"Entirely God-Breathed." *The Reflections of Bryn MacPhail.* Web. 11 Dec. 2010. <http://www.reformedtheology.ca/2tim3bb.htm>.

Farris, Michael. *From Tyndale to Madison*, B&H Publishing Group, Nashville, TN 2007.

Fuller, David Otis. *Counterfeit or Genuine Mark 16? John 8?* Grand Rapids International Publications, Grand Rapids, MI. 1975.

Fuller, David Otis. *True or False?* Grand Rapids International Publications, Grand Rapids, MI. 1973, 1975 flyleaf.

Fuller, David Otis. *Which Bible.* Grand Rapids International Publications, Grand Rapids, MI. 1970.

Gipp, Sam. *Is Our English Bible Inspired?* Daystar Publishing, Miamitown, OH. 2004.

Gipp, Samuel C. *The Answer Book.* Bible & Literature Missionary Foundation, Shelbyville, TN. 1989.

"God-Breathed Scripture." *PBC.* Web. 11 Dec. 2010. <http://www.pbc.org/files/messages/7727/4606.html>.

Grady, William. *Final Authority; The Christian's Guide to the King James Bible.* Grady Publications, Schererville, IN. 1993.

Henry, Matthew. *Matthew Henry's Commentary on the Whole Bible.* (1998) P C Study Bible (Version 2.11) [Computer Software]. Seattle, WA: Biblesoft.

Hills, Edward F. *Believing Bible Study Key to the Space Age.* The Christian Research Press: Des Moines, IA. 1967, 1977.

Hills, Edward F. *The King James Version Defended.* The Christian Research Press, Des Moines, IA. 1973, 1979.

International Standard Bible Encylopaedia, Electronic Database Copyright (C) 1996 by Biblesoft).

Is the Headcovering Really an Issue? A Serious and Indepth Study (2nd. Edition-revised 1997, 1999 R.J. Vogel) Web. 11 Nov, 2010. < http://www.montanasat.net/rickv/Headcovering_Veiling.html>

Jamieson, Fausset, and Brown Commentary. (1998) P C Study Bible (Version 2.11) [Computer Software]. Seattle, WA: Biblesoft.

Jones, Floyd Nolen. *Which Version Is The Bible.* KingsWord Press, Goodyear, AZ. 1989, 2006.

Keil, Carl Friedr., and Franz Delitzsch. *Biblischer Commentar Über Das Alte Testament: Carl Friedr..* Leipzig: Dörffling Und Franke, 1870. Electronic.

Kirkpatrick, Paul. *"Baptism" In The King James Version.* Tabernacle Baptist Church, Lubbock, TX. Tract #218.

"...Let her Be Veiled." *An in-depth study of 1 Corinthians 11:1-16* edited by Tom Shank, Torch Publications, Kootenai Christian Fellowship. Web. 11 Nov. 2010. <http://truthinheart.com/EarlyOberlinCD/CD/Doctrine/BeVeiled.htm#Chapter%201>

Lindsell, Harold. *The Battle For the Bible.* Zondervan Publishing House, Grand Rapids, MI. 1976.

MacArthur, John. *By the Way.* "Our God-Breathed Bible." *Bible Bulletin Board.* Web. 11 Dec. 2010. http://www.biblebb.com/files/mac/55-17.htm>.

McClure, Alexander. *Translators Revived.* Maranatha Publications, Worthington, PA.

McClure, A.W. *Translators Revived,* Maranatha Publications Worthington, Pa – reprint.

McCord, By Hugo. "God-Breathed Scriptures." *TheBible.net.* Web. 11 Dec. 2010. <http://www.thebible.net/modules.php?name=Read&itemid=99&cat=3>.

Moorman, Jack. *Forever Settled.* The Dean Burgeon Society Press, Collingswood, NJ. 1999.

Moulton, Harold K. ed, *The Analytical Greek Lexicon Revised,* Zondervan Publishing House, Grand Rapids, MI. 1977.

Nelson's Illustrated Bible Dictionary. (1998) P C Study Bible (Version 2.11) [Computer Software]. Seattle, WA: Biblesoft.

"Origen | Christian History." *ChristianityToday.com | Magazines, News, Church Leadership & Bible Study.* Web. 13 Dec. 2010. <http://www.christianitytoday.com/ch/131christians/scholarsandscientists/origen.html>.

Perschbacher, Wesley J. The New Analytical Greek Lexicon.

Pfeiffer, Charles and Harrison, Everett. ed. *The Wycliffe Bible Commentary.* (1962) Moody Press. P C Study Bible (Version 2.11) [Computer Software]. Seattle, WA: Biblesoft.

Pride, Mary. *The Way Home: Beyond Feminism, Back to Reality.* Wheaton, Illinois: Crossway Books, 1985.

Ray, Jasper James. *God Wrote Only One Bible.* The Eye Opener Publishers, Eugene, OR. 1955.

Rice, John R. *Our God-Breathed Book – The Bible.* Sword of the Lord Publishers, Murfreesboro, TN., 1969.

Riplinger, G.A. *Hazardous Materials: Greek & Hebrew Study Dangers.* (A.V. Publications, Corp., Ararat, VA. 2008.

Riplinger, G.A. *In Awe of Thy Word, Understanding the King James Bible.* A.V. Publications, Ararat, VA. 2003.

Riplinger, G.A. *New Age Bible Versions,* AV Publications, Munroe Falls, OH. 1993

Riplinger, Gail. *The Language of the King James Bible.* A. V. Publications, Ararat, VA. 1998.

Robertson, A.T. *Robertson's Word Pictures of the New Testament* (1998) P C Study Bible (Version 2.11) [Computer Software]. Seattle, WA: Biblesoft.

Sargent, Robert J. *Landmarks of English Bible: Manuscript Evidence.* Bible Baptist Church Publications, Oak Harbor, WA. 1989.

Shakespeare, William. Hamlet. Act 3, scene 2, lines 222–230.

Sorenson, David H. *Touch Not The Unclean Thing The Text Issue and Separation.* Northstar Baptist Ministries, Duluth, MN. 2001.

Strong, James. *The Exhaustive Concordance of the Bible.* Holman Bible Publishers, Nashville, TN.

Strong, James. *Strong's Concordance, A Concise Dictionary.* Holman Bible Publishers, Nashville, TN.

Tenney, Merrill C. Zondervan's *Pictorial Encyclopedia of the Bible* (Vols.1-5). Grand Rapids, MI: Regency Reference Library. Vol.3.

The American Heritage® Dictionary of the English Language, Fourth Edition copyright ©2000 by Houghton Mifflin Company. Updated in 2009.

The Compact Oxford English Dictionary, Second Edition. Oxford University Press, 1989 (reprint 1999)

The Online Bible Thayer's Greek Lexicon And Brown Driver & Briggs' Hebrew Lexicon. 1993, Woodside

Bible Fellowship, Ontario, Canada. Licensed from the Institute for Creation Research.

The Wesley Center Online: Home. Web. 11 Dec. 2010. <http://wesley.nnu.edu/biblical_studies/tyndale/2ti.txt>.

The Wesley Center Online: Home. Web. 11 Dec. 2010. <http://wesley.nnu.edu/biblical_studies/wycliffe/2ti.txt>.

The Random House College Dictionary, Revised Edition. Random House, Inc., New York, NY. 1975.

Vance, Laurence M. *Archaic Words and the Authorized Version,* Vance Publications, Pensacola, Fl. 1996, 1999.

"Vestments." *Merriam-Webster Dictionary. Dictionary and Thesaurus - Merriam-Webster Online*. Web. 13 Dec. 2010. <http://www.merriam-webster.com/dictionary>.

Vincent's Word Studies of the New Testament (1997) P C Study Bible (Version 2.11) [Computer Software]. Seattle, WA: Biblesoft.

Vine's Expository Dictionary of Biblical Words (1998) P C Study Bible (Version 2.11) [Computer Software]. Seattle, WA: Biblesoft.

Waite, D.A. *Defending The King James Bible A Fourfold Superiority.* The Bible For Today Press, Collingswood, NJ. 1992.

Waite, Donald A. *Fundamentalist Mis-Information on Bible Versions,* The Bible For Today Press, Collingswood, NJ. 2000.

Walker, David E. *The Bible Believer's Guide to Dispensationalism.* Daystar Publishing, Miamitown, OH. 2005.

Webster's 1828 Dictionary. Christian Technologies, Inc. Version 2.2004.

"Vestment." *Wikipedia, the Free Encyclopedia*. Web. 11 Dec. 2010. <http://en.wikipedia.org/wiki/Vestment>.

"Walter Freeman." *Wikipedia, the Free Encyclopedia*. Web. 11 Dec. 2010. <http://en.wikipedia.org/wiki/Walter_Freeman>.

Wile, Jay L. & Durnell, Marilyn F. *Exploring Creation With Biology.* Apologia Educational Ministries, Inc., Anderson, IN. 1998.

"The Wycliffe Bible Commentary." *Biblesoft - Buy PC Study Bible Direct and Save!* Web. 13 Dec. 2010. <http://store.biblesoft.com/ProductDetails.asp?ProductCode=Wycliffeb00214>.